Silverlight™ 3 Programmer's F

Silverlight™ 3

Programmer's Reference

Silverlight™ 3
Programmer's Reference

J. Ambrose Little
Jason Beres
Grant Hinkson
Devin Rader
Joseph Croney

WILEY

Wiley Publishing, Inc.

Silverlight™ 3 Programmer's Reference

Published by
Wiley Publishing, Inc.
10475 Crosspoint Boulevard
Indianapolis, IN 46256
www.wiley.com

ISBN: 978-0-470-38540-1

Manufactured in the United States of America

10 9 8 7 6 5 4 3 2 1

Library of Congress Cataloging-in-Publication Data is available from the publisher.

For general information on our other products and services please contact our Customer Care Department within the United States at (800) 762-2974, outside the United States at (317) 572-3993 or fax (317) 572-4002.

Non nobis, Domine, non nobis, sed nomini Tuo da gloriam.

— Ambrose Little

I dedicate this book to my beautiful wife, Sheri, and amazing daughter, Siena, who put up with my crazy schedule and who forgive me every time I need to do things like write a book chapter or two when I really should be having fun with them.

— Jason Beres

To Ania, my wife and best friend, for supporting me through the long hours and late nights.

— Grant Hinkson

For Kyle

— Devin Rader

To Laura, my loving wife, and my two children, Joey and Annabelle, whose beaming smiles and endless support give me the inspiration and strength to tackle big challenges.

— Joseph Croney

About the Authors

Ambrose Little lives in central New Jersey and works there for Infragistics, where he is working mainly on new product development. As an INETA speaker and Microsoft MVP, he's been known to show up occasionally at user groups and write the occasional article and book. He's been designing and developing real business applications for more than 10 years.

Jason Beres is the director of product management for Infragistics, the world's leading publisher of presentation layer tools. Jason is also one of the founders of Florida .NET User Groups, the founder of the New Jersey .NET User Group, a Visual Basic .NET MVP, on the INETA Speakers Bureau, and on the INETA board of directors. Jason is the author of several books on .NET development, an international speaker, and a frequent columnist for several .NET publications. He also keeps very active in the .NET community.

Grant Hinkson is director of the experience design group at Infragistics. He is passionate about design, usability, and technology and is rewarded by working with a team of people who share similar passions. Grant is a Microsoft Expression MVP, a contributing author of *Silverlight 1.0*, published by Wrox, and *Foundation Fireworks CS4*, published by Friends of Ed, and a contributing author on Adobe DevNet. He has spoken at Adobe MAX, Microsoft ReMIX, and DevScovery and is active in the WPF, Silverlight, and Fireworks communities. He has authored several utilities for the designer/developer community, including the Fireworks to XAML exporter. When not coding or designing, Grant enjoys playing both the piano and the organ.

Devin Rader is a product manager on the Infragistics Web Client team, responsible for leading the creation of Infragistics Silverlight and Data Visualization products. Devin is also an active proponent and member of the .NET developer community, being a cofounder of the St. Louis .NET User Group, an active member of the New Jersey .NET User Group, a former board member of the International .NET Association (INETA), and a regular speaker at user groups. He is also a contributing author on the Wrox titles *Professional ASP.NET 2.0*, *Professional ASP.NET 3.5*, and *Wrox Silverlight 1.0*, as well as a technical editor for many other Wrox publications. He has also written columns for *ASP.NET Pro* magazine and .NET technology articles for MSDN Online. You can find more of Devin's ramblings at www.geekswithblogs.com/devin.

Joseph Croney is director of product development at Infragistics, where he leads a worldwide team of engineers that delivers cutting-edge software components for Silverlight, WPF, and ASP.NET. He is a former Microsoft program manager, who led feature teams in the MSN, Mobility, and Developer divisions. After leaving Microsoft, Joseph founded Calabash Technologies, a U.S. Virgin Islands Technology start-up, which successfully built and introduced a revolutionary handheld GPS Tour Guide. While CEO of Calabash, Joseph found time to share his passion for Computer Science with the next generation of technology leaders as an advanced-placement computer science teacher. Joseph has spoken at a wide range of events, including Microsoft PDC, ASP.NET Connections, Microsoft TechEd, and the College Board's National Convention.

Credits

Executive Editor
Bob Elliott

Senior Development Editor
Tom Dinse

Technical Editors
Jess Chadwick
Ed Blankenship
Todd Snyder
Ben Hoelting
Steven Murawski

Senior Production Editor
Debra Banninger

Copy Editors
Cate Caffrey
Foxxe Editorial Services

Editorial Manager
Mary Beth Wakefield

Production Manager
Tim Tate

Vice President and Executive Group Publisher
Richard Swadley

Vice President and Executive Publisher
Barry Pruett

Project Coordinator, Cover
Lynsey Stanford

Associate Publisher
Jim Minatel

Compositor
Craig Johnson, Happenstance Type-O-Rama

Proofreader
Nancy Carrasco

Indexer
J & J Indexing

Acknowledgments

Thanks first to my wife, Christiane, and four munchkins — Bridget, John, Brendan, and Thomas — for letting me disappear down into the basement for so many hours to work on this book, being patient, understanding, and supportive. Thanks to my coauthors for their hard work despite our ridiculously busy schedules; to Tom, Debra, and Bob at Wrox for sponsoring and coordinating; and to all our editors, technical and otherwise, who helped make this book better. It has been a tremendous team effort.

— *Ambrose Little*

I would like to take this opportunity to thank the Wrox team, especially Tom Dinse, who kept this book on track and made sure we all did what we needed to do to keep our tight schedule. I would also like to shout out a very special thanks to the great author team — Devin, Ambrose, Joe, and Grant — for making this book happen. It was awesome doing this book and even more awesome working with you guys at Infragistics every day.

— *Jason Beres*

First, thanks to my wife, Ania, for your constant support and encouragement on yet another after-hours project. Thanks also to my family for constantly encouraging and supporting me along the way. Finally, thanks to my coauthors and fellow XDGer's at Infragistics — it's a pleasure working with you all!

— *Grant Hinkson*

I thank my wife, Kathleen, for putting up with the late nights and working weekends. Once again, I say this is the last one. Thanks also to my Mom and Dad for all of your support and advice.

Thanks to my coauthors who put so much time and effort into the book, who were a bit wiser this time and yet still signed on. Thanks to all of those at Wiley, especially Bob Elliott and Jim Minatel, for giving us the opportunity to do this book and for keeping us moving in the right direction through its creation.

— *Devin Rader*

I would like to take a moment to recognize all the people who contributed to making this book a success. First and foremost, I want to thank my coauthors and the staff at Wrox, who spent countless hours dedicating their time and talent to the project. I also want to recognize my Silverlight development team, especially Stephen Zaharuk, whose technical expertise and support proved invaluable while I was exploring the depths of Silverlight. Finally, I thank my family for making the personal sacrifices that allowed me the time to focus on making this book a reality.

— *Joseph Croney*

Contents

Contents

Contents

Contents

Contents

Contents

Contents

Contents

Introduction

To abuse an already abused cliché, we are at a tipping point for the Web and application development in general. The last several years have seen a notable shift away from basic full-page-based, postback-intensive web applications that minimized the use of JavaScript in favor of server-side code for maximum browser compatibility. Today, some amount of AJAX is assumed for any new web application, and every day we see new "Web 2.0" applications and companies popping up.

At the same time, and in part because of this shift, the old "thin client" versus "rich client" dichotomy has increasingly faded. It is entirely possible, and, indeed, it is often the case, for a Web-based application using AJAX to truly have a richer experience than most desktop-based applications, be they Windows Forms, Java, or MFC. In fact, one might say that web applications today set the bar (excluding games, of course).

Enter Windows Presentation Foundation (WPF), the long-awaited, updated Microsoft desktop-application user interface (UI) framework. WPF borrowed from what has been learned on the Web (such as markup-based interface declaration and good separation of UI concerns), unified multiple Windows graphics APIs, and introduced new capabilities to Windows-based applications and new platform features (such as the enriched dependency property system, commanding, triggers, declarative animations, and more). WPF re-established the desktop as the new "rich client," although not without contest from fairly rich Internet applications (RIAs) that were based on AJAX.

But this book is not about AJAX. Nor is it about WPF, at least not directly. It's about bringing together these two worlds of RIAs and rich WPF-based desktop applications, and that's where Silverlight comes in.

Silverlight was originally codenamed *WPF/e*, meaning "WPF everywhere." And that's a pretty good tagline for Silverlight — bringing the good stuff from WPF to all the major platforms today, including OS X and flavors of Linux (via the Linux "Moonlight" implementation).

Silverlight 1.0 was an initial salvo. It brought with it the rich media, the rich UI declarative model, and a subset of WPF's presentation layer capabilities. But it still depends on JavaScript for the development environment and browsers' JavaScript execution engines. It does not have many of the basic application development facilities that developers today have come to expect and rely on, such as a control model (and controls), data binding facilities, and a solid development environment with reliable IntelliSense and debugging. Building a truly rich application for Silverlight 1.0 was only marginally better than using AJAX — the key advantages were in the high-quality media player and, of course, animation facilities.

The fall of 2008 brought Silverlight 2 and now, just a few months later, we're seeing a respectable update with Silverlight 3. Silverlight 3 and up will inevitably become the de facto Microsoft RIA development platform, and not just for Internet but also (in this author's opinion) for line-of-business solutions, except in cases where the functional or experiential demands call for the greater power of WPF. That said, although dramatically improved over Silverlight 1.0 and light-years better than building on AJAX frameworks, in many ways, even Silverlight 3 is still something of a fledgling RIA platform. But hey, that's more because RIAs and the necessary infrastructure to support them are still relatively young.

Introduction

Silverlight 3, in a broad sense, brings pretty much all the goodness of the .NET development platform to the browser. Almost everything you need from the .NET Frameworks that would apply in a browser environment is at your disposal. Oh, and did I mention, that includes a CLR especially crafted for RIAs?

So, why say that it is a fledgling RIA platform? Well, apart from the fact that what was essentially the real 1.0 version of what Silverlight needs to be as a RIA platform (Silverlight 2) was just released last fall, RIAs in themselves introduce a not-exactly-new but new-to-many-developers application model. You are essentially forced into a three-tier model that many, perhaps most, Microsoft developers have only given lip service to. You can no longer simply write ADO.NET code to directly access a database — you must go through a network service, be that HTTP or TCP-based, and for many developers, this will no doubt be a stumbling block. However, for those who have been developing true three-tier applications, while it may not be a stumbling block, they will appreciate the added complexity that this model imposes. Silverlight 3 does little to alleviate this burden, although when .NET RIA Services come to fruition, they will go a long way toward ameliorating this extra complexity.

On the flip side (architecturally speaking), there are no doubt client-side facilities that can and will mature. Silverlight 2 added isolated storage, which is essentially a sandboxed local filesystem, and that's a great start. But there are architectural facilities — such as those provided by Enterprise Library (e.g., enhanced exception handling and reporting, tracing, logging, caching) and those such as identity authentication and authorization — that need to be developed for this application model and platform.

Certainly there will also be new facilities whose need emerges as more and more RIAs are built as well with a focus on simplifying UI development itself. The raw power is there today, but it will require skill sets that historically have been relegated to high-end software development. (We're speaking here of various kinds of designers, particularly visual designers and interaction designers.) Because, as they say, with great power comes great responsibility, end-users have and will continue to expect more and better user experiences that the RIA platforms can provide.

Yet, despite how far there is to go to mature Silverlight into the rich application platform it needs to be, Silverlight 3 is, as noted, light-years ahead of developing RIAs on AJAX. In some ways, Silverlight does not add much in the way of experiential capability over a rich AJAX framework (or a combination of them). A lot of the basic and not-so-basic animations and, of course, asynchronous capabilities can be had without Silverlight, and certainly it is easier today to build rich AJAX-based applications than in even very recent years past.

But it is still terribly difficult not only to build but also to maintain a truly rich Internet application on AJAX. Although we developers might enjoy the immense technological challenge; the exciting intellectual stimulation of dancing between CSS, HTML, XML, and JavaScript; the sheer joy of screaming at the monitor when the beautiful set of functionality you finally got working in Firefox totally falls apart in Internet Explorer; the exhilaration of dealing with angry customers who have somehow disabled (or had disabled by corporate policy) one of the several technical puzzle pieces your application relies on — we, in the end, could be putting our collective intelligence and valuable time into far more valuable and rewarding — for *everybody* — enterprises.

And this is one of the chief areas where Silverlight 3 rushes to the rescue. By giving you a reliable CLR; .NET Frameworks; the WPF-based presentation core (including controls, data binding, and much more); a better networking stack; local, isolated storage; a rich IDE with rich debugging, IntelliSense, and LINQ (and even a Dynamic Language Runtime, DLR); Silverlight makes developing rich *interactive* applications far more feasible for everybody, especially our patrons (businesses), who are concerned with the total cost of ownership, not just what's technically feasible. And for developers, except for those few die-hard JavaScripters, Silverlight will undoubtedly be a source of newfound joy in productivity and empowerment.

Why Write This Book?

So that's all fine and dandy. Silverlight is just awesome. But why bother writing a book about it?

The reason is simple. Silverlight 2 was the first and biggest step toward fundamentally changing the future of web (and, indeed, all) application development, and Silverlight 3 carries that forward. It is one of the first pure Internet (*cloud*, if you will) development platforms. It is the culmination of years of technological evolution toward a new future where computing will truly be ubiquitous. It will be a key enabler in this new world of better user experiences with ubiquitous computing devices.

It is obviously just one piece of that puzzle, but it is a crucial one. The world is moving away from the desktop, and therefore we can't be restricted to it for rich software experiences. We want to help developers make this crucial step toward that future.

Will learning Silverlight make you magically able to develop these great experiences? No. There are other skills to learn and certainly other professionals who will need to take part in making that future. But Silverlight (and platforms like it) is the future of software, and if you don't want to get left behind, this is about as good a place to go next as you can pick.

This book will help you take that step. We propose to cover most, if not all, of this new platform as it stands in its current incarnation. While doubtless, given the rapid nature of change, some of this book will soon become obsolete, nearly all of it will be applicable as the Silverlight platform matures.

You may not need to use Silverlight today, but you will soon. What this book provides both by way of tutorial and reference will be an invaluable guide from seasoned developers and designers. It will help you see past the fluff and the marketing hype to the real challenges and problems that you as a programmer will face in developing applications on the Silverlight platform.

So what are you waiting for? Don't become the next COBOL dinosaur — dive into this book and make yourself relevant now and for years to come!

Who This Book Is For

This book embodies the Wrox philosophy of programmer to programmer. We are experienced programmers writing for other programmers. We wrote the book with the average business application developer in mind. Certainly, others can derive value — anyone trying to build on or even just understand the architectural concerns and realities of Silverlight — but this is at its heart a true *programmer's reference*.

What This Book Covers

While other books on Silverlight may spend inordinate amounts of time on the finer points of shapes, brushes, and styling — the fancy UI glitz that WPF and Silverlight do, indeed, bring to the table — we recognize that most application developers need a more holistic understanding of this new platform and what it offers and does not offer for building real, especially business-oriented, applications. We do cover the UI glitz (which is really great), but at a fundamental level that most devs need; what we strive to do is put that in perspective and offer not only the technical details, but also a sort of wisdom that we hope will help you better build on this platform.

This book, obviously, focuses in on Silverlight 3 (Build 40522), but we cover related technologies and concerns that developers will need to know about when building on Silverlight 3, and, as noted previously, most of what is covered here will remain relevant even as the platform matures.

How This Book Is Structured

This book is broken into four main parts. The first part is an introduction and provides an overview of Silverlight 3 and how to get started with it. It's safe to say that if you read nothing else, you'd probably want to read this part, but the other parts are where this book's value really shines.

Part 2 covers the essentials of what Silverlight 3 gives developers in the box. Its focus is on the presentation core of Silverlight, which is more or less the "new" stuff in Silverlight that most .NET developers will have to learn in terms of new APIs, objects, services, and concepts.

Part 3 builds on the basics from the first parts but does not necessarily presume that you have read it. The purpose of this third part is to walk through the various concerns that an application developer would have in building a real application on Silverlight. This is the real meat of the book. While we do reference relevant parts of an application called *Lumos* throughout, we do not assume that you have read prior chapters in most parts. The book is more like a generic front-to-back application tutorial, so if you only need to read up on or reference how certain application-building concerns (e.g., data binding) can be addressed in Silverlight, you can safely dive into that particular chapter or section with minimal difficulty. The chapters are ordered more or less in terms of how you should think about building applications, starting with architectural, cross-cutting concerns and moving through the other concerns in a manner that would make sense to a developer building a real application on this platform.

Part 4 contains reference Appendixes. These are for your use when you need to consult a specific API. We try to add value here over the MSDN library reference, and certainly we focus in on Silverlight-specific APIs.

The high-level approach we suggest is to read Parts 1 and 2 once through. This will give you a good foundation to start playing around in Silverlight. Part 3 is especially valuable as a holistic application building reference — you can jump to sections you are currently dealing with in the applications you are building; however, it can (and perhaps should) be read straight through to give you a more holistic understanding of what it takes to build solid applications in Silverlight. Part 4 is not intended to be read through; we recommend just using it as needed, but it may offer insights and details that the other parts only touch on, so you shouldn't ignore it!

What You Need to Use This Book

You need your hands and eyes to use this book unless, of course, you have the highly secret audio version! Seriously, we try to list all relevant code along with supplemental text to explain it, so you don't need to lug a computer with you to get value from reading this. We even have color for most of the book to make the code listings that much easier to read and to give you a better sense of what the underlying code results in when run. (This is a rich UI technology, after all!)

But if you do have your computer handy, you can download the samples (or recreate them) using the tools outlined in Chapter 4. In short, there's nothing required that you shouldn't be able to download freely from the Internet.

Conventions

To help you get the most from the text and keep track of what's happening, we've used several conventions throughout the book.

> **Boxes like this one hold important, not-to-be forgotten information that is directly relevant to the surrounding text.**

Notes, tips, hints, tricks, and asides to the current discussion are offset and placed in italics like this.

As for styles in the text:

- ❑ We *highlight* new terms and important words when we introduce them.
- ❑ We show keyboard strokes like this: [Ctrl]+A.
- ❑ We show URLs and code within the text like so: `persistence.properties`.
- ❑ We present code in two different ways:

```
We use a monofont type with no highlighting for most code examples.
We use highlighting to emphasize code that's particularly important in the
present context.
```

Also, Visual Studio's code editor provides a rich color scheme to indicate various parts of code syntax. That's a great tool to help you learn language features in the editor and to help prevent mistakes as you code. To reinforce Visual Studio's colors, the code listings in this book are colorized using colors similar to what you would see on screen in Visual Studio working with the book's code. In order to optimize print clarity, some colors have a slightly different hue in print from what you see on screen. But all of the colors for the code in this book should be close enough to the default Visual Studio colors to give you an accurate representation of the colors.

Source Code

As you work through the examples in this book, you may choose either to type in all the code manually or to use the source code files that accompany the book. All of the source code used in this book is available for download at www.wrox.com. Once at the site, simply locate the book's title (either by using the Search box or by using one of the title lists), and click on the Download Code link on the book's detail page to obtain all the source code for the book. \

> *Because many books have similar titles, you may find it easiest to search by ISBN; this book's ISBN is 978-0-470-38540-1.*

Once you download the code, just decompress it with your favorite compression tool. Alternatively, you can go to the main Wrox code download page at www.wrox.com/dynamic/books/download.aspx to see the code available for this book and all other Wrox books.

Errata

We make every effort to ensure that there are no errors in the text or in the code. However, no one is perfect, and mistakes do occur. If you find an error in one of our books, like a spelling mistake or faulty piece of code, we would be very grateful for your feedback. By sending in errata, you may save another reader hours of frustration, and at the same time, you will be helping us provide even higher quality information.

To find the errata page for this book, go to www.wrox.com and locate the title using the Search box or one of the title lists. Then, on the Book Details page, click on the Book Errata link. On this page, you can view all errata that have been submitted for this book and posted by Wrox editors. A complete book list including links to each book's errata is also available at www.wrox.com/misc-pages/booklist.shtml.

If you don't spot "your" error on the Book Errata page, go to www.wrox.com/contact/techsupport.shtml, and complete the form there to send us the error you have found. We'll check the information and, if appropriate, post a message to the book's Errata page and fix the problem in subsequent editions of the book.

p2p.wrox.com

For author and peer discussion, join the P2P forums at p2p.wrox.com. The forums are a Web-based system for you to post messages relating to Wrox books and related technologies and interact with other readers and technology users. The forums offer a subscription feature to e-mail you topics of interest of your choosing when new posts are made to the forums. Wrox authors, editors, other industry experts, and your fellow readers are present on these forums.

At http://p2p.wrox.com, you will find several different forums that will help you not only as you read this book, but also as you develop your own applications. To join the forums, just follow these steps:

1. Go to p2p.wrox.com and click on the Register link.
2. Read the terms of use and click Agree.

3. Complete the required information to join as well as any optional information you wish to provide, and click Submit.

4. You will receive an e-mail with information describing how to verify your account and complete the joining process.

You can read messages in the forums without joining P2P, but in order to post your own messages, you must join.

Once you join, you can post new messages and respond to messages that other users post. You can read messages at any time on the Web. If you would like to have new messages from a particular forum emailed to you, click on the "Subscribe to This Forum" icon by the forum name in the forum listing.

For more information about how to use the Wrox P2P, be sure to read the P2P FAQs for answers to questions about how the forum software works as well as many common questions specific to P2P and Wrox books. To read the FAQs, click the FAQ link on any P2P page.

Silverlight™ 3

Programmer's Reference

Part I: Getting Started

Introduction to Silverlight

Silverlight 3, the third iteration of the Silverlight platform, continues to deliver on the promise of Adobe Flash–like and Flex-like rich Internet applications (RIAs) built using a standards-based, open approach with HTML and XAML using tools like Visual Studio 2008 and Microsoft Expression Blend. Silverlight 3 adds more excitement to RIA development with the inclusion of a subset of the Base Class Libraries (BCLs) from the .NET Framework, new user interface controls, and new libraries for building line-of-business applications. The result is that not only do you have the rich, XAML markup to describe expressive user interfaces, but you also have the power of the .NET Framework and your language of choice (C#, VB, etc.) to build Silverlight applications. Even with the .NET Framework libraries, Silverlight still retains the cross-browser and cross-platform compatibility that it has had since the beginning. This includes Windows 2000, Windows XP, Windows Vista, Windows 7, Macintosh, and, through the Mono Project, various Linux distributions. You can build a Silverlight application and run it in a Safari Web browser on an Apple Macintosh, while being served up from an Apache Web Server running on Linux. There is a lot to learn about Silverlight, and you'll gain more and more insight with each chapter in this book.

This chapter does two basic things:

- ❑ It gives you an introduction to Silverlight.
- ❑ It sets the groundwork, with the essentials on creating Silverlight applications, that will help you move on to the next chapter and the rest of the book.

What Is Silverlight?

Silverlight is a Web-based platform for building and running RIAs. The Web-based platform part of that equation is essentially the plug-in that runs inside the Web browser. Silverlight applications execute within an ActiveX browser plug-in that installs onto the local machine via the Web browser in the exact same manner that you install Adobe Flash to run Flash-based animations on Web pages. The Silverlight plug-in supports the entire wow factor that you'd expect from an RIA, such as vector-based graphics and animations and full video integration, including Digital Rights Management

(DRM) secured audio/video and hi-definition video, as well as the tools for building rich line-of-business applications. You can boil down the coolness of Silverlight to the following points:

❑ Silverlight is a cross-platform, cross-browser platform for delivering rich interactive applications.

❑ Silverlight 3 applications can be built using Expression Blend, Visual Studio, or Eclipse on Windows, and with Eclipse on Apple Macintosh computers.

❑ Silverlight supports playback of native Windows Media VC-1/WMA (with Digital Rights Management) as well as MPEG-4-based H-264 and AAC audio on PCs and Macs with no dependency on Windows Media Player.

❑ Silverlight supports playback of 720p+ full-screen HD Video.

❑ Using XAML, HTML, JavaScript, C#, VB (or your managed language of choice, including dynamic languages like Ruby and Python), Silverlight delivers rich multimedia, vector graphics, animations, and interactivity beyond what AJAX can deliver.

❑ With the Base Class Libraries (BCLs), you have access to common classes for generics, collections, and threading that you are accustomed to using in Windows client development.

❑ There are more than 60 controls in the toolbox, with many more from third-party vendors.

❑ You can deliver out-of-browser experiences that can run any Silverlight 3 application as a desktop application with complete network detection for graceful exception handling.

❑ The installation package is less than 6 MB on Windows and less than 12 MB on Macintosh.

❑ Almost all of the same XAML created for Silverlight can be used in WPF applications with no changes.

The Silverlight player (or *plug-in*, or *control* — those terms are used interchangeably in the book and you will see those variances when others talk about Silverlight as well) itself is a completely stand-alone environment; there is no dependency version of the .NET Framework on the client or the server to run Silverlight 3 applications. When developing applications for Silverlight 3, you are using tools (like Visual Studio 2008 or Expression Blend) that require or are based on a version of the Common Language Runtime (CLR), but the compiled Intermediate Language (IL) of your Silverlight applications that is parsed by the Silverlight 3 player is not using a specific client version of the .NET Framework. The BCL for Silverlight is entirely self-contained within the player itself. The XAML and BCL used by the Silverlight 3 player are both subsets of their counterparts that are used when building full desktop-based WPF applications.

You might ask why Microsoft is pushing out another Web-based, client-side technology when there is already ASP.NET, ASP.NET AJAX Extensions, and, with CLR 3.5 and Visual Studio 2008, specific project types that target the ASP.NET AJAX Framework. The simple answer is that users are demanding an even richer experience on the Web. Even though AJAX does a lot for improved user experience — the postback nightmare of Web 1.0 is finally going away — it does not do enough. There is demand for a richer, more immersive experience on the Web. This has been accomplished with Windows Presentation Foundation (WPF) on the Windows client side. WPF provides a unified approach to media, documents, and graphics in a single run time. The problem with WPF is that it is a 30-MB run time that runs only on the Windows OS. Microsoft needed to give the same type of experience that WPF offers, only in a cross-platform, cross-browser delivery mechanism. So what Microsoft did was take the concept of a plug-in model like Adobe Flash, mix it with the .NET Framework and the WPF declarative language in XAML, and they came up with a way to develop highly rich, immersive, Web 2.0 applications.

The big picture of Silverlight from an architecture perspective is shown in Figure 1-1. Each area is covered in more detail as you read along in the book.

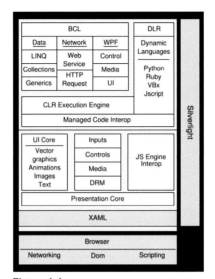

Figure 1-1

As mentioned earlier, Silverlight can conceivably be fully supported across multiple browsers and operating systems. The current status for browser and OS support is identified in the following table:

Browser	Internet Explorer 6, 7, and 8 on Windows
	Safari, Firefox on Windows and Mac
	Firefox 2 and Firefox 3 on Linux
Operating Systems	Windows 2000, Windows 2003, Windows XP, Windows Vista, Windows 7
	Mac OS 10.4/10.5 Intel
	SUSE Linux Enterprise Desktop, openSUSE 11.0, openSUSE 11.1, Ubuntu 8.04, Fedora Core 9 via the Mono Project's Moonlight implementation of the Silverlight 2 player (a Silverlight 3 implementation of the Moonlight player is not available as of this writing).

Silverlight Versions Explained

If you have been following Silverlight, you might be a little confused over the versions that are available:

❑ **Silverlight 1.0** — This is the first version of Silverlight and supports the JavaScript programming model. This means that your language choice is simple — JavaScript. You use JavaScript to interact with Silverlight objects that are executing within the Silverlight player in the browser. There is no managed language support in Silverlight 1.0, which means no BCL for Silverlight 1.0.

❑ **Silverlight 2** — Released in late 2008, Silverlight 2 brought the ability to create RIA applications with the familiar code-behind programming model used in Windows Forms, ASP.NET, and WPF development. Starting with Silverlight 2, you can use any CLR language to code Silverlight applications, and you have the power of the .NET Framework to interact with Silverlight objects. The ability to use the base class libraries and your .NET language of choice to build Silverlight applications truly revolutionized the way developers and designers looked at this new RIA platform.

❑ **Silverlight 3** — This is the third version of Silverlight and the topic of this book, following the release of Silverlight 2 in late 2008. Silverlight 3 supports the familiar code-behind programming model used in Windows Forms, ASP.NET, and WPF development. You can use any CLR language to code Silverlight applications, and you have the power of the .NET Framework to interact with Silverlight objects. Silverlight 3 includes extensive enhancements to Silverlight 2 for building line-of-business applications as well as richer support for graphics and media.

Silverlight uses an auto-update model for the player. When a new version of Silverlight is released, the player running in the browser is updated to the latest version automatically. There is also the commitment of backward compatibility, so your applications will not break when the player moves from version 1.0 to 2, or 2 to 3, and so on.

Application Development Scenarios

When building Silverlight applications, there are two basic scenarios that occur:

❑ Your entire application is written in Silverlight, the player takes up 100 percent of the height and width of the browser, and all UI interaction is done through Silverlight.

❑ You implement an "Islands of Richness" scenario, in which your application is an ASP.NET application (or any other type of HTML-rendered application), and you build islands of your UI with Silverlight. Thus, you are adding richness to your web applications but not building the entire interaction using Silverlight.

I see the "Islands of Richness" scenario as being a very common way for Silverlight to find its way into most applications. Silverlight is a simple way to add audio, video, or interactive data visualization to a Web page without having to rebuild or re-design existing applications on a new platform. The area surrounded with the red box in Figure 1-2 is an example of an "Islands of Richness" scenario in which Silverlight has been added to an existing web application. In this case, the image strip is a Silverlight control that will play a video in-page when an item is clicked on. Silverlight 3 enhances the "Islands of

Richness" scenarios by allowing multiple Silverlight plug-ins and an easy way to communicate with each other in the browser. This also works across browsers; for example, a Silverlight 3 application running in a Firefox browser can talk to a Silverlight 3 application running in Internet Explorer 8 on the same machine.

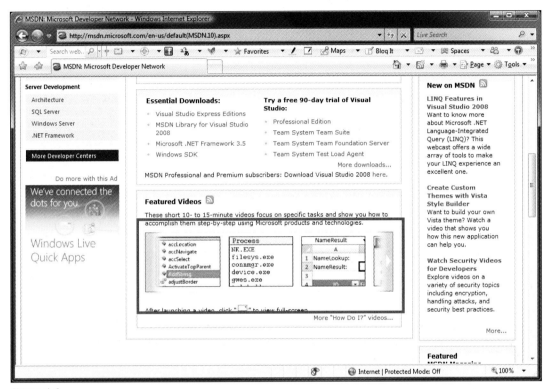

Figure 1-2

Getting the Silverlight Plug-In

The first time you navigate to a Web page that contains a Silverlight application, the Silverlight player is not installed automatically; the installation is similar to the Adobe Flash experience. There is a nonintrusive image on the page where the Silverlight content is placed to run that gives a link to download the player. Silverlight has two different prompts for installation — the standard install and the in-place install.

In a *standard install*, the Get Microsoft Silverlight image tells you that you need to install Silverlight to complete the experience on the Web page you have arrived at. Figure 1-3 illustrates a page with the standard install images.

Once you click on the Get Microsoft Silverlight Installation image, one of two scenarios takes place. You are taken to the Silverlight Installation page on the Microsoft site, as Figure 1-4 demonstrates.

Figure 1-3

Figure 1-4

Or you are prompted to install Silverlight *in place* with a download prompt, as shown in Figure 1-5.

After the Silverlight player is installed, you never have to install it again. Silverlight also has built into it the knowledge of updates, so once a new version of Silverlight is available, you are asked if you would like to install the update to get the latest version of the player. Once you refresh the browser, the Silverlight content will be rendered correctly in the browser, as Figure 1-6 shows.

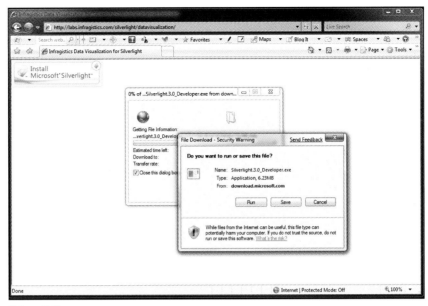

Figure 1-5

Figure 1-6

Getting the Silverlight SDK

To build Silverlight applications, you need more than the Silverlight player. If you have not arrived at a page where you are prompted to install the Silverlight run time, you can easily get it on the Silverlight SDK page. There are also supporting files, help files, samples, and quick starts in the Silverlight Software Development Kit (SDK), which will give you the files you need to start building Silverlight applications. To get the SDK, go to www.silverlight.net/getstarted/default.aspx, as shown in Figure 1-7.

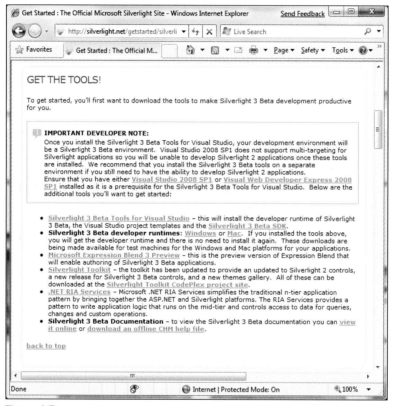

Figure 1-7

On the Get Started page, you can download all of the tools that you need to create Silverlight 3 applications:

- ❑ Silverlight run times for Mac and Windows operating systems
- ❑ Silverlight tools for Visual Studio 2008
- ❑ The latest version of Microsoft Expression Blend
- ❑ A trial version of Visual Studio 2008

More importantly, this page has links to dozens of videos, tutorials, and samples that will help you learn Silverlight.

Building Silverlight Applications

Now that you have the Silverlight player installed and you know how to get the tools for Visual Studio that will give you the project templates, you can start building Silverlight applications. There are several ways to create Silverlight applications:

❑ Visual Studio 2008 Silverlight project templates, which include Silverlight Application, Silverlight Navigation Application, and Silverlight Class Library, as well as Silverlight Business Application if you have .NET RIA Services installed

❑ Expression Blend 3

❑ Eclipse using the Eclipse plug-in. There is an Eclipse plug-in for both Windows- and Apple Macintosh–based operating systems.

In the next chapter, you will get a better understanding of the details for how to build applications using Visual Studio 2008 and Expression Blend.

Silverlight 3 Tour

Silverlight 3 continues the improvements that Silverlight 2 delivered over Silverlight 1.0. In the next section, we'll look at some of the more important features of Silverlight 3, including:

❑ XAML

❑ .NET Framework support

❑ Graphics and animations

❑ Page layout and design

❑ User interface controls

❑ Audio and video

❑ Local data storage

❑ Out-of-browser capability

❑ Navigation Framework

❑ Ink support

❑ Network access

❑ Data binding

❑ Deep Zoom technology

Throughout the book, you will learn about each of the items listed in much more detail. The following sections are designed to set the stage for what's to come as you explore the full capability of Silverlight 3.

XAML

If you are not familiar with WPF, you are probably not familiar with XAML. Since the dawn of Visual Studio, there has always been code and user interface design separation. This means that a developer can write code, while a designer just works on the design and layout aspects of an application. This had never been realized, mostly because developers and designers were always using different tools and different languages. With the introduction of XAML, however, there was finally a unified markup that could not only describe what a control is and how it fits into a page but also how layout and, more importantly, the overall look and feel of the controls on a page are defined. A designer can use XAML to create a mockup of a page or an application, and a developer can take that XAML markup and use it directly in his project files. Because partial classes and code-behind files in Visual Studio 2008 allow you to separate the code logic from the layout and control definitions, using XAML gives you the opportunity to have this separation of the design from the code.

XAML elements are objects that map to classes in the Silverlight run time. So when you declare a XAML `TextBlock` like this:

```
<TextBlock />
```

you are actually creating a new instance of the `TextBlock` class like this:

```
TextBlock t = new TextBlock();
```

The following code demonstrates a XAML snippet from a Silverlight application that shows *Hello World* in a `TextBlock`:

```
<Canvas>
    <TextBlock>Hello World</TextBlock>
</Canvas>
```

The next code listing shows how the XAML can get more complex, demonstrating adding animations to the `TextBlock` element. In this example, a `RotateTransform` is being applied to a `TextBlock` control via a `DoubleAnimation` in a `StoryBoard` object. This action is triggered when the `UserControl` loads, through the `RoutedEvent Canvas.Loaded`. If you run the XAML, you will see that the text *Hello World* rotates in a 360-degree circle.

In Chapter 9, you will learn how animations work in Silverlight and how they are used to bring your application to life in the Silverlight player.

```
<StackPanel Margin="4"
            HorizontalAlignment="Center"
            Orientation="Horizontal">
    <TextBlock Width="200" Height="150"
               FontSize="24">Hello World

        <TextBlock.Triggers>
            <EventTrigger RoutedEvent="Canvas.Loaded">
                <EventTrigger.Actions>
                    <BeginStoryboard>
                        <Storyboard BeginTime="0"
                                    RepeatBehavior="Forever">
                            <DoubleAnimation
```

```
                                        Storyboard.TargetName="rotate"
                                        Storyboard.TargetProperty="Angle"
                                        To="360"
                                        Duration="0:0:10"/>
                            </Storyboard>
                        </BeginStoryboard>
                    </EventTrigger.Actions>
                </EventTrigger>
            </TextBlock.Triggers>

            <TextBlock.RenderTransform>
                <RotateTransform x:Name="rotate"
                                 Angle="0"
                                 CenterX="300"
                                 CenterY="200"/>
            </TextBlock.RenderTransform>
        </TextBlock>
    </StackPanel>
```

In Chapter 2, you will get a more in-depth explanation of XAML and how you can use it to define and create your Silverlight applications. You will also be getting your fair share of XAML throughout the book, because it is how you will create most of the examples and applications that we have created. Tools like Microsoft Expression Blend and Visual Studio 2008 are all Rapid Application Development (RAD) tools that you can use to create your Silverlight applications. As you will learn when you start building Silverlight applications using Visual Studio 2008, Microsoft Expression Blend is the only tool that gives you a nice design-time experience, where you can drag-and-drop controls onto the design surface and switch between the designer view and the XAML view. Visual Studio 2010 will have rich support for RAD development of Silverlight 3 applications. At the time of this writing, Visual Studio 2010 is still in beta. Besides using Expression Blend or Visual Studio 2008, you can look to other XAML tools like XAMLPad or Kaxaml to help you learn XAML. In Chapter 4, you will learn more of the specifics on building Silverlight 3 applications using Visual Studio.

.NET Framework Support

Two key aspects of Silverlight 3, and probably the most exciting aspects of this technology, are its support for the CLR and BCL of the .NET Framework. Although they are not the exact set of class libraries you are familiar with using on the desktop and the CLR might handle memory management and optimizations slightly differently than on the desktop or server, the fundamental capabilities of the .NET Framework do exist for you to use to build rich Silverlight applications.

Execution of content targeting the Silverlight player is handled by the CoreCLR. The CoreCLR is a smaller, refactored version of the CLR used in full .NET desktop applications. Although the Microsoft Intermediate Language (MSIL) is exactly the same between the CLRs, the CoreCLR is stripped of the unnecessary scenarios that are not needed for Silverlight 3 development. The CLR is still responsible for managing memory in Silverlight applications, as well as enforcing the common type system (CTS). Some examples of the differences in the CoreCLR versus the full CRL are:

❑   The JIT Compiler in the CoreCLR is enhanced for fast startup time, while the full CLR is enhanced for more complex optimizations.

❑   In ASP.NET applications, the garbage collection mode is tuned for multiple worker threads, while the CoreCLR is tuned for interactive applications.

Both the CoreCLR and CLR can run in the same process; therefore, for example, you can have an embedded Silverlight player running in an Office Business application that also includes a full .NET 3.5 plug-in. The isolation of the CoreCLR is why you can run Silverlight applications on machines that do not have any versions of the .NET Framework installed; this is further highlighted by the fact that Silverlight can run on Macintosh operating systems.

The namespaces that contain all of the classes that you interact with in your Code window are the Base Class Libraries, as you have learned. The Silverlight BCL does not contain namespaces and classes that do not make sense for client development, such as code-access security, ASP.NET Web Server–specific classes, and many others.

Chapter 3 delves into the specifics of the CoreCLR.

Graphics and Animations

A big part of why Silverlight is an exciting technology is that it provides a rich, vector-based drawing system as well as support for complex animations. Some of the new additions in Silverlight 3 include:

❑   Perspective 3D graphics

❑   Pixel-Shader effects, including `Blur` and `DropShadow`

❑   Bitmap Caching to increase the rendering performance

❑   Animation effects like `Spring` and `Bounce`

❑   Local font usage for rendering text

For vector-based drawing, Silverlight supports `Geometry` and `Shape` objects that include support for rendering shapes, such as ellipse, line, path, polygon, polyline, and rectangle. These classes give you the ability to render any type of visual display. For example, the following XAML displays an image in its normal, square shape:

```
<Canvas>
    <Image
        Source="Images/elk.jpg"
        Width="200" Height="150">
    </Image>
</Canvas>
```

Using the `EllipseGeomtry` class, you can clip the image into whatever shape you desire. This XAML clips the image into an oval:

```
<Canvas>
    <Image
        Source="Images/elk.jpg"
        Width="200" Height="150">
        <Image.Clip>
            <EllipseGeometry
                RadiusX="100"
                RadiusY="75"
                Center="100,75"/>
```

```
        </Image.Clip>
      </Image>
    </Canvas>
```

with the results displayed in Figure 1-8.

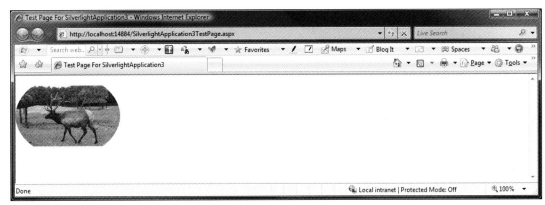

Figure 1-8

Once you render your geometries or shapes into something meaningful, you can use `Brushes`, `VideoBrushes`, or `Transforms` to further give life to your UI rendering. The following XAML takes a basic `TextBlock` and adds a `LinearGradientBrush` for some nice special effects:

```
<TextBlock
  Canvas.Top="100"
  FontFamily="Verdana"
  FontSize="32"
  FontWeight="Bold">
    Linear Gradient Brush
    <TextBlock.RenderTransform>
      <ScaleTransform ScaleY="4.0" />
    </TextBlock.RenderTransform>
    <TextBlock.Foreground>
      <LinearGradientBrush StartPoint="0,0" EndPoint="1,1">
        <GradientStop Color="Red" Offset="0.0" />
        <GradientStop Color="Blue" Offset="0.2" />
        <GradientStop Color="Green" Offset="0.4" />
        <GradientStop Color="Olive" Offset="0.6" />
        <GradientStop Color="DodgerBlue" Offset="0.8" />
        <GradientStop Color="OrangeRed" Offset="1.0" />
      </LinearGradientBrush>
    </TextBlock.Foreground>
</TextBlock>
```

You can also use an `ImageBrush` to paint an image on your `TextBlock`, as the following code demonstrates:

```
<StackPanel>
    <!--TextBlock without an ImageBrush -->
```

```
    <TextBlock
        FontSize="72"
        FontFamily="Verdana"
        FontStyle="Italic"
        FontWeight="Bold">
            Rhino Image
    </TextBlock>

    <!--TextBlock with an ImageBrush -->
    <TextBlock
        FontSize="72"
        FontFamily="Verdana"
        FontStyle="Italic"
        FontWeight="Bold">
            Rhino Image
        <!-- Add an Image as the foreground -->
        <TextBlock.Foreground>
        <ImageBrush ImageSource="Images/rhino.jpg"
                Stretch="Fill"/>
        </TextBlock.Foreground>
    </TextBlock>
</StackPanel>
```

The resulting content looks like Figure 1-9.

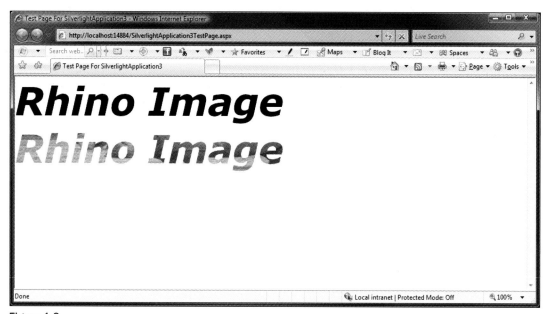

Figure 1-9

Later in this section, you will see a `VideoBrush` applied to text. In Chapter 9, we'll cover graphics and animations in full detail.

Page Layout and Design

Silverlight 3 includes several options for doing rich, resolution independent layout using a Canvas, DockPanel, Grid, StackPanel, and WrapPanel element. These five major layout panels can be described as:

❑ Canvas — An absolute positioning panel that gives you an area within which you can position child elements by coordinates relative to the Canvas area. A Canvas can parent any number of child Canvas objects.

❑ DockPanel — Is used to arrange a set of objects around the edges of a panel. You specify where a child element is located in the DockPanel with the Dock property.

❑ Grid — Similar to an HTML table, a Grid is a set of columns and rows that can contain child elements.

❑ StackPanel — A panel that automatically arranges its child elements into horizontal or vertical rows

❑ WrapPanel — Allows the arrangement of elements in a vertical or horizontal list and have elements automatically wrap to the next row or column when the height or width limit of the panel is reached.

One you decide how you are going to lay out your page using one of the layout types, you can use other means of positioning individual elements as well. For example, you can change margins, set the ZOrder or Border of an object, or perform RotateTranforms to change the position of an object. Chapter 7 covers all layout options in greater detail. Here we'll look at the Canvas object and how it behaves.

The Canvas essentially becomes the container for other child elements, and all objects are positioned using their X- and Y-coordinates relative to their location in the parent canvas. This is done with the Canvas.Top and Canvas.Left attached properties, which provide the resolution-independent pixel value of a control's X- and Y-coordinates. The following code shows a Canvas object with several child elements absolutely positioned within the Canvas.

```
<Canvas>
    <Rectangle
    Canvas.Top ="30"
    Canvas.Left="30"
    Fill="Blue"
    Height="100" Width="100"/>

    <Rectangle
    Canvas.Top ="75"
    Canvas.Left="130"
    Fill="Red"
    Height="100" Width="100"/>

    <Ellipse
    Canvas.Top ="100"
    Canvas.Left="30"
    Fill="Green"
    Height="100" Width="100"/>
</Canvas>
```

This XAML is explained in more detail in Figure 1-10, which shows the location of the objects in the canvas.

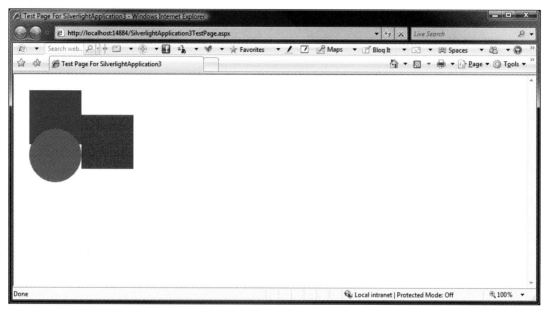

Figure 1-10

In the following example from the SDK, you can see how a DockPanel can be configured to return the results shown in Figure 1-11.

```
<StackPanel x:Name="LayoutRoot" Background="White">
    <TextBlock Margin="5" Text="Dock Panel" />
    <Border BorderBrush="Red" BorderThickness="2" >
        <controls:DockPanel LastChildFill="true"
                            Height="265">
            <Button Content="Dock: Left"
                    controls:DockPanel.Dock ="Left" />
            <Button Content="Dock: Right"
                    controls:DockPanel.Dock ="Right" />
            <Button Content="Dock: Top"
                    controls:DockPanel.Dock ="Top" />
            <Button Content="Dock: Bottom"
                    controls:DockPanel.Dock ="Bottom" />
            <Button Content="Last Child" />
        </controls:DockPanel>
    </Border>
</StackPanel>
```

In Figure 1-11, notice the position of the elements based on the TextBlock and Border controls that wrap the DockPanel in the XAML.

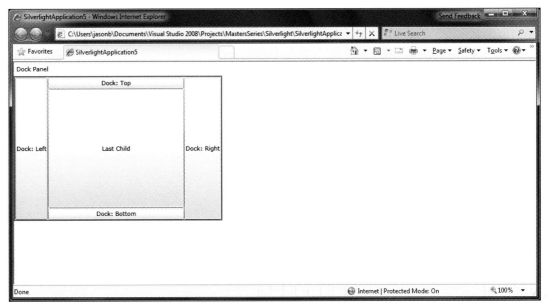

Figure 1-11

User Interface Controls

Silverlight 3 adds an even greater number of controls to the Toolbox for creating user interfaces. The Toolbox in Visual Studio 2008 is now filled with controls that can be dragged onto forms to build the user interface. The following controls are included for use by the core Silverlight 3 player:

AutoCompleteBox	DatePicker	Label	StackPanel
Border	DockPanel	ListBox	TabControl
Button	Expander	MediaElement	TextBlock
Calendar	Grid	MultiScaleImage	TextBox
Canvas	GridSplitter	Popup	TreeView
CheckBox	HeaderedContentControl	RadioButton	ViewBox
ContentControl	HeaderedItemsControl	RepeatButton	WrapPanel
DataForm	HyperlinkButton	ScrollBar	
DataGrid	Image	ScrollViewer	
DataPager	InkPresenter	Slider	

In addition to the aforementioned controls, the Silverlight Toolkit, which is a separate download from CodePlex, contains several very useful additions to the core list.

When working with any of the controls, remember they are just like any other control model: The XAML controls in Silverlight can be instantiated in code, and properties can be retrieved or set on them. Over the next several chapters, you will learn about the controls in more detail, as well as how they can be used with Visual Studio 2008 or Expression Blend.

Using Media in Silverlight

One could argue that the entire reason for Silverlight was to provide rich, multimedia experiences on Web pages, which essentially means audio and video on Web pages. If you take a look at the top 100 trafficked web sites on the Internet, almost all of them have video playing on the home page or use video prevalently throughout. Silverlight 3 continues to add first-class media capability to the player.

Adding Video to Web Pages

To add video or audio to a Web page, you set the `Source` property on the `MediaElement` object. The following code demonstrates playing the video file car.wmv automatically when the canvas is loaded:

```
<UserControl x:Class="SilverlightApplication3.Page"
    xmlns="http://schemas.microsoft.com/winfx/2006/xaml/presentation"
    xmlns:x="http://schemas.microsoft.com/winfx/2006/xaml"
    Width="600" Height="300">
    <Grid x:Name="LayoutRoot" Background="White">
        <MediaElement Source="Images/video1.wmv" />
    </Grid>
</UserControl>
```

The `Source` property is the URI of a valid video or audio file. In the preceding code example, the source file is located in the deployment directory of your Silverlight application. Your media files can be located in various locations, including the web-site folder structure you are running the page from, or from a remote site. In either case, in order to maintain cross-platform support, you must use "/" in place of "\" in your URIs. For example:

```
<MediaElement Source="..\..\car.wmv"></MediaElement>
```

should read:

```
<MediaElement Source="../../car.wmv"></MediaElement>
```

If the `Source` property is pointing to a file on a Windows Media Server using the MMS protocol, the player will automatically attempt to stream the video down to the client. The default behavior is a progressive download, which means that the audio or video will begin playing immediately and background-load as you are playing the media. The drawback to progressive downloads is that even if you pause the video, it still downloads the media file, even if you never intended to continue playing it. With streaming media, the only data that is downloaded is the data that you actually play, which is a more efficient use of network resources.

Microsoft Live Services offers a free media streaming service for Silverlight applications, named Silverlight Streaming Services. *Using Silverlight Streaming Services, anyone can upload up to 4 GB of Silverlight content to stream to their pages. To get a free account for this service, visit* https:// silverlight.live.com.

Supported Audio and Video Formats

The `MediaElement` supports the Advanced Stream Redirector (ASX) playlist file format, as well as the audio and video formats listed in the following table:

Video Formats	Audio formats
WMV1: Windows Media Video 7	WMA 7: Windows Media Audio 7
WMV2: Windows Media Video 8	WMA 8: Windows Media Audio 8
WMV3: Windows Media Video 9	WMA 9: Windows Media Audio 9
WMVA: Windows Media Video Advanced Profile, non-VC-1	WMA 10: Windows Media Audio 10
WMVC1: Windows Media Video Advanced Profile, VC-1	AAC: Advanced Audio Coding — Can only be used for progressive download, smooth streaming, and adaptive streaming. AAC is the LC variety and supports sampling frequencies up to 48 kHz.
H.264 — Can only be used for progressive download, smooth streaming, and adaptive streaming. Supports Base, Main, and High Profiles.	MP3: ISO/MPEG Layer-3 with the following features:
	❑ Input — ISO/MPEG Layer-3 data stream
	❑ Channel configurations — Mono, stereo
	❑ Sampling frequencies — 8, 11.025, 12, 16, 22.05, 24, 32, 44.1, and 48 kHz
	❑ Bitrates — 8–320 Kbps, variable bitrate
	❑ Limitations — "Free format mode" (ISO/IEC 11172-3, subclause 2.4.2.3) is not supported.

Local Data Storage

Using the *isolated storage* concept in the full .NET Framework, you can use a client-side cache location to store data. This means that you can take commonly needed data, and, instead of always having to go back to the server to retrieve it, you can store it locally and access it locally. Examples might be a list of states or countries, or buddy lists for instant messenger clients. This data is commonly needed for fast access but does not change often enough to warrant constant round-trips back to the server to retrieve it.

By default, Silverlight gives you 1 MB of local storage. This can be increased by prompting the user to allow for more local storage or can be accessed via the Silverlight Configuration screen. As its name implies, this is isolated storage, so you cannot access the end-user's filesystem or do anything that would break the partial trust sandbox that Silverlight runs in. Storage is granted per application, so, for example, you might have `www.someapp.com`, which is using 10 MB of storage, and another application running on the same client computer from a different domain that has its own 20 MB of isolated storage. The storage areas are independent of each other; there is no limit to the number of applications that can have isolated storage on a client machine.

Out-of-Browser Experiences

With the new Out-of-Browser capability of any Silverlight application, an end-user can save your application to the desktop on their Windows or Apple Macintosh computer. There is no need to install any special assemblies or controls to make this work — it is part of the native Silverlight 3 experience. With the new network detection APIs in Silverlight 3, an out-of-browser application can intelligently determine if it is connected to the network and react accordingly. In Chapter 11, you'll learn how easy it is to actually create this out-of-browser experience.

Navigation Framework

Silverlight 3 adds two new controls that enable complete browser-journal back/forward integration with your application. Using the new `Frame` and `Page` controls, you can partition your views into separate XAML files (instead of separate `UserControl` objects as you did in Silverlight 2) and navigate to each view as simply as you would previously a Web page. The Navigation Framework also allows you to implement deep linking support in your Silverlight application, which builds on the SEO (Search Engine Optimization) enhancements added in Silverlight 3.

The following XAML shows the navigation control added to a `UserControl`:

```
<navigation:Frame x:Name="Frame"
                  Source="/Views/HomePage.xaml"
                  HorizontalContentAlignment="Stretch"
                  VerticalContentAlignment="Stretch"
                  Padding="15,10,15,10"
                  Background="White"/>
```

And the following code demonstrates the `Navigate` method of the `Frame` class, which is how you move from `Page` to `Page`.

```
private void NavButton_Click(object sender, RoutedEventArgs e)
{
    Button navigationButton = sender as Button;
    String goToPage = navigationButton.Tag.ToString();
    this.Frame.Navigate(new Uri(goToPage, UriKind.Relative));
}
```

As well as `Navigate`, the `Frame` class includes other useful methods such as `Navigated`, `NavigationFailed`, and `NavigationStopped` that give you complete control over the navigation life cycle of your `Page` object. Chapter 11 talks more about the `Navigation` and `Frame` classes.

Annotation and Ink

Like WPF, Silverlight has full support for ink input in the player. Using the `InkPresenter` object, you can give users an input area where they can use the mouse or an input device to handwrite. Using the application interface for the `InkPresenter` object, the application developer collects the `Stroke` objects that are written and persists them to a location on the server for later use. An example of where ink might be cool on a Web page is a simple blog, where text and ink can combine to create a great visual output for whatever the blog is about. The XAML in the following code shows how to create an InkPresenter object:

```
<InkPresenter x:Name="inkInput" Cursor="Stylus"
    MouseLeftButtonDown="inkInput_MouseLeftButtonDown"
    MouseMove="inkInput_MouseMove"
    MouseLeftButtonUp="inkInput_MouseLeftButtonUp"/>
```

Notice that events are wired up for the various mouse behaviors. Each action of the mouse — the Move, LeftButtonUp, and LeftButtonDown — has a method in the code-behind that acts on the strokes of the input device. The following code gives an example of how you would collect the strokes from the InkPresenter:

```
private Stroke MyStroke = null;

private void inkInput_MouseLeftButtonDown
    (object sender, MouseButtonEventArgs e)
{
    inkInput.CaptureMouse();
    StylusPointCollection
        MyStylusPointCollection = new StylusPointCollection();
    MyStylusPointCollection.Add
        (e.StylusDevice.GetStylusPoints(inkInput));
    MyStroke = new Stroke(MyStylusPointCollection);
    inkInput.Strokes.Add(MyStroke);
}

private void inkInput_MouseMove
    (object sender, MouseEventArgs e)
{
    if (MyStroke != null)
    {
        MyStroke.StylusPoints.Add
            (e.StylusDevice.GetStylusPoints(inkInput));
        txtBlock.Text =
            "" + e.StylusDevice.GetStylusPoints(inkInput)[0].X;
        txtBlock.Text =
            "" + e.StylusDevice.GetStylusPoints(inkInput)[0].Y;
    }

}

private void inkInput_MouseLeftButtonUp
    (object sender, MouseButtonEventArgs e)
{
    MyStroke = null;
}
```

Once you have the ink data collected, you can store it locally on the client machine, put it into a database, or even save the ink as an image.

Accessing the Network

To access network resources in Silverlight, you have the classes in the System.Net namespaces and the System.Net.Sockets namespace. The namespace you choose would depend on the type of network access you are trying to achieve. For basic HTTP or HTTPS access to URI-based resources, you can use the WebClient class in the System.Net namespace. Some examples of this type of network access are:

❑   Retrieving XML, JSON, RSS, or Atom data formats from a URI then parsing it on the client

❑   Downloading resources such as media or data to the browser cache

Using WebClient, you can perform the types of asynchronous operations that are common in browser-based applications. The following code demonstrates a simple method that grabs an image file from a network resource and downloads it to the browser cache:

```
void DownloadFile(string imgPart)
{
    WebClient wc = new WebClient();
    wc.OpenReadCompleted +=
        new OpenReadCompletedEventHandler
        (wc_OpenReadCompleted);
    wc.OpenReadAsync(new Uri("imgs.zip",
        UriKind.Relative), imgPart);
}
```

If you need more flexibility in how you access HTTP or HTTPS resources, you can use the HttpWebRequest and HttpWebResponse classes.

If you need more direct and constant access to network resources or if you are working in a situation in which multiple clients are "listening" for the same server data, you would choose to use the classes in the System.Net.Sockets namespace. Although both Sockets and WebClient allow asynchronous communication using the TCP protocol, Sockets gives you the ability to write "push-style" applications, where the server can communicate with the client in a more client-server manner. Imagine the unnecessary overhead when using basic AJAX timers (polling) to look for updated data on the server. If you were using sockets instead of this type of timer-based polling, you would reduce the amount of wasted bandwidth and would achieve tighter control of the data passing between the client and the server.

No matter how you choose to work with the network, both the System.Net and System.Net.Sockets namespaces support the ability to access network resources from other URIs than the originating domain. By default, a Silverlight 3 application can always access resources from its originating domain. Using a policy file, an application can access resources from different domains from the one containing its original URL. This cross-domain access is controlled by policy files that dictate the type of network domain access an application has. For WebClient requests, the same format used by Adobe Flash is supported. The next code is an example of a crossdomain.xml file:

```
<?xml version="1.0"?>
<! DOCTYPE cross-domain-policy
    SYSTEM "http://www.macromedia.com/xml/dtds/cross-domain-policy.dtd">
<cross-domain-policy>
    <allow-access-from domain="*" />
</cross-domain-policy>
```

In Chapters 11 and 13, you will be fully exposed to various ways of accessing network resources.

Data Binding

Similarly to the data-binding features in WPF, Silverlight supports data-bound controls, XAML markup extensions, and support for data context binding. Most of the time, your bindings will be set up in XAML, which is where the markup extensions come into play. In the following XAML, the Text property of the TextBlock element is using the Binding markup extension to bind the Title field from the data source:

```
<TextBlock x:Name="Title"
 Text="{Binding Title, Mode=OneWay}" />
```

The field Title from the original data source is retrieved from the data content of the control's parent element; in this case, the TextBlock could be contained in a Canvas or Grid object. Once you set the DataContext property for the parent element, the data contained in that object is available for binding to anything it contains. A more complete example of this data binding looks like this:

```
<Canvas x:Name="rootCanvas" Background="White" >
    <TextBlock x:Name="Title"
    Text="{Binding Title, Mode=OneWay }" />

    <TextBlock x:Name="Name"
    Text="{Binding Title, Mode=OneWay }" />
</Canvas>
```

You would then set the context in the code like this:

```
LayoutRoot.DataContext = dataList;
```

where the dataList object is an object that contains the data you are binding to the controls. In the case of simple TextBlock objects, you would have to handle the navigation between elements yourself. If you want a richer, tabular data display, you could use the Grid that is included with Silverlight. The XAML for the DataGrid control looks like this:

```
<data:DataGrid x:Name="dataGrid1"
    Height="120" Width="450"
    AutoGenerateColumns="True" />
```

The same dataList object can be bound to the grid in code like this:

```
dataGrid1.ItemsSource = dataList;
```

All of the binding could be accomplished in code, but using the combination of XAML and code gives you greater flexibility when building Silverlight applications. An interesting area of data binding in Silverlight is where the data actually comes from. Since the Silverlight player is a complete client-side solution, you are not creating connections to SQL Server or other data sources, then dumping that data into a data set in your code-behind. You are going to be using technologies like WCF to access services on the Internet and then putting the data you retrieve into objects that are bound to controls in Silverlight. In Chapter 14, you will learn about the various types of data access, how to interact with different data formats, and how the data-binding mechanism works in Silverlight.

Deep Zoom Graphics

Deep Zoom is a multi-scale image-rendering technology that partitions a very large image, or set of images, into smaller *tiles* that are rendered on demand to the Silverlight player. When an image is first loaded, it is in the lowest-resolution tiles. As the user zooms into the image using the mouse wheel or keyboard, higher-resolution images are loaded based on the area that is being zoomed into. The wow factor of Deep Zoom was shown off at Mix '08 in April 2008. The Hard Rock Cafe created a Deep Zoom collection of their memorabilia. You can explore the site yourself at `http://memorabilia.hardrock.com`. In Figure 1-12, you can see the initial page loaded into the browser.

Once you start zooming in with the mouse wheel, you can get from the lower-resolution images to jthe higher-resolution images. Figure 1-13 shows the detail of a portion of the larger image seen in Figure 1-12.

To build a Deep Zoom application, you don't even need Visual Studio or Expression Blend. You can do it all with the Deep Zoom Composer tool. To get a complete tutorial on how to use the Deep Zoom Composer and integrate your own images into Deep Zoom, visit this URL: `http://community.infragistics.com/redirects/silverlight/deepzoom.aspx`.

Figure 1-12

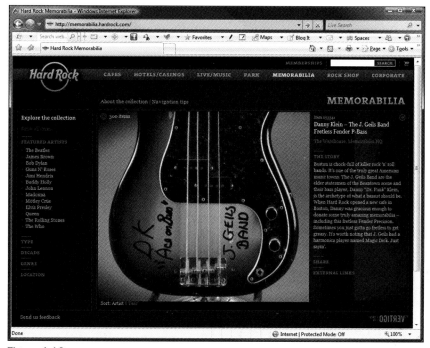

Figure 1-13

Summary

Silverlight brings a lot to the table for rich Internet application development. It has progressed from its original release into much more than a simple media player. Silverlight is a platform for developing rich line-of-business applications that have the data and input capability of ASP.NET with the media and interactive capabilities usually reserved for Adobe Flex applications.

2

XAML Basics

Chapter 1 exposed you to the fundamentals of building Silverlight applications. You were introduced to XAML, which is the glue between the interactive user interfaces you create and managed code you write. This chapter explores more details of XAML and will give you the basics that you need to understand the richer XAML concepts throughout the book.

Introducing XAML

As was indicated in Chapter 1, XAML finally provides a unified markup that can describe not only what a control is and how it fits into a page, but also how layout and, more importantly, the overall look and feel of the controls on a page are defined. A designer can use XAML to create a mockup of a page or an application, and a developer can take that XAML markup and use it directly in his project files. Because partial classes and code-behind files in Visual Studio allow you to separate the code logic from the layout and control definitions, using XAML gives the opportunity to have this separation of the design from the code. Let's look at the following XAML example, which demonstrates an animation on a `TextBlock` element:

```
<Canvas
    Width="640" Height="480"
    Background="White">
        <Canvas.Triggers>
            <EventTrigger RoutedEvent="Canvas.Loaded">
                <BeginStoryboard>
                    <Storyboard x:Name="Timeline1"/>
                </BeginStoryboard>
            </EventTrigger>
        </Canvas.Triggers>

        <TextBlock Width="349" Height="67"
            Canvas.Top="140" Text="Hello World"
            TextWrapping="Wrap"
            RenderTransformOrigin="0.5,0.5"
            x:Name="textBlock">
            <TextBlock.RenderTransform>
```

```
                <TransformGroup>
                    <ScaleTransform ScaleX="1" ScaleY="1"/>
                </TransformGroup>
            </TextBlock.RenderTransform>
        </TextBlock>
    </Canvas>
```

This XAML may seem daunting, but learning XAML is like learning HTML; there are a lot of details, but for most of your applications, you are using tools to build the XAML and not hand-coding it yourself. The reason that it is important to understand XAML is the same reason that it is important to know HTML if you are a web developer. There are times when you need to inspect the HTML of a file to understand or debug a page, just as there will be times when you are looking at XAML and you need to understand why something is happening in your Silverlight application.

Microsoft Expression Blend and Visual Studio are both Rapid Application Development (RAD) tools that you can use to create the XAML in your Silverlight applications. However, as of this writing, Microsoft Expression Blend is really the only tool that gives you a nice design-time experience, where you can drag-and-drop controls onto the design surface and switch between the designer view and the XAML view as you design your user interface. Your options will get better as the platform and tools mature, but it's important that you understand XAML now so you can save time later if you run into problems and really need to dig into larger, more complex XAML files.

Before we delve deeper into XAML, there is an issue that's important to understand: When using XAML in Silverlight versus using XAML in WPF, not all things are created equal. Because Silverlight is optimized for speed and the fast delivery of rich, interactive applications to the browser, the XAML available to Silverlight applications is a subset of the XAML that can be used in a full desktop-based WPF application. In WPF, each XAML element maps directly to a corresponding class in the .NET Framework. In Silverlight, the XAML parser is part of the Silverlight player, so there is no dependency on the .NET Framework for it to run. To you this means that if you are working in WPF now and you are wondering why certain things are not working in Silverlight, you need to reference Appendix A, which lists all of the objects that are available to you in Silverlight. The list is shorter than what a WPF developer expects. Trade-offs needed to be made in order to keep a small run time, so the XAML available is not as complete.

Silverlight XAML Basics

XAML is a case-sensitive declarative language, based on XML that lets you design the user interface of a Silverlight application in descriptive markup. Similar to the way ASP.NET or Windows Forms work with the concept of a code-behind file, XAML files map to managed-code partial classes where you can write in your language of choice. XAML is important for the evolution of how you create the user interface because the user interface is separate from the code files. This means that a designer using tools like Expression Blend can create a UI using XAML, and that same XAML can be used in Visual Studio and integrated into a larger project. As a matter of fact, Expression Blend and Visual Studio share the same project structure, so the .csproj and .vbproj files can be opened by either tool. The ability for a designer to express a user interface and have it directly used without alteration in an application is something that has never been possible with Microsoft tools. There has always been a large amount of throwaway art work, because developers would get a mockup and try to duplicate it.

XAML files have a .xaml extension and, at first glance, might be confused with an XML data file. This makes sense, because XML (Extensible Markup Language) is the basis for XAML (Extensible Application Markup Language). The following code shows the default Silverlight XAML file when you create a new Silverlight application using Visual Studio, which is also broken down in the table that follows the code:

```
<UserControl x:Class="SilverlightApplication6.Page"
    xmlns="http://schemas.microsoft.com/winfx/2006/xaml/presentation"
    xmlns:x="http://schemas.microsoft.com/winfx/2006/xaml"
    Width="400" Height="300">
<Grid x:Name="LayoutRoot" Background="White">

</Grid>
</UserControl>
```

The following table describes the preceding code:

XAML	Description
`<UserControl x:Class="SilverlightApplication6.Page"`	Opening object tag of the root UserControl
`xmlns="http://schemas.microsoft.com/winfx/2006/xaml/presentation"`	Default Silverlight namespace mapping
`xmlns:x="http://schemas.microsoft.com/winfx/2006/xaml"`	Default XAML namespace mapping
`Width="400" Height="300">`	Default Height and Width properties of the UserControl
`<Grid x:Name="LayoutRoot" Background="White">`	Opening tag for the Grid layout element
`</Grid>`	Closing tag for the Grid layout element
`</UserControl>`	Closing tag for the root UserControl object

In Chapter 1, you learned about the namespace declaration in Visual Studio for other assemblies than the core Silverlight and code Silverlight XAML namespaces. If you had a compiled user control or class file that you wanted to include in your opening UserControl declaration, you would use a custom prefix and point to the fully qualified namespace and object you are adding to the page. For example, if you need to access features in the System.Windows assembly, you would add the following namespace declaration to your page:

```
xmlns:vsm="clr-namespace:System.Windows;assembly=System.Windows"
```

where vsm is your custom prefix (which can be whatever prefix you would like), the clr-namespace you are using is System.Windows, and the actual assembly name is System.Windows. Later in this chapter, we will talk about the XAML namespace, whose objects are prefixed with the default x: identifier.

Declaring Objects in XAML

You can use either the object element syntax or the attribute syntax to declare objects in XAML:

❑ **Object Element Syntax** — Uses opening and closing tags to declare an object as an XML element. You can use this syntax to declare root objects or set complex property values.

❑ **Attribute Syntax** — Uses an inline value to declare an object. You can use this syntax to set the value of a property.

Object or Content Element Syntax

Most elements are created using the object (or content) element syntax, which is used in the "Introducing XAML" section earlier in this chapter to create the TextBlock object:

```
<TextBlock>Hello World</TextBlock>
```

This syntax maps to:

```
<ObjectName> … </ObjectName>
```

where ObjectName is the name of the object that you are trying to instantiate. The following example uses object element syntax to declare a Canvas:

```
<Canvas>
</Canvas>
```

Some objects, such as Canvas, can contain other objects, such as Rectangle or TextBlock:

```
<Canvas>
    <TextBlock>
    </TextBlock>
</Canvas>
```

If an object does not contain other objects, you can declare it using one self-enclosing tag instead of two:

```
<Canvas>
    <Rectangle />
</Canvas>
```

When you are creating objects, there really is no bad or good way. The hierarchy of the XAML documents, which is covered later in this chapter, does not change.

Attribute Element Syntax

XAML also supports the less verbose attribute syntax for setting properties. The following markup creates a rectangle that has a green background (or `Fill` as the attributed property is named):

```
<Rectangle Fill="Green" Height="100" Width="100" />
```

Property Element Syntax

Attribute syntax is not possible on certain object properties because the object or information necessary to provide the property value cannot be adequately expressed as a simple string. For these cases, the property element syntax can be used. Property element syntax sets the referenced property of the containing element with a new instance of the type that the property takes as its value, for example:

```
<objectName>
    <objectName.property>
        <setter propertyValue = "" />
    </objectName.property>
</objectName>
```

The following code uses property element syntax to add a `Stroke` with a `LinearGradientBrush` to a `Rectangle` element:

```
<Rectangle Width="485" Height="60"
        Canvas.Left="99" Canvas.Top="55">
    <Rectangle.Stroke>
        <LinearGradientBrush EndPoint="1,0.5" StartPoint="0,0.5">
            <GradientStop Color="#FF483333" Offset="0.308"/>
            <GradientStop Color="#FF514C4C" Offset="0.1070303"/>
        </LinearGradientBrush>
    </Rectangle.Stroke>
    <Rectangle.Fill>
        <LinearGradientBrush EndPoint="1,0.5" StartPoint="0,0.5">
            <GradientStop Color="#FF000000" Offset="0"/>
            <GradientStop Color="#FFFFFFFF" Offset="1"/>
        </LinearGradientBrush>
    </Rectangle.Fill>
</Rectangle>
```

You can set properties on objects declared using object element syntax. You have three ways to set properties in XAML:

❑ Using implicit collection syntax

❑ Using attribute syntax

❑ Using property element syntax

Setting a Property Using Implicit Collection Syntax

When a property takes a collection, you can omit the collection element and simply specify its contents instead. This is known as *implicit collection syntax*. The following code shows how you can omit the

GradientStopCollection for a LinearGradientBrush and simply specify its GradientStop objects. The GradientStopCollection is included in the first LinearGradientBrush but omitted from the second. The results are shown in Figure 2-1.

```
<Rectangle Width="100" Height="100"
  Canvas.Left="0" Canvas.Top="30">
    <Rectangle.Fill>
        <LinearGradientBrush>
            <LinearGradientBrush.GradientStops>

                <!-- Here the GradientStopCollection tag is used. -->
                <GradientStopCollection>
                    <GradientStop Offset="0.0" Color="Red" />
                    <GradientStop Offset="1.0" Color="Blue" />
                </GradientStopCollection>
            </LinearGradientBrush.GradientStops>
        </LinearGradientBrush>
    </Rectangle.Fill>
</Rectangle>


<Rectangle Width="100" Height="100"
  Canvas.Left="100" Canvas.Top="30">
    <Rectangle.Fill>
        <LinearGradientBrush>
            <LinearGradientBrush.GradientStops>

                <!-- Notice that the GradientStopCollection tag
             is omitted. -->
                <GradientStop Offset="0.0" Color="Red" />
                <GradientStop Offset="1.0" Color="Blue" />
            </LinearGradientBrush.GradientStops>
        </LinearGradientBrush>
    </Rectangle.Fill>
</Rectangle>
```

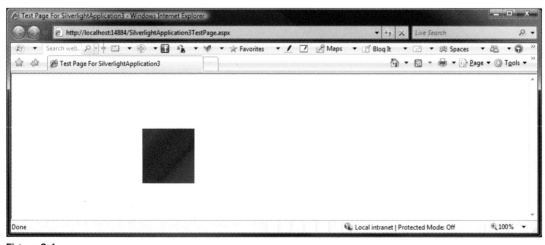

Figure 2-1

There are times when the property collection indicates the type of collection being parsed. In these cases, you can omit both the collection element and the property element tags, as the following code demonstrates:

```
<Rectangle Width="100" Height="100"
   Canvas.Left="200" Canvas.Top="30">
     <Rectangle.Fill>
        <LinearGradientBrush>
           <GradientStop Offset="0.0" Color="Red" />
           <GradientStop Offset="1.0" Color="Blue" />
        </LinearGradientBrush>
     </Rectangle.Fill>
</Rectangle>
```

Deciding When to Use Attribute or Property Element Syntax to Set a Property

So far, you have learned that all properties support either the attribute or property element syntax. Some properties, however, support other syntax, which is dependent on the type of object property it accepts.

Primitive types, such as a `Double`, `Integer`, or `String`, support only the attribute element syntax. The following example uses attribute element syntax to set the width of a rectangle. The `Width` property supports attribute syntax because the property value is a `Double`.

```
<Rectangle Width="100" />
```

Whether or not you can use attribute syntax to set a property depends on whether the object you use to set that property supports attribute syntax. The following example uses attribute syntax to set the fill of a rectangle. The `Fill` property supports attribute syntax when you use a `SolidColorBrush` to set it because `SolidColorBrush` supports attribute syntax.

```
<Rectangle Fill="Blue" />
```

Whether or not you can use property element syntax to set a property depends on whether the object you use to set that property supports object element syntax. If the object supports object element syntax, the property supports property element syntax. The following example uses property element syntax to set the fill of a rectangle. The `Fill` property supports attribute syntax when you use a `SolidColorBrush` to set it because `SolidColorBrush` supports attribute syntax.

```
<Rectangle>
    <Rectangle.Fill>
        <SolidColorBrush Color="Blue"  />
    </Rectangle.Fill>
</Rectangle>
```

XAML Hierarchy

When you add XAML objects to the Silverlight control, you are defining a hierarchical tree structure with a root object. All XAML files have a root element. In Silverlight, the root element is always the container that has the `x:Class` attribute. The following XAML example creates an object hierarchy containing a root `UserControl` object in the `SilverlightApplication6` namespace `Page` class. When the XAML is parsed by the player, the `Canvas` object, which has `Rectangle` and `TextBlock` elements, is resolved, as well as the additional `TextBlock` element in the file. When the parsing is complete, there is a tree-structured hierarchy of the elements in the file.

```
<!-- The top-most object in the XAML hierarchy is -->
<!-- referred to as the root object. -->
<UserControl x:Class="SilverlightApplication6.Page"
    xmlns="http://schemas.microsoft.com/winfx/2006/xaml/presentation"
    xmlns:x="http://schemas.microsoft.com/winfx/2006/xaml"
    Width="400" Height="300">

    <!-- Canvas objects can be a child of another Canvas object. -->
    <Canvas
      Canvas.Left="20" Canvas.Top="20">
        <Rectangle
          Width="200" Height="35"
          Fill="Red" />
        <TextBlock
          Canvas.Left="25" Canvas.Top="5"
          Foreground="White" FontFamily="Verdana"
          FontSize="18" FontWeight="Bold"
          Text="Child Canvas TextBlock" />
    </Canvas>

    <TextBlock
      Canvas.Left="40" Canvas.Top="60"
      Foreground="Black" FontFamily="Verdana"
      FontSize="18" FontWeight="Bold"
      Text="Hello Silverlight" />
</UserControl>
```

When the Silverlight player attempts to render the XAML content, it is converted into a hierarchical tree structure with a root object. The tree structure determines the rendering order of Silverlight objects. The order of traversal starts with the root object, which is the topmost node in the tree structure — in this case, the `UserControl` object. The root object's children are then traversed, from left to right. If an object has children, its children are traversed before the object's siblings. This means the content of a child object is rendered in front of the object's own content. Figure 2-2 shows the rendered output from the previous XAML example, showing the rendering order sequence.

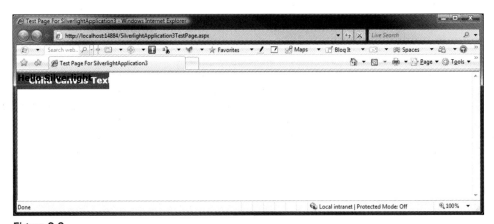

Figure 2-2

Events and the Silverlight Control

The Silverlight object model defines a set of objects that allow you to create a Silverlight application. In the unmanaged Silverlight 3 programming model, the Silverlight player itself had a limited number of events that you could respond to in JavaScript functions, such as mouseMove, mouseLeftButtonUp, and so forth. In the managed programming model of Silverlight 3, these same events, along with richer events based on the type of object, are handled in the code-behind of the partial class that is associated with the XAML file your objects are in. All interaction with the browser is handled through the normal interaction processing of the browser, where inputs are accepted client-side. In the case of Silverlight, the player responds to events and routes them to the appropriate event handler that you have defined.

This section discusses the Silverlight objects; how you reference them; and how you handle, add, and remove events on those objects. Because you cannot create fully interactive applications in XAML alone, it is important to understand how all of the elements — the objects in XAML, the HTML, and your code-behind — work together to deliver the richness that Silverlight offers.

Event Handlers and Partial Classes

In Silverlight, the association of the XAML file with a code-behind file is set up with the x:Class attribute at the top of your XAML files. The x: prefix indicates that the Class object is part of the XAML namespace, and the Class object is declared as an attribute off the root element of a XAML file. The x:Class attribute cannot be used on child elements in a page hierarchy; it can only be declared once and on the root element. The syntax for declaring the x:Class is the same as for any other type declaration in Silverlight:

```
<object x:Class="namespace.classname;assembly=assemblyname"...>
  ...
</object>
```

In default cases when you add new pages to your application, the assembly is left off and assumed to be the current projects assembly.

```
<UserControl x:Class="SilverlightApplication1.Page"
```

When you build your Silverlight application, the compiler builds the XAML, parses the XAML, and creates instance objects of all of the uniquely identified elements in the file using x:Name. The association of the class defined in the x:Class attribute and its partial class occur during the compile, and the references for all of the objects with an x:Name are created so that they can be referenced at run time. The x:Name attribute is used as a unique identifier to the elements you define. Similar to HTML, where the id attribute denotes the uniqueness of an element, Silverlight needs a way to isolate and reference elements in XAML so that they can be referenced in the code-behind files. In Silverlight 1.0, there were no code-behind files because all coding was handled via JavaScript. But by using <script> tags in HTML pages, you can define what code files should be able to access DOM for the page in which you are running the Silverlight control. In Silverlight, the partial class files contain your managed code, and thus they contain your event handlers. Objects are defined in XAML with an x:Name attribute, and corresponding fields are created in the partial class, which can have event handlers that respond to the input event.

The naming rules for the `x:Name`, `x:Class`, and `x:Key` attributes are:

❑ They can contain numbers, letters, or underscore.

❑ They cannot begin with a number.

❑ Unicode characters are not supported.

The `x:Key` attributes are used in the child elements of `ResourceDictionary` objects. The child elements are basically keyed by the XAML processor and can be used by the `StaticResource` markup extension, which we cover later in this chapter.

The following XAML demonstrates a file where a `button` element has a unique identifier. Although both `x:Name` and `x:Key` enforce uniqueness, you will get a compile error if you have an `x:Name` and `x:Key` object using the same name.

```
<Grid x:Name="LayoutRoot" Background="White">
   <Button x:Name="button1" Click="button1_Click"></Button>
</Grid>
```

In the code-behind for this XAML file, the event handler looks like this:

```
private void button1_Click(object sender, RoutedEventArgs e)
{

}
```

In Visual Studio, the XAML Editor will give you hints for the attributes for the object that you are typing against, including the object's corresponding events. This makes it easier to wire events from XAML to your code-behind. You can also manually wire events to objects:

```
button1 += new MouseButtonEventHandler(button1_Click);
```

And in Visual Basic, you can use the `Handles` keyword to associate XAML elements with class functions:

```
Private Sub button1_Click(ByVal sender As Object, _
        ByVal e As System.Windows.RoutedEventArgs) _
        Handles button1.Click

End Sub
```

Your event handlers can be public or private. Objects with the `x:Name` attribute are scoped to the page they are in. Similar to the way events are handled in ASP.NET or Windows Forms, the event handlers in Silverlight have two parameters:

❑ `sender` — Identifies the Silverlight object that generated the event. You can retrieve the type value of the object by calling the object's API.

❑ `args` — Identifies the set of argument values for the specific event. An event, such as the `Loaded` event, does not define any event arguments, so the value of `eventArgs` is null.

The next table is an example of the event parameters for the KeyDown event of the Silverlight player. This example is typical of how you will see events described in the Silverlight 3.0 SDK.

Event Parameter	Description
sender	Object Identifies the object that invoked the event.
KeyEventArgs	Object keyEventArgs.key — Integer that indicates that a key is pressed. This value is not operating-system-specific. keyEventArgs.platformKeyCode — Integer that indicates that a key is pressed. This value is operating-system-specific. keyEventArgs.shift — Boolean value that indicates whether the [Shift] key is down. keyEventArgs.ctrl — Boolean value that indicates whether the [Ctrl] key is down.

As an example of the KeyDown event, the following code demonstrates how you would define the event on the Canvas element in XAML:

```
<TextBox Height="100" Width="200"
        KeyDown="TextBox_KeyDown"></TextBox>
<TextBlock x:Name="results"></TextBlock>
```

Next, the code here demonstrates the code-behind in Visual Basic that is used to handle the KeyDown event on the Button object:

```
Private Sub TextBox_KeyDown(ByVal sender As System.Object, _
        ByVal e As System.Windows.Input.KeyEventArgs)

        results.Text = e.Key & "-" & e.PlatformKeyCode
End Sub
```

When you wire the event directly in the XAML to the method in your code-behind, the approach is no different than if you were building a Windows Forms application.

Defining Events in JavaScript

If you choose not to use a managed programming model, which is the case if you omit the x:Class attribute on your XAML file, then you must handle all events in JavaScript. When adding or removing event handlers via JavaScript, you will use the AddEventListener and RemoveEventListener methods on the elements on which you want to add or remove events. You use the following syntax:

```
Element.addEventListener("EventName", "EventHandler");
```

For example, the following code demonstrates adding the onMouseEnter and onMouseLeave event handlers to the TextBlock element named Status.

The following JavaScript example shows how to add events to a `TextBlock` object:

```
function onLoaded(sender, eventArgs)
{
    textBlock = sender.findName("Status");
    textBlock.addEventListener("MouseEnter", "onMouseEnter");
    textBlock.addEventListener("MouseLeave", "onMouseLeave");
}
```

To remove an existing event handler function, use the `RemoveEventListener` method, as demonstrated next.

```
function removeEvents()
{
    textBlock.removeEventListener("MouseEnter", "onMouseEnter");
    textBlock.removeEventListener("MouseLeave", "onMouseLeave");
}
```

Finding a XAML Object Using findName

In JavaScript, you use the `findName` method and reference the object's `x:Name` attribute value. The `findName` function will search the entire object hierarchy of the DOM running in the Silverlight control, so the location of an element in the hierarchy does not matter. If the element passed to the `findName` function cannot be found, a null value is returned. The next code demonstrates using the `findName` function as well as how to properly check if the object being sought exists:

```
function onLoaded(sender, eventArgs)
{
    // Retrieve the object corresponding to the x:Name attribute value.
    var canvas = sender.findName("rootCanvas");

    // Determine whether the object was found.
    if (canvas != null)
    {
        alert(canvas.toString());
    }
    else
    {
        alert("Object not found");
    }
}
```

Event Bubbling

Since Silverlight supports the same routed event model that WPF uses, the concept of *event bubbling* becomes important for some events. A *routed event* is an event that traverses the object hierarchy from the root element that triggers the event up to each of its parent objects. Events are *bubbled* up.

The framework elements that support routed events are:

❑   KeyDown

❑   KeyUp

- ❏ MouseEnter
- ❏ MouseLeftButtonDown
- ❏ MouseLeftButtonUp
- ❏ MouseMove
- ❏ BindingValidationError

The following code demonstrates an example in which event bubbling might come into play. Notice there are MouseMove events on the root UserControl, as well as the child elements in the user control:

```
<UserControl x:Class="SilverlightApplication1.Page"
 xmlns="http://schemas.microsoft.com/winfx/2006/xaml/presentation"
  xmlns:x=http://schemas.microsoft.com/winfx/2006/xaml
   Loaded="onLoaded"
   MouseMove="rootCanvasMouseMove">


    <Rectangle
      x:Name="rect1"
      MouseMove="rect1MouseMove"
      Width="100" Height="100"
      Fill="PowderBlue" />

    <Rectangle
      x:Name="rect2"
      MouseMove="rect2MouseMove"
      Canvas.Top="50" Canvas.Left="50"
      Width="100" Height="100"
      Fill="Gold" Opacity="0.5" />

    <TextBlock
      x:Name="statusTextBlock"
      Canvas.Top="180" />

 </UserControl>
```

Event bubbling means that there are multiple MouseMove events defined for an object and its ancestors. The event is received by each object in the ancestor hierarchy, starting with the object that directly receives the event.

The next code demonstrates this in a different fashion. Because both Rectangle elements have a MouseMove event defined and the Canvas element has a MouseMove event defined, if the mouse is moved over either rectangle, the onRectMouseMove event is fired. And because the Canvas is looking for a MouseMove event, the mouse move over the rectangles is bubbled up through the object hierarchy to the Canvas element.

```
<Canvas
  MouseMove="onCanvasMouseMove"
```

```
Loaded="onLoaded">

  <Rectangle
    x:Name="RectA"
    MouseMove="onRectMouseMove"
    Width="100" Height="100" Fill="Red" />

  <Rectangle
    x:Name="RectB"
    MouseMove="onRectMouseMove"
    Width="100" Height="100" Fill="Blue"
    Canvas.Top="25" Canvas.Left="25" Opacity="0.5" />

</Canvas>
```

Markup Extensions

Since you can create static or instance objects in XAML, you need a way to use those objects as properties on other XAML elements. This is where XAML markup extensions come in. Using an opening and a closing curly brace "{}" syntax, you can reference static object resources created elsewhere in your application using an attribute or property element syntax. For example, if you created a static `Style` resource that you planned to use to target multiple elements in your application, you would use the markup extension syntax to set the style property on the target element. The following code is an example of a static style resource:

```
<Style x:Key="MainButton" TargetType="Button">
    <Setter Property="Width" Value="80" />
    <Setter Property="Height" Value="35" />
    <Setter Property="FontSize" Value="18" />
</Style>
```

To apply this resource to a target element, in this case the `TargetType` Button, you would use the attribute syntax shown here:

```
<Button x:Name="Button1" Style="{StaticResource MainButton}" ... />
<Button x:Name="Button2" Style="{StaticResource MainButton}" ... />
```

When the XAML is parsed, the presence of the curly brace indicates that this is an extension and to process the type of markup extension and the string value that follows the type. Silverlight supports three markup extensions:

❑   `Binding`

❑   `StaticResource`

❑   `TemplateBinding`

We'll look at `Binding` and `StaticResource` in this chapter and `TemplateBinding` in Chapter 8.

Binding Markup Extensions

In Chapter 8, you will learn the details of data binding. In this section, we'll look at the basic XAML syntax. To understand the binding markup extension, you'll need to understand how data retrieved in a managed function ends up being displayed in XAML. Before we go into an example, let's go over the basic syntax. There are several ways you can set binding using the `Binding` markup extension:

```
<object property="{Binding}" .../>

<object property="{Binding propertyPath}" .../>

<object property="{Binding oneOrMoreBindingProperties}" .../>

<object property="{Binding propertyPath, oneOrMoreBindingProperties}" .../>
```

In all cases, `object` is an element such as a `TextBlock`, and `property` is an attribute property on that element, such as `Text`. The remaining options are how you specify the properties of the binding, such as the binding `Mode` (`OneTime`, `OneWay`, or `TwoWay`), `Converter`, `Path`, and so forth.

When you retrieve or build data, you normally set the data source to the `DataContext` of a XAML element, such as a `Canvas` or `Grid` object, so it can be used by the containers' child elements. For example, if you had a basic `Grid` element named `LayoutRoot`, it would look something like this:

```
<Grid x:Name="LayoutRoot" Background="White">

    <!-- grid definition, XAML children -->

</Grid>
```

In your code-behind, to bind data to the child elements of LayoutRoot, you would set the data source in your code-behind to the DataContext of LayoutRoot:

```
LayoutRoot.DataContext = dataRecords;
```

In this case, `dataRecords` is a custom object that has various properties like `Name`, `Address`, and `Email` that I set through code. Once the `DataContext` is set, the child elements have access to fields on the data context of the parent element, as the following code demonstrates:

```
<Grid x:Name="LayoutRoot" Background="White">

    <!-- Grid definition -->

    <Grid.RowDefinitions>
        <RowDefinition MaxHeight="30" />
        <RowDefinition MaxHeight="30" />
        <RowDefinition MaxHeight="70" />
        <RowDefinition MaxHeight="30" />
        <RowDefinition MaxHeight="40" />
        <RowDefinition MaxHeight="50" />
    </Grid.RowDefinitions>
```

```xml
    <Grid.ColumnDefinitions>
        <ColumnDefinition MaxWidth="150"/>
        <ColumnDefinition MaxWidth="200" />
    </Grid.ColumnDefinitions>

    <!-- XAML children -->

    <TextBlock x:Name="NameLabel" Text="Name:    "
        VerticalAlignment="Bottom"
        HorizontalAlignment="Right"
        Grid.Row="0"  Grid.Column="0" />

    <TextBlock x:Name="Name"
        Text="{Binding Name, Mode=OneWay }"
        VerticalAlignment="Bottom"
        HorizontalAlignment="Left"
        Grid.Row="0" Grid.Column="1" />

    <TextBlock x:Name="AddressLabel" Text="Address: "
        VerticalAlignment="Bottom"
        HorizontalAlignment="Right"
        Grid.Row="1"  Grid.Column="0" />

    <TextBlock x:Name="Address"
        Text="{Binding Address, Mode=OneWay }"
        VerticalAlignment="Bottom"
        HorizontalAlignment="Left"
        Grid.Row="1" Grid.Column="1" />

<TextBlock x:Name="EmailLabel" Text="Email:    "
        VerticalAlignment="Bottom"
        HorizontalAlignment="Right"
        Grid.Row="2" Grid.Column="0"  />

  < TextBlock x:Name="Email"
        Text="{Binding  Email, Mode=OneWay}"
        VerticalAlignment="Bottom"
        HorizontalAlignment="Left"
        Height="60" Width="200"
        Grid.Row="2" Grid.Column="1" />

</Grid>
```

When the application runs, the data from the custom object is bound to the Grid element, and the grid's child TextBlock elements consume the available data by using the binding markup extension.

StaticResource Markup Extensions

The StaticResource markup extension is used to set the x:Key attribute on an object that is defined in a ResourceDictionary object.

```xml
<Style x:Key="MainButton" TargetType="Button">
    <Setter Property="Width" Value="80" />
```

The x:Key attribute is applied to the Style object to give it the unique name MainButton. This Style object is in a ResourceDictionary, which in Silverlight is normally the outermost XAML element of your XAML file:

```
<UserControl.Resources>
  <Style x:Key="MainButton" TargetType="Button">
    <Setter Property="Width" Value="80" />
    <Setter Property="Height" Value="35" />
    <Setter Property="FontSize" Value="18" />
  </Style>
</UserControl.Resources>
```

x:Key gives the resource its uniqueness, so it can be applied to objects in the XAML file using the StaticResource markup extension syntax you learned about earlier:

```
<Button x:Name="Button1" Style="{StaticResource MainButton}" ... />
```

In this case, the properties defined in the MainButton Style will be applied to any Button object using the StaticResource markup extension.

Summary

This chapter gave you a good foundation for the various aspects of using XAML in Silverlight. There are a few takeaways about Silverlight XAML that you need to remember:

❑ Silverlight XAML is a subset of WPF XAML, so theoretically an application in Silverlight can move up to WPF. However, moving an application from WPF to Silverlight will not work (in most cases).

❑ The Silverlight player is an ActiveX browser plug-in, so the XAML you are using is built into the player; it is not based on .NET Framework objects.

❑ XAML alone cannot build Silverlight applications. You need HTML to host the Silverlight player, which, in turn, hosts the XAML, and you need to use the managed coding model in Silverlight 3 or the unmanaged coding model in Silverlight 1.0 to interact with the XAML.

❑ XAML opens the doors for designers and developers to work closely together, because the same language (XAML) that is used to style applications is also used to define the user interface.

❑ The X in XAML stands for extensible — so as Silverlight matures, with the capabilities of the player such that you can add your own extensions, your applications will become more powerful.

3

Silverlight Architectural Tour

Before diving too deeply into any one particular area of Silverlight 3, it'll be helpful to get an overall understanding of its architecture — the core building blocks, frameworks, and execution environments. In this chapter, you'll take a look at these and come away with a high-level understanding of Silverlight capabilities along with a good grasp of how all the pieces fit and play together.

Figure 3-1 gives a very high-level overview of the layout of a Silverlight application with respect to major Silverlight architectural layers. Of course, Silverlight lives as a plug-in inside a browser host. There is then a presentation core layer that takes care of both presenting and animating visuals (images, text, video, and audio), as well as receiving input from the user in the form of keyboard, mouse, or ink. It's also responsible for the Digital Rights Management (DRM) capabilities of Silverlight.

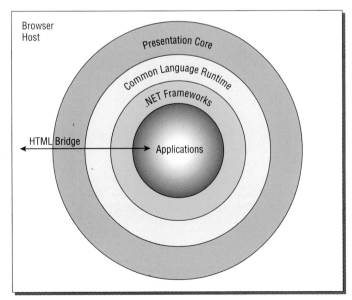

Figure 3-1

On top of the presentation core, Silverlight includes .NET features, chiefly the Common Language Runtime (CLR), which is the execution environment for the .NET code (as it is with standard .NET applications). It's sometimes called the *CoreCLR*, as it is a selected subset deemed to be the core necessary for Silverlight applications. And on this CLR hang all of the various .NET-based libraries that developers can use to create rich, .NET-based applications in Silverlight.

The following sections delve into these in more depth.

Browser Host

Silverlight is technically just a browser plug-in. As such, it lives inside the browser host and is subject to all that entails in terms of application activation, sandboxing, and deactivation.

Application Services

Silverlight has a few application-level facilities that help developers deal with application deployment and life-cycle issues.

Installation and Updates

Silverlight scripts or the Silverlight ASP.NET controls can be used to detect if Silverlight is available in the current browser and provide an installation experience. This can be the default, plain blue badge, but it is recommended that developers customize this to provide a better experience, including a preview and instructions.

Once installed, Silverlight will update itself if that is allowed by the host environment.

Out-of-Browser Experience

Silverlight gives end-users the option to install properly configured applications to their desktops and Start menus as local applications. Using the new network APIs in Silverlight 3, you can detect network availability in code to create a connected and disconnected experience of your out-of-browser applications.

Activation

How a Silverlight application gets activated depends largely on the browser host, but there is a common means of activating it: either by using the OBJECT or EMBED tags in HTML or by creating the object in JavaScript. Because it is activated in this way, Silverlight relies on the browser to parse the HTML or JavaScript when it sees fit and do the loading at that time.

This implies, unfortunately, that you cannot count on an offline activation model; that is, you can't count on users being able to pull up the URL to a Silverlight application while offline and have it load, as you can for technologies like ClickOnce or Adobe AIR. No doubt Microsoft is investigating this problem and will have a solution in due time. If it is important to you, be sure to make your voice heard.

Deactivation

As with activation, deactivation is largely dependent on the browser, but in general, once the page that references the Silverlight object is disposed, so will the Silverlight object be. This means that if you have data in volatile memory that you want to persist, you should consider using isolated storage for caching.

Networking

As with previous Silverlight versions and with AJAX, the browser facilities for HTTP requests and responses are still available and can definitely be used with your applications. This will be a common scenario for hybrid applications in which you are using AJAX and Silverlight side-by-side.

BOM and DOM

The Browser Object Model (BOM) and Document Object Model (DOM) are exposed through interop so that you can manipulate and interact with the browser from managed code and vice versa. You can even attach managed event handlers to DOM events. This tight integration capability between managed code and Silverlight is a huge benefit for hybrid applications.

JavaScript

As with the BOM and DOM, JavaScript is still a first-class citizen for Silverlight 3 development, if you want it to be. You can handle certain Silverlight object events like load, unload, and error in JavaScript to create better experiences for your users and more meaningful integration with surrounding, more typical client-side stuff in the browser.

Presentation Core

The Silverlight *presentation core* is the unmanaged (native) run time that much of the Silverlight low-level, UI-oriented code executes in. This can't be managed because it has to live on multiple platforms with differing execution environments. From a developer perspective, this is pretty much anything you can do, either with JavaScript or XAML, that does not require .NET code. Everything in this section can be thought of as running in that execution environment.

Display

Although the presentation core is not .NET or WPF (Windows Presentation Foundation) per se, it has many of the features that WPF provides. In fact, if you are familiar with WPF, you can think of Silverlight as a subset of WPF in terms of its presentation layer capabilities.

In addition to occupying a place in the browser page, Silverlight supports a full-screen mode that will take up the full screen of the monitor that the browser is in.

Vector and Bitmap Graphics

What UI technology would be complete without support for graphics? Silverlight has support for a broad range of bitmap graphics (what most developers think of as images — JPEG, GIF, BMP, etc.), and it loads them in familiar ways (by referencing their location), although the way it resolves image locations is different from what most web developers may be used to, so pay close attention to Chapter 8, which discusses this topic.

In addition to bitmap image support, Silverlight is itself vector-based. The most notable benefit of this is the ability to scale (grow bigger) without *pixelation* (loss of quality where images look blurry and blocky).

So any visuals you use in Silverlight (the built-in shapes, brushes, geometries, paths, controls, etc.) will scale well by default, as will, of course, external vector-based images.

Bitmap Caching

Rendering performance is greatly enhanced in Silverlight 3 with the ability to cache vector content, text, and controls into bitmaps. When elements are cached, they are passed to the GPU (Graphics Processing Unit) for re-rendering, which can double or even triple the FPS (frames per second) when rendering content.

Three Dimensions (3D)

The addition of perspective three dimensions (3D) in Silverlight 3 enables you to put any element on a 3D place and manipulate its X-, Y-, and Z-axis. Enabling 3D requires no code — it is completely declarative.

Text

The text facilities in Silverlight are pretty basic, especially when compared to WPF or even HTML and CSS. You aren't going to run out and convert all your HTML content to Silverlight any time soon. That said, it does have a fairly sufficient set of text facilities for less content-oriented needs.

Designers will definitely appreciate the ability to embed custom fonts, which are stored in the XAP file and referenced there by the text controls, of which you have `TextBlock` (for text display) and `TextBox` (for text input).

Text formatting is supported through the use of properties on the text objects or via styles.

Layout Engine

Silverlight layout functions very similarly to WPF, although there are differences, the details of which are covered in Chapter 7. This engine handles the positioning of visuals based on several considerations such as size, alignment, transforms, and, of course, the kind of layout, which is determined by the different layout controls.

Transforms

Transforms are likely a new concept to a lot of business application developers. The general idea is that you can *change the form* (hence *transform*), which means changing the way a UI element looks without altering its base configuration. So you can set, for example, a base width and height, and then you can use a scale transform to make it bigger or smaller without actually changing the width and height properties.

Some transforms do things that you can't do using properties on most objects (like skew and rotate). Probably the most common use for transforms is in animations.

Animations

We all understand animations at a gut level — making things come alive, usually moving, growing, shrinking, fading, or otherwise dynamically altering the visual aspects of things. A good way to think of it in terms of programming is changing the value of a property over time. Animation support in Silverlight is huge in terms of helping take applications to the next level of richness for users; it really starts to leverage the capabilities, from a UI point of view, that computers have to enhance interactions that are otherwise static, uninteresting, and often difficult to use. Developers would be wise to invest time in this area of Silverlight as it is one of the prime capabilities for enabling better user experiences.

XAML

Although XAML came into its own in WPF in .NET 3.0, it's not inherently a .NET thing — it's application markup. And since it was used as the declarative UI specification language of WPF, it's only natural that it be used in Silverlight, which is a subset of WPF when it comes to its UI capabilities.

Input

As covered in detail in Chapter 16, Silverlight provides the standard input mechanisms that you've come to expect in modern application platforms.

Mouse

Silverlight supports the standard mouse events like mouse enter, move, and leave as well as the left-button `click` events. Notable exceptions are no right (or other) button `click` events and no scroll events, although you can get past that through the browser interop bridge.

Keyboard

Silverlight supports the common key-down and -up events that enable keyboard input and control. These are restricted to navigational keys when in full-screen mode because of security concerns.

Ink

Silverlight has an ink/stylus-based input mechanism including a familiar object model (for those who are familiar with other ink OMs) to rationalize the user input as discrete objects that can be serialized and re-drawn, which opens up interesting possibilities, for example, text recognition. Although it isn't inherently supported, you could do it via a service-based approach.

File

Silverlight provides a File Open dialog to facilitate the input of files from the user's OS into an application as well as a File Save dialog.

Controls

There is a base set of common controls in the presentation core that supports all of the various presentation functionalities from a developer perspective. In terms of the presentation core, these are created primarily through XAML, although the new .NET facilities provide a managed API to do so. Both JavaScript and .NET can manipulate the various UI controls, although custom .NET controls require additional work to make them accessible via JavaScript.

Styling

The presentation core supports the styling framework that enables developers to share property settings among multiple instances of controls to ease maintenance and help ensure consistency. Silverlight 3 adds the ability to theme entire applications at run times using an external XAML file called a

`ResourceDictionary`. Also new to Silverlight 3 is the ability to create a style based on another style, using the `BasedOn` property.

Templating

As with styling, Silverlight has a WPF-based templating model that enables the complete re-design of visual controls as well as the basic binding facilities for data-based templates.

Media

Unlike traditional web technologies (HTML, CSS, JavaScript), media is a first-class citizen in Silverlight; it is, in fact, one of the primary motivators for the creation of Silverlight, as evidenced by Version 1, and that doesn't go away with Silverlight 3.

For both audio and video, Silverlight provides playback control, timeline markers, and server-side playlists, as well as Digital Rights Management. These can be progressively downloaded or downloaded on demand via direct streaming using Windows Media Server.

Audio and Video

The audio and video formats in the following table are supported:

Video Formats	Audio Formats
WMV1 — Windows Media Video 7	**WMA 7** — Windows Media Audio 7
WMV2 — Windows Media Video 8	**WMA 8** — Windows Media Audio 8
WMV3 — Windows Media Video 9	**WMA 9** — Windows Media Audio 9
WMVA — Windows Media Video Advanced Profile, non-VC-1	**WMA 10** — Windows Media Audio 10
WMVC1 — Windows Media Video Advanced Profile, VC-1	**AAC** — Advanced Audio Coding. Can only be used for progressive download, smooth streaming, and adaptive streaming. AAC is the LC variety and supports sampling frequencies up to 48 kHz.
H.264 — Can only be used for progressive download, smooth streaming, and adaptive streaming. Supports Base, Main, and High Profiles.	**MP3** — ISO/MPEG Layer-3 with the following features:
	❑ **Input** — ISO/MPEG Layer-3 data stream
	❑ **Channel Configurations** — Mono, stereo
	❑ **Sampling Frequencies** — 8, 11.025, 12, 16, 22.05, 24, 32, 44.1, and 48 kHz
	❑ **Bitrates** — 8–320 Kbps, variable bitrate
	❑ **Limitations** — "Free format mode" (ISO/IEC 11172-3, subclause 2.4.2.3) is not supported.

Protocols

Silverlight essentially just supports HTTP(S), all of which, except for MMS, will default to progressive downloading:

❑ HTTP

❑ HTTPS

❑ mms (falls back to HTTP, but tells Silverlight to try streaming first)

❑ rtsp (falls back to HTTP)

❑ rstpt (falls back to HTTP)

Digital Rights Management

The Silverlight client can use two forms of DRM encryption/decryption: the traditional Windows Media Digital Rights Management 10 (WMDRM 10) and the newer PlayReady with AES encryption. This enables existing content encrypted using the WMDRM 10 SDK to play back within both Silverlight and other Windows Media playback software that supports DRM (such as Windows Media Player), and Silverlight-only media to offer a higher degree of security. Silverlight DRM only supports Windows Media Audio (WMA), Windows Media Video (WMV), and PYA/PYV files for PlayReady.

For more information, go to www.microsoft.com/playready.

.NET

The previous section covered all the core facilities that are part of the native presentation core. In this section, you'll explore all that .NET for Silverlight has to offer, which sometimes is more like .NET facades and other times like true .NET-specific value adds. By far, making the .NET platform (even the subset that it is) available to run inside the popular, modern browsers is the biggest thing to hit web development since, well, since maybe the browser itself, in our opinion.

Common Language Runtime (CoreCLR)

The CLR is a distinct run time from what most .NET developers have come to know and love. This is an important point — it is not the same CLR as is in the main .NET platform. A nickname has emerged for it — the *CoreCLR*, which may be just right in terms of communicating its difference from the full .NET CLR.

Microsoft has built a CoreCLR to run on top of Windows as well as Mac OS X. Microsoft is working with the Linux community to support its efforts to develop the CLR for Moonlight, the Linux version of the Silverlight run time, so that it hits a broad majority of current Internet users. In addition, Microsoft is working on a Mobile version.

Now, having established that the CoreCLR is distinct from the main CLR, you can forget about it (or at least file it away). From a developer perspective, there is little discernable difference, although it surely will have implications in tricky debugging scenarios.

The following sections outline at a high level what you can expect from the CoreCLR.

Memory Management

The CoreCLR provides familiar garbage-collection memory management for .NET developers.

Common Type System and Type Safety

One of the benefits of using strong typing is the ability to specify types and rely on the run time to enforce that for you, and it's no different with the CoreCLR. The CLR relies on the common type system to provide a framework for understanding types and ensuring that they play well together. This also includes generics, which have become essential for .NET development since they were introduced in .NET 2.0.

Exception Handling

You get the same, familiar try-catch-finally semantics for exception handling.

Threading

You get familiar threading experiences, although most developers should rarely need to go very deep with this. It is a multithreaded environment, and the BCL provides classes for creating and controlling threads as well as familiar synchronization mechanisms. That said, most work will be done on the UI thread except when calling network services, which are asynchronous by default in Silverlight (as they are, essentially, in AJAX). There is also a relatively easy API to do intensive work on the background thread via the `BackgroundWorker` class.

Code Security

Good-bye, Code Access Security (CAS), and good riddance! While CAS was certainly one of the more innovative aspects of .NET, it caused no end of confusion and headache for developers, particularly when they were going to deploy applications and when they were trying to run them in the browser (e.g., XBAP for WPF).

Silverlight does away with all that by simply limiting the libraries, that is, the things developers can do, inherently. There is no way to request or demand elevated privileges — developers are completely sandboxed. So there is no need for CAS. This greatly reduces one of the big pains in deployment and troubleshooting.

There are certain attributes that code can use to get at protected resources, but the use of these is limited to Microsoft libraries; thus essentially, developers get free, invisible code security.

Base Class Library (BCL)

The Base Class Library (BCL) is quite a monster, but it provides the lifeblood of .NET applications. Microsoft has gone through it with a fine-toothed comb to pick out the facilities that developers need to develop rich applications on the Web, and that's what you get in Silverlight.

Strings and Other Base Types

As you certainly should expect, the BCL gives you all the common base types that you've grown accustomed to doing in .NET development — strings, integers, DateTime, TimeSpan, floating points, decimal, and so on. As far as your code is concerned, not much should change here; however, there are some minor distinctions on some of the utility methods for converting and parsing, for example. That said, you do get pretty much all of the conversion and parsing utilities you're used to for the common base types.

Input/Output

For input/output (I/O), you're pretty much limited to in-memory I/O streams, readers, and writers, as well as the new Isolated Storage API for accessing a sandboxed filesystem. The nice thing is that working with the Isolated Storage API is very much like working with the standard filesystem API.

Cryptography

Cryptography is, of course, an important consideration for Silverlight since it is an inherently network-based application platform. The BCL doesn't let you down here, providing the standard symmetric and asymmetric encryption/decryption algorithms you're used to, as well as standard hashing algorithms. The APIs should be familiar to .NET developers currently using them.

Reflection

The Silverlight BCL has support for standard .NET reflection over the Silverlight for a .NET type system. No surprises there; however, you need to be aware of the boundaries such as when you cross over from .NET to JavaScript or unmanaged types — you'll get limited information in those cases.

The Silverlight BCL also supports the dynamic creation of new types and assemblies through the `Reflection.Emit` classes as in the standard BCL.

Collections

As noted in the CLR section, .NET for Silverlight supports generics and is thus able to support all that entails, including the new 3.5 language features like LINQ. This means that you can use generic collections and their built-in enumerators to easily group like types and perform queries over them, which is a big leap over standard for-each approaches.

The main collections are arrays, lists, dictionaries, queues, and stacks, and the BCL has both the generic and non-generic versions of these. Choosing between them is no different in Silverlight from in standard .NET.

Globalization

The globalization services are covered in more detail in Chapter 16, but suffice it to say here that Silverlight supports the facilities that .NET developers have grown used to in terms of customized sorting, formatting, parsing, and culture info types, including calendaring.

Serialization

Whether or not serialization belongs under the Base Class Library is debatable, depending on what is meant. Silverlight supports essentially two kinds of serialization formats — XML and JSON. Of course, XML has two options: POX and SOAP. The reasoning here, one can only assume, is that being a client-side technology with access to only isolated storage, XML is pretty much the only format one needs, although we can imagine a desire for binary blobs cached in isolated storage. In any case, you control your two basic serialization formats using the Windows Communication Foundation (WCF) approach of data contracts (and also message contracts), or you can use the new Silverlight "opt out" model, which is reminiscent of the old standard XML serialization based on type/member names and access modifiers (public/private). The converse of this is that there are no `ISerializable`, `XmlElement`, or Array of type `XmlNode` or `IXmlSerializable` types that can be used in Silverlight 3 data contracts. In other words, Silverlight is simplifying because it doesn't require as high a degree of backward compatibility (because it can, and it's the right thing to do). New to Silverlight 3 is the ability to use a binary serialization for service data. Using binary writers and readers should further optimize the payloads from server to client and increase the overall performance of service calls.

Silverlight Class Library (SCL)

Don't bother live-searching for *SCL*; we made *Silverlight Class Library (SCL)* up to describe the new libraries that Silverlight provides to do new "Silverlighty" things. If you like it, blog about it, so it'll catch on.

Isolated Storage

As covered in more detail in other chapters of the book, Silverlight provides an isolated space on the disk and exposes it via a virtual filesystem emulating the Windows filesystem that should be familiar to .NET developers — it supports just simple single-file access (stored in a root folder) as well as a hierarchical tree of folders.

The actual location of the files will vary based on the Silverlight hosting environment. In terms of space, all applications on a domain (e.g., `wrox.com`) share a single quota group, and applications must ask the user to increase it if need be. By default, the quota is 1 MB.

Browser Interop

One of the big advantages of Silverlight is the tight integration with the browser and the ability to automate and execute code across the plug-in boundary; that is, JavaScript can fiddle around with managed objects, respond to managed events, and call managed methods, and vice versa. This is done via this thing they're calling the *HTML bridge*. Not only is it a great tool for applications that are integrating HTML-based stuff and Silverlight, but also it is currently the means of communication between Silverlight instances on a page.

Packaging

Silverlight 3 deployment entails packaging the application and, potentially, related resources into a single .xap file. The current format of the XAP file is simple ZIP packaging and compression, and Silverlight supplies APIs to deal with this as well as accessing other resources and packages. This facilitates the ability to split up the application into chunks to reduce initial download size if so desired. There is also support for splash screen customization.

To reduce the size of the XAP file in Silverlight 3, Microsoft has enabled the caching of System assemblies used for multiple projects on the client. You can set this up through your project's Properties options, and from then on, the Microsoft assemblies will be downloaded once from Microsoft, and they will not be included in the XAP for your application.

Networking

Given that Silverlight lives in a browser, it comes naturally for it to rely heavily on HTTP for communications and understand the common wire formats. In addition to HTTP, Silverlight provides sockets.

Some general HTTP networking restrictions to keep in mind are:

❑ Silverlight uses the browser's networking stack, so authentication and things like cookies are managed by the browser.

❑ Similarly, the number of open connections available is limited by the browser. Keep that in mind, especially if you're using duplex binding, which essentially will tie up one of those.

Windows Communication Foundation (WCF)

The BCL section touched on some aspects of what could be considered part of Windows Communication Foundation (WCF); the thing is that for serialization in Silverlight, WCF is not an add-on but really the foundation, and, of course, serialization doesn't have to be geared toward communication, although it often is. This section highlights the features of WCF that are in Silverlight.

Silverlight uses WCF-based Web services clients for services that conform to the WS-I Basic Profile 1.0, that is, SOAP 1.1 over HTTP. The bindings supported are BasicHttpBinding, BinaryHttpBinding (the new default binding), and a derivative duplex binding for polling-based duplex services. There are a few other notable limitations for SOAP-based and .NET-based services:

❑ No other version of SOAP or any other WS-* protocols are inherently supported, so you could, for example, insert authentication headers into the message.

❑ DataSets are right out. You can use direct HTTP access and get them as XML, but Microsoft does not recommend that.

❑ Watch out for types that use the `SerializableAttribute` and the `ISerializable` interface; these may not be consumable by Silverlight applications.

❑ ASP.NET AJAX WCF services need to have a basic HTTP binding added along with metadata publishing.

❑ ASMX AJAX services using `Dictionary<string, object>` for arbitrary JSON data must be re-done to not use that approach.

❑ Page methods and update panel-related services are not supported.

HTTP Request and Response

Silverlight provides generic HTTP `request` and `response` objects for accessing non-SOAP-based services. In addition, the `WebClient` type provides a simplified wrapper that will serve most common scenarios.

REST and POX

Silverlight uses the basic HTTP request/response or `WebClient` objects and then parses the data appropriately using XML deserialization, XLINQ, or the generic XML reader.

RSS/Atom Syndication

Silverlight provides special classes to make consuming feeds easier.

JSON

Silverlight has special classes for handling JSON deserialization using data contract attributes and also supplies special classes for dealing with weakly typed JSON as well.

Sockets

Silverlight provides a managed implementation of the appropriate sockets interface for the platform it is run on (e.g., Winsock on Windows and the BSD UNIX interface on OS X). This enables you to have full duplex communication over TCP using DNS or IP-based endpoints in the range of ports between 4502 and 4534.

Data

No application would be complete without data, and Silverlight has support for various kinds.

Objects — LINQ

Applications using custom objects or client proxies generated by service references can take full advantage of LINQ to perform queries over those objects.

XML — LINQ to XML (XLINQ)

As noted in the networking and serialization sections, there are a few ways to deal with XML in Silverlight. You have the basic XML readers, the XML deserializer for known types, and XLINQ for more advanced free-form XML exploration and manipulation.

JSON

As noted in the networking section, Silverlight provides a few classes to manipulate JSON-based data objects without needing to deserialize them to strongly typed objects.

ADO.NET (or .NOT)

Being the browser-based technology it is and living in that sandbox, currently there is zero support for ADO.NET in Silverlight. Just glance over the list of namespaces in the MSDN Library class reference — it is conspicuously missing `System.Data`. This means absolutely no direct connections to databases and also no data readers, no data sets, no data adapters, and the like. Get used to it! So how would you ADO.NET? Look to ADO.NET Data Services (formerly known as *Astoria*) to give you a solid data option for your applications.

Windows Presentation Foundation (WPF)

Most of what Windows Presentation Foundation provides is built into the presentation core, but in terms of what you might consider more specifically in the .NET layer, Silverlight provides several controls to help out.

Layout

Silverlight 2 had the `Canvas` for absolute positioning, `StackPanel` for basic stack-based layout, and `Grid` for everything else (well, for grid-based layout). Silverlight 3 has added the `DockPanel` and `WrapPanel`, so the combined five layout options pretty much cover all of the scenarios for basic layout. Look to third-party vendors for docking controls, animated layout controls, and other layout derivatives.

Data Binding

Data templates are provided so you can have reusable UI templates for your data-bound elements. As in WPF, Silverlight uses the DataContext approach for data binding, and, since ADO.NET does not exist in Silverlight, you're always binding to objects or XML. New in Silverlight 3 is the element-to-element binding found in WPF. For example, a bound value property of a `Slider` control can be linked (bound) declaratively via XAML to filter values in a data grid. All of this can happen without a need to use code-behind or any server calls.

Other Controls

There are many other controls that have been added in Silverlight 3 based on the new control model. These are usually more complex controls like textboxes, date pickers, calendars, and so on targeted at making full-fledged interactive applications more feasible in Silverlight. These will continue to be built-out in add-on packs by Microsoft as time progresses and can be opted into, but there is a core set that is installed in the Silverlight run time.

Dynamic Language Runtime (DLR)

The last area to think about in this whirlwind tour of Silverlight is the Dynamic Language Runtime (DLR). This is an additive run time that sits on top of the CLR to interpret dynamic languages. Out-of-the-box, though, you have to opt into both the DLR and languages in your applications. Microsoft is providing IronPython, IronRuby, and Managed JScript.

Summary

That completes this 30,000-foot overview of Silverlight capabilities and how they all play together. The three highest-level components are:

- ❑ The Browser Host
- ❑ The Silverlight Presentation Core
- ❑ .NET for Silverlight

Within the last one, there are two main divisions — the run times (CLR and DLR) and the frameworks that empower .NET developers to create rich web applications, leveraging the experience they've gained over the last several years building .NET applications. If you've learned WPF, you have an even bigger head start, and that's a huge value proposition when considering Silverlight over other rich web application technologies like Flash, Flex, and JavaFX.

You can see how Silverlight delivers the power of a rich interactive application platform that runs cross-browser and cross-platform and will in the long run (and possibly in the short run) drastically reduce TCO. For the rest of the book, you'll be diving into the various components of Silverlight to learn how you can build applications for this great platform.

4

Silverlight Developer Toolbox

Microsoft has a long history of supporting developers not only by providing innovative and powerful development platforms, but also through the significant investment it has made in providing developers with amazing development tools. These tools empower developers to make the most of their chosen development platform, lower the barriers to developers learning a new platform, and make developers dramatically more productive on their platform.

This tradition continues with the Silverlight 3 platform, which Microsoft has made available with several developer productivity tools. Microsoft has also recognized the importance of user experience in the platform and the role that designers are playing in software development, so they have expanded their platform to include tools specifically designed for designers. Expression Blend 3 extends the already impressive Blend design tools into the Silverlight 3 platform, allowing designers to easily contribute their usability and design talents to a software development team. Finally, media is becoming such an important part of the Web, and because Silverlight 3 includes amazing media capabilities, Microsoft offers Expression Encoder as an easy-to-use tool for readying your media assets for the Web.

In this chapter, you will learn what you need to get started developing Silverlight 3–based applications, as well as learn about the tools available to you, whether you are a developer, a designer, or wear both hats. The chapter gets started by discussing the minimum requirements for creating a basic Silverlight 3 development or design environment. Next, the chapter introduces you to the Silverlight 3 development tools available for Visual Studio 2008, then the Silverlight 3 designer tool Expression Blend. Finally, the chapter walks you through a basic overview of the Expression Encoder media-encoding application.

Silverlight 3 Tools

As with most other software platforms, there are several tools you need to download and install before you can begin creating your own Silverlight 3 applications. Microsoft has packaged the Silverlight platform tools in various ways that can be somewhat confusing, so the first section of this chapter will walk you through the different options for acquiring and installing the basic tools required for Silverlight 3 development.

Silverlight 3 Tools for Visual Studio 2008

If you are a developer using Visual Studio 2008, then the first and easiest option you have for setting up a Silverlight 3 development environment is to download and install the Silverlight 3 Tools for Visual Studio 2008 SP1. This installation provides all of the tools you need to start creating Silverlight 3 applications inside Visual Studio 2008, all in one convenient download available at the following URL: http://sn.im/ezw20.

The "Silverlight 3 Tools for Visual Studio 2008 SP1" package installs the Silverlight 3 Developers Runtime, Silverlight 3 SDK, and, as the name implies, several developer tools that plug into Visual Studio 2008 SP1. You will learn more about the tools provided later in this chapter.

Before installing the Silverlight 3 Tools for Visual Studio 2008 SP1, be aware that because Visual Studio 2008 does not support multitargeting for Silverlight projects, if you install the Silverlight 3 tools for Visual Studio 2008, you will no longer be able to create applications that target Silverlight 2. If you open an existing project written using the *Silverlight 2* Tools for Visual Studio 2008 SP1, Visual Studio will prompt you to upgrade those projects to *Silverlight 3*.

Developers can install the Silverlight 3 Tools for the Visual Studio 2008 SP1 package with any version of Visual Studio 2008 SP1, or with Visual Web Developer 2008 Express with SP1.

Expression Blend 3

For designers, the easiest way to get a Silverlight 3 design environment up and running is to download and install Blend 3, which is available at the following URL: http://sn.im/ezw2u.

Expression Blend 3 adds support for Silverlight 3 applications and provides user interface (UI) designers with a familiar environment in which they can easily style Silverlight 3 applications. You will learn more about the tools provided by Blend 3 later in this chapter.

Silverlight Runtime and SDK

Finally, for developers who want to use a different IDE or prefer a more lightweight development environment, Microsoft does allow you to download the different Silverlight development components individually.

To do this, begin by downloading and installing the Silverlight 3 Developers Runtime, using this URL: http://sn.im/ezw39.

The standard Silverlight 3 run time is highly optimized in order to keep the download size of the player to an absolute minimum. This comes at some cost to developers because part of the optimizations includes the removal of things that are helpful to developers such as exception messages. The Developers Runtime differs from the standard runtime installation in that it can provide you with more detailed debugging and error information but is a slightly larger download size.

Next, download and install the Silverlight 3 SDK using the following URL: http://sn.im/ezw3q.

The SDK includes tools, libraries, documentation, and samples needed to develop for Silverlight 3. By default, the SDK installs itself to C:\Program Files\Microsoft SDKs\Silverlight\v3.0. The SDK installs the following folders:

❑ **Libraries** — Contains both Client and Server libraries. The Client libraries contain all of the Silverlight Extensions and User Controls. The Server libraries contain Silverlight Server Controls.

❑ **SDK Help** — Help using and navigating the SDK

❑ **Tools** — Contains several useful tools including a debug instance of the Silverlight client script file (silverlight.js) and an instance of the Silverlight 3 service reference proxy generation utility.

The Developer Runtime and SDK are the minimum requirements needed in order to build and package Silverlight 3 applications. Once you have that installed, you can use your favorite editor (such as Notepad) to begin creating Silverlight 3 applications.

Developing with Silverlight 3 Tools for Visual Studio 2008 SP1

For developers who are using Visual Studio 2008 SP1, the Silverlight 3 Tools for Visual Studio 2008 SP1 currently offer the best development Silverlight 3 environment. Furthermore, because they simply extend the existing functionality of Visual Studio, which you probably are already familiar with, the tools let you get started building applications quickly.

The Silverlight 3 Tools for Visual Studio 2008 SP1 contain all of the pieces you need to get started developing Silverlight 3 applications. Included in the installation package are:

❑ Silverlight 3 Developers Runtime

❑ Silverlight 3 SDK

❑ Visual Studio 2008 project templates

❑ Visual Studio development tools

You can install the tools with any version of Visual Studio 2008 SP1 or with Visual Web Developer Express with SP1.

> *For developers who have installed any beta versions of the Silverlight 3 Tools for Visual Studio 2008 SP1, you will need to make sure you completely uninstall them before installing the release version of the tools.*

Let's take a look at creating new Silverlight applications and the tools that Silverlight 3 Tools for Visual Studio 2008 SP1 provides to you so that you will be familiar with them as you move through the rest of the book.

Silverlight Project Templates

Once you have the Silverlight Tools for Visual Studio 2008 SP1 installed, you can get started creating your first Silverlight application. When you open the Visual Studio New Project dialog, shown in Figure 4-1, you will see a new Silverlight project type in the "Project types" tree. Choosing the Silverlight project type, you can see three Silverlight project templates: Silverlight Application, Silverlight Class Library, and Silverlight Navigation Application.

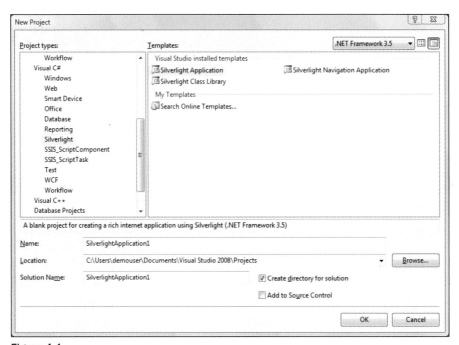

Figure 4-1

The *Silverlight Application* project template sets up a new Silverlight application, which compiles to the XAP file for deployment to your Web Server. A XAP file is the deployment package used by Silverlight 3, which generally contains all of the assemblies and resources used by an application, as well as a manifest file, which tells Silverlight about the contents of the XAP.

> *A XAP file is simply a ZIP archive. You can simply change the extension of the XAP file from .xap to .zip, and you can then open the archive using your favorite ZIP utility.*

The *Silverlight Class Library* project template sets up a basic Silverlight class library. A *class library* allows you to create assemblies that are compiled against the Silverlight libraries and that you can reference in other Silverlight application projects. When an external assembly is referenced by a Silverlight application, it is by default automatically included in the XAP file generated by the Silverlight application.

A Silverlight class library may appear to be very similar to a standard Class Library project; however, there is one significant difference. The Silverlight class library references libraries that are specific to Silverlight, so even though both projects have references to identically named assemblies (such as System *and* System.Core*), these references actually point to different assemblies. You can see this by looking at the* Path *property of the assembly references. This is important because you cannot simply reference an existing .NET class library in a Silverlight application. It must be explicitly compiled against the Silverlight 3 framework assemblies.*

The *Silverlight Navigation Application* project template sets up a new Silverlight application, but uses a template that provides you with a project that leverages Silverlight 3's new navigation framework. The project's main page includes the new Frame element, and the Views folder is where you would create new XAML pages that should be included in your application's navigation.

Generally, when beginning a new Silverlight project, you will want to start by choosing the Silverlight Application or Silverlight Navigation Application project templates. Once you choose either of these project types, provide a name for the project, and click OK, Visual Studio will provide you with the opportunity to associate a new Silverlight application with a Web project. Because Silverlight applications are hosted as objects inside a Web page, associating a Silverlight application with a Web project allows you to develop and debug both applications seamlessly.

The New Silverlight Application dialog, shown in Figure 4-2, allows you to configure exactly how the Silverlight application should be hosted.

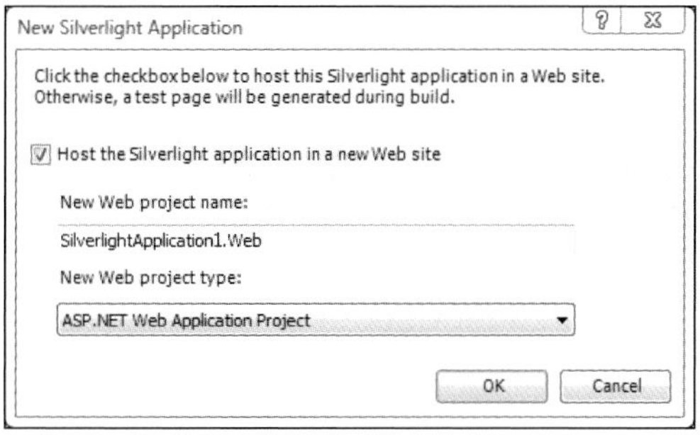

Figure 4-2

By default, Visual Studio assumes that you want to create a new ASP.NET Web Application Project within your solution; however, you can have Visual Studio generate a new ASP.NET web site, or even to not associate the Silverlight application with any Web project and simply have Visual Studio dynamically generate a host Web page when you run the application.

Once you choose the web-site association, you are done configuring the Silverlight application and it will be loaded in Visual Studio. Figure 4-3 shows the solution structure of a newly created Silverlight Application Project type. In this case, a new Web Application Project has also been created and added to the solution.

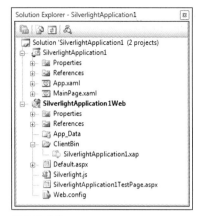

Figure 4-3

You can see that the Silverlight Application project template sets up a standard Silverlight application, including default App.xaml and MainPage.xaml files. The web application created with Silverlight Application includes an ASP.NET test host page, as well as a ClientBin folder, which is where Visual Studio places the Silverlight Applications–compiled XAP file.

Should you ever want to change the Silverlight application associated with a Web project, or even associate additional Silverlight applications with a Web project, you can do this by accessing the Silverlight Applications section of the Web projects Properties dialog, which is shown in Figure 4-4.

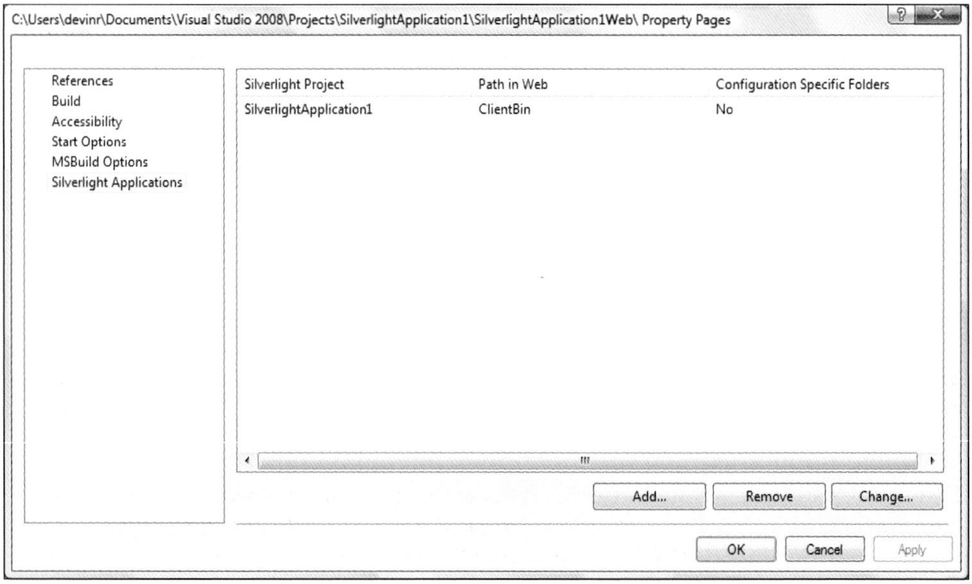

Figure 4-4

Visual Studio Silverlight Development Tools

As part of the Silverlight 3 Tools for Visual Studio 2008 SP1, several new developer tools are installed inside Visual Studio that will help you be more productive in creating Silverlight applications. Tools like the XAML Editor and Toolbox all are shown once a Silverlight application is opened in Visual Studio.

XAML Editor

The Silverlight XAML Editor allows you to edit your application's XAML markup. To assist you in writing the markup, the Editor includes IntelliSense, which will automatically show the properties of any assemblies or objects referenced in the XAML markup. If you are familiar with the WPF XAML Editor, the Silverlight XAML Editor may look and feel very familiar to you, however, remember that Silverlight is considered a subset of WPF. When editing XAML in a Silverlight application, the XAML Editor is smart enough to only display and allow you to enter Silverlight-specific markup, and attempting to enter markup that may be valid in WPF but not in Silverlight will cause the Editor to display errors.

By default, the XAML IntelliSense will work automatically for all of the native Silverlight objects; however, there will be times where you have created your own custom objects that you want to refer to in the XAML. To do this, you need to make sure that you add a namespace reference to the top of your `UserControl`. Doing this tells Silverlight about this new reference and assigns it a unique namespace within the XAML markup.

Figure 4-5 demonstrates how Visual Studio assists you in adding additional namespace references to a `UserControl`'s XAML.

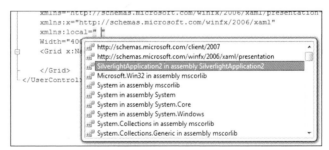

Figure 4-5

The Editor will display namespace information for all .NET namespaces that are included as project references as well as in the project itself. In this case, Figure 4-5 demonstrates adding a namespace reference to an object stored in the local project.

Once the namespace reference is added to the `UserContol`, the XAML Editor is able to offer IntelliSense for that object automatically. Figure 4-6 demonstrates how, once the local namespace is added, IntelliSense displays all of the objects in that namespace.

Figure 4-6

The XAML Editor can also assist you in creating event handlers within your XAML. Figure 4-7 demonstrates how, when you add the `Click` event to the `Button` object in XAML, the Editor automatically offers to create a new event handler for you in the XAML code-behind.

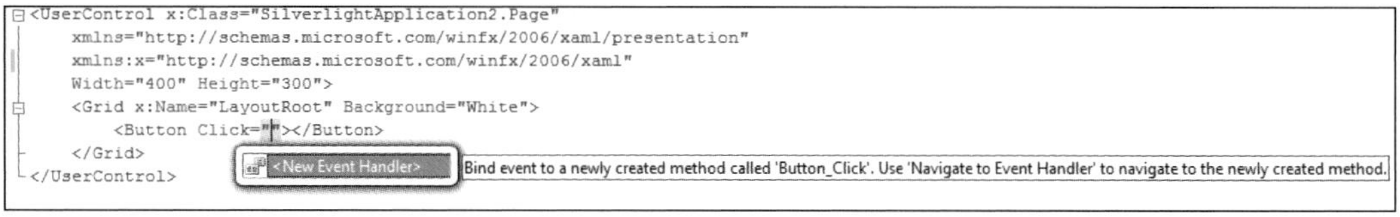

```
<UserControl x:Class="SilverlightApplication2.Page"
    xmlns="http://schemas.microsoft.com/winfx/2006/xaml/presentation"
    xmlns:x="http://schemas.microsoft.com/winfx/2006/xaml"
    Width="400" Height="300">
    <Grid x:Name="LayoutRoot" Background="White">
        <Button Click="|"></Button>
    </Grid>
</UserControl>
```
`<New Event Handler>`   Bind event to a newly created method called 'Button_Click'. Use 'Navigate to Event Handler' to navigate to the newly created method.

Figure 4-7

Designing with Expression Blend 3

Expression Blend is a design tool that was originally targeted to user interface and interaction designers working with the WPF (Windows Presentation Foundation) platform. It is designed to provide a familiar tool for designers who are transitioning to the XAML-based platforms that Microsoft now offers. Because WPF and Silverlight share a common user interface definition language (XAML), it made sense that Microsoft would simply extend Blend to support the design of Silverlight applications. With the release of Blend 3, Blend now supports projects that target all of Microsoft's XAML-based platforms: the rich-client WPF platform, the original Silverlight 1.0 platform, and the new Silverlight 3 platform.

In this chapter, you will get a quick overview of the basic capabilities of Blend 3. Chapter 8 provides a far more in-depth lesson on using the design tools provided by Blend to design your Silverlight applications.

Creating Projects

To get started using Blend to design your Silverlight 3 application, you first need to make sure that you have the Silverlight run time installed. Although Blend installs the portions of the Silverlight SDK needed to create Silverlight applications, it does not install the actual Silverlight player. Running an application without having the player installed will result in the normal installation prompts to occur in the browser. However, Blend users can download and install the Silverlight 3 Developers Runtime, as described earlier in this chapter, rather than using the standard run time in order to receive better debugging and exception information from the run time.

Once you have the run time installed, you can install Blend 3. Once you have the Service Pack installed, you will see a new project type called *Silverlight 3 Application* added to its New Project dialog, shown in Figure 4-8.

Figure 4-8

Choose this new project type to create a new Silverlight 3–based application.

Once you create a new Silverlight 3 application in Blend, you will immediately notice that Blend offers much of the same tooling for Silverlight 3 applications as it does for other supported platforms, including a simple design surface, property editor, and toolbox. The default Blend user interface with a Silverlight 3 application loaded is shown in Figure 4-9.

A quick survey of the Blend tools includes the Project Explorer, which displays the files included in the project, an interactive Silverlight 3 design surface, a XAML Editor, a powerful Properties pane, and a toolbox that includes all of the drawing tools you will need to build your application.

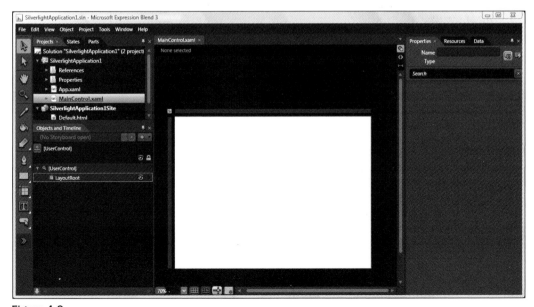

Figure 4-9

If you are collaborating with a developer who is using Visual Studio 2008, Blend 2 uses the same Solution and Project structure as Visual Studio, so sharing projects between the two environments is possible. Either the designer or the developer can use his or her environment to create a new project.

Blend 3 includes integration for Microsoft's Visual Studio Team System source control system, so designers working in organizations using this to store their application resources can access and work with resources stored in source control. Currently, Team System is the only source control system with integrated Blend 3 support. If your team is using some other type of source control system, you will need to use an external source control management application in order to work with resources stored in source control.

Getting around Blend

Once you open a project inside Blend, you can start working with the design surface to create your application's user interface. The toolbox allows you to simply double-click on controls like the `Grid` and `Button` to add them to your design surface. Once a control is added to the design surface, you can use the Properties tool pane to change the style and behavior of the control, as well as create event handlers for the controls.

When creating event handlers, if you have Visual Studio 2008 also installed, Blend will attempt to open the Silverlight application project in a new instance of Visual Studio to allow you to work with the event-handling code right away. You can configure this behavior of Blend in the Options dialog.

Additionally, Blend 3 supports an improved code-editing experience, providing IntelliSense in XAML view.

Generating Video Using Expression Encoder

The role of audio and video on the Web has exploded in recent years, and Silverlight is designed to make the integration of media assets a snap. Part of the process of getting media on the Web involves encoding raw media files into a format that is suitable for the Web, and to help in this process, Microsoft has introduced the Expression Encoder 2 application. Expression Encoder gives you the power to ready your media files for the Web, including encoding media files at various bitrates based on your needs, adding pre-rollers and post-rollers, overlaying images, adding marker information, and even publishing files directly to the Microsoft Silverlight Streaming service. In this chapter, you will get a brief introduction to Expression Encoder, and Chapter 10 will provide more detailed information on the product.

Using Expression Encoder

To begin getting your media ready for distribution with Expression Media Encoder, you first need to download and install the application, which can be done using the following URL: http://sn.im/ezw58.

Once you have Encoder installed, take a quick look around its fairly simple UI. The primary focus of the interface is the Preview area in the middle. The Preview area allows you to step through your media frame-by-frame, using the Timeline and VCR buttons as well as the Preview function, and even lets you compare the original video with a sample of encoded video side-by-side. The timeline allows you to insert new markers, clip the media length, and add leaders and trailer video clips.

Below the Preview area is the Media Content List. This area lists all of the media files that are included in your current encoding project. You can choose to import media (Encoder supports importing from

17 different video formats and seven different audio formats), or you can choose to encode directly from a live media feed such as a video camera. Figure 4-10 shows the Encoder application with a single media file imported.

With a media file imported or a live stream configured, Encoder now allows you to choose how you encode the files. There are 14 predefined video encoding profiles and seven predefined audio profiles that allow you to select an encoding specific to your needs, whether that is high-quality HD video or bandwidth-frugal audio. Of course, you can always customize the encoding settings and save them as your own custom profile.

Publishing Encoded Video

Once your video has completed encoding, you next need to find some way to publish the video for others to view. Microsoft has introduced a streaming video service that offers a simple and free way to publish your videos to the Web.

> *For more information on the Microsoft Streaming Media service, check out* `http://sn.im/ezw5z.`

Encoder takes advantage of this service by offering the Silverlight Streaming Publishing plug-in for Expression Encoder, which can be downloaded from the following URL: `http://sn.im/ezw6h.`

Once installed, this simple plug-in allows you to encode your video and then publish it as a Silverlight application directly to the Streaming service, allowing others to view it online.

Figure 4-10

Summary

In this chapter, you have been introduced to the tools that allow you to create amazing Silverlight applications and that will be demonstrated in greater detail through the rest of this book. The chapter started by introducing you to the most basic tools needed to create a Silverlight development environment, including the Silverlight Developers Runtime and Silverlight 3 SDK.

You then looked at some of the more advanced tools available for developers and designers of Silverlight 3 applications. For developers, the Silverlight 3 Tools for Visual Studio 2008 SP1 offer a great set of tools that plug directly into the Visual Studio 2008 development environment, which most .NET developers should already be familiar with. The project templates and XAML Editor all allow a developer to get up and be coding new Silverlight 3 applications quickly.

Expression Blend 3 has added support for Silverlight 3 projects that allows designers to contribute their talents to the creation of new Silverlight 3 applications easily. Because it offers many of the familiar styling tools for Silverlight that are used for WPF, designers using Blend should be able to transition easily into Silverlight.

Finally, as media continues to play a more dominant role in delivering content over the Web, Expression Encoder provides even novice users with a simple and understandable way to encode video and audio media elements, including live streams, into formats that can easily be delivered using the Silverlight platform. Coupled with the Silverlight Streaming plug-in, Encoder is a compelling tool for readying your media assets for online use.

Part II: Using Silverlight 3 Essentials

Chapter 5: Controls

Chapter 6: Silverlight Text

Chapter 7: Layout

Chapter 8: Styling Your App and Dealing with Resources

Chapter 9: Using Graphics and Visuals

Chapter 10: Making It Richer with Media

Chapter 11: Using the Services

5

Controls

While Silverlight 1.0 focused on many of the core features of Silverlight such as XAML, Silverlight 2 took the platform to the next level by adding a managed-code framework, and a benefit of that is the ability to introduce controls to the platform. Silverlight 3 continues that trend by adding several new controls.

For developers who need to be productive, controls provide encapsulated reusable chunks of behavior and a UI that make it easy to add common user interface patterns to your application. Rather than being responsible for drawing every minor detail and coding every behavior, controls allow you to focus more on the specific requirements of your application and less on developing those lower-level capabilities.

This chapter will introduce you to many of the common and more complex controls that are included in the default Silverlight 3 toolbox. The chapter is not intended to be an in-depth guide to every single control included in Silverlight 3, simply because many of the controls are fairly self-explanatory (e.g., Checkbox). Additionally, some controls such as MediaElement are discussed in detail in other, more applicable chapters in this book.

Text Input

Silverlight 3 includes a TextBox control, which provides the same basic text input capabilities you are used to receiving from the HTML <input> element. The control offers single-format, multiline input capabilities with automatic text wrapping, as well as integration with the clipboard. An undo/redo stack is also included. The following code demonstrates using the TextBox:

```
<UserControl x:Class="SilverlightApplication4.SilverlightControl13"
    xmlns="http://schemas.microsoft.com/winfx/2006/xaml/presentation"
    xmlns:x="http://schemas.microsoft.com/winfx/2006/xaml"
    Width="400" Height="300">
    <Grid x:Name="LayoutRoot" Background="White">
        <TextBox Text="Lorum Ipsum" />
    </Grid>
</UserControl>
```

For those creating applications for international audiences, the control supports IME Level 3 when run on Windows and Level 1 when run on a Mac. It also includes international keyboard support.

As you might expect, the TextBox exposes a TextChanged event that you can use to be notified when the user changes the TextBox's text.

Also included in Silverlight 3 is the PasswordBox. Related to the TextBox, the PasswordBox gives you a convenient way to allow users to enter a password into your application. The control allows you to change the password character displayed to the end-user. The following code demonstrates the use of the PasswordBox:

```
<UserControl x:Class="SilverlightApplication4.SilverlightControl14"
    xmlns="http://schemas.microsoft.com/winfx/2006/xaml/presentation"
    xmlns:x="http://schemas.microsoft.com/winfx/2006/xaml"
    Width="400" Height="300">
    <Grid x:Name="LayoutRoot" Background="White">
        <PasswordBox PasswordChar="#" Password="password" />
    </Grid>
</UserControl>
```

As shown above, you can get or set the value of the PasswordBox by using the control's Password property.

Unlike the TextBox, the PasswordBox accepts only a single line of text, but like the TextBox, it includes a PasswordChanged event that you can use to be notified when the end-user changes the PasswordBox value.

DataGrid

Perhaps most important for application developers building line-of-business controls, Silverlight 3 includes a powerful DataGrid control. This control allows you to easily bind a collection of data to it and have it automatically display the data and allow the end-user to edit the data and manipulate the data display.

Data Binding

To get started using the DataGrid, you simply need to provide it with some data by setting its ItemsSource property to some type of enumerable object, either in XAML or in code. The code that follows shows how to set the property in XAML, using a StaticResource containing a list of employees:

```
<UserControl
xmlns:data="clr-namespace:System.Windows.Controls;
    assembly=System.Windows.Controls.Data"
x:Class="SilverlightApplication4.SilverlightControl16"
    xmlns="http://schemas.microsoft.com/winfx/2006/xaml/presentation"
    xmlns:x="http://schemas.microsoft.com/winfx/2006/xaml"
    xmlns:local="clr-namespace:SilverlightApplication4"
    Width="400" Height="300">
    <UserControl.Resources>
        <local:EmployeeData x:Key="myData" />
    </UserControl.Resources>
```

```
<Grid x:Name="LayoutRoot" Background="White">
    <data:DataGrid
        ItemsSource="{Binding Source={StaticResource myData},
                      Path=EmployeeDataCollection}" />
    </Grid>
</UserControl>
```

Once you set the `ItemsSource` property, the `DataGrid` control will automatically interrogate the data source and generate the appropriate column structure based on public members exposed by the objects on the data source. The rendered `DataGrid` is shown in Figure 5-1.

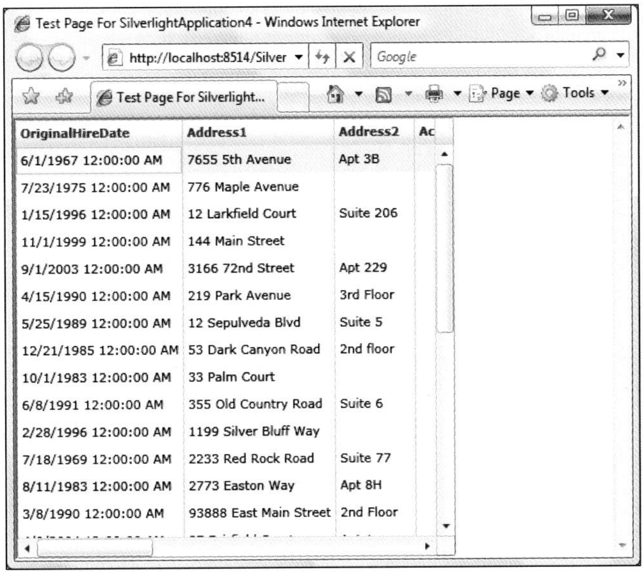

Figure 5-1

Of course, you can also set the `ItemsSource` property in code.

You can control whether or not the control automatically generates columns for you by using the `AutoGenerateColumns` property. If you choose to set this property to false, then you will need to manually define a set of columns for the `DataGrid` to display, using the control's `Columns` collection.

The control also exposes the `AutoGeneratingColumn` event, which allows you to plug your own logic into the column generation process. Using this event, you can access the column currently being created and alter its properties.

The control also exposes the `RowLoading` event, which allows you to access each row as it is being created in the grid.

Note that when the grid is rendered, it takes advantage of UI virtualization in order to maintain a high level of performance. UI virtualization means that the control will only create the UI elements that are needed to display information on the screen. If a row moves out of the visible area of the control, its resources are freed.

The grid also supports the selection of rows in the grid, supporting Single and Extended Selection modes. *Single Selection mode* allows end-users to select only a single row at any given time. *Extended Selection mode* allows them to select multiple rows by holding the [Ctrl] or [Shift] keys while clicking rows. You can change the current selection mode by setting the control's SelectionMode property, as well as access the currently selected item(s) by using the SelectedItem or SelectedItems properties.

Grid Columns

The DataGrid control includes three different column types that you can add to the Columns collection: Text, CheckBox, and Template. Each column allows you to bind a field from the data source to it, using the Binding property.

The next code snippet shows how you can use the Columns collection to display data in the DataGrid using the DataGridTextBoxColumn:

```
<data:DataGrid
    ItemsSource="{Binding Source={StaticResource myData},
                Path=EmployeeDataCollection}"
    AutoGenerateColumns="False" >
        <data:DataGrid.Columns>
            <data:DataGridTextColumn Binding="{Binding EmployeeName}" />
            <data:DataGridTextColumn Binding="{Binding Address1}" />
            <data:DataGridTextColumn Binding="{Binding Address2}" />
            <data:DataGridTextColumn Binding="{Binding City}" />
        </data:DataGrid.Columns>
    </data:DataGrid>
```

Each column exposes a DisplayIndex property that allows you to control the order in which columns are displayed.

Each column also exposes a Header property that allows you to provide text content for the column header. Unfortunately, the DataGrid does not provide a DataTemplate for the header, but if you do want to change the default style of a column header, you can create your own DataGridColumnHeader style and assign it to the column's HeaderStyle property.

If you are manually defining your own columns, you can also do this by using the DataGridCheckBoxColumn in your Columns collection, as shown in the next listing, or if AutoGenerateColumns is set to true, the control will automatically display a checkbox for properties that return a Boolean type:

```
<data:DataGrid
    ItemsSource="{Binding Source={StaticResource myData},
                Path=EmployeeDataCollection}"
    AutoGenerateColumns="False" >
    <data:DataGrid.Columns>
        <data:DataGridCheckBoxColumn Binding="{Binding City}" />
        <data:DataGridTextColumn Binding="{Binding EmployeeName}" />
        <data:DataGridTextColumn Binding="{Binding Address1}" />
        <data:DataGridTextColumn Binding="{Binding Address2}" />
        <data:DataGridTextColumn Binding="{Binding City}" />
    </data:DataGrid.Columns>
</data:DataGrid>
```

Figure 5-2 shows the checkbox column in the DataGrid.

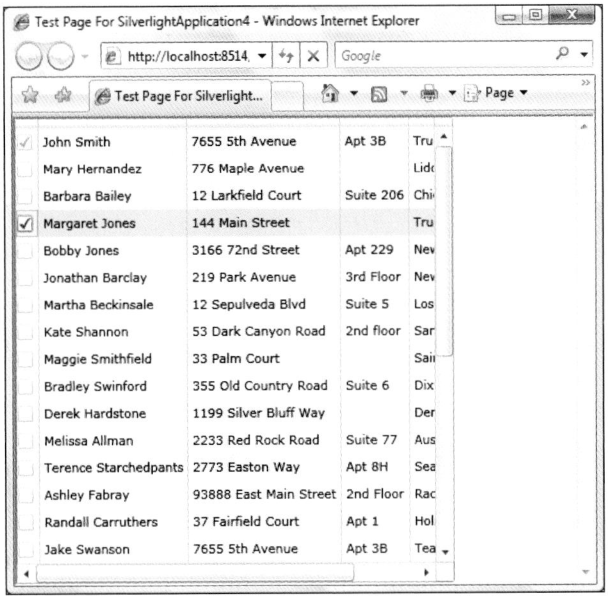

Figure 5-2

The DataGridCheckBoxColumn not only allows you to use a standard two-state checkbox, but also by setting the IsThreeState property, you can have the checkbox behave like a tri-state checkbox. This allows you to set the IsChecked property to true, false, or null.

Finally, if you want total control over the display of the contents of a column, you can use the DataGridTemplateColumn in your Columns collection. This column type allows you to use its CellTemplate property to set a DataTemplate that the column can use to define the cells' display.

The following code snippet shows the use of the DataGridTemplateColumn:

```
<UserControl
xmlns:data="clr-namespace:System.Windows.Controls;
    assembly=System.Windows.Controls.Data"
x:Class="SilverlightApplication4.SilverlightControl6"
    xmlns="http://schemas.microsoft.com/winfx/2006/xaml/presentation"
    xmlns:x="http://schemas.microsoft.com/winfx/2006/xaml"
    xmlns:local="clr-namespace:SilverlightApplication4"
    >
    <UserControl.Resources>
        <local:EmployeeData x:Key="myData" />
        <DataTemplate x:Key="myCellTemplate">
            <Button Content="{Binding State}" />
        </DataTemplate>
    </UserControl.Resources>
    <Grid x:Name="LayoutRoot" Background="White">
```

```
<data:DataGrid
    ItemsSource="{Binding Source={StaticResource myData},
                  Path=EmployeeDataCollection}"
    AutoGenerateColumns="False" >
    <data:DataGrid.Columns>
        <data:DataGridCheckBoxColumn Binding="{Binding Active}" />
        <data:DataGridTextColumn Binding="{Binding EmployeeName}" />
        <data:DataGridTextColumn Binding="{Binding Address1}" />
        <data:DataGridTextColumn Binding="{Binding Address2}" />
        <data:DataGridTextColumn Binding="{Binding City}" />
        <data:DataGridTemplateColumn
            CellTemplate="{StaticResource myCellTemplate}" />
    </data:DataGrid.Columns>
</data:DataGrid>
</Grid>
</UserControl>
```

The `DataGridTemplateColumn` also includes a `CellEditingTemplate` property that allows you to specify a `DataTemplate` that the column should display when a cell enters Edit mode.

When running the `DataGrid` even in the simplest configuration, such as the one shown in the previous listing, you will notice that it provides you with a lot of capabilities right out-of-the-box. For example, clicking on a column header sorts the column data; dragging a column header allows you to change the column display order; hovering over the edge of a column header allows you to resize the column width; and double-clicking a cell places that cell into Edit mode, allowing you to change the cell data. As you will see as you read through the rest of this section, the `DataGrid` exposes properties that allows you to control all of these behaviors both at the control level and on a per-column level.

Sorting

As shown previously, the grid by default enables column sorting. Out-of-the-box, the user can sort individual columns, or by holding down the [Ctrl] or [Shift] keys, the user can click on successive columns, sorting each.

`DataGrid` exposes various properties that allow you to control the grid's sorting behavior. At the root level, you can change whether or not you want to enable sorting in the entire grid by using the `CanUserSortColumns` property. You can also control the sorting behavior on an individual column, using the column's `CanUserSort` property.

Overriding the `DataGridColumnHeader` style as described earlier, you can also control the sort indicator shown in the column header.

Finally, using `SortMemberPath`, you can configure a column to sort a column based on a different data source field than the one configured in the column's `Binding` property.

Column Resizing

`DataGrid` includes properties that allow you to set column widths on each column and heights on rows. Like the standard Grid panel included in Silverlight, `DataGrid` gives you a number of different options for specifying size units. When setting size properties on the `DataGrid`, you can give the `Height` and `Width` properties a value from the `DataGridLength` object.

The `DataGridLengrth` object includes four different size options:

❑   `Auto` — This option sizes the column or row to the size of the largest visible header or cell.

Because the `DataGrid` virtualizes its row UI, it, therefore, cannot know ahead of time what the largest cell contents will be in the entire grid. This means that, as you scroll the rows, if the grid encounters a cell with larger content, you may notice the column or row size increase. Once the size has increased, however, the grid will not revert back to a smaller size once the row has scrolled out of view.

❑   `Size To Header` — Sizes the column or row to the size of the header, ignoring the size of the cell contents.

❑   `Size To Cell` — Sizes the column or row to the size of the largest visible cell. This option also behaves like the Auto option, meaning that the column or row size may change as rows are scrolled.

❑   `Numeric` — Allows you to set a specific pixel base value.

You, the developer, can set sizes on columns, but the `DataGrid` allows not only you but also end-users to resize columns at run time. Since this capability is on by default, you can control this behavior for the entire grid by setting the `CanUserResizeColumns` property on the `DataGrid`. You can also control this on a per-column basis by setting the `CanUserResize` property on an individual column.

The `DataGrid` also allows you to set minimum and maximum column width values, again both at the grid level, using the `DataGrid`'s `MinColumnWidth` and `MaxColumnWidth` properties, and on the column level, using the `MinWidth` and `MaxWidth` properties.

Column Freezing

The `DataGrid` supports freezing columns in the grid. This behavior replicates the Excel frozen columns behavior, which allows you to freeze, or fix, a certain number of columns to the left side of the `DataGrid`. This means that if the grid is displaying a horizontal scrollbar, the frozen columns will remain fixed to the left side of the grid, while the remaining columns are free to scroll horizontally.

You can set the number of columns you want to be included in the freeze using the grid's `FrozenColumnCount` property. The grid will then freeze that number of columns, starting from the left side of the grid.

Column Moving

As described earlier, `DataGrid` allows you to set the order in which columns are displayed by using the `DisplayIndex` property. The control, also by default, allows users to reorder columns in the grid at run time. To do this, the user simply clicks on and drags a column header to a new position in the headers. They are given visual cues to help then determine where the column will be inserted when dropped.

If the user reorders columns at run time, this will reset the `DisplayIndex` property of all other grid columns.

You can control this behavior for the entire grid by using the control's `CanUserReorderColumns` property on the root control or individually on a column, using its `CanUserRender` property. You can also use the series of events exposed by the `DataGrid` to be notified when the end-user initiates and completes a column move.

Row Details

As shown earlier in the chapter, the DataGrid control includes three column types that you can use to control how data is shown. Often, though, you may only want to show summary information in a grid row and to have a separate area for displaying more detailed information about the currently selected row. DataGrid includes a built-in mechanism for this, called the RowDetailsTemplate. This feature allows you to specify a DataTemplate in which you can include additional details for the currently selected row.

The following code demonstrates using the RowDetailsTemplate:

```
<UserControl
xmlns:data="clr-namespace:System.Windows.Controls;
    assembly=System.Windows.Controls.Data"
x:Class="SilverlightApplication4.SilverlightControl15"
    xmlns="http://schemas.microsoft.com/winfx/2006/xaml/presentation"
    xmlns:x="http://schemas.microsoft.com/winfx/2006/xaml"
        xmlns:local="clr-namespace:SilverlightApplication4"
            Width="500"
    >
    <UserControl.Resources>
        <local:EmployeeData x:Key="myData" />
        <DataTemplate x:Key="myCellTemplate">
            <TextBlock Text="{Binding State}" />
        </DataTemplate>
        <DataTemplate x:Key="myRowDetailsTemplate">

            <Grid>
                <Grid.RowDefinitions>
                    <RowDefinition />
                    <RowDefinition />
                    <RowDefinition />
                    <RowDefinition />
                    <RowDefinition />
                </Grid.RowDefinitions>
                <Grid.ColumnDefinitions>
                    <ColumnDefinition />
                    <ColumnDefinition />
                    <ColumnDefinition />
                    <ColumnDefinition />
                </Grid.ColumnDefinitions>

                <TextBlock Grid.Column="0" Grid.Row="0">
                    Original Hire Date:</TextBlock>
                <TextBlock Grid.Column="1" Grid.Row="0"
                    Text="{Binding OriginalHireDate}" />
                <TextBlock Grid.Column="0" Grid.Row="1">Cell Number:</TextBlock>
                <TextBlock Grid.Column="1" Grid.Row="1"
                    Text="{Binding CellNumber}" />
                <TextBlock Grid.Column="0" Grid.Row="2">Phone Number:</TextBlock>
                <TextBlock Grid.Column="1" Grid.Row="2"
                    Text="{Binding PhoneNumber}" />
```

```xml
            <TextBlock Grid.Column="2" Grid.Row="0">Street:</TextBlock>
            <TextBlock Grid.Column="3" Grid.Row="0"
                Text="{Binding Address1}" />
            <TextBlock Grid.Column="2" Grid.Row="1"></TextBlock>
            <TextBlock Grid.Column="3" Grid.Row="1"
                Text="{Binding Address2}" />
            <TextBlock Grid.Column="2" Grid.Row="2">City:</TextBlock>
            <TextBlock Grid.Column="3" Grid.Row="2" Text="{Binding City}" />
            <TextBlock Grid.Column="2" Grid.Row="3">State:</TextBlock>
            <TextBlock Grid.Column="3" Grid.Row="3" Text="{Binding State}" />
            <TextBlock Grid.Column="2" Grid.Row="4">Zip Code:</TextBlock>
            <TextBlock Grid.Column="3" Grid.Row="4" Text="{Binding Zip}" />
        </Grid>

    </DataTemplate>

</UserControl.Resources>
<Grid x:Name="LayoutRoot" Background="White">
    <data:DataGrid FrozenColumnCount="3"
        RowDetailsTemplate="{StaticResource myRowDetailsTemplate}"
        RowDetailsVisibilityMode="VisibleWhenSelected" AutoGenerateColumns="False"
        ItemsSource="{Binding Source={StaticResource myData},
            Path=EmployeeDataCollection}" >
        <data:DataGrid.Columns>
            <data:DataGridCheckBoxColumn Binding="{Binding Active}">

            </data:DataGridCheckBoxColumn>
            <data:DataGridTextColumn Binding="{Binding EmployeeName}"  />
            <data:DataGridTextColumn Binding="{Binding Department}" />
            <data:DataGridTextColumn Binding="{Binding Email}" />
            <data:DataGridCheckBoxColumn Binding="{Binding Active}" />
        </data:DataGrid.Columns>
    </data:DataGrid>

</Grid>
</UserControl>
```

Using the `RowDetailsVisibilityMode` property, the `DataGrid` allows you to configure when this template is shown, having it be either always collapsed for every row, always visible for every row, or only visible for the currently selected row. You can also use the `RowDetailsVisibilityChanged` event to be notified when the `RowDetailsTemplate` is changed.

ListBox, ComboBox, and TabControl

Despite their quite different user interfaces, the `ListBox`, `ComboBox`, and `TabControl` controls are all derived from the same base class (`System.Windows.Controls.ItemsControl`) and allow you to display a list of items and select items in that list. Because they all share the same base class, the controls share many of the same properties and basic behaviors.

The `ListBox` control allows you to display items in a single flat list, specifying the list items either manually or bound from a data source, using the control's `ItemsSource` property. The number of items visible is dictated by the size of the control.

By default, when items are bound using `ItemsSource`, the control will simply output the objects in that list as strings. You can, however, create a `DataTemplate` and provide a far more complex layout for each list item using the `ItemTemplate` property. The next code listing demonstrates the use of the `ListBox`, including the use of a `DataTemplate` to define the list items display:

```xml
<UserControl x:Class="SilverlightApplication4.SilverlightControl1"
    xmlns="http://schemas.microsoft.com/winfx/2006/xaml/presentation"
    xmlns:x="http://schemas.microsoft.com/winfx/2006/xaml"
         xmlns:local="clr-namespace:SilverlightApplication4"
    Width="400" Height="300">
    <UserControl.Resources>
        <local:EmployeeData x:Key="myData" />
        <DataTemplate x:Key="myTemplate">
            <Grid>
                <TextBlock Text="{Binding EmployeeName}" />
            </Grid>
        </DataTemplate>
    </UserControl.Resources>
    <Grid x:Name="LayoutRoot" Background="White">
        <ListBox ItemTemplate="{StaticResource myTemplate}"
            ItemsSource="{Binding Source={StaticResource myData},
                        Path=EmployeeDataCollection}" />
    </Grid>
</UserControl>
```

Another interesting feature of the `ListBox` is the `ItemsPanel` property. This property allows you to specify the layout panel you want the `ListBox` to use when arranging its children. By default, the `ListBox` uses a simple `StackPanel`, but you can create your own layout panel and provide it to the `ListBox`. The code below demonstrates this by providing the `ListBox` with a new `StackPanel` with its `Orientation` property changed:

```xml
<UserControl x:Class="SilverlightApplication4.SilverlightControl1"
    xmlns="http://schemas.microsoft.com/winfx/2006/xaml/presentation"
    xmlns:x="http://schemas.microsoft.com/winfx/2006/xaml"
         xmlns:local="clr-namespace:SilverlightApplication4"
    Width="400" Height="300">
    <UserControl.Resources>
        <local:EmployeeData x:Key="myData" />
        <DataTemplate x:Key="myTemplate">
            <Grid>
                <TextBlock Text="{Binding EmployeeName}" />
            </Grid>
        </DataTemplate>
    </UserControl.Resources>
    <Grid x:Name="LayoutRoot" Background="White">
        <ListBox ItemTemplate="{StaticResource myTemplate}"
            ItemsSource="{Binding Source={StaticResource myData},
                        Path=EmployeeDataCollection}">
            <ListBox.ItemsPanel>
                <ItemsPanelTemplate>
                    <StackPanel Orientation="Horizontal" />
                </ItemsPanelTemplate>
```

```
        </ListBox.ItemsPanel>
      </ListBox>
    </Grid>
</UserControl>
```

The `ComboBox` works much in the same way as the `ListBox`, although rather than displaying items in a flat list, the `ComboBox` displays them in a pop-up display.

The following code demonstrates the user of the `ComboBox` control using the same data source as the previous code listing, and also using the same `DataTemplate`:

```
<ComboBox x:Name="ComboBox1" VerticalAlignment="Top" HorizontalAlignment="Center"
            ItemsSource="{Binding Source={StaticResource myData},
                          Path=EmployeeDataCollection}"
            DisplayMemberPath="Address1">
</ComboBox>
```

You can access the currently selected item of either control by using the `SelectedItem` property, and both controls can also notify you when the current selected item changes, using the `SelectionChanged` event.

The `TabControl` again works much the same way as the `ComboBox` and `ListBox` controls. By using the `ItemsSource` property, you can assign a list of objects as the control's tabs. However, unlike `ListBox` and `ComboBox`, `TabControl` does require a bit of extra work. By default, `TabControl` does not know how to convert the objects in your list into tabs. To help it out, you can create `ValueConverter`, which is shown in the following code:

```
using System.Windows.Data;
using System.Collections.Generic;
using System.Windows.Controls;
using System;
using SilverlightApplication4;
using System.Collections.ObjectModel;
using System.Windows;

namespace SilverlightApplication4
{
    public class TabConverter : IValueConverter
    {
        public object Convert(object value,
            Type targetType, object parameter, System.Globalization.CultureInfo culture)
        {
            ObservableCollection<Employee> source =
                value as ObservableCollection<Employee>;

            FrameworkElement root =
                (FrameworkElement)Application.Current.RootVisual;

            if (root!=null)
            {
                DataTemplate template = (DataTemplate)root.Resources["myTemplate"];
```

```
            if (source != null)
            {
                List<TabItem> result = new List<TabItem>();
                foreach (Employee e in source)
                {
                    result.Add(new TabItem()
                    {
                        Header = e.EmployeeName,
                        ContentTemplate = template,
                        DataContext = e
                    });
                }
                return result;
            }
        }
        return null;
    }

    public object ConvertBack(object value,
        Type targetType, object parameter, System.Globalization.CultureInfo culture)
    {
        throw new NotImplementedException();
    }
}
```

The `ValueConverter` control converts each object in your collection into a tab and assigns the header text, the `DataTemplate`, and a `DataContext` to each tab.

Once you have created the `TabConverter`, you can use it to bind your data to the `TabControl`. This is shown in the following code:

```
<basics:TabControl
    ItemsSource="{Binding Converter={StaticResource myConverter},
                  Source={StaticResource myData},
                        Path=EmployeeDataCollection}"
    ItemTemplate="{StaticResource myTemplate}">

</basics:TabControl>
```

Of course, as with the `ListBox` and `ComboBox` controls, you can also create tabs manually. The following code demonstrates creating tabs directly in XAML using the `TabItem` object:

```
<basics:TabControl>
    <basics:TabControl.Items>
        <basics:TabItem Header="ADSASDA" Content="asdasd" />
    </basics:TabControl.Items>
</basics:TabControl>
```

As with `ComboBox` and `ListBox`, `TabControl` exposes a `SelectedItem` property that allows you to determine which tab is selected, as well as an event that allows you to be notified when the selected tab changes.

Button, HyperLinkButton, and ToggleButton

Silverlight includes the requisite `Button` control, and it offers the same basic behaviors that you would expect a button to, such as Normal, Hover, Pressed, and Click states, and a `click` event, but like other Silverlight controls, the `Button` control uses the power of XAML to allow you to transform the normal gray button into something completely different.

You can first see this if you try to find a `Text` property on the button, which you would expect to be there in order to allow you to set the button's text. This is where the power of Silverlight begins to kick in. Rather than a basic text property, the `Button` control offers a `Content` property that, unlike `Text`, which only accepts a `String`, accepts a more generic `Object`. Using this, you can set the `Content` property to very complex elements such as a checkbox or even another button!

A more realistic example might be placing an image as the button content rather than text. In platforms like Windows Forms, you would need to draw this yourself, or in HTML, you would have to use an `Image` button, both of which have significant drawbacks. The following code demonstrates using the `Content` property to use an `Image` as the button's content:

```
<Button>
    <Button.Content>
        <Image Source="/imagebutton.png" Height="23" Width="50" />
    </Button.Content>
</Button>
```

This example only replaces the content area of the button, but the power of XAML will actually allow you to replace the entire default user interface for `Button`.

Another interesting feature of the `Button` control is the `ClickMode` property. Using this property, you can set when the button's `click` event should fire, when the mouse is hovered, when the mouse is pressed, or when the mouse is released.

Silverlight also includes two additional controls that extend the basic capabilities of the `Button` — the `HyperlinkButton` and the `ToggleButton`.

The `HyperlinkButton`, as the name suggests, allows you to provide the button with a URL value using the `NavigateUri` property. When the `Button` is clicked, Silverlight will automatically navigate the browser to the provided URL.

The next code demonstrates the use of the `HyperlinkButton`:

```
<HyperlinkButton
    ClickMode="Release" NavigateUri="http://www.silverlight.net">
    <HyperlinkButton.Content>
        <TextBlock Text="Click Me!" TextDecorations="Underline" />
    </HyperlinkButton.Content>
</HyperlinkButton>
```

Silverlight also contains a new `ToggleButton` control. This control combines the basic behaviors of a button with the behavior of a checkbox, allowing your `Button` control to have a `Checked` state.

The following code demonstrates the use of the `ToggleButton`:

```
<ToggleButton Content="No, Click ME!" IsChecked="true" />
```

The `ToggleButton` control serves as the base for other controls that have a checked state such as `Check box` and `RadioButton` and therefore supports the same capabilities, including supporting a three-state checked option.

Calendar **and** DatePicker

Silverlight includes two controls that allow you to add date selection to your application — the `Calendar` control and the `DatePicker` control.

The `Calendar` control, as the name implies, renders a calendar, which by default shows a Month view, as shown in Figure 5-3.

Figure 5-3

The control also supports both Year and Decade calendar views, which can be set using the control's `DisplayMode` property. You can also control the selection behavior of the control by setting the `SelectionMode` property. The control supports No Selection, Single Date Selection, Single Date Range Selection, and Multiple Date Range Selection modes. Also, as with other controls, the control exposes a variety of events that allow you to be notified when the currently displayed date changes, a selected date changes, or the display mode changes.

The `DatePicker` control displays a simple `TextBox` entry with an attached calendar pop-up. This is shown in Figure 5-4.

Unlike the `Calendar` control, which allows date ranges to be selected, the `DatePicker` control allows for only a single date to be selected at one time. As with `Calendar`, there are events you can use to be notified when the selected date changes.

```
<M/d/yyyy>                                                    15
```

	◄	**November, 2008**	►			
Su	Mo	Tu	We	Th	Fr	Sa
26	27	28	29	30	31	1
2	3	4	5	6	7	8
9	10	11	12	13	14	15
16	17	18	19	20	21	22
23	24	25	26	27	28	29
30	1	2	3	4	5	6

Figure 5-4

GridSplitter

The Grid panel, which is discussed in detail in Chapter 7, is a great way to lay out your application's user interface. A common pattern when using a Grid is to allow the user to resize grid columns or rows. While the Grid panel itself does not have this capability, Silverlight includes the GridSplitter control, which allows you to add this capability to it.

The following code demonstrates the use of the GridSplitter control, splitting a column containing two columns:

```
<UserControl
    xmlns:basics="clr-namespace:System.Windows.Controls;
        assembly=System.Windows.Controls"
    x:Class="SilverlightApplication4.SilverlightControl16"
    xmlns="http://schemas.microsoft.com/winfx/2006/xaml/presentation"
    xmlns:x="http://schemas.microsoft.com/winfx/2006/xaml"
    Width="400" Height="300">
    <Grid x:Name="LayoutRoot" Background="White">
        <Grid.ColumnDefinitions>
            <ColumnDefinition />
            <ColumnDefinition />
        </Grid.ColumnDefinitions>
        <basics:GridSplitter></basics:GridSplitter>
    </Grid>
</UserControl>
```

To control the orientation of the GridSplitter control, use its horizontal and vertical alignment properties. If HorizontalAlignment is set to Stretch, then the grid will split between rows; if VerticalAlignment is set to Stretch, then the control will split columns. The following code demonstrates using the GridSplitter control in two different configurations, one splitting a grid vertically, and one splitting a grid horizontally:

```
<Grid x:Name="hLayout" Background="Gray"
    Width="258" Margin="0,67,47,230" HorizontalAlignment="Right">
<Grid.RowDefinitions>
<RowDefinition />
<RowDefinition />
</Grid.RowDefinitions>
<basics:GridSplitter
        VerticalAlignment="Bottom"
        HorizontalAlignment="Stretch" />
</Grid>
<Grid x:Name="vLayout" Background="Gray"
    Width="253" HorizontalAlignment="Left" Margin="47,76,0,230">
<Grid.ColumnDefinitions>
<ColumnDefinition />
<ColumnDefinition />
</Grid.ColumnDefinitions>
<basics:GridSplitter
        VerticalAlignment="Stretch"
        HorizontalAlignment="Right" />
</Grid>
```

If both are set to `Stretch` and `GridSplitter` has an actual height less than its actual width, then it will split rows. If the actual height is greater than the width, then columns will be split.

Setting the alignment properties to `Left`, `Right`, `Top`, or `Bottom`, you can control the direction in which the splitter will resize its column or row. Setting a property to `Center` means to resize in both directions.

`GridSplitter` always drags the entire `Column` or `Row`, even if it only visually appears in one cell. You can use the Grid's `RowSpan` and `ColumnSpan` properties on the `GridSplitter` to make it appear in multiple cells.

Also, by default, when the `GridSplitter` is repositioned, the content of the grid is resized in real time. You can use the `GridSplitter`'s `ShowsPreview` property to configure the control to show a preview first of the new `GridSplitter` position, then resize it when the user releases the splitter.

Silverlight Controls Toolkit

In addition to the controls that Microsoft includes in the Silverlight SDK, it offers an additional set of controls through the Silverlight Controls Toolkit. These controls are made available outside the Silverlight release cycle and are made available with full source code via the Microsoft Codeplex web site: `www.codeplex.com/Silverlight`.

Having a separate set of controls outside of Silverlight allows Microsoft to release new controls more frequently and at differing levels of quality that are required for control in the SDK. Controls in the toolkit include `DataForm`, `HeaderedContentControl`, `AutoCompleteBox`, `Chart`, `Accordian`, `ImplicitStyleManager`, `TimePicker`, and 11 professionally designed themes.

Summary

This chapter has introduced you to many of the most important and complex controls that are available in Silverlight. From the Silverlight `TextBox`, which makes it easy to begin to take data input from end-users, to perhaps the most complex control, the `DataGrid`, you learned how you can take advantage of all of these controls to make your applications more useful and make you more productive in your development.

6

Silverlight Text

Although the graphical browser has made the Web a powerful platform for expressing ideas using complex imagery, a core function of the Web remains to disseminate information, and text remains a primary mechanism to achieve this function. The basic text capabilities of HTML and CSS have improved dramatically, allowing designers significant control over the layout and appearance of the text displayed in their web sites. Silverlight provides a designer with many of the same powerful capabilities of HTML and CSS, and extends those basic capabilities with even more functionality that can dramatically enhance designers' abilities to control, to a fine point, the way their web sites deliver their textual information.

This chapter looks at the basic mechanisms included in Silverlight for displaying and formatting text.

Text Support in Silverlight

Silverlight provides basic support for text directly in the platform. By default, Silverlight uses the Portable User Interface font, which is a composite font that uses several different fonts to implement characters for the full range of international languages supported by Silverlight. The font is primarily composed of Lucida Grand, which is used for most Western writing systems, and many other fonts used for East Asian support.

Silverlight also includes support for 10 other local system Latin fonts (see Figure 6-1).

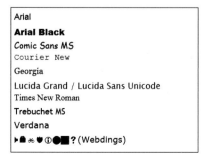

Figure 6-1

Use of these local system fonts requires no files to be hosted on the Web Server or downloaded as part of the application but does require that these fonts be available on the local system.

In addition to the 10 fonts in Figure 6-1, which are used primarily for Western languages, Silverlight includes native support for 31 different East Asian fonts. A full list of natively supported East Asian fonts can be found on Microsoft's MSDN web site.

Displaying Text with `TextBlock`

The basic mechanism for displaying text in Silverlight is the `TextBlock` element. This basic element encapsulates text display and serves as the core means of manipulating the text display. The following code shows the most basic use of the `TextBlock` element in Silverlight:

```
<TextBlock>Lorem ipsum dolor sit amet, consectetuer adipiscing elit.
    Fusce porttitor, tellus id tristique viverra, ligula pede pulvinar
    purus, nec hendrerit urna justo et nulla. Cras condimentum nulla
    at ipsum. Nullam nulla. Sed elit lectus, hendrerit rhoncus,
    gravida id, tristique quis, justo. Vivamus et enim. Nunc accumsan.
    Curabitur ultrices dui ac tortor. Nunc mollis, turpis quis
    consequat laoreet, nisl quam laoreet justo, a euismod magna nisi
    sed orci. Etiam nec dui egestas elit pretium sodales.
    Etiam felis.</TextBlock>
```

Figure 6-2 shows this `TextBlock` rendered in a default Silverlight `UserControl`.

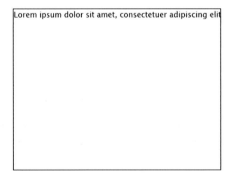

Lorem ipsum dolor sit amet, consectetuer adipiscing elit

Figure 6-2

The `TextBlock` control also includes a `Text` property, shown in the following sample, that you can use to provide the element's content:

```
<TextBlock Text="Lorem ipsum dolor sit amet,
    consectetuer adipiscing elit. Fusce porttitor, tellus id tristique
    viverra, ligula pede pulvinar purus, nec hendrerit urna justo et
    nulla. Cras condimentum nulla at ipsum. Nullam nulla. Sed elit
    lectus, hendrerit rhoncus, gravida id, tristique quis, justo.
    Vivamus et enim. Nunc accumsan. Curabitur ultrices dui ac tortor.
    Nunc mollis, turpis quis consequat laoreet, nisl quam laoreet
```

```
                justo, a euismod magna nisi sed orci. Etiam nec dui egestas elit
                pretium sodales. Etiam felis."></TextBlock>
```

Note that there is a slight difference in the behavior of the TextBlock, depending on whether you provide the text content using the Text property or as inline content. Using the Text property, the TextBlock ignores any leading or trailing white space that may be present; however, this is preserved by providing the content inline.

The TextBlock includes a variety of properties that allow you to control various font-related properties such as the family, weight, style, and size. The following code shows the TextBlock with additional font-related properties set:

```
<TextBlock FontFamily="Times New Roman" FontSize="24"
    FontStyle="Italic" FontWeight="Bold">Lorem ipsum dolor sit amet,
    consectetuer adipiscing elit. Fusce porttitor, tellus id tristique
    viverra, ligula pede pulvinar purus, nec hendrerit urna justo et
    nulla. Cras condimentum nulla at ipsum. Nullam nulla. Sed elit
    lectus, hendrerit rhoncus, gravida id, tristique quis, justo.
    Vivamus et enim. Nunc accumsan. Curabitur ultrices dui ac tortor.
    Nunc mollis, turpis quis consequat laoreet, nisl quam laoreet
    justo, a euismod magna nisi sed orci. Etiam nec dui egestas elit
    pretium sodales. Etiam felis.</TextBlock>
```

The FontFamily property allows you to specify the specific family of fonts that the TextBlock should use to display the text. A *font family* is a group of typefaces with the same name but differing in features such as Bold or Italic.

You can provide a list of fallback fonts by providing a comma-delimited list of font family names:

```
<TextBlock
    FontFamily="My Favorite Font, Times New Roman" FontSize="24">
```

In the preceding sample, if the font family named My Favorite Font cannot be found on the client, Silverlight will automatically fall back to using Times New Roman as the font for this TextBlock.

The FontStyle property allows you to specify a style to apply to the font. Currently, Silverlight supports two FontStyle values: Normal, which is the default, and Italic.

The FontWeight property allows you to specify that a font be displayed as Bold.

Silverlight also includes the ability to algorithmically render Italic and Bold fonts, when a true Italic or Bold font set is not available. If the FontStyle is set to Italic or the FontWeight is set to Bold, Silverlight will first attempt to locate an Italic or Bold font set on the local system. If none is found, then it will fall back to algorithmic font rendering and generate Italic and/or Bold glyphs for display. Unlike most applications, which measure font size in points, the FontSize property in Silverlight is a numeric value that represents the font size in pixels. This is done in order to maintain compatibility with Windows Presentation Foundation (WPF); however, it can cause some confusion if you try to compare a font size set in an application like Microsoft Word against the font size rendered by Silverlight. For example, setting the FontSize property to 24 will not render a font of *24 points* as you might expect; instead, this value represents *24 pixels*, which Silverlight converts to a point value. This is shown in Figure 6-3, which shows a 24-point font rendered in Word (top) and a 24-pixel font rendered in Silverlight (bottom).

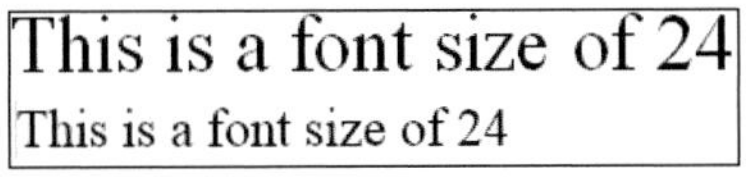

This is a font size of 24
This is a font size of 24

Figure 6-3

Notice how much smaller the 24-pixel font appears in Silverlight because of the pixels-to-points conversion. Silverlight renders text at a default 14.666 pixels, which converts to exactly 11 points.

The calculation from pixels to points is one of the few areas of Silverlight that contains a fixed value. To run this conversion, Silverlight needs to know a dots-per-inch (dpi) value, which is hard-coded at 96 dpi.

In addition to font properties, the `TextBlock` also allows you to set the foreground of its text. Unlike many other platforms, where you are limited to simply setting the foreground color of the font, Silverlight allows you to provide any standard `Brush` type as the `Foreground` properties value. The following sample demonstrates using a simple `SolidColorBrush` to change the foreground color:

```
<TextBlock Foreground="Aqua">
```

Notice that you can simply provide the property with a named color, and it will automatically convert it to the appropriate brush.

If you want to get more complex, you can provide more complex brushes such as a gradient brush or even image or video brushes. The following code demonstrates how to provide a `LinearGradientBrush` for the the `TextBlock`'s foreground property:

```
<TextBlock TextWrapping="Wrap" >
    <TextBlock.Foreground>
        <LinearGradientBrush EndPoint="0,0" StartPoint="1,1">
            <GradientStop Color="#FFFF2300"/>
            <GradientStop Color="#FFFB00FF" Offset="1"/>
            <GradientStop Color="#FFF0FF00"
                Offset="0.25900000333786011"/>
            <GradientStop Color="#FF1CFF00"
                Offset="0.51800000667572021"/>
            <GradientStop Color="#FF0B07FF"
                Offset="0.75900000333786011"/>
        </LinearGradientBrush>
    </TextBlock.Foreground>
    Lorem ipsum dolor sit amet, consectetuer adipiscing elit. Fusce
    porttitor, tellus id tristique viverra, ligula pede pulvinar purus,
    nec hendrerit urna justo et nulla. Cras condimentum nulla at ipsum.
    Nullam nulla. Sed elit lectus, hendrerit rhoncus, gravida id,
    tristique quis, justo. Vivamus et enim. Nunc accumsan. Curabitur
    ultrices dui ac tortor. Nunc mollis, turpis quis consequat laoreet,
    nisl quam laoreet justo, a euismod magna nisi sed orci. Etiam nec
    dui egestas elit pretium sodales. Etiam felis.
</TextBlock>
```

Figure 6-4 shows what your text will looks like after setting the `Foreground` to a `LinearGradientBrush`.

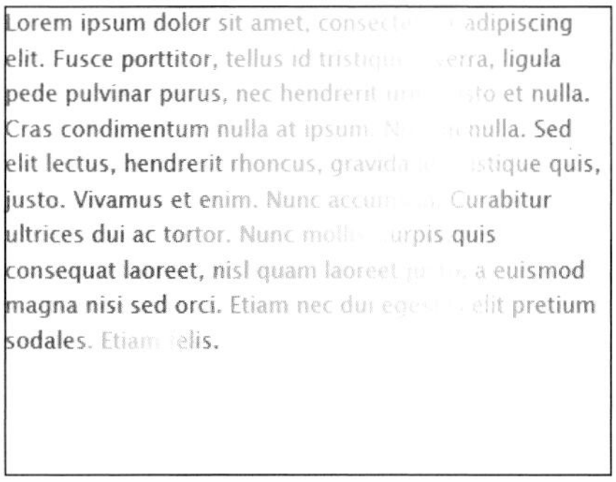

Figure 6-4

Controlling Text Layout in `TextBlock`

The `TextBlock` element also includes a series of properties that allow you to influence the layout of text in the `TextBlock`. `TextWrapping`, `LineHeight`, and `LineStackingStrategy` are all properties that give you fine-grained control over the layout of the `TextBlock`'s text.

The `TextWrapping` property allows you to indicate if you want the text within the `TextBlock` to automatically wrap based on the size of the `TextBlock`. As you have seen in previous samples in this chapter, by default, if your `TextBlock`'s text exceeds its container, it is simply clipped. To instead set the text to wrap, simply set the `TextWrapping` property to `Wrap`, as shown in the previous code and again here:

```
<TextBlock TextWrapping="Wrap">Lorem ipsum dolor sit amet, consectetuer
    adipiscing elit. Fusce porttitor, tellus id tristique viverra,
    ligula pede pulvinar purus, nec hendrerit urna justo et nulla. Cras
    condimentum nulla at ipsum. Nullam nulla. Sed elit lectus,
    hendrerit rhoncus, gravida id, tristique quis, justo. Vivamus et
    enim. Nunc accumsan. Curabitur ultrices dui ac tortor. Nunc mollis,
    turpis quis consequat laoreet, nisl quam laoreet justo, a euismod
    magna nisi sed orci. Etiam nec dui egestas elit pretium sodales.
    Etiam felis.</TextBlock>
```

Enabling text wrapping allows the `TextBlock` to intelligently wrap the text to fit it within the width of its container, as shown in Figure 6-5.

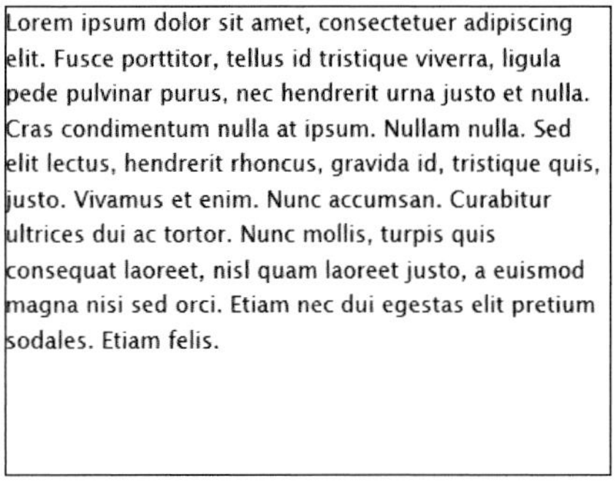

Figure 6-5

Note that even though the `TextBlock` will wrap text horizontally, if the wrapped text exceeds the vertical height available to the `TextBlock`, the text will continue to be clipped.

For East Asian text, Silverlight correctly uses Kinsoku line-breaking rules when wrapping is enabled.

Also keep in mind that when you enable text wrapping, you will alter the values returned from the `TextBlock`'s `ActualWidth` and `ActualHeight` properties. When text wrapping is disabled, the `ActualWidth` property returns a value that is equal to the width of the `TextBlock`'s container. When text wrapping is enabled, the `ActualWidth` will be the length of the longest wrapped line in the `TextBlock`.

`LineHeight` and `LineStackingStrategy` give you control over the height given to each line of text and how lines are stacked when wrapped.

`LineStackingStrategy` offers two options: `MaxHeight` says that Silverlight should use the smallest value that contains all of the inline elements on that line that are aligned properly. `BlockLineHeight` says that the stack height is determined by the block element's `LineHeight` property, which by default is determined according to the font characteristics.

Text Decorations

`TextBlock` also allows you to supply a text decoration. *Text decorations* are visual ornaments that can be applied to text such as underline, overline, or strike-through. Whereas in WPF you can apply any of these different types of text decorations, in Silverlight you are limited to only the underline text decoration. To apply the decoration, simply use the `TextDecorations` property and provide it with a value of `Underline`, as shown in the following sample:

```
<TextBlock TextDecorations="Underline">
```

Inline Text Formatting

So far in this chapter, we have looked at how changing the different formatting properties on a `TextBlock` affects the format of the text within; however, there are many times when you want to format only a portion of a larger block of text. Thankfully, Silverlight supports formatting blocks of text within a larger body of text.

`TextBlock` allows you to specify specific runs of `Text` that need unique formatting options by using the `Run` element. The following code demonstrates using the `Run` element within a `TextBlock` to create three discrete text sections, each of which has its own unique font styling:

```
<TextBlock TextWrapping="Wrap">
    Lorem ipsum dolor sit amet, consectetuer adipiscing elit.
    <Run FontFamily="Courier New">Fusce porttitor, tellus id
    tristique viverra, ligula pede pulvinar purus, nec hendrerit
    urna justo et nulla.</Run> Cras condimentum nulla at ipsum.
    <Run Foreground="Red">Nullam nulla.</Run> Sed elit lectus,
    hendrerit rhoncus, gravida id, tristique quis, justo. Vivamus
    et enim. Nunc accumsan. <Run FontWeight="Bold">Curabitur
    ultrices dui ac tortor.</Run> Nunc mollis, turpis quis
    consequat laoreet, nisl quam laoreet justo, a euismod magna nisi
```

```
sed orci. Etiam nec dui egestas elit pretium sodales.
Etiam felis.</TextBlock>
```

Figure 6-6 shows the output of this `TextBlock`.

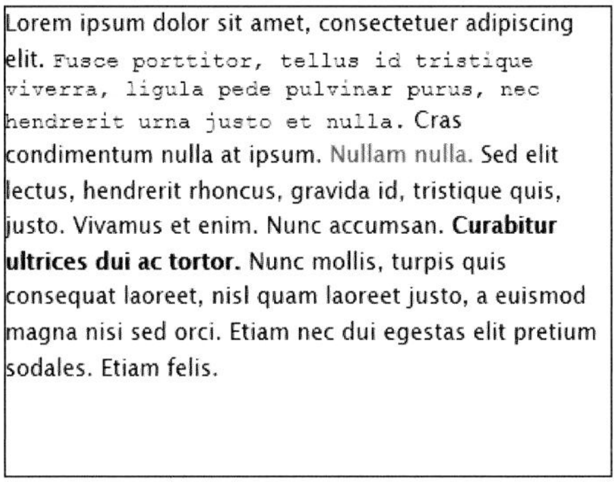

Lorem ipsum dolor sit amet, consectetuer adipiscing
elit. Fusce porttitor, tellus id tristique
viverra, ligula pede pulvinar purus, nec
hendrerit urna justo et nulla. Cras
condimentum nulla at ipsum. Nullam nulla. Sed elit
lectus, hendrerit rhoncus, gravida id, tristique quis,
justo. Vivamus et enim. Nunc accumsan. **Curabitur
ultrices dui ac tortor.** Nunc mollis, turpis quis
consequat laoreet, nisl quam laoreet justo, a euismod
magna nisi sed orci. Etiam nec dui egestas elit pretium
sodales. Etiam felis.

Figure 6-6

Setting styling properties in a discrete `Run` element overrides the style properties set on the `TextBlock` for that specific `Run`.

The `TextBlock` also allows you to explicitly insert line breaks into the text content using the `LineBreak` element. Using the `LineBreak` element gives you explicit control over the location where the `TextBlock` breaks a line of text, as shown here:

```
<TextBlock TextWrapping="Wrap">
    Lorem ipsum dolor sit amet, consectetuer adipiscing elit.
    <Run FontFamily="Courier New">Fusce porttitor, tellus id
    tristique viverra, ligula pede pulvinar purus, nec hendrerit
    urna justo et nulla.</Run>
    <LineBreak />
    Cras condimentum nulla at ipsum.
    <Run Foreground="Red">Nullam nulla.</Run> Sed elit lectus,
    hendrerit rhoncus, gravida id, tristique quis, justo. Vivamus
    et enim. Nunc accumsan. <Run FontWeight="Bold">Curabitur
    ultrices dui ac tortor.</Run>
    <LineBreak />
    Nunc mollis, turpis quis
    consequat laoreet, nisl quam laoreet justo, a euismod magna nisi
    sed orci. Etiam nec dui egestas elit pretium sodales.
    Etiam felis.
</TextBlock>
```

Figure 6-7 shows the text rendered with the line breaks.

Using `Run` and `LineBreak` still allows the `TextBlock` to control the rendering of the text as a single unified object; therefore, as your application is resized, the `TextBlock` can intelligently reorganize the text it contains, regardless of how that text may be formatted.

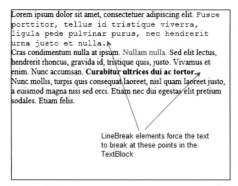

Figure 6-7

Using Embedded Fonts

As discussed earlier in the chapter, Silverlight natively supports 10 Western language fonts and 31 East Asian fonts, but the world of fonts is vast, and designers should not be limited to this tiny handful. Thankfully, Silverlight includes support for embedding fonts in the application, allowing designers to use any font they wish in their application design.

To use an embedded font with the TextBlock, you simply provide the FontFamily property with a special font URI that tells Silverlight the name of the TrueType font file you want to use and the specific TypeFace from that file to use. This is shown in the following sample:

```
<TextBlock FontFamily="[FontFile]#[TypeFace]" />
```

So, for example, if you want to use the font file named *MyFavoriteFont.ttf*, which contains a typeface named *My Favorite Font Normal*, you can configure a TextBlock to use this font using this syntax:

```
<TextBlock FontFamily="segoesc.ttf#Segoe Script" />
```

Figure 6-8 shows the text in the TextBlock using the embedded font.

Lorem ipsum dolor sit amet, consectetuer adipiscing elit. Fusce porttitor, tellus id tristique viverra, ligula pede pulvinar purus, nec hendrerit urna justo et nulla.
Cras condimentum nulla at ipsum. Nullam nulla. Sed elit lectus, hendrerit rhoncus, gravida id, tristique quis, justo. Vivamus et enim. Nunc accumsan. **Curabitur ultrices dui ac tortor.**
Nunc mollis, turpis quis consequat laoreet, nisl quam laoreet justo, a euismod magna nisi sed orci. Etiam nec dui egestas elit pretium sodales. Etiam felis.

Figure 6-8

Note that if you are embedding fonts in your Silverlight application, this may be considered distributing a font with your application. If you are using a licensed font, you may need to ensure that you have the appropriate distribution rights.

Chapter 9 contains an in-depth review of embedding fonts into your Silverlight application.

Glyphs

Silverlight also allows a designer to render individual font glyphs. The advantage of using the Glyphs element is that you do not have to embed an entire font file into your application. Instead, using the FontUri property, you can specify a font that is hosted on your Web Server. The Glyphs element also can use an expanded set of fonts that is located on the client system.

As shown in the following code, using the Glyphs element, you can render specific glyphs contained in a font:

```
<Glyphs
    Fill = "SteelBlue"
    FontUri="/LANDMARK.ttf"
    FontRenderingEmSize = "36"
    UnicodeString = "Hello">
</Glyphs>
```

In the preceding sample, only the glyphs needed to render the UnicodeString are retrieved from the font on the server. Also note that, unlike TextBlock, the default Fill value for Glyphs is null, and the FontRenderingEmSize is zero; therefore, you should make sure to provide values for both of these properties in order to render the text. If you want to use a font that is on the local client system, you can use the Silverlight plug-in's JavaScript to enumerate the local system fonts and then assign that font as the Glyphs font source. This is shown in the code listing below:

```
function handleLoad(sender, args) {
    var plugIn = sender.get_element();

    var gtc = plugIn.settings.GetSystemGlyphTypefaces();

    for (i = 0; i < gtc.count; i++) {

        gtf = gtc.getItem(i);

        if (gtf.FontUri == "comic.ttf") {
            var glyph = plugIn.content.root.findName("glyph");
            glyph.SetFontSource(gtf, ""); //must include ""
        }
    }
}
```

This listing shows how you can use the GetSystemGlyphTypefaces function of Silverlight's JavaScript API to get a list of the local systems' fonts, then, using the Glyphs element's SetFontSource function, assign the glyph a font typeface.

You can use the `Glyphs` element's `Indices` property to specify specific glyph indices in the font. You can also use the `Indices` property to control the spacing of characters in the `UnicodeString`. The `Indices` property accepts a semicolon-delimited list of glyph indices and spacing information. Each index can be defined using the following format:

```
[GlyphIndex][,[Advance][,[uOffset][,[vOffset]]]]
```

Each portion of this format is optional. More information on using the `Indices` property to control font spacing can be found at `http://msdn.microsoft.com/en-us/library/ms748985.aspx`.

Transforming Text with `RenderTransforms`

The last area that this chapter looks at is using `RenderTransforms` with the Silverlight `TextBlock` element. Silverlight contains a series of transforms that allows you to transform the rendering of UI elements using various schemes such as `Rotation`, `Skewing`, or `Scaling`. You can easily apply these transforms to `TextBlocks` in your application simply by setting the `RenderTransform` property of the `TextBlock`.

The `Rotate` transform, as the name implies, allows you to rotate a `TextBlock`. You can add a `Rotate` transform to a `TextBlock` by setting the element's `RenderTransform` property, as shown here:

```
<TextBlock TextWrapping="Wrap">
    Lorem ipsum dolor sit amet, consectetuer
    adipiscing elit. Fusce porttitor, tellus id tristique viverra,
    ligula pede pulvinar purus, nec hendrerit urna justo et nulla. Cras
    condimentum nulla at ipsum. Nullam nulla. Sed elit lectus,
    hendrerit rhoncus, gravida id, tristique quis, justo. Vivamus et
    enim. Nunc accumsan. Curabitur ultrices dui ac tortor. Nunc mollis,
    turpis quis consequat laoreet, nisl quam laoreet justo, a euismod
    magna nisi sed orci. Etiam nec dui egestas elit pretium sodales.
    Etiam felis.
    <TextBlock.RenderTransform>
        <RotateTransform Angle="45" CenterX="200" CenterY="150" />
    </TextBlock.RenderTransform>
</TextBlock>
```

The `Rotate` transform allows you to specify the angle of rotation as well as set the rotation center of the element.

Other transforms available to you include the `ScaleTransform`, which allows you to scale the `TextBlock` horizontally and vertically:

```
<ScaleTransform ScaleX="1.5" ScaleY="1.5" />
```

The `SkewTransform` allows you to skew the `TextBlock` along the X- or Y-axis:

```
<SkewTransform AngleY="25" />
```

The `TranslateTransform` allows you to offset the text from along its X- or Y-axis:

```
<TranslateTransform X="7" Y="13" />
```

Finally, the `MatrixTransform` allows you to create custom transforms, which the previously mentioned transforms provide:

```
<MatrixTransform Matrix="1, 0, 0, -1, 0, 0"/>
```

Transform Groups

While the `RenderTransform` property allows you to provide a single transform to the `TextBlock`, there will be times when you want to apply more than one transform to the element. To do this, you can use the `TransformGroup` property, which allows you to add multiple transforms. The following code demonstrates the use of the `TransformGroup`, adding both a `RotateTransform` and a `SkewTransform` to the `TextBlock`:

```
<TextBlock TextWrapping="Wrap">
    Lorem ipsum dolor sit amet, consectetuer
    adipiscing elit. Fusce porttitor, tellus id tristique viverra,
    ligula pede pulvinar purus, nec hendrerit urna justo et nulla. Cras
    condimentum nulla at ipsum. Nullam nulla. Sed elit lectus,
    hendrerit rhoncus, gravida id, tristique quis, justo. Vivamus et
    enim. Nunc accumsan. Curabitur ultrices dui ac tortor. Nunc mollis,
    turpis quis consequat laoreet, nisl quam laoreet justo, a euismod
    magna nisi sed orci. Etiam nec dui egestas elit pretium sodales.
    Etiam felis.
    <TextBlock.RenderTransform>
        <TransformGroup>
            <RotateTransform Angle="90" />
            <SkewTransform AngleX="25" />
        </TransformGroup>
    </TextBlock.RenderTransform>
</TextBlock>
```

Summary

As the Internet moves toward even more rich media content, text remains a central way to convey information to end-users. Silverlight puts significant new capabilities into the hands of web developers and frees web designers from many of the constraints imposed on them by traditional HTML text display.

This chapter looks at the core mechanism used to display text in Silverlight, the `TextBlock`. This versatile element gives you amazing power to style and display text. Choose from the set of native fonts or provide your own font set to differentiate your site from others.

The chapter also explored more advanced text options such as using the `Glyphs` element to display individual font glyphs, as well as using text transforms to transform text.

7

Layout

Controlling the layout of an application's user interface is a problem that has long plagued developers. Over the years, rich client developers have written thousands of lines of code solely devoted to the repositioning of user interface elements in the application as its window size changes. Web developers have long struggled with the multitude of positioning schemes available to them, starting with HTML tables and progressing to CSS layout, and — adding insult to injury — dealing with different browser interpretations of these layout schemes.

Microsoft looked to address many of the basic problems in application user interface layout with Windows Presentation Foundation by creating a powerful, yet flexible and highly extensible new layout system, and, thankfully, they have brought most of those layout concepts into the world of Silverlight. Through the use of layout containers and panels, the Silverlight layout system gives you a level of layout control that was previously difficult, if not impossible, to achieve.

In this chapter, you will look at the basics of the Silverlight layout system and how you can use it to create flexible application user interfaces. This chapter walks you through the core concepts of the layout system, then looks at the panels included in the Silverlight that implement these concepts. You will also learn how simple it is to take advantage of the layout system by building your own custom panel that includes your own layout logic. Finally, the chapter also looks at how external influences such as browser rendering can influence the layout of your Silverlight application.

Measure, Then Arrange

The basis of the Silverlight layout system is to measure, arrange, and then draw elements. Every element that can be drawn in Silverlight is included as part of the application's visual tree. When the application begins a layout pass, it uses the visual tree as a map, enumerating the leaves in the tree to first measure, then arrange, and finally draw the UI element.

The first pass of the system, the Measure pass, asks each element in the visual tree to determine how much space it would like to have by calling its `Measure` method. Starting with the root UI element, each child determines its size, usually based on the size of its content or a hard-coded `Height` or `Width` value. This measurement is known as the element's `DesiredHeight` and `DesiredWidth` because although an element may desire a specific size, other factors in the UI may cause the element to be rendered with a different size.

The second pass of the system, called *Arrange*, is where the logic of a `Panel` is used to position elements. As with the Measure pass, during the Arrange pass the Silverlight layout system enumerates the members of the visual tree, this time calling each element's `Arrange` method. The `Arrange` method accepts a rectangle as a parameter. This rectangle defines the coordinate position of the element within its parent, as well as the size of the element. Once this pass is completed, you can query for the element's `ActualHeight` and `ActualWidth`. When querying an element for its current size, you should always use the `ActualHeight` and `ActualWidth` properties since the element's parent can alter the element's height and width regardless of any explicit height and width values that might be set.

Also note that each time a UI element changes position, it has the potential to trigger a new pass by the layout system, which can become an expensive process, depending on the complexity of your application.

Bounding Box

In order to simplify the layout system, Silverlight surrounds every UI element with a bounding box. When the layout system attempts to position an element, it is in reality positioning a rectangle, also called a *layout slot*, which contains the element.

The size of the layout slot is determined by the layout system, giving consideration to the amount of available screen space, constraints like margin and padding, and the unique behavior of the parent `Panel`. It is up to the parent container to determine the size of the layout for each of its children.

If an element extends outside of its allocated layout slot, the layout system will begin to clip the element. You can get the dimensions of the visible portion of the element by calling the `GetLayoutClip` method.

Element Sizing Characteristics

Every UI element includes several properties that can help the element influence its own size and position within the layout container.

Width and Height

Every UI element can have an explicit pixel width and height set on it. Depending on the element's layout container, these values will generally override any other sizing properties set on the element. By default, elements have their `Width` and `Height` properties set to `Double.NaN`, which is interpreted by the layout system as "Auto." The Auto layout generally means that the layout system should size the element to the available size in the layout, rather than to any specific pixel value.

> *Although not necessary, you can explicitly set a `Width` or `Height` to Auto in XAML. Additionally, if you have previously assigned an explicit height or width to an element, and wish to set the value back to Auto, simply assign the property a value of `Double.NaN` in code.*

As shown in the following code sample, the effect of the Auto size value is most clearly seen by adding a button to a grid:

```
<UserControl x:Class="RotatePanelSample.GridTest"
    xmlns="http://schemas.microsoft.com/winfx/2006/xaml/presentation"
    xmlns:x="http://schemas.microsoft.com/winfx/2006/xaml"
    Width="400" Height="300">
    <Grid x:Name="LayoutRoot" Background="White">
        <Button Content="Button 1" Width="Auto" />
    </Grid>
</UserControl>
```

In this sample, the Button's width has been explicitly set to Auto, although we could have completely omitted the property, since this is the default Width property value. The results of the Auto value are shown in Figure 7-1.

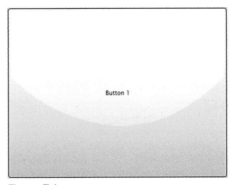

Figure 7-1

You can clearly see that, as expected, the Button control has sized itself to take all available size in its layout container. Because, in this case, the Button is the only element in the Grid, it consumes all available space in the Grid.

Also note that the Grid itself has Width and Height properties set to Auto by default, which explains why the Grid is consuming all available space of its layout container, the UserControl. It is only the UserControl that has an explicit height and width set.

Setting an explicit width on the Button will constrain it within the Grid, as shown in Figure 7-2, where the Button now has its Width property set to 150.

Note that leaving a control's Height or Width as Auto does allow the Panel to influence how a control is ultimately rendered. For example, if you take the code from the previous listing and substitute a StackPanel for the Grid as the Button's layout container, you will see that the Button's height is rendered differently. We will explain this in greater detail when we examine the StackPanel layout container later in this chapter.

Figure 7-2

In addition to setting height and width values, every element can have height and width thresholds set on it. Using an element's MinWidth, MinHeight, MaxWidth, and MaxHeight properties, you can dictate to the element's layout container that the element should never exceed certain height or width values, even if the element's Width or Height properties are explicitly set to values outside the minimum or maximum range.

In cases in which the available size given to the layout container is less than the MinWidth or MinHeight of the element, the container will begin to clip the element rather than reduce the element's size.

Alignment

Elements can have a horizontal or vertical alignment set on them. The alignment properties include the standard alignment values — Left, Right, and Center for horizontal alignment and Top, Center, and Bottom for vertical alignment — but by default, an element's alignment is set to a fourth option, called Stretch. Stretch tells the element that it should attempt to fill its parent's entire layout slot.

Margin and Padding

Finally, every object derived from FrameworkElement includes a Margin, and every object derived from Control includes a Padding property. Margins allow you to add space to the outside of the element between the element and other elements that surround it, be they peer elements or even an element's parent.

The Margin property allows you to set this spacing for all four sides of the elements, as shown in Figure 7-3.

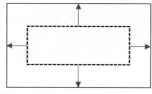

Figure 7-3

If the element container has no size constraints, the margins will push the container boundaries outward. This is shown in Figure 7-4, where a Button has been placed in a Grid that has no explicitly set height or width. The Grid's Background has been set to LightGray and the HorizontalAlignment and VerticalAlignment properties have been set to Center. The Button has explicit height and width properties set, and has had a margin size of 40 set on each side. You can see that the margin is pushing the Grid outward beyond the boundaries of the Button, where it would normally be.

If the layout system determines that space is not available, the system will attempt to constrain, or even clip, the element's content in order to display the full margins. This is shown in Figure 7-5, where the Grid now has an explicit height and width set along with the Button; therefore, the content of its child is now clipped when a margin is added.

If the element having margins applied to it does not have an explicit size set, Silverlight will attempt to constrain the element content in order to display the full margins.

The Padding property allows you to add space around the inside of an element, as shown in Figure 7-6.

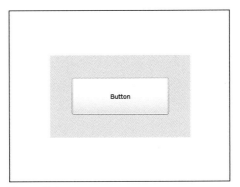

Figure 7-4

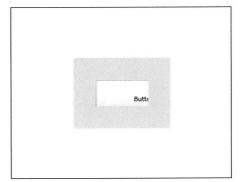

Figure 7-5

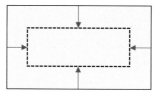

Figure 7-6

Figure 7-7 demonstrates this by showing a `Border` control that contains a rectangle. The `Border` has had its `Padding` property set to increase the buffer between it and the child rectangle.

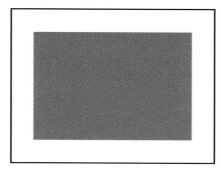

Figure 7-7

As with the `Margin` properties, if the parent element has no explicit size set, the element will increase in size in order to accommodate the padding.

`Margin` and `Padding` are cumulative, meaning that if the parent element has `Padding` defined and the inner element has `Margin` defined, Silverlight will display both.

Layout Panels

Now that you have a basic understanding of how the Silverlight layout system works, you can begin to use some of the Panels built into Silverlight that leverage this system. Silverlight includes a variety of built-in Panels that each provides a unique layout mechanism you can leverage in your application.

Canvas

The `Canvas` panel provides you with a way to position elements using an explicit coordinate system. Elements contained in the `Canvas` are positioned relative to the top-left corner of the panel, which is considered position 0,0.

While this layout panel may feel the most familiar to developers who are coming from the Windows Forms world, for the most part, you should avoid using `Canvas` in your applications (or at least use it sparingly) because it forces you to do most of the work to control the position of your UI elements, rather than allowing the layout system to do this for you.

An excellent explanation of why the use of Canvas should be avoided can be found here: http://blogs .msdn.com/devdave/archive/2008/05/21/why-i-don-t-like-canvas.aspx.

To position elements on the Canvas, you can use the Canvas's Top and Left attached properties on its child elements. An example of using Canvas is shown next:

```
<UserControl x:Class="RotatePanelSample.CanvasText"
    xmlns="http://schemas.microsoft.com/winfx/2006/xaml/presentation"
    xmlns:x="http://schemas.microsoft.com/winfx/2006/xaml"
    Width="400" Height="300">
    <Grid x:Name="LayoutRoot" Background="White">
        <Canvas>
            <Button Canvas.Left="0" Canvas.Top="0" Content="Button1" />
            <Button Canvas.Left="50" Canvas.Top="25" Content="Button1" />
            <Button Canvas.Left="100" Canvas.Top="50" Content="Button1" />
            <Button Canvas.Left="150" Canvas.Top="75" Content="Button1" />
            <Button Canvas.Left="200" Canvas.Top="100" Content="Button1" />
            <Button Canvas.Left="250" Canvas.Top="125" Content="Button1" />
        </Canvas>
    </Grid>
</UserControl>
```

Rendering this as shown in Figure 7-8 results in the buttons being absolutely positioned within the Canvas.

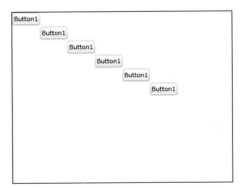

Figure 7-8

While Canvas is useful when you need to explicitly position elements in your user interface — for example, if your application performs some type of physics-based rendering or drawing — it does mean that your user interface becomes less dynamic and will not be able to properly scale as the available space in the UI changes. Canvas does not consider some of the basic element characteristics like HorizontalAlignment and VerticalAlignment when positioning children because Canvas is based on absolute positioning.

StackPanel

As the name implies, the StackPanel simply stacks elements vertically or horizontally. The next code sample demonstrates the use of the StackPanel:

```
<UserControl x:Class="RotatePanelSample.StackPanelTest"
    xmlns="http://schemas.microsoft.com/winfx/2006/xaml/presentation"
```

```
    xmlns:x="http://schemas.microsoft.com/winfx/2006/xaml"
    Width="400" Height="300">
    <Grid x:Name="LayoutRoot" Background="White">
        <StackPanel>
            <Button Content="Button" />
            <TextBlock>Lorum Ipsum</TextBlock>
            <Slider></Slider>
            <HyperlinkButton Content="HyperlinkButton" />
            <CheckBox />
        </StackPanel>
    </Grid>
</UserControl>
```

As you can see in Figure 7-9, when child elements are added to the StackPanel, the panel simply stacks them in its default vertical orientation. Using the StackPanel's Orientation property, you can change the panel to stack elements horizontally.

Figure 7-9

Because the stack panel internally sets its available width or height (depending on the current value of Orientation) to infinity, if no explicit height has been set on a child element of the StackPanel, it will take as much space as is available to it in the StackPanel.

Additionally, as with every other element, StackPanel can have its height and width set. If no width is set, the StackPanel will be as wide as its widest child. If no height is set, it will take enough height to display all of its children.

Grid

Perhaps the most powerful layout container in Silverlight is the Grid panel. As the name implies, the Grid panel allows you to define a grid of rows and columns in which you can position child elements.

The following code demonstrates a simple Grid layout container:

```
<UserControl x:Class="RotatePanelSample.SilverlightControl3"
    xmlns="http://schemas.microsoft.com/winfx/2006/xaml/presentation"
    xmlns:x="http://schemas.microsoft.com/winfx/2006/xaml"
    Width="400" Height="300">
    <Grid x:Name="LayoutRoot" Background="White" ShowGridLines="True">
        <Grid.RowDefinitions>
```

```
            <RowDefinition />
            <RowDefinition />
        </Grid.RowDefinitions>
        <Grid.ColumnDefinitions>
            <ColumnDefinition />
            <ColumnDefinition />
        </Grid.ColumnDefinitions>

        <TextBlock Text="Grid Cell 1" Grid.Row="0" Grid.Column="0" />
        <TextBlock Text="Grid Cell 1" Grid.Row="0" Grid.Column="1" />
        <TextBlock Text="Grid Cell 1" Grid.Row="1" Grid.Column="0" />
        <TextBlock Text="Grid Cell 1" Grid.Row="1" Grid.Column="1" />
    </Grid>
</UserControl>
```

In the above sample, a grid structure consisting of two rows and two columns is created using the Grid's RowDefinitions and ColumnDefinitions collections. Once the structure is defined, a TextBlock is added to each grid cell. The placement of the TextBlocks is achieved by using the Grid's Row and Column attached properties, which allow you to dictate which grid cell an element should be positioned in.

The Grid also exposes RowSpan and ColumnSpan attached properties that you can use to alter how an element is positioned in the Grid. The next listing demontrates the use of these attached properties:

```
<UserControl x:Class="RotatePanelSample.SilverlightControl3"
    xmlns="http://schemas.microsoft.com/winfx/2006/xaml/presentation"
    xmlns:x="http://schemas.microsoft.com/winfx/2006/xaml"
    Width="400" Height="300">
    <Grid x:Name="LayoutRoot" Background="White" ShowGridLines="True">
        <Grid.RowDefinitions>
            <RowDefinition />
            <RowDefinition />
        </Grid.RowDefinitions>
        <Grid.ColumnDefinitions>
            <ColumnDefinition />
            <ColumnDefinition />
        </Grid.ColumnDefinitions>

        <TextBlock Grid.Row="0" Grid.Column="0"
                Grid.ColumnSpan="2" TextWrapping="Wrap">
            Lorem ipsum dolor sit amet, consectetuer adipiscing elit.
            Sed ultricies lectus et dui. Quisque vulputate facilisis nisl.
            Nulla sed turpis. Pellentesque ultricies mi ac velit. Praesent
            id turpis. Nunc mattis pharetra enim. In leo eros, sollicitudin
            vitae, ultricies accumsan, luctus quis, justo.
        </TextBlock>
        <TextBlock Text="Grid Cell 1" Grid.Row="1" Grid.Column="0" />
        <TextBlock Text="Grid Cell 1" Grid.Row="1" Grid.Column="1" />
    </Grid>
</UserControl>
```

The Grid also allows you to set properties on the individual rows and columns that affect their layout. The RowDefinition and ColumnDefinition classes expose properties that allow you to set Height and Width properties.

Unlike a standard element's `Width` and `Height` properties, which only accept pixel measurements or the `Auto` keyword, Grid Row and Column size properties accept a type called `GridLength`. This special type not only offers the standard size units (`Pixels` or `Auto`), but also includes an additional measurement type call `Star`. The `Star` unit allows you to provide a value that expresses a size as a weighted proportion of available space. To specify a `Star` value, you simply provide the literal `*` character as the value for the `Width` property. You can also specify a factor by placing an integer preceding the `*`, for example, `3*`.

The following listing demonstrates the use of the `Star` sizing in a `Grid`:

```
<UserControl x:Class="RotatePanelSample.SilverlightControl3"
    xmlns="http://schemas.microsoft.com/winfx/2006/xaml/presentation"
    xmlns:x="http://schemas.microsoft.com/winfx/2006/xaml"
    Width="400" Height="300" Loaded="UserControl_Loaded">
    <Grid x:Name="LayoutRoot" Background="White" ShowGridLines="True">
        <Grid.RowDefinitions>
            <RowDefinition />
            <RowDefinition />
        </Grid.RowDefinitions>
        <Grid.ColumnDefinitions>
            <ColumnDefinition Width="100" />
            <ColumnDefinition Width="*" />
            <ColumnDefinition Width="2*" />
            <ColumnDefinition Width="*" />
        </Grid.ColumnDefinitions>

    </Grid>
</UserControl>
```

In this sample, the first `ColumnDefinition` has an explicit pixel width set, while the rest use `Star` size values. The third `ColumnDefinition` includes a factorial value that specifies that the width given to this column should be two times that given to the other columns. Figure 7-10 shows the resulting grid rendered.

In this case, the `Grid` has had its `ShowGridLines` property set to `True` in order to show the column widths.

Figure 7-10

Custom Panels

As was stated earlier in the chapter, the layout system included in Silverlight is not only highly flexible but also very extensible. It is quite easy to leverage the layout system to create your own custom layout panels that contain your own unique layout logic. In order to show this, this section demonstrates how to create a simple Wrap Panel control. The layout logic for the Wrap Panel will stack its child elements from left to right, starting in the upper-left corner of the panel. When the child elements begin to exceed the width of the panel, the panel will automatically begin to wrap the elements to a new row.

To get started creating a custom panel, simply create a new Silverlight Class Library in your project. Once the class file has been created, change the class so that it derives from the base `Panel` object. This is shown in the following code:

```
using System;
using System.Windows;
using System.Windows.Controls;

namespace RotatePanelSample
{
    public class SimpleStackPanel : Panel
    {
    }
}
```

Next, you need to override two methods from the base `Panel` — `MeasureOverride` and `ArrangeOverride` — as follows:

```
public class SimpleStackPanel : Panel
{
    protected override Size MeasureOverride(Size availableSize)
    {
    }

    protected override Size ArrangeOverride(Size finalSize)
    {
    }
}
```

That's all that is required to set up your own custom layout panel. Now all that is left is for you to implement your own custom layout logic in the `Measure` and `Arrange` methods. As an example, this chapter demonstrates how to create a panel that wraps UI elements that exceed the width of the panel to a new row.

The following code shows the overriden `MeasureOverride` method for this custom panel:

```
protected override Size MeasureOverride(Size availableSize)
{
    Size size = new Size();

    availableSize.Height = double.PositiveInfinity;
    availableSize.Width = double.PositiveInfinity;

    foreach(UIElement element in this.Children)
```

```
        {
            if (element != null)
            {
                element.Measure(availableSize);
                Size desiredSize = element.DesiredSize;

                size.Width = Math.Max(size.Width, desiredSize.Width);
                size.Height += desiredSize.Height;
            }
        }

        return size;
    }
```

The first step in this method is to take the availableSize parameter, which represents the amount of space that the layout system says is initially available to the panel, based on the element's size characteristics (as described earlier in the chapter), and set its Width and Height properties to Infinity. We do this in order to get any of the panel's children that do not have explicitly set Width and Height values to return a desired size that reflects the size defined in their default template. If we did not do this, some controls like Button would attempt to fill all available space because by default their heights and widths are set to Auto.

The next step in the method is to loop through all of the panel's child elements and call Measure on each one of them, passing in the availableSize parameter. This will cause the child elements to calculate their own desired sizes.

Finally, using the loop, the Panel control also attempts to identify the amount of space needed by the panel for the layout. This is calculated by finding the width of the widest element in the panel and by calculating the sum height of all elements in the panel. Once the size is determined, it is returned as the result of the method.

Once the layout system has completed the Measure pass, it will then execute its arrange. The Arrange pass is when the the Panel control actually positions its child elements in the final space allocated to the panel by the layout system. The positioning of the child elements is done by calling the Arrange method on each child of the Panel, passing the child its final desired size and position by using a Rectangle object.

The following code shows the panel's ArrangeOverride method, which includes the positioning logic for the panel:

```
protected override Size ArrangeOverride(Size finalSize)
{
    Point point = new Point(0, 0);
    Rect finalRect =
        new Rect(point, new Point(finalSize.Width, finalSize.Height));

    double maxheight = 0.0;
    double rowheight = 0.0;
    double width = 0.0;

    foreach (UIElement element in this.Children)
    {
        if (element != null)
```

```
        {
                finalRect.X += width;
                width = element.DesiredSize.Width;

                //Check to see if this element will be rendered outside of
                //the panels width and if so, create a new row in the panel
                if ((finalRect.X + element.DesiredSize.Width) > finalSize.Width)
                {
                    finalRect.X = 0.0;

                    maxheight += rowheight;
                    finalRect.Y = maxheight;
                    rowheight = 0.0;
                }

                //Find the tallest element in this row
                if (element.DesiredSize.Height > rowheight)
                    rowheight = element.DesiredSize.Height;

                finalRect.Width = width;
                finalRect.Height = element.DesiredSize.Height;

                element.Arrange(finalRect);
            }
        }

        return finalSize;
    }
```

The logic in the `Arrange` method for this panel is relatively simple. To start, a new `Rectangle` object is created, which will be used to provide the panel's children with the information they need to position themselves within the panel.

Next, several internal members are defined, which will help the `Panel` track information about the positioned elements. The `Panel` needs to track three things: the cumulative width of all elements it has positioned in the current row, the height of the tallest element in the current row, and the cumulative height of all rows in the panel.

The cumulative width is used to correctly position the next element in the row. The tallest element in the current row is used to determine the overall row height. As each element is positioned, the `Panel` checks to see if its height is greater than any other element that has been positioned in the row before it. The cumulative row height of all rows in the panel is used to determine the position of the next row.

Next, the method begins to enumerate each child element of the panel, calculating the position for each child element and calling its `Arrange` method. As the `Panel` enumerates each element, it sets the `Width` and `Height` and `X` and `Y` properties of the positioning rectangle using the data from the internal members.

The `Panel` also checks to determine if the element, when positioned, will exceed the width of the panel. If this is found to be true, the `Panel` resets the `Rectangle`'s `X` and `Y` properties to reposition the element onto a new row.

Finally, the child elements' `Arrange` method is called. and the `Rectangle` is passed as the parameter.

Figure 7-11 shows the results of the panel once it is rendered.

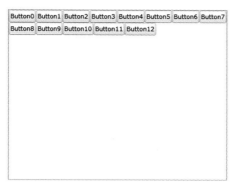

Figure 7-11

While the Wrap Panel is a simple example of a custom panel, every panel that you create will follow the same basic Measure and Arrange principles.

Silverlight Plug-In Sizing and Position

As has been described in the book, at its core, Silverlight is a browser plug-in, which is added to the page using a standard HTML `<object>` tag. This means that when mixed into a page that contains other HTML, CSS, and JavaScript, the specific way the browser renders this content can have significant influence over how the Silverlight plug-in is sized and positioned.

To control the size of the browser plug-in, you can set a `height` and `width` attribute on the object tag in HTML, as shown in the following code:

```
<object data="data:application/x-silverlight-2,"
    type="application/x-silverlight-2" width="100%" height="100%">
<param name="source" value="ClientBin/MySample.xap"/>
<param name="onerror" value="onSilverlightError" />
<param name="background" value="white" />
<param name="minRuntimeVersion" value="2.0.31005.0" />
<param name="autoUpgrade" value="true" />
<a href="http://go.microsoft.com/fwlink/?LinkID=124807"
            style="text-decoration: none;">
<img src="http://go.microsoft.com/fwlink/?LinkId=108181"
            alt="Get Microsoft Silverlight" style="border-style: none"/>
</a>
</object>
```

As with other HTML `height` and `width` attributes, you can either provide percent values, like those shown in the sample, or fixed pixel values.

If you are using the ASP.NET XAML control, you can set its `Height` and `Width` properties:

```
<asp:Silverlight ID="Xaml1" runat="server"
    Source="~/ClientBin/MySample.xap" MinimumVersion="2.0.31005.0"
    Width="100%" Height="100%" />
```

These properties will be added as `Height` and `Width` properties on the object tag rendered by the control.

Summary

Silverlight provides a new and innovating user interface layout system that allows you to create highly flexible user interfaces that easily adjust and accommodate changes in application and content size. This chapter introduced you to the basics of this new layout system, starting with an overview of the new Measure, Arrange, and Render pattern used by Silverlight to intelligently render UI elements. This two-pass system allows Silverlight first to evaluate the amount of space that each UI element needs, and then to arrange each of these elements in the actual amount of space available.

The layout system allows you to influence this process by setting various sizing characteristics such as the height, width, alignment, and margin on UI elements.

The chapter then introduced you to the available `Panel` control, which is responsible for most of the element arrangement that happens in Silverlight. You can choose a panel that uses a layout scheme that meets your layout needs, be it `Grid`, `StackPanel`, or `Canvas`, or as the chapter showed, you can create your own custom panel with your own custom layout scheme.

Finally, the chapter looked briefly at how the browser itself can influence how Silverlight renders its content and how you can use the object tag to configure the Silverlight object size.

8

Styling Your App and Dealing with Resources

Creating beautiful, highly styled web-based applications is a core promise of the Silverlight platform. Rarely have we seen Microsoft promote ugly Silverlight apps. Generally, they've been through the user experience and visual design machines of top-notch companies who specialize in creating beautiful software. However, learning to take advantage of the power of the platform and thus deliver on the promise of the platform starts at a technical, and somewhat *unbeautiful*, level. I'm not even going to try to teach you to create a thing of great beauty — I'm just going to empower you to apply your artistic talents to a platform that embraces them.

In this chapter, I'll teach you how to customize the look and feel of the core controls you were introduced to in previous chapters. I'll discuss the ways you can target controls for styling, present approaches for organizing your styles and resources, and teach you what a *resource* actually is. When we're finished, you should have a solid understanding of how to make your app look the way you want it to.

Getting Started

Before we jump into styling, I want to define a small set of core terminology that will be used throughout this chapter. I also want to define a testing environment that you can use to follow the examples that are coming up. Let's get started!

Core Terminology

We'll start with five key concepts that will be used throughout this discussion. There are many more concepts that we'll cover along the way; these will provide us with just enough common ground to move ahead.

- ❑ **Brush** — A `Brush` object in Silverlight is used to paint elements with solid colors, linear gradients, radial gradients, and images. The brush can be applied to elements such as rectangles, circles, text, and panels.

- ❑ **Resource** — A *resource* is a static instance of some type of object. *Brush*-based types are frequently defined as resources for use within an application.

- ❑ `ResourceDictionary` — A `ResourceDictionary` contains a collection of resources. A `ResourceDictionary` can be defined inline in a Silverlight page (i.e., Page.xaml) or externally as a stand-alone XAML file.

- ❑ **Style** — A `Style` is a special type of object that contains a collection of property `Setters`. A `Style` is defined within a `ResourceDictionary` and targets a particular type of control, like a `TextBox`. It is commonly used to set properties like `Foreground`, `FontStyle`, and `FontFamily`. Remember and repeat to yourself: *A Style is a collection of Setters*.

- ❑ `ControlTemplate` — A `ControlTemplate` is the `VisualTree` of elements that make up the look of a control. These elements can range from a series of nested `Borders` (like the default button) to a combination of paths with complex gradient fills. A `ControlTemplate` is generally applied by a `Style` in a `Setter` that sets the `Template` property.

The term styling encompasses many ideas, from the `Foreground` color and `FontStyle` of a `TextBlock`, to the default hover animation applied to a button. I'm going to start from the ground up, first showing you how to set visual properties inline, at the control level. We'll then look at how resources, such as `SolidColorBrushes`, are defined and consumed by elements in a `Page`, then move on to defining `Styles` that set multiple properties on a particular type of control. Finally, we'll look at retemplating controls to completely customize their appearance. In the end, you should understand the "big picture" of styling in Silverlight.

Defining the Working Environment: A XAML-Based Approach

As we start our styling journey, let's establish a common working environment so that you can easily follow the examples. You can work either in Visual Studio 2008 or in Blend 3; the environment you choose is really not important at this point. (I'll be using Blend as I step through this chapter, so the screenshots you see will likely be taken in the Blend environment.)

Create a new Silverlight 3.0 Project, and add a `UserControl` to your project. Figure 8-1 demonstrates how to do this in both Blend and Visual Studio by right-clicking on the Project node in Solution Explorer. Once you've added the `UserControl`, double-click on its XAML file to make it the active document, and then switch to XAML view.

To ensure that your new `UserControl` is the page that you see when you debug, open App.xaml.cs and edit the `OnStartup` method created by the Silverlight Project starter template. Change the line highlighted in the following code to match the name of your new `UserControl`:

```
private void OnStartup(object sender, StartupEventArgs e)
    {
        // Load the main control here
```

```
        this.RootVisual = new UserControl1(); // Change this control
}
```

Now, with that little bit of housecleaning out-of-the-way, let's get started.

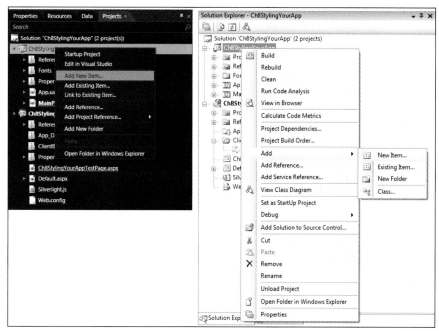

Figure 8-1

Local Styling (Inline Styling)

Local styling is no more than setting properties on an instance of a control. This may sound a bit obvious, but it's crucial that you see this basic piece of the bigger puzzle. Let's assume that you want to customize the look of a `TextBlock`, setting its `Foreground` to red (#FF0000 in hexadecimal), its `FontStyle` to Arial, and its `FontWeight` to bold. The following code demonstrates how to do this in XAML:

```
<TextBlock Text="My Red Bold Arial Label" Foreground="#FF0000" FontFamily="Arial"
FontWeight="Bold" />
```

The `Foreground` property above accepts an inline hexadecimal value that represents a `SolidColorBrush`. We can also use the longhand version and set the `Foreground` property by explicitly declaring a `SolidColorBrush` object:

```
<TextBlock Text="My Red Bold Arial Label" FontFamily="Arial" FontWeight="Bold">
    <TextBlock.Foreground>
        <SolidColorBrush Color="#FF0000" />
    </TextBlock.Foreground>
</TextBlock>
```

I'm showing you this longhand version so that you see the underlying object type needed to set the `Foreground` property. We've just encountered the first definition — *Brush*, in this case, the `SolidColorBrush`. Let's suppose now that you want to create a `Rectangle`, painted with the same red `SolidColorBrush`. You can do it inline just as we did with the `TextBlock`:

```
<Rectangle Width="100" Height="100">
    <Rectangle.Fill>
        <SolidColorBrush Color="#FF0000" />
    </Rectangle.Fill>
</Rectangle>
```

Let's now assume that you always want your `TextBlock` `Foreground` to match the `Fill` of this `Rectangle`, and let's pretend that your mood just changed from red to green. Let's also add to our layout 10 additional `TextBlocks` and three additional `Rectangles` and demand that they abide by the same color rules. You could step through your XAML (or Blend or Visual Studio) and manually change property values every time you change your mind . . . or you can use resources.

Styling with Resources

Let's resolve our color-sync nightmare through the use of resources. We'll first define the resource, then reference that resource inline on each of our `TextBlocks` and `Rectangles`. The XAML snippet below shows our `UserControl` prior to defining any resources:

```
<UserControl
    xmlns="http://schemas.microsoft.com/winfx/2006/xaml/presentation"
    xmlns:x="http://schemas.microsoft.com/winfx/2006/xaml"
    xmlns:d="http://schemas.microsoft.com/expression/blend/2008"
    xmlns:mc="http://schemas.openxmlformats.org/markup-compatibility/2006"
    mc:Ignorable="d"
    x:Class="Silverlight2BookSamples.UserControl1"
    d:DesignWidth="640" d:DesignHeight="480">

    <Grid x:Name="LayoutRoot" Background="White" >
        <Rectangle Height="84" HorizontalAlignment="Left" Margin="8,35,0,0"
VerticalAlignment="Top" Width="84" Fill="#FFFF0000" Stroke="#FF000000"/>
        <TextBlock HorizontalAlignment="Left" VerticalAlignment="Top"
Text="TextBlock" TextWrapping="Wrap" Margin="8,12.4630002975464,0,0"/>
    </Grid>
</UserControl>
```

Resources are housed in a `ResourceDictionary`, commonly in the outermost element of your XAML file. All `UIElement`-derived classes have a `Resources` property of type `ResourceDictionary`, and `UserControl` is no exception. The code below shows a new `SolidColorBrush` added to the `UserControl` `.Resources` `ResourceDictionary`:

```
<UserControl
    xmlns="http://schemas.microsoft.com/winfx/2006/xaml/presentation"
    xmlns:x="http://schemas.microsoft.com/winfx/2006/xaml"
    xmlns:d="http://schemas.microsoft.com/expression/blend/2008"
    xmlns:mc="http://schemas.openxmlformats.org/markup-compatibility/2006"
    mc:Ignorable="d"
```

```
     x:Class="Silverlight2BookSamples.UserControl1"
     d:DesignWidth="640" d:DesignHeight="480">
   <UserControl.Resources>
           <SolidColorBrush x:Key="SharedBrush" Color="#FFFF0000"/>
   </UserControl.Resources>
   ...
```

Notice that the definition of the brush is exactly the same as the inline definition, only it now includes an x:Key property value. When applying this resource, you will reference it by the key value *SharedBrush*. To reference a resource in XAML, you use the {StaticResource keyName} markup extension. The following shows both the Rectangle's Fill property and the TextBlock's Foreground property referencing the new resource named SharedBrush:

```
<UserControl
 xmlns="http://schemas.microsoft.com/winfx/2006/xaml/presentation"
 xmlns:x="http://schemas.microsoft.com/winfx/2006/xaml"
 xmlns:d="http://schemas.microsoft.com/expression/blend/2008"
 xmlns:mc="http://schemas.openxmlformats.org/markup-compatibility/2006"
 mc:Ignorable="d"
 x:Class="Silverlight2BookSamples.UserControl1"
 d:DesignWidth="640" d:DesignHeight="480">
 <UserControl.Resources>
         <SolidColorBrush x:Key="SharedBrush" Color="#FFFF0000"/>
 </UserControl.Resources>

 <Grid x:Name="LayoutRoot" Background="White" >
         <Rectangle Height="84" HorizontalAlignment="Left" Margin="8,35,0,0"
 VerticalAlignment="Top" Width="84" Fill="{StaticResource SharedBrush}"
 Stroke="#FF000000"/>
         <TextBlock HorizontalAlignment="Left" VerticalAlignment="Top"
 Text="TextBlock" TextWrapping="Wrap" Margin="8,12.4630002975464,0,0"
 Foreground="{StaticResource SharedBrush}"/>
 </Grid>
</UserControl>
```

The key thing to notice in the XAML is the statement Fill="{StaticResource SharedBrush}". This statement basically reads, assign the resource named SharedBrush to the Fill property.

The curly braces are required when referencing a resource.

You've now seen how to define a resource and reference that resource. Try changing the Color property of your SharedBrush resource and rerun your application. You should see that both the foreground of the text and the fill of the rectangle have been updated, reflecting your new color value.

As I pointed out in the definitions section at the beginning of the chapter, a resource is a static instance of *some type* of object. You're not limited to creating Brush resources. The following code shows two additional resources, CornerRadiusX and CornerRadiusY, both of type System:Double (note that I added a namespace definition for System). These are referenced by the Rectangle's CornerX and CornerY properties.

```
<UserControl
 xmlns="http://schemas.microsoft.com/winfx/2006/xaml/presentation"
```

```
xmlns:x="http://schemas.microsoft.com/winfx/2006/xaml"
xmlns:d="http://schemas.microsoft.com/expression/blend/2008"
xmlns:mc="http://schemas.openxmlformats.org/markup-compatibility/2006"
xmlns:System="clr-namespace:System;assembly=mscorlib"
mc:Ignorable="d"
x:Class="Silverlight2BookSamples.UserControl1"
d:DesignWidth="640" d:DesignHeight="480">
<UserControl.Resources>
        <SolidColorBrush x:Key="SharedBrush" Color="#FFFF0000"/>
        <System:Double x:Key="CornerRadiusX">9</System:Double>
        <System:Double x:Key="CornerRadiusY">9</System:Double>

</UserControl.Resources>

<Grid x:Name="LayoutRoot" Background="White" >
        <Rectangle Height="84" HorizontalAlignment="Left" Margin="8,35,0,0"
VerticalAlignment="Top" Width="84" Fill="{StaticResource SharedBrush}"
Stroke="#FF000000" RadiusX="{StaticResource CornerRadiusX}"
RadiusY="{StaticResource CornerRadiusY}"/>
        <TextBlock HorizontalAlignment="Left" VerticalAlignment="Top"
Text="TextBlock" TextWrapping="Wrap" Margin="8,12.4630002975464,0,0"
Foreground="{StaticResource SharedBrush}"/>
</Grid>
</UserControl>
```

If you're keeping your local project in sync with this running sample, your UserControl should now look like Figure 8-2.

TextBlock

Figure 8-2

Carrying this idea further, we can define resources for the FontFamily, FontSize, FontWeight, and FontStyle properties of our TextBlock. And while this approach still satisfies our goal of centralizing shared values, the following code demonstrates how messy this approach can become:

```
<UserControl.Resources>
        <SolidColorBrush x:Key="SharedBrush" Color="#FFFF0000"/>
        <System:Double x:Key="CornerRadiusX">9</System:Double>
        <System:Double x:Key="CornerRadiusY">9</System:Double>
        <FontFamily x:Key="SharedFont">Portable User Interface</FontFamily>
        <System:Double x:Key="SharedFontSize">14.666666984558106</System:Double>
        <FontWeight x:Key="SharedFontWeight">Normal</FontWeight>
        <FontStyle x:Key="SharedFontStyle">Normal</FontStyle>

</UserControl.Resources>
```

```
...

<TextBlock
            HorizontalAlignment="Left"
            VerticalAlignment="Top"
            Text="TextBlock"
            TextWrapping="Wrap"
            Margin="8,12.4630002975464,0,0"
            Foreground="{StaticResource SharedBrush}"
            FontFamily="{StaticResource SharedFont}"
            FontSize="{StaticResource SharedFontSize}"
            FontWeight="{StaticResource SharedFontWeight}"
            FontStyle="{StaticResource SharedFontStyle}"/>

...
```

We're now referencing resources for a large number of properties on this `TextBlock` control. We'll have to do the same thing for every other `TextBlock` in our layout that we want to share this same look. Not only will this make our XAML hard to read, but it will also become a nightmare to maintain. What if we decide to synchronize another property, such as `TextWrapping`? With this model, we'll need to define another resource and update all of our `TextBlocks` to point to this new resource. This is quickly becoming a problem. Fear not — the `Style` object is here to save the day!

Working with the `Style` Object

When I defined *style* at the beginning of this chapter, I asked you to remember that *a Style is a collection of Setters*. Furthermore, a `Style` is a keyed resource that contains a collection of `Setters` that target properties and specify values for a particular type of control (such as `TextBlock`). The previous code listing shows what can happen when we try to centralize values for several different properties on a control. A large number of resources are defined, one for each property. Then, on each instance of the control (`TextBlock` in the example), we have to use a `StaticResource` reference for each centralized property value. It becomes a real mess! The following code shows you how this problem is solved, using a `Style` object defined in the same `ResourceDictionary`:

```
<UserControl.Resources>
<Style x:Key="TextBlockStyle" TargetType="TextBlock">
            <Setter Property="FontFamily" Value="Verdana"/>
            <Setter Property="FontSize" Value="14"/>
            <Setter Property="FontWeight" Value="Bold"/>
            <Setter Property="FontStyle" Value="Normal"/>
            <Setter Property="Foreground" Value="#FFFF0000"/>
        </Style>

</UserControl.Resources>

<Grid x:Name="LayoutRoot" Background="White" >
    <TextBlock
            HorizontalAlignment="Left"
            VerticalAlignment="Top"
            Text="TextBlock" TextWrapping="Wrap"
            Style="{StaticResource TextBlockStyle}"/>
</Grid>
```

control's properties is independent from the actual look of the control. The look of the control is defined in XAML and is applied at compile time.

Why Define a Custom Template?

Acknowledging that Silverlight controls are lookless is one thing, but understanding *why* they are lookless is another. Because a control is lookless, you can completely replace its visual appearance. Let's consider the Button for a moment. The Button control is probably the most commonly retemplated control in both Silverlight and WPF. Consider the immersive Web experiences or applications you've encountered over the years. A core action of your experience is clicking. You click, click, click — text, images, custom artwork — anything is fair game. Generally, the item you are clicking responds to the MouseOver and MousePressed events, providing you with visual feedback to your interaction.

If I ask you to picture different button styles that you've encountered, your mind probably fills will different shapes, colors, and textures — imprints left by the many visually diverse experiences you've had in your travels. If your mind didn't fill with images, at least consider the differing appearance between a Windows Vista button and an OS X button. The two buttons react to the same interaction (MouseOver, MousePressed, Disabled) and generally fire the same events for developers (e.g., Click), but their appearance is markedly different.

Your application will likely need the functionality provided by Buttons, ListBoxes, RadioButtons, and CheckBoxes, but your *brand* may require a look other than the default look provided by Silverlight. By retemplating the controls, you get the same functionality provided out-of-the-box with the added benefit of having your custom look applied.

Defining and Applying a Custom Template

Before we retemplate the Button, let's add a default-styled Button to the page for comparison. Figure 8-3 shows the default Silverlight Button on the stage in Blend. All of the visual elements that make up the look of the button reside in the Button's default template. Later, we'll look at the XAML that makes up the default button; for now, I want to call out a few key elements. Notice the single-pixel gray border with rounded corners — that's defined by a Border element. In the foreground of that Border element is another border with a gradient fill. In the foreground of that element is a rounded piece of artwork that simulates a highlight. Finally, there is an element that displays the Content we have specified on the button. It is center-aligned both vertically and horizontally.

Figure 8-3

A custom template is defined using the same layout panels and controls you've been introduced to throughout this book. Everything in your Silverlight arsenal is fair game for a control's template. The following code shows a simple Style that sets the Template property of a Button control, replacing the default template with a Grid containing a nested red Rectangle:

```
<Style x:Key="customStyle" TargetType="Button">
  <Setter Property="Template" >
```

```
        <Setter.Value>
            <ControlTemplate TargetType="Button">
                <Grid>
                    <Rectangle Fill="#FF0000" />
                </Grid>
            </ControlTemplate>
        </Setter.Value>
    </Setter>
</Style>
```

Here, for the first time in this chapter, you're seeing the more verbose way of setting the Value property of a Setter. Because the value we are supplying is much more complex than a single string value, we have to set the Value property by using <Setter.Value />. The value of the Template property is always a ControlTemplate object whose TargetType property matches the value of the Style object it is defined within. The ControlTemplate object accepts a single child element whose value is always some type of Panel; in this case, it's a Grid.

> Unlike WPF, the value of the TargetType **property is just a string and does not**
> **require the** {x:Type ControlName} **syntax.**

Applying this Style to a Button is achieved by setting the Style property, just like we did for the TextBlock example before:

```
<Button Style="{StaticResource customStyle}" Content="Click Me!"
        HorizontalAlignment="Center" VerticalAlignment="Center"/>
```

Applying this Style to a Button results in a button that looks like a flat, red rectangle like the button depicted in Figure 8-4. We've completely replaced the default template of the button with a single rectangle.

Figure 8-4

Not too exciting, eh? And where is the text "Click Me!" as specified on the Content property? Since we have completely replaced the template of the Button with a Grid and nested Rectangle, we have eliminated the Button's ability to display its own content! See, the Template property really *is* the most powerful property of all. As we define the template of a control, we have to think about how we want the control's property values to affect the way the control actually looks. Let's deal with the content issue first.

The **ContentPresenter**

The ContentPresenter control, just as its name indicates, is used to display *content*. All controls derived from ContentControl have a Content property. Button happens to be derived from ContentControl, which is why you set its Content property instead of its Text property. The Content property is of type UIElement, which means pretty much any visual element can be thrown at it, even another Button.

129

In order to display the text "Click Me!" as set on our `Button`'s `Content` property, we need to add a `ContentPresenter` to our custom template defined in `customStyle`. The following XAML shows this `ContentPresenter` in place:

```
<Style x:Key="customStyle" TargetType="Button">
    <Setter Property="Template" >
        <Setter.Value>
            <ControlTemplate TargetType="Button">
                <Grid>
                    <Rectangle Fill="#FF0000" />
                        <ContentPresenter Margin="5,5,5,5" />
                </Grid>
            </ControlTemplate>
        </Setter.Value>
    </Setter>
</Style>
```

That's all there is to it. It's actually deceptively simple. The `ContentPresenter`, when dropped into a `ContentControl`, automatically detects the type of content that has been set and displays it accordingly. When the content is text, as in this example, a `TextBlock` is automatically created whose `Text` property is set to the value specified.

Try setting the `Content` of the button to different types of objects (`Circles`, `Rectangles`, `ComboBoxes`, etc.) and notice how each of these objects is displayed inside the custom template. Figure 8-5 shows some of the variations that are possible. And remember, you can affect the layout of the `ContentPresenter` by using the `HorizontalAlignment`, `VerticalAlignment`, and `Margin` properties (or any other layout properties) as with any other control.

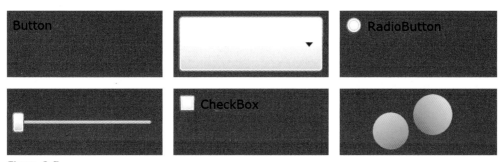

Figure 8-5

TemplateBinding

In the previous section, you saw how to present the `Content` of a `ContentControl` by using the `ContentPresenter`. In this section, we'll look at how you can use other properties defined on the control you're templating, using `TemplateBinding`.

`TemplateBinding` is a special type of binding that lets you access the value of properties defined on a control from within the template you're authoring. The first template we created consisted of a `Grid` with a nested `Rectangle`. At run time, all `Buttons` whose `Style` was set to `customStyle` looked exactly the same, regardless of their property settings. If the `Background` property was set to green, the `Rectangle` in the template was still red. In fact, those buttons couldn't even present their own content. We took care of the content situation by adding a `ContentPresenter` to the template. We now want to take advantage of the `Background` property, empowering the template to set the `Rectangle`'s color to the value of the `Button`'s `Background` property.

The following XAML demonstrates how to use the `TemplateBinding` syntax to assign values set on the control to elements within its template:

```xml
<Style x:Key="customStyle" TargetType="Button">
    <Setter Property="Template" >
        <Setter.Value>
            <ControlTemplate TargetType="Button">
                <Grid>
                    <Rectangle Fill="{TemplateBinding Background}" />
                        <ContentPresenter />
                </Grid>
            </ControlTemplate>
        </Setter.Value>
    </Setter>
</Style>
```

The `Rectangle`'s `Fill` property is now bound to the `Button`'s `Background` property. I happened to choose the `Background` property in this example, but I could just as easily have chosen the `BorderBrush` property, because they're both of type `Brush`. If I were authoring a template for another control that defined more `Brush` properties, I could have chosen those properties as well.

Try creating several instances of `Button`, setting each instance's `Style` property to `customStyle`, then set each `Button`'s `Background` property to a different color value. When you run the sample, you should see your `Background` properties honored on each `Button` instance. It's important to note that the value supplied by the `TemplateBinding` is the runtime value of each control's instance. `TemplateBinding` does not synchronize values across controls; it just gives you a way to pump property values into your control's template.

More **TemplateBinding**

In the previous example, we used `TemplateBinding` to bind the `Button`'s `Background` property to the `Fill` property of a `Rectangle` nested within the `Button`'s `ControlTemplate`. Every single property defined on `Button` can be bound to an element within the template using `TemplateBinding`. It's through `TemplateBinding` that the properties of this lookless control come to life and start to have meaning.

Let's attach a few more properties. I'm going to start with `Padding`. *Padding* is typically used to define the amount of space surrounding an object's content. In comparison, an object's *margin* is the amount of space preserved around the control itself. Both the `Margin` and `Padding` properties are of type `Thickness` and are defined using four double values that represent Left, Top, Right, and Bottom. The most meaningful way for us to use the `Padding` property is by applying it as the `Margin` of the `ContentPresenter`. The following code demonstrates how this is achieved:

```xml
<Style x:Key="customStyle" TargetType="Button">
    <Setter Property="Template" >
        <Setter.Value>
            <ControlTemplate TargetType="Button">
                <Grid>
                    <Rectangle Fill="{TemplateBinding Background}" />
                        <ContentPresenter Margin="{TemplateBinding Padding}" />
```

```
            </Grid>
          </ControlTemplate>
        </Setter.Value>
      </Setter>
    </Style>
```

The previous code and Figure 8-6 demonstrate various `Padding` values and their resulting visuals. Note how the space around the content changes as the `Padding` value changes.

Figure 8-6

```
<!--Red Button with 5 Pixel Margin on All Sides-->
<Button
    Style="{StaticResource customStyle}"
    Content="Click Me!"
    Background="#FF0000"
    HorizontalAlignment="Left"
    VerticalAlignment="Top"
    Margin="10,10,0,0"
    Padding="5,5,5,5" />

<!--Green button with 5 pixel Margin on Top and Bottom-->
<Button
    Style="{StaticResource customStyle}"
    Content="Click Me!"
    Background="#00FF00"
    HorizontalAlignment="Left"
    VerticalAlignment="Top"
    Margin="10,60,0,0"
    Padding="0,5,0,5" />

<!--Blue Button with 5 pixel Margin on Left and Right-->
<Button
    Style="{StaticResource customStyle}"
    Content="Click Me!"
    Background="#0000FF"
    HorizontalAlignment="Left"
    VerticalAlignment="Top"
    Margin="10,120,0,0"
    Padding="5,0,5,0" />
```

I'm now going to add `HorizontalAlignment` and `VerticalAlignment` property settings to the `ContentPresenter` and set their values to `HorizontalContentAlignment` and `VerticalContentAlignment` using `TemplateBinding`. The following XAML demonstrates the updated `Style`:

```xml
<Style x:Key="customStyle" TargetType="Button">
    <Setter Property="Template" >
        <Setter.Value>
            <ControlTemplate TargetType="Button">
                <Grid>
                    <Rectangle Fill="{TemplateBinding Background}" />
                    <ContentPresenter
                        Margin="{TemplateBinding Padding}"
                        HorizontalAlignment="{TemplateBinding
                        HorizontalContentAlignment}"
                        VerticalAlignment="{TemplateBinding
                        VerticalContentAlignment}" />
                </Grid>
            </ControlTemplate>
        </Setter.Value>
    </Setter>
</Style>
```

Now that we've hooked these properties up in the template, they will actually have an effect when set on each `Button` instance. We can now specify both the padding and internal alignment of the content of each `Button` that uses the `customStyle` style.

I'm not going to keep stepping through each property on `Button` and show you how to hook it up via `TemplateBinding`; instead, you can just keep repeating the same process, experimenting to your heart's content. I *will* point out that you can `TemplateBind` to the same property multiple times in a template. For example, I could have two nested `Borders`, each of whose `Padding` property is bound to the `Button`'s `Padding` property. Similarly, I could have multiple `TextBlocks`, each of whose `Text` property is bound to the `Button`'s `Content` property, achieving the drop shadow effect shown in Figure 8-7.

Figure 8-7

Without `TemplateBinding`, properties set on individual control instances would have no visual effect at all. `TemplateBinding` provides a path into the template of a control by means of simple property settings at the control-instance level. The `Styles` and `Templates` defined for the default Silverlight controls have made extensive use of `TemplateBinding`. Try changing the `Background`, `BorderBrush`, `HorizontalContentAlignment`, and `Padding` properties of the default `Button`. As you change these properties, the button's appearance changes accordingly. The author(s) of the default `Styles` had to employ `TemplateBinding` throughout the default `Styles` in order to enable the behavior that you expect when interacting with the control.

Preserving the Essence of Your Style

If you've experimented with the default Silverlight `Button` control, you should have noticed that as you set its `Background` property, the overall look and feel, or *essence*, of the control remains the same. For example, if you set the Background property to a green SolidColorBrush, the button does not actually appear flat green. Instead, it looks almost the same, only now it has a green hue. The oval highlight in the foreground remains, and the background color appears to fade vertically to white. Figure 8-8 shows the default Silverlight button, without a custom background color, and two additional buttons, each of whose Background property has been set.

Figure 8-8

In order to achieve this effect, the Template must include more than a single rectangle, as we've been using up to this point. The default template employs several elements, layered in the foreground of a base element that is template-bound to the Background property. The foreground elements are partially transparent to allow the base element to shine through. As the Style author, it is up to you to define how various property settings affect the final look of your control. You can choose to completely ignore local settings, by not using TemplateBinding at all, or you can choose to strategically apply TemplateBinding to elements within your Template to maintain the essence of your design, while providing a degree of flexibility.

The code listing below displays the XAML for the default Silverlight button. I've added comments throughout the template to hopefully shed some light on the techniques employed.

```xml
<Style x:Key="DefaultButtonStyle" TargetType="Button">
    <!-- ===================================== -->
    <!-- Default Brushes Defined At Style Level  -->
    <!-- ===================================== -->
    <Setter Property="Background" Value="#FF1F3B53"/>
    <Setter Property="Foreground" Value="#FF000000"/>
    <Setter Property="Padding" Value="3"/>
    <Setter Property="BorderThickness" Value="1"/>
    <Setter Property="BorderBrush">
        <Setter.Value>
            <LinearGradientBrush EndPoint="0.5,1" StartPoint="0.5,0">
                <GradientStop Color="#FFA3AEB9" Offset="0"/>
                <GradientStop Color="#FF8399A9" Offset="0.375"/>
                <GradientStop Color="#FF718597" Offset="0.375"/>
                <GradientStop Color="#FF617584" Offset="1"/>
            </LinearGradientBrush>
        </Setter.Value>
    </Setter>
    <Setter Property="Template">
        <Setter.Value>
            <ControlTemplate TargetType="Button">
                <Grid>
                    <!-- ================================================================ -->
                    <!-- VisualStateManager Defined as Child of First Template Element -->
                    <!-- ================================================================ -->
                    <vsm:VisualStateManager.VisualStateGroups>
                        <vsm:VisualStateGroup x:Name="CommonStates">
```

```xml
            <vsm:VisualState x:Name="Normal"/>
            <!-- =============== -->
            <!-- MouseOver State -->
            <!-- =============== -->
            <vsm:VisualState x:Name="MouseOver">
                <Storyboard>
                    <DoubleAnimationUsingKeyFrames
                        Storyboard.TargetName="BackgroundAnimation"
                        Storyboard.TargetProperty="Opacity">
                        <SplineDoubleKeyFrame KeyTime="0" Value="1"/>
                    </DoubleAnimationUsingKeyFrames>
                    <ColorAnimationUsingKeyFrames
                        Storyboard.TargetName="BackgroundGradient"
Storyboard.TargetProperty="(Rectangle.Fill).(GradientBrush.GradientStops)[1].
(GradientStop.Color)">
                            <SplineColorKeyFrame KeyTime="0"
                                Value="#F2FFFFFF"/>
                    </ColorAnimationUsingKeyFrames>
                    <ColorAnimationUsingKeyFrames
                        Storyboard.TargetName="BackgroundGradient"
Storyboard.TargetProperty="(Rectangle.Fill).(GradientBrush.GradientStops)[2].
(GradientStop.Color)">
                            <SplineColorKeyFrame KeyTime="0"
                                Value="#CCFFFFFF"/>
                    </ColorAnimationUsingKeyFrames>
                    <ColorAnimationUsingKeyFrames
                        Storyboard.TargetName="BackgroundGradient"
Storyboard.TargetProperty="(Rectangle.Fill).(GradientBrush.GradientStops)[3].
(GradientStop.Color)">
                            <SplineColorKeyFrame KeyTime="0"
                                Value="#7FFFFFFF"/>
                    </ColorAnimationUsingKeyFrames>
                </Storyboard>
            </vsm:VisualState>
            <!-- ============= -->
            <!-- Pressed State  -->
            <!-- ============= -->
            <vsm:VisualState x:Name="Pressed">
                <Storyboard>
                    <ColorAnimationUsingKeyFrames
                        Storyboard.TargetName="Background" Storyboard.
TargetProperty="(Border.Background).(SolidColorBrush.Color)">
                            <SplineColorKeyFrame KeyTime="0"
                                Value="#FF6DBDD1"/>
                    </ColorAnimationUsingKeyFrames>
                    <DoubleAnimationUsingKeyFrames
                        Storyboard.TargetName="BackgroundAnimation"
                        Storyboard.TargetProperty="Opacity">
                        <SplineDoubleKeyFrame KeyTime="0" Value="1"/>
                    </DoubleAnimationUsingKeyFrames>
                    <ColorAnimationUsingKeyFrames
                        Storyboard.TargetName="BackgroundGradient"
Storyboard.TargetProperty="(Rectangle.Fill).(GradientBrush.GradientStops)[0].
(GradientStop.Color)">
                            <SplineColorKeyFrame KeyTime="0"
                                Value="#D8FFFFFF"/>
```

```xml
                        </ColorAnimationUsingKeyFrames>
                        <ColorAnimationUsingKeyFrames
                            Storyboard.TargetName="BackgroundGradient"
Storyboard.TargetProperty="(Rectangle.Fill).(GradientBrush.GradientStops)[1].
(GradientStop.Color)">
                            <SplineColorKeyFrame KeyTime="0"
                                Value="#C6FFFFFF"/>
                        </ColorAnimationUsingKeyFrames>
                        <ColorAnimationUsingKeyFrames
                            Storyboard.TargetName="BackgroundGradient"
Storyboard.TargetProperty="(Rectangle.Fill).(GradientBrush.GradientStops)[2].
(GradientStop.Color)">
                            <SplineColorKeyFrame KeyTime="0"
                                Value="#8CFFFFFF"/>
                        </ColorAnimationUsingKeyFrames>
                        <ColorAnimationUsingKeyFrames
                            Storyboard.TargetName="BackgroundGradient"
Storyboard.TargetProperty="(Rectangle.Fill).(GradientBrush.GradientStops)[3].
(GradientStop.Color)">
                            <SplineColorKeyFrame KeyTime="0"
                                Value="#3FFFFFFF"/>
                        </ColorAnimationUsingKeyFrames>
                    </Storyboard>
                </vsm:VisualState>
                <!-- =============== -->
                <!-- Disabled State  -->
                <!-- =============== -->
                <vsm:VisualState x:Name="Disabled">
                    <Storyboard>
                        <DoubleAnimationUsingKeyFrames
                            Storyboard.TargetName="DisabledVisualElement"
                        Storyboard.TargetProperty="Opacity">
                            <SplineDoubleKeyFrame KeyTime="0" Value=".55"/>
                        </DoubleAnimationUsingKeyFrames>
                    </Storyboard>
                </vsm:VisualState>
            </vsm:VisualStateGroup>
            <vsm:VisualStateGroup x:Name="FocusStates">
                <!-- =============== -->
                <!-- Focused State   -->
                <!-- =============== -->
                <vsm:VisualState x:Name="Focused">
                    <Storyboard>
                        <DoubleAnimationUsingKeyFrames
                            Storyboard.TargetName="FocusVisualElement"
                            Storyboard.TargetProperty="Opacity">
                            <SplineDoubleKeyFrame KeyTime="0" Value="1"/>
                        </DoubleAnimationUsingKeyFrames>
                    </Storyboard>
                </vsm:VisualState>
                <vsm:VisualState x:Name="Unfocused"/>
            </vsm:VisualStateGroup>
```

```xml
        </vsm:VisualStateManager.VisualStateGroups>
        <!-- ===================================================== -->
        <!-- Base Border (BorderBrush and BorderThickness TemplateBound) -->
        <!-- ===================================================== -->

        <Border x:Name="Background" Background="White"
        BorderBrush="{TemplateBinding BorderBrush}"
        BorderThickness="{TemplateBinding BorderThickness}" CornerRadius="3">
            <!-- ===================================================== -->
            <!-- Grid (Background TemplateBound to Button.Background) -->
            <!-- ===================================================== -->
            <Grid Margin="1" Background="{TemplateBinding Background}">
                <Border x:Name="BackgroundAnimation" Opacity="0"
                    Background="#FF448DCA"/>
                <Rectangle x:Name="BackgroundGradient">
                    <Rectangle.Fill>
                        <LinearGradientBrush EndPoint=".7,1"
                            StartPoint=".7,0">
                            <GradientStop Color="#FFFFFFFF" Offset="0"/>
                            <GradientStop Color="#F9FFFFFF"
                                Offset="0.375"/>
                            <GradientStop Color="#E5FFFFFF"
                                Offset="0.625"/>
                            <GradientStop Color="#C6FFFFFF" Offset="1"/>
                        </LinearGradientBrush>
                    </Rectangle.Fill>
                </Rectangle>
            </Grid>
        </Border>
        <!-- ===================================================== -->
        <!-- ContentPresenter (Content and ContentTemplate
        <!-- Property Settings Not Necessary)               -->
        <!-- ===================================================== -->
        <ContentPresenter x:Name="contentPresenter"
            HorizontalAlignment="{TemplateBinding HorizontalContentAlignment}"
            Margin="{TemplateBinding Padding}"
            VerticalAlignment="{TemplateBinding VerticalContentAlignment}"
            Content="{TemplateBinding Content}"
            ContentTemplate="{TemplateBinding ContentTemplate}"/>
        <Rectangle x:Name="DisabledVisualElement" Fill="#FFFFFFFF"
            RadiusX="3" RadiusY="3" IsHitTestVisible="false"
            Opacity="0"/>
        <Rectangle x:Name="FocusVisualElement" Stroke="#FF6DBDD1"
            StrokeThickness="1" RadiusX="2" RadiusY="2" Margin="1"
            IsHitTestVisible="false" Opacity="0"/>
        </Grid>
    </ControlTemplate>
  </Setter.Value>
 </Setter>
</Style>
```

If you look at the first grid defined in the template, you'll see that its `Background` property is set to `{TemplateBinding Background}`:

```
<!-- ====================================================== -->
<!-- Grid (Background TemplateBound to Button.Background) -->
<!-- ====================================================== -->
<Grid Margin="1" Background="{TemplateBinding Background}">
```

The second child of that grid is a rectangle that uses a `LinearGradientBrush` as its `Fill`. The `Color` values of each `GradientStop` are white, each with varying shades of opacity. This lets the containing grid's background brush bleed through. The foreground rectangle is used to create a shading effect. When the `Background` property of the control is set, the essence of the button remains the same because it's really the foreground rectangle that's responsible for creating the gradient effect.

Try replacing the white foreground gradient with a black-based gradient. You should see that the template still responds to the `Background` setting, only now the button is much darker than the default Silverlight Style.

Limitations of **TemplateBinding**

I just pointed out that the default button lets you change its background color by specifying a custom value for its `Background` property. But what if you want to change the button's hover color? There isn't a `BackgroundHover` property. Likewise, if you want the `HorizontalContentAlignment` to change when the button is in a hover state, you won't find a property specific to the hover state. Or maybe you just want to turn off the default button's oval highlight artwork — it's in these cases of interaction and customization where the control author can either choose to add additional properties (such as a `DisplayHighlight` property) or require you to edit the default template. In most cases, you'll need to edit the default template.

You can see that once your customization needs step beyond just the basics, you have to create a custom `Style` and override the default template. To anticipate even a minor level of template-level customization, a large number of properties would need to be added to the control. Consider once again, just for a moment, the ways you might want to customize the button when it's in a hover state. How about turning off the highlight and changing the border color, the background color, the foreground color of the text, and the text's `FontWeight`? This would all require custom properties to be defined on the control that you could then `TemplateBind` to. And what if the template itself had no highlight artwork? What good would our highlight-based property(ies) be then?

I hope you see that properties defined simply to point directly into the template can be quite arbitrary in nature and often won't hold up across the many uses a control might find itself in. There are certainly cases in which it makes sense to add properties (such as an `AlternateRowBackground` brush property for a grid), but they should not be added on a whim. Fortunately, Silverlight provides a model that allows us to react to state changes from within the template itself.

Visual State Manager: Reacting to State Changes within a Template

So far you've seen how to define the look of a control by creating a custom `ControlTemplate`. But the examples so far result in a static visual, with no interaction whatsoever. The control looks the same whether it has focus or doesn't have focus, whether the mouse is over it or not, and even whether it is pressed or not. For a personal project, this may be fine, but for interactive Silverlight applications, your users are going to expect visual feedback. Enter the `VisualStateManager`.

If you paid close attention to the previous code listing, you may have noticed the `VisualStateManager` definition (`<vsm:VisualStateManager />`) defined within the button's `ControlTemplate`. The `VisualStateManager` is used to define how controls react visually to changes in state, such as `MouseOver` or `Pressed`. You use the `Visual State Manager` (VSM) to define different `VisualStates` for the control whose template you're authoring.

It is up to the control author to define both the control's `VisualStateGroups` and the `VisualStates` of each group. The control author is also responsible for transitioning from state to state throughout the life of the control. The default Silverlight controls all employ this *State Model* and use the `TemplateVisualState` attribute:

```
[TemplateVisualState(Name = "MouseOver", GroupName = "CommonStates")]
```

Microsoft Expression Blend looks for this attribute on controls and presents all `VisualStateGroups` and `VisualStates` defined when in template editing mode. Figure 8-9 shows how Blend exposes these states.

Figure 8-9

Editing state transitions is most commonly done in Blend, but I'll break down the default button's `VisualStateManager` XAML so that you have a firm grasp of what's being generated behind the scenes. The following XAML defines two `VisualStateGroups` — CommonStates and FocusStates:

```
<vsm:VisualStateManager.VisualStateGroups>
        <vsm:VisualStateGroup x:Name="CommonStates"></vsm:VisualStateGroup>
        <vsm:VisualStateGroup x:Name="FocusStates"></vsm:VisualStateGroup>
</vsm:VisualStateManager.VisualStateGroups>
```

To the `VisualStateGroups`, we will add `VisualStates`:

```
<vsm:VisualStateManager.VisualStateGroups>
        <vsm:VisualStateGroup x:Name="CommonStates">
            <vsm:VisualState x:Name="Normal" />
            <vsm:VisualState x:Name="MouseOver" />
            <vsm:VisualState x:Name="Pressed" />
            <vsm:VisualState x:Name="Disabled" />
        </vsm:VisualStateGroup>
```

```
    <vsm:VisualStateGroup x:Name="FocusStates">
        <vsm:VisualState x:Name="Focused" />
        <vsm:VisualState x:Name="Unfocused" />
    </vsm:VisualStateGroup>
</vsm:VisualStateManager.VisualStateGroups>
```

These are all of the states that have been defined for the `Button` control by the Silverlight engineering team. You can add additional `VisualStates` to the XAML, but they will never be accessed because the control is not looking for them. This is another reason it's a good idea to start from the default control XAML when skinning controls.

Now that we have the default `VisualStateGroups` and `VisualStates` defined, let's add a simple `Storyboard` to the `MouseOver` state:

```
<vsm:VisualStateManager.VisualStateGroups>
    <vsm:VisualStateGroup x:Name="CommonStates">
        <vsm:VisualState x:Name="Normal" />
        <vsm:VisualState x:Name="MouseOver">
            <Storyboard>
                <ColorAnimation Storyboard.TargetName="LinearBevelDarkEnd"
                    Storyboard.TargetProperty="Color" To="#FF000000" Duration="0" />
            </Storyboard>
        </vsm:VisualStatep>
        <vsm:VisualState x:Name="Pressed" />
        <vsm:VisualState x:Name="Disabled" />
    </vsm:VisualStateGroup>
    <vsm:VisualStateGroup x:Name="FocusStates">
        <vsm:VisualState x:Name="Focused" />
        <vsm:VisualState x:Name="Unfocused" />
    </vsm:VisualStateGroup>
</vsm:VisualStateManager.VisualStateGroups>
```

The `ColorAnimation` added targets a `GradientStop` with the name `"LinearBevelDarkEnd"` defined in the default button's XAML and animates the value of the `GradientStop`'s `Color` property to black (#FF000000). This `Storyboard` is started when the control enters the `MouseOver` state. The `Duration` of the `ColorAnimation` is set to `0`, which essentially means "Take 0 seconds to get to your destination." If you wanted the `GradientStop` value to slowly change to black, you could have entered `"00:00:05.00"` for a 5-second animation. The animation continues to have an effect even after the `Duration` has been reached and will remain at the destination value until another animation is started. In this case, the `GradientStop` value will remain black until the control changes state.

A control can only be in one state *per* `VisualStateGroup` at a time. So, based on the XAML above, this means that the `Button` cannot be in both a `Normal` state and a `MouseOver` state at once. If you look at the states that have been defined, I think you'll see this makes sense. However, a control *can* be in multiple states across `VisualStateGroups`. For example, the `Button` can be in both a `MouseOver` and `Focused` state at the same time.

Empty `VisualStates` *have an effect on the control: as a control changes state, if a matching* `VisualState` *is found, any previous animations that were started as a result of previous* `VisualStates` *will be stopped. Empty* `VisualStates` *will essentially reset a control to its base state when triggered.*

Defining Transitions

The `VisualStateManager` lets you define `Transition Storyboards` that are played as the control transitions between states. The animations do not replace the `VisualState Storyboards`; they just serve as interludes between them. The following XAML adds to the `VisualStateManager` a `VisualTransition` that will be played as the control leaves the `MouseOver` state and enters the `Normal` state:

```xaml
<vsm:VisualStateManager.VisualStateGroups>
    <vsm:VisualStateGroup x:Name="CommonStates">
        <vsm:VisualStateGroup.Transitions>
            <vsm:VisualTransition From="MouseOver" To="Normal"
                Duration="0:0:0.2">
                <Storyboard>
                    <ColorAnimation
                        Storyboard.TargetName="LinearBevelDarkEnd"
                        Storyboard.TargetProperty="Color" To="#FFFFFFFF" />
                </Storyboard>
            </vsm:VisualTransition>
        </vsm:VisualStateGroup.Transitions>

        <vsm:VisualState x:Name="Normal" />
        <vsm:VisualState x:Name="MouseOver">
          <Storyboard>
            <ColorAnimation Storyboard.TargetName="LinearBevelDarkEnd"
                Storyboard.TargetProperty="Color" To="#FF000000" Duration="0" />
          </Storyboard>
        </vsm:VisualStatep>
        <vsm:VisualState x:Name="Pressed" />
        <vsm:VisualState x:Name="Disabled" />
    </vsm:VisualStateGroup>
    <vsm:VisualStateGroup x:Name="FocusStates">
        <vsm:VisualState x:Name="Focused" />
        <vsm:VisualState x:Name="Unfocused" />
    </vsm:VisualStateGroup>
</vsm:VisualStateManager.VisualStateGroups>
```

Over a period of 0.2 seconds, the same `GradientStop` we've been targeting will animate to a white color, before returning to its base state. Because the `"Normal"` `VisualState` is empty, all previously applied `Storyboards` will be stopped. The final result of this `VisualStateManager` definition: Mousing over the `Button` will result in the `GradientStop` named `LinearBevelDarkEnd` animating to black immediately (Duration: 0). As the mouse leaves the control, the same `GradientStop` will animate to white over a 0.2-second duration, then immediately return to its original, base state.

The default `Button` XAML defines additional `Storyboards` and transitions that we didn't cover here. It's really just more of the same, but now you can read the XAML and actually decipher what you see!

Text-Related Properties

Text properties in Silverlight behave differently than their fellow non-text properties. Unlike properties such as `Fill` and `HorizontalAlignment`, the following properties cascade from the top down in the `VisualTree`:

- ❑ FontFamily
- ❑ FontWeight

141

❑   FontStyle

❑   FontSize

❑   FontStretch

When set at any level, these property settings are inherited by all children in the `VisualTree` of the element where the properties are set. Only set these properties locally when you want to intercept this inheritance and override those values. Keep this in mind when you are defining `Styles` for controls — font settings on the `Style` will take precedence over those defined at an application or page level, intercepting application-level font settings.

Defining and Organizing Resources

Resources can be defined almost anywhere. Because all `FrameworkElement`-derived objects have a .Resources collection, you can dangle resources off your base `UserControl` (UserControl.Resources), in nested `Grids` (Grid.Resources), in nested `Buttons` (Button.Resources), and any number of other elements. In addition to defining resources within a single `UserControl`, resources can also be defined in App.xaml and in external `ResourceDictionaries`. With all of these locations capable of housing resources, it's important to define some best practices and understand how these resources are scoped.

Defining Stand-Alone `ResourceDictionaries`

Silverlight provides us with a mechanism for housing resources outside of `UserControls`. These stand-alone `ResourceDictionaries` are simply XAML files whose outermost element is a `ResourceDictionary`. Both Blend and Visual Studio have `ResourceDictionary` templates that can be accessed by right-clicking on the project, selecting "Add New Item," and selecting "ResourceDictionary" from the dialog that appears. In both applications, you'll be prompted to provide a name for the new `ResourceDictionary`. The following XAML shows a simple stand-alone `ResourceDictionary` with a single `SolidColorBrush` resource defined:

```
<ResourceDictionary
    xmlns="http://schemas.microsoft.com/winfx/2006/xaml/presentation"
    xmlns:x="http://schemas.microsoft.com/winfx/2006/xaml">
    <SolidColorBrush x:Key="SharedBrush" Color="#FFFF0000"/>
</ResourceDictionary>
```

Merged Dictionaries

Much like CSS's `@import` statement for referencing additional CSS files, Silverlight's `ResourceDictionary` .MergedDictionaries collection lets you reference external `ResourceDictionaries`. Each `ResourceDictionary` has a `MergedDictionaries` collection, so you can reference external dictionaries from any location where resources can be defined. The following XAML demonstrates how a `ResourceDictionary` containing button resources (Resources/Buttons.xaml) can be referenced at the `UserControl` level:

```
<UserControl x:Class="SilverlightBookSamples.Resources"
    xmlns="http://schemas.microsoft.com/winfx/2006/xaml/presentation"
    xmlns:x="http://schemas.microsoft.com/winfx/2006/xaml"
```

```
        Height="300" Width="300">
    <UserControl.Resources>
        <ResourceDictionary>
            <ResourceDictionary.MergedDictionaries>
                <ResourceDictionary Source="Resources/Buttons.xaml" />
                <!-- Additional Resource Definitions Here -->
            </ResourceDictionary.MergedDictionaries>
        </ResourceDictionary>
    </UserControl.Resources>
    <Grid>

    </Grid>
</UserControl>
```

When using the `MergedDictionaries` collection, you have to explicitly declare a `ResourceDictionary` object with the container .Resources collection. If you refer to previous resource definitions in the chapter, the `<ResourceDictionary />` tag was not required.

Resource Scope

The location where a resource is defined and/or referenced determines the scope within which it can be used. The following are the locations where resources may be defined:

❑ App.xaml

❑ Themes/generic.xaml (for defining custom controls)

❑ Custom UserControl.xaml

❑ External `ResourceDictionaries` (.xaml files within the project)

App.xaml

Resources defined or referenced at the App.xaml level can be used anywhere in your Silverlight application. When you're synchronizing the look of an application across multiple `UserControls`, you'll want to define your resources here. Any external `ResourceDictionaries` referenced at this level will also be available throughout your application.

Custom Controls — Themes/generic.xaml

In projects in which you define custom controls, a `myButton` control, for example, the default style for that custom control is defined in generic.xaml. Both Blend and Visual Studio will automatically add this file to your project when you add a custom control to the project using their starter templates. When your project is compiled and your control is used either in the same project or another project, the style defined in generic.xaml will be applied. You should not house application-level styles or resources in this file. The resources defined in generic.xaml should be specifically for custom controls you are defining.

Local Resources — UserControl.xaml

When you don't need your resources to have a full application-wide scope, you can define them within the current `UserControl` you're authoring. In these cases, you will likely add the resources to `<UserControl.Resources>`:

```
    <!-- Add Resources Here -->
    </UserControl.Resources>
```

All resources defined in `<UserControl.Resources />` will be available throughout your `UserControl`. If you want to further scope your resource definitions to a particular area within your `UserControl`, this is a possibility as well. Each `FrameworkElement`-derived object in Silverlight has a `Resources` collection. So just as you can access the `UserControl`'s resources collection via `UserControl.Resources`, you can access the `Grid`'s resources collection via `Grid.Resources`:

```
<Grid x:Name="LayoutRoot">
    <Grid.Resources>
        <!-- Add Local Resources Here. Only items within this Grid have
             access to these resources -->
    </Grid.Resources>
</Grid>
```

Littering your `UserControl` with localized `Resources` is generally not the best approach. You'll end up with resources scattered throughout your page and have a hard time tracking down your styling bugs. However, for those times when you need to scope your resources, you now know that you have localized resources at your disposal.

Thus, the discussion of organization is really a discussion of scope. If you want your entire Silverlight application to have access to a resource, you need to add that resource to App.xaml. Every page loaded in your Silverlight application will have access to resources defined in App.xaml.

External `ResourceDictionaries`

External `ResourceDictionaries` do not have an inherent scope. Their scope is determined by the scope of the MergedDictionary where they're referenced. If they are referenced in App.xaml, they will have an Application-wide scope. Likewise, if they are referenced by a `Grid` defined within UserControl2.xaml, they will be scoped to that `Grid`.

Organizing Resources

We've already looked at where resources can be defined; now let's look at one approach for organizing your resources within those locations. Often, the organization of resources is an afterthought, something that you come back to as part of your cleanup phase once you have everything working. When you choose to organize your resources is really dependent on your workflow requirements. If you're a single developer working on a project, the resource organization is more for your own sanity than the sanity of others, so you can do this when you please. If you're a member of a team, collaborating with both designers and developers, it makes sense to organize your resources early, providing both consistency and clarity for team members.

In applications with a large number of resources, it generally makes sense to organize your resources into external `ResourceDictionaries`. Start by creating a Resources folder in your project, and then group your resources by shared type or shared purpose:

Define common brushes in one `ResourceDictionary`.

Define non-`Style` or non-`Template` related resources (i.e., `CornerRadius`, `Thickness`, etc.) in their own `ResourceDictionary`.

Define `Styles`, grouped by control type (i.e., all `Buttons` together).

Define `Styles` for related controls (i.e., `ComboBox` and its subcontrols).

Below is a sample folder structure to give you a better idea:

```
\[ProjectName]\
        \Resources
                \Brushes.xaml
                \Buttons.xaml
                \CommonControls.xaml
                \MainMenuBrushes.xaml
                \MainMenuControls.xaml
```

It's important to get into the habit of creating centralized styles and brushes for use throughout your application. It may feel like extra work at first, but in the end, it empowers you and your team to refine the application much more quickly than they could if everything were defined inline.

Resource Naming

Just as there are best practices for naming variables within an application, there are *best practices* for naming resources. And, just like strategies for naming variables, with a little Web searching, you can find some heated debates as to which approach is the *best*. As I did with the previous section on organization, I'm just going to present you with a few guidelines to get you started. How you evolve this and make this work within your organization is entirely up to you.

Brush Naming: Template/Style-Specific Brushes

When naming brushes that are specific to certain `Styles` and `Templates`, try to tie the name of the brush to the `Style`, to elements within the `Style`, and to the state of the control represented by the brush. For example:

```
ControlNameStateElementNameFill
```

Here are three hypothetical brushes used by the `PlayButton` style:

```
PlayButtonNormalOuterBorderFill
PlayButtonHoverOuterBorderFill
PlayButtonPressedOuterBorderFill
```

Here are three additional brushes that will be applied to the `BorderBrush` of the `OuterBorder` element contained within the `PlayButton` template:

```
PlayButtonNormalOuterBorderBorderBrush
PlayButtonHoverOuterBorderBorderBrush
PlayButtonPressedOuterBorderBorrderBrush
```

Brush Naming: Non-Template Brushes

Name brushes for elements within your applications in a way that makes sense to you and your team. Using the name `BackgroundBrush`, for example, is quite vague. Instead, use the name `ApplicationBackgroundBrush` or `MainMenuBackgroundBrush`. It's important that your brush naming map to the element-naming conventions you've decided on for your application. Consistency here is key. If you have a `UserControl` named `MenuArea`, don't name the brush that is applied as the `MenuArea`'s background `BackgroundRegionMenu`; instead, name it `MenuAreaBackground`. Furthermore, name additional `MenuArea` brushes and resources with the `MenuArea` prefix: `MenuAreaForeground`, `MenuAreaCornerRadius`, and so forth.

Again, consistency is key here. Define a naming convention that is logical for your team, that is repeatable, and that is readable; and follow that convention religiously.

Style/Template Naming

When naming styles, include the control's `TargetType` in your key (`PlayButtonStyle`, `PlayButtonTemplate`, `VolumeSliderStyle`). This lets you quickly identify the control type without having to rely on additional information that the IDE might provide you with (via an icon or additional label).

Summary

You should now have a solid mental image of what the term styling means in the context of Silverlight. We started with the very basic approach of setting properties on controls. We then replaced those property values with resources that represented the property type (a `SolidColorBrush` resource was the first). From there, we looked at setting more and more properties with inline `StaticResource` references and welcomed the clarity, and brevity, that the `Style` object provides. With all of our property setters moved to a centralized `Style`, we considered the highest degree of control customization possible: template editing. We saw how powerful template editing is and learned how `TemplateBinding` ties specific elements within the template to the properties of our *lookless* control. We concluded our journey with a brief examination of resource scope and naming/organization conventions.

As I mentioned at the start of this chapter, learning to style Silverlight apps starts at a technical, and somewhat unbeautiful, level. I've laid the groundwork for your technical understanding; it's now up to you to make something of it!

Using Graphics and Visuals

Silverlight includes all of the core primitive elements you would expect in a platform designed to provide a compelling visual experience. These basic elements include the `Rectangle`, `Ellipse`, `Path`, `Image`, and `MediaElement` controls. When listed, these controls can seem basic and boring, yet impressively complex visuals can be created from this simple toolset. In addition to these base controls, Silverlight 3 adds bitmap effects, support for HLSL shaders, and Perspective 3D. These last three items can empower a limitless array of visual effects in your applications. In this chapter, we'll start by covering the basic building block controls and how they are defined in XAML to provide a firm foundation of understanding. Along the way, you'll see how to use Blend to save some time manually creating these elements. We'll then see how both effects and 3D can fit into your application and look at the tooling that supports them. We'll wrap up our discussion by looking at design tools other than Blend and discuss how those tools can fit into your Silverlight workflow.

The Basics

Let's get started by looking at the core Silverlight controls at your disposal to create visuals. We'll look at each control individually and cover XAML composition of that control. Along the way, I'll try to point out things you need to be aware of when working with particular controls.

Rectangles and Borders

The `Rectangle` control can serve as a foundation for many UI elements. Most controls that you interact with on a daily basis are rectangular in nature: buttons, scrollbars, header element background, and so forth. Generally, these controls are not composed of a single rectangle, but multiple layered rectangles, each with varying shades of opacity, margins, and fills. Together these rectangles form the visuals you have come to expect from modern operating systems and applications. Figure 9-1 calls out the nested rectangles used to create the Office 2007 Ribbon control and the default Silverlight button.

Figure 9-1

The following XAML defines a lime-green `Rectangle` that is 100 pixels wide by 20 pixels tall:

```
<Rectangle Width="100" Height="20" Fill="#FFCCFF00" />
```

Rounded Corners

You should have noticed in Figure 9-1 that both examples had rounded corners. This is easily achieved in Silverlight by setting the `RadiusX` and `RadiusY` properties on the `Rectangle` control. The following XAML defines a `Rectangle` with uniformly rounded corners, each with a 5-pixel corner radius:

```
<Rectangle Height="20" Width="100" Fill="#CCFF00" RadiusX="5" RadiusY="5" />
```

Both the `RadiusX` and `RadiusY` properties have the same value as in the previous example. These values do not have to be the same, however. By increasing the value on either axis, you'll see that the corner begins to skew either horizontally or vertically, depending on which property value is greater. Figure 9-2 demonstrates the effect on each axis when one corner radius value is greater than the other.

Figure 9-2

Pixel-Based Values

It's important to note once again that the corner radius values are pixel-based and not percentage-based. So, if you set the corner radius to 5, the amount of curvature on each corner will remain the same whether your rectangle is 100 pixels wide or 100 pixels high. Some design programs store the corner radius as a percentage of the object's size, so a corner radius of 10 would be 10 pixels for a rectangle 100 pixels wide and 100 pixels for a rectangle 1,000 pixels wide. That is always frustrating for me, so I'm glad Silverlight implements these as pixel values rather than percentage values.

Rectangle versus Border

You may be wondering why `Border` is included in a discussion about drawing primitives. The `Border` control is actually a `FrameworkElement`-derived control that can accept child content, and not a primitive drawing element. The `Border` control provides a key feature that the `Rectangle` control does not — individual control over each corner's radius! This means that you can have a "rectangle" whose top-left and top-right corners are rounded, while its bottom corners remain square. With the `Rectangle` control, it's an all-or-nothing proposition. The following XAML defines a lime-green `Border` that is 100 pixels wide by 20 pixels tall, with its top-left and top-right corners rounded on a 5-pixel radius:

```
<Border Width="100" Height="20" Background="#FFCCFF00"
CornerRadius="5,5,0,0" />
```

The Border's `CornerRadius` property provides the corner-by-corner flexibility that makes this control so useful. The `CornerRadius` property has four properties that let you specify the corner radius for each corner: `TopLeft`, `TopRight`, `BottomRight`, and `BottomLeft`. The previous XAML demonstrates how these properties can be set inline with comma-delimited values. The following pseudo-XAML represents the order in which these values are applied to each corner:

```
<Border CornerRadius="TopLeft, TopRight, BottomRight, BottomLeft" />
```

Additional Notes

The `Border` element, unlike the `Rectangle`, has a `Child` property and supports nested content. This means that you can create a series of nested `Border`s housed by a single parent `Border`. You set the `Padding` property on each `Border` to create inset effects with each child `Border`. The following XAML demonstrates how three nested `Border`s can be used to create a shiny button, as shown in Figure 9-3:

```
<Border
        Opacity="1"
        HorizontalAlignment="Left"
        VerticalAlignment="Top"
        Margin="281.031005859375,250,0,0"
        CornerRadius="14.805,14.805,14.805,14.805"
        Background="#ccff00" Width="208" Height="63" Padding="2,2,2,2">
    <Border
        Opacity="1"
        HorizontalAlignment="Stretch"
        VerticalAlignment="Stretch"
        CornerRadius="14.1,14.1,14.1,14.1">
        <Border.Background>
            <LinearGradientBrush
                StartPoint="0.5098039215686274,0.35"
                EndPoint="0.5098039215686274,1.0478118896484374">
                <LinearGradientBrush.GradientStops>
                    <GradientStopCollection>
                        <GradientStop
                            Color="#00ccff00"
                            Offset="0" />
                        <GradientStop
                            Color="#FF5e7500"
                            Offset="1" />
                    </GradientStopCollection>
                </LinearGradientBrush.GradientStops>
            </LinearGradientBrush>
        </Border.Background>
        <Border
        Opacity="1"
        HorizontalAlignment="Stretch"
        VerticalAlignment="Stretch"
        Margin="0,0,0,27"
        CornerRadius="13.8,13.8,13.8,13.8">
        <Border.Background>
            <LinearGradientBrush
                StartPoint="0.3872549019607843,-0.08571428571428572"
```

```
                    EndPoint="0.3872549019607843,1.2612723214285715">
                    <LinearGradientBrush.GradientStops>
                        <GradientStopCollection>
                            <GradientStop
                                Color="#FFffffff"
                                Offset="0" />
                            <GradientStop
                                Color="#00ffffff"
                                Offset="1" />
                        </GradientStopCollection>
                    </LinearGradientBrush.GradientStops>
                </LinearGradientBrush>
            </Border.Background>
        </Border>
        </Border>
    </Border>
```

Figure 9-3

So, you now have two tools in your arsenal to create rectangle-based shapes. The `Rectangle` is a lighter control, so you'll probably want to go with it for most cases, but, when you need to specifically target individual corners, the `Border` is your best friend.

Ellipses

The `Ellipse` control is used to define both circles and ellipses and is just as easy to define as the `Rectangle`. In fact, the following XAML is the same XAML we started with for `Rectangle` but with the term *Ellipse* instead of *Rectangle*:

```
<Ellipse Width="100" Height="20" Fill="#FFCCFF00" />
```

This XAML results in an oval 100 pixels wide by 20 pixels high, as shown in Figure 9-4.

Figure 9-4

To create a circle, just set the `Height` and `Width` to the same value.

Paths

While the `Rectangle` and `Ellipse` controls are used to customize predefined, familiar shapes, the `Path` control is used to represent *any* shape. Like the `Rectangle` and `Ellipse`, the `Path` control includes `Height` and `Width` properties, but unlike `Rectangle` or `Ellipse`, the `Path` control has a `Data` property that is used to define the point data that makes up the shape. And while you can hand-code the path data, you'll likely only do that in the most basic of cases, and only then for simple shapes or purely intellectual exercises. Generally, you'll rely on a tool like Expression Blend (or one of several design tools discussed later).

Let's start by looking at simple path data, then move on to additional properties on the `Path` control that define the way the shape is ultimately rendered. The following XAML defines a 10 × 10 square purely using path data:

```
<Path
    HorizontalAlignment="Left" VerticalAlignment="Top"
    Stroke="#FF000000" Data="M0,0 L10,0 L10,10 L0,10 L0,0 z"/>
```

Figure 9-5 shows this `Path` rendered in Expression Blend.

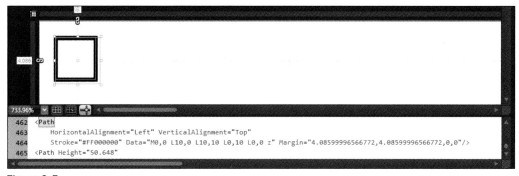

Figure 9-5

The path data `"M0,0 L10,0 L10,10 L0,10 L0,0 z"` may look a little cryptic at first, but once you know the basic structure, I think you'll find it quite readable. All paths consist of a starting point (defined by an X,Y-coordinate pair), followed by a series of subsequent points. In the data string for this rectangle path, try replacing *M* with "MoveTo" and *L* with "LineTo." The result reads more like a sentence: `"MoveTo 0,0 LineTo 10,0 LineTo 10,10 LineTo 0,10 LineTo 0,0 z"`. The z closes the path.

The next XAML defines a circle purely using path data:

```
<Path Fill="#FFCCFF00" Stretch="Fill" Stroke="#FF000000"
    Data="M50.147999,25.323999 C50.147999,39.033916 39.033916,50.147999
25.323999,50.147999 C11.614083,50.147999 0.5,39.033916 0.5,25.323999 C0.5,11.614083
11.614083,0.5 25.323999,0.5 C39.033916,0.5 50.147999,11.614083 50.147999,25.323999
z" />
```

Figure 9-6 shows this path rendered in Expression Blend.

Figure 9-6

Whereas the rectangle's path data consists of a series of straight lines, the circle consists of a series of curves. Instead of a simple X,Y pair representing each point on the path, the circle's points are represented by three X,Y pairs to define a Bezier point. The first and third X,Y pairs define the tension handles, while the second pair defines the anchor point. Figure 9-7 shows a selected point in Expression Blend. The selected point is solid blue, with its two tension points denoted by circles drawn at the end of the tangent line.

The path data `"M50.147999,25.323999 C50.147999,39.033916 39.033916,50.147999 25.323999,50.147999 C11.614083,50.147999 0.5,39.033916 0.5,25.323999 C0.5,11.614083 11.614083,0.5 25.323999,0.5 C39.033916,0.5 50.147999,11.614083 50.147999,25.323999 z"` for the circle is a bit more complex than that of the rectangle, but again we'll do a little string substitution and the data will read like a sentence. This time, replace *M* with "MoveTo" and *C* with "CurveTo." You'll end up with a sentence that reads like `"MoveTo x,y CurveTo x,y x,y x,y CurveTo x,y x,y x,y…"`.

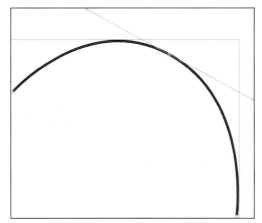

Figure 9-7

The following XAML mixes things up a bit by combining both `LineTo` and `CurveTo` points:

```
Data="M74.833336,76.333336 L85.5,76.333336 C85.5,76.333336 87.666351,83.250168
80.083427,83.250168 C72.500504,83.250168 74.833336,76.333336 74.833336,76.333336 z"
```

With your new understanding of the path data syntax, you can now recognize that this path starts with a line segment, followed by two Bezier points. However, unless you're some type of savant, you probably can't read the data and immediately picture the path that will be rendered. That's why, as I said before, you'll likely use a design tool to define paths.

> **Try removing the closing z and see what your Path looks like. Its absence will be more noticeable if you've set both the Stroke and StrokeThickness properties and if your last point is a considerable distance away from your starting point.**

Defining the Path Resize Behavior

When we defined the rectangle as a `Path`, the first point of our path data was (0,0). However, when we drew the circle, the starting point was approximately (75,76). When the circle was rendered on the screen, it didn't actually start at the point (75,76). Instead, Silverlight drew the circle artwork based on several properties on the `Path` control, taking into account the `Path`'s `Width`, `Height`, `HorizontalAlignment`, `VerticalAlignment`, and `Margin`. The underlying path data was normalized to the top-left corner of the `Path` control.

When the `Path` control is resized, the actual size of the control will differ from that of the underlying path data. You can define how the underlying data is rendered by setting the `Stretch` property. The `Stretch` property accepts one of the following values:

❑　`Fill` (Default) — The artwork is stretched both vertically and horizontally, filling the `Path` control. This is the behavior you most likely expect if you are coming to Silverlight from the design world.

❑　`None` — The underlying artwork does not stretch at all.

In practice, the behavior when set to None is the same as when set to Fill.

❑　`Uniform` — The underlying artwork maintains its original shape and aspect ratio, while scaling to fit within the control. With this mode the shape is always drawn in its entirety.

❑　`UniformToFill` — The underlying artwork maintains its original shape and aspect ratio, although if the aspect ratio of the containing `Path` control differs from the underlying path data, the path will be clipped.

Figure 9-8 demonstrates how these different stretch modes affect the final rendering of a `Path`.

None

Fill

Uniform

UniformToFill

Figure 9-8

Images and Media

Images and media are dealt with similarly in Silverlight. Each has a specialized control that points to a source image or media file. The image or media can be either a file included in the project or an external file, possibly residing on a remote server. We'll start by looking at the Image control, then move on to the MediaElement control. Once we've covered the Image control, there will just be a few more things to add to bring you up to speed with MediaElement.

Images

Even though Silverlight provides a vector-based rendering and layout engine, you're likely to use Images in your Silverlight applications. Whether you're creating a photo-browser, using an existing image-based icon library, or working with artwork from your design team, I'm sure you'll encounter the need to use an image at some point in your Silverlight career.

Image Control

The Image control is used to display bitmap images in your Silverlight applications. The following XAML demonstrates how to display a photo that is 640 × 480 pixels in dimension, positioned 25 pixels from the left and top of its parent Grid:

```
<Image
    Source="myPhoto.jpg"
    HorizontalAlignment="Left"
    VerticalAlignment="Top"
    Margin="25,25,0,0"
    Stretch="Uniform" Width="640" />
```

Notice that the Image control has a Stretch property, just like the Path control. And, like the Path control, the available values for Stretch are Fill, None, Uniform, and UniformToFill. See the previous section, "Defining the Path Resize Behavior," to understand how these values affect the way the Image is resized.

If the Height and Width are not set or other sizing constraints (such as Margins) are not in place, the Image will be displayed at the native size of the underlying source image.

Referencing Images

Images referenced via the Image control can be images compiled into the containing assembly, images that live inside the XAP file as siblings to your compiled assembly, images compiled as resources in other assemblies, loose images on your server (outside of the XAP), or images on a remote server. Let's look at how each of these approaches is achieved and the pros and cons of each.

Compiled Images

An image is compiled into your project's assembly when its Build Action is set to Resource. This is the default approach taken by Blend when you first reference an image.

This is the same behavior you see in Flash when an image is imported and dragged onto the stage. It is compiled into the swf file and does affect file size.

Adding an Image in Blend

The `Image` control in Blend is not exposed in the main toolbox. You have to open the Asset Library, expand Controls, and select All, as shown in Figure 9-9. Select Image to make it the active control. You can now draw an `Image` control on the canvas, just like you create a rectangle, or you can double-click on the Image icon to add a default-sized `Image` to the canvas.

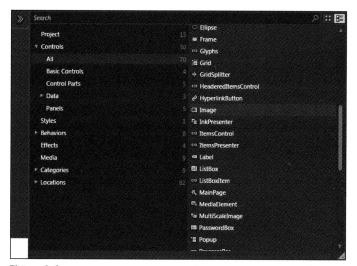

Figure 9-9

Setting the Image Source

Once you've added an `Image` control to the surface, you need to set its `Source` property using the Property panel. The `Source` property is found in the Common Properties category. If you've already added images to your project, those images should appear in the Source combobox. In Figure 9-10, you can click on the ellipses to launch a File Browser dialog.

Figure 9-10

Once you've selected an image, that image will be copied to your project directory and added to the root folder of your project. Behind the scenes, the file's Build Action will be set to `Resource`. This is not something that you can change via the Blend interface, but you can do so in Visual Studio. Figure 9-11 highlights both the Build Action and the Copy to Local Directory properties that are available in Visual Studio's Properties Window when a file is selected. The scenarios that follow will require that you change these properties.

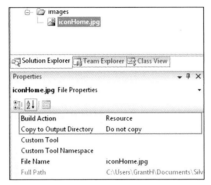

Figure 9-11

Referencing the Image in XAML

Reference an embedded image using a relative URL. If the image is in the root folder of your project, you simply type its name. If the image is in a subfolder, such as *Images*, include the entire relative path. For example, the following XAML references an image stored in the Images/Icons subfolder of the project directory:

```
<Image HorizontalAlignment="Left" Margin="10,10,0,0" Width="72"
    Source="images/icons/iconHome.jpg"/>
```

You can also use a path that explicitly references the assembly this image is housed in. If your Silverlight project name is *MyProject*, then the previous XAML could be replaced by the following:

```
<Image HorizontalAlignment="Left" Margin="10,10,0,0" Width="72"
    Source="MyProject;component/images/icons/iconHome.jpg"/>
```

The text in bold is key: `MyProject;component/`.

The text `MyProject` should be replaced with the name of your project, but `;component/` should remain at all times.

❑   **Pros** — Image is available immediately; simple relative path references; no security issues.

❑   **Cons** — Large images or large numbers of small images can bloat the assembly size and increase page load time.

XAP File Images

An image is included in the XAP file and is not compiled into the assembly when its Build Action is set to Content. When configured as Content, image files do not bloat the size of your project assembly, but they do continue to bloat the size of the XAP file. You might want to do this if you will be reusing the project assembly, but not the resources.

Referencing the Image in XAML

When images are included this way, you need to add a forward slash "/" before the path to the image:

```
<Image HorizontalAlignment="Left" Margin="10,10,0,0" Width="72"
    Source="/images/icons/iconHome.jpg"/>
```

❑ **Pros** — Image is available immediately; simple relative path references; no security issues; assembly size is reduced.

❑ **Cons** — Large images or large numbers of small images can bloat the XAP size and increase page load time.

Loose Images

You can add images to your project that are not compiled into the project assembly or added to the XAP file. These files do not bloat either the assembly or the XAP file. To achieve this scenario, set the Build Action of your image to None and "Copy to Local Directory" to "Copy Always" or "Copy if Newer."

Referencing the Image in XAML

Use the same syntax that you used with XAP File Images, adding a forward slash to the URI:

```
<Image HorizontalAlignment="Left" Margin="10,10,0,0" Width="72"
    Source="/images/icons/iconHome.jpg"/>
```

❑ **Pros** — Assembly size is reduced; XAP size is reduced (faster page load time).

❑ **Cons** — Image is not loaded at page load; image loads asynchronously after the XAP is downloaded.

Use this scenario when you want to create a very lightweight, quick-loading application. You can then use the `WebClient` to download the image asynchronously and provide a "loading" experience.

Images in Other Assemblies

Just as images can be compiled in your main project assembly, images can be compiled in additional resource assemblies. These could be assemblies that you create yourself or they could be third-party assemblies. And, just like referencing images embedded in the project assembly, images in other assemblies can be referenced in XAML using a special syntax.

Referencing the Image in XAML

The following XAML references an image named *alienFace.png* defined in an assembly named `AlienImages.dll`:

```
<Image HorizontalAlignment="Left" Margin="10,10,0,0" Width="72"
    Source="AlienImages;component/images/alienFace.png"/>
```

This syntax should look familiar to you — it's the same *alternative* syntax shown in the "Compiled Images" section previously. The only thing that has changed is the assembly name. It should be comforting to know that the URI for referencing resources is the same whether it is defined in the main project assembly or a referenced assembly.

❑ **Pros** — Assembly size is reduced; XAP size is (potentially) increased, as referenced assemblies grow in size; separates visuals from application logic.

❑ **Cons** — Images can be renamed or removed if you are not in control of the resource assembly; increases the number of projects you must maintain (if you are in control of the resource assembly).

Images on Other Domains

When you want to access an image on a remote server (like flickr or photobucket, or a friend's site), you can use the fully qualified URL to access the image:

```
<Image HorizontalAlignment="Left" Margin="10,10,0,0"
    Source="http://www.remotewebsite.com/images/targetImage.png"/>
```

However, Silverlight's security policies will prevent the remote image from loading if the remote site does not have a security manifest file in place that grants you access. For all the gory details on security policies, see Chapter 11.

❑ **Pros** — Enables your cross-domain needs.

❑ **Cons** — Cannot rely on image being at URI; requires security policies.

Image Summary

Which Build Action you choose is ultimately up to the priorities and reliance on images of your application. If you are using just a few images relatively small in size, embedding the images in your assembly probably makes sense. If your project is image-intensive and intended to load gracefully for users with limited bandwidth, going with a loose image solution is probably the right move for you. It will let you create a fast startup experience that then relies on asynchronous image-loading.

MediaElement

Adding video to your Silverlight application is just as easy as adding an image using the `Image` control. Only, instead of using the `Image` control, you use the `MediaElement` control. With the exception of a few additional properties and methods, working with media is practically the same as working with images. In fact, you can pretty much re-read the previous section about images and replace `Image` with `MediaElement`.

Adding a Video in Blend

Like the `Image` control, the `MediaElement` control is accessed by launching Blend's Asset Library, expanding Controls, and selecting All. Figure 9-12 shows the `MediaElement` control in the Asset Library.

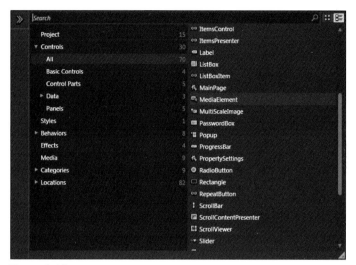

Figure 9-12

Create an instance of the `MediaElement` by dragging a rectangle on the design surface or double-clicking on the control's icon once selected. With the `MediaElement` selected on the design surface, you can select a Source file by clicking the ellipses next to the `Source` property. Figure 9-13 shows the `Source` property in Blend's Media category.

Figure 9-13

Once you've selected a supported media file, it will be added to your project with a Build Action of Content and a "Copy to Output Directory" setting of "Copy if Newer." You can modify these settings in Visual Studio to meet your needs. See the previous section, "Referencing Images," to understand the various options afforded to you by changing the values of these two properties.

This section on `MediaElement` just touches on adding a `MediaElement` to your page. For a much more in-depth look at this control, see Chapter 10.

Brushes

In Silverlight, brushes are used to paint elements on your page. These brushes can be solid color values, linear or radial gradients, or even images. In this section, we'll look at the base XAML definitions for each of these, then look at how you can define and edit brushes in Expression Blend.

SolidColorBrush

The `SolidColorBrush` is used to paint elements with a (surprise, surprise) solid color. The following XAML shows how to define a `SolidColorBrush` and set its color property:

```
<SolidColorBrush Color="#FFCCFF00"/>
```

Generally, when applying a solid color to an object, you just set its appropriate `Brush` property (`Fill`, `Stroke`, `Background`, or `Border`) inline:

```
<Rectangle Height="20" Width="100" Fill="#CCFF00" />
```

You would only need to use the full `SolidColorBrush` definition when you are creating Resources of type `SolidColorBrush`. However, you can use the full syntax:

```
<Rectangle Height="20" Width="100">
    <Rectangle.Fill>
        <SolidColorBrush Color="#FFCCFF00"/>
    </Rectangle.Fill>
</Rectangle>
```

LinearGradientBrush

Gradients are used in applications of every flavor (desktop, Web, mobile) to create a modern, polished experience. Through skilled techniques, artists can create glass effects, reflection effects, and subtle transitions that draw the eye from one area to the next. In Silverlight, you'll use the `LinearGradientBrush` to achieve such feats. The following XAML defines a (boring) black-to-white, vertical gradient:

```
<LinearGradientBrush StartPoint="0.5,0" EndPoint="0.5,1">
    <GradientStop Color="#FF000000" Offset="0"/>
    <GradientStop Color="#FFFFFFFF" Offset="1"/>
</LinearGradientBrush>
```

To define the direction of the gradient, you must specify both a `StartPoint` and an `EndPoint`. The value of each of these properties is an ordered pair that specifies a point in a normalized 1 × 1 square, where 1 actually represents 100 percent. When the control is rendered, this imaginary square stretches from the top-left corner of the object's bounding box (0,0) to the lower-right corner of the object's bounding box (1,1).

Figure 9-14 shows what the directional handles look like for the previous `LinearGradientBrush`.

0.5, 0

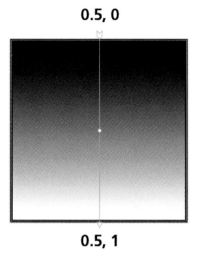

0.5, 1

Figure 9-14

In addition to defining the `StartPoint` and `EndPoint` for the brush, you also define a collection of `GradientStops`. Each `GradientStop` consists of a `Color` and `Offset`. The `Color` property accepts a `Color` using the #AARRGGBB notation, just like the `SolidColorBrush`, and the `Offset` accepts a double-precision value between 0 and 1. The `Offset` is used to define the order of the each `GradientStop`.

> *When two* `GradientStops` *share the same* `Offset` *value, the Silverlight renderer relies on the order in which the* `GradientStops` *appear in XAML when drawing the gradient.*

RadialGradientBrush

The `RadialGradientBrush` can be used to define both radial and elliptical gradients. Like the `LinearGradientBrush`, the `RadialGradientBrush` accepts a collection of `GradientStops`. The following XAML creates a radial gradient that goes from blue in the center to white:

```
<RadialGradientBrush>
    <GradientStop Color="#FF65BADA" Offset="0"/>
    <GradientStop Color="#FFFFFFFF" Offset="1"/>
</RadialGradientBrush>
```

By default, the radial gradient is drawn from the center of the object it is being applied to in a symmetrical fashion. However, by adjusting the following properties, you can achieve a wide range of variations:

❑ `Center`

❑ `RadiusX`

❑ `RadiusY`

❑ `GradientOrigin`

The first three properties work together to define an ellipse within which a gradient is drawn. Just like the LinearGradientBrush, you need to imagine a 1 × 1 normalized box that starts at the top-left corner of the target object's bounding box and stretches to the lower-right corner of the target object's bounding box. The values of all four of these properties lie within the 0 . . . 1 range and are applied across this imaginary box. Figure 9-15 demonstrates how changing the values of Center, RadiusX, and RadiusY affect the ellipse within which the gradient is drawn.

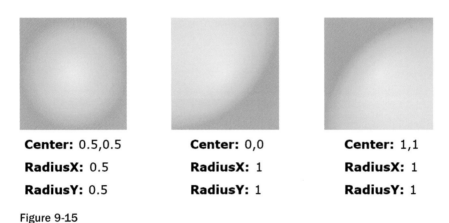

Center: 0.5,0.5   **Center: 0,0**   **Center: 1,1**

RadiusX: 0.5   **RadiusX: 1**   **RadiusX: 1**

RadiusY: 0.5   **RadiusY: 1**   **RadiusY: 1**

Figure 9-15

By default, Center is set to 0.5,0.5, and both RadiusX and RadiusY are set to 0.5. This is the first example shown in Figure 9-15. Once you've defined the ellipse, you need to specify a GradientOrigin.

You can think of the GradientOrigin almost like a light source, with the GradientStops radiating from the GradientOrigin to the edge of the ellipse defined by the Center, RadiusX, and RadiusY properties. Each *ray* is drawn from the GradientOrigin (offset 0) to the edge of the ellipse (offset 1). Figure 9-16 shows how various values of GradientOrigin affect the final rendering.

Center: 0.5,0.5
RadiusX: 0.5
RadiusY: 0.5

GradientOrigin: 0.5,0.5   **GradientOrigin: 0,0**   **GradientOrigin: 1,1**

Figure 9-16

ImageBrush

The ImageBrush is used to paint objects with images. You can use an ImageBrush for any Brush-derived property, like the Path's Fill property or the TextBlock's Foreground property. When applied, the image referenced by the ImageBrush is painted within the bounds of the object. The following XAML defines an ImageBrush resource whose ImageSource property references a wood-textured image:

```
<Grid
 Height="Auto"
 Background="{x:Null}"
 VerticalAlignment="Top" HorizontalAlignment="Left"
 Margin="29,30,0,0" Width="Auto">
 <Grid.Resources>
    <ImageBrush
       x:Key="Brush1"
       Stretch="UniformToFill"
       ImageSource="wood.png"
    />
 </Grid.Resources>
 <Border
    Opacity="1"
    HorizontalAlignment="Left"
    VerticalAlignment="Stretch"
    Margin="0,0,0,0"
    Background="{StaticResource Brush1}" Width="125" Height="125" />
 <Ellipse HorizontalAlignment="Left" Margin="147,0,-126,-1"
    Width="125" Fill="{StaticResource Brush1}" Stroke="#FF000000"
    Height="125"/>
 <TextBlock HorizontalAlignment="Left" Margin="285,62,0,0"
    VerticalAlignment="Center" FontFamily="Arial Black" FontSize="48"
    Text="WOOD" TextWrapping="NoWrap"
    Foreground="{StaticResource Brush1}"/>
</Grid>
```

Figure 9-17 shows the result of the previous XAML — an ImageBrush applied to Border, Ellipse, and TextBlock objects.

Figure 9-17

Just like the Image control, the ImageBrush control has a Stretch property that defines the way the source image is rendered when the object being painted is not the same size as the underlying image. And, as we've seen before, the values for Stretch can be None, Fill, Uniform, and UniformToFill.

VideoBrush

Just as you can paint an object with an image, you can paint an object with video! While a lot of the samples demonstrating this may seem a bit frivolous (like animated text with video painted on it), being able to paint elements with video can enable some really interesting visual effects. Just for fun, I'll show you how to paint text with video anyway.

Instead of simply setting a `Source` property on the `VideoBrush` (as we did with `ImageBrush`), you first have to define a `MediaElement` and give it a name. You then consume the `MediaElement` with the `VideoBrush` by setting its `SourceName` property to the name of the `MediaElement` you just created. You can then apply the `VideoBrush` to your target object just like any of the previous brushes we've looked at.

The following XAML defines a `MediaElement` and sets its name to *sourceMediaElement*:

```
<MediaElement
    x:Name="sourceMediaElement"
    Source="SampleVideo.wmv" IsMuted="True" Opacity="0"
    IsHitTestVisible="False" />
```

In addition to giving the `MediaElement` a name, I also set `Opacity` to 0, `IsHitTestVisible` to `False`, and `IsMuted` to `True`. Together these properties ensure that the `MediaElement` itself is neither seen nor heard nor able to intercept mouse clicks. The following XAML defines a `VideoBrush` that references this `MediaElement`. The `VideoBrush` is then applied to the `Foreground` of a `TextBlock`:

```
<TextBlock
    FontFamily="Arial Black" FontSize="48" Text="VIDEO"
    TextWrapping="NoWrap">

    <TextBlock.Foreground>
        <VideoBrush SourceName="sourceMediaElement"
            Stretch="UniformToFill" />
    </TextBlock.Foreground>
</TextBlock>
```

Editing Brushes in Blend

You've now seen how to define the various brush types by hand. Now it's time to take a look at how these same brushes can be created using Microsoft Expression Blend. Blend provides a brush-editing experience similar to other design programs you may have experienced before, reducing the labor of hand-typing `GradientStops` to simple, familiar user-interface conventions. Don't feel that the previous XAML-focused exercise was a waste, however — you now have a solid understanding of what's happening behind the scenes, and you're prepared to hand-tweak the designer-generated brushes when they just don't follow your every need.

Using the Brush Editor

Properties such as `Fill`, `Background`, `Stroke`, and `Foreground` all accept values of type `Brush`. We've just seen how Silverlight supports brushes of type `SolidColorBrush`, `LinearGradientBrush`, `RadialGradientBrush`, `ImageBrush`, and `VideoBrush`. A simple text field will obviously not work for this type of property. Enter the Brush editor, a tool that should look familiar to users of modern design programs.

In Figure 9-18, an ellipse is selected on the canvas whose Fill property is set to a LinearGradientBrush. On the right, the Brushes category is expanded (select the Properties tab in Blend if you haven't already). Notice the list of brush properties at the very top of this category. You'll see the Fill, Stroke, and OpacityMask brush properties listed. You can tell that Fill is the active property because it's highlighted with a light-gray background. Pay attention to two other details here also: the brush preview drawn adjacent to the property name, and the white marker directly next to the preview.

Figure 9-18

You can use the preview to glance and quickly determine the brush values that are applied to the currently selected object. The white box is known as a *marker* and launches a context menu for the property. Clicking it reveals a menu that lets you reset the property value, among other things. You can see that neither the Stroke nor the OpacityMask properties in Figure 9-18 have values set because their markers are both grayed out.

Applying a Brush Value

The Brush editor is divided into four tabs, one for each brush type available. Click on the first tab to clear the brush value. Click on the second tab to specify a SolidColorBrush, click on the third tab to specify a GradientBrush, and click on the fourth tab to select a brush resource.

Solid Color Brushes

When you specify a SolidColorBrush, the Brush editor interface appears as shown in Figure 9-19.

Although this editor may appear a little complicated at first glance, it is actually quite simple and just provides multiple ways to achieve the same task. You can quickly change the color by clicking anywhere in the large color area, indicated by the mouse cursor in Figure 9-19. Change the hue by dragging the Hue slider or clicking anywhere along the hue range.

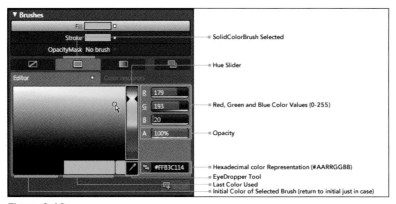

Figure 9-19

As you change the hue or choose different colors, the R, G, and B values will be updated accordingly. These are the Red, Green, and Blue color components of the selected color, respectively. Each component has a range from 0 to 255. The "A" entry listed beneath R, G, and B stands for *Alpha* (Transparency) and has a value range from 0 percent to 100 percent, where 0 represents fully transparent and 100 represents fully opaque. You can also specify the color by typing in an #AARRGGBB hexadecimal representation. The hexadecimal box will accept RRGGBB values if you paste in from a paint program that doesn't include an Alpha value, so it's a quick way to bring over color values if you have them elsewhere.

Gradient Brushes

Click on the third tab in the Brush editor to specify a GradientBrush. By default, a LinearGradientBrush will be applied to your selected object. You can toggle between LinearGradientBrush and RadialGradientBrush by clicking either of the two "Gradient Type" buttons located in the lower-left corner of the editor (as shown in Figure 9-20).

Figure 9-20

The `GradientBrush` editor builds on the `SolidColorBrush` editor by adding a gradient preview rectangle. The preview includes draggable swatches that represent `GradientStops`. Simply click a swatch to make it the active swatch. In Figure 9-20, the rightmost swatch is active, indicated by its black border.

❑ **Adding Stops** — Add additional `GradientStops` by clicking anywhere in the preview rectangle that does not already include a stop.

❑ **Moving Stops** — Change the position and order of stops by pressing and dragging the target stop.

❑ **Deleting Stops** — Remove `GradientStops` by dragging the stop down and away from the rectangle preview. Release when the stop disappears.

❑ **Precision Editing** — When editing gradients that require extreme precision, such as the sharp highlight shown in Figure 9-21, you may find that the visual editor is not precise enough for you.

Figure 9-21

In Figure 9-22, the second stop from the left is actually two stops. Their offsets are so close that they appear to be a single stop. Achieving this level of precision is frustrating if not impossible using the editor itself. Fortunately, you can actually edit the `GradientStops` in XAML. Jump directly to the XAML for your selected rectangle by right-clicking on it in the Object tree and selecting "View XAML" from the context menu.

Figure 9-22

The following code shows the XAML used to define the gradient shown in Figure 9-22:

```
<Rectangle
      Opacity="1"
      Canvas.Left="689"
      Canvas.Top="114"
      Width="128"
      Height="35t">
      <Rectangle.Fill>
            <LinearGradientBrush
                  StartPoint="0.9334821701049805,0.05263148716517857"
                  EndPoint="0.9334821701049805,0.9473685128348214">
                  <LinearGradientBrush.GradientStops>
                        <GradientStopCollection>
```

```
                                        <GradientStop
                                                Color="#FFd3ddab"
                                                Offset="0" />
                                        <GradientStop
                                                Color="#FF819d35"
                                                Offset="0.49" />
                                        <GradientStop
                                                Color="#FF739221"
                                                Offset="0.49" />
                                        <GradientStop
                                                Color="#FF678822"
                                                Offset="0.79" />
                                        <GradientStop
                                                Color="#FFBBC749"
                                                Offset="0.92t" />
                                        <GradientStop
                                                Color="#FFdbde58"
                                                Offset="1" />
                            </GradientStopCollection>
                        </LinearGradientBrush.GradientStops>
                    </LinearGradientBrush>
            </Rectangle.Fill>
        </Rectangle>
```

Notice the two stops with `Offset` values of 0.49. Remember, when two stops have the same `Offset` value, they are rendered in the order they're defined in XAML. This gives you the ability to create sharp lines in your gradients. Achieving this level of precision is just not possible with the current Gradient editor. Any time you find yourself having troubles getting your gradient to look exactly right, jump to the XAML and manually tweak the `Offset` values.

ImageBrushes

`ImageBrushes` can be quickly created from existing `Images` on the design surface in Blend. First, create an instance of the `Image` control and set its `Source` property to an image you want to use as an `ImageBrush`. With the `Image` selected, navigate to "Make ImageBrush Resource" on the main menu, as shown in Figure 9-23.

```
Tools > Make Brush Resource > Make ImageBrush Resource...
```

Figure 9-23

After selecting "Make ImageBrush Resource," you will be prompted to specify both a Key and a location for the `ImageBrush` resource. In Figure 9-24, I gave my brush the name *tiledImageBackgroundBrush* and selected `UserControl` as the location where I want the resource defined.

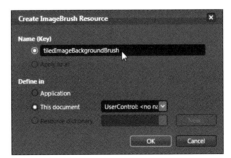

Figure 9-24

After clicking OK, it appears as if nothing has happened. The selected control is still an `Image`, and my design surface remains unchanged. Behind the scenes, a new `ImageBrush` resource was created in the location you specified, either in App.xaml or in the current `Page`'s resources collection (`UserControl.Resources`).

We can now apply this new resource using the fourth tab of the Blend Brush editor. First, draw a `Rectangle` on the stage, and then switch to the Properties tab if you have not already done so. With the rectangle selected, click on the `Fill` property in the Brush editor to make it the active brush property. Now, select the Brush resources tab, the fourth tab next to the Gradient Brush tab. Figure 9-25 shows the Brush Resources tab selected.

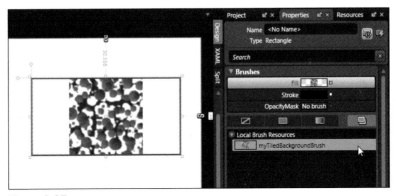

Figure 9-25

With the rectangle selected, clicking on the name of the `ImageBrush` you just defined applies the brush to the active brush property, in this case, `Fill`. By default, the image used by the `ImageBrush` is scaled uniformly within the object it is being applied to. But, just like the `Image` and several other controls we've looked at along the way, the `ImageBrush` has a `Stretch` property that lets you define the stretching and scaling behavior of the image.

In order to edit the `Stretch` property of the `ImageBrush`, you have to switch to the Resources tab of Blend. Figure 9-26 shows the Resources tab selected and `UserControl` expanded to reveal the `ImageBrush` named *myTiledBackgroundBrush*.

Figure 9-26

Click on the down arrow next to the brush preview to reveal the Brush editor and set the `Stretch` property, as shown in Figure 9-27.

Figure 9-27

The two other important properties of the `ImageBrush`, `ViewportUnits`, and `Viewport` are not exposed in the version of Blend at the time of this writing. You'll have to jump to XAML to edit those properties. (See, I told you the XAML section wasn't a waste!)

VideoBrush

Blend does not currently provide authoring support for `VideoBrush`. For now, you'll have to define your `VideoBrush` resources by hand.

Fonts and Font Embedding

Silverlight ships with several "system" fonts built-in. I put "system" in quotation marks, because these are included in the Silverlight run time and do not fall back to the operating system, so you can count on these core fonts whether you are running your Silverlight application on Windows, OS X, or Linux. Figure 9-28 shows a preview of these always-available fonts.

These fonts should all be familiar to you — they've shipped as standard fonts with Windows since Windows XP. Well, maybe not *Portable User Interface*. What is that, anyway? The *Portable User Interface* designation is really a fallback to the default Lucida Sans Unicode. It's the font you get when you don't specify a `FontFamily`.

Figure 9-28

Font Embedding

If you've selected a TextBlock in Blend, you'll see these default fonts listed at the top of the FontFamily dropdown (see Figure 9-29). The blue Silverlight logo next to these fonts indicates that they are embedded.

Figure 9-29

If you want to use a font other than one of the defaults, you'll have to embed that font in your project (or a referenced assembly). This is easy in Blend, simply select the font you wish to apply and check the "Embed" box in the Text properties panel. Blend will automatically create a *Fonts* folder, copy the required fonts files to that folder, and set their Build Action. It will also write the FontFamily syntax required for referencing embedded fonts so you can go about your business designing. If you're not using Blend you'll have to do these steps manually. Let's take a look at the manual process now.

To get started, find a font file on your system that you want to use in your Silverlight application. In Blend, you can add the font to the project by right-clicking on either the project itself or a folder within the project and selecting "Add Existing Item," as shown in Figure 9-30.

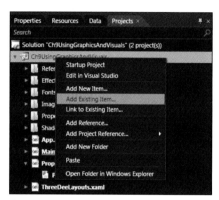

Figure 9-30

As with images, when Blend adds external font files, it automatically sets the Build Action to Resource. If you add the file using Visual Studio, you will need to manually set the Build Action to Resource (see Figure 9-31).

Once the font is included in your project as a resource, you can apply it via XAML by setting the FontFamily property:

```
<TextBlock FontFamily="Fonts/DistrictThin.ttf#DistrictThin"
    Text="Custom Font: District Thin" />
```

Let's break down the value of FontFamily so that you understand exactly how this works. First, you specify the actual font file path within your project. In this case, it's "Fonts/DistrictThin.ttf". Next, you specify the actual name of the font, preceded by the # symbol. Here, it's "#DistrictThin". It's important to note that the *name* of the font may be different from the *filename* of the font. An easy way to find the *name* of the font is by double-clicking on the font file in Windows Explorer and taking a look at the Font name declaration at the top of the preview window. Figure 9-32 shows this preview window for the example font DistrictThin.

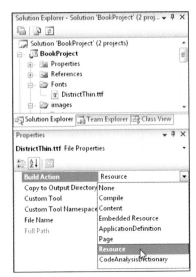

Figure 9-31

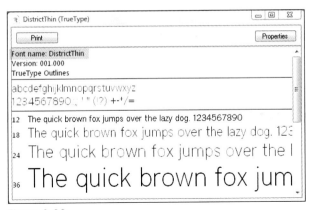

Figure 9-32

In the previous XAML, the font file was referenced just like we reference image resources in the project. And, just as we saw with image references, you can add a notation to the FontFamily font source path that specifies which assembly the font file resides in. The following XAML explicitly declares the project (assembly) name:

```
<TextBlock FontFamily="BookProject;component/Fonts/DistrictThin.ttf#DistrictThin"
        Text="Custom Font: District Thin" />
```

This means that you can embed font resources in other assemblies and still reference them via XAML, using a familiar syntax that is consistent with the syntax used by other controls.

Effects and Perspective 3D

So far in this chapter, we've looked at the fundamental building blocks used to define an application's interface.

Effects

Effects are used through the design industry — from print to the Web to desktop applications to motion video. These effects are used to add realism (subtle glows), create a sense of depth (drop shadows), simulate a real-world phenomenon (rippling water), and achieve a wide variety of additional visualizations. The core Silverlight run time includes a couple of common effects (`Blur` and `DropShadow`) but also supports custom PixelShader-based effects. This support essentially delivers the potential for an infinite number of effect possibilities.

Applying Effects

All objects derived from `UIElement` have a property of type `Effect` that happens also to be named `Effect`. To apply an effect to an object, you simply set the value of this property to an object that derives from `Effect`. The sample XAML defines two buttons, one with and one without a `BlurEffect` applied:

```
<StackPanel Orientation="Horizontal" HorizontalAlignment="Center">
    <Button Content="I'm Not Blurred"
        HorizontalAlignment="Center"
        VerticalAlignment="Center"
        Margin="0,0,10,0">
    </Button>
    <Button Content="I'm Blurred"
        HorizontalAlignment="Center"
        VerticalAlignment="Center">
    <Button.Effect>
        <BlurEffect Radius="4" />
    </Button.Effect>
    </Button>
</StackPanel>
```

The previous XAML results in a layout that looks like that shown in Figure 9-33.

Figure 9-33

Currently only a single effect can be applied to an object at a time. In order to apply multiple effects to the same visual, you will need to wrap the target element with additional panels (such as a `Border`) and progressively apply effects to each wrapper panel.

Native Effects

Silverlight 3 includes two native effects that are included as part of the core run time — BlurEffect and DropShadowEffect. These two effects alone may not seem like much, but the DropShadowEffect can also be used to create what is traditionally known as a glow effect as well. Together, these three effects are probably the most commonly used effects when creating user interface artwork.

BlurEffect

Using the BlurEffect is extremely simple and only includes a single customization property — Radius. The radius is used to determine how blurry the target element is: the higher the radius value, the blurrier your target. The default value for this property is 5 (in device-independent units of 1/96 of an inch).

Figure 9-34 shows the same target element with varying degrees of blur applied:

Figure 9-34

Common Uses for the BlurEffect

❑   Blur the main body of your application to draw focus to modal dialogs in the foreground.

❑   Apply BlurEffects over time in animations to simulate motion blur.

❑   Emphasize disabled items by slightly blurring them.

❑   Create a sense of depth by applying varying degrees of blur to layers in your application.

DropShadowEffect

The DropShadowEffect can be used to create both drop shadow and glow effects. Unlike the BlurEffect, this effect includes more than one property for customization. The following XAML defines a DropShadowEffect that results in a green glow around a custom button (Style is defined in the previous chapter):

```
<Button Style="{StaticResource ButtonWithDropShadow}"
    Width="130" Content="GLOW" Height="45">
    <Button.Effect>
        <DropShadowEffect ShadowDepth="0" BlurRadius="20" Opacity="1"
            Color="#FF25DFCE" Direction="315"/>
    </Button.Effect>
</Button>
```

It's by setting the ShadowDepth property to 0 that this effect essentially becomes a glow effect. The other properties all affect the way the final "shadow" is drawn. Figure 9-35 shows several DropShadowEffect configurations and their resulting visuals. The first sample shown is the result of the previous XAML.

Figure 9-35

When using the `DropShadowEffect` for user interfaces, I generally find subtle techniques, such as the *Soft Shadow* or *Radiosity* samples above, more effective than "in your face" options like *Hard Shadow* and *Top Shadow*. I hope you see that a wide variety of visualizations can be achieved with this single effect.

Applying Effects in Blend

You don't have to manually apply effects in XAML if you're using Blend 3. Figure 9-36 shows the Asset Library expanded with the Effects tab selected.

Figure 9-36

To apply an effect, press and hold your mouse over the effect you wish to apply, and drag the effect to the target object either on the design surface or in the Object tree. The behavior will appear in the Object tree as shown in Figure 9-37.

Figure 9-37

Editing the properties of an effect is no different from editing the properties of any other selected object on the stage. You can either select the effect in the Object tree directly and edit the effect's properties in the Property panel, or you can select the parent object (in this case Image) and expand the `Effect` property in the Property panel. Figure 9-38 shows the Property panel when the effect is selected directly (on the left) and shows the `Effect` property expanded when the parent `Image` is selected.

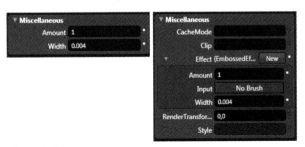

Figure 9-38

Custom Effects

Silverlight opens up a world of creativity possibilities by supporting custom High Level Shading Language (HLSL)–based effects. HLSL is the shader language used to define DirectX effects and was introduced with DirectX 8. Because HLSL has been around for a while, you can find a large number of articles and free resources (read: "free effects") that you can take advantage of. Start by visiting `http://msdn.microsoft.com/en-us/library/bb509561(VS.85).aspx` to learn more about HLSL, then do a Web search on *HLSL* to find a wealth of resources on this topic.

In order to use HLSL-based effects in Silverlight, you have to create a proxy class derived from `ShaderEffect`. It's in this derived class that you load precompiled HLSL bytecode and define proxy properties between your class and the underlying HLSL effect. In the walk-through that follows, you'll first learn how to use freely available tools to tweak and compile HLSL shaders, and then see how to consume those effects in custom classes that can be used in your Silverlight projects in the same way as native effects.

Getting the Tools

In order to compile HLSL shaders, you'll need the DirectX SDK, freely available on the Microsoft web site. In addition to the SDK, I also recommend downloading Walt Ritscher's Shazzam Shader Editing Tool. Shazzam is delivered as a WPF ClickOnce application and provides a nice interface for editing and testing HLSL shaders.

❏ **DirectX SDK** — `http://msdn.microsoft.com/en-us/directx/aa937788.aspx`

❏ **Shazzam** — `http://shazzam-tool.com/publish.htm`

Viewing and Compiling Shaders with Shazzam and the DirectX SDK

Start by downloading and installing the latest version of the DirectX SDK. (Be warned, it's a fairly hefty 400+ MB download.) Once you've installed the SDK, install and run Shazzam. The first time you run Shazzam, you'll probably need to update its settings to ensure that it knows the correct location of the

DirectX FX compiler. Do this by expanding the Settings panel and clicking on the "Change Path" button, shown expanded in Figure 9-39:

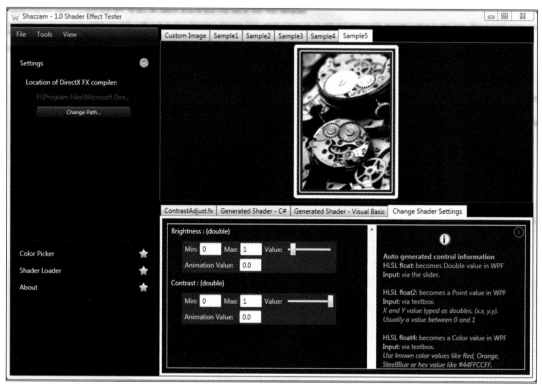

Figure 9-39

The default installation path required by Shazzam will be something like C:\Program Files\ Microsoft DirectX SDK (March 2009)\Utilities\bin\x86\fxc.exe. This path will vary slightly based on the version of the SDK you've installed and whether or not you've changed the default installation path. Once you've set the correct path, you can move on to the fun stuff — testing and compiling shaders.

Shazzam ships with several default shaders that you can play with by expanding the Shader Loader panel. Click on the "Sample Shaders" button, and then select a shader from the list. The shader will be loaded in an uncompiled state as the first tab. Press [F5] or select Tools ➪ Apply from the main menu to compile and test the results. When you compile a shader in Shazzam, several important things happen:

❑ ShaderEffect-derived classes are auto-generated in both C# and Visual Basic for use in your own projects.

❑ The "Change Shader Settings" tab is either added or updated, providing you with an interface for modifying the shader input values.

❑ The new effect is applied to all of the sample images in the tabbed preview area.

Figure 9-40 shows the Embossed.fx shader selected, compiled, and applied to the Sample5 image.

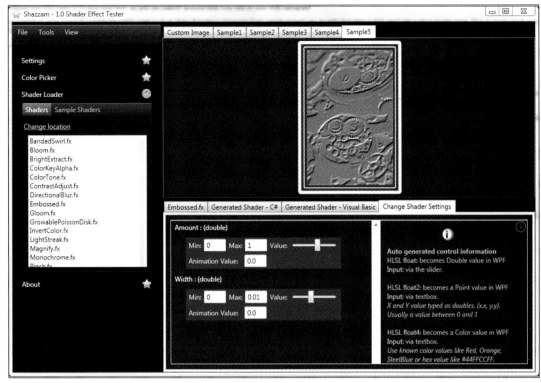

Figure 9-40

I've set the value of the Amount parameter to .57 and the value of the Width parameter to .004. For many of the sample effects, the default value range of the sliders is not effective. For example, I changed the Max value of Width to .01 for this Embossed effect. If you compile a shader and feel like it's not working, it's likely that you just haven't found an appropriate combination of input values yet.

Creating a Custom Shader Effect

With the custom shader tweaked and compiled, it's now time to create a custom ShaderEffect class that can be consumed by our Silverlight applications. Shazzam has already taken a lot of the guesswork out of the process by compiling the .fx shader and generating a starter effect class for us. We now have to add the compiled effect to our Visual Studio project and customize the starter class for Silverlight. (Shazzam currently generates WPF code.)

Add the Compiled Shader to Visual Studio

Select Tools ⇨ View Compiled Shaders from the main menu in Shazzam. This will open the GeneratedShaders folder in Windows Explorer. You will see a number of .ps files, one for each Sample Shader you've compiled and tested. In this sample, I'm going to use the Embossed shader. Create a folder inside your Visual Studio project named *Shaders*, and then drag Embossed.ps from Windows Explorer to the Visual Studio folder. Figure 9-41 shows the file Embossed.ps added to the Shaders folder inside the Visual Studio project. Make sure you set the Build Action of your shader file to Resource.

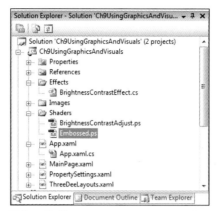

Figure 9-41

Create the Effect Class

With the shader in place in the project, it's now time to create our proxy effect class. Start by creating an Effects folder in Visual Studio. Add an empty class to that folder with the filename *EmbossedEffect.cs*. Now, switch back to Shazzam and select the "Generated Shader — C#" tab (or "Visual Basic" if you're trying this in VB). Copy all of the auto-generated code to the new `EmbossedEffect` class you just added to Visual Studio.

Below is the initial code generated by Shazzam:

```
namespace Shazzam.Shaders
{
    using System.Windows;
    using System.Windows.Media;
    using System.Windows.Media.Effects;


    public class AutoGenShaderEffect : ShaderEffect
    {

        public static DependencyProperty InputProperty =
ShaderEffect.RegisterPixelShaderSamplerProperty("Input", typeof(AutoGenShaderEffect), 0);
        public static DependencyProperty AmountProperty =
DependencyProperty.Register("Amount", typeof(double), typeof(AutoGenShaderEffect),
new System.Windows.UIPropertyMetadata(new double(), PixelShaderConstantCallback(0)));
        public static DependencyProperty WidthProperty =
DependencyProperty.Register("Width", typeof(double), typeof(AutoGenShaderEffect), new
System.Windows.UIPropertyMetadata(new double(), PixelShaderConstantCallback(1)));

        public AutoGenShaderEffect(PixelShader shader)
        {
            // Note: for your project you must decide how to use the generated
            // ShaderEffect class (Choose A or B below).
            // A: Comment out the following line if you are not passing in the shader
```

```
            // and remove the shader parameter from the constructor

            PixelShader = shader;

            // B: Uncomment the following two lines - which load the *.ps file
            // Uri u = new Uri(@"pack://application:,,,/bandedswirl.ps");
            // PixelShader = new PixelShader() { UriSource = u };

            // Must initialize each DependencyProperty that's affliated with a shader register
            // Ensures the shader initializes to the proper default value.
            this.UpdateShaderValue(InputProperty);
            this.UpdateShaderValue(AmountProperty);
            this.UpdateShaderValue(WidthProperty);
        }

        public virtual System.Windows.Media.Brush Input
        {
            get
            {
                return ((System.Windows.Media.Brush)(GetValue(InputProperty)));
            }
            set
            {
                SetValue(InputProperty, value);
            }
        }

        public virtual double Amount
        {
            get
            {
                return ((double)(GetValue(AmountProperty)));
            }
            set
            {
                SetValue(AmountProperty, value);
            }
        }

        public virtual double Width
        {
            get
            {
                return ((double)(GetValue(WidthProperty)));
            }
            set
            {
                SetValue(WidthProperty, value);
            }
        }
    }
}
```

The generated code includes a class derived from ShaderEffect and dependency properties for each of the shader's input fields. We now need to make a few tweaks to get this working in Silverlight. Start by updating the generated namespace so that it's similar to `ProjectName.Effects`. Now, right-click on the class name and select Refactor ➯ Rename from the context menu. Enter **EmbossedEffect** and click OK.

Two of the three `DependencyProperties` use a class named `UIPropertyMetadata`. In Silverlight, this class is simply `PropertyMeta`. Drop the *UI* from the two `DependencyProperties` using this class, and your project and this class should now compile (compile but not work).

We need to add a parameterless constructor that loads the Embossed.ps shader resource we added in the previous step; otherwise, this is just an empty effect with a few meaningless input properties. In the following code, a new URI object (found in the `System` namespace) has been defined that references the .ps resource (using the *ProjectName;*component syntax introduced earlier in this chapter).

```
public EmbossedEffect()
{
    Uri u = new Uri(@"Ch9UsingGraphicsAndVisuals;component/Shaders/Embossed.ps",
                    UriKind.Relative);
    PixelShader = new PixelShader() { UriSource = u };

    this.UpdateShaderValue(InputProperty);
    this.UpdateShaderValue(AmountProperty);
    this.UpdateShaderValue(WidthProperty);
}
```

The `PixelShader` property (defined on `ShaderEffect`) is initialized to a new instance of `PixelShader` whose `UriSource` is the URI just defined. This is the magic hookup that ties the HLSL shader to a Silverlight-supported `ShaderEffect`. The last three lines of this constructor ensure that the shader values are initialized the first time it is applied. The following code shows the `EmbossedEffect` class after our updates (I've omitted the `Input`, `Amount`, and `Width` property definitions as they did not change):

```
namespace Ch9UsingGraphicsAndVisuals.Effects
{
    using System.Windows;
    using System.Windows.Media;
    using System.Windows.Media.Effects;
    using System;

    public class EmbossedEffect : ShaderEffect
    {
        public static DependencyProperty InputProperty =
ShaderEffect.RegisterPixelShaderSamplerProperty("Input", typeof(EmbossedEffect), 0);
        public static DependencyProperty AmountProperty =
DependencyProperty.Register("Amount", typeof(double), typeof(EmbossedEffect),
new System.Windows.PropertyMetadata(new double(), PixelShaderConstantCallback(0)));
        public static DependencyProperty WidthProperty =
DependencyProperty.Register("Width", typeof(double), typeof(EmbossedEffect),
new System.Windows.PropertyMetadata(new double(), PixelShaderConstantCallback(1)));

        public EmbossedEffect()
        {
            Uri u = new Uri(@"Ch9UsingGraphicsAndVisuals;component/Shaders/Embossed.ps",
                            UriKind.Relative);
            PixelShader = new PixelShader() { UriSource = u };

            this.UpdateShaderValue(InputProperty);
```

```
        this.UpdateShaderValue(AmountProperty);
        this.UpdateShaderValue(WidthProperty);
    }
    // Input, Amount, and Width Properties here
}
```

Before moving on to actually applying the custom effect, I want to recap what is a fairly simple process:

1.   Test and compile shader in Shazzam.

2.   Add compiled .ps file to Visual Studio and set its Build Action to Resource.

3.   Add new Effect-named class to your project.

4.   Copy Shazzam-generated effect code to your new class.

5.   Update the namespace.

6.   Refactor ➪ Rename the class name.

7.   Change `UIPropertyMetaData` to `PropertyMetaData`.

8.   Create a `Uri` that references the .ps file (using `System` is required).

9.   Add a parameter-less constructor that initializes the `PixelShader` property.

Applying the Custom Effect

With the custom effect defined, we can now apply it via XAML just like we apply the `Blur` and `DropShadow` effects. The only additional thing required is a namespace mapping to our custom effects namespace. The following XAML defines a `localEffects` namespace and applies the `EmbossedEffect` to a sample image:

```
<UserControl
    xmlns:localEffects="clr-namespace:Ch9UsingGraphicsAndVisuals.Effects"
    ...
<Image Source="Images/sampleImage.jpg">
    <Image.Effect>
        <localEffects:EmbossedEffect Width=".003" Amount="1" />
    </Image.Effect>
</Image>
```

Figure 9-42 shows the sample image with and without the `EmbossedEffect` applied.

Figure 9-42

We can easily enable real-time adjustments of the effect input values by binding `Slider` controls to the effect instance itself, just as Shazzam generates automatically. The following XAML adds an `x:Name` attribute to the `EmbossedEffect` instance and binds a `Slider`'s `Value` property to the `EmbossedEffect`'s `Width` property:

```
<Image Source="Images/sampleImage.jpg">
  <Image.Effect>
    <localEffects:EmbossedEffect x:Name="EmbossedEffect"
       Width=".003" Amount="1" />
  </Image.Effect>
</Image>
<Slider Value="{Binding ElementName=EmbossedEffect, Path=Width, Mode=TwoWay}"
      Minimum="0" SmallChange=".001" Maximum=".01" />
```

When you compile and run, you can drag the slider and adjust the `Width` parameter of the `EmbossedEffect` in real time — Nice!

Summary

I hope you are now starting to see the power of shader-based custom effects in Silverlight. There are so many creative possibilities here. If you're interested in seeing more effects than those that ship with Shazzam, be sure to check out the open-source WPF/Silverlight Shader Effects Library at Codeplex: `http://wpffx.codeplex.com`. In addition to providing a large number of predefined effects, this solution also demonstrates how to share a code base between Silverlight and WPF projects.

Perspective 3D

Silverlight gives you the ability to rotate every `UIElement` in your application in its own three-dimensional (3D) space simply by setting the `Projection` property. Unlike true 3D environments wherein multiple elements live in a shared 3D space, objects in Silverlight each have their own space. 3D in Silverlight is really a 3D transform applied to individual objects and not a true all-encompassing 3D environment that supports 3D objects and materials. For example, you can't import a 3ds model of a fighter jet and have it fly across the screen, but you *can* flip a configuration panel up from the bottom of the screen or rotate an image into view.

While this level of support may sound limited compared to a full 3D environment, it actually supports a wide array of user interface scenarios and is more flexible than you might at first think. Let's start by looking at a simple sample, then move on to some of the configuration options that demonstrate flexibility. The following XAML defines two images. The first is displayed normally, while the second is rotated about the X- and Y-axes:

```
<Image Height="116" Margin="241,317,0,0" VerticalAlignment="Top"
    Source="Images/sampleImage.jpg" Stretch="Fill" Width="154"
    HorizontalAlignment="Left"/>
<Image Source="Images/sampleImage.jpg" Stretch="Fill" Width="154"
    VerticalAlignment="Top" Height="116" HorizontalAlignment="Left"
    Margin="421,317,0,0">
  <Image.Projection>
    <PlaneProjection RotationX="-17" RotationY="-34"/>
  </Image.Projection>
</Image>
```

All we had to do was set the `Projection` property of the `Image` to an instance of the `PlaneProjection` object. It's on the `PlaneProjection` where we customize all of the rotation properties. This sample uses an `Image`, but `Image` could just as easily have been a `Button`, `Grid`, `Border`, `Rectangle`, or any other control you felt needed to be rotated. Figure 9-43 shows the `Image` both with and without the transform.

Figure 9-43

By default, the image is rotated about its center on all three axes. You can customize the center of rotation by adjusting the `CenterOfRotationX`, `CenterOfRotationY`, and `CenterOfRotationZ` properties on the `PlaneProjection` object. The following XAML sets both the X and Y center to 0 (top, left corner) of the image and rotates –60 degrees about the Y-axis:

```
<Image Height="116" Margin="241,317,0,0" VerticalAlignment="Top"
    Source="Images/sampleImage.jpg" Stretch="Fill" Width="154"
    HorizontalAlignment="Left"/>
<Image Source="Images/sampleImage.jpg" Stretch="Fill" Width="154"
    VerticalAlignment="Top" Height="116" HorizontalAlignment="Left"
    Margin="421,317,0,0">
    <Image.Projection>
        <PlaneProjection RotationX="0" RotationY="-60" CenterOfRotationX="0"
            CenterOfRotationY="0" CenterOfRotationZ="0"/>
    </Image.Projection>
</Image>
```

In Figure 9-44, you can see how the image appears to be swinging back, almost like a door on its hinge.

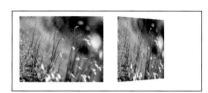

Figure 9-44

You can simulate a true 3D environment by synchronizing the initial position of a number of objects and synchronizing their `CenterOfRotation` properties. Figure 9-45 shows 200 procedurally generated `Rectangles`, all positioned in the center of a container Grid, with a `CenterOfRotationZ` property set to –300. When the `RotationX` and `RotationY` properties are set, it's as if these images are being moved around the surface of a sphere.

Figure 9-45

Each rectangle has its own `PlaneProjection` and is rotated in its own 3D space, but by synchronizing the initial positions and `CenterOfRotationZ` property, we have achieved a deceptive result. The following code shows how this visual was created:

```
public ThreeDeeLayouts()
{
        // Required to initialize variables
        InitializeComponent();

    GenerateSphere();
}

int rowCount = 10;
int columnCount = 20;
int rectHeightWidth = 30;

private void GenerateSphere()
{
    for (var i = 0; i < rowCount; i++)
    {
        for (var j = 0; j < columnCount; j++)
        {
            // Create Rectangle
```

```
Rectangle rect = new Rectangle();
rect.Height = rect.Width = rectHeightWidth;

// Create PlaneProjection and Initialize CenterOfRotationZ
PlaneProjection projection = new PlaneProjection();
projection.CenterOfRotationZ = -300;

// Set RotationX and RotationY based on current row and column
projection.RotationX = -90 + ((180 / rowCount) * i);
projection.RotationY = (360 / columnCount) * j;

// Assign PlaneProject to Rectangle's Projection property
rect.Projection = projection;

// Set the Rectangle's Fill property
rect.Fill = new SolidColorBrush(Color.FromArgb(150,255,255,255));

// Add the Rectangle to a XAML-defined Grid (named "sphere")
this.sphere.Children.Add(rect);
        }
    }
}
```

This sample just defines and applies a 3D transformation to a collection of rectangles. You could extend this sample and make it more interactive by responding to mouse position and updating all of the 3D transforms, creating a sense of interactive 3D space. I'll leave that up to you, though; you are now armed with the basic understanding of what is required to take it further.

Adjusting **PlaneProjections** in Blend

Blend 3 adds support in the Properties panel for adjusting the values of a PlaneProjection applied to an object. Select an object on the stage, and then scroll to the Transform category of the Properties panel. By default, the Project property is hidden in the "Advanced properties" section. Click the down arrow to reveal the editor shown in Figure 9-46.

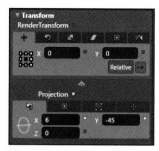

Figure 9-46

You can manually define rotation values for the X-, Y-, and Z-axes, or you can click and drag the circle-based sphere icon to do a freeform rotation. Additional tabs in this editor expose the Center of Rotation, Global Offset, and Local Offset property categories. We did not look at these last two property groups in the previous exercise. These additional value categories let you adjust the positions of items in 3D space, much like applying a `TranslateTransform` in 2D space. These properties can be used to further simulate a true 3D environment much as our previous sphere example demonstrated.

Importing Artwork from Additional Design Tools

You may be wondering why you would even need to work with artwork created outside of Blend, considering that Blend provides practically all of the tools you need to design a user interface. I think there are two clear answers to this question:

1. Most of you already have preexisting artwork created in other applications that you would like to reuse.

2. Many of you are already very familiar with your own design tools and can simply work faster in your design tool of choice.

Based on my experience, you will initially be inclined to export to XAML from your favorite tool, staying in your design comfort zone. Then, as you become more and more familiar with Blend, you will find yourself starting in Blend for most tasks and jumping back to your other program only for specialty design needs.

Designing with Blend/Silverlight in Mind

If you're doing the designing, exporting, and integrating yourself, you have the luxury (or responsibility) of designing with exporting in mind. This means that you can anticipate the needs of your application layout and design so that achieving your intended results is as easy as possible. If you're a designer working in a third-party tool delivering artwork to a fellow developer using Blend, you can strengthen your work relationship by exporting your artwork in a way that makes the developer's job easier.

There are several questions you need to keep in mind when designing artwork:

❑ Are bitmaps acceptable? (If so, can you use all the effects you want?)

❑ Does the piece you're working on need to stretch? (Horizontally, vertically, or both?)

❑ Will pieces of the user interface animate? (Like panel backgrounds or buttons?)

We'll take a look at each of these scenarios and discuss certain techniques you can use that will make your life (or your coworkers' lives) easier.

Are Bitmaps Acceptable?

There are several factors that affect the answer to this question, many of which go beyond the scope of this book. However, we'll try to cover a few key scenarios here.

File Size

The first, and possibly most obvious, aspect of including bitmaps in your project is file size. Silverlight is a Web-based platform, which means that bandwidth is a very real concern. Even with growing numbers of broadband connections in homes, keeping the download footprint of your application to a minimum is still a necessary evil. There are times when the XAML required to represent your artwork could actually be larger than a representative bitmap, and if the other considerations listed next don't contradict your file size requirement, exporting your artwork as a bitmap may be the best option.

Scaling

At the heart of Silverlight is a high-performance, vector-based rendering engine. This means vector-based artwork, represented by XAML, can be rendered without loss at virtually any size. If the artwork you are designing is intended to scale, exporting to bitmaps is not the way to go. When bitmaps are resized in the Silverlight player, you'll begin to see pixelation as the artwork increases in size and blurriness as the artwork decreases in size.

Dynamic Changes

Artwork in Silverlight applications can be updated dynamically at run time. For example, you could change the brush that is used to paint the background of a button when the mouse moves over it. If the artwork you are creating will be used in this type of scenario, exporting as a bitmap is not an option.

Techniques That Require a Bitmap Export

Most design programs are platform-agnostic and export to various flattened file formats. When authoring for Silverlight, you have to consider the features of the Silverlight rendering engine. The following techniques are not supported by the Silverlight player and will require that you export your artwork as a bitmap. If exporting to bitmaps is not an option for your application, you can either scale back the visuals or recraft your artwork using other techniques.

❑ **Effects** — Currently, the Silverlight player does not support live bitmap effects (drop shadows, blurs, glows, etc.), so any time you need to achieve these types of effects, you will have to export your artwork as a bitmap.

❑ **Blending Modes** — If the visuals you're creating use Blending modes (Screen, Add, Subtract, Saturation, etc.), you will have to export your artwork as a bitmap or choose alternative techniques. The Silverlight player does not currently include support for Blending modes.

Which Bitmap File Type Is Best?

If you find that you do have to include bitmaps in your project, your first step is to determine which file type is right for you. If you need to composite the bitmap with a transparent background, exporting as a 32-bit PNG with a transparent background is the best choice. If transparency isn't a requirement, finding the right balance between file size and quality is your next step. The same rules that apply to traditional Web design apply here. If you're exporting a photo, a JPEG is the obvious choice. Just play with the quality settings until you achieve the right balance. If you're exporting artwork, experiment with JPEG quality and PNG bit depths until you reach a compromise that meets your needs. Most modern design applications provide live previews that help you find this quality/file size balance quickly.

Does the Piece You're Working on Need to Stretch?

You need to consider whether the artwork you're working on needs to scale vertically, horizontally, or both. You need to anticipate how the artwork is going to scale and export your artwork accordingly. If you have rounded corners, how are you going to design so that the XAML you export behaves correctly?

Will you use a single `Border` object and set the `CornerRadius` property, or will you "slice" your artwork, much as traditional Web designers would slice the artwork they export? You may have to work through your layout a few times before you come to an acceptable solution.

If you as a designer don't consider how the application is going to behave, you'll end up with artwork in Blend that isn't functional. Regardless of the size of the team you're working on, it's important to establish open lines of communication between design and development. And if you're wearing both hats, design with interactivity in mind — you'll save yourself lots of extra rework in the end.

Exporting to XAML in Other Tools

When I first started working with XAML (way back in the spring of 2005), I was pretty much stuck with Notepad and a handful of cobbled-together converters and exporters. I would create artwork in Adobe Illustrator, save to an Illustrator SVG file, and then convert the SVG to XAML using the Xamlon SVG to XAML Converter. I would then hand-tweak the generated XAML and copy it into my application and cross my fingers. If things weren't quite right, I'd step through the process again … and again … and again. …

Fortunately, things have matured considerably since then. Blend 3 now has native Adobe Photoshop and Adobe Illustrator importers. There are also a number of third-party exporters and converters for a variety of popular design applications and file types. Mike Swanson, a technical evangelist at Microsoft, created a freely available Illustrator to a XAML plug-in that many of us began using early on. During the summer of 2006, I spent my nights and weekends creating the Fireworks to XAML Exporter, a panel for Adobe Fireworks that I still use in practically every WPF and Silverlight project. There are many other passionate people out there who have created similar plug-ins for their tools of choice, and we've provided the following list of those tools. We've also included in the list some commercial applications that you may need to help round out your toolset.

- ❑ **Microsoft Expression Design** (`www.microsoft.com/expression`) — Included in the Microsoft Expression Suite and available as a trial download. Supports WPF and Silverlight-specific XAML export.

- ❑ **Adobe Fireworks to WPF/XAML Exporter** by Grant Hinkson (`www.granthinkson.com/tools/fireworks`) — A free extension for Adobe Fireworks CS4. This panel lets you copy XAML directly to the clipboard or save XAML to a file.

- ❑ **Adobe Illustrator to WPF/XAML Export Plug-In** by Mike Swanson (`www.mikeswanson.com/XAMLExport`) — A free plug-in for Adobe Illustrator that adds XAML as an export format

- ❑ **XamlXporter for Illustrator** by Pavan Podila (`www.codeplex.com/Wiki/View.aspx?ProjectName=xamlxporter`) — An open-source, C#-based exporter for Adobe Illustrator

- ❑ **SWF2XAML: A Flash to XAML Conversion Tool** by Mike Swanson (`www.mikeswanson.com/SWF2XAML`) — A free converter for Adobe Flash SWF files. Opens exported SWF files and converts each frame to XAML.

- ❑ **theConverted–SWF to XAML Edition** by Debreuil Digital Works (`theconverted.ca`) — A commercial SWF to XAML converter

- ❑ **Kaxaml** by Robby Ingebretsen (`www.kaxaml.com`) — A free, lightweight XAML Editor for WPF and Silverlight.

Summary

We started this chapter by examining the core set of controls at your disposal for creating interesting visuals in Silverlight. You were exposed to the XAML syntax first so that you would have a solid understanding of what's happening behind the scenes. After covering the XAML, we jumped to Blend and used a design surface to do the same things we had just done by hand. In some cases, Blend was able to do everything for us (and was practically necessary for tasks such as creating complex paths). In other cases, Blend didn't provide tooling for certain control features (such as setting `ViewportUnits` on an `ImageBrush`), and we had to return to the XAML to achieve just what we wanted.

We also looked at how to reference and include binary assets (images, fonts, videos, etc.) and how to use Visual Studio to set the Build Action. You also learned that Blend doesn't provide a way to change the Build Action itself and that you *have* to use Visual Studio (or edit the .csproj file by hand). We then shifted focus to effects and 3D support offered by Silverlight and even stepped through creating our own custom effect. You should now have an understanding of how the various tools at your disposal — whether raw XAML, design tools such as Blend and Fireworks, or development environments such as Visual Studio — all have their place in the Silverlight ecosystem and are really co-dependent. You can use one or two exclusively, but ultimately you need to be familiar with a number of design and development tools.

10

Making It Richer with Media

Silverlight supports MP3 audio, H.264 Video, AAC Audio, and several Windows Media Audio and Windows Media Video formats, giving you the ability to create media-rich, Web-based experiences. And even if you're not creating a photo browser or interactive video application, you can use Silverlight's media capabilities to add subtle `MouseOver` sound effects to buttons in your application to add that next level of polish. In this chapter, you'll look at the capabilities of the Silverlight `MediaElement` control and the file formats it supports. You'll see how to define the control both in XAML and in Blend and see how to respond to the events it raises. You'll also be introduced to Expression Media Encoder 2 and learn how to prepare your media for use in your Silverlight app. We'll conclude the chapter by looking at the free live.com-based Silverlight Streaming service and the new Smooth Streaming feature of IIS7 for delivering high-definition live video.

Supported Formats

Before we even take a look at including media in our Silverlight apps, let's take a look at the file formats and codecs supported natively by the Silverlight player. Media can be encoded using several of the Windows Media Video and Windows Media Audio codecs, as well as the MP3 and AAC audio codecs and H.264 video codec. Windows Media Audio and Video are more than just two codecs. Both of these formats include various versions and use-specific codecs (such as Windows Media Screen and Windows Media Voice). Silverlight supports a subset of the broad array of Windows Media codecs. Listed below are the versions supported by the player. These formats are supported, regardless of the file extension of the encoded file. Silverlight ignores the file extension when the source media file is referenced.

Video

❑ **WMV1** — Windows Media Video 7

❑ **WMV2** — Windows Media Video 8

❑ **WMV3** — Windows Media Video 9

- ❑ **WMVA** — Windows Media Video Advanced Profile, non-VC-1

- ❑ **WMVC1** — Windows Media Video Advanced Profile, VC-1

- ❑ **H.264**

- ❑ Can only be used for progressive download, smooth streaming, and adaptive streaming

- ❑ Supports Base, Main, and High Profiles.

Audio

- ❑ **WMA 7** — Windows Media Audio 7

- ❑ **WMA 8** — Windows Media Audio 8

- ❑ **WMA 9** — Windows Media Audio 9

- ❑ **WMA 10** — Windows Media Audio 10

- ❑ **AAC** — Advanced Audio Coding

- ❑ Can only be used for progressive download, smooth streaming, and adaptive streaming

- ❑ AAC is the LC variety and supports sampling frequencies up to 48 kHz.

- ❑ **MP3** — ISO/MPEG Layer-3

  - ❑ **Input** — ISO/MPEG Layer-3 data stream

  - ❑ **Channel Configurations** — Mono, stereo

  - ❑ **Sampling Frequencies** — 8, 11.025, 12, 16, 22.05, 24, 32, 44.1, and 48 kHz

  - ❑ **Bitrates** — 8–320 Kbps, variable bitrate

  - ❑ **Limitations** — "Free format mode" (see ISO/IEC 11172-3, subclause 2.4.2.3) is not supported.

Unsupported Windows Media Formats

The following Windows Media–based formats are not supported by the Silverlight `MediaElement` control:

- ❑ Interlaced video content

- ❑ Windows Media Screen

- ❑ Windows Media Audio Professional

- ❑ Windows Media Voice

- ❑ Combination of Windows Media Video and MP3 (WMV video + MP3 audio)

- ❑ Windows Media Video using odd (not divisible by two) dimensioned frames; for example, 127×135

H.264 and AAC Support

H.264 is a popular codec for encoding high-definition video. This format is used widely across several devices and applications and has been made popular by the iTunes store and family of supported devices. Many consumer camcorders now encode video natively to H.264 so that the video can be immediately uploaded to media-sharing web sites such as YouTube.com and Vimeo.com. The Silverlight player can access H.264 videos directly via the MediaElement or via IIS7 Smooth Streaming (enabled through the Media Services 3.0 extension for IIS7 available at www.iis.net/extensions/SmoothStreaming). H.264 video cannot be delivered via Windows Media Server streaming.

AAC is the audio codec counterpart to H.264; most videos encoded with the H.264 codec have an accompanying audio stream encoded using the AAC codec. AAC is also the audio format natively used by iTunes.

Silverlight does not currently support DRM (Digital Rights Management) for H.264 encoded video.

Using the MediaElement Control

Media is displayed in Silverlight applications by using the MediaElement control. Just like the Image control, the MediaElement control has a Source property that points to the source media. The source media can be an internal resource, compiled into your Silverlight assembly, a resource compiled into a referenced assembly, a loose file sitting on the host server, a file residing on a remote server, or a playlist served up from a local or remote server. In short, the MediaElement can reference a file that resides just about anywhere.

The following XAML defines a MediaElement control and references a loose video on the server, located as a sibling to the XAP file:

```
<MediaElement
    Width="320"
    Height="240"
    HorizontalAlignment="Left"
    VerticalAlignment="Bottom"
    Margin="50,50,0,0"
    Source="SampleVideo.wmv" />
```

This particular MediaElement is 320 pixels wide × 240 pixels tall and is aligned to the top-left corner of the page with both a top and left margin of 50 pixels (Margin="50,50,0,0", where Margin="TL,TR, BR, BL"). Pretty simple, right? The layout principles introduced in Chapter 9 apply here, too.

Build Actions and Referencing Media

Just like images or other binary files, media files can reside just about anywhere and can even be included in your project in a number of ways. Let's take a look at the various approaches available, examine the pros and cons of each, and see how the approach alters the way the media is referenced via XAML.

Each of the following sections mentions the term *Build Action*. *Build Action* refers to a property available in Visual Studio (and not available in Blend) that dictates how the file is treated when the project is compiled. Figure 10-1 shows the Visual Studio Property panel when a media file has been selected in the Solution Explorer.

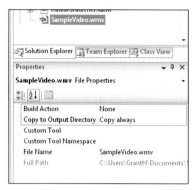

Figure 10-1

Assembly Resource Media

A media file is compiled into your project's assembly when its Build Action is set to *Resource*. This should only be done for short clips that you want to be available immediately when your application or assembly is loaded. Files included as `Resources` are compiled into the application assembly and can greatly increase the assembly's file size.

Referencing the Media in XAML

Reference an embedded media file using a relative URL. If the file is in the root folder of your project, you simply type its name. If the file is in a subfolder, such as Media, include the entire relative path. For example, the following XAML references a video stored in the media/stockfootage subfolder of the project directory:

```
<MediaElement
    Width="320"
    Height="240"
    HorizontalAlignment="Left"
    VerticalAlignment="Bottom"
    Margin="50,50,0,0"
    Source="media/stockfootage/Bear.wmv" />
```

You can also use a path that explicitly references the assembly that the video is housed in. If your Silverlight project name is *MyProject*, then the previous XAML could be replaced by the following:

```
<MediaElement
    Width="320"
    Height="240"
    HorizontalAlignment="Left"
    VerticalAlignment="Bottom"
    Margin="50,50,0,0"
    Source="MyProject;component/media/stockfootage/Bear.wmv" />
```

The text in bold is key: `MyProject;component/`.

The text `MyProject` should be replaced with the name of your project, but `;component/` should remain at all times.

❑ **Pros**

    ❑ Media is available immediately.

    ❑ Simple relative path references

    ❑ No security issues

❑ **Cons**

    ❑ Large media files can bloat the assembly size and increase page load time.

XAP File Media

A media file is included in the XAP file and is not compiled into the assembly when its Build Action is set to *Content*. When configured as `Content`, media files do not bloat the size of your project assembly, but they do continue to bloat the size of the XAP file. You might take this approach if you want your media files available immediately but do not want to bloat the size of your assembly.

Referencing the Media in XAML

When media is included this way, you need to add a forward slash (/) before the path to the file:

```
<MediaElement
    Width="320"
    Height="240"
    HorizontalAlignment="Left"
    VerticalAlignment="Bottom"
    Margin="50,50,0,0"
    Source="/media/stockfootage/Bear.wmv" />
```

❑ **Pros**

    ❑ Media is available immediately.

    ❑ Simple absolute path references

    ❑ No security issues

    ❑ Assembly size is reduced.

❑ **Cons**

    ❑ Large media files can bloat the XAP size and increase page load time.

Loose Files

You can add media files to your project that are not compiled into the project assembly or added to the XAP file. These files neither bloat the assembly nor the XAP file. To achieve this scenario, set the Build Action of your file to *None*, and "Copy to Local Directory" to *Copy Always* or *Copy if Newer*.

Referencing the Image in XAML

Use the same syntax as you used with XAP File Images, adding a forward slash to the URI:

```
<MediaElement
    Width="320"
    Height="240"
    HorizontalAlignment="Left"
    VerticalAlignment="Bottom"
    Margin="50,50,0,0"
    Source="/media/stockfootage/Bear.wmv" />
```

❑ **Pros**

    ❑   Assembly size is reduced.

    ❑   XAP size is reduced (faster page load time).

❑ **Cons**

    ❑   Media is not loaded at page load; instead, it loads asynchronously after the XAP is downloaded.

Use this scenario when you want to create a very lightweight, quick-loading application. The media will begin streaming from the server to the `MediaElement` control as soon as it is referenced.

Media in Other Assemblies

Media does not have to be housed in your main project's assembly for you to reference it. Media files can be compiled as resources into separate assemblies either created by you or a third party. When referencing images in assemblies other than the main project, you are required to use the `ProjectName;component/` syntax introduced a couple of sections back.

Referencing the Media in XAML

The following XAML references a video named *cloudTexture.wmv* defined in an assembly named `BackgroundVideoTextures.dll`:

```
<MediaElement
    Width="320"
    Height="240"
    HorizontalAlignment="Left"
    VerticalAlignment="Bottom"
    Margin="50,50,0,0"
    Source="BackgroundVideoTextures;component/cloudTexture.wmv" />
```

❑ **Pros**

    ❑ Assembly size is reduced.

    ❑ XAP size is (potentially) increased; as referenced assemblies grow in size, separates visuals from application logic.

❑ **Cons**

    ❑ Media cannot be renamed or removed if you are not in control of the resource assembly.

    ❑ Increases the number of projects you must maintain (if you are in control of the resource assembly).

Media on Other Domains

When you want to access audio or video on a remote server, you can use the fully qualified URI to access the image:

```
<MediaElement
    Width="320"
    Height="240"
    HorizontalAlignment="Left"
    VerticalAlignment="Bottom"
    Margin="50,50,0,0"
    Source="http://www.remotewebsite.com/publicvideo.wmv" />
```

However, Silverlight's security policies will prevent the remote file from loading if the remote site does not have a security manifest file in place that grants you access. For all the gory details on security policies, see Chapter 11.

❑ **Pros**

    ❑ Allows you to host media on remote, high-capacity servers.

❑ **Cons**

    ❑ You don't have control of the remote server.

    ❑ The integrity of the application is dependent on third-party server performance.

    ❑ Requires security policies.

Adding a `MediaElement` in Blend

While it's important to know how to define the `MediaElement` by hand in XAML, it's also quite likely that you'll use Blend to add, position, and size media. The `MediaElement` control is accessed by launching Blend's Asset Library and checking the "Show All" checkbox. Figure 10-2 shows the `MediaElement` control in the Asset Library.

Figure 10-2

Create an instance of the `MediaElement` by first selecting the `MediaElement` control from the Asset Library and then dragging a rectangle on the design surface to define its initial position and size. You can also double-click on the control's icon in the toolbar. With the `MediaElement` selected on the design surface, you can specify a Source file by either clicking the dropdown arrow or clicking the ellipsis next to the `Source` property. Clicking the dropdown arrow will reveal any media files already added to the project.

Clicking the ellipsis will launch a File Browser dialog. Once you've selected a supported media file, it will be added to your project with a Build Action of *Content* and a "Copy to Output Directory" setting of *Copy if Newer*. You can modify these settings in Visual Studio to meet your needs.

Figure 10-3 shows the `Source` property in Blend's Media category.

Figure 10-3

Sizing Video and Setting the Stretch Behavior

The `MediaElement` control does not have to be the same size as the source video. Just like any element in your `VisualTree`, you are in charge of its positioning and size. Just like the `Image` and `Path` control that we examined in Chapter 9, the `MediaElement` control has a `Stretch` property that dictates the way the underlying video is drawn as its container `MediaElement` control is sized and resized. The following values can be set on `MediaElement.Stretch`:

- ❏ `Fill` — The video is stretched both vertically and horizontally, filling the `MediaElement` control. With this setting, video can feel distorted.

- ❏ `None` — The underlying artwork does not stretch at all.

   In practice, the behavior when set to `None` *is the same as when set to* `Fill`.

- ❏ `Uniform (Default)` — The underlying video maintains its original aspect ratio while scaling to fit within the control. With this mode, the video is always drawn in its entirety.

- ❏ `UniformToFill` — The underlying video maintains its original aspect ratio; although unlike `Uniform`, it always scales to fit the longest axis. The resulting video is never distorted, although it may be clipped.

Figure 10-4 demonstrates how the various values of `Stretch` affect the final rendering of the `MediaElement`.

None   **Fill**   **Uniform**   **UniformToFill**

Figure 10-4

The `Stretch` property lets you control the behavior of the `MediaElement` when the source video is a different size from the `MediaElement` control. What if you always want to draw the `MediaElement` at the exact same size as the underlying video? Fortunately, the `MediaElement` control provides a couple of properties that expose the native height and width of the loaded file. You can use `NaturalVideoHeight` and `NaturalVideoWidth` to get the original height and width of the source video, then update the `Height` and `Width` properties (and any additional layout properties) of your `MediaElement` to display your video in the size it was intended to be viewed.

The following method handles the `MediaOpened` event for our sample video. Once this event has been raised, we have access to the `NaturalVideoHeight` and `NaturalVideoWidth` properties. This event handler uses these two properties to update the `Height` and `Width` properties of the `MediaElement` that raised the event:

```
<MediaElement
    Width="320"
    Height="240"
    x:Name="meSampleVideo"
    MediaOpened="SetNaturalDimensions"
    Source="/SampleVideo.wmv" />

private void SetNaturalDimensions(object sender, RoutedEventArgs e)
{
```

```
MediaElement media = sender as MediaElement;
media.Height = media.NaturalVideoHeight;
media.Width = media.NaturalVideoWidth;
...
```

Transforming Video

Just like any `FrameworkElement`-derived object, the `MediaElement` can be positioned, sized, transformed, and clipped in a myriad of ways to meet your layout needs. I'll show you a few examples here, just to get your creative juices flowing, but this is in no way an exhaustive demonstration of what can be achieved.

Let's start by rotating a `MediaElement`. On the Blend design surface, shown in Figure 10-5, I can simply mouse over one of the corners of my selected `MediaElement` until I get the rotate icon, then rotate to the desired angle.

Figure 10-5

Figure 10-6 shows the RenderTransform Editor in the Blend Properties panel that lets you adjust rotation (and all of the other transform properties) with numerical precision.

Figure 10-6

Behind the scenes, the `RenderTransform` property of the `MediaElement` has been set. When editing any of the transform properties in Blend, a `TransformGroup` containing each of the transform types is applied to the `RenderTransform` property. The following XAML shows what Blend has applied behind the scenes:

```
<MediaElement
    Width="320"
    Height="240"
    HorizontalAlignment="Left"
    VerticalAlignment="Stretch"
    x:Name="meSampleVideo"
    Source="/SampleVideo.wmv" RenderTransformOrigin="0.5,0.5" >
        <MediaElement.RenderTransform>
                <TransformGroup>
                    <ScaleTransform/>
                    <SkewTransform/>
                    <RotateTransform Angle="9.862"/>
                    <TranslateTransform/>
                </TransformGroup>
        </MediaElement.RenderTransform>
</MediaElement>
```

Rotating Video in 3D

After realizing that you can apply a RenderTransform to video, it's only natural to consider rotating the video in three-dimensional (3D) space. Fortunately, 3D transformations can be applied to `MediaElements` just as easily as they can be applied to other `UIElements`, by setting the `Projection` property. The following XAML "swings" the video back just like the Image sample shown in Chapter 9 (Figure 9-44):

```
<Image Source="Images/sampleImage.jpg" Stretch="Fill" Width="154"
    VerticalAlignment="Top" Height="116" HorizontalAlignment="Left"
    Margin="421,317,0,0">
    <Image.Projection>
        <PlaneProjection RotationX="0" RotationY="-60" CenterOfRotationX="0"
            CenterOfRotationY="0" CenterOfRotationZ="0"/>
    </Image.Projection>
</Image>
```

Figure 10-7 shows the resulting `MediaElement`.

Figure 10-7

With the ability to apply true 3D transformations to video, Silverlight is empowering creative and media professionals to create truly stunning interfaces that were previously only capable on desktop and gaming platforms. And it's easy to do, too!

Clipping Video

Again, just like any `FrameworkElement`-derived object, the `MediaElement` can be clipped using a clipping path. To clip the `MediaElement`, you set the `Clip` property using the same path data syntax you were introduced to in Chapter 9. Blend makes creating clipping paths easy. Simply define a path using the Blend drawing tools, and then size and position the path over the `MediaElement` you want to clip. Once you have the path where you want it, select both the `Path` and the `MediaElement` (hold down the [Shift] key to select multiple objects); then, from the main menu, select Object ➪ Path ➪ Make Clipping Path. Figure 10-8 shows both a `MediaElement` and `Path` selected on the design surface with the command exposed on the main menu.

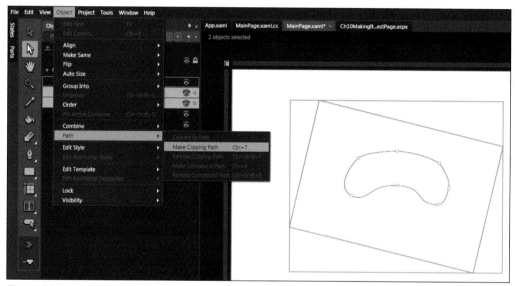

Figure 10-8

Notice that the `Path` is positioned directly over the `MediaElement` that I want to clip. You need to position the `Path` exactly where you want the visible area of the video to be before using the `Make Clipping Path` command. Blend normalizes the values of the `Path` data to be relative to the top-left corner of the element being clipped. With clipping masks, (0,0) represents the top-left corner of the object being clipped, not the top-left corner of the design surface. Figure 10-9 shows the `MediaElement` after it has been clipped.

Figure 10-9

In the following XAML, you can see that the `Clip` property accepts the same path data syntax that you should be vaguely familiar with now. Try hand-editing a few points to see how the clipping mask is affected:

```
<MediaElement
    Width="320"
    Height="240"
    x:Name="meSampleVideo"
    Source="/SampleVideo.wmv"
    RenderTransformOrigin="0.5,0.5"
    Clip="M89.626343,47.989033 C89.626343,47.989033 1.9381521,109.92341
54.496151,126.16163 C107.05415,142.39984 88.938194,90.738899 141.32475,105.99192
C193.71132,121.24493 205.15047,87.790825 202.15236,82.222031 C199.15424,76.653236
186.56322,39.257092 151.01031,33.257763 C115.45742,27.258436 89.626343,47.989033
89.626343,47.989033 z" >
</MediaElement>
```

Painting Elements with the `VideoBrush`

Using the `VideoBrush`, you can paint any element on your design surface with video. The classic example is text painted with video; however, you can paint any custom artwork with a video brush to create a variety of really interesting effects. You could, for example, have cloud-shaped paths, painted with subtly moving fluffy textures, floating across your page. Let's stick with convention, though, and paint some text with video!

The `VideoBrush` is not completely self-contained. Instead, it needs a reference to an existing `MediaElement` defined within your page. The following XAML defines a `MediaElement` that references a WMV file named *texture.wmv*:

```
<MediaElement
    Width="320"
    Height="240"
    x:Name="textureVideo"
    Opacity="0"
    IsMuted="True"
    IsHitTestVisible="False" />
```

I've highlighted several properties above that you'll likely want to set when defining a `MediaElement` for use by a `VideoBrush`. First, I've set `Opacity` to 0 so that the source video won't be seen except when used by the `VideoBrush`. Second, I've set `IsMuted` to `True`. I don't really want to hear any audio playing in the background if this video has an audio track. I just want the video. Last, I've set `IsHitTestVisible` to `False` so that the `MediaElement` doesn't erroneously capture my mouse clicks. These three properties together keep the `MediaElement` quiet and prevent it from making itself known in ways other than how I've intended.

The following XAML defines a `TextBlock` and sets its `Foreground` property with a `VideoBrush` that references the `MediaElement` just defined. Note that the name of the `MediaElement` is "textureVideo" (x:Name="textureVideo").

```
<TextBlock
    Text="VideoBrush"
    FontFamily="Arial"
    FontSize="72"
    FontWeight="Bold">
```

```
        <TextBlock.Foreground>
            <VideoBrush
                SourceName="textureVideo" Stretch="UniformToFill" />
        </TextBlock.Foreground>
    </TextBlock>
```

The VideoBrush is applied just as you apply a SolidColorBrush, LinearGradientBrush, or ImageBrush. I've highlighted the SourceName property above. The SourceName property accepts a string with the name of the source MediaElement, in this case, *textureVideo*. Because VideoBrush is derived from TileBrush (like ImageBrush), it has a Stretch property. Use the Stretch property to define how the video is applied as it fills the target element.

Simulating Video Reflections

It's likely you've seen Silverlight media samples that simulate reflected video. This technique is easy and fast to achieve once you know the basics. You can apply this same technique to any other element in your Page as well. To achieve the effect, we'll use:

- ❑ Two MediaElements, both using the same Source
- ❑ ScaleTransform
- ❑ OpacityMask

First, start by creating two MediaElements and set their Source property to the same video. Then, position them one on top of the each other as shown in Figure 10-10.

Figure 10-10

You can use whatever layout panel works best for you here — positioning absolutely using the Canvas control, or via the StackPanel with its Orientation set to Vertical. Next, we need to flip the bottom video using a ScaleTransform. The following XAML shows how to do this by setting the ScaleY property to -1 to "flip" the video on the Y-axis:

```
<MediaElement
    Height="320"
    Width="240"
```

```
        x:Name="videoReflection"
        Source="/SampleVideo.wmv" RenderTransformOrigin="0.5,0.5">
        <MediaElement.RenderTransform>
            <TransformGroup>
                <ScaleTransform ScaleY="-1"/>
            </TransformGroup>
        </MediaElement.RenderTransform>
    </MediaElement>
```

You can achieve this with a single button click in the Blend transform editor. Just select the second video and select the last tab in the transform editor. Figure 10-11 shows the "Flip Y axis" button that automatically applies the `ScaleTransform` for you.

Figure 10-11

The last step in simulating a reflection is applying a `LinearGradientBrush` as an `OpacityMask` to the second video. The following XAML defines a vertical `LinearGradientBrush` that starts at 50 percent opacity (4C in Hexadecimal) and fades to 0 percent opacity (00 in Hexadecimal):

```
<MediaElement
    Height="320"
    Width="240"
    x:Name="videoReflection"
    Source="/SampleVideo.wmv" RenderTransformOrigin="0.5,0.5">
    <MediaElement.RenderTransform>
        <TransformGroup>
            <ScaleTransform ScaleY="-1"/>
        </TransformGroup>
    </MediaElement.RenderTransform>
    <MediaElement.OpacityMask>
        <LinearGradientBrush EndPoint="0.5,1" StartPoint="0.5,0">
            <GradientStop Color="#00FFFFFF"/>
            <GradientStop Color="#4CFFFFFF" Offset="1"/>
        </LinearGradientBrush>
    </MediaElement.OpacityMask>
</MediaElement>
```

Note that the order of the stops feels reversed, with the first stop representing 0 percent opacity and the second stop representing 30 percent opacity. This is because the `OpacityMask` is applied to the `MediaElement` before it is flipped.

So, that's all there is to it! Create two videos. Position them. Flip the second. Apply an `OpacityMask`. Easy, easy! Now you can spend time adjusting the `OpacityMask` until you achieve the final effect you're after. Try wrapping the two `MediaElement`s with a container panel (such as `Grid`) and apply a 3D transform — reflected, 3D-rotated video in just a few steps!

Enabling GPU Hardware Acceleration

When rendering high-definition video (or any video for that matter), you may want to enable hardware acceleration to offload the processing to your GPU. You first have to enable this at the plug-in level. The following ASPX enables this on the ASP Silverlight component:

```
<asp:Silverlight ID="Silverlight1"
    EnableGPUAcceleration="true"
    EnableCacheVisualization="true"
    runat="server" Source="~/ClientBin/Ch10MakingItRicherWithMedia.xap"
    MinimumVersion="3.0.40307.0"
    Width="100%" Height="100%" />
```

You can also set these parameters using the `<param />` tag when using an `<object />` instead of the Silverlight ASP control:

```
<object data="data:application/x-silverlight-2,"
    type="application/x-silverlight-2" width="100%" height="100%">
    <param name="source" value="ClientBin/Ch10MakingItRicherWithMedia.xap"/>
    <param name="EnableGPUAcceleration" value="true" />
    <param name="EnableCacheVisualization" value="true" />
    <param name="background" value="white" />
    <param name="minRuntimeVersion" value="3.0.40307.0" />
</object>
```

The first parameter, `EnableGPUAcceleration`, enables the option of GPU acceleration at the plug-in level. Note that at this point no elements in the player will actually be GPU-accelerated. The second parameter, `EnableCacheVisualization`, will apply a red overlay to all elements *not* GPU-accelerated. If you run your project at this point, everything should be red because you haven't explicitly turned on acceleration for any objects. `EnableCacheVisualization` is a great tool for understanding what is actually being offloaded to the GPU.

Now that you've enabled GPU acceleration at the plug-in level, you have to turn on GPU acceleration for specific elements in your application. The following XAML enables GPU acceleration by setting the `CacheMode` property to `BitmapCache` on a `MediaElement`:

```
<MediaElement x:Name="sampleVideo"
    Source="media/sampleVideo.m4v"
    CacheMode="BitmapCache"
    />
```

If you test now, you should see that your video is no longer red (meaning that the GPU is rendering it). When you're satisfied with your caching settings, either delete the `EnableCacheVisualization` parameter or set its value to `false`.

Audio Settings

The Blend interface exposes some of the common properties you might want to set when initializing your media. Three of the properties seen in Figure 10-3 deal with audio: `Balance`, `IsMuted`, and `Volume`. These properties can be set via XAML, via the Blend property panel, or at run time via code.

❑ Balance — The `Balance` property accepts a value between –1 and 1, where –1 represents the left channel of audio, and 1 represents the right channel. By default, this value is centered with a value of 0.

- ❏   `IsMuted` — Toggle the value of this property to turn the volume of the `MediaElement` on or off, while preserving the value of the `Volume` property.

- ❏   `Volume` — The `Volume` property accepts a value between 0 and 1, where 0 represents no volume, and 1 represents full volume.

Buffering

By default, the `MediaElement` will buffer 5 seconds of the target source file before playback starts. You can adjust this value by setting the `BufferingTime` property. This property is of type `TimeSpan` and accepts a value in the following format:

```
[days.]hours:minutes:seconds[fractionalSeconds]
```

Both `days` and `fractionalSeconds` are optional. The following XAML instructs the `MediaElement` to buffer 1 minute and 30.5 seconds of video:

```
<MediaElement
    Width="320"
    Height="240"
    BufferingTime="00:01:30.5"
Source="/media/stockfootage/Bear.wmv" />
```

As the buffer is loaded, the `BufferingProgress` property of the `MediaElement` is updated. The value of this property, like other properties representing a percentage, is 0 to 1. When this value reaches 1, it means that 100 percent of the media specified by the `BufferingTime` has been downloaded, not 100 percent of the media itself. Every time the `BufferingProgress` value is updated by 0.05 or more, the `MediaElement` raises the `BufferingProgressChanged` event. The following XAML demonstrates how to specify an event handler for the `BufferingProgressChanged` event:

```
<MediaElement
    x:Name="meSampleVideo"
    BufferingProgressChanged="meSampleVideo_BufferingProgressChanged"
    Width="320"
    Height="240"
    BufferingTime="00:01:30.5"
Source="/media/stockfootage/Bear.wmv" />
```

The following code represents the `meSampleVideo_BufferingProgressChanged` event handler, referenced by the previous XAML. When called, this method sets the `Text` property of the `TextBlock` named `tbBufferProgress` with a meaningful message, based on the value of the `MediaElement`'s `BufferingProgress` value:

```
private void meSampleVideo_BufferingProgressChanged(object sender, RoutedEventArgs e)
{
    tbDownloadProgress.Text = (meSampleVideo.BufferingProgress *
                        100).ToString() + "% Buffered";
}
```

Detecting Download Progress

Just as you can detect the amount of video that has been buffered, you can detect the amount of the total video that has been downloaded. The MediaElement's DownloadProgress property represents the percentage of video that has been downloaded in the value range of 0 to 1. As the value of this property increases by 0.05, the DownloadProgressChanged event is raised by the MediaElement. The following XAML demonstrates how to specify an event handler for the DownloadProgressChanged event:

```
<MediaElement
    x:Name="meSampleVideo"
    DownloadProgressChanged="meSampleVideo_DownloadProgressChanged"
    Width="320"
    Height="240"
    BufferingTime="00:01:30.5"
Source="/media/stockfootage/Bear.wmv" />
```

The following code represents the meSampleVideo_DownloadProgressChanged event handler, referenced by the previous XAML. When called, this method sets the Text property of the TextBlock named tbDownloadProgress with a download status message based on the MediaElement's DownloadProgress property:

```
private void meSampleVideo_DownloadProgressChanged(object sender, RoutedEventArgs e)
{
        tbBufferProgress.Text = (meSampleVideo.DownloadProgress *
                                100).ToString() + "% Downloaded";
}
```

Notice that I'm multiplying the DownloadProgress value by 100 to obtain a percentage-based value.

Detecting Playback Quality

The MediaElement control exposes two properties, DroppedFramesPerSecond and RenderedFramesPerSecond, that you can use to detect the video quality being rendered at any point in time. If the framerate has dropped to a really low number, or the number of frames being dropped per second is close to the framerate of your video, you could choose to change the Source of the MediaElement to a stream encoded at a lower bitrate.

Controlling Playback

The MediaElement exposes several common methods that you can use to control the playback of the loaded media.

Pause()

When called, the Pause method pauses playback at the current position. Playback can be resumed from the Pause position by calling the Play method. If Pause is called but not available, the call will simply be ignored. The MediaElement exposes a Boolean CanPause property that you can access to determine whether or not pausing is available for the currently loaded media. Even though the Pause method will be ignored when CanPause is false, you can take advantage of this property to update your user interface, potentially disabling or hiding your pause button.

The following code represents the Click event handler for a Button named btnPause:

```
private void btnPause_Click(object sender, RoutedEventArgs e)
{
    if (meSampleVideo.CanPause)
        meSampleVideo.Pause();
}
```

Play()

When the Play method is called, the media is either started (if media was loaded with AutoPlay set to false) or playback resumes from the current position (if paused). If the media is already playing, calling this method has no effect. The following code represents the Click event handler for a Button named btnPlay:

```
private void btnPlay_Click(object sender, RoutedEventArgs e)
{
    meSampleVideo.Play();
}
```

Stop()

When called, the Stop method stops playback and resets the Position property to 00:00:00. If the media was paused when Stop was called, the Position is simply reset. If playback was already stopped, the method is ignored. The following event handler stops playback of MediaElement named meSampleVideo:

```
private void btnStop_Click(object sender, RoutedEventArgs e)
{
    meSampleVideo.Stop();
}
```

SetSource()

Generally, you will set the value of the MediaElement's Source property directly, specifying a valid URI. However, if you already have access to a media file via a Stream or MediaSourceStream (potentially obtained asynchronously using the WebClient), you can use the SetSource method to change the media stream. The following code hints at how this might be achieved:

```
private void btnLoadStream_Click(object sender, RoutedEventArgs e)
{
    // Load media using a stream obtained via WebClient
    // meSampleVideo.SetSource(WebClient stream here);
}
```

Seeking

The MediaElement does not expose a method for seeking to a particular location within the loaded media. You can, however, set the value of the Position property, which achieves the desired result. Just like pausing, seeking is not available when the media source is a live stream. You can detect whether or not seeking is available for the loaded media by accessing the CanSeek property.

The following XAML specifies an event handler for the `MediaElement`'s `MediaOpened` event:

```
<MediaElement
    Width="320"
    Height="240"
    x:Name="meSampleVideo"
    MediaOpened="UpdateScrubberVisibility"
    Source="/SampleVideo.wmv" />
```

The following code handles the `MediaOpened` event and toggles the visibility of a `Slider` named *Scrubber* based on the value of the `MediaElement`'s `CanSeek` property:

```
private void UpdateScrubberVisibility(object sender, RoutedEventArgs e)
{
    MediaElement media = sender as MediaElement;

    if (media.CanSeek)
    {
        Scrubber.Visibility = Visibility.Visible;
    }
    else
    {
        Scrubber.Visibility = Visibility.Collapsed;
    }
}
```

Responding to Video Markers

Windows Media files can be encoded with "Markers" throughout their timelines that can represent either text or some type of script at a specified point on the timeline. You can use these markers to create a higher level of interactivity with the media currently playing. For example, consider a recorded presentation that includes a set of coordinating slides. As the video plays, you would like to change the active slide at different points in the video to coincide with the appropriate narration. You can achieve this feat by encoding your video with markers at each point along the timeline where you want the slide to change. The section "Encoding Media with Expression Encoder" later in this chapter describes how to add markers to video.

The Markers Property

When media is loaded via the `MediaElement` control, the `MediaElement.Markers` property is cleared and then loaded with any markers defined in the currently loaded media. This property is available once the `MediaOpened` event is raised.

The `Markers` property is of type `TimelineMarkerCollection`, a collection of `TimelineMarker` objects. Each timeline marker has a `Text`, `Time`, and `Type` property. Generally, with video encoded for Silverlight applications, the value of the `Type` property will be `"Name"`, with the value of `Text` representing the *Name* of the particular marker. The `Time` property is of type `TimeSpan` and represents the location along the media's timeline where the marker occurs.

Using the `Markers` collection, you can retrieve all of the names of each marker for the currently loaded video and create an interface that lets you jump directly to a particular scene. The following code loops through all of the markers for a MediaElement that has just been opened and writes the value of each marker's Text property to the debug window:

```
private void TraceMarkers(object sender, RoutedEventArgs e)
{
    MediaElement mediaElementWithMarkers = sender as MediaElement;
    foreach (TimelineMarker marker in mediaElementWithMarkers.Markers)
    {
        Debug.WriteLine("Marker Found: " + marker.Text);
        Debug.WriteLine("              > " + marker.Time.ToString());
    }
}
```

You can also use the Time property of a particular marker to seek to a position in the loaded media. The following code jumps to the position of the last marker in the Markers collection:

```
private void SeekLastMarker(MediaElement mediaElement)
{
    // Get Index of Last Marker
    int lastMarkerIndex = mediaElement.Markers.Count - 1;

    // Seek to Position of Last Marker
    mediaElement.Position = mediaElement.Markers[lastMarkerIndex].Time;
}
```

Remember, the MediaElement does not contain a Seek() method; instead, you simply set the value of the Position property directly.

The MarkerReached Event

The Markers property gives you all of the information you need to jump directly to a predefined point in your media. However, if you want to enable the synchronized video + slideshow scenario described at the beginning of this section, you'll need to respond to the MarkerReached event of the MediaElement. The MarkerReached event is raised any time a marker is reached during playback. The following XAML demonstrates how to assign an event handler to the MarkerReached event:

```
<MediaElement
    Width="320"
    Height="240"
    x:Name="meSampleVideo"
    MarkerReached="OnMarkerReached"
    Source="/SampleVideo.wmv" />
```

Similar to the TraceMarkers method we saw earlier, the following OnMarkerReached method displays the Text and Time of the marker that was just reached:

```
private void OnMarkerReached(object sender, TimelineMarkerRoutedEventArgs e)
{
    Debug.WriteLine("Marker Reached: " + e.Marker.Text);
    Debug.WriteLine("               > " + e.Marker.Time.ToString());
}
```

The `TimelineMarkerRoutedEventArgs` object includes a `Marker` property that you use to get information about the marker that has just been reached. The previous simple event handler just writes the `Text` and `Time` to the Debug window. A more realistic sample might update an image and modify the text of a label. The following example does just that:

```
private void OnMarkerReached(object sender, TimelineMarkerRoutedEventArgs e)
{
    // Set Slide Title
    txtSlideTitle.Text = e.Marker.Text;

    // Update Slide Image
    imgSlide.Source = new BitmapImage(new Uri("images\\"
                    + e.Marker.Text
                    + ".png", UriKind.Relative));
}
```

In the previous example, we create a new `BitmapImage` (`System.Windows.Media.Imaging` namespace), assuming that there is a PNG image available that matches the string contained within the `Marker.Text` property. In practice, you could have some type of data structure that matches the marker's text or offset with the source video file and provides any number of fields you need to support your UI.

Windows Media files support multiple streams, each of which can have their own set of markers. The `MediaElement.Markers` property only contains the markers embedded in the main file header, not the additional streams. However, the `MediaElement` will still raise the `MarkerReached` event as these additional markers are reached.

Handling Failed Media

We'd all like to think that nothing we create will ever fail, but you and I both know that's just not reality. When you're setting the source file of the `MediaElement` to a URL on a remote web site, you can only hope that it will always be there. If you're not in control of the server, you can never truly count on its existence, or the availability of the server, for that matter. Fortunately, the `MediaElement` control will let us know when a referenced media file doesn't load, isn't supported, or "errors out" during playback.

The following XAML demonstrates how to assign an event handler to the `MediaFailed` event:

```
<MediaElement
    Width="320"
    Height="240"
    MediaFailed="OnMediaFailed"
    Source="/SampleVideo.wmv" />
```

When this unfortunate event occurs, you can either try to load another file or present the user with some type of meaningful message or experience. The following code updates a `TextBlock` and displays an error image:

```
private void OnMediaFailed(object sender, RoutedEventArgs e)
{
```

```
// Set Slide Title
txtSlideTitle.Text = "An error occurred while trying to load the
                     selected video.";

// Update Slide Image
imgSlide.Source = new BitmapImage(new Uri("images\\errorSlide.png",
                                     UriKind.Relative));
}
```

Responding to State Changes

The MediaElement has a CurrentState property that can be accessed at any point during the life of the control to determine its state. The CurrentState property is of type MediaElementState, an enum type with the following values:

❑   Closed

❑   Opening

❑   Individualizing

❑   AcquiringLicense

❑   Buffering

❑   Playing

❑   Paused

❑   Stopped

The MediaElement also raises a CurrentStateChanged event that you can handle and respond to. The following XAML demonstrates how to assign an event handler to this event:

```
<MediaElement
    Width="320"
    Height="240"
    CurrentStateChanged="OnCurrentStateChanged"
    Source="/SampleVideo.wmv" />
```

The following code handles this event and writes the current state of the MediaElement to the debug window:

```
private void OnCurrentStateChanged(object sender, RoutedEventArgs e)
{
    MediaElement media = sender as MediaElement;
    Debug.WriteLine("Current State: " + media.CurrentState);
}
```

You can use your knowledge of the current state of the MediaElement to update playback controls in your application. For example, if the current state changes to *Playing*, you probably want to show a Pause button and vice versa.

Media Playlists

In certain scenarios, playing a single media file is not enough. Consider an online news program that consists of several news segments interspersed with commercials. Or consider on online radio program that consists of a number of audio tracks, framed at the beginning and the end with commentary. In both of these scenarios, a media playlist is desirable.

Silverlight supports both Server Side Playlist (SSPL) and Advanced Stream Redirector (ASX) playlist files to enable the scenarios described previously.

Server-Side Playlist Files

SSPL files are XML-based and use the .wsx file extension. These files are used by a Microsoft Media Server of some flavor (Windows Server 2003, Windows Server 2008, Windows Web Server 2008, etc.). Microsoft has a server comparison guide to help illustrate the differences between their different server offerings at the following URL: `www.microsoft.com/windows/windowsmedia/forpros/server/version.aspx`.

You'll see that the Standard Edition of Windows Server 2003 does not support Advanced Fast Start or Advanced Fast Forward/Rewind, whereas the Enterprise and DataCenter versions of those servers do. There are several other features such as this that you don't get with the non-Enterprise version of the servers.

Why Use a Media Server and SSPL

Below are some common advantages offered by the Media Server technologies. Access the previously referenced web site to get a full understanding of the capabilities offered by Microsoft Media Servers.

❑ **Dynamic Generation** — SSPL files can be created either statically or, more attractively, dynamically. This means that you can serve up a dynamic playlist based on a user's authentication level or the time of day the playlist is being requested. You can even edit the playlist after it has been accessed by a client, giving you an extreme level of control over the served-up content.

❑ **Loading/Startup Experience** — When broadcasting a live event, it's common for users to sign in before the event has started. To provide a better experience for the early birds, you can specify a media file to loop prior to the broadcast.

❑ **Fine-Grained Control** — The SSPL supports various configuration options that give you a high level of control over each media file in your playlist. For example, you can define alternative video streams or files should another video fail. You can also display a subclip of a video instead of the entire video, by setting the `clipBegin` and `clipEnd` properties.

Creating and Consuming a WSX File

The .wsx file is an XML-based file that can be easily defined by hand. Once defined and saved, the file must be published using a Windows Media Server. When a .wsx file is published, a *publishing point* will be defined. It is this publishing point that will be consumed by the `MediaElement` control, just like a standard media file:

```
myCustomPlaylist.wsx => publish => mms://MyMediaServer:8081/myCustomPlaylist
```

The following shows a simple WSX file definition:

```
<?wsx version="1.0"?>
<smil>
  <seq id="debateSeq">
    <media id="introVideo" src="intro.wmv" />
    <media id="debate" src="debate.wmv" />
    <media id="summaryVideo" src="summary.wmv" />
  <seq>
</smil>
```

Consuming the WSX is just as easy as consuming a single media file. You simply set the `Source` property of `MediaElement` to the URI of your published playlist:

```
<MediaElement
    Width="320"
    Height="240"
    HorizontalAlignment="Left"
    VerticalAlignment="Bottom"
    Margin="50,50,0,0"
    Source="mms://MyMediaServer:8081/myCustomPlaylist" />
```

The SSPL currently supports a number of features that Silverlight *does not* support. To see the latest list of Silverlight-supported attributes visit the Audio and Video ⇨ Server-Side Playlists section of the Silverlight Developer Center (`http://msdn.microsoft.com/en-us/library/cc645037(VS.95).aspx`).

Advanced Stream Redirector (ASX) Files

In addition to SSPL files, Silverlight supports ASX-based playlist files. Like WSX files, ASX files are XML-based and can be easily defined by hand or programmatically on the server. Unlike WSX files, ASX files can reside on a standard Web Server and do not have to be published via Windows Media Server. This capability may make ASX files more attractive to you when the power (and extra overhead) of Windows Media Server is too much for your needs. The following URL covers in depth all aspects of the ASX file format: `http://msdn.microsoft.com/en-us/library/ms925291.aspx`.

Key Features of ASX

The following are a few key features of the ASX playlist that may help you decide between SSPL and ASX:

❑ **Server Independent** — ASX files do not require a Windows Media Server. They are stand-alone files that can reside loosely on a server or as part of your Silverlight project.

❑ **Dynamic Generation** — ASX files can be created either statically or, more attractively, dynamically. This means you can serve up a dynamic playlist based on a user's authentication level or the time of day the playlist is being requested. You could achieve this dynamic approach by creating an ASPX page that returns ASX content. Set the `Source` property of your `MediaElement` to the ASPX page's path.

❑ **Fine-Grained Control** — The ASX file format offers various configuration options for each entry in the playlist. For example, the `STARTMARKER` attribute lets you specify the start time of a particular entry. Most of these features of ASX are not currently supported by Silverlight 3, although I wanted to call this ASX feature out should they be implemented at some point in the future.

Creating and Consuming an ASX File

A simple ASX file contains a single root ASX element and a list of child Entry elements. Each Entry represents an item in the playlist. The following is a simple example that defines a playlist with a single item:

```
<ASX version = "3.0">
<!--A simple playlist with entries to be played in sequence.-->
    <Title>Playlist Title</Title>
    <Entry>
        <Title>Sample Show Title</Title>
        <Author>ABC Video</Author>
        <Copyright>(c) 2008 ABC Video</Copyright>
        <Ref href="Bear.wmv" />
    </Entry>
</ASX>
```

Reference the ASX playlist just as you would a single media element:

```
<MediaElement
    Width="320"
    Height="240"
    HorizontalAlignment="Left"
    VerticalAlignment="Bottom"
    Margin="50,50,0,0"
    Source="MyCustomPlaylist.asx" />
```

Not all of the capabilities of the ASX format are supported by Silverlight 3. The following table identifies those features and describes the behavior of the player when unsupported features are encountered:

ASX Feature	Description
PreviewMode attribute	This attribute is found on the root ASX object. It is not supported and will raise a MediaError with AG_E_ASX_UNSUPPORTED_ATTRIBUTE.
BannerBar attribute	This attribute is found on the root ASX object. It is not supported and will raise a MediaError with AG_E_ASX_UNSUPPORTED_ATTRIBUTE.
SkipIfRef	This attribute is found on the root ENTRY object. It is not supported and will raise a MediaError with AG_E_ASX_UNSUPPORTED_ATTRIBUTE.
PARAM element	This is not supported and will raise a MediaError with AG_E_ASX_UNSUPPORTED_ELEMENT.
REPEAT element	This is not supported and will raise a MediaError with AG_E_ASX_UNSUPPORTED_ELEMENT.
EVENT element	This is not supported and will raise a MediaError with AG_E_ASX_UNSUPPORTED_ELEMENT.

ASX Feature	Description
STARTMARKER element	This is not supported and will raise a MediaError with AG_E_ASX_UNSUPPORTED_ELEMENT.
ENDMARKER element	This is not supported and will raise a MediaError with AG_E_ASX_UNSUPPORTED_ELEMENT.
Invalid content	If a valid ASX tag has content that is not accepted (e.g., a MOREINFO tag contains a REF tag), a MediaFailed error is raised.
Fallback URLs	If an ENTRY tag has multiple REF children, only the first one is read. Unlike WMP, Silverlight will not attempt to open additional REF URLs in case the first one fails, and a MediaFailed error is raised.

Encoding Media with Expression Encoder

Now that you know how to do practically everything you can with the MediaElement, let's take a look at how to prepare media for use by the MediaElement. We'll use Microsoft Expression Encoder 2, available as a trial download from www.microsoft.com/expression (Note: Be sure to download and install Expression Encoder Service Pack 1 or later for H.264 and ACC support — http://www.microsoft.com/downloads/details.aspx?FamilyId=A29BE9F9-29E1-4E70-BF67-02D87D3E556E&displaylang=en). Expression Encoder is designed with Silverlight exporting in mind. It lets you quickly trim videos, add markers, and render to a format natively supported by Silverlight. It even includes publishing templates that generate Silverlight-based layouts (that include MediaElements, of course) to quickly present your media on the Web.

In this walk-through, I'll step you through a common encoding scenario to get you up-and-running quickly; I won't cover Expression Encoder in great detail. If you really need to dig deep, the Expression Encoder Help should do the trick. So, here's a quick glance at what we'll cover:

❑   Importing a media file

❑   Trimming the media

❑   Adding markers

❑   Setting encoder settings

❑   Defining metadata

❑   Publishing the video

Let's get started. Figure 10-12 shows Expression Encoder right after it's been launched.

The default workspace is mostly disabled at startup. To get going, click on the Import button in the lower-left corner of the screen (see Figure 10-13), or select File ➪ Import from the main menu.

Clicking Import will launch the File Browser dialog and let you select a file of any of the supported media types, a fairly exhaustive list that should meet most of your needs (see Figure 10-14).

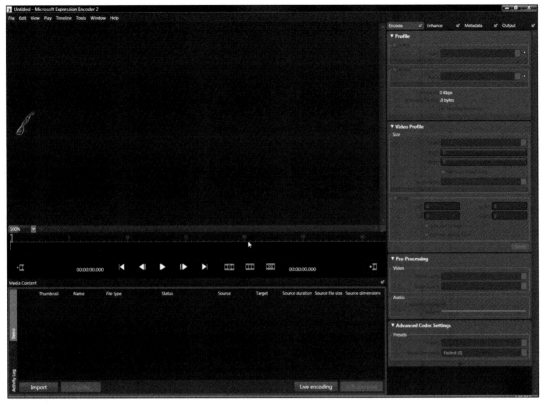

Figure 10-12

Figure 10-13

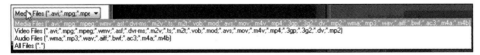

Figure 10-14

Once you've selected a media file, it will be added to the Media Content panel, shown in Figure 10-15. I selected the file Bear.wmv from the Windows Vista Videos folder as an example.

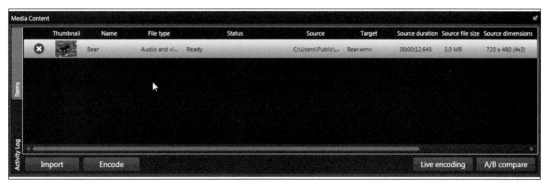

Figure 10-15

Once you've imported the file, Expression Encoder detects some features of the file, such as File type, duration, file size, and dimensions. These are displayed inline as a quick reference for you. You can import any number of media files by clicking on the Import button again. Just select the media element in the Content panel's list to make it the active element on the edit surface, as seen in Figure 10-16.

Figure 10-16

Timeline Controls

The timeline and transport controls appear directly beneath a video once it is selected. The interface is broken into six key regions, highlighted in Figure 10-16:

❏   Timeline

❏   Timeline Viewing controls

❏   Playback controls

❏   Editing buttons

❏   "Add leader" button

❏   "Add trailer" button

Timeline

The Timeline is where you will trim the beginning and ending of your video, cut segments from your video, and add media markers. You navigate the Timeline by dragging the "playhead" (orange box icon) to a desired position. As you drag (or *scrub*, as it's also known), the position indicator and video preview will update (see Figure 10-17).

Figure 10-17

Trimming Video

Mouse over the beginning or ending of the timeline until your cursor changes, and you'll see the icons shown in Figure 10-18. Once you see the icon, press and drag to the right or left to trim the beginning or ending of the video.

Figure 10-18

Cutting Video/Editing along the Timeline

You can cut segments from the middle of the timeline by adding an *edit*. Do this by positioning the scrubber at the location where you want to make the edit, then click on the "Add an edit at the play-head" button, as shown in Figure 10-19.

Once you've added an edit, you can trim the beginning or ending of the new segment just like you trimmed the entire timeline (see Figure 10-20).

Figure 10-19

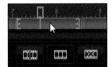

Figure 10-20

The third of the editing buttons lets you remove the segment currently beneath the playhead. This lets you cut out an entire segment of video. If you want to control your edits with an extra level of precision, select the Enhance tab on the right of the screen (Window ➪ Enhance if it's not available). Here, as shown in Figure 10-21, you will see the "Start Time" and "End Time" for all of the edits you have added.

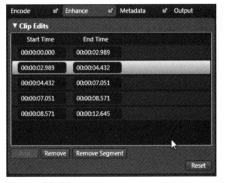

Figure 10-21

Adding Markers

Markers can be added to the Timeline by right-clicking at the location of the playhead and selecting "Add Marker," or by positioning the playhead and pressing [Ctrl]+M on your keyboard. Once you've added a marker, it appears on the Timeline as a white rectangle (see Figure 10-22).

Figure 10-22

Once you've added markers on the Timeline, you can edit their properties using the Markers panel, available on the Metadata tab (Window ➪ Metadata). Figure 10-23 shows the Markers tab open with a single marker added.

Figure 10-23

You can hand-tweak the time, provide a `Value`, specify whether or not to encode this as a keyframe, and specify whether or not to generate a thumbnail for this particular marker. If you click on the Thumbnail checkbox, a .jpg image will be created from the video at the position of the marker. This is useful if you want to create a DVD-style navigation that displays images for different jump points in your media.

Timeline Viewing Controls

The Timeline Viewing controls are directly beneath the start of the Timeline, on the left-hand side of the screen. The first item in this set is a toggle button that lets you toggle the visibility of segments in the video that have been cut. In Figure 10-24, this feature is turned on, revealing a section in red that has been cut. The second button toggles between the current zoom level (set by the zoom slider at the end of this set) and a zoom level that shows the Timeline in its entirety. Use the zoom slider to set the zoom factor, sliding it to the right to zoom in for more precise editing.

Figure 10-24

Playback Controls

The playback controls are positioned right in the middle of the Timeline area, making it easy to navigate your timeline quickly. The leftmost and rightmost buttons, commonly used to navigate to the previous and next track on a media player, are here used to navigate from edit point to edit point or marker to marker. The next set of buttons, second from the left and second from the right, let you step through your video frame-by-frame. The middle button lets you toggle between Play and Pause. If you ever forget the meaning of practically any element in the interface, just hover for a few moments to see the control's tooltip (see Figure 10-25).

Figure 10-25

Editing Buttons

See the previous section, "Cutting Video/Editing along the Timeline."

Add Leader/Add Trailer Buttons

Expression Encoder lets you quickly set an opening (*leader*) and closing (*trailer*) video to your currently selected media by clicking on either the "Add Leader" or "Add Trailer" button. This is useful if you have a standard branding that you want to apply to the beginning, end, or both, of all of the videos you produce.

You cannot edit or trim either the leader or trailer. You'll have to edit those separately, encode them, and then set them as a leader or trailer if you need to perform any editing on those videos.

Editing Metadata

Select the Metadata tab (Window ⇨ Metadata) to edit properties such as `Title`, `Author`, `Copyright`, `Rating`, and the like that will be included with your encoded media file. If the encoded file is opened with Windows Media Player, you will see this information displayed. The metadata properties listed by default are only the most commonly used fields. Click the down arrow beneath the Description field to see all of the supported fields. You can access this metadata in Silverlight using the `MediaElement` `.Attributes` property (see Figure 10-26).

Figure 10-26

Encoding Settings

Select the Encode tab (Window ⇨ Encode) to customize the way your video and audio will be encoded. At the beginning of this chapter, we looked at a list of codecs supported by Silverlight. Now, we actually encounter them. Figure 10-27 shows the Profile panel of the Encode tab. The first two sections let you specify a video profile and an audio profile by selecting from a dropdown list of options. You can think of these as presets, each of which sets a codec, bitrate, height, width, and several other properties.

Figure 10-27

If you click the down arrow beneath the Video combobox, you'll see all of the properties each item in the combobox is setting. Figure 10-28 shows all of the sections contained within the Profile panel expanded, revealing all available property settings. Try changing your combobox selection to see how property settings are updated.

Figure 10-28

If you want to get a feeling for how your video will look with your current encoding settings, click on the "A/B compare" button in the lower-right corner of the Media Content area, as shown in Figure 10-29.

Figure 10-29

When you select "A/B compare," the video preview area goes into a split mode, with the original video on the left and a preview of the encoding video on the right. You first have to click on the "Generate preview" link positioned in the right-hand area of the video. When the preview area goes blank, don't worry — the preview is being rendered. You will see a progress bar in the Media Content List for the currently selected item. Once the preview has been rendered, you should see a preview similar to the one in Figure 10-30.

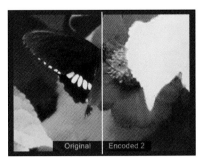

Figure 10-30

Exit the Preview mode by clicking on the same A/B button you pressed to enter this mode. Its label has changed to "Exit A/B compare."

Additional Encoding Features

The Encode tab also includes three other panels: Video Profile, Pre-Processing, and Advanced Codec Settings. Use the Video Profile panel to resize and crop your video prior to encoding it. The Pre-Processing panel includes options for de-interlacing your video, adjusting the resize quality, and normalizing the level of you audio. The Advanced Codec Settings panel provides several options that let you tweak the way the video is processed when it is being encoded. For more information about all of these features, consult the Expression Media Help.

Adding a Video Overlay

Expression Media lets you quickly add an overlay image to your encoded video. This could be useful if you want to watermark your video with a transparent logo, or even if you wanted to simulate a television-style footer. You can supply either a static overlay, in the form of an image, or a motion overlay, in the form of another video file or even XAML!

To add an overlay, select the Enhance tab (Window ➪ Enhance), and then scroll down to the Overlay panel, as shown in Figure 10-31.

Figure 10-31

Click on the ellipsis button next to File to browse for an overlay file. For still image overlays, you can use a JPG, BMP, PNG, or GIF file. I recommend using a 32-bit PNG file, as it supports a full alpha channel (meaning real transparency). If you want to use a video overlay, you can select any of the many video types that Expression supports for encoding. Expression also supports QuickTime files with full alpha channels, giving you the ability to add animated overlays full alpha-channel transparency (see Figure 10-32).

As mentioned earlier, you can also provide XAML-based overlays. This puts the full power of the Silverlight rendering and animation engine at your disposal for creating video overlays.

You'll need to use a `Canvas`*-based layout when creating your overlay.*

Figure 10-32

Output Settings

The Output tab (Window ⇨ Output) lets you customize thumbnail encoding options (file type, image dimensions, etc.) and, most importantly, lets you specify where you want to render your media and whether or not you want to publish using a Silverlight template. Figure 10-33 shows the Job Output panel. The first property listed is Template. By default (None) is selected. If you wish to publish your video with a Silverlight media player template, select an item from the dropdown list. As you change your selection, the preview below the dropdown will change. Selecting one of these presets does not affect your render settings; it just adds to the number of files that are generated and copied to your destination folder. With "None" selected, only the .wmv or .wma is generated. With a template, the .wmv or .wma *plus* several supporting files are generated.

Figure 10-33

Encoding Media

Once you've finished customizing the Output Settings, Encoding Options, and optional overlay, you're ready to encode. So, click on the large Encode button in the lower left-hand corner of the screen, and watch the progress bar work its way to 100 percent. That's it! (See Figure 10-34.)

Figure 10-34

Using the Silverlight Streaming Service

Microsoft offers a free media hosting service at `http://silverlight.live.com` known as *Microsoft Silverlight Streaming by Windows Live*. Once you've created an account, you have 10 GB of storage at your disposal for publishing Silverlight applications. That 10 GB may sound great, but you don't actually get a 10-GB free-for-all. Your video files must be smaller than 105 MB in size. That's approximately 10 minutes of video encoded at a bitrate of 1.4 Mbps. Once you've created your account and logged in, you'll see a menu similar to the one shown in Figure 10-35.

Figure 10-35

The first thing you want to do is click "Manage Applications." On the next screen, you'll click "Upload an application," as shown in Figure 10-36.

Figure 10-36

After clicking "Upload an application," you'll be prompted to give your new application a name. Enter a name, and then click Create (see Figure 10-37).

Application Name

Sample Silverlight Application

Create

Figure 10-37

Once you've named your application, you'll be prompted to upload a zipped version of your published app. I browsed to my bin/Release folder, selected All files, then right-clicked and chose Send To ⇨ Compressed (Zipped) Folder. With my project zipped, I then browsed to the zip using the Browse dialog in the Web page (see Figure 10-38).

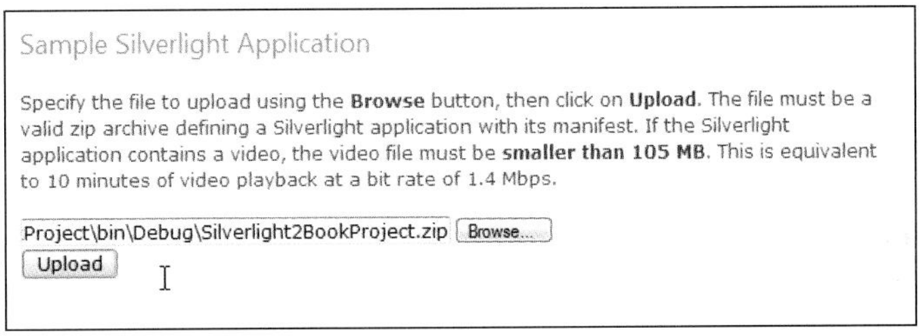

Sample Silverlight Application

Specify the file to upload using the **Browse** button, then click on **Upload**. The file must be a valid zip archive defining a Silverlight application with its manifest. If the Silverlight application contains a video, the video file must be **smaller than 105 MB**. This is equivalent to 10 minutes of video playback at a bit rate of 1.4 Mbps.

Project\bin\Debug\Silverlight2BookProject.zip   Browse...

Upload

Figure 10-38

After your application has finished uploading, you'll be taken to the Application Properties page for your newly created application. You can reaccess this page at any time by selecting "Manage Applications" on the main menu, then selecting the desired project. Figure 10-39 shows the Application Properties page for my newly created application named *SampleStreaming*.

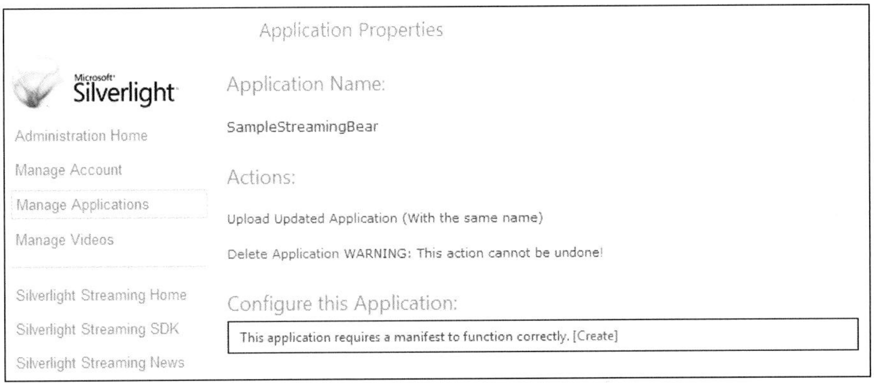

Application Properties

Microsoft
Silverlight

Administration Home

Manage Account

Manage Applications

Manage Videos

Silverlight Streaming Home

Silverlight Streaming SDK

Silverlight Streaming News

Application Name:

SampleStreamingBear

Actions:

Upload Updated Application (With the same name)

Delete Application WARNING: This action cannot be undone!

Configure this Application:

This application requires a manifest to function correctly. [Create]

Figure 10-39

On this page, you can choose from the options: Update the application by uploading a new version of the zip file with the same name, delete the application, or configure the application by creating or editing its manifest. If the service cannot detect the settings of your embedded manifest file, it lets you create one inline and edit those settings, as shown in Figure 10-40.

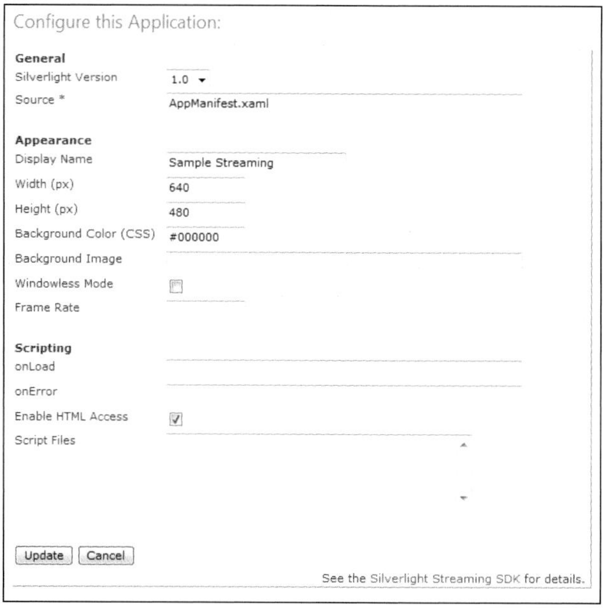

Figure 10-40

Once you have a valid manifest file, the service provides directions for adding your uploaded application to a Web page. As of this writing, you can embed the application as a frame in your page or use a live control (see Figure 10-41).

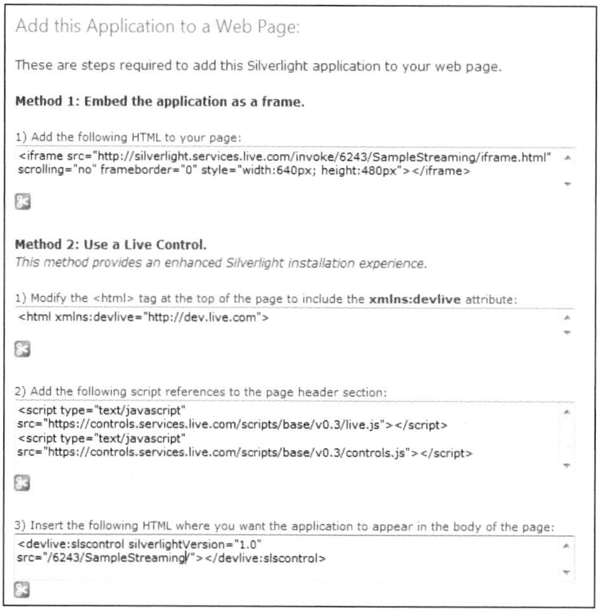

Figure 10-41

The Silverlight Streaming service gives you a location to host your Silverlight applications (whether they include media or not) on a large network or redundant servers to reduce the load on your own server. This is a great way to save costs if your application is going to be bandwidth-intensive or if you expect to receive high-volume traffic on your application.

Smooth Streaming and IIS7

Smooth Streaming is an IIS Media Services extension, available for download at www.iis.net/extensions/SmoothStreaming. This technology dynamically switches between various encodings of the same media content based on the detected bandwidth of the requesting PC. Via this dynamic switching, Smooth Streaming can enable near-instant seeking of video: A low-quality version of the video is immediately sent to the PC upon seeking so that playback can begin. In the background, the next higher-quality feed is being cached. When available, the video steps up to the next level of quality. This process continues until the PC's bandwidth no longer supports the next higher encoding.

In order to deliver Smooth Streaming video, the video must be encoded at a number of target quality levels to support the various levels of bandwidth encountered. Expression Encoder 2 with Service Pack 1 includes Smooth Streaming support that makes encoding for this powerful feature as easy as selecting a single profile. If you don't have Service Pack 1 installed, you'll need to download it and install it before proceeding (www.microsoft.com/downloads/details.aspx?FamilyId=A29BE9F9-29E1-4E70-BF67-02D87D3E556E).

Figure10-42 shows the Encode tab in Expression Encoder. To generate a collection of files to enable Smooth Streaming, select the "Adaptive Streaming" profile from the Video dropdown, and select "Adaptive Streaming Audio" from the Audio dropdown.

Figure 10-42

Like any of the other presets, you can customize individual properties once the preset has been selected. Once you're satisfied with your settings, you can complete the Publish section to publish your rendered files directly to a Smooth Streaming IIS7 server. Select "WebDAV" from the "Publish To" dropdown in the Publish category shown in Figure 10-43.

Figure 10-43

Click on the Encode button and step away for a coffee or a good night's rest, depending on the length of your footage.

Summary

The media capabilities offered by the Silverlight player empower you to create true multimedia experiences. You now know how to respond to all of the events raised by the MediaElement and interact with its properties to create interactive, media-rich applications. You learned how to use Microsoft Expression Media Encoder to prepare media files for consumption by your Silverlight applications and saw how the Microsoft Silverlight Streaming service can be used to help carry your bandwidth burden. I hope your mind is now racing with ideas for exciting media applications!

11

Using the Services

In this chapter, you'll look at the services Silverlight provides out-of-the-box and get an understanding of how to use them in your applications. Here we use the term *services* generically — facilities that do something for you. We've categorized these roughly into three groups: communications, storage, and installation and updates; and we'll cover these, some in depth and some at a high level, while referencing other parts of the book that delve into them in more detail.

Communications

Silverlight, at a high level, gives you essentially two forms of network communications: HTTP-based and TCP-based sockets. Before diving into those, it is worthwhile to consider some URL access restrictions that affect how you can use these services.

URL Access Restrictions

Silverlight has a few URL access restrictions. For the most part, they're what you'd expect from a browser-based technology, but they are worth discussing briefly. They apply both to HTTP-based classes and to other facilities in the framework that internally use HTTP — for example, images, media, font files, XAML source files, and streaming media.

At a high level, there are three kinds of restrictions: those based on schemes (i.e., HTTP, HTTPS, and FILE); those based on domains, for which Silverlight loosens the standard browser restrictions to enable cross-domain access; and those based on zone access (in Internet Explorer).

For zone-based access, the rule is that you can't access resources in a zone that is more trusted; for example, you can't get a resource in Trusted Sites if your application is running in the Internet zone. This zone-based security will override cross-domain policies, so keep this in mind if you find yourself trying to access a site that you *know* has the correct cross-domain policy; you also need to check to ensure that it's not in a more trusted zone.

The following table gives a good outline of how the restrictions affect the various kinds of access in Silverlight.

	WebClient and HTTP Classes	Image, MediaElement (Non-Streaming)	XAML Source Files	Font Files	Streaming Media
Allowed Schemes	HTTP, HTTPS	HTTP, HTTPS, FILE	HTTP, HTTPS, FILE	HTTP, HTTPS, FILE	HTTP
Cross-Scheme Access	No	No	No	No	Not from HTTPS
Cross-Domain Access	Only with security policy; not HTTPS-HTTPS	Not HTTPS-HTTPS	Not HTTPS-HTTPS	No	Not HTTPS-HTTPS
Cross-Zone Access (in IE)	Same or less restrictive	Same or less restrictive	Same or less restrictive	Same or less restrictive	Same or less restrictive
Re-Direction Allowed	Same site/ scheme or cross-domain with a policy	Not cross-scheme	No	No	No

Other network and security considerations are covered in Chapter 13.

HTTP-Based Communications

HTTP-based communications are those that you use to — surprise — communicate over HTTP in a broad sense. This includes the simplified WebClient as well as the more generic but more powerful HttpWebRequest/Reponse. Within these, you have a few libraries to help you with particular scenarios, such as RSS/syndication, duplex communications, and downloading.

Obviously, the most common scenario you'll have is accessing some kind of Web service from Silverlight. You may have a formal service with WSDL (Web Services Description Language); if that's the case, you can generate a client proxy for that service and access it using the proxy. Another very common scenario is to access a service that is just Plain-Old XML (POX) and Representational State Transfer (REST) services. For both of these, you can just use the WebClient or HttpWebRequest/Response classes, although Silverlight does provide some facilities for REST, particularly for ADO.NET Data Services. These topics are covered in depth in Chapter 14, and, in general, HTTP-based communication is covered throughout the book, so we won't dig into that here.

Downloader

In Silverlight 1.0, there was a special Downloader service that simplified downloading items with HTTP GET. In Silverlight 2, the Downloader was replaced by the `WebClient` class, which is a more general-purpose web client (as its name implies). You can use this class to download all sorts of things (XAML, XML, media, fonts, packages, additional assemblies, etc.) asynchronously over HTTP.

In addition to starting and receiving, it can also be used to monitor progress; the `DownloadProgressChangedEventArgs` has various members such as bytes and total bytes to receive as well as a nifty progress percentage member that you can use to display meaningful progress to users.

If you are downloading a package, you use the `OpenReadAsync` method in conjunction with the `System .Windows.Resources.StreamResourceInfo` class and the `System.Windows.Application.GetResourceStream` overload that takes the `StreamResourceInfo` instance to extract different parts of the downloaded package. This can be extremely useful for minimizing bandwidth usage by zipping things up into coherent packages.

Because the `WebClient` class is so multipurpose (and useful), it is used throughout this book and elsewhere; therefore, this chapter will not cover it in depth.

Duplex Communication

Duplex communication is a special facility that enables Silverlight clients to connect to a server and effectively keep a channel of communication open so that the server can send updates (sometimes called *push*) to clients without their having to repeatedly poll for updates. This is especially helpful in cases such as instant communications clients (IMs/chat services) as well as server-based monitoring.

> **Note that under the covers, there is intermittent polling going on, but it is effectively two-way as the server will keep the poll connection open until it responds (or times out).**

The following sample illustrates the basics of setting up duplex (two-way) communications. Be prepared to be mystified if this sort of thing is new to you; it requires jumping through a lot of hoops and does not provide most of the WCF service niceties (like client generation) that you're used to. First, you'll want to set up your Silverlight application as usual and add a web site (or link to an existing one).

Setting Up the Duplex Service

On the server side, you need to add a reference (in addition to standard WCF references) to `System .ServiceModel.PollingDuplex.dll`, which can be found in the server-side Evaluation folder in the Silverlight SDK (e.g., C:\Program Files\Microsoft SDKs\Silverlight\v3.0\Libraries\Server). It should show up in the .NET tab of the "Add Reference" dialog in Visual Studio.

Create a Services folder in your Web project and right-click to add an item. I recommend just adding a text file and calling it *Notifications.svc* because the current state of things with duplex makes it easier than clearing out stuff that doesn't apply. In that file, add the following at the top:

```
<%@ ServiceHost Language="C#" Debug="true"
    Factory="Wrox.Silverlight3.Services.NotificationsHostFactory" %>
```

237

We'll get to the service factory eventually. For now, add a Notifications.cs code file to your App_Code directory (you might need to add that special ASP.NET folder to your web site). In that file, add the following to define your contracts. In this sample, keep it simple. The service will simply be set up for client subscriptions to arbitrary server notifications, which you'll use to just send the server time down, but it establishes the basic principles that you could use to build other duplex services.

```
using System;
using System.Linq;
using System.Runtime.Serialization;
using System.ServiceModel;
using System.ServiceModel.Activation;
using System.ServiceModel.Channels;
using System.Threading;
using System.Collections.Generic;

namespace Wrox.Silverlight3.Services
{
    #region Contracts
    [ServiceContract(Namespace = "http://wrox.com/Silverlight3/Services",
      CallbackContract = typeof(IReceiveNotifications))]
    public interface ISendNotifications
    {
        [OperationContract(IsOneWay = true)]
        void Subscribe(Message message);
    }

    [ServiceContract(Namespace ="http://wrox.com/Silverlight3/Services")]
    public interface IReceiveNotifications
    {
        [OperationContract(IsOneWay = true)]
        void Notify(Message message);
    }
    #endregion
}
```

ISendNotifications is the server-side contract, and IReceiveNotifications defines the client-side contract. What is really important here is the ServiceContract namespace, as that is how WCF will map the messages sent back and forth to the corresponding code operations. On the server, you just define a Subscribe that clients can call to subscribe to server notifications; the client defines a Notify that the server will use to send notifications to clients. Note the CallbackContract on ISendNotifications; this indicates the client-side contract that WCF will expect for duplex communication.

Now add an implementation of the server-side contract (as you normally would):

```
#region Service Implementation
[ServiceBehavior(InstanceContextMode = InstanceContextMode.Single)]
public class Notifications : ISendNotifications
{
    Dictionary<string,IReceiveNotifications> _Clients =
      new Dictionary<string, IReceiveNotifications>();
    object _SyncRoot = new object();

    Timer _ServerTimer;

    public Notifications()
```

```
    {
      _ServerTimer = new Timer(GenerateNotification, null, 0, 1000);
    }

    public void Subscribe(Message message)
    {
      lock (_SyncRoot)
      {
        OperationContext.Current.Channel.Closing += Channel_Closing;
        _Clients[OperationContext.Current.Channel.SessionId] =
          OperationContext.Current.
            GetCallbackChannel<IReceiveNotifications>();
      }
    }

    void GenerateNotification(object clientMessage)
    {
      Message notification = Message.CreateMessage(MessageVersion.Soap11,
        "http://wrox.com/Silverlight3/Services/ISendNotifications/Notify",
          "Server Time: " + DateTimeOffset.Now.ToString());
      lock (_SyncRoot)
      {
        foreach (IReceiveNotifications client in _Clients.Values)
          client.Notify(notification);
      }
    }

    void Channel_Closing(object sender, EventArgs e)
    {
      lock (_SyncRoot)
      {
        IContextChannel channel = (IContextChannel)sender;
        _Clients.Remove(channel.SessionId);
      }
    }
  }
#endregion Service Implementation
```

All this code simply sets up a service that will send 1-second updates to subscribed clients, telling them what the current server time is. The timer is just there to facilitate the updates; normally, you wouldn't do this — you would have something more meaningful to send back to the client that would more likely be event-based than timer-based.

The code uses a simple generic dictionary to keep track of subscribed clients by using the SessionId on the client context as the key. This is used in the Closing event handler to remove those clients that close their connections (or time out) from the list of clients to notify.

You use the System.ServiceModel.Channels.Message class to send messages back and forth. The Create method has a few overloads; the code above uses the one that takes a message version (duplex only supports SOAP 1.1 right now), the action (remember that this is mapped to the service namespace, service, and operation names), and the content of the message — you can only send string-based messages, so you have to serialize and deserialize your objects yourself.

Next, you have to create your own factory (that was specified in the .svc file, if you recall):

```
#region Service Host Factory
public class NotificationsHostFactory : ServiceHostFactoryBase
{
  public override ServiceHostBase CreateServiceHost(
    string constructorString, Uri[] baseAddresses)
  {
    ServiceHost service =
      new ServiceHost(typeof(Notifications), baseAddresses);
    PollingDuplexHttpBinding binding = new PollingDuplexHttpBinding()
    {
      ServerPollTimeout = TimeSpan.FromSeconds(60),
      InactivityTimeout = TimeSpan.FromMinutes(10)
    };

    service.AddServiceEndpoint(typeof(ISendNotifications),
      binding, "");

    return service;
  }
}
#endregion Service Host Factory
```

Although this is doubtless gobbledygook to those not steeped in WCF-ology, the basic thing here is to create the PollingDuplexHttpBinding, set its time-out values, and add the endpoint on a service of the Notifications type that you just created.

So that's it for the server side; you should be able to right-click and open Notifications.svc in the browser without error at this point, although it won't supply metadata because you didn't specify a metadata exchange endpoint. Hopefully, once the infrastructure is fully baked, you'll be able to let Visual Studio take care of all this for you and/or even use web.config instead of coding the factory.

Setting Up the Duplex Client

The server is pretty straightforward compared to the client interface. This is where you better make sure you have a cup of Joe handy and your best focus music going before diving into this convoluted mess. In this sample, you'll just create two buttons, one for telling the client to subscribe to server notifications and one to unsubscribe, as well as a textbox to display messages in, so the XAML looks like this:

```
<Grid x:Name="LayoutRoot" Background="White">
  <StackPanel>
    <Button Content="Subscribe" x:Name="SubscriptionButton"
      Click="SubscriptionButton_Click" />
    <Button Content="Unsubscribe" x:Name="UnsubscriptionButton"
      Click="UnsubscriptionButton_Click" />
    <TextBlock x:Name="SusbscriptionInfo" TextWrapping="Wrap" />
  </StackPanel>
</Grid>
```

Before moving on, you will need a few extra references. Add references in your Silverlight project to `System.ServiceModel`, `System.ServiceModel.PollingDuplex`, and `System.Runtime.Serialization`. Then, in your code-behind, you will need to use some of those namespaces:

```
using System.Threading;
using System.ServiceModel;
using System.ServiceModel.Channels;
```

Next, you need to set up a few class members to make coding a bit easier:

```
SynchronizationContext _UiThread;
IDuplexSessionChannel _Channel;
bool IsChannelOpen { get { return _Channel != null; } }
```

Now, in your `SubscriptionButton_Click` handler, add the following code:

```
if (IsChannelOpen)
{
  AppendServerMessage("Already subscribed.");
  return;
}
AppendServerMessage("Subscribing to server notifications...");
_UiThread = SynchronizationContext.Current;

PollingDuplexHttpBinding binding = new PollingDuplexHttpBinding()
{
  InactivityTimeout = TimeSpan.FromMinutes(10)
};

IChannelFactory<IDuplexSessionChannel> factory =
    binding.BuildChannelFactory<IDuplexSessionChannel>(new
        BindingParameterCollection());

IAsyncResult factoryOpenResult =
    factory.BeginOpen(OnFactoryOpenComplete, factory);
if (factoryOpenResult.CompletedSynchronously)
{
  FactoryOpenComplete(factoryOpenResult);
}
```

The first thing this does is check to see if there is already a channel set up and open (it assumes, as you'll see, that if there is a channel instance, it is effectively open). This keeps the channels open to one, which is important because this will use one of the two available IE connections that you have available (if you're using IE, of course, although, no doubt, most other browsers have similar limitations).

The `AppendServerMessage` is just a helper function to add text to the textbox you set up; it will be used from background threads to post messages via the `SynchronizationContext`'s `Post` method, and that's also why you grab a reference to the UI thread's context. Here's what it looks like:

```
void AppendServerMessage(object messagePayload)
{
  string message = messagePayload as string;
```

```
    if (!string.IsNullOrEmpty(message))
      this.SusbscriptionInfo.Text += message + Environment.NewLine;
}
```

Next, you get to the actual client binding code. Much as you did on the server, you create a PollingDuplexHttpBinding and set its time-outs. Here we're just setting the inactivity time-out, which is an additive time-out that determines how long the client will keep its session open without any real messages from the server. The code above sets it to 10 minutes to wait before timing out because of inactivity; this needs to vary based on your needs and usage patterns.

Then you set up a duplex channel factory to create your channel from. This is where the craziness really starts — pretty much every communication method has an asynchronous capability but could also execute synchronously, so you need to supply an asynchronous callback as well as a synchronous handler. The general pattern, as you will see, is that the asynchronous callback method checks to see if the call was completed synchronously, and only if it wasn't, will it then call the synchronous handler.

```
void OnFactoryOpenComplete(IAsyncResult result)
{
  if (!result.CompletedSynchronously)
    FactoryOpenComplete(result);
}

void FactoryOpenComplete(IAsyncResult result)
{
  IChannelFactory<IDuplexSessionChannel> factory =
      (IChannelFactory<IDuplexSessionChannel>)result.AsyncState;

  factory.EndOpen(result);

  _Channel = factory.CreateChannel(new EndpointAddress(
     "http://localhost:1045/ServicesWeb/Services/Notifications.svc"));

  IAsyncResult channelOpenResult =
     _Channel.BeginOpen(OnChannelOpenComplete, null);
  if (channelOpenResult.CompletedSynchronously)
  {
    ChannelOpenComplete(channelOpenResult);
  }
}
```

Whether or not it completed asynchronously, you need to call the corresponding End method to continue. Once you have created the factory, you then create a channel using the endpoint for your service. (Obviously, in a real app, you won't want to hard-code the URI to your endpoint.) Now you have a channel, so you can open it using BeginOpen and the corresponding completion handlers:

```
void OnChannelOpenComplete(IAsyncResult result)
{
  if (!result.CompletedSynchronously)
    ChannelOpenComplete(result);
}

void ChannelOpenComplete(IAsyncResult result)
{
```

```
_Channel.EndOpen(result);
Message message =
    Message.CreateMessage(MessageVersion.Soap11,
"http://wrox.com/Silverlight3/Services/ISendNotifications/Subscribe",
  string.Empty);
IAsyncResult sendResult =
    _Channel.BeginSend(message, OnSendComplete, null);
if (sendResult.CompletedSynchronously)
{
  SendComplete(sendResult);
}
ReceiveNotifications();
}
```

After opening the channel, you are free to send messages to the server to your heart's content. What the code above does is send a subscribe message to the server (effectively calling the `ISendNotifications` `.Subscribe` method on your contract implementation). Remember the mapping of the service namespace to actual code operations. If you get it wrong, the correct server code won't work. This is another case in which you'd typically want to refactor so that you're not hard-coding the operation strings in your code (e.g., a `MessageHelper` static class with constant strings for message operations).

You send off that message and move on with life to the `ReceiveNotifications` method to go ahead and prepare the client to receive messages. The send completion handlers look like this — nothing special:

```
void OnSendComplete(IAsyncResult result)
{
  if (!result.CompletedSynchronously)
    SendComplete(result);
}

void SendComplete(IAsyncResult result)
{
  _Channel.EndSend(result);
  _UiThread.Post(AppendServerMessage, "Waiting for notifications...");
}
What's more interesting is the preparation to receive messages from the server.
void ReceiveNotifications()
{
  IAsyncResult result =
    _Channel.BeginReceive(OnReceiveComplete, null);
  if (result.CompletedSynchronously)
    ReceiveComplete(result);
}
```

OK, so it isn't that interesting in itself, but what this does is initiate the poll/wait on the server for a message. When the client receives a message, your completion handlers will be called:

```
void OnReceiveComplete(IAsyncResult result)
{
  if (!result.CompletedSynchronously)
    ReceiveComplete(result);
}

void ReceiveComplete(IAsyncResult result)
```

243

```
{
  try
  {
    Message receivedMessage = _Channel.EndReceive(result);

    if (receivedMessage == null)
    {
      _UiThread.Post(AppendServerMessage, "Server disconnected.");
      this.Close();
    }
    else
    {
      string text = receivedMessage.GetBody<string>();
      _UiThread.Post(AppendServerMessage, text);
      ReceiveNotifications();
    }
  }
  catch (CommunicationObjectFaultedException)
  {
    _UiThread.Post(AppendServerMessage, "Server notifications timed out.");
  }
}
```

The `EndReceive` method on the channel returns the `Message` that the server sent, and that's what you have to use to dive into the response. A typical thing to do is use the `GetBody` method to retrieve the message body, and this is where your custom deserialization code would come into play if you were shipping serialized custom objects around. In this case, you're just getting a string message, which is immediately posted to the UI thread. Last, you set up the client to receive again by calling `ReceiveNotifications` again.

You will note a few conditions here. First, if the message is null, it is best to assume that the connection has been severed in some way, so you want to handle that accordingly. In the preceding code, it just posts a message to that effect and cleans up the channel. The other condition is a fault condition that should be triggered if a time-out occurs.

What's left is the code `Close` and cleaning up the channel:

```
void Close()
{
  if (IsChannelOpen)
  {
    IAsyncResult result =
        _Channel.BeginClose(OnCloseChannel, null);
    if (result.CompletedSynchronously)
    {
      CloseChannel(result);
    }
  }
}

void OnCloseChannel(IAsyncResult result)
{
  if (!result.CompletedSynchronously)
```

```
        CloseChannel(result);
    }

    void CloseChannel(IAsyncResult result)
    {
      if (IsChannelOpen)
      {
        _Channel.EndClose(result);
        _UiThread.Post(AppendServerMessage, "Unsubscribed.");
        _Channel = null;
      }
    }
```

As you can see, it pretty much follows the pattern used thus far, calling the `BeginClose` and `EndClose` methods on the channel and clearing out the channel reference. And that makes way for the final bit of code in this sample, the `UnsubscriptionButton_Click` handler, which just closes the channel:

```
    void UnsubscriptionButton_Click(object sender, RoutedEventArgs e)
    {
      this.Close();
    }
```

The problem with where things are right now is that you're left to do a lot of the grunt work yourself to do duplex communication. No doubt this will be made easier as it is developed, but if you need it sooner, you can and should refactor your duplex code into a separate class or set of classes to encapsulate it better both for reuse and for cleaner, more maintainable code.

Sockets

Like the HTTP-based duplex communication just covered in the previous section, sockets are likely going to appeal to a limited audience, but they're very useful for those who need them. Silverlight's sockets implementation uses Windows Sockets (Winsock) on Windows and BSD UNIX's sockets on OS X to provide a standard, managed interface. If you need true, real-time duplex communication and can use TCP, then this is your solution in Silverlight. The challenge, of course, is that it uses ports (4502–4532 and 943 for policy) that are less likely to be open in firewalls, so the application of a sockets solution may be limited because of that.

The example that follows is a simple implementation of essentially the same scenario covered in the duplex HTTP section, that is, server notifications. The first thing you'll need to do is create a server; probably the easiest way to do this is via a console application, so you can just add a `Console` application to your solution and call it `SocketsServer` to get started.

Setting Up the Policy Server

Now, because sockets require a call access security file (even for site-of-origin calls), you first need to set up a policy server listener. To do this, add a new class file to your console application, calling it `PolicyServer`. You'll need to use a few namespaces to make things more manageable:

```
using System.IO;
using System.Net;
using System.Net.Sockets;
```

Most of the socket's functionality you'll need will, of course, be in `System.Net.Sockets`. We have I/O included because we want to read the policy XML file from the local filesystem, as you'll see shortly. `System.Net` has the network endpoint classes you'll be using. Now, create a few class members:

```
Socket _Listener;
byte[] _PolicyData;
```

The `Socket`, of course, is the listener socket you'll set up; the policy data will be in an in-memory byte buffer of your policy file data to be shared across connections. Now define a constructor that takes a file path to the location of your policy file:

```
public PolicyServer(string policyFile)
{
  using (FileStream policyStream =
    new FileStream(policyFile, FileMode.Open))
  {
    _PolicyData = new byte[policyStream.Length];
    policyStream.Read(_PolicyData, 0, _PolicyData.Length);
  }
}
```

As you can see, this simply reads the policy file data into the aforementioned byte buffer. The policy file you'll use can be added to your project and called whatever you like; since you're going to allow all access, you might call it *allow-all.xml*. You could create different policies in different files then and just use some mechanism to specify which policy should apply at any particular time. The allow-all access XML file looks like the following:

```
<?xml version="1.0" encoding ="utf-8"?>
<access-policy>
  <cross-domain-access>
    <policy>
      <allow-from>
        <domain uri="*" />
      </allow-from>
      <grant-to>
        <socket-resource port="4502-4532" protocol="tcp" />
      </grant-to>
    </policy>
  </cross-domain-access>
</access-policy>
```

The two key things here are the `allow-from` with the * URI, which means any URI can call it, and the port specification, which here is just as open as Silverlight itself, although you could use this to further constrain the allowable ports.

Back to the policy server. You will want to add a `Start` method of some sort that will create the socket listener and start listening for requests:

```
public void Start()
{
  Console.WriteLine("Starting policy server...");
```

```
_Listener = new Socket(AddressFamily.InterNetwork, SocketType.Stream, ProtocolType.Tcp);
_Listener.Bind(new IPEndPoint(IPAddress.Any, 943));
_Listener.Listen(10);
_Listener.BeginAccept(OnConnection, null);
Console.WriteLine("Policy server waiting for connections...");
}
```

Silverlight limits the kinds of sockets you can create — pretty much streams over TCP. Since this is the policy server, you need to bind to the well-known port 943, and the Listen method starts it listening on that port, allowing up to 10 connections in the queue, which is more than enough in this sample. Finally, you attach a handler to the BeginAccept event, such as the OnConnection method:

```
void OnConnection(IAsyncResult res)
{
  Socket client = null;
  try
  {
    client = _Listener.EndAccept(res);
  }
  catch (SocketException)
  {
    return;
  }
  Console.WriteLine("Policy client connected.");

  PolicyConnection policyConnection =
    new PolicyConnection(client, _PolicyData);
  policyConnection.NegotiatePolicy();

  _Listener.BeginAccept(OnConnection, null);
}
```

The first thing this handler does is get a reference to the client socket, which will be used to send the policy file. To facilitate this, you need to create a PolicyConnection class as follows. In that class, you need to use a couple of namespaces:

```
using System.Net.Sockets;
using System.Text;
```

The Sockets namespace is, of course, for the sockets work, and the Text namespace facilitates using the text encoding to read a string from a byte array. Now add a few class members:

```
Socket _Connection;
byte[] _PolicyRequestBuffer;
int _NumBytesReceived;
byte[] _PolicyData;
static string _PolicyRequest = "<policy-file-request/>";
```

In this case, the Socket will be the connection to the client. The policy request buffer will be used to compare the connection request with the expected request, identified in the shared policy request string — this is what Silverlight clients will send when looking for a policy file. The number of bytes received is just used to track that the full request is received, as you'll see, and the policy data byte array will be a reference to the given policy file data.

```
public PolicyConnection(Socket client, byte[] policy)
{
  _Connection = client;
  _PolicyData = policy;
  _PolicyRequestBuffer = new byte[_PolicyRequest.Length];
  _NumBytesReceived = 0;
}
```

As you might expect, the constructor initializes the class members appropriately:

```
public void NegotiatePolicy()
{
  Console.WriteLine("Negotiating policy.");
  try
  {
    _Connection.BeginReceive(_PolicyRequestBuffer, 0,
      _PolicyRequest.Length, SocketFlags.None, OnReceive, null);
  }
  catch (SocketException)
  {
    _Connection.Close();
  }
}
```

This is the method you called from the PolicyServer's OnConnection handler to negotiate the policy for the current connection. It simply starts receiving the request from the client into the buffer, using the OnReceive method as the completion event handler:

```
private void OnReceive(IAsyncResult res)
{
  try
  {
    _NumBytesReceived += _Connection.EndReceive(res);
    if (_NumBytesReceived < _PolicyRequest.Length)
    {
      _Connection.BeginReceive(_PolicyRequestBuffer, _NumBytesReceived,
        _PolicyRequest.Length - _NumBytesReceived, SocketFlags.None,
        OnReceive, null);
      return;
    }
    string request = Encoding.UTF8.GetString(
      _PolicyRequestBuffer, 0, _NumBytesReceived);
    if (StringComparer.InvariantCultureIgnoreCase.Compare(
        request, _PolicyRequest) != 0)
    {
      _Connection.Close();
      return;
    }
    Console.WriteLine("Policy successfully requested.");
    _Connection.BeginSend(_PolicyData, 0, _PolicyData.Length,
      SocketFlags.None, OnSend, null);
  }
```

```
      catch (SocketException)
      {
        _Connection.Close();
      }
    }
```

OK, so this is where dealing with sockets can be a little more archaic than what the average .NET dev is probably used to. Because there is no guarantee that the entire request that you are expecting was sent in the first go, you may want to take this approach. Calling `EndReceive` will tell you how many bytes were received. You can then compare that with what you are expecting to see if you're done. In the preceding code, you're expecting to receive a request with the length of the policy request length; if it isn't there yet, you call `BeginReceive` again to (hopefully) get the rest of what you're looking for.

Once you have something that is at least the right length, the next step is to compare that to what you are expecting; however, you first need to read the received bytes into a UTF8 string. You can then compare the actual request contents with the well-known policy request string. If it doesn't match, you just close the connection — this server only handles negotiating server policy according to the Silverlight policy negotiation protocol. If, on the other hand, it is the expected request, you then just send the server policy data down to the client.

The last thing to do for the policy server is to set it up when the console application starts, so go into your `Main` method (in the `Program` class file, assuming that you used the standard VS Console Application template), create a policy server instance, and start it up like this:

```
    static void Main(string[] args)
    {
      PolicyServer ps = new PolicyServer("allow-all.xml");
      ps.Start();
    }
```

See, here you're passing in the path to your policy file. This is hard-coded for simplicity; you'd probably want to let the policy file be passed in via command-line arguments or some other fancier mechanism in real-world code. Also, note that you can simply add that file as a text file to your project and set its Build Action to Content and the "Copy to Output Directory" to "Copy if newer" so that you can manage the file in your project and have it be in the output location to be consumed while you are running and debugging it.

Unfortunately, that's a lot of boilerplate code that you have to deal with just to enable Silverlight clients to connect to your *real* sockets server, that is, the one that is doing your domain work. On the positive side, your policy server should be the same (code) for all sockets apps, so you can reuse it across them and just tweak your policy files as needed.

Setting Up the Application Sockets Server

In this sample case, the real sockets server will just send notifications, so set that up next by adding a `SocketsServer` class file to your project and using the following namespaces:

```
    using System.Collections.Generic;
    using System.Text;
    using t = System.Timers;
    using System.Net.Sockets;
```

```
using System.Net;
using System.Threading;
using System.Diagnostics;
```

It's a lot of namespaces, but there's no need to get overwhelmed. You'll only be using a few things from each. Next thing to do is set up your class fields:

```
t.Timer _ServerTimer;
Socket _Listener;
ManualResetEvent _ThreadCoordinator = new ManualResetEvent(false);
List<Socket> _Clients = new List<Socket>();
object _SyncRoot = new object();
```

Since there is a System.Threading timer and a System.Timers timer, it is helpful to disambiguate using the namespace alias set up in the using statements, that is t. The thread coordinator, sync root, and clients list are all there to facilitate tracking multiple connections and coordinating between them. Next, add a Start method as you did with the policy server to set things off:

```
public void Start()
{
  _ServerTimer = new t.Timer(1000);
  _ServerTimer.Enabled = false;
  _ServerTimer.Elapsed += ServerTimer_Elapsed;

  _Listener = new Socket(AddressFamily.InterNetwork,
    SocketType.Stream, ProtocolType.Tcp);
  IPEndPoint serverEndpoint = new IPEndPoint(IPAddress.Any, 4502);
  _Listener.Bind(serverEndpoint);
  _Listener.Listen(2);

  while (true)
  {
    _ThreadCoordinator.Reset();
    _Listener.BeginAccept(AcceptClient, null);
    Console.WriteLine("Waiting for clients...");
    _ThreadCoordinator.WaitOne();
  }
}
```

The first thing here is the creation of the timer. Note that it is disabled initially — no need for it to be running while no clients are connected. Also, keep in mind that this is just used for simulation purposes; it's safe to assume that you would have more meaningful events and notifications to send to real-world clients than timer-based ones.

The next block of code should look familiar; it is setting up the server socket listener. One thing that is different is that it is listening on port 4502 — one of the ports allowed by Silverlight and not the policy negotiation port of 943. Also, the code is (arbitrarily) limiting queued connections to two; you need to adjust this to what makes sense for your expected usage and capacity.

The last block here sets up the listener loop. The ManualResetEvent that here is called _ThreadCoordinator is used as a simple way for threads to signal that they're doing or not doing something. Reset tells all the threads to hold on while the current thread does its thing. `WaitOne` tells the current thread to chill until it gets a signal that says "Go ahead." In between, you set up the `AcceptClient` method to take the next connection that comes in:

```csharp
void AcceptClient(IAsyncResult result)
{
    try
    {
        _ThreadCoordinator.Set();

        Socket clientSocket = _Listener.EndAccept(result);
        lock (_SyncRoot)
            _Clients.Add(clientSocket);
        Console.WriteLine("Client connected.");


        if (!_ServerTimer.Enabled)
            _ServerTimer.Enabled = true;
    }
    catch (ObjectDisposedException ex)
    {
        Trace.WriteLine("Socket closed: " + ex.ToString());
    }
    catch (SocketException ex)
    {
        Console.WriteLine(ex.Message);
    }
}
```

In this method, the first thing is to say, "Yo, all y'all can go ahead now" to the waiting threads that were previously blocked. Then it goes on to get a reference to the connected client socket, synchronizes access to the current list of clients, and adds this one to the list of subscribed clients. The next thing is to go ahead and enable the server timer now that clients are connected and waiting for notifications. If you'll recall, you attached the `ServerTimer_Elapsed` method to the timer's `Elapsed` method back in the `Start` method.

```csharp
void ServerTimer_Elapsed(object sender,
    System.Timers.ElapsedEventArgs e)
{
    byte[] serverTimeBytes = Encoding.UTF8.GetBytes(
        DateTimeOffset.Now.ToString());
    Console.WriteLine("Sending server time.");
    lock (_SyncRoot)
    {
        List<Socket> refreshedList = new List<Socket>(_Clients.Count);
        foreach (Socket client in _Clients)
        {
            if (client.Connected)
            {
                try
                {
                    client.Send(serverTimeBytes);
                }
```

```
        catch (Exception ex)
        {
          if (!(ex is SocketException) ||
            ((SocketException)ex).SocketErrorCode !=
                SocketError.ConnectionReset)
            Console.WriteLine("Client Send Error: " + ex.ToString());
          else
            Console.WriteLine("Client disconnected.");
          client.Close();
          return;
        }
        refreshedList.Add(client);
      }
    }
    _Clients = refreshedList;
    if (_Clients.Count == 0)
      _ServerTimer.Enabled = false;

  }
}
```

This method does the actual sending of notifications to clients, but remember that this is completely arbitrary — you could send updates to clients based on any number of server-side events. Since this sample is timer-based, it makes sense to just send the server time, so that first bit is grabbing the current server time into a byte buffer to be sent to the clients.

The next block goes ahead and synchronizes access to the client list by locking on the sync root object. It then creates a new list of clients that will be used to refresh the list of currently connected clients — in this way, when clients fall off or unsubscribe, we let go of them on the server side and let their resources get cleaned up. Then, for every client that is still connected, you add them to the new list and try to send them the message (the server time).

The last bit of code in this method updates the _Clients reference with the new, refreshed list of clients and then checks to see if any clients are still connected. If not, it disables the timer until new clients connect.

The final thing you need to do on the server is to create an instance of this class and start it up, so go back to your Main method and add it like this:

```
static void Main(string[] args)
{
  PolicyServer ps = new PolicyServer("allow-all.xml");
  ps.Start();

  SocketsServer s = new SocketsServer();
  s.Start();
}
```

Setting Up the Sockets Client

Now that your server is all set, you need to create a client. To do this, you can copy the XAML from the duplex HTTP sample into a new Sockets.xaml user control. Then, in the code-behind, you need to set up some stuff. This is where, if you ask me, sockets are easier than duplex HTTP — it feels like far fewer methods and far less trouble to accomplish the same scenario. So first, adding the following namespace includes:

```
using System.Threading;
using System.Net.Sockets;
using System.Text;
```

Then add these class members:

```
SynchronizationContext _UiThread;
Socket _Channel;
DnsEndPoint _RemoteEndPoint;
bool Connected {get{ return _Channel != null && _Channel.Connected; }}
```

This is fairly similar to the duplex HTTP sample, and, in fact, you can copy the AppendServerMessage from that sample as well as the button click event-handler signatures, the first of which is the SubscriptionButton_Click handler:

```
void SubscriptionButton_Click(object sender, RoutedEventArgs e)
{
  if (Connected)
  {
    AppendServerMessage("Already subscribed.");
    return;
  }

  AppendServerMessage("Subscribing to server notifications...");
  _UiThread = SynchronizationContext.Current;

  _Channel = new Socket(AddressFamily.InterNetwork,
    SocketType.Stream, ProtocolType.Tcp);
  _RemoteEndPoint =
    new DnsEndPoint(Application.Current.Host.Source.DnsSafeHost, 4502);

  SocketAsyncEventArgs args = new SocketAsyncEventArgs();
  args.RemoteEndPoint = _RemoteEndPoint;
  args.Completed += SocketConnectCompleted;
  _Channel.ConnectAsync(args);
}
```

The first part of this should look familiar from the duplex HTTP, just ensuring only one subscription for this client at a time and grabbing a reference to the UI thread context. Assuming that it is not already connected, this will create a new socket and set up a DnsEndPoint to the site of origin (that's the Application .Current.Host.Source bit) on port 4502. The important thing here, of course, is to connect on the port that the server is listening on, so if this were a real-world app, you'd have to publish that information to your clients somehow. Here, we're hard-coding for simplicity.

Now Silverlight uses the SocketAsyncEventArgs class as a sort of general socket communication facility, so you go ahead and create an instance, set the remote endpoint to the one just created, attach to the Completed event with the SocketConnectCompleted handler, and call ConnectAsync on the socket. When the connection completes, it will call SocketConnectCompleted:

```
void SocketConnectCompleted(object sender, SocketAsyncEventArgs args)
{
  if (!_Channel.Connected)
  {
    _UiThread.Post(AppendServerMessage,
      "Could not connect to server.");
    _Channel.Dispose();
    _Channel = null;
    return;
  }

  args.Completed -= SocketConnectCompleted;
  args.Completed += ReceiveData;
  args.SetBuffer(new byte[2048], 0, 2048);
  _Channel.ReceiveAsync(args);
  _UiThread.Post(AppendServerMessage, "Waiting for notifications...");
}
```

If the result of the connection attempt is not successful, you dispose of the socket and send a message to the user letting them know that. If it does succeed, you move on to the next step — receiving data. Again, the SocketAsyncEventArgs class is used; in fact, you can reuse it to conserve resources as done here. First, remove the SocketConnectCompleted event handler and attach instead the ReceiveData handler. Set up a buffer to specify how much to receive at a time; in this case, 2048 is rather arbitrary and actually way more than you need since you know that the server is just sending the server time. What you'd want to do is set it up to something reasonable that would handle most messages but that is not so large that it ties up too many resources. Then it goes ahead and puts itself into a state to receive data from the server.

Remember that once this client connected, if the server will enable its timer (if no other clients were already connected) and start sending server time updates every second, the ReceiveData method should be called almost immediately:

```
void ReceiveData(object sender, SocketAsyncEventArgs e)
{
  if (Connected)
  {
    string notification = Encoding.UTF8.GetString(
      e.Buffer, e.Offset, e.BytesTransferred);
    _UiThread.Post(AppendServerMessage, notification);
    _Channel.ReceiveAsync(e);
  }
}
```

This method just grabs the bytes sent as a UTF8 string, posts those to the UI thread, and tells the socket to receive again (using the same `SocketAsyncEventArgs` instance). This loop will continue as long as the server keeps sending data and, of course, as long as the socket remains open, which leads us to the `UnsubscriptionButton_Click` handler:

```
void UnsubscriptionButton_Click(object sender, RoutedEventArgs e)
{
  if (Connected)
  {
    _Channel.Dispose();
    _Channel = null;
    AppendServerMessage("Unsubscribed.");
  }
  else
    AppendServerMessage("Not subscribed.");
}
```

If connected, this will dispose of the socket, clear out the reference to it, and notify the user accordingly.

So that about wraps it up for the communications services. As noted, you're going to see a lot of samples in this book using the standard HTTP- and WCF-style communications, so those were omitted here, but you did cover the duplex HTTP and sockets in enough depth to give you a good understanding of what is involved in using them. If you have a need for duplex, real-time communication, those are your two best options in Silverlight. If the application is meant to run over the Web, your best bet is duplex HTTP; however, if you can require your clients to open up the right ports, sockets may be a more dependable solution, perhaps even a simpler solution.

Storage

A really great service that Silverlight provides is what they call *isolated storage*. The general idea is that you get a quota of disk space and a virtual filesystem to work with within that quota. The default quota that applications get is 100 KB, but you can request that the application be given more space, up to `System.Int64.MaxValue` in bytes, which is more than any Silverlight app should ever need. This is done by calling the `IncreaseQuotaTo` method on the desired store (which is an instance of the `IsolatedStorageFile` class) and providing it with the size, in bytes, that you want. The size must be larger than the current quota, so you need to check that.

> **It is worth highlighting that you will get an exception if you try to request an increase to the quota when not in a user-initiated event handler method, such as a button `click` handler. You need to be proactive about managing the quota.**

While there is an API to simply store application settings using the `IsolatedStorageSettings` class, you can imagine that it would not be ideal to store settings in isolated storage because they will only be persisted for the current machine the user is using (so users will have to reconfigure settings on each new machine). From a user experience perspective, this is bad. Instead, you should consider using, for example, the ASP.NET profile service to store user application settings as outlined in Chapter 16. You could still use the local settings for simple name–value pairs that you want to store under the covers persistently, but I'm having trouble thinking of a good scenario in which storing them on the server wouldn't be better.

That said, where isolated storage really shines is in providing a persistent local cache. To facilitate better performance in networked applications, it is often helpful to get and send data to and from the server in chunks. Imagine an e-mail program that had to go and get the user's e-mails again from the server every time it loaded up. This would be less than ideal on many levels — user experience, bandwidth usage, server utilization, and so forth. Instead, caching data locally would make the app perform better and use fewer resources.

The key when using isolated storage is to keep usage of it in the background, indiscernible to the user as much as possible. The user shouldn't know if you're caching or not — they should just know that they like how well your application performs and how reliable it is when, for example, the browser crashes for some reason, and they can get right back in to what they were doing on the application.

Interacting with isolated storage is very (and intentionally) reminiscent of using the normal .NET file-system APIs. The only particularly isolated *storagey* thing about it is getting to the store in the first place, but once you have a reference to the store, you can list, create, delete, and get info about directories and files in essentially the same way. To illustrate this, take the sockets sample from earlier in this chapter and enhance it to include some basic logging.

Using Isolated Storage for Local Logging

You could create a new user control or simply copy the existing sockets' user control and rename the files and class. Once you do that, add a few extra namespaces:

```
using System.Text;
using System.IO.IsolatedStorage;
using System.IO;
```

You can already get an inkling from these that you'll be dealing with familiar APIs — the only new one is IsolatedStorage. Next, go ahead and add a couple more class members:

```
IsolatedStorageFile _UserStore;
IsolatedStorageFile UserStore
{
  get
  {
    if (_UserStore == null)
      _UserStore = IsolatedStorageFile.GetUserStoreForApplication();
    return _UserStore;
  }
}
const string LOG_FILE = "ServerNotification.log";
```

Here you see basically the only particularly isolated storagey thing you'll be doing in this sample. You call the GetUserStoreForApplication method on IsolatedStorageFile, which will return the user's isolated store for the current application. You can think of this as a (initially very small) disk drive on the computer.

The LOG_FILE is just there so that you don't repeat yourself in specifying the log file. It is interesting to note that there's really no firm reason to bother with file extensions here because these files are not exposed directly in the host filesystem. However, you may as well give it one in case you should ever want to ship it up to the server without extra intervention and just because folks are used to seeing file extensions.

Now add a method to log messages to this log file:

```
void LogMessage(string message)
{
  using (IsolatedStorageFileStream log =
    UserStore.OpenFile(LOG_FILE, FileMode.Append,
      FileAccess.Write, FileShare.ReadWrite))
  {
    using (StreamWriter sw = new StreamWriter(log))
      sw.WriteLine(message);
  }
}
```

So there is a specialized file stream type for isolated storage; but for all intents and purposes, it doesn't matter. You see that you just call OpenFile as you likely have on the standard filesystem APIs, and the parameters are essentially the same as well. Then you use a standard System.IO.StreamWriter to write stuff to the log file. Add a call to this method at the end of the AppendServerMessage method, which was created in (and copied from) the sockets and duplex HTTP examples.

Once you do this and run it, you will be writing the same messages that appear on the screen to the log file on the users' computers. You can imagine that this is a useful scenario for tracing and even for exception handling — you could log locally and then periodically (preferably with the users' consent) ship these logs up to the server for analysis.

Now you have a working log, but why not go ahead and do a little bit more with it here? Add a new button to your XAML to show the log contents:

```
<Button Content="Show Log" x:Name="ShowLogButton"
  Click="ShowLogButton_Click" />
```

Here's what the click handler looks like:

```
void ShowLogButton_Click(object sender, RoutedEventArgs e)
{
  using (IsolatedStorageFileStream log =
    UserStore.OpenFile(LOG_FILE, FileMode.OpenOrCreate,
      FileAccess.Read, FileShare.ReadWrite))
  {
    using (StreamReader sr = new StreamReader(log))
      this.SusbscriptionInfo.Text = sr.ReadToEnd();
  }
}
```

Again, same stuff you're used to. It's good to use "using" statements to ensure that the resources get closed and released, particularly on the `StreamWriter` (in the previous snippet), because if you don't do that or call `Flush`, it won't actually write to the underlying stream. But it's just generally good practice to call `Dispose` (which is what the using block will do for you — even if there's an exception) on classes that implement `IDisposable`. Implementing that is supposed to be a signal that the class uses unmanaged resources that you will want to release when you're done with them (such as a file on the filesystem).

Last, why not have the ability to clear the log file? To do this, just add another button and corresponding `click` handler as follows:

```
<Button Content="Clear Log" x:Name="ClearLogButton"
  Click="ClearLogButton_Click" />

void ClearLogButton_Click(object sender, RoutedEventArgs e)
{
  if (UserStore.FileExists(LOG_FILE))
    UserStore.DeleteFile(LOG_FILE);
  this.SusbscriptionInfo.Text = string.Empty;
}
```

Here again, you see the familiar methods like `FileExists` and `DeleteFile`. As you can see, interacting with isolated storage is a breeze if you're familiar with the .NET filesystem APIs. The real trick is to use it wisely and in a way that will have the most positive effect on user experience. Along those lines, it's not clear yet how users will respond to requests for quota increases, but let's hope that as Silverlight applications become more common, they will become comfortable with them enough so that it won't be a problem. Use it wisely in any case.

Out-of-Browser Applications

To bring Web-based RIAs closer to the feel of a desktop application, Silverlight 3 introduces Out of Browser Applications (OOBAs). An OOBA is essentially the exact same application that you would run from a URL in the browser, except that it is started from a desktop icon or an icon from the Start Menu. This is enabled via a configuration file in your Silverlight application, which displays the desktop installation option via the right-click menu of your running Silverlight application. This desktop-deployed application still runs in the Silverlight plug-in in the browser; it just has the ability to be launched via the desktop or the Start Menu via an icon, just like any other desktop application. That being said, there are some interesting scenarios that you can implement with this new capability. For example, since you have the ability to check the state of the network, as well as the ability to store a file locally with the `IsolatedStorage` API's, you can create a very rich, desktop-like experience using Silverlight because the OOBA can run without being connected to the Internet or your local network.

To enable an OOBA, follow these steps:

1. In Visual Studio, right-click on your Silverlight project to select Properties from the context menu. This will bring up the Project Properties page in Visual Studio, as Figure 11-1 shows.

2. Check the box that reads "Enable running Silverlight application out of the browser".

Once you do this, a configuration file named OutOfBrowserSettings.xml is added to your project under the Properties folder, as demonstrated in Figure 11-2, and the *.proj* file is updated to point to this configuration file so the build knows to include the OOBA capabilities.

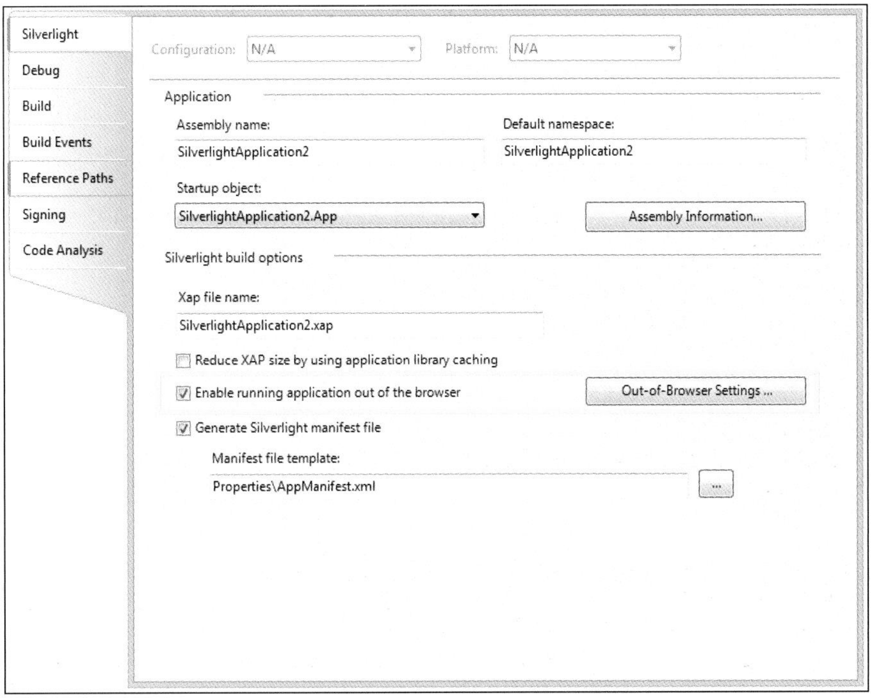

Figure 11-1

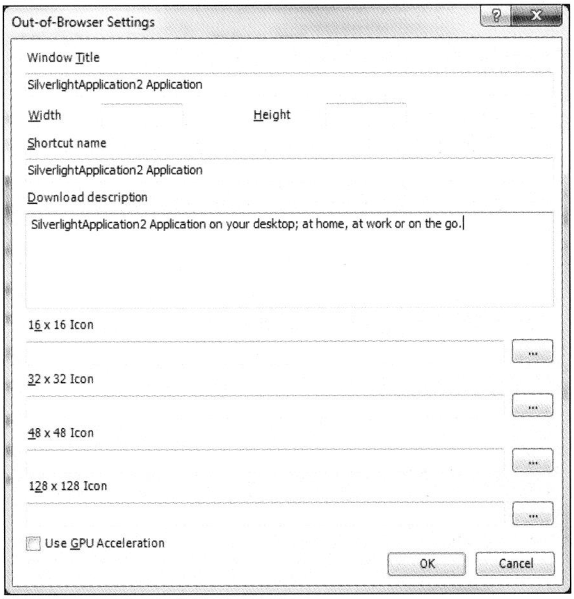

Figure 11-2

This XML configuration file is all that is needed to enable your application to be installed to the desktop with the default settings. If you open this file, you'll see something like this:

```
<OutOfBrowserSettings
                  ShortName="SilverlightApplication2 Application"
                  EnableGPUAcceleration="False"
                  ShowInstallMenuItem="True">
  <OutOfBrowserSettings.Blurb>
    SilverlightApplication2 Application on your desktop; at home, at work or on the
go.
  </OutOfBrowserSettings.Blurb>
  <OutOfBrowserSettings.WindowSettings>
    <WindowSettings Title="SilverlightApplication2 Application" />
  </OutOfBrowserSettings.WindowSettings>
  <OutOfBrowserSettings.Icons />
</OutOfBrowserSettings>
```

You'll also notice the "Out-of-Browser Settings ..." button on the Project Properties page shown in Figure 11-1. This button, which displays the model Out-of-Browser Settings dialog, shown in Figure 11-3, allows you to change the various properties allowed in an OOBA experience, instead of hand-coding the XML configuration file.

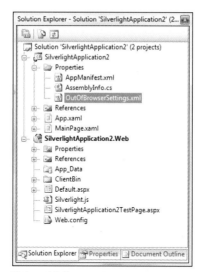

Figure 11-3

These properties, located in the `OutOfBrowserSettings` class in the `System.Windows` namespace, are detailed in the following list:

❑   `Blurb` — Gets a short description of the application.

❑   `EnableGPUAcceleration` — Gets a value that indicates whether to use graphics processor unit hardware acceleration for cached compositions, which potentially results in graphics optimization.

❏   Icons — Gets a collection of Icon instances (16×16, 32×32, 48×48, and 128×128) associated with the application. If you do not specify icon files, default icons are displayed at runtime.

❏   ShortName — Gets the short version of the application title.

❏   ShowInstallMenuItem — Gets a value that indicates whether the application right-click menu includes an install option.

❏   WindowSettings — Gets the settings applied to the application window.

When you run an application that is properly configured, you'll see the right-click option shown in Figure 11-4.

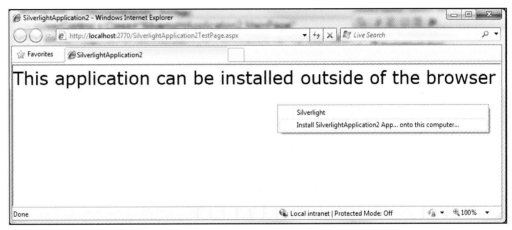

Figure 11-4

Once you click the menu item to install the application to the desktop, the Install Application dialog, shown in Figure 11-5, gives the option to confirm the install to the Start menu by default, and the Desktop as an option.

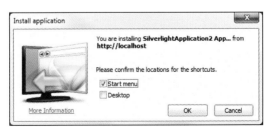

Figure 11-5

Once the OK button is clicked, the application icon will appear in the Start menu or Desktop and the application can be run locally. To uninstall the application, the right-click Install option is replaced with a Remove option, as shown in Figure 11-6.

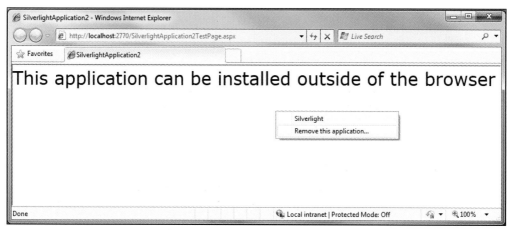

Figure 11-6

When the application is brought offline, the following happens:

1. An application request is sent to the server, and the XAP for the application is sent back to the browser and stored in a low-trust location (a round-trip occurs here).

2. Metadata is stored along with the XAP, which includes the original URI of the application, and time-stamp information on the XAP file (the ETag of the HttpRequest).

The `Application.InstallState` property contains the enumeration of states that you can programmatically check to determine if an application is installed locally and subsequently install the application locally via code. The values for `InstallState` are:

❑   `NotInstalled` — The application is running within its host Web page.

❑   `Installing` — The application is in the process of being installed to run outside the browser.

❑   `Installed` — The application is running outside the browser.

❑   `InstallFailed` — The application could not be installed to run outside the browser.

This code would check the install state of an application and install it locally:

```
if (Application.Current.InstallState == InstallState.NotInstalled)
{
    Application.Current.Install();
}
```

You cannot uninstall an application programmatically; this must be initiated by the end user via the right-click option.

Detecting Network State

The OOBA experience wouldn't be completely useful unless there was a way to detect whether the local application was online. Checking the results of the `NetworkInterface.GetIsNetworkAvailable` method in the `NetworkChange.NetworkAddressChanged` event, you can check the state of the current network connection.

```
if ( NetworkInterface .GetIsNetworkAvailable())
```

At the application level, in the App.Xaml.Cs file, you can determine whether an application is running outside the browser by checking the `IsRunningOutOfBrowser` property:

```
if (Application.Current.IsRunningOutOfBrowser)
```

Checking for Application Updates

To check for and retrieve an update to OOBA, you can call the `CheckAndDownloadUpdateAsync` method and handle the `Application.CheckAndDownloadUpdateCompleted` event. In order for the updated application to be used, you can check the `UpdateAvailable` property in this event handler, and if it returns `true`, you can prompt the user to restart the application. In the case where an update is available, but the update is using a newer version of Silverlight, the `UpdateAvailable` will return `false`, and the update will not download. Note that OOBA will *not automatically* check for an updated application, you need to deal with that yourself.

Installation and Updates

One last area where Silverlight helps out a lot is in installation and updates. Of course, for your applications, Silverlight follows the Web model, ensuring that users are always using the latest version, almost invisibly. You are responsible, though, for ensuring a reasonable download and startup time for your applications. If you have large applications, think about breaking them up into multiple Silverlight projects and downloading them either on demand or in the background after an initial download, or even just placing different "areas" of your application in different locations on your server (e.g., you could have a `/users` directory with one Silverlight project that deals with managing user information and a `/projects` directory that deals with managing projects).

New in Silverlight 3 is the ability to improve the overall download size of your application by letting Silverlight keep a global cache of the Silverlight-specific assemblies in the client for all Silverlight applications. This means that when you compile your application, the XAP will not contain any of the necessary System.* DLLs or 3rd party vendor DLLs that Silverlight needs. Instead, the manifest will point to a URL at Microsoft.com for the Silverlight specific DLLs or the appropriate vendors website for 3rd party DLLs to download the files if they are not already on the local machine. You can enable this assembly-caching feature by selecting the "Reduce Xap size by using application library caching" option in the Properties window for your application, as shown in Figure 11-7.

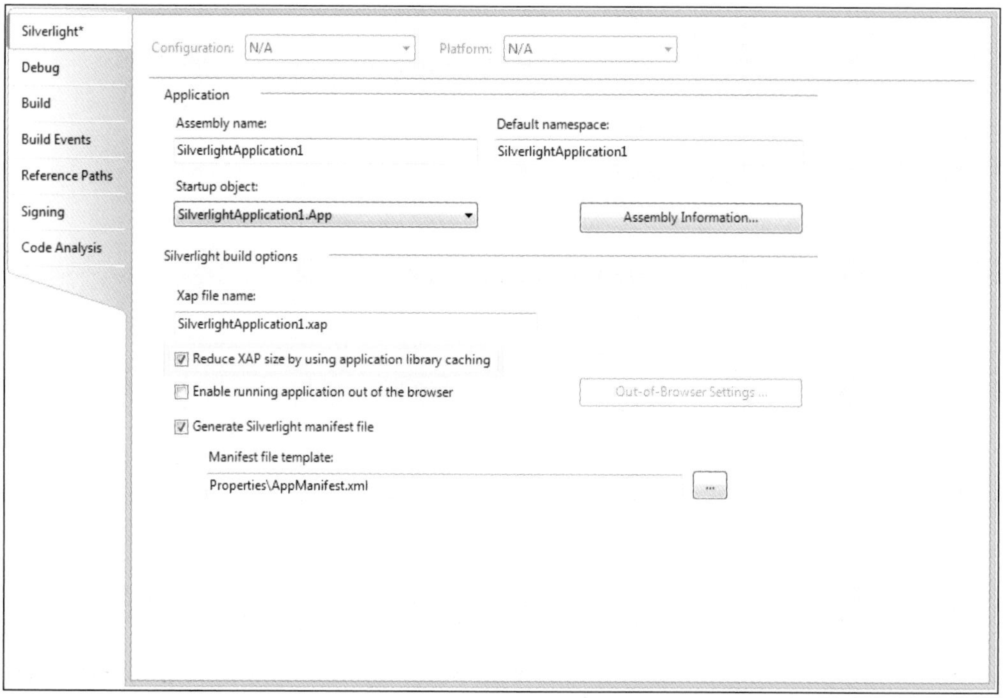

Figure 11-7

But as far as the Silverlight run time itself is concerned, Microsoft handles the distribution, installation, and updates for you. As you doubtless have seen and will see elsewhere in the book, you can and should supply the standard blue Silverlight badge (or whatever color it becomes in the future) so that it is familiar (and thus increases trust). You can, and should, supply a preview image of your application and encourage users to choose to install to get that functionality. But the hard part of distributing, downloading, installing, and updating is taken care of for you.

If the browser and OS will allow it, Silverlight wants to do automatic updates for users; however, this is configurable even in the cases in which it is allowed via the Silverlight Configuration dialogs that users can access by right-clicking on any Silverlight instance. There is an Updates tab, as shown in Figure 11-8, that users can use to change how Silverlight updates. In this instance, it is running on Vista under User Account Control (UAC), so automatic updates are not allowed.

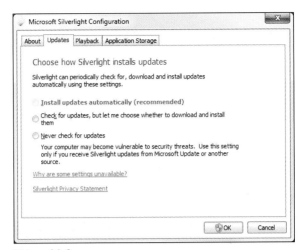

Figure 11-8

Summary

In this chapter, you covered various services that Silverlight provides to make application development and maintenance easier and, in some cases, possible for certain user scenarios. You looked first at communications services such as HTTP-based services, including duplex communication over HTTP, and also at sockets communications. You then looked at storage services, which, in Silverlight, take the form of isolated storage; and, finally, you read about Out of Browser applications and the basic facilities that Silverlight provides to manage installation and updates for you.

Part III: Building Applications

12

Silverlight, the Browser, and the Server

Prepare yourself for a fun ride through the rapids. This chapter will gear you up with an understanding of where Silverlight sits in relation to the browser and the server, two foundational relationships that you need to know inside and out. First, you'll take a brief tour of the knobs that Silverlight offers to configure the run time and your applications and then go on to how to deal with various non-executing resources. After that, you dig deep into Silverlight's relationship with the browser, which, as you'll see, is quite extensive and powerful thanks to the HTML bridge. Finally, you'll wrap up with a look at Silverlight's relationship with the server, with particular focus on the facilities that ASP.NET brings to the table to make your life easier.

Silverlight All by Its Lonesome

It is strange to think about it this way, but Silverlight is in itself an entire development and runtime platform for applications. Microsoft has created a specialized managed run time, set of libraries, and a common translation layer so that it can run on multiple operating systems, much like Java. Some have called Silverlight just a *player* or just another applet or plug-in, and it *is* those, but it is selling Silverlight short to leave it at that.

It's important to draw this out because you really need to think of it as a full-fledged run time apart from the browser, the server, and the operating system. It is its own ecosystem, a mini-universe for developers to play in, to create anything from a simple animated ad to a full-fledged accounting system. It is true that, as of Silverlight 2, it is dependent on a browser host, but there is nothing inherent in Silverlight that should keep it in the browser, much like Flash and Flex have moved out of the browser with the Adobe Integrated Runtime (AIR). I have no doubt that Silverlight will get there, and thus it will do developers good to think about Silverlight in these terms, as a full-scale application platform on its own.

Having said this, there are certainly considerations that you must keep in mind relating Silverlight to the browser and the server, which you will cover later in this chapter.

Configuration

The current configuration model relies on the HTML object tag attributes and parameters. Here is an example of a Silverlight object declaration:

```
<div id="silverlightControlHost">
<object data="data:application/x-silverlight-2,"
  type="application/x-silverlight-2" width="100%" height="100%">
  <param name="source" value="ClientBin/SilverlightApplication2.xap"/>
  <param name="onError" value="onSilverlightError" />
  <param name="background" value="white" />
  <param name="minRuntimeVersion" value="3.0.40603.0" />
  <param name="autoUpgrade" value="true" />
  <a href="http://go.microsoft.com/fwlink/?LinkID=149156&v=3.0.40603.0"
              style="text-decoration:none">
        <img src="http://go.microsoft.com/fwlink/?LinkId=108181"
              alt="Get Microsoft Silverlight"
              style="border-style:none"/>
  </a>
</object><iframe id="_sl_historyFrame"
        style="visibility:hidden;height:0px;width:0px;border:0px"></iframe>
</div>
```

The full list of attributes is:

❑   id — Specifies an identifier that can be used to reference the runtime instance in script.

❑   data — Helps with the instantiation; it is recommended that the value be the standard Silverlight MIME type, data:application/x-silverlight.

❑   type — This is the specific MIME type and is used to specify which version of Silverlight should be loaded.

❑   height — Specifies the height of the runtime instance in either pixels (integer) or percentage.

❑   width — Specifies the width of the runtime instance in either pixels (integer) or percentage.

You're typically going to want to specify all of these. The parameters are a bit more involved, but they're still few enough to be easily digested. They're broken up into data and event parameters.

Data Parameters

The data parameters include:

❑   source — This is required and specifies the path to the application, which typically will be a XAP file. You can also use the hash (#) followed by a DOM ID to point to some inline XAML, but that is not supported by managed code.

❑   enableHtmlAccess — Specifies whether or not this Silverlight instance can access the HTML bridge, as covered later in this chapter.

❑   allowHtmlPopupWindow — Specifies whether or not code in the Silverlight instance can use the HtmlPage.PopupWindow method to create a new browser window.

❑   background — This lets you specify a background color for the Silverlight instance, and it defaults to fully opaque white (#FFFFFFFF).

❑ minRuntimeVersion — Specifies the minimum version you need for your application to run correctly.

❑ autoUpgrade — Lets you specify that Silverlight should try to auto-update if its version is less than the minimumRuntimeVersion.

❑ maxFramerate — Allows you to specify the desired maximum framerate. The default is 60, and the actual framerate will vary by the system load and processing power.

❑ windowless — This only applies for Windows (other systems are always windowless). The default is false, and that improves performance on Windows, but if you need to layer HTML on top of the Silverlight instance, you need to set this to true.

The parameters thus far configure the Silverlight run time itself, but you get a couple of parameters that let you tweak the behavior a bit and pass information to the application that runs in the instance:

❑ splashScreenSource — This enables you to customize the loading screen while the application referred to by the source parameter is downloaded. By default, Silverlight provides a generic download progress bar, but you may want to enhance your User Experience (UX) by customizing it, especially if you expect anything more than a few seconds of download time.

❑ initParams — Used to pass in custom parameters to your application. This is the closest thing to what you get with application settings in .NET, but it is woefully basic.

The last couple of data parameters are for debugging only and should not, as you could infer, be used in production applications.

❑ enableRedrawRegions — This adds a special adornment to illuminate which regions are being re-drawn with each frame, which can be useful if something isn't visually updating as you expect it to do.

❑ enableFramerateCounter — This one only works in IE on Windows, but it will show the actual framerate in the status bar of the browser, which can help you debug issues with visual latency.

Event Parameters

Event parameters are those that let you specify unmanaged JavaScript methods to handle events coming from the Silverlight runtime instance:

❑ onError — This is used to handle both error events in the run time itself and those caused by user code that are not handled in user code as dealt with in Chapter 16.

❑ onResize — This event occurs when the actual height and width of the runtime instance changes.

❑ onLoad — Occurs when the runtime instance is loaded and everything in the root visual is loaded.

❑ onfullscreenchanged — Fires when a change to the FullScreen property occurs.

❑ onSourceDownloadComplete — Occurs when the source referenced by the source parameter is fully downloaded.

❑ onSourceDownloadProgressChanged — Occurs while the source download progresses.

Application Configuration

Unfortunately, beyond the `initParams` parameter, there is no built-in application-level configuration. An alternative to using `initParams` is to use JavaScript variables to store configuration that can be accessed via the HTML bridge as done in Chapter 16. You could take this a step further and have your server-side code emit such a configuration based on server-side configuration, which would let you take advantage of the .NET configuration system to manage your settings. But the fact is that you're on your own on this point.

Resources

First, be aware that there are multiple kinds of resources when dealing with Silverlight. There are Silverlight resources, which are things like styles and templates referenced via resource dictionaries. These are covered in Chapter 8. The resources referred to here are application resources, which are any non-executable files (XAML, XML, images, media, etc.) that are used by your application. Within these, there are basically three categories: embedded resources, content resources, and site-of-origin resources.

Embedded Resources

Embedded resources should be familiar to most developers — these are resources that are packaged up in the assemblies themselves. To use these in Visual Studio (or MSBuild), you mark the file as a *Resource* in the Properties pane or as a `Resource` element in the MSBuild file. These will then be packaged in with the assembly when it is compiled and will be downloaded along with the assembly when the assembly is downloaded.

You can reference these kinds of resources by URI, using XAML attribute values such as the `Source` attribute on the `Image` control:

```
<Image Source="MyEmbeddedImage.png" />
```

Alternatively, you can specify them in code using the `Uri` class:

```
Uri myUri = new Uri("/MyEmbeddedImage.png", UriKind.Relative);
```

These are resolved relative to the running code, so if you need to reference an image from another assembly, you have to use this special syntax:

```
Uri myUri = new Uri("/OtherAssembly;component/MyEmbeddedImage.png",
  UriKind.Relative);
```

The first bit followed by `;component` tells the resolution mechanism to find that assembly and then look for the resource relative to it.

Content Resources

Content resources are functionally similar to embedded resources in that they are packaged up and downloaded with the application package itself. The distinction is that they are not embedded in one particular assembly, so this is a good option to share resources between assemblies more naturally and not bloat assembly size.

To use these, mark the files as `"Content"` in the VS property grid or use the `Content` element in the MSBuild specification. When the package is built, they will be included in the generated XAP file but not embedded in particular assemblies.

You reference them in basically the same way as embedded resources; however, you need to start with a leading slash (/) to specify where the resource is relative to the package root.

Site-of-Origin Resources

"Site-of-origin resources" is a fancy way of saying resources that are located outside of the package and assembly, typically on a Web Server. In VS, you mark these as *None* and use the `None` element in MSBuild (assuming that they're in your project), and then you'll likely want to specify that they be copied to your output directory, which is configurable in the VS Property grid as well as by using the `CopyToOutputDirectory` attribute in the MSBuild specification.

You reference these resources in exactly the same way that you reference content resources, with the leading slash (/), which is relative to the location of the application source.

Choosing Resource Type

The decision of which resource type to choose depends on your usage scenario and, to some extent, on the size of the resource. The general rule is that if you must have the resource for the application to run successfully, you should package it either in the assembly or the package as embedded resources or content resources, respectively. As noted, choosing between those two depends largely on whether or not you intend to share the resource between assemblies or if, for instance, you have a library assembly that always needs its resources — in that case, you'd want to embed the resources with the assembly. Otherwise, I would generally suggest content resources.

If you don't need to have the resource, that is, if you can meaningfully execute the application without it, you should probably consider hosting that resource outside of the package to limit downloading time for the package itself — this is your best option for download-on-demand scenarios, and this is likely the best approach for large multimedia files, unless you have a good reason to embed those.

Silverlight with the Browser

The previous section talked about Silverlight itself and how you can configure it and handle its resources. In this section, you'll explore in more depth what Silverlight provides in terms of interaction with the browser and browser technologies. The name that Microsoft seems to prefer for talking about this stuff is the *HTML Bridge*, so if you see that term, it means "the facilities that enable communication between managed code and the browser/JavaScript." Remember that everything in the chapter up to and including this section is independent of the server-side technology.

Interacting with the Browser Object Model (BOM)

The *Browser Object Model* (BOM) is the set of objects that allow applications to understand and manipulate browser facilities such as window-, location-, navigator-, and frames-related functionality. It also provides access to the currently loaded document, which gets you into the Document Object Model and is usually the object that receives the most focus and efforts of DHTML development.

In terms of browser-level interaction, Silverlight provides a few facilities. First, there is the HtmlPage
.BrowserInformation member. This gets you environmental information about the browser, as shown
in Figure 12-1. Pretty much all of the HTML bridge/browser stuff is in the System.Windows.Browser
namespace, so if you do much with it, you'll want to import/use that namespace.

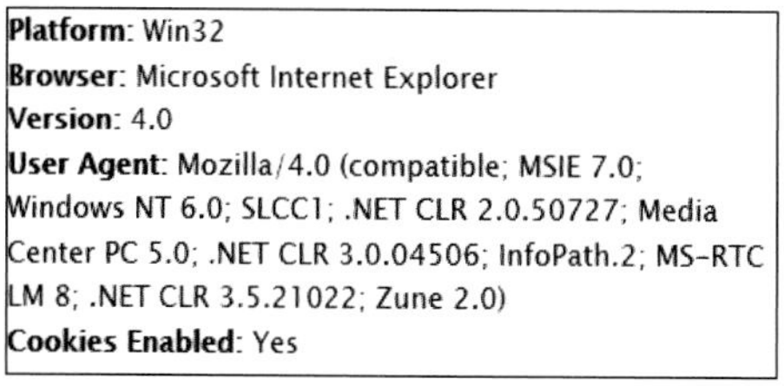

Platform: Win32
Browser: Microsoft Internet Explorer
Version: 4.0
User Agent: Mozilla/4.0 (compatible; MSIE 7.0;
Windows NT 6.0; SLCC1; .NET CLR 2.0.50727; Media
Center PC 5.0; .NET CLR 3.0.04506; InfoPath.2; MS-RTC
LM 8; .NET CLR 3.5.21022; Zune 2.0)
Cookies Enabled: Yes

Figure 12-1

The code that produces this is fairly straightforward, as you might expect:

```
void Page_Loaded(object sender, RoutedEventArgs e)
{
    this.SetBrowserInfo();
}

void SetBrowserInfo()
{
    this.AddLine(this.BrowserInfo, "Platform",
        HtmlPage.BrowserInformation.Platform);
    this.AddLine(this.BrowserInfo, "Browser",
        HtmlPage.BrowserInformation.Name);
    this.AddLine(this.BrowserInfo, "Version",
        HtmlPage.BrowserInformation.BrowserVersion.ToString());
    this.AddLine(this.BrowserInfo, "User Agent",
        HtmlPage.BrowserInformation.UserAgent);
    this.AddLine(this.BrowserInfo, "Cookies Enabled",
        (HtmlPage.BrowserInformation.CookiesEnabled ? "Yes" : "No"));
}

private void AddLine(TextBlock block, string label, string value)
{
    Run r = new Run();
    r.FontWeight = FontWeights.Bold;
    r.Text = label + ": ";
    block.Inlines.Add(r);
    r = new Run();
    r.Text = value;
    block.Inlines.Add(r);
    block.Inlines.Add(new LineBreak());
}
```

I'd expect this kind of information to be less valuable in Silverlight than it is in standard web development, where you often need to do special stuff based on browser information, but it could certainly be
helpful information to log in error handling.

Of course, your window (pun intended) into the world of the browser is the Window object that hangs off the HtmlPage type (i.e., HtmlPage.Window). You have most of the stuff you've come to know and loathe in JavaScript as follows.

Alerts, Confirms, and Prompts, Oh Dear!

In the following sections, you'll see how to use standard JavaScript user message/input facilities. For alerts that are triggered from the server, Silverlight 3 introduces the MessageBox class, which provides a static Show method that you can use to display a message in a simple dialog box. The dialog box is modal and provides an OK button. There is an overload of the Show method that enables you to specify a title bar caption and an optional Cancel button. If you display a Cancel button, you can use the return value of the method to determine the user's response. The next several sections will only discuss the JavaScript message and input facilities.

Alert

You can, as an extremely lazy and unpleasant (but sometimes useful) approach, use Window.Alert to show the standard JavaScript Alert window, passing in whatever string you want displayed. For instance, add a Button and set its Click property to Alert_Demo in XAML, and then use this code for that handler:

```
private void Alert_Demo(object sender, RoutedEventArgs e)
{
    Exception ex = new Exception("I didn't get handled well.");
    HtmlPage.Window.Alert(ex.ToString());
}
```

That will give you what you see in Figure 12-2, as you should expect.

Figure 12-2

In terms of user experience, this is less than ideal. Ideally, you'll create an area of your UI or create a nicely styled user control to display these kinds of messages to users. For example, you could create a TransientMessage control that is styled in accord with the application and fades in and out to show certain messages. Don't require your users to click anything to dismiss such messages; it's just extra work for them.

The `TransientMessage` control is essentially a `UserControl` that has a few borders (for styling) and a `TextBlock` (to display the message). You then add a `StoryBoard` to the `UserControl.Resources` that looks something like the following:

```
<Storyboard x:Name="ShowTimeline">
  <DoubleAnimationUsingKeyFrames Storyboard.TargetName="LayoutRoot"
    Storyboard.TargetProperty="Opacity" BeginTime="00:00:00">
    <SplineDoubleKeyFrame KeyTime="00:00:00" Value="0"/>
    <SplineDoubleKeyFrame KeyTime="00:00:00.8000000" Value="1"/>
    <SplineDoubleKeyFrame x:Name="StartHideFrame"
      KeyTime="00:00:04.8" Value="1"/>
    <SplineDoubleKeyFrame x:Name="EndHideFrame"
      KeyTime="00:00:05.600000" Value="0"/>
  </DoubleAnimationUsingKeyFrames>
</Storyboard>
```

`LayoutRoot` is the standard `Grid` you start with when creating a `UserControl` — it's just the root visual element on this control. The `StoryBoard` targets the `Opacity` property in order to fade in and out. Using keyframes enables you to have more discrete control over how the animation works. To allow the control to be displayed for user-configured durations, you need to add names to the last two frames to change them in code via, for example, a `ShowDuration` property:

```
public static DependencyProperty ShowDurationProperty =
    DependencyProperty.Register("ShowDuration", typeof(double),
    typeof(TransientMessage), null);
public double ShowDuration
{
    get
    {
        return (double)this.GetValue(ShowDurationProperty);
    }
    set
    {
        this.SetValue(ShowDurationProperty, value);
        this.StartHideFrame.KeyTime =
          KeyTime.FromTimeSpan(TimeSpan.FromSeconds(value + .8d));
        this.EndHideFrame.KeyTime =
          KeyTime.FromTimeSpan(TimeSpan.FromSeconds(value + 1.6d));
    }
}
```

You see here that in the setter, you reset the `KeyTime` on the `StartHideFrame` (the one that controls when to start fading out) to be 0.8 second after the requested duration. This is because the storyboard has a 0.8-second fade-in, so you want to show at 100 percent opacity for the specified duration. Then you set the `EndHideFrame`'s `KeyTime` to be 1.6 seconds after the desired duration, so the overall effect is to fade in for 0.8 second, show for the desired duration, and then fade out for 0.8 second.

You can, of course, add other features, but at a minimum, you need to add a `Message` property to let users set the text of the message:

```
public string Message
{
```

```
get
{
    return this.MessageBlock.Text;
}
set
{
    this.MessageBlock.Text = value;
}
}
```

This simply sets the Text property on the TextBlock you have defined in your XAML (we called it *MessageBlock*, but you can call it whatever you want). Then you will want to add a Show method as follows:

```
public void Show()
{
    this.LayoutRoot.Visibility = Visibility.Visible;
    this.ShowTimeline.Begin();
}
```

This sets the visibility to Visible, meaning that it will take up space and display, all other things (like Opacity) being equal. Then simply start your storyboard, which handles the fading in and out for you.

That reminds me, you have some setting up to do in your constructor:

```
public TransientMessage()
{
    InitializeComponent();

    this.LayoutRoot.Visibility = Visibility.Collapsed;
    this.LayoutRoot.Opacity = 0;
    this.ShowDuration = 4d;
    this.ShowTimeline.Completed +=
        new EventHandler(ShowTimeline_Completed);
}
```

Here you set the visibility on your root visual to Collapsed (which means that it won't take up space and won't show) and default to zero Opacity (which makes it invisible, even if it were not collapsed, a good starting point for fading in). Then default the ShowDuration to whatever makes sense, such as 4 seconds. Finally, attach a Completed event handler to your storyboard.

Now when your storyboard completes, your ShowTimeline_Completed method is called:

```
void ShowTimeline_Completed(object sender, EventArgs e)
{
    this.LayoutRoot.Visibility = Visibility.Collapsed;
}
```

This just resets the Visibility so that it is no longer taking up space, which may or may not matter depending on your layout.

Now to use the control, you first (as always) need to define an XML namespace for it:

```
xmlns:l="clr-namespace:BrowserAndStuff"
```

Then use it in your layout where it makes sense, but given that objects defined later have a higher default z-index, it's usually good to put it at the bottom, so it will be on top by default.

```
<l:TransientMessage x:Name="ServiceError"
    MaxHeight="90" MaxWidth="350"
    ShowDuration="5" Message="There was a problem getting your information. Please
        try again later. If this keeps happening, please let us know." />
```

It's good to define a `Height` and `Width` (or `MaxHeight` and `MaxWidth`) because if it is in a `Grid`, it will expand to take up the entire `Grid`, which is likely the entire control (or page, if you're using Silverlight with 100% height/width). Set the duration for a reasonable time for users to read the message, and then you set the message itself.

This one is an error message that you could show when calling your services, so in the completed handler for your call to the service, if there is an error, essentially do this:

```
this.ServiceError.Show();
```

That results in the user seeing Figure 12-3.

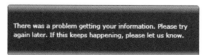

Figure 12-3

Of course, you could use this approach for non-error messages as well, informational, whatever. You might also add an overload to `Show` that lets you change the message, so you could use it similarly to the `Window.Alert`, and that would have a lot better UX than the built-in Alert approach. If you're building real apps, you should also think about the different kinds of messages.

It's pretty common to at least have two kinds of message (error and information); sometimes you need a warning, but those (like confirmations as discussed below) should be avoided if possible. In distinguishing between these types of messages, you should follow standard approaches, particularly for errors, in terms of clearly communicating an error state (unlike what was done with the `TransientMessage` above). I recommend exploring the Windows Vista UX Guidelines for error messages on this point as a good starting point for crafting (or better yet, avoiding) your error messages.

Confirm

Like `Alert`, `Window` allows you to bridge into the `Confirm` JavaScript function. The following code shows an example of that, assuming that you have a button that uses it for its `Click` event:

```
private void Confirm_Demo(object sender, RoutedEventArgs e)
{
```

```
        if (HtmlPage.Window.Confirm(
            "Are you sure you want to hurt your users like this?"))
    {
        // you're unbelievably cruel
    }
}
```

And like `Alert`, this is a really shoddy user experience that you should avoid. First off, you should avoid confirmations in general. A better pattern to follow is `Undo`, that is, allowing users to easily undo actions. It encourages users to explore functionality and not be anxious about actions they might take, which makes them more comfortable with the application. Similarly, most of the time when a user does something, he really means to do it, which means that, say, 80 percent of the time, you're just bothering him with a confirmation dialog. Last, as you see in Figure 12-4, the standard confirm dialogs are just ugly and almost certainly do not share the look and feel of your application. Slightly extending the `TransientMessage` approach, you can easily imagine how you could design a confirmation dialog with a much better experience.

Figure 12-4

Prompt

Any hall of shame for bad UX wouldn't be complete without the JavaScript prompt dialog, as shown in Figure 12-5.

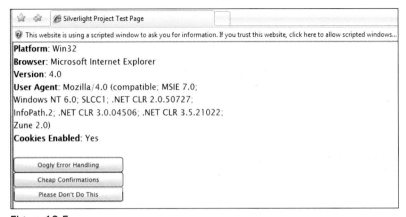

Figure 12-5

279

Oh wait, I couldn't show you this in Figure 12-5 because I first had to tell IE that it was OK to show prompt dialogs. Let's try Figure 12-6.

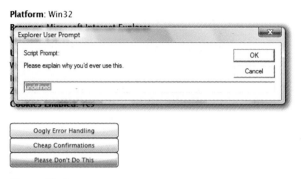

Figure 12-6

I hope I don't have to go into detail as to why this is a bad idea and should never be used. Just don't do it! But if you must, here's how:

```
private void Prompt_Demo(object sender, RoutedEventArgs e)
{
    string reason =
        HtmlPage.Window.Prompt(
            "Please explain why you'd ever use this.");
}
```

Navigation

OK, enough of the no-no's. A facility that you will likely need and want to use on the Window object is the ability to navigate or open new windows. You can do this with the Window.Navigate method (and overloads). There three overloads:

❑   Window.Navigate(*Uri navigateToUri*)

❑   Window.Navigate(*Uri navigateToUri, string target*)

❑   Window.Navigate(*Uri navigateToUri, string target, string targetFeatures*)

Of course, that maps pretty closely to the JavaScript window.Open method. The point is that you use this to change the current window location as well as open new ones (or target frames). As you might guess, the Uri is where you want to go, the target is the target frame or window, and the features are the same features you can use with window.Open.

So let's just drop a Button into the page like this:

```
<Button
    Width="200"
    HorizontalAlignment="Left"
    Content="Feeling Lucky!"
    Click="Feeling_Lucky" />
```

and add the handler vis-à-vis what's in the XAML:

```
private void Feeling_Lucky(object sender, RoutedEventArgs e)
{
    HtmlPage.Window.Navigate(
        new Uri("http://www.wrox.com", UriKind.Absolute),
        "NavWindow", "toolbars=no,address=no,width=800,height=600");
}
```

And this will, of course, result in something like what you see in Figure 12-7.

Figure 12-7

Microsoft supplies you with the `HyperlinkButton` control, so you may rarely need to use this approach, but it's there if you do need to. One nice thing is that as long as you navigate to a new window in response to a user click, you should get by pop-up blockers — just don't try to do it on the sly.

`Window` also gives you `NavigateToBookmark` (method) and `CurrentBookmark` (property), which lets you change the hash value (aka, bookmark) of the current URL. This can be very useful for enabling what is sometimes called *deep linking*, that is, URLs that will link directly/deeply into an Ajax, Flash, Silverlight, or similar application. The accompanying samples for the chapter have a utility class that shows how you might simplify working with this kind of approach, but setting and getting are fairly straightforward, so much so that one wonders, why even have the method, since it just sets the property?

Silverlight 3 adds a new content control, a `Frame`, that handles navigation between `Page` objects. This new control will also handle the updating of the browser journal history, which means that there is complete integration of page navigation between Silverlight pages and the browser.

Window Events

Using `Window` events between script and managed code is covered in Chapter 16, but note that there is an `AttachEvent` and `DetachEvent` set of methods on `Window` that lets managed code subscribe to and unsubscribe from JavaScript events. Both of these have an overload that takes the method name as string as the first parameter and either `EventHandler` or `EventHandler<HtmlEventArgs>` as the second. These are derived from the `HtmlObject` type, which is covered more fully later in this chapter.

Frames

Frames have generally fallen out of favor, and I can only guess that's why they're not explicitly supported on the `Window` object. If you're using inline frames, you can use the `GetProperty` method to get a reference to the frame.

Interacting with the Document Object Model (DOM)

In the previous section, you saw the facilities for interacting with BOM; in this section, you'll see the facilities provided for interacting with the DOM, which is what you'll want to do if you need to control or get information about visual elements in the browser that are outside the Silverlight instance.

The first, and most obvious, way to get at the DOM is through the `Document` object itself, and Silverlight provides a super-easy way to do that: `System.Windows.Browser.HtmlPage.Document`. The `Document` property gets you an `HtmlDocument` instance, which is a derivative of `HtmlObject`, the class that defines the basic behaviors for dealing with all HTML elements in managed code such as attaching and detaching events (which is covered in depth in Chapter 16).

`HtmlDocument` has some interesting behaviors that you should expect if you've done any scripting with the `Html.Document` object.

- ❑ `CreateElement(string elementName)` — Creates the specified element and returns a managed reference to it. The element will be stand-alone; that is, it won't have a parent until you add it somewhere in the DOM.
- ❑ `GetElementById(string id)` — Gets the HTML element with the matching ID.
- ❑ `GetElementsByTagName(string tagName)` — Gets a `ScriptObjectCollection` of all elements of the specified tag name (essentially getting HTML elements by their type).
- ❑ `Submit(string formId)` — Posts the form specified by `formId`; there is also an overload with no parameters that will post the first form in the document.

In addition to these behaviors, the `HtmlDocument` object has some interesting additional properties:

- ❑ `Body` — Gets a reference to the HTML document's body element (as an `HtmlElement`).
- ❑ `Cookies` — Lets you read or set the browser's cookie string.
- ❑ `DocumentElement` — Gets an `HtmlElement` reference to the `HtmlDocument` element.

❑   `DocumentUri` — Gets you the `Uri` instance for the current document — sure to be a very commonly used property on the `Document`.

❑   `IsReady` — Lets you figure out if all elements on Silverlight's host page have been parsed, that is, that it is ready to start programming against. This is a good gate flag to keep you from running into unexpected errors while hacking away at the DOM.

❑   `QueryString` — This is a nifty Read Only dictionary of the current query string values. If you need to modify them, you need to use the `Navigate` methods as outlined in the BOM section of this chapter — modifying the query string is considered a navigational action.

Finally, the `HtmlDocument` object has a handy `DocumentReady` event that you can use to simplify your code by holding off your hacking until it is done (a good alternative to manually checking `IsReady`), but be aware that this event could fire before you subscribe to it, so probably the best thing would be to use something like the following in your application initialization:

```
if (!System.Windows.Browser.HtmlPage.Document.IsReady)
    System.Windows.Browser.HtmlPage.Document.DocumentReady +=
        new EventHandler(Document_DocumentReady);
```

Then in `Document_DocumentReady`, do whatever DOM hacking you need to do up front. Depending on your level of confidence in how quickly the page will parse, you may want to check `IsReady` in your DOM manipulation code.

So that's the `HtmlDocument` "Document" property on the page that gives you a nice "in" into the DOM, but normally, when manipulating the DOM, you are dealing with HTML elements, and that's where the `HtmlElement` class comes in, providing you with what DOM programmers are used to, such as these extra behaviors:

❑   `AppendChild(HtmlElement element)` — If the element allows children, this sticks the given element on the end of the children collection. If you want to insert it, you use the overload that takes a second `HtmlElement`, and then the new element will be stuffed in before that element.

❑   `RemoveChild(HtmlElement element)` — Removes the given element from the children collection if it is in it.

❑   `Focus()` — Need more be said?

❑   `GetAttribute(string name)` — Gets the specified attribute value; it returns null if the attribute is not specified.

❑   `GetStyleAttribute(string name)` — Same as above, only for CSS styles

❑   `RemoveAttribute(string name)` — Removes the specified attribute if it exists or just clears out the attribute value, depending on the browser (e.g., in Firefox it just clears it out).

❑   `RemoveStyleAttribute(string name)` — This is similar to the above; however, different browsers behave differently if they don't understand the named style.

❑   `SetAttribute(string name, string value)` — Sets the given attribute to the provided value.

❑   `SetStyleAttribute(string name, string value)` — Sets the given CSS style attribute to the provided value. The same caveats that apply to removing style attributes apply here.

In addition, there are some interesting properties on `HtmlElement`:

❑ `Children` — Gets you a Read Only `ScriptObjectCollection` of any children that the element has; it'll be empty if there are no children.

❑ `CssClass` — Lets you get or set the CSS class value for the element; recall that you can have more than one class on an element according to the rules of CSS.

❑ `Id` — Gets the HTML element's `id` value or an empty string if it isn't set.

❑ `Parent` — Gets you an `HtmlElement` reference to the HTML element's parent if it has one; otherwise, you get null.

❑ `TagName` — Gets you the HTML tag name, which is essentially its type.

The following example shows DOM access and manipulation in action. First off, add a new `Button` to the existing `BrowserAndStuff` sample like this:

```
<Button
    Width="200"
    HorizontalAlignment="Left"
    Content="Add Selector"
    Click="AddSelector_Click" />
```

and then add this code in that handler:

```
void AddSelector_Click(object sender, RoutedEventArgs e)
{
    HtmlDocument doc = HtmlPage.Document;
    HtmlElement selector = doc.CreateElement("select");
    HtmlElement item = doc.CreateElement("option");
    item.SetAttribute("innerText", "-- Choose One --");
    item.SetProperty("textContent", "-- Choose One --");
    item.SetAttribute("value", "");
    selector.AppendChild(item);
    item = doc.CreateElement("option");
    item.SetAttribute("innerText", "Option 1");
    item.SetProperty("textContent", "Option 1");
    item.SetAttribute("value", "1");
    selector.AppendChild(item);
    item = doc.CreateElement("option");
    item.SetAttribute("innerText", "Option 2");
    item.SetProperty("textContent", "Option 2");
    item.SetAttribute("value", "2");
    selector.AppendChild(item);
    doc.Body.AppendChild(selector);
}
```

It should be pretty readable, but just to be explicit, it gets a reference to the HTML document, creates a select element, then adds a few options to that, and finally adds that select element to the document body. The only slightly odd thing is that you still have to account for browser disparity here — IE likes the `innerText` property for the option text, and the standard XML DOM likes `textContent`. Also note that using `SetAttribute` doesn't work for `textContent`; you have to use `SetProperty`, which is a way to execute JavaScript, as covered in more detail in Chapter 13.

Sadly, at least the current version of Silverlight (and probably future versions as well) doesn't do much to hide away the browser inconsistencies, so you're still left fending for yourself in that regard. An interesting thought: If you do intense DOM manipulation, you could create an invisible Silverlight instance and let it do the DOM manipulation for you. About the only way I can see this being good is if you extend the managed API to provide strongly typed objects based on HTML element tag names, so you'd get type checking at least on the tag-specific properties. It's probably not worth the effort, but it's a thought. If, however, you're using a dynamic language or if you can wait for the C# 4 dynamic features, this option may become more palatable, as it improves on interop.

That about wraps it up for manipulating the DOM. You should be able to do pretty much everything you can do in script, but the key scenarios will be enabling Silverlight integration with HTML elements. For instance, you could use an HTML overlay to integrate Live Maps (Virtual Earth). You can see how, with these APIs, you can get some pretty rich, almost invisible integration between Silverlight and the DOM.

Calling Script from Managed Code

This section covers the basics of calling script from managed code. As when dealing with the BOM and DOM, the API for calling script is located in the `System.Windows.Browser` namespace and is facilitated by just a few classes, some of which have already been touched on in this chapter and are used in Chapter 16 as well. The main item in this space for dealing with script on the managed side is the `ScriptObject` type, which is actually the base class for most of the types in this space. It gives you some tools that are pretty handy for dealing with all that stuff, like:

❏   `CheckAccess()` — Same as usual; tells you if you're on the UI thread.

❏   `ConvertTo(Type targetType, bool allowSerialization)` — (Tries to) convert the `ScriptObject` to the given type, with optional support for serialization, which, if true, tries to serialize the JavaScript object to JSON and then back out into the desired managed object. There's a generic overload `ConvertTo<T>()` that essentially calls the main overload with serialization support and casts the result back for you. This is very handy if you want a managed copy (or reference to an existing managed object) of a script object.

❏   `GetProperty(string name)` — Gets the value of the specified property by name. There is an integer overload that goes by the ordinal number of the property (since properties can be enumerated in JavaScript).

❏   `SetProperty(string name, object value)` — Sets the value of the specified property by name. As with the getter, you can use an integer ordinal instead of the name.

❏   `Invoke(string name, params object[] args)` — One of the most useful methods, this will invoke the named method on the current object and allow you to (optionally) pass in arguments.

❏   `InvokeSelf(params object[] args)` — This is likely one of the least useful methods; it will assume that the current script object is a method and invoke it with the given arguments. The thing is that, in most cases, you don't want to reinvoke a method that you have a reference to because, in order to get a reference to a method in the first place, you have to call `Invoke` on `HtmlWindow`, and the method has to return itself. In other words, it needs to be a JavaScript *class* constructor, in which case, you wouldn't want to call it again for the same instance.

In addition to the methods, you get a couple of potentially useful properties:

❑   `Dispatcher` — The same as usual; gets you the UI Dispatcher, which you can use to invoke stuff on the UI thread if need be, that is, if you have a `ScriptObject` on a background thread. It seems unlikely that this would happen much, but it's there if you need it.

❑   `ManagedObject` — If you have a case in which you have passed a reference type to JavaScript (or created one from JavaScript) and get an untyped `ScriptObject` reference to it in managed code, you can use just this property and cast it to the right type rather than, for example, using `ConvertTo`.

The following example illustrates some of these. The use of `GetProperty`, `SetProperty`, and `Invoke` is shown at various points in the book, as these are likely the most common uses — those you might use, for example, when interacting with the Live Maps JavaScript API. The example here shows a slightly more complex scenario, creating a JavaScript *class* (there are no real classes in JavaScript — they're emulated using functions that have members) and then calling a member on that instance, passing in a scriptable managed type.

First, create a JavaScript *class* definition as follows in a script block on your HTML page used in your handy-dandy `BrowserAndStuff` project:

```
function MyFancyJavaScriptObject(someConstructionParameter)
{
    this._constructorParam = someConstructionParameter;

    if (typeof _MyFancyJavaScriptObjectInitialized == 'undefined')
    {
        this.someMethod = function(baseBaseBase)
        {
            alert(baseBaseBase.All + baseBaseBase['Your'] +
                baseBaseBase.Base + this._constructorParam);
        }
        _MyFancyJavaScriptObjectInitialized = true;
    }
    return this;
}
```

This is about as basic as it gets for a JavaScript type. It takes one constructor parameter, which it just saves for later reference.

> **The `typeof` ... block is there just as a good practice element for perf — it ensures that the `someMethod` function is only defined once; otherwise, every time you construct a `MyFancyJavaScriptObject`, it would re-define it. This doesn't matter much here, but if it were many and/or large methods, it could have a deleterious effect on performance.**

Next, add a new `Button` to your Page.xaml:

```
<Button
    Width="200"
```

```
        HorizontalAlignment="Left"
        Content="Create JS Object And Do Stuff"
        Click="CallJavaScript" />
```

Now you can write your handler for that `Click` event as follows:

```
void CallJavaScript(object sender, RoutedEventArgs e)
{
    ScriptObject fancyScriptObject =
        (ScriptObject)HtmlPage.Window.Invoke("MyFancyJavaScriptObject",
                        "are belong to us.");
    fancyScriptObject.Invoke("someMethod", new AllYourBase());
}
```

So you see here that you call `Invoke` on the window to create an instance of your JavaScript type, passing in the constructor parameter (`"are belong to us."`). Then you can invoke methods on your JavaScript object, again using the `Invoke` method, and pass in a new instance of the managed `AllYourBase` type. This type should be defined like this:

```
[ScriptableType]
public class AllYourBase
{
    public string All { get { return "All "; } }
    public string Your { get { return "your "; } }
    public string Base { get { return "base "; } }
}
```

Marking a type with the `ScriptableTypeAttribute` makes all public properties and methods accessible from script. When the object is passed to script, a dictionary-based wrapper is created, so you can either use the properties as defined or you can access properties via a string indexer. Both approaches are illustrated in the `someMethod` implementation — the `All` and `Base` are accessed via properties, and `Your` is accessed via the indexer.

If you're not familiar with "all your base," you should Google it.

Calling Managed Code from Script

The last part of the previous section introduced a key aspect of calling managed code from script — using the `ScriptableTypeAttribute`. There's another one you can use, `ScriptableMemberAttribute`, if you want finer-grained control of what type members are exposed to script. Marking up your types to indicate how they can be scripted is a good first step, but you need to take another to make your types available to be used from JavaScript directly (i.e., not passed to JavaScript from managed code as they were in the previous sample). The `HtmlPage` class's static members illuminate this further:

❑   `RegisterScriptableObject(string scriptKey, object instance)` — This is what you use to expose a managed object instance to script. The script key is used to provide a handle to access that instance on the script side, which is slapped onto the `Content` object of the Silverlight runtime instance.

287

❑ RegisterCreateableType(*string scriptAlias, Type type*) — Exposes a type to script via the given alias. In script, you use the alias with the Content.services.createObject method to create managed types from script.

❑ UnregisterCreateableType(*string scriptAlias*) — If, for some reason, you want to prevent further script creation of a type, you can use this to do that.

So how about putting all this wondrous knowledge to some use? Go ahead and grab that BrowserAndStuff project, and in the Page.xaml.cs, add this method to your Page class:

```
[ScriptableMember]
public AllYourBase GiveMeYourBase()
{
    return new AllYourBase();
}
```

What that will do is specifically expose that method to script, assuming we register it somehow. Next, to enhance your AllYourBase class a bit, add this method to it:

```
public void SayIt(AllYourBase baseBaseBase)
{
    HtmlPage.Window.Alert(
        baseBaseBase.All + baseBaseBase.Your +
        baseBaseBase.Base + "ARE belong to us!");
}
```

Nothing special here — we just added a method that uses the HTML bridge's Alert method (that one that you should really not use), but hang with me. Now, go to your App.xaml.cs, and, in the app startup handler, add the following registrations so that it ends up looking like this:

```
private void Application_Startup(object sender, StartupEventArgs e)
{
    this.RootVisual = new Page();
    HtmlPage.RegisterScriptableObject("thePage", this.RootVisual);
    HtmlPage.RegisterCreateableType("AllYourBase", typeof(AllYourBase));
}
```

Note that you are registering the new *instance* of the Page class that is your root visual and providing a handle of "thePage" so that your script can access it (the handle can be whatever you like). The next line registers the *type* of AllYourBase as a script-creatable type and assigns it the alias of "AllYourBase", which again could be whatever you want, but it seems to me that a good practice would be to match the .NET type (you might even use namespace, depending on how complex your app is). At this point, you should be all set to use these new things in script, so flip on over to your HTML page and add an HTML button like this:

```
<button
    onclick="javascript: return UltimateBaseDemo();">DO It!</button>
```

Then define the UltimateBaseDemo function as follows:

```
function UltimateBaseDemo()
{
```

```
    var slRuntime = document.getElementById('silverlightRuntime');
    var allYerBase = slRuntime.content.thePage.GiveMeYourBase();
    var theRealDealYo =
      slRuntime.content.services.createObject('AllYourBase');
    theRealDealYo.SayIt(allYerBase);
}
```

Now you may need to kick your noggin into overdrive to follow this. When you run and click on the "DO It!" button, this function will get a reference to the Silverlight runtime instance. At that point, it uses the `Content` property (it is case-insensitive because it is a property on the plug-in object) to access the handle you set up in the app start handler (`"thePage"`). This handle is a script wrapper over your root visual `Page` instance, and, if you recall, you set up the `GiveMeYourBase` method as a scriptable member, so you can call it from script to get a script wrapper around a new instance of the `AllYourBase` type.

Next, the code again uses the `Content` property, this time accessing the `Services` property to call the helper `createObject` method, passing in the alias you set up in the app start handler so that it returns another wrapped instance of the `AllYourBase` type. Finally, it calls the `SayIt` method on this second instance, passing in the first; and that method, if you'll glance back, simply shows a JavaScript alert (calling back into script from managed code, which was called from script using a script wrapper of a managed type!). Pretty crazy, huh? The results are what you'd expect, as shown in Figure 12-8.

Figure 12-8

Truly, all your base *ARE* belong to us.

Silverlight and JavaScript Marshaling

A note on marshaling types between script and managed code: while the basic scenarios (and even not-so-basic ones) should go off without a hitch following the principles illustrated here, there are actually a lot of sticky details in terms of how stuff gets sent back and forth between script and managed code. If you're going to do a lot of this, you should consult the MSDN documentation on this topic. The basic rules are:

❑ Managed types are wrapped by reference to JavaScript. This is why, for instance, you can get a `ScriptObject` and use the `ManagedObject` reference to get that reference back.

❑ JavaScript types that are passed as data (e.g., as parameters to methods and property setters) have to be converted to a corresponding managed wrapper, which is what is passed to code.

Exceptions between Managed Code and Script

There is limited support for passing exceptions between managed code and script. You should reference Chapter 13, on cross-cutting concerns, for details on exception handling. The key things to know here are that exceptions thrown to JavaScript from managed code are reported as a `ManagedRuntimeError`, and only the top-level exception information (not nested) is passed to JavaScript. Also, exceptions that occur in managed code called from a JavaScript event handler (e.g., a button's `click` handler) are silently ignored.

JavaScript exceptions are passed to the calling managed code as `InvalidOperationException` instances, and if you have a chain of calls from, for example, managed code that was called by JavaScript, which was called by managed code, you will not get the original managed-code details — they're lost in translation. Last, because all browsers have their own way of reporting messages, you can't always count on getting good info in managed code to parse/handle specially, and, specifically, Safari may not return an exception at all, so you need to be extra careful with any JavaScript code that is called from managed code to effectively handle it in JavaScript as much as possible.

HTML Bridge Scenarios

Here are a few more interesting scenarios to think about that are enabled thanks to this truly advanced HTML bridge:

- ❏ **Silverlight to Silverlight** — You can have two instances of Silverlight on one page and communicate between them using the bridge or the new Local Connection API. This could be useful in scenarios in which you need to coordinate data between them (such as multiple Silverlight Web Parts in a portal) as well as situations in which you need more advanced layering than is supported out-of-the-box, for example, a background Silverlight layer, a middle HTML layer for rich HTML overlays, and another, top Silverlight layer, for Silverlight overlays that need to be placed on top of the HTML.

- ❏ **Silverlight to Flash or *<insertnamehere>*** — If you have existing Flash or other plug-in-based technology, you can use the bridge to communicate with those.

- ❏ **Silverlight to Ajax** — This will likely be the most common scenario, in which you have a fairly rich Ajax-based app that you want to add a Silverlight "island of richness" to, so you use the bridge to facilitate that.

Silverlight with the Server

The last section in this chapter deals very briefly with Silverlight's relationship with the server. Unlike ASP.NET and other HTML-generating server-side technologies, Silverlight is a pure client play, which means that you can run it just fine in a plain old HTML page; however, the chances of that happening without some server-side platform are probably kind of low. It is more likely that you will want to plug your Silverlight into some server-side framework.

The good news is that because it is pure client side, you can pick and choose your server-side technology. You can run it with PHP, Perl, Python, Ruby, Java, and even CGI if you like. What's more, because of the CLR, Silverlight can support other languages, and Microsoft, in addition to VB and C#, is adding

IronRuby, IronPython, and Managed JScript (along with the necessary DLR infrastructure). So if, say, Ruby's your thing, you can use Ruby on Rails on the server and IronRuby in Silverlight: pretty awesome setup if you're into that. Get all the power of Silverlight, including some Visual Studio tooling and debugging, along with your favorite language and server-side framework.

Silverlight with ASP.NET

Of course, it's one thing to say that you can run Silverlight with other server platforms, but there is no doubt that the biggest developer audience will be using ASP.NET. And in addition to specialized Silverlight support for WCF and ADO.NET Data Services on the client, Microsoft is providing a couple of facilities to make using Silverlight on ASP.NET even easier. These are:

❑ `System.Web.UI.SilverlightControls.MediaPlayer` — This control empowers developers to easily add rich media capabilities to their ASP.NET applications by handling the details of creating a Silverlight player. It supports some nice-looking built-in skins as well as the ability to supply custom skins and use the output of Expression Media Encoder.

❑ `System.Web.UI.SilverlightControls.Silverlight` — This control simplifies adding Silverlight applications to ASP.NET pages.

Silverlight Control

Essentially, the `Silverlight` control provides a server-side facility for declaring and configuring a Silverlight instance. It exposes the various configuration knobs as properties on the server control and handles the details of appropriately creating an instance based on browser support. Thus, there isn't much more to say. Here's what a simple declaration will look like (generated for test pages when you create new Silverlight web projects):

```
<asp:Silverlight ID="Xaml1" runat="server"
  Source="~/ClientBin/SilverlightAndAspNetBff.xap"
  MinimumVersion="2.0.31005"
  Width="100%" Height="100%" />
```

You will see this used throughout this book as well as in any number of Silverlight samples in other learning resources. One thing to note is that you will need to register the `Silverlight` controls tag prefix either in the web.config or on your pages:

```
<%@ Register Assembly="System.Web.Silverlight"
    Namespace="System.Web.UI.SilverlightControls"
    TagPrefix="asp" %>
```

MediaPlayer Control

The `MediaPlayer` control drastically simplifies adding media to ASP.NET applications. All you have to do is add a reference to the System.Web.Silverlight.dll (same thing for the Silverlight control itself), register the tag prefix as shown previously, and then declare it on your ASPX as follows:

```
<asp:MediaPlayer ID="MyMediaPlayer" runat="server"
  MediaSource="~/Media/Butterfly.wmv" Width="100%" Height="100%" />
```

Of course, you have to add your media, and it's best if you encode it using Expression Encoder, but that's all there is to it. Figure 12-9 shows the outcome of this.

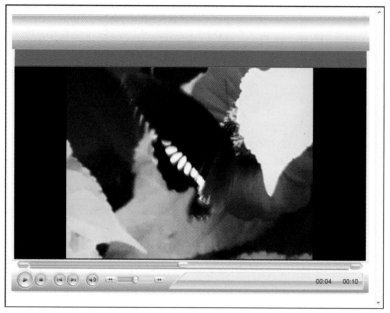

Figure 12-9

That skin isn't the most beautiful, though, but never fear! If you switch into design view and select the smart tag, you can just use the Import Skin option to pick one of the several prebaked skins. See Figure 12-10 to see what I'm talking about.

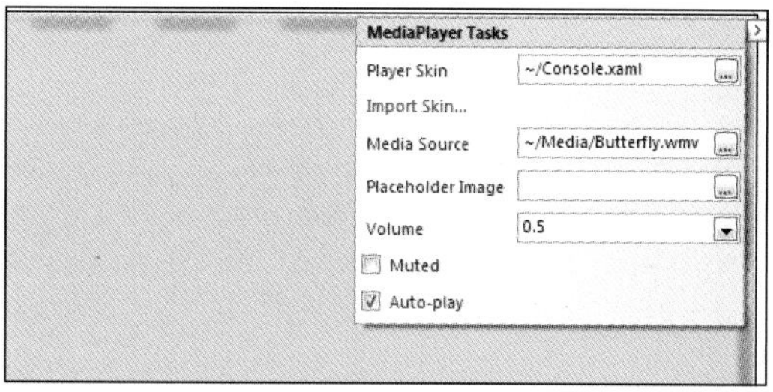

Figure 12-10

I kind of like the Console skin, so I picked it. That does two things: it copies Console.xaml from the Silverlight 3 SDK (typically found at C:\Program Files\Microsoft SDKs\Silverlight\v3.0\Libraries\ Server\MediaPlayerSkins) to the web app and sets the `MediaSkinSource` property to that file, so if you flip back to source view, your `MediaPlayer` definition now looks like this:

```
<asp:MediaPlayer ID="MyMediaPlayer" runat="server"
    MediaSource="~/Media/Butterfly.wmv" Width="100%" Height="100%"
    MediaSkinSource="~/Console.xaml" />
```

And if you run this, you'll see something like Figure 12-11.

Figure 12-11

That's all there is to it! And another nice thing about this is that clients only need Silverlight 1.0 to add the rich media player to your ASP.NET apps. Naturally, however, there's a lot more to multimedia in Silverlight, and that's already covered in depth in Chapter 10.

Summary

After reading this chapter, you should have a good basic understanding of Silverlight as a complete application platform in its own right, an in-depth understanding of how Silverlight relates to the browser, and how to get the two to play nicely together; finally, you should be aware of how Silverlight lives vis-à-vis the server, particularly with ASP.NET. At this point, you're ready to dig in to deeper cross-cutting concerns that you should think about when setting out to build your own Silverlight applications.

13

First Things First: Handling Cross-Cutting Concerns

Cross-cutting concerns are those system design issues that cut across the various areas of an application and are typically foundational system services that you need to consider before diving into building an application. Most common among these are security, exception handling, and logging. In this chapter, you'll get an understanding of how to address these in your applications, particularly how these concerns change in the context of a Silverlight application.

Security

In this section, you'll look at the various aspects of security that you'll need to think about for Silverlight applications.

Code Access Security Model

Silverlight 3 completely rips out the familiar .NET Code Access Security (CAS) model and replaces it with a straightforward, invisible model. Because it is targeted strictly at web applications and runs in the browser, it more or less inherits the browser/AJAX security model in terms of what it allows applications to do. So, in a sense, the burden of security, particularly code security, is removed from the developer — no worrying about attributes, asserts, demands, and that sort of thing.

Under the covers it is more complicated than that, of course. Platform (Microsoft) code has the ability to do things that aren't what you'd call *sandboxed*, things like accessing the host filesystem. To do this, Silverlight has essentially three layers of security. The first is the transparent, which is where your application code will run (and always will run — you can't elevate or demand). The third, if you will, is the critical code that actually talks to the host system. And in between the two, the second, is the safe critical code.

This intermediate layer is the most interesting for Silverlight because it acts as the gatekeeper. It's not literally a separate layer — just conceptually — but the thing it does is perform checks to ensure that the application is in an acceptable state and validating parameters before performing critical operations. Again, this is only the Microsoft libraries that can do this — applications are prevented from doing so.

Network Access Security Model

By default, Silverlight applications can only access the server that they were deployed to (and downloaded from), a.k.a., their *site of origin*. If you don't do anything special, this is the extent of the communication allowed, much as in AJAX applications; however, Silverlight 3 also has the capability to make cross-domain calls, that is, calls to servers in other domains, which is essential for enabling mashups.

To do this, Silverlight has a security policy system. This means that calls using the WebClient and HTTP classes in `System.Net` will require a policy file to be downloaded first before accessing other network resources on the target server for calls to non-site-of-origin servers — they don't require the policy for site-of-origin access. On the other hand, all socket connections will require a policy, regardless of whether the call is to the site of origin or not.

At a high level, the way this works for HTTP-based calls is that Silverlight will look for a Silverlight-based clientaccesspolicy.xml file in the root of the target domain. If one is returned, it will use this policy for the duration of the application session. If one can't be found, it falls back to asking for the Flash cross-domain policy file, crossdomain.xml, and it will use that. This is great for accessing all the existing sites enabled for Flash cross-domain access, but *it must enable access to all domains to be used by Silverlight*.

Sockets work a bit differently, given their nature. The client connects on port 943 and sends a special `<policy-file-request />` message and waits for the policy file to be returned. Once this file is successfully parsed, and assuming its policy is met, it will open a connection to the target. It will not fall back to the Flash policy file/format.

> **Socket connections in Silverlight are limited to the port range of 4502–4534.**

Check out Chapters 11 and 14 for examples of cross-domain calls.

Cryptography

Silverlight 3 provides a subset of the .NET Framework's cryptography capabilities, which is likely more than enough for most Silverlight applications. With these, you can do both symmetric and asymmetric encryption, handle hashes, and generate random numbers.

The thing is that, in most cases, you'll want to do your cryptography on the server because there's no terribly safe place to keep things like keys on the client. One possible work-around for that would be to require the user to authenticate to a service that will then supply a session key for the client code to use for encrypted communications. More likely, you'll rely on SSL for secure communications between the client and the server.

In any case, here's a basic class you could use as a starting point for cryptography in your application. It simplifies interaction with the boorish framework security classes.

```csharp
using System;

namespace AppServices.Security
{
  public static class Crypto
  {
    static System.Security.Cryptography.AesManaged _Cryptor = null;
    static System.Security.Cryptography.AesManaged Cryptor
    {
      get
      {
        if (_Cryptor == null)
        {
          _Cryptor = new System.Security.Cryptography.AesManaged();
          _Cryptor.GenerateIV();
          _Cryptor.GenerateKey();
        }
        return _Cryptor;
      }
    }

    public static string Encrypt(string value)
    {
      using (System.IO.MemoryStream encryptionStream =
        new System.IO.MemoryStream())
      {
        using (System.Security.Cryptography.CryptoStream encrypt =
         new System.Security.Cryptography.CryptoStream(
            encryptionStream, Cryptor.CreateEncryptor(),
            System.Security.Cryptography.CryptoStreamMode.Write))
        {
          byte[] utfD1 =
            System.Text.UTF8Encoding.UTF8.GetBytes(value);
          encrypt.Write(utfD1, 0, utfD1.Length);
          encrypt.FlushFinalBlock();
          encrypt.Close();

          return
            Convert.ToBase64String(encryptionStream.ToArray());
        }
      }
    }

    public static string Decrypt(string value)
    {
      byte[] encryptedData = Convert.FromBase64String(value);

      using (System.IO.MemoryStream decryptionStream =
        new System.IO.MemoryStream())
      {
        using (System.Security.Cryptography.CryptoStream decrypt =
          new System.Security.Cryptography.CryptoStream(
            decryptionStream,Cryptor.CreateDecryptor(),
            System.Security.Cryptography.CryptoStreamMode.Write))
```

```
        {
            decrypt.Write(encryptedData, 0, encryptedData.Length);
            decrypt.Flush();
            decrypt.Close();

            byte[] decryptedData = decryptionStream.ToArray();
            return
                System.Text.UTF8Encoding.UTF8.GetString(decryptedData, 0,
                decryptedData.Length);
        }
    }
}

public static string Hash(string value)
{
    byte[] inBytes =
        System.Text.UTF8Encoding.UTF8.GetBytes(value);

    System.Security.Cryptography.SHA256Managed hasher =
        new System.Security.Cryptography.SHA256Managed();

    byte[] outBytes = hasher.ComputeHash(inBytes);

    return Convert.ToBase64String(outBytes);
}

    }
}
```

The encryption code here takes advantage of the auto-generation of keys and initialization vectors built into the cryptography classes; however, most likely you'll want to modify it to supply the class with a key derived from some other source, such as the aforementioned server.

This chapter's sample includes a sample control called CryptoSample.xaml that shows how to use this wrapper class, but it is very straightforward — just call the appropriate method and supply the value.

Authentication

Silverlight 3 has no built-in authentication services, but you can use the ASP.NET services for Windows Communication Foundation (WCF) to provide ASP.NET-based authentication. The following goes over how you can go about doing that.

First, create a Silverlight application, if you don't have one already. The code in this sample uses a project, including an accompanying web site, called AppServices.

Next, set up some users. You can do that by selecting the web site in Solution Explorer and clicking Website ⇨ ASP.NET Configuration from the menu in Visual Studio. Then, in the admin web site that comes up, go to Security and Create a user or two, as shown in Figure 13-1. This is standard ASP.NET.

> **By default, ASP.NET wants to use SQL Express for web site configuration. If you don't have that installed, you will need to configure a different provider as outlined here:** http://weblogs.asp.net/scottgu/archive/2005/08/25/423703.aspx.

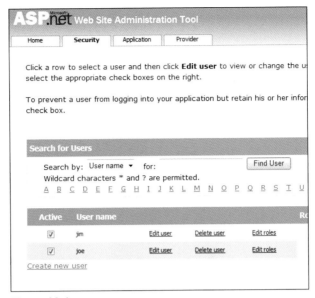

Figure 13-1

While you're in there, go and set your app to use Forms authentication (choose "Select authentication type" and then "From the Internet"), or you can add it in the system.web section in web.config yourself:

```
<authentication mode="Forms" />
```

Next, add a Services folder, as shown in Figure 13-2. You don't have to do this, but it is a nice way to cordon off your services.

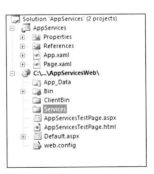

Figure 13-2

Then add a new Authentication service to the Services folder, as shown in Figure 13-3. Because you're using pre-baked services, it's easiest to pick the text file type and just change the filename.

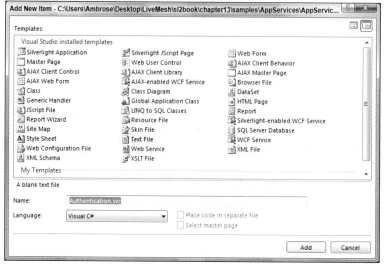

Figure 13-3

Open the .svc file and update it to point to the built-in `AuthenticationService` type as follows:

```
<%@ ServiceHost Language="C#"
  Service="System.Web.ApplicationServices.AuthenticationService" %>
```

Now configure the web.config to enable the service:

```
<system.serviceModel>
  <services>
    <service
      name="System.Web.ApplicationServices.AuthenticationService"
      behaviorConfiguration="AuthenticationServiceTypeBehaviors">
      <endpoint
        contract="System.Web.ApplicationServices.AuthenticationService"
        binding="basicHttpBinding" bindingConfiguration="userHttp"
        bindingNamespace="http://asp.net/ApplicationServices/v200"/>
    </service>
  </services>

  <bindings>
    <basicHttpBinding>
      <binding name="userHttp">
        <security mode="None"/>
      </binding>
    </basicHttpBinding>
  </bindings>

  <behaviors>
    <serviceBehaviors>
      <behavior name="AuthenticationServiceTypeBehaviors">
```

```
            <serviceMetadata httpGetEnabled="true"/>
          </behavior>
        </serviceBehaviors>
      </behaviors>

      <serviceHostingEnvironment aspNetCompatibilityEnabled="true"/>
    </system.serviceModel>
```

The first section adds the service, specifying the behavior, contract, and binding information; then you add a `basicHttpBinding` definition with a security mode of none (you'd probably use HTTPS in real app scenarios). Add a behavior definition to match what you specified for the service, and last turn on ASP.NET compatibility to run this inside ASP.NET.

Next add a system.web.extensions section to enable the new extensions service:

```
<system.web.extensions>
  <scripting>
    <webServices>
      <authenticationService enabled="true" requireSSL="false"/>
    </webServices>
  </scripting>
</system.web.extensions>
```

Now you should be able to verify the service setup by right-clicking on the svc file and choosing "View in Browser." It should look something like Figure 13-4.

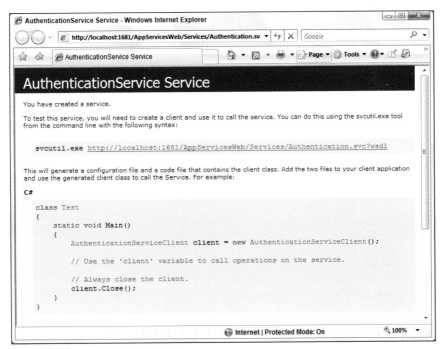

Figure 13-4

301

Now, on the client side, you need to get ready to use it. First, add a Controls folder, and in the folder, add a new `SignIn` user control, as in Figure 13-5.

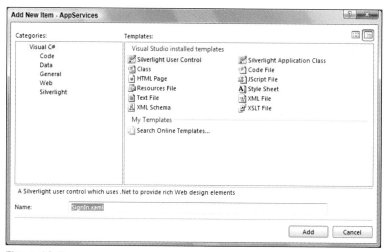

Figure 13-5

At a minimum, add a username and password `TextBox` as well as a "Sign-In" button (you'll probably need a "Cancel/Close" button, too). Here's an example of how you might do this with a little styling and simple animation (for fade in/out).

```xml
<UserControl x:Class="AppServices.Controls.SignIn"
    xmlns="http://schemas.microsoft.com/winfx/2006/xaml/presentation"
    xmlns:x="http://schemas.microsoft.com/winfx/2006/xaml"
    Width="294" Height="163">
  <UserControl.Resources>
    <Storyboard x:Name="ShowMe">
      <DoubleAnimation Storyboard.TargetName="LayoutRoot"
            Storyboard.TargetProperty="Opacity"
            Duration="0:0:0.5" To="1" />
    </Storyboard>
    <Storyboard x:Name="CloseMe">
      <DoubleAnimation Storyboard.TargetName="LayoutRoot"
            Storyboard.TargetProperty="Opacity"
            BeginTime="0:0:0.5"
            Duration="0:0:0.5" To="0" />
    </Storyboard>
  </UserControl.Resources>
  <Grid x:Name="LayoutRoot">
    <Border CornerRadius="4,4,4,4">
      <Border.Background>
        <LinearGradientBrush EndPoint="0.5,1" StartPoint="0.5,0">
          <GradientStop Color="#FF000000" Offset="0.071"/>
          <GradientStop Color="#FFFFFFFF" Offset="0"/>
          <GradientStop Color="#FF070707" Offset="0.933"/>
```

```xml
              </LinearGradientBrush>
            </Border.Background>
        <Canvas Height="157" Width="289">
            <TextBlock Height="25" Width="115" Foreground="#FFFFFFFF"
              Text="Sign In" TextWrapping="Wrap" Canvas.Left="3"
              Canvas.Top="2" x:Name="TitleLabel"/>
            <Path Height="1" Width="86.016"
                    Canvas.Left="1" Canvas.Top="23"
                    Data="M20.647833,63 L142.66422,63" Stretch="Fill">
              <Path.Stroke>
                <LinearGradientBrush
                  EndPoint="0.5,1" StartPoint="0.5,0">
                  <GradientStop
                    Color="#FF000000" Offset="1"/>
                  <GradientStop
                    Color="#FFFFFFFF" Offset="0"/>
                </LinearGradientBrush>
              </Path.Stroke>
            </Path>
            <TextBlock Height="21" Width="94" FontSize="12"
              Foreground="#FFFFFFFF" Text="Username"
              Canvas.Top="31" Canvas.Left="24" x:Name="UsernameLabel" />
            <TextBox Height="Auto" Width="130"
              FontFamily="Verdana" FontSize="10"
              Canvas.Left="24" Canvas.Top="46.5"
              KeyUp="SignIn_KeyUp"
              x:Name="Username"/>
            <TextBlock Height="21" Width="94" FontSize="12"
              Foreground="#FFFFFFFF" Text="Password"
              Canvas.Top="73" Canvas.Left="24" x:Name="PasswordLabel"/>
            <PasswordBox Height="Auto" x:Name="Password" Width="130"
              FontFamily="Verdana" FontSize="10"
              Canvas.Left="24" Canvas.Top="88.5"
              KeyUp="SignIn_KeyUp" />
            <TextBlock Height="111.5" Width="121" FontSize="10"
              Foreground="#FFFFFFFF" TextWrapping="Wrap"
              x:Name="UserMessage" Margin="0,0,0,0"
              Canvas.Left="160" Canvas.Top="30"/>
            <Button Height="23" Width="73.5"
              Canvas.Left="24" Canvas.Top="118.5"
              Content="Sign In!" x:Name="SignInButton"
              Click="SignInButton_Click"/>
            <Button Height="16" Width="17" FontSize="9"
              Canvas.Left="264" Canvas.Top="8"
              Content="X" x:Name="CloseButton"
              Click="CloseButton_Click"/>
        </Canvas>
      </Border>
    </Grid>
</UserControl>
```

You'll want to implement the Show/Close functionality. At a minimum, you can just use the `Visibility` property, but it is often a nice experience to use some subtle animations (such as a quick fade in and out). Here is what the code for that looks like:

```csharp
public partial class SignIn : UserControl
{
  public SignIn()
  {
    InitializeComponent();
    this.Visibility = Visibility.Collapsed;
    this.LayoutRoot.Opacity = 0;
    this.ShowMe.Completed += ShowMe_Completed;
    this.CloseMe.Completed += CloseMe_Completed;
  }

  public void Show()
  {
    this.Visibility = Visibility.Visible;
    this.ShowMe.Begin();
  }

  void ShowMe_Completed(object sender, EventArgs e)
  {
    this.Username.Focus();
  }

  public void Close()
  {
    this.CloseMe.Begin();
  }

  void CloseMe_Completed(object sender, EventArgs e)
  {
    this.Visibility = Visibility.Collapsed;
    this.Username.Text = string.Empty;
    this.Password.Password = string.Empty;
    this.UserMessage.Text = string.Empty;
  }

  private void SignInButton_Click(object sender, RoutedEventArgs e)
  {
    this.DoSignIn();
  }

  private void CloseButton_Click(object sender, RoutedEventArgs e)
  {
    this.Close();
  }

  private void SignIn_KeyUp(object sender, KeyEventArgs e)
  {
    if (e.Key == Key.Enter)
```

```
        this.DoSignIn();
    }

    void DoSignIn()
    {
    }
}
```

There are definitely a few nice-to-haves in this code. In addition to the show and close animations, the code in the Show Completion handler will set the focus on the username, so users can immediately start typing. The `SignIn_KeyUp` handler, which is attached to both input boxes, will attempt a sign-in if the [Enter] key is pressed (so users don't have to reach for the mouse and click on the "Sign-In" button). The last nicety is the `UserMessage TextBox`; this is a very basic approach to enable feedback to the user as to what is going on with their sign-in attempts, as you will see.

Then you can use this on your `Page` by defining an XML namespace and declaring it. You need a login button of some sort, too. Here's an example of that:

```
<UserControl
  x:Class="AppServices.Page"
  xmlns="http://schemas.microsoft.com/winfx/2006/xaml/presentation"
  xmlns:x="http://schemas.microsoft.com/winfx/2006/xaml"
  xmlns:l="clr-namespace:AppServices.Controls"
    >
    <Grid x:Name="LayoutRoot">
    <HyperlinkButton
      x:Name="LoginButton"
      HorizontalAlignment="Right" VerticalAlignment="Top"
      Content="Login" Click="LoginButton_Click" />
    <l:SignIn x:Name="SignInBox" />
  </Grid>
</UserControl>
```

Here's the code for the login button `click` handler:

```
private void LoginButton_Click(object sender, RoutedEventArgs e)
{
    this.SignInBox.Show();
}
```

And when you click on the Login button, you'll see something like what is shown in Figure 13-6.

Figure 13-6

Now you're ready to consume the authentication service, so right-click on your Silverlight project and choose "Add Service Reference." Choose Discover, and the program should find your local authentication service and automatically select it. Then you can give it a namespace — I like using *Services* to group services, so specify Services.Authentication for this reference, as in Figure 13-7.

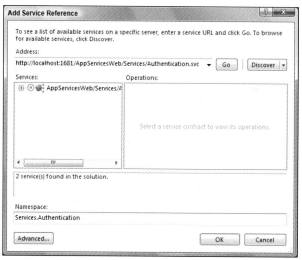

Figure 13-7

Now that you have the service client, you can use it in your DoSignIn method on the SignIn user control. Update your SignIn code-behind like this:

```
void DoSignIn()
{
  Services.Authentication.AuthenticationServiceClient auth =
    new Services.Authentication.AuthenticationServiceClient();
  auth.LoginCompleted += LoginCompleted;
  auth.LoginAsync(this.Username.Text, this.Password.Password,
    string.Empty, false, this.Username.Text);
  this.UserMessage.Text = "Attempting to sign in...";
}

void LoginCompleted(object sender,
  Services.Authentication.LoginCompletedEventArgs e)
{
  if (e.Error != null)
    this.UserMessage.Text = "There's a technical problem preventing " +
      "sign in at this time. Please try again later and let us know " +
      "if the problem continues.";
  else
  {
    bool success = e.Result;
    if (!success)
      this.UserMessage.Text = "We could not sign you in with the " +
        "username and password you supplied. Please double-check " +
        "and try again.";
```

```
    else
    {
      this.UserMessage.Text = "Signed in successfully!";
      App.CurrentUser =
        new Security.AppPrincipal((string)e.UserState, true);
      this.Close();
    }
  }
}
```

The code creates an authentication client, adds a completion handler for the Login method, starts a login (asynchronously, of course), and lets the user know that this is occurring. Once you get a result back from the server, it does very basic error checking, letting the user know if there is an error. Then it checks the result, which is a Boolean indicating success. If the sign-in attempt failed, the code lets the user know; otherwise, it tells the user that he or she logged in successfully, creates a corresponding AppPrincipal (which will be discussed shortly), and closes the dialogue.

> Closing automatically is, in itself, a good experience — don't make users click when they don't have to. Also, the CloseMe animation is set up to pause for half a second to let the user see the success message before fading out.
>
> If this were a real app, you should consider a "working" animation (such as a spinning cycle or bar) that shows while contacting the server, and you should consider using visual language (such as color) to indicate failure and success, but I didn't want to further distract from the core issue here, which is authentication using the ASP.NET service.

Now you should be wondering what this AppPrincipal thing is. That's a custom class that implements the System.Security.Principal.IPrincipal interface. Silverlight 3 does not have built-in support for standard principals, which is fine as you probably would want to extend it in most cases anyway. But we do get the usual IIdentity and IPrincipal interfaces as a good starting point.

To use this is pretty simple:

First, create an AppIdentity class, putting it in a Security folder in your app. Have that class inherit from IIdentity and implement the members, adding a relevant constructor as follows:

```
public class AppIdentity : IIdentity
{
  public AppIdentity(string name, bool authenticated)
  {
    _Name = name;
    _IsAuthenticated = authenticated;
  }

  #region IIdentity Members
  public string AuthenticationType
  {
    get { return "ASP.NET Services"; }
```

```
    }

    bool _IsAuthenticated;
    public bool IsAuthenticated
    {
      get { return _IsAuthenticated; }
    }

    string _Name;
    public string Name
    {
      get { return _Name; }
    }
    #endregion
  }
```

Next, create an AppPrincipal class in the same folder, inheriting from IPrincipal and implementing in a similar fashion:

```
public class AppPrincipal : IPrincipal
{

  public AppPrincipal(string name,
    bool authenticated)
    : this(name, authenticated,
        new string[0]{}) { }

  public AppPrincipal(string name,
    bool authenticated, string[] roles)
  {
    _Identity = new AppIdentity(name, authenticated);
    _Roles = roles;
  }

  string[] _Roles;

  #region IPrincipal Members

  IIdentity _Identity;
  public IIdentity Identity
  {
    get
    {
      return _Identity;
    }
  }

  public bool IsInRole(string role)
  {
    return _Roles.Contains(role);
  }

  #endregion
}
```

You'll need to use/import `System.Linq` to use the `Contains` extension method and also `System` `.Security.Principal` for both classes. The next thing is to create a shared/static member to serve as the current principal/user reference, and it just makes sense to stick it on the `App` class that is part of the usual VS project template:

```
static Security.AppPrincipal _CurrentUser;
internal static Security.AppPrincipal CurrentUser
{
  get
  {
    if (_CurrentUser == null)
      _CurrentUser =
        new Security.AppPrincipal(string.Empty, false);
    return _CurrentUser;
  }
  set
  {
    if (_CurrentUser != value &&
      (_CurrentUser == null || value == null ||
      (value.Identity.Name != _CurrentUser.Identity.Name)))
    {
      _CurrentUser = value;
      if (CurrentUserChanged != null)
        CurrentUserChanged(App.Current, new EventArgs());
    }
  }
}

public static event EventHandler CurrentUserChanged;
```

There are a few things going on here. First, if the current user is not set and it is accessed, the system generates a default, unauthenticated principal, so you don't have to worry about null checking in relation to this.

The next thing is the `CurrentUserChanged` event. This can be used by various observers in the app to know when the authenticated user is changed, and with that, the setter checks to see if the current user is different from the new user value before setting it and then raising the event.

Before moving on, you may want to add one more authentication feature — a `SignInStatus` control. The idea is, much as with the ASP.NET `LoginStatus`, to display a `Sign In` command if the user is *not* authenticated, and to display a simple authenticated user message and a `Sign Out` command if the user *is* authenticated. Most of the hard work is already done.

First, create a `SignInStatus` user control in your Controls directory. Now, copy the XML namespace declaration for your custom controls from your Page.xaml to the SignInStatus.xaml, and then you can cut and paste the sign-in hyperlink button and the sign-in box from your page (with the corresponding code) to the new control. Then you can add a `StackPanel` with a `TextBlock` and another `HyperlinkButton` to end up with something like the following:

```
<UserControl x:Class="AppServices.Controls.SignInStatus"
    xmlns="http://schemas.microsoft.com/winfx/2006/xaml/presentation"
    xmlns:x="http://schemas.microsoft.com/winfx/2006/xaml"
    xmlns:l="clr-namespace:AppServices.Controls">
```

```
<Grid x:Name="LayoutRoot">
  <HyperlinkButton
      x:Name="SignInButton"
      HorizontalAlignment="Right" VerticalAlignment="Top"
      Content="Sign In" Click="LoginButton_Click" />
  <StackPanel x:Name="SignOutPanel" Visibility="Collapsed"
    HorizontalAlignment="Right" VerticalAlignment="Top"
    Orientation="Horizontal">
    <TextBlock x:Name="StatusMessageBlock" />
    <HyperlinkButton x:Name="SignOutButton"
      Content=" [Sign Out]" Click="SignOutButton_Click" />
  </StackPanel>
  <l:SignIn x:Name="SignInBox" />
</Grid>
</UserControl>
```

The code for this control is pretty simple, as you might expect:

```
public partial class SignInStatus : UserControl
{
  public SignInStatus()
  {
    InitializeComponent();
    App.CurrentUserChanged += App_CurrentUserChanged;
    this.StatusMessageBlock.FontFamily = this.SignOutButton.FontFamily;
    this.StatusMessageBlock.FontSize = this.SignOutButton.FontSize;
  }

  void App_CurrentUserChanged(object sender, EventArgs e)
  {
    this.UpdateStatus();
  }

  public void UpdateStatus()
  {
    if (App.CurrentUser.Identity.IsAuthenticated)
    {
      this.StatusMessageBlock.Text = "Welcome, " +
        App.CurrentUser.Identity.Name + "!";
      this.SignInButton.Visibility = Visibility.Collapsed;
      this.SignOutPanel.Visibility = Visibility.Visible;
    }
    else
    {
      this.SignInButton.Visibility = Visibility.Visible;
      this.SignOutPanel.Visibility = Visibility.Collapsed;
    }
  }

  private void LoginButton_Click(object sender, RoutedEventArgs e)
  {
    this.SignInBox.Show();
  }

  private void SignOutButton_Click(object sender, RoutedEventArgs e)
```

```
    {
        App.CurrentUser = null;
    }
}
```

Now see? You're already taking advantage of that `CurrentUserChanged` event! It allows for nice, loose coupling for things that need to be aware of authentication status. The next two lines in the constructor are just synchronizing the font properties so the message and the sign-out command look similar. The `LoginButton_Click` does the same thing as before, and the `SignOutButton_Click` simply sets the current user for the app to `null` (which, of course, will trigger the `CurrentUserChanged`, which will, in turn, call `UpdateStatus` from our handler.

`UpdateStatus` checks to see if the user is authenticated. If so, it displays a simple Welcome message and a "Sign-Out" button (along with hiding the "Sign-In" button). If not, it will hide the message and sign-out command in favor of the sign-in command. Figure 13-8 shows what it looks like just after the user is authenticated, right before the Sign-In box fades out.

Figure 13-8

Now you're all set with a basic authentication infrastructure; the next step in security is authorization.

Authorization

Authorization is about ensuring that an actor (usually a person/user) is authorized to do something. ASP.NET carries forward the concept of role-based authorization. This is superior to the common level-based authorization (e.g., user, superuser, admin) because it allows for more fine-grained control, based on the role that a user is in. It is somewhat similar to groups in NT file access security, although there is no built-in grouping of other roles. Role-based authorization is limited, though, and usually needs to be supplemented by further authorization based on assignment, ownership, or (generically speaking) responsibility.

This latter is when you, for instance, have a role such as Project Managers that determines a user can perform project management functions, but you need a further authorization level to restrict what projects a particular user can manage. Usually there is some level of responsibility implied here. In any case, you have to implement that level of responsibility-based authorization yourself, but you can take advantage of the ASP.NET role-based authorization for more coarse-grained authorization.

Adding support for ASP.NET role-based authorization is very similar to using ASP.NET authentication in that you start by adding a service for it to your Web project. Remember to pick the text file type and rename it to *Authorization.svc*, and then add the following to that file:

```
<%@ ServiceHost Language="C#"
    Service="System.Web.ApplicationServices.RoleService" %>
```

Next, open that web.config file, find the system.serviceModel/services section, and add this code there:

```
<service name="System.Web.ApplicationServices.RoleService"
         behaviorConfiguration="RoleServiceTypeBehaviors">
  <endpoint contract="System.Web.ApplicationServices.RoleService"
            binding="basicHttpBinding" bindingConfiguration="userHttp"
            bindingNamespace="http://asp.net/ApplicationServices/v200"/>
</service>
```

And add the behavior to the system.serviceModel/behaviors section:

```
<behavior name="RoleServiceTypeBehaviors">
  <serviceMetadata httpGetEnabled="true"/>
</behavior>
```

Then enable the role manager service for ASP.NET in the system.web section, as follows.

```
<roleManager enabled="true"/>
```

The last thing in web.config is to enable the role manager to be exposed via the services. To do that, find the system.web.extensions/scripting/webServices section and add the following:

```
<roleService enabled="true"/>
```

Now you can right-click and view in the browser to ensure that the new service is functional, at least to the extent that you didn't make a goof in the configuration. Good? OK, now if you don't have roles already set up, go into the Website ➪ ASP.NET Configuration for the web site and go to Security ➪ Create or Manage Roles. There, you can add a few roles, such as Project Managers and Account Executives, as shown in Figure 13-9.

Assign them to your users in Security ➪ Manage users. On the admin interface, you click "Edit Roles" for each user and check the ones you want. We set Jim to be an Account Executive (AE) and Joe to be a Project Manager (PM).

Now that the server side is set up, you can add a service reference just like you did for authentication: Just use `Services.Authorization` for the namespace on this reference.

Next, you need to use this new service to cache the roles for the user. You need to consider that caching means that changes in roles on the server will not be reflected until the user signs out and in again. That usually won't be a problem, but if you have scenarios that would make it problematic, such as the user can do something that would change his or her role, you would want to update their roles at that point as well.

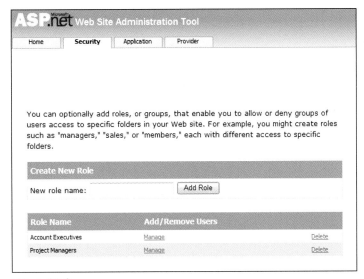

Figure 13-9

So open SignIn.xaml.cs, which you created in the Authentication section. Modify the sign-in success as follows. (Remove the line that updates the user message — we're going to move that later.)

```
Services.Authorization.RoleServiceClient rsc =
  new Services.Authorization.RoleServiceClient();
rsc.GetRolesForCurrentUserCompleted +=
  rsc_GetRolesForCurrentUserCompleted;
rsc.GetRolesForCurrentUserAsync(e.UserState);
```

This sets up the roles service client, attaches a completion handler for role retrieval, and tells it to go get the roles for the user. Add the rsc_GetRolesForCurrentUserCompleted method like this:

```
void rsc_GetRolesForCurrentUserCompleted(object sender,
  Services.Authorization.GetRolesForCurrentUserCompletedEventArgs e)
{
  if (e.Error != null)
  {
    this.UserMessage.Text =
    "Sorry! There's a technical problem preventing " +
    "sign in at this time. Please try again later and let us know " +
    "if the problem continues.";
  }
  else
  {
    this.UserMessage.Text = "Signed in successfully!";
    App.CurrentUser =
     new Security.AppPrincipal((string)e.UserState, true,
       e.Result.ToArray());
    this.Close();
  }
}
```

After checking for an error, this will let the user know that sign-in was OK (see, we moved it down here) and then set up the new principal just as before; only this time, you're adding the third parameter, which will be the list of roles for that user as a string array.

So now your user principal object will be set up with the basics of authentication and authorization. We recommend adding a few convenience and maintenance facilities. First, you may want to add a static `Roles` class to your app to centralize the string names for your roles. To do that, just go into App.xaml. cs and add the following somewhere in the `App` class definition.

```
public static class Roles
{
    public const string ProjectManager = "Project Managers";
    public const string AccountExecutive = "Account Executives";
}
```

The value here is that it is easy to reference these whenever you need to do an authorization against known roles, as you'll see shortly.

Next, you can optionally add an `Extensions` class to the root of your project. .NET 3.5 adds the ability to have extension methods, which enable you, in practice, to add your own instance methods to types that you don't necessarily have control over. It's a compiler trick, really, because you're not modifying the types but, rather, adding static methods that the compiler will let you use as if they were instance methods. The one we added was an authorization checker to the `FrameworkElement` type that lets you easily modify any `FrameworkElement`'s `Visibility` based on whether or not the user is in a given role. Here's what it looks like:

```
public static class Extensions
{
    public static void AuthorizeVisibility(this FrameworkElement fe,
        string role)
    {
        fe.Visibility = App.CurrentUser.IsInRole(role) ?
            Visibility.Visible : Visibility.Collapsed;
    }

}
```

The trick for extension methods is as follows:

1. Declare a static class.

2. Use the `this` keyword for the first parameter to a static method to indicate the type that the method should extend/be attached to.

3. Use the namespace that your class is in for any calling code.

Since we put this in the root (AppServices), it shows up for most code in the project without trying.

At this point, you're pretty much there in terms of setting up the authorization service infrastructure. Now you should add some authorization checking in the application against these roles. What we did was just add a couple of buttons to the main Page.xaml under the sign-in control:

```
<StackPanel>
  <l:SignInStatus x:Name="SignInStatus" />
  <Button x:Name="ManageProjects"
    Width="200" Height="30"
    Content="Manage Projects" Visibility="Collapsed" />
  <Button x:Name="ManageAccounts"
    Width="200" Height="30"
    Content="Manage Accounts" Visibility="Collapsed" />
</StackPanel>
```

By default, these buttons are hidden. To show them, add some code to do the authorization. In the Page .xaml.cs constructor, add a handler to handle the user-changed event on the application:

```
App.CurrentUserChanged += App_CurrentUserChanged;
That method then updates the authorization:
void App_CurrentUserChanged(object sender, EventArgs e)
{
   this.ManageProjects.AuthorizeVisibility(App.Roles.ProjectManager);
   this.ManageAccounts.AuthorizeVisibility(App.Roles.AccountExecutive);
}
```

You see here that we use the two facilities added to make maintenance and readability better. The `AuthorizeVisibility` method is the extension method we defined to extend `FrameworkElement` (and buttons are derivatives of that, so they can use those, just as you'd expect for normal type inheritance of methods). It takes a role, so the code passes in the role, using the string constants set up off the `App` class.

Now, when you run the application, it will update the visibility of the buttons based on the current user's roles. Jim will only see the "Manage Accounts" button because he's an Account Executive, and Joe will only see the "Project Manager" button. You can imagine how you can easily extend this for your own authorization of users.

Exception Handling and Logging

The next common cross-cutting concern is exception handling, and logging often goes hand-in-hand with that (at least in the sense that the most common logging is exception logging). Now I hope your mind immediately goes to the Microsoft Enterprise Library when the topic of .NET exception handling and logging comes up. Unfortunately, as of the time of writing, there are no Silverlight-based EntLib libraries, and since Silverlight is not binary-compatible, you can't just drop EntLib into your Silverlight projects.

Of course, if you talk to the EntLib creators and aficionados, they'll scoff to think you need them to provide you with binaries — they'd prefer that folks customize EntLib for their particular needs rather than use the binaries directly. And if you're in that camp, by all means, enjoy porting what you can to Silverlight. If you are among the other 99 percent of Microsoft developers, you can either wait for the Patterns and Practices group to produce some Silverlight libraries or do some footwork for yourself. I've not heard of any plans to specifically port EntLib to Silverlight, though, so that probably means creating some basic facilities yourself.

The nice thing is that you can lean on the server to do the heavy lifting and just focus on some minimal work on the client. If you want instrumentation/tracking of usage, you'll have a bit more work cut out for you, but for basic exception handling and logging, there's not too terribly much. Essentially, you can use EntLib on your server, create an exception logging service, and log your exceptions to that service, which is what you'll do here, except that we won't dive into EntLib — that's beyond the scope of this book, and what we're building isn't necessarily EntLib-specific.

So first, create a logging service by right-clicking on your Services directory in the AppServices web site, choosing "Add New Item," selecting "Silverlight-enabled WCF Service," and calling it *Logging.svc*. That will automatically create a Logging.cs file in your App_Code directory (and should open it for you). It has some default goo, which is OK; you just need to change the default method signature to something like this:

```
[OperationContract]
public void LogException(ExceptionInfo info)
{
    // do something to log message on the server
    System.Diagnostics.Debug.WriteLine(info.Details);
}
```

As noted, this chapter won't cover what you do with it on the server, as that's no different from .NET today. You could use EntLib, ELMAH, Log4Net, or any number of other exception/logging frameworks. The ExceptionInfo type is a custom class defined as follows:

```
[DataContract]
public class ExceptionInfo
{
    [DataMember]
    public string Application { get; set; }
    [DataMember]
    public DateTimeOffset TimeOfOccurrence { get; set; }
    [DataMember]
    public string ClientInfo { get; set; }
    [DataMember]
    public string UserInfo { get; set; }
    [DataMember]
    public string FullTypeName { get; set; }
    [DataMember]
    public string Details { get; set; }
}
```

That's it for the server side. You might want to right-click and view the new service in your browser to ensure that it comes up. Then flip over to the client side and add a service reference (as you did with the authentication and authorization); we used Services.Logging for the namespace, as in Figure 13-10.

Now you have a service to log to, so you just need to decide how you're going to handle and log. In our example, we just handle the unhandled exceptions using the System.Windows.Application .UnhandledException event in our App.xaml.cs class. It's actually handled by default in the VS Silverlight application template. You can delete the generated code and add the following:

```
private void Application_UnhandledException(object sender,
    ApplicationUnhandledExceptionEventArgs e)
{
```

```
try
{
    CurrentPage.PromptException(e.ExceptionObject);
    e.Handled = true;
}
catch (Exception)
{
}
}
```

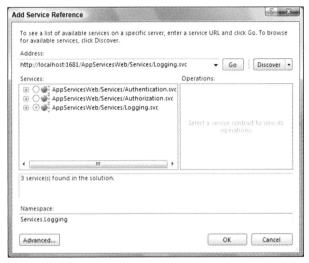

Figure 13-10

The `CurrentPage` is a static property we already defined that just casts the App's `RootVisual` as our `Page` class. Now you can add a `PromptException` method on your `Page` class.

```
public void PromptException(Exception ex)
{
    this.ExceptionPrompt.Prompt(ex);
}
```

OK, enough infrastructure! Now on to the actual handling code, which we've encapsulated in an `ExceptionPrompt` user control. So go ahead and add an `ExceptionPrompt.xaml` user control in the Controls directory. On that, you'll want to put a message to the user, letting them know there was a problem, and because this is client side, the polite thing to do is ask them if they want to report it, so you can add a question to the user asking that and provide a "Send" or "Don't Send" button.

We got a little fancy in this sample, adding a nice fade and slide in (which, of course, you can't see in a book), but Figure 13-11 shows the end result — it acts like a modal dialogue by putting a layer over everything that is dark and mostly opaque and slides the message in from the top (all in less than 1 s). Pretty smooth; you should check it out.

Problem with AppServices

An unexpected problem happened with the AppServices application. If it keeps happening, please don't hesitate to give us an earful about it.

Would you like to report this to us?

Send Report   Don't Send

Figure 13-11

We're following several of the Vista UX best practices for error handling here — making the title clear that there is a problem, telling them what application is the source, showing a big error icon, and letting them report it or not, and the like. You'll want to, of course, customize this and maybe even make the style match your app style — just make it obvious that it is an error and not just info or a warning.

If the user chooses Don't Send, our code is just hiding the prompt and moving on with life. That may or may not make sense for your application. If you're doing a good job, standard exception-handling best practices still apply; that is, try to handle exceptions and keep the app moving, so if it gets this far (to a generic unhandled exception handler), it may be safe to assume the app can't continue, in which case, you may want to redirect to some contact page or something to give the user some direction on what to do next. But you could use this prompt approach for other errors that are non-fatal but that may be useful to report, telling the user to try again or whatever makes sense for the context.

If the user chooses to Send, that's where we engage our logging code, like this:

```
Services.Logging.ExceptionInfo _ExInfo;
public void Prompt(Exception exception)
{
  _ExInfo = new Services.Logging.ExceptionInfo();
  _ExInfo.TimeOfOccurrence = DateTimeOffset.Now;
  _ExInfo.FullTypeName = exception.GetType().FullName;
  _ExInfo.Details = exception.ToString();
  _ExInfo.Application = "AppServices";
  _ExInfo.ClientInfo =
    "Platform: " +
    System.Windows.Browser.HtmlPage.BrowserInformation.Platform +
    "\r\nBrowser: " +
    System.Windows.Browser.HtmlPage.BrowserInformation.Name +
    "\r\nVersion: " +
    System.Windows.Browser.HtmlPage.
      BrowserInformation.BrowserVersion.ToString() +
    "\r\nCookies: " +
    (System.Windows.Browser.HtmlPage.BrowserInformation.CookiesEnabled
        ? "Yes" : "No") +
    "\r\nUser Agent: " +
    System.Windows.Browser.HtmlPage.BrowserInformation.UserAgent +
    "\r\nUser Culture: " +
    System.Globalization.CultureInfo.CurrentUICulture.Name;
```

```
      _ExInfo.UserInfo =
        "Authenticated: " + (App.CurrentUser.Identity.IsAuthenticated
          ? "Yes" : "No") +
        "\r\nUsername: " + App.CurrentUser.Identity.Name +
        "\r\nRoles: " + App.CurrentUser.Roles;
      this.Visibility = Visibility.Visible;
      this.Show.Begin();
    }
```

Recall that this is the method being called from the Page.xaml.cs `PromptException` method. It creates an instance of your service reference's proxy `ExceptionInfo` class and sets a bunch of stuff on it. The idea here, of course, is to log as much as you can to help your debugging efforts on the back end. This is just a simplistic capture — you'd want to customize it to provide whatever context and debugging information makes sense for your app.

At the very end, we go ahead and show the dialogue (nothing's been sent yet). See Figure 13-11 again to see what shows at that point. Now here's the code for `Send`:

```
    private void Send_Click(object sender, RoutedEventArgs e)
    {
      if (_ExInfo != null)
      {
        try
        {
          Services.Logging.LoggingClient logger =
            new Services.Logging.LoggingClient();
          logger.LogExceptionAsync(_ExInfo);
        }
        catch (Exception ex)
        {
          // maybe log to isolated storage
          System.Diagnostics.Debug.WriteLine(ex.ToString());
        }
        finally { _ExInfo = null; }
        this.Hide.Begin();
      }
    }
```

Pretty simple. Just create an instance of the Logging client proxy and send the `ExceptionInfo` instance created in the `Prompt` method. It might be worthwhile handling the `LogExceptionCompleted` method and checking for an error, depending on how robust you want your logging to be — you could fall back to logging to isolated storage. Finally, the code clears out the info so that it doesn't hang around, and then it hides the dialogue (the Show and Hide are storyboards we created that are not listed here; see the sample code for details).

And that's pretty much it. You can extend this concept, elaborate it, and make it more robust for your applications as needed. You could use a similar approach to log feature usage of your app — just be sure that you don't blow up when logging, as the user won't know what's going on, and you should probably ask the user if it is OK to log that sort of thing, like the many "Customer Experience Improvement Program" dialogues you see in things like Office, Visual Studio, and the like.

Similarly, if you need to do general auditing (outside of data auditing), you could save audit logs to the local isolated storage and periodically send them to the server in batch updates. Your data-level auditing will need to be done as you normally do it and sent along to the server with the data updates themselves, as you might expect.

Summary

In this chapter, you saw how to deal with the most common cross-cutting concerns for applications — security, exception handling, and logging. You covered the basics of the Silverlight security models for code access and network access, touched on cryptography, and dug into how to take advantage of the ASP.NET authentication and authorization services. (Chapter 16 builds on that to add personalization using the ASP.NET profile service.) After looking at those services, you saw an example of how to handle and log exceptions and some brief thoughts on best practices in that area. Now you should be ready to take this infrastructure and start building out your application experience.

14

Dealing with Data

One of the most prominent and compelling aspects of rich Internet applications is unfettered access to data. It should, therefore, be no surprise that Silverlight provides a rich, pervasive model that allows you to create dynamic data-driven applications. Silverlight provides a host of facilities for retrieving, displaying, manipulating, and storing data from a variety of data sources.

In this chapter you will discover:

❑   How to expose data from a server and retrieve it from a Silverlight application

❑   How to present data via the XAML-binding syntax

❑   How to store data on the client

Getting Data to Your Application

If you are accustomed to using classes within `Sytem.Data` to query databases directly, you are in for a rude surprise with Silverlight, as none of these services are available. Instead, the `WebClient` class is provided to make network requests to arbitrary URI data endpoints. Fortunately, Microsoft also provides the infrastructure to generate WCF proxy client classes, which take care of the details needed to access data you expose through WCF services.

Fetching Data with the `WebClient` Class

You can use the `WebClient` class to retrieve data from a wide variety of endpoints including POX-, JSON-, RSS-, and REST-based services. All requests are performed asynchronously in Silverlight, which enables your application to respond even while loading data.

Depending on the format of the data returned by a server, you then choose the appropriate class to parse it into a format for your application to consume. For example, the `XmlReader` class can be used to quickly access data returned from the server in Plain Old XML (POX).

Initiating the Download Request

Once you have created a WebClient object and added an event handler for the DownloadStringCompleted event, you are ready to retrieve data:

```
public partial class Page : UserControl
{
  public Page()
  {
    InitializeComponent();
    this.Loaded += new RoutedEventHandler(Page_Loaded);
  }

  void Page_Loaded(object sender, RoutedEventArgs e)
  {
    // Construct a new WebRequest object
    WebClient client = new WebClient();

    // Configure an event handler for when the Download is complete
    client.DownloadStringCompleted += new
      DownloadStringCompletedEventHandler(client_DownloadCompleted);

    // Request an XML document located adjacent to the XAP
    Uri xmlUri = new Uri("Destinations.xml", UriKind.Relative);
    client.DownloadStringAsync(xmlUri);
  }

  void client_DownloadCompleted(object sender,
    DownloadStringCompletedEventArgs e)
  {
    // If no error, sends results to a text block
    if (e.Error == null)
    {
      ResultsTextBlock.Text = e.Result;
    }
  }
}
```

In this case, an XML file located adjacent to the XAP is being accessed, which makes for a very simple endpoint URI.

Reusing a Single **WebClient** Object

If you want to download a set of data files but do not want to create a separate WebClient object and event handler for each, you can choose to reuse a single WebClient. Although each download request is made asynchronously, the WebClient class does not support simultaneous requests. You can, however, make additional calls to DownloadStringAsync once previous calls have completed.

Since each WebClient object has a single DownloadStringCompleted event, you need a way to distinguish exactly what request has completed in your event handler. This can be achieved by specifying some state with each call to DownloadStringAsync through the userToken parameter:

```
public partial class Page : UserControl
{
```

```csharp
// Construct a new WebRequest object as a private member
WebClient _client = new WebClient();

public Page()
{
  InitializeComponent();
  this.Loaded +=new RoutedEventHandler(Page_Loaded);
}

void Page_Loaded(object sender, RoutedEventArgs e)
{
  // Configure an event handler for when the Download is complete
  _client.DownloadStringCompleted += new
    DownloadStringCompletedEventHandler(client_DownloadCompleted);

  // construct a URI based on files with an indexed naming scheme
  Uri targetUri = new Uri("Destinations1.xml", UriKind.Relative);

  // iniate the download passing an integer as the userToken
  _client.DownloadStringAsync(targetUri, 1);
}

void client_DownloadCompleted(object sender,
  DownloadStringCompletedEventArgs e)
{
  // if no error, process the result      if (e.Error == null)
  {
    // retrieve the state we originally specified
    int count = (int)e.UserState;
    // Set the text of the apporpriate textbox based on
    // our integet userToken
    switch (count)
    {
      case 1:
        ResultsTextBlock1.Text = e.Result;
        break;
      case 2:
        ResultsTextBlock2.Text = e.Result;
        break;
      case 3:
        ResultsTextBlock3.Text = e.Result;
        break;
    }
    // Fire off requests until we have retrieved 3 files
    if (count++ < 3)
    {

      Uri targetUri = new Uri("Destinations" + count + ".xml",
          UriKind.Relative);

      // iniate the download passing an integer as the userToken
      _client.DownloadStringAsync(targetUri, count);
    }
  }
}
}
```

Cross-Domain Access

Silverlight enables access to any services that are contained in the same domain as the application. If you wish to access services that are located on a different domain, then a policy file is required. Assuming that you have root access to your deployment server, adding a Silverlight policy file is actually quite simple.

Many domains have already been configured to allow cross-domain access from Flash clients via a crossdomain.xml policy file. Thankfully, Silverlight supports the Silverlight (clientaccesspolicy.xml) policy format and the subset of Flash (crossdomain.xml) and policy formats.

clientaccesspolicy.xml

The following Silverlight policy file will enable classes in `System.Net` such as `WebClient` as well as classes in the `System.Net.Sockets` classes to access all available resources located in the domain:

```xml
<?xml version="1.0" encoding="utf-8"?>
<access-policy>
  <cross-domain-access>
    <policy>
      <allow-from http-request-headers="*">
        <domain uri="*"/>
      </allow-from>
      <grant-to>
        <resource path="/" include-subpaths="true"/>
      </grant-to>
    </policy>
  </cross-domain-access>
</access-policy>
```

crossdomain.xml

The following Flash-based policy file will allow Silverlight to make cross-domain calls to resources on the server from `WebClient` and other HTTP classes in the `System.Net` namespace:

```xml
<?xml version="1.0"?>
<!DOCTYPE cross-domain-policy SYSTEM
    "http://www.macromedia.com/xml/dtds/cross-domain-policy.dtd">
<cross-domain-policy>
  <allow-http-request-headers-from domain="*" headers="*"/>
</cross-domain-policy>
```

Processing XML Data

While a developer might actually enjoy seeing XML presented directly in an application, it is far more likely that you will need to massage the XML data into some strongly typed objects that will be presented to the user. For instance, you would probably not want to expose the end-user to the following raw XML:

```xml
<?xml version="1.0" encoding="utf-8" ?>
<destinations>
  <destination name="St. Croix" population="70,000"
               averageAirfare="300" averageHotel="300"
               bestKnownFor="Beaches" />
```

```
    <destination name="St. Barths" population="8,450"
                  averageAirfare="600" averageHotel="800"
                  bestKnownFor="Shopping"  />
    <destination name="St. Lucia" population="160,765"
                  averageAirfare="400" averageHotel="400"
                  bestKnownFor="Rainforests"  />
</destinations>
```

Silverlight provides both the low-level XMLReader class and LINQ to XML for working with raw XML. Either framework can be used to transform XML into a strongly typed class that represents the data. In this example, we have a Destination class, which exposes some of the important factors you might consider when deciding where to spend your next vacation.

```
public class Destination
{
  public string Name { get; set; }
  public int Population { get; set; }
  public double AverageAirfare { get; set; }
  public double AverageHotel { get; set; }
  public string BestKnownFor { get; set; }
}
```

Let's take a look at how we can use both LINQ to XML and the XMLReader classes to grab the information found in XML and create a set of Destination objects.

LINQ to XML

LINQ to XML provides a clean, consistent syntax for accessing XML data. Begin by adding references to System.Xml and System.Xml.Linq. Once WebClient completes downloading the data, you will need to construct a new XDocument for LINQ to query. From there, you can map the XML file to a list of strongly typed objects.

```
void Page_Loaded(object sender, RoutedEventArgs e)
{
  // Construct a new WebRequest object
  WebClient client = new WebClient();

  // Configure an event handler for when the Download is complete
  client.DownloadStringCompleted += new
    DownloadStringCompletedEventHandler(client_DownloadCompleted);

  // Request an Xml document located adjacent to the XAP   Uri xmlUri = new
Uri("Destinations.xml", UriKind.Relative);
  client.DownloadStringAsync(xmlUri);
}

// private member for holding destinations
private IEnumerable<Destination> _destinationsList;

void client_DownloadCompleted(object sender,
  DownloadStringCompletedEventArgs e)
{
```

```
    // If no error, sends results to a text block  if (e.Error == null)
    {
      parseDestinationsXml(e.Result);
    }
}

void parseDestinationsXml(string xmlContent)
{
  // Create an Xml document from the conteent
  XDocument doc = XDocument.Parse(xmlContent);

  // Create a Linq query which maps to Destination objects  _destinationsList =
    from destination in doc.Descendants("destination")
    select new Destination
    {
      Name = (string)destination.Attribute("name"),
      Population = (int)destination.Attribute("population"),
      AverageAirfare = (double)destination.Attribute
                        ("averageAirfare"),
      AverageHotel = (double)destination.Attribute("averageHotel"),
      BestKnownFor = (string)destination.Attribute("bestKnownFor")
    };
  DestinationsListBox.ItemsSource = _destinationsList;
}
```

XML Reader

You are also free to parse the data through the XMLReader API; just don't expect all the bells and whistles of LINQ:

```
public partial class Page : UserControl
{
  // private member for holding destinations
  private List<Destination> _destinationsList;

  public Page()
  {
    InitializeComponent();
    this.Loaded += new RoutedEventHandler(Page_Loaded);
  }

  void Page_Loaded(object sender, RoutedEventArgs e)
  {
    // Construct a new WebRequest object
    WebClient client = new WebClient();

    // Configure an event handler for when the Download is complete
    client.DownloadStringCompleted += new
      DownloadStringCompletedEventHandler(client_DownloadCompleted);

    // Request an xml document located adjacent to the XAP
    Uri xmlUri = new Uri("Destinations.xml", UriKind.Relative);
    client.DownloadStringAsync(xmlUri);
  }

  void client_DownloadCompleted(object sender,
```

```
        DownloadStringCompletedEventArgs e)
  {
     // If no error, sends results to a text Block
     if (e.Error == null)
     {
       parseDestinationXml(new StringReader(e.Result));
     }
  }

  void parseDestinationXml(StringReader xmlContent)
  {
     // Create a list to hold our destinations
     _destinationsList = new List<Destination>();

     // Create a new XmlReader to walk through the document
     XmlReader reader = XmlReader.Create(xmlContent);

     while (reader.Read())
     {
       if (reader.NodeType == XmlNodeType.Element)
       {
         if (reader.Name == "destination")
         {
           Destination d = new Destination
           {
             Name = reader["name"],
             Population = int.Parse(reader["population"]),
             AverageAirfare = double.Parse(reader["averageAirfare"]),
             AverageHotel = double.Parse(reader["averageHotel"]),
             BestKnownFor = reader["bestKnownFor"]
           };
           _destinationsList.Add(d);
         }
       }
     }
     DestinationsListBox.ItemsSource = _destinationsList;
  }
}
```

Accessing Data through WCF

Visual Studio .NET provides relatively seamless integration of WCF services into your Silverlight application. A huge benefit of leveraging WCF is automatic type serialization and deserialization between the server and client for a wide variety of types.

Taking advantage of WCF can be factored into several key steps, including:

1. Creating business objects that correspond to your data

2. Exposing WCF services for working with those objects

3. Referencing the WCF service from your Silverlight project and creating proxy classes

4. Accessing the services from your Silverlight application

Factoring Out Business Objects for Your Data

For many developers who have been working with Web services or following formal tiered architectures, it might be a foregone conclusion that they will have to factor out business objects; however, many ASP.NET developers choose to include SQL queries directly in their presentation layer and have found no need to factor out business objects. If you fall into the latter category, get ready for a major context switch! The time spent making this adjustment is well worth it, since your developer skills and the applications you build will be greatly improved.

Since Silverlight does not provide any classes for accessing SQL databases directly, you are forced to create a server-side layer that exposes the data to the client. While you are free to use a variety of server-side data access technologies, it is strongly advisable to create objects that represent that data that is essential to your application.

This could be as straightforward as creating a set of objects that mirror your SQL table structure, or might be more involved depending on the architecture of your application.

In this example, we are going to reuse the Destination object:

```
public class Destination
{
    public string Name { get; set; }
    public int Population { get; set; }
    public double AverageAirfare { get; set; }
    public double AverageHotel { get; set; }
    public string BestKnownFor { get; set; }
}
```

Serialization

At some point, WCF is going to need to serialize your types, so you should take a moment to consider what is the most appropriate for your application's types. The four built-in serialization mechanisms are:

❑   XmlSerializer

❑   DataContractSerializer

❑   NetDataContractSerializer

❑   DataContractJsonSerializer

By default, WCF will use DataContractSerializer, while classic ASMX services default to XmlSerializer. This disconnect may lead to some confusion if you are transitioning between the two service platforms.

If you are using built-in types and don't have particularly complicated objects, you should not need to spend much time digging through MSDN's serialization documentation.

Exposing a WCF Service

Start by adding a new "Silverlight-enabled WCF service" to your web application in Visual Studio. You might be wondering why we selected the Silverlight Enabled WCF service instead of creating a standard WCF service. The primary difference is the transport enabled for the service. Silverlight supports only `basicHttpBinding`, and a quick look at your web.config will show that this has been configured automatically for the new service:

```
<system.serviceModel>
    <behaviors>
        <serviceBehaviors>
            <behavior name="Wrox.Silverlight30.Data.WCFService.Web.
DestinationsServiceBehavior">
                <serviceMetadata httpGetEnabled="true" />
                <serviceDebug includeExceptionDetailInFaults="false" />
            </behavior>
        </serviceBehaviors>
    </behaviors>
    <serviceHostingEnvironment aspNetCompatibilityEnabled="true" />
    <services>
        <service behaviorConfiguration="Wrox.Silverlight30.Data.WCFService.Web.
DestinationsServiceBehavior"
            name="Wrox.Silverlight30.Data.WCFService.Web.DestinationsService">
                <endpoint address="" binding="basicHttpBinding"
    contract="Wrox.Silverlight30.Data.WCFService.Web.DestinationsService" />
                <endpoint address="mex" binding="mexHttpBinding"
contract="IMetadataExchange" />
        </service>
    </services>
</system.serviceModel>
```

After selecting an appropriate `ServiceContract` namespace and class name, you will want to create a set of methods that are flagged with the `OperationContract` attribute.

In this case, one service is offered for retrieving a list of the U.S. Virgin Islands:

```
[ServiceContract(Namespace = "Wrox.Silverlight30.Data.WCFService.Web")]
[AspNetCompatibilityRequirements(RequirementsMode =
AspNetCompatibilityRequirementsMode.Allowed)]
public class DestinationsService
{
  [OperationContract]
  public List<Destination> GetIslands()
  {
    List<Destination> destinations = new List<Destination>();
    destinations.Add(new Destination { Name = "St. Croix" });
    destinations.Add(new Destination { Name = "St. John" });
    destinations.Add(new Destination { Name = "St. Thomas" });
    return destinations;
  }
}
```

Referencing the WCF Service from Silverlight

Now that you have a WCF service to offer up, it is time to set up the hooks so that you can access it from the client. To make consuming services easy, Visual Studio is capable of generating proxy classes for accessing the service.

This process begins by selecting "Add Service Reference" from the Project menu. You can select services by URI or by finding them in other solution projects. Visual Studio's interface allows you to drill into the service to verify that it exposes the operations you expect.

Take a moment to consider the appropriate namespaces Visual Studio is about to create for consuming and working with the data provided by the service. Once a service is selected, choose a namespace for the proxy objects through which you will access the service.

A host of advanced options, which control the proxy classes that Visual Studio generates, are available by selecting the Advanced button. If you are wondering why the return type of collection objects exposed through the service doesn't align with what is found in the generated proxy class, take a quick look at the Advanced settings. One option that may catch you by surprise is that the proxy class will expose collections offered through service operations as ObservableCollections. Later in this chapter, we will discuss the advantages of using this collection when binding a collection to the presentation layer.

Accessing the Service from Silverlight

Having created and exposed a WCF service, you are now set up to consume it from Silverlight. Each time you add a service reference, Visual Studio creates several classes for facilitating communication with the service. The ServiceClient is the key class for calling into the service and is named the same as the service with *ServiceClient* appended. In this example, we have created a service.

The **ServiceClient** Class

Similarly to the WebClient class, ServiceClient-derived classes are built around asynchronous calls to the server. A quick inspection of the ServiceClient-derived class named DestinationsServiceClient created for the Destinations service reveals unique asynchronous methods and matching event handlers for each method in the service. This is the pattern you will find in all ServiceClient classes.

To invoke a method in the WCF service, you need to create a new instance of the ServiceClient, attach an event handler for the method you wish to call, and, finally, invoke the service:

```csharp
public partial class Page : UserControl
{
  public Page()
  {
    InitializeComponent();
    this.Loaded += new RoutedEventHandler(Page_Loaded);
  }

  void Page_Loaded(object sender, RoutedEventArgs e)
  {
    // Instantiate the Service Client
    DestinationsServiceClient client = new DestinationsServiceClient();

    // Invoke a service method
    client.GetIslandsAsync();

  }
}
```

Waiting for the Service to Respond

The `ServiceClient` class provides an event for each service method, which will fire after a service method has been invoked. In our service, we will listen to the `GetIslandsCompleted` event. Access to the return data from the service is provided in a strongly typed manner through the `Result` property of the custom `EventArgs` objects created for each service method.

```
public partial class Page : UserControl
{
  public Page()
  {
    InitializeComponent();
    this.Loaded += new RoutedEventHandler(Page_Loaded);
  }

  void Page_Loaded(object sender, RoutedEventArgs e)
  {
    // Instantiate the Service Client
    DestinationsServiceClient client = new DestinationsServiceClient();

    // Hook up listener for completion of inoking a service method
    client.GetIslandsCompleted +=
      new EventHandler<GetIslandsCompletedEventArgs>(client_GetIslandsCompleted);

    // Invoke a service method
    client.GetIslandsAsync();
  }

  void client_GetIslandsCompleted(object sender, GetIslandsCompletedEventArgs e)
  {
    if (e.Error == null)
    {
      DestinationsListBox.ItemsSource = e.Result;
    }
  }
}
```

Binding a User Interface to Data

Silverlight provides a flexible data-binding model for connecting a user interface to data objects. Built around the `Binding` object, it facilitates both presenting and processing updates to data. The binding model is not tied to a specific data provider; instead, it is centered around connecting a property from a source object to a property on a target object. Silverlight's architecture enables and encourages a high degree of separation between the presentation and business layers of an application.

Establishing a Data-Binding Connection

To establish a binding, you need to specify both the object that will communicate via the binding and the properties on those objects that should be connected. Bindings can be established at run time through code or can be specified statically in XAML markup.

Before diving into the details, consider a simple scenario of binding a few TextBlock elements to a single object. We will continue to use the Destination object discussed earlier in this chapter. Begin by adding binding statements to the properties on the target object that map to select properties on the source object:

```
<Grid x:Name="LayoutRoot" Background="White">
  <StackPanel>
    <TextBlock Text="{Binding Name}"></TextBlock>
    <TextBlock Text="{Binding Population}"></TextBlock>
  </StackPanel>
</Grid>
```

Next, provide the source object for both TextBlocks by specifying the DataContext for the StackPanel:

```
public partial class Page : UserControl
{
  public Page()
  {
    InitializeComponent();
    this.Loaded += new RoutedEventHandler(Page_Loaded);
  }

  void Page_Loaded(object sender, RoutedEventArgs e)
  {
    Destination d = new Destination { Name = "St. Croix", Population = 70000 };
    LayoutRoot.DataContext = d;
  }
}
```

In the preceding case, each TextBlock is the target of a binding, and a single Destination object acts as the source.

Valid Binding Target Types

Silverlight's binding model is able to establish communication among a wide variety of objects. While the binding source can be of any type for one-way and one-time binding, the target must be both a member of a FrameworkElement object and a dependency property. This restriction is of greater concern when building custom controls because it is essential for supporting data binding.

Specifying the Source Object

Since a binding's target must be a FrameworkElement, you can take advantage of the DataContext property to specify the source object for a binding. DataContext is inherited from parents in the object tree, which eliminates the need to specify the source for a group of UI elements that present information for the same data object. This is why, in our first example, we only needed to specify the DataContext for the StackPanel instead of on each TextBlock element.

If you do not want the binding source to be inherited by children, you can specify the source property on the binding object itself. In this example, we establish the binding in code:

```
<Grid x:Name="LayoutRoot" Background="White">
  <StackPanel>
```

```
    <TextBlock x:Name="NameTextBlock"></TextBlock>
    <TextBlock x:Name="PopulationTextBlock"></TextBlock>
  </StackPanel>
</Grid>

public partial class Page : UserControl
{
  public Page()
  {
    InitializeComponent();
    this.Loaded += new RoutedEventHandler(Page_Loaded);
  }

  void Page_Loaded(object sender, RoutedEventArgs e)
  {
    // The object which will be used as the source
    Destination d = new Destination { Name = "St. Croix", Population = 70000 };

    // Create a Binding in code for the Name
    System.Windows.Data.Binding nameBinding = new Binding("Name");
    nameBinding.Source = d;
    nameBinding.Mode = BindingMode.OneTime;

    // Connect the binding to the TextBox's Text property
    NameTextBlock.SetBinding(TextBlock.TextProperty, nameBinding);

    // Create a Binding in code for the Population
    System.Windows.Data.Binding popBinding = new Binding("Population");
    popBinding.Source = d;
    popBinding.Mode = BindingMode.OneTime;
    PopulationTextBlock.SetBinding(TextBlock.TextProperty, popBinding);
  }
}
```

Selecting a Property from the Source Object

The binding object's Path property allows you to specify the property from the Source object. For members on the Source object, you can simply specify the name of the property.

```
<Binding Path="SourceProperty" />
```

Since Path is of type PropertyPath, it also allows for specifying properties of subobjects on the source as well as collections. In Silverlight, you can traverse subobjects through the use of a period in between the property names.

```
<Binding Path="SourceProperty.SubObjectProperty" />
```

If your Source object offers collection properties that have additional collections nested beneath them, you can use a forward slash to traverse the relationship:

```
<Binding Path="SourceCollectionProperty/SubCollectionProperty"
```

Binding to Collections with `ItemsControl`

Up to this point, we have looked at bindings in the context of a single source data object. An equally common, and more interesting, use case is binding to collections of data. Any `ItemsControl` can be used to apply a `DataTemplate` for presenting each item in a `Source` object's collection. `IEnumerable` is all that is required on the `Source` object for basic collection-binding behavior.

The `ItemsSource` property on `ItemsControl` is used to specify the `Collection` to which the control is bound. This can be specified programmatically or set through a binding. If no `ItemTemplate` is provided for the control, you can take advantage of the `DisplayMemberPath` property to select which source property will be rendered. The following `ItemsControl` will be bound to a collection found in the effective `DataContext` and render the `Name` property of each item in that collection:

```
<Grid x:Name="LayoutRoot" Background="White">
  <ItemsControl ItemsSource="{Binding}" DisplayMemberPath="Name" />
</Grid>
```

Accessing the source collection through the `ItemsSource` will give you only Read access; if you wish to modify the source collection, make sure to do so through a direct reference.

Since we have created a binding for the `ItemsSource`, the `ItemsControl` will honor the effective `DataContext`, so creating the binding is straightforward:

```
public partial class Page : UserControl
{
  public Page()
  {
    InitializeComponent();
    this.Loaded += new RoutedEventHandler(Page_Loaded);
  }

  void Page_Loaded(object sender, RoutedEventArgs e)
  {
    List<Destination> destinations = new List<Destination>();
    destinations.Add(new Destination { Name = "St. Croix" });
    destinations.Add(new Destination { Name = "St. John" });
    destinations.Add(new Destination { Name = "St. Thomas" });

    LayoutRoot.DataContext = destinations;
  }
}
```

Specifying an `ItemTemplate`

If you wish to override the default rendering for each item, you can create a `DataTemplate` and set it as the `ItemsTemplate` for the `ItemsControl`. Note that the source of each `Binding` defined within the `Template` will be an item in the `Collection` to which the `ItemsControl` is bound.

```
<Grid x:Name="LayoutRoot" Background="White">
  <ItemsControl ItemsSource="{Binding}" >
    <ItemsControl.ItemTemplate>
```

```
        <DataTemplate>
          <StackPanel Orientation="Horizontal">
            <TextBlock Text="{Binding Name}" ></TextBlock>
            <TextBlock Text="{Binding Population}" ></TextBlock>
          </StackPanel>
        </DataTemplate>
      </ItemsControl.ItemTemplate>
    </ItemsControl>
  </Grid>

public partial class Page : UserControl
{
  public Page()
  {
    InitializeComponent();
    this.Loaded += new RoutedEventHandler(Page_Loaded);
  }

  void Page_Loaded(object sender, RoutedEventArgs e)
  {
    List<Destination> destinations = new List<Destination>();
    destinations.Add(new Destination { Name = "St. Croix", Population = 70000 });
    destinations.Add(new Destination { Name = "St. John", Population = 5000 });
    destinations.Add(new Destination { Name = "St. Thomas", Population = 50000 });

    LayoutRoot.DataContext = destinations;
  }
}
```

Providing a Custom **ItemsPanel**

By default, ItemsControl uses a Vertical StackPanel to arrange the elements rendered for each item. Continuing to highlight the Silverlight pattern of flexibility, you can adjust this by setting the ItemsPanel to a custom ItemsPanelTemplate:

```
<Grid x:Name="LayoutRoot" Background="White">
  <ItemsControl ItemsSource="{Binding}" >
    <ItemsControl.ItemTemplate>
      <DataTemplate>
        <StackPanel Orientation="Horizontal">
          <TextBlock Text="{Binding Name}" ></TextBlock>
          <TextBlock Text="{Binding Population}" ></TextBlock>
        </StackPanel>
      </DataTemplate>
    </ItemsControl.ItemTemplate>
    <ItemsControl.ItemsPanel>
      <ItemsPanelTemplate>
        <StackPanel Orientation="Horizontal"></StackPanel>
      </ItemsPanelTemplate>
    </ItemsControl.ItemsPanel>
  </ItemsControl>
</Grid>
```

Using a Relative Source Binding

Silverlight 3 introduces the ability to specify the source of a `Binding` relative to the target. For instance, you can create a `Binding` with the source specified as the target's `TemplatedParent`. The following example demonstrates using a `RelativeSource` binding to bind the `Text` property of a `TextBlock` to the content of the parent `Button` element:

```
<Grid x:Name="LayoutRoot" Background="White">
    <StackPanel>
        <Button Content="SampleContent">
            <Button.Template>
                <ControlTemplate>
                    <StackPanel>
                        <TextBlock Text="{Binding RelativeSource=
                        {RelativeSource TemplatedParent},
                        Path=Content}" />
                    </StackPanel>
                </ControlTemplate>
            </Button.Template>
        </Button>
    </StackPanel>
</Grid>
```

Element-to-Element Binding

Silverlight 3 also introduces the ability to specify an element as the source for a `Binding` through the `ElementName` property. This easily used feature can come in handy when building interactive interfaces where one `Element` should reflect changes to another. Currently, the target of such binding must be a `FrameworkElement`. The following example demonstrates binding the text property of a `TextBlock` to the current value of a `Slider`:

```
<Grid x:Name="LayoutRoot" Background="White">
    <StackPanel>
        <Slider x:Name="Slider1" Minimum="0" Maximum="100" />
        <TextBlock Text="{Binding ElementName=Slider1, Path=Value}" />
    </StackPanel>
</Grid>
```

Handling Data Updates

Silverlight's binding object provides three distinct binding modes, which determine the way that data flows between the source and target objects.

- ❑ OneWay — Changes to the `Source` are reflected on the `Target` as they occur.

- ❑ OneTime — The `Target` property is only set when the binding is initialized.

- ❑ TwoWay — Changes to the `Source` are reflected on the `Target`, and updates to the `Target` are propagated to the `Source`.

Both `OneWay` and `TwoWay` functionality comes at the cost of restricting the types of object that can participate in the binding. Silverlight relies on the `DependencyObject` infrastructure and several Notification-based interfaces to support the processing of `DataBinding` updates.

INotifyPropertyChanged Interface

The INotifyPropertyChanged interface offers a single event to broadcast when a property has been modified on the object. The expectation is that this will be triggered anytime that a property is adjusted.

Here we have an IslandTimer class, which reflects a slower pace of life. Note that it fires PropertyChanged events both from within the Name property and from the Read Only ElapsedTime property, a value that is managed internally.

```
public class IslandTimer : INotifyPropertyChanged
{

  private TimeSpan _elapsedTime;
  private DispatcherTimer _timer;
  private string _name;

  public event PropertyChangedEventHandler PropertyChanged;

  public TimeSpan ElapsedTime
  {
    get { return _elapsedTime; }
  }

  public string Name
  {
    get
    {
      return _name;
    }
    set
    {
      _name = value;
      OnPropertyChanged("Name");
    }
  }

  public IslandTimer()
  {
    _elapsedTime = new TimeSpan();

    // Create a timer which fires every few seconds
    _timer = new DispatcherTimer();
    _timer.Interval = TimeSpan.FromSeconds(2);
    _timer.Tick += new EventHandler(timer_Tick);
  }

  public void StartTimer()
  {
    if (!_timer.IsEnabled)
    {
      _timer.Start();
    }
  }

  public void StopTimer()
  {
```

```
      _timer.Stop();
    }

    private void timer_Tick(object sender, EventArgs e)
    {
      _elapsedTime += TimeSpan.FromSeconds(1);
      OnPropertyChanged("ElapsedTime");
    }

    // Helper method to fire PropertyChanged Events
    private void OnPropertyChanged(string propName)
    {
      if (PropertyChanged != null)
        PropertyChanged(this, new PropertyChangedEventArgs(propName));
    }
  }
```

Collection Update Notifications

The INotifyCollectionChanged interface is implemented on interfaces that wish to participate in full data binding. Similarly to INotifyPropertyChanged, it exposes one event for when the collection is modified, CollectionChanged.

Thankfully, Silverlight includes ObservableCollection<T>, which is a generic collection that implements this interface. If you have a collection that you expect to be updated during the life of your application, it is highly recommended that you use this type.

OneTime Bindings

The simplest and most performant binding mode, OneTime, specifies that the binding should only be applied when the application starts or when the effective DataContext is adjusted. This is most appropriate when the source object is not manipulated during the life of the application and when the target object does not accept user input.

OneWay Bindings

If you anticipate that the source object may change during the life of the application, you can rely on Silverlight data binding to automatically update target object properties when in the OneWay mode.

Now that we have an object capable of letting Silverlight know that its properties are changing, we can attach it as the source for a OneWay binding:

```
<Grid x:Name="LayoutRoot" Background="White">
  <StackPanel>
    <Button x:Name="StartButton" HorizontalAlignment="Center">
      <TextBlock>Start Timer</TextBlock>
    </Button>
    <StackPanel Orientation="Horizontal" HorizontalAlignment="Center">
      <TextBlock>Elapsed Island Time: </TextBlock>
      <TextBlock Text="{Binding ElapsedTime, Mode=OneWay}" />
    </StackPanel>
  </StackPanel>
</StackPanel>
```

```
    </Grid>

public partial class Page : UserControl
{
  IslandTimer _timer;
  public Page()
  {
    InitializeComponent();
    this.Loaded += new RoutedEventHandler(Page_Loaded);
    _timer = new IslandTimer() { Name = "MyTimer" };

    StartButton.Click += new RoutedEventHandler(StartButton_Click);
  }

  void Page_Loaded(object sender, RoutedEventArgs e)
  {
    LayoutRoot.DataContext = _timer;
  }

  void StartButton_Click(object sender, RoutedEventArgs e)
  {
    _timer.StartTimer();
  }
}
```

TwoWay Binding

TwoWay bindings are the most powerful mode and offer bidirectional update support for property value changes. They make sense in scenarios in which you use controls that accept users' inputs and are bound to dynamic data objects.

Here, we allow the user to adjust the name of the Timer. Note the use of static bindings to configure the bindings completely in XAML.

```
<Grid x:Name="LayoutRoot" Background="White">
  <StackPanel>
    <Button x:Name="StartButton" HorizontalAlignment="Center">
      <TextBlock>Start Timer</TextBlock>
    </Button>
    <StackPanel Orientation="Horizontal" HorizontalAlignment="Center">
      <TextBlock>Elapsed Island Time:</TextBlock>
      <TextBlock Text="{Binding ElapsedTime, Mode=OneWay}"></TextBlock>
    </StackPanel>
    <StackPanel Orientation="Horizontal" HorizontalAlignment="Center">
      <TextBlock>Timer Name:</TextBlock>
      <TextBox Text="{Binding Name, Mode=TwoWay}" Width="100" />
    </StackPanel>
  </StackPanel>
</Grid>
```

Validating Data

Data Validation is driven by the binding framework's capability to capture exceptions that take place while a binding is in process. Silverlight 3 extends this with a set of controls with distinct VisualStates that visually indicate that a validation error has occurred.

Handling Binding Exceptions

In a `TwoWay` binding, exceptions can occur as data flows from the `Target` back to the `Source` property. The `Binding` object provides two properties that allow you to adjust the way these exceptions are handled:

- ❏   `ValidatesOnExceptions`
- ❏   `NotifyOnValidationError`

If `ValidatesOnExceptions` is set to true, any exceptions thrown by the setter of the source property or by a converter will be handled by the `Binding` object.

If `NotifyOnValidationError` is also true, then the `Binding` will raise the `BindingValidationError` as exceptions are encountered. Somewhat counterintuitive, the `BindingValidationError` event will also fire once the binding is able to successfully send the data to the source property. You can therefore use this event to determine both when a validation error has occurred and when it has been resolved.

The `Action` property of the `ValidationEventArgs` indicates the state of the `Validation` error. As a binding encounters exceptions when applying the data updates, the `Action` will be `VaidationErrorEventAction.Added`. Once the binding is able to successfully update the source object, the event will be raised with `VaidationErrorEventAction.Removed`.

In the following example, we adjust the foreground color of the target object based on the `Action` of the `ValidationError`. Since the `ValidationErrorEvent` is routed up the chain of parent elements, we are able to catch it from the `LayoutRoot`.

```
<Grid x:Name="LayoutRoot"
    BindingValidationError="LayoutRoot_BindingValidationError" Background="White" >
  <Grid.RowDefinitions>
        <RowDefinition Height="0.113*"/>
        <RowDefinition Height="0.887*"/>
  </Grid.RowDefinitions>
  <Grid.ColumnDefinitions>
        <ColumnDefinition Width="0.462*"/>
        <ColumnDefinition Width="0.538*"/>
  </Grid.ColumnDefinitions>
  <TextBlock Text="Destination Name"/>
  <TextBlock Grid.Column="1" Text="Population" />
  <TextBlock Text="{Binding Name, Mode=OneWay}" Grid.Row="1" />
  <TextBox Text="{Binding Population, Mode=TwoWay,
        ValidatesOnExceptions=true, NotifyOnValidationError=true}"
        VerticalAlignment="Top" Grid.Column="1" Grid.Row="1" Width="200" />
</Grid>
```

When executed, the application will adjust the color of the TextBox when an error is encountered converting the text value to the integer value expected by the destination's Population property.

```
public partial class Page : UserControl
{
  public Page()
  {
    InitializeComponent();
    this.Loaded += new RoutedEventHandler(Page_Loaded);
  }

  void Page_Loaded(object sender, RoutedEventArgs e)
  {
    Destination d = new Destination { Name = "St. Croix", Population=70000 };
    LayoutRoot.DataContext = d;
  }

  void LayoutRoot_BindingValidationError(object sender, ValidationErrorEventArgs e)
  {
    // Adjust the foreground color base on the Action
    if (e.Action == ValidationErrorEventAction.Added)
    {
      TextBox tb = (TextBox)e.OriginalSource;
      tb.Foreground = new SolidColorBrush(Colors.Red);
    }
    else
    {
      TextBox tb = (TextBox)e.OriginalSource;
      tb.Foreground = new SolidColorBrush(Colors.Black);
    }
  }
}
```

Visual States That Reflect Validation Errors

Silverlight 3 enhances a variety of core controls so that they can indicate when a binding validation exception has occurred. This is enabled through the Validation class, which offers attached properties for data validation that are then used to determine the appropriate visual state of the control.

A common scenario for offering a visual indicator when a validation error occurs is on a data entry form. Since the Silverlight 3 TextBox contains visual states that respond to validation errors, all that is required is establishing the binding with ValidatesOnExceptions set to true.

```
public partial class MainPage : UserControl
{
  public MainPage()
  {
    InitializeComponent();
    this.Loaded += new RoutedEventHandler(Page_Loaded);
  }
  void Page_Loaded(object sender, RoutedEventArgs e)
  {
    Destination d =
        new Destination { Name = "St. Croix", Population = 70000 };
```

```
        LayoutRoot.DataContext = d;
    }
}

<Grid x:Name="LayoutRoot" Background="White">
  <StackPanel>
    <TextBlock x:Name="DestinationName" Text="{Binding Name}" />
    <TextBox x:Name="PopulationTextBox"
     Text="{Binding Population, Mode=TwoWay,
           ValidatesOnExceptions=true}"
    />
    <Button Content="Ok" />
  </StackPanel>
</Grid>
```

Converting Data Types

There are many instances in which the source and destination property types will not align. In these cases, the binding will attempt to perform a data conversion that may result in a format that is less than ideal. Fortunately, Silverlight provides a baked-in mechanism for converting data as it passes through a binding.

DateTime objects often call for some conversion to display them in a meaningful way to the user. To demonstrate this, we will add the PeakSeasonStart property to the Destination object and bind it to a TextBlock. Without a converter, this will result in a string such as 12/1/2009 12:00:00 AM:

```
public class Destination
{
  public string Name { get; set; }
  public int Population { get; set; }
  public double AverageAirfare { get; set; }
  public double AverageHotel { get; set; }
  public string BestKnownFor { get; set; }
  public DateTime PeakSeasonStart { get; set; }
}

<Grid x:Name="LayoutRoot" Background="White">
  <TextBlock Text="{Binding PeakSeasonStart}" />
</Grid>

public partial class Page : UserControl
{
  public Page()
  {
    InitializeComponent();
    this.Loaded += new RoutedEventHandler(Page_Loaded);
  }

  void Page_Loaded(object sender, RoutedEventArgs e)
  {
    Destination d = new Destination() { Name = "St. Croix",
      PeakSeasonStart = new DateTime(2009, 12, 1) };
    LayoutRoot.DataContext = d;
  }
}
```

To adjust this behavior, we need to take several steps:

1. Create a class that implements IValueConverter.

2. Include an instance of that class in a Resource.

3. Specify a Converter in the binding.

IValueConverter

The IValueConverter interface defines two straightforward methods to enable conversion: Convert and ConvertBack. As their names suggest, they allow conversion back and forth between two types. If all that you need to support is OneWay binding, the ConvertBack method is not invoked.

Here, you see a basic implementation of IValueCOnverter that adjusts the way that a DateTime object is converted to a String:

```
// Class for converting between DateTime and string objects
public class DateConverter : IValueConverter
{
  // Convert DateTime to a string without time info
  public object Convert(object value, Type targetType,
    object parameter, System.Globalization.CultureInfo culture)
  {
    DateTime date = (DateTime)value;
    return (date.ToShortDateString());
  }

  public object ConvertBack(object value, Type targetType,
    object parameter, System.Globalization.CultureInfo culture)
  {
    string s = (string)value;
    return (DateTime.Parse(s));
  }
}
```

Adding the Converter to a Binding

The Binding object provides a Converter property for specifying the object that should serve as the intermediary between the source and target. Here, we include the Converter as a resource and reference it from the binding for the binding between a DateTime source and String target object. The following will provide a slightly more pleasing representation of our date, which omits the time information:

```
<UserControl x:Class="Wrox.Silverlight30.Data.Convertion.Page"
    xmlns="http://schemas.microsoft.com/winfx/2006/xaml/presentation"
    xmlns:x="http://schemas.microsoft.com/winfx/2006/xaml"
    xmlns:data="clr-namespace:Wrox.Silverlight30.Data.Convertion"
    Width="400" Height="300">
  <UserControl.Resources>
    <data:DateConverter x:Key="DateConverter" />
  </UserControl.Resources>
  <Grid x:Name="LayoutRoot" Background="White">
    <TextBlock Text="{Binding PeakSeasonStart,
        Converter={StaticResource DateConverter}}" />
```

```
    </Grid>
  </UserControl>
```

Using the `ConverterParameter`

The `Binding` object provides an additional property, which allows you to feed a parameter to the `IValueConverter`. This can be useful if you want to employ a converter in several related scenarios that are slightly different. Those familiar with formatting strings in .NET should be no stranger to the variety of `FormatStrings` available for built-in data types. The following example leverages the `ConverterParameter` to provide a `FormatString`.

The following example passes in the .NET short date format string `'{0:d}'` for display of the destination's start of peak season:

```csharp
// Class for converting to a string based on the provided FormatString
public class FormatStringConverter : IValueConverter
{
  public object Convert(object value, Type targetType,
    object parameter, System.Globalization.CultureInfo culture)
  {
    string formatString = (string)parameter;
    return String.Format(formatString, value);
  }

  public object ConvertBack(object value, Type targetType,
    object parameter, System.Globalization.CultureInfo culture)
  {
    throw new NotImplementedException();
  }
}
```

```xml
<UserControl x:Class="Wrox.Silverlight30.Data.Convertion.Page"
    xmlns="http://schemas.microsoft.com/winfx/2006/xaml/presentation"
    xmlns:x="http://schemas.microsoft.com/winfx/2006/xaml"
    xmlns:data="clr-namespace:Wrox.Silverlight30.Data.Convertion"
    Width="400" Height="300">
  <UserControl.Resources>

    <data:FormatStringConverter x:Key="FormatStringConverter" />
  </UserControl.Resources>
  <Grid x:Name="LayoutRoot" Background="White">
    <StackPanel>
      <TextBlock Text="{Binding PeakSeasonStart,
        Converter={StaticResource FormatStringConverter},
        ConverterParameter='{0:d}'}" />
    </StackPanel>
  </Grid>
</UserControl>
```

Persisting Data in Isolated Storage

Silverlight's isolated storage infrastructure allows you to securely cache data on the client, opening up a range of options to improve user experiences. Each application is given access to a virtual filesystem through which files can be managed. The core Isolated Storage API is very similar to what is offered in the `System.Data File` and `FileStream` classes, which makes it easy to approach.

In this section we will cover the basics of:

❑ Getting a reference to the `IsolatedStore`

❑ Creating a new file in the store

❑ Reading and writing to files

Accessing the Isolated Store

The `IsolatedStorageFile` class provides several static methods for obtaining a reference to `Isolated Storage`. The isolated store can be scoped to the application or site level and is accessed uniformly across any assemblies in your application.

Once you have an instance of the `IsolatedStorageFile`, you can perform basic file operations such as checking if a file exists.

```csharp
public partial class Page : UserControl
{
  public Page()
  {
    InitializeComponent();
    this.Loaded += new RoutedEventHandler(Page_Loaded);
  }

  void Page_Loaded(object sender, RoutedEventArgs e)
  {
    IsolatedStorageFile store;
    store = IsolatedStorageFile.GetUserStoreForApplication();

    if (store.FileExists("destinations.xml"))
    {
      // app logic
    }
  }
}
```

Managing the Size of the Store

Microsoft arbitrarily decided on a default file store quota of 1 MB per application. Fortunately, they offered a simple API for detecting the size of the store and a convenient way to prompt users for more space.

A common case in which you might need to request additional space is if you detect that you are approaching the threshold of the quota for your application:

```
public partial class Page : UserControl
{
  private IsolatedStorageFile _store;

  public Page()
  {
    InitializeComponent();
    this.Loaded += new RoutedEventHandler(Page_Loaded);
  }

  void Page_Loaded(object sender, RoutedEventArgs e)
  {
    _store = IsolatedStorageFile.GetUserStoreForApplication();
    CheckAvailableSpace();
  }

  private void CheckAvailableSpace()
  {
    // See if the store is over 90% full
    if (_store.AvailableFreeSpace < .1 * _store.Quota)
    {
      // Request the user for permission to
      // increase the quota by a megabyte
      _store.IncreaseQuotaTo(_store.Quota + 1048576);
    }
  }
}
```

Creating a New File

The Isolated Storage API allows you to create directories and reference files via a virtual path. Before creating a new file, you are going to want to see if it already exists:

```
public partial class Page : UserControl
{
  private IsolatedStorageFile _store;

  public Page()
  {
    InitializeComponent();
    this.Loaded += new RoutedEventHandler(Page_Loaded);
  }

  void Page_Loaded(object sender, RoutedEventArgs e)
  {
    _store = IsolatedStorageFile.GetUserStoreForApplication();
    CreateFile();
  }

  private void CreateFile()
```

```
    {

      // Create a new directory for data related files
      if (!_store.DirectoryExists("data"))
      {
        _store.CreateDirectory("data");
      }

      // Add a new file if it does not already exist
      if (!_store.FileExists("data\\destinations.xml"))
      {
        _store.CreateFile("data\\destinations.xml");
      }
    }
  }
```

Reading and Writing to a File

Access to each file is provided through stream objects, which are returned by the store. Each
IsolatedStorageFileStream can be configured with different parameters, which control how the file is
accessed and how the stream should handle file existence.

Once you have a reference to the FileStream, you can perform the normal stream operations to read
and write data. If you want to store an object that was already sent across the wire via a Web service,
you should be able to serialize it without much headache. For instance, the XML serialize command
will suffice for our collection of Destination objects. Note that XML serialization requires a reference
to the System.Xml.Serializaiton assembly.

The following example creates an XML file containing a list of destinations and then reads that back in
before it is bound to the DataContext:

```
public partial class Page : UserControl
{
  private IsolatedStorageFile _store;
  List<Destination> _destinations;

  public Page()
  {
    InitializeComponent();
    this.Loaded += new RoutedEventHandler(Page_Loaded);
  }

  void Page_Loaded(object sender, RoutedEventArgs e)
  {
    _store = IsolatedStorageFile.GetUserStoreForApplication();
    CheckAvailableSpace();
    CreateFile();
    ReadDestinations();
    LayoutRoot.DataContext = _destinations;
  }

  private void CheckAvailableSpace()
```

```
  {
    // See if the store is over 90% full
    if (_store.AvailableFreeSpace < .1 * _store.Quota)
    {
      // Request from the user permission to
      // increase the quota by one megabyte
      _store.IncreaseQuotaTo(_store.Quota + 1048576);
    }
  }

  private void CreateFile()
  {
    // Create a new directory for data-related files
    if (!_store.DirectoryExists("data"))
    {
      _store.CreateDirectory("data");
    }

    // Add a new file if it does not already exist
    if (!_store.FileExists("data\\destinations.xml"))
    {
      _store.CreateFile("data\\destinations.xml");
      WriteDestinations();
    }
  }

  private void WriteDestinations()
  {
    // Open up a file stream
    IsolatedStorageFileStream fs;
    fs = _store.OpenFile("data\\destinations.xml", System.IO.FileMode.Open);

    // Create a bunch of Desination objects
    List<Destination> destinations = new List<Destination>();
    destinations.Add(new Destination { Name = "St. Croix", Population = 70000 });
    destinations.Add(new Destination { Name = "St. John", Population = 5000 });
    destinations.Add(new Destination { Name = "St. Thomas", Population = 50000 });

    // Use XML serialization to write out the destinations list
    XmlSerializer serializer;
    serializer = new XmlSerializer(destinations.GetType());
    serializer.Serialize(fs, destinations);
    fs.Close();
  }

  private void ReadDestinations()
  {
    // Open up a file stream
    IsolatedStorageFileStream fs;
    fs = _store.OpenFile("data\\destinations.xml", System.IO.FileMode.Open);

    XmlSerializer serializer = new XmlSerializer(typeof(List<Destination>));
    _destinations = (List<Destination>)serializer.Deserialize(fs);
  }
}
```

Summary

Silverlight truly provides the core infrastructure needed to allow pervasive data in your applications. Silverlight makes few assumptions about where your data lives and the format it takes, which opens up exciting opportunities to work with data across a variety of platforms and from disparate providers.

You should now be able to retrieve data from Silverlight, provide compelling data bound interfaces with bindings, and cache data in the Isolated File Store. The core options for accessing, manipulation, and storing data presented in this chapter are a great foundation for exploring the wealth of options available to all Silverlight developers.

15

Designing and Styling the User Interface

Designing and styling the user interface (UI) of your Silverlight application can be one of the most exciting and satisfying parts of the process. It is through design and styling that you give your application a personality. That personality can feel corporate and reserved (ready to get things done without any frills) or young and hip (not afraid to get a little sidetracked on the way to accomplishing the task at hand). All of the UI building blocks that we've discussed in previous chapters now come together in an infinite array of possibilities to meet your vision.

This concept is so large that this chapter could really be represented by a completely separate book that brings together software-planning concepts, user-experience concepts, and visual-design concepts. Countless books *have* already been written on these topics, and each caters to a different target audience, from single designers/developers to small software development teams, to large enterprise-scale application development teams. Instead of getting sidetracked by all of the many variations along the way, I'm going to present a single workflow that takes you from concept to implementation. Instead of focusing on the details of requirements gathering, because each of you probably goes about it in a little bit different way, I'll just say "after gathering requirements," then move along.

Let's start by looking at a team organization model that works well in both Silverlight and WPF. We'll review each team's role, responsibilities, and the tools they use to achieve their tasks.

The Players

In Silverlight and WPF development, it is common to organize product team members by development roles, designer roles, and integrator roles. For large projects, this could be three separate departments of individuals; for small projects and companies, this could be three individuals. Sometimes, these three roles are even played by two people or one person. Let's take a look at these three roles and get an understanding of how they fit into the big picture.

Developers

I imagine most of you reading this book fit into the Developer role. The Developer role is responsible for … developing! Imagine that. OK, more specifically, the *developer* is primarily concerned with all things technical and architectural. You should not concern yourself with things like color, layout, or animation, except in cases in which you are supporting the design teams with properties, events, and transitions to enable their vision.

This should be welcome news to you as a developer — you don't have to think about design. You get to focus on what you're good at — coding. Now, sometimes designers will try to do some really crazy things, like paint the entire background of an application with video, or apply tiled `ImageBrushes` to every object on the page. When your once-lightning-fast application comes to a crawl because of design decisions, you get to have a say in design. But instead of scolding, you should really play a troubleshooting and enabling role, working to come to a compromise that benefits both performance and artistic integrity. This Brave New World where designers are actually working directly in your projects is going to take some getting used to, and you're going to have to play your part in reducing tension and establishing trust. Once both sides trust each other's skill set, the level of quality and creativity can increase.

Tools Used

The developer will spend most of her time in Visual Studio because 99 percent of her time should be code-focused. However, there are many things that are simply faster in Blend than they are in Visual Studio, such as layout, data binding, and setting brushes. For those tasks, a basic level of Blend competence can really speed the developer's tasks along.

- ❏ Visual Studio 2008 (or later)
- ❏ Blend 3 (or later)

Designers

Designers breathe personality into Silverlight applications, taking them from purely functional to engaging, branded experiences. Silverlight designers need to be technically oriented designers, but they don't need to have programming skills. These designers will traditionally be familiar with tools like Adobe Illustrator, Fireworks, Photoshop, and Flash. Those who have worked in Flash often make the fastest transition because they are already familiar with integrated animation and coding concepts.

Ultimately, these designers will need to learn XAML, just as web designers ultimately need to learn XHTML and CSS to become highly proficient at their job. In this world, artwork is not just sliced and thrown over a wall; it is integrated directly into the application, so having an understanding of the underlying technology is really helpful.

Tools Used

Silverlight designers will ultimately spend a lot of time in Blend, either designing artwork completely in that tool, or integrating artwork they've created in other design tools. In addition to working with design tools, designers will also need to become familiar with Visual Studio for advanced control of project assets. For example, Blend cannot currently change the Build Action of an asset or easily move items (such as images) once they have been added to a project.

- ❏ Blend 3 (or later)
- ❏ Microsoft Expression Design

- ❏ Adobe Fireworks, Illustrator, Photoshop, and the like
- ❏ Visual Studio 2008 (or later)

Integrators

The *integrator* is a special breed of person who has both technical and design skills. This person acts as a bridge between the strict worlds of design and development. In reality, these people are hard to find, and the role is often played by one of the more technical designers or one of the more visually aware developers. Still, thinking of this person in a purest sense provides clarity, and they do actually exist!

The integrator understands the language of developers and asks the development team precisely for what the design team needs in a language that the development team respects and understands. For example, instead of the designer saying to the developer, "I want to fade out the login screen when the user has logged in," the integrator will say "Upon successful login, please start a storyboard named `sbLoginSuccess`. Go ahead and create a dummy storyboard, and let me know where it is defined when you have it in place." Now, instead of the developer coming up with a procedural way of fading out the login container element, she will anticipate the need for a storyboard and start it at the appropriate time in the application's life cycle.

The integrator is also responsible for taking the original artwork created by the design team and translating it into XAML (if it was defined outside of Blend). He will create custom Styles based on the original artwork and apply those Styles to the representative controls in the real application.

Tools Used

Silverlight integrators will use all of the tools listed for both developers and designers, although they'll likely spend the majority of their time in Blend.

- ❏ Visual Studio 2008 (or later)
- ❏ Blend 3 (or later)
- ❏ Microsoft Expression Design
- ❏ Adobe Fireworks
- ❏ Additional Design Tools (Illustrator, Photoshop, etc.)

Gathering Requirements

Before we start pushing pixels around on the screen, we need to have some sort of end goal in mind. Your end goal could be to migrate your existing ASP.NET web application to Silverlight, taking advantage of the new layout and animation capabilities of the platform. Or maybe you're coming to Silverlight from a WPF or Windows Forms application, looking forward to easing deployment issues used in a Web-based technology. In both of these cases, it's highly likely that you already have a clear understanding of what your application needs to do, how it needs to do it, and a few areas in which it could do a bit better. Assuming that you're not completely reinventing your app, you're likely just considering how you can take advantage of Silverlight (and work within its limitations) to meet your end goal.

If you aren't migrating an app, you're creating something from scratch. And depending on where you work, your requirement-gathering can range from scribbled notes on a napkin to months of planning, analysis, meetings, more meetings, and still more meetings and planning. This is where we're going to skip the details and just agree that requirements were gathered and that a set of features were agreed on.

For demonstration purposes, we're going to walk through creating an interface for a simple application called *schtüff*. This app lets you keep track of all of your "stuff" online, in case you tragically need to take advantage of your insurance policy. After a quick napkin-based requirements-gathering process, I arrived at the following set of requirements for the application:

Primary Objective

Help people keep track of what they own, what those things are worth, and when they were purchased.

Features

- ❑ Account-based login/authentication

- ❑ Define properties/locations (e.g., Home, Office, Vacation Home).

- ❑ Add items to each location.

- ❑ Items represented by title, value, purchase date, description (optional), and an image (maybe multiple images in v2)

- ❑ Show total values by Property.

Additional Thoughts

- ❑ Should I be able to assign a UPC/ISBN number to items using my old CueCat barcode scanner?

- ❑ Should I be able to categorize items?

- ❑ Should I support exporting the database to Excel or CSV?

- ❑ Should I charge for the service and integrate some type of payment service?

Before I move on to the next stage, I define a simple database structure to support my Properties and Items. Figure 15-1 shows the two tables I'll use to store my data.

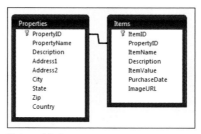

Figure 15-1

UI Brainstorming/UX Sessions

With a firm understanding of *what* my application should do, it's now time to consider *how* it should do it. For personal projects, I start with my favorite pen and idea pad and start drawing. If I'm developing an interface with a team of collaborators, we'll use a large whiteboard instead. Start at a high level, and try to capture what you consider to be all of the screens or states of your application. Some people recommend doing this with Post-it notes or index cards. Once you've identified all of your states, try to get a feel for the transitions between these states. Figure 15-2 shows a hand-drawn starting point for *schtüff*, the login screen.

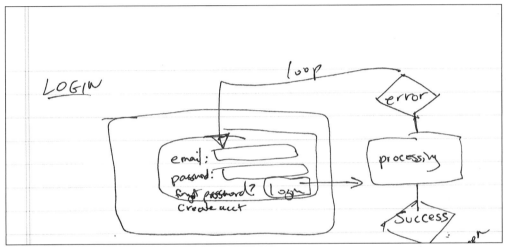

Figure 15-2

Figure 15-3 represents the home screen seen after a successful login.

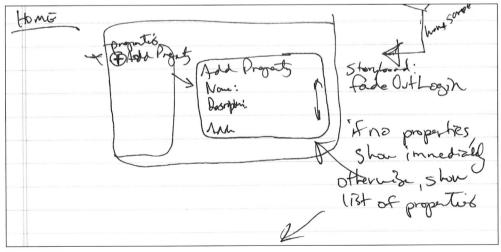

Figure 15-3

In my login success transition, I've made a note: "storyboard: fadeOutLogin." This is a callout early in the process that I want to fade the login dialog out of view after a successful login. I've also noted that "if no properties have been defined (i.e., home, office), show the Add Property dialog immediately; otherwise, show the list of defined properties.

Once a property has been defined and selected, it's time to define a list of items. The mockup in Figure 15-4 shows a property named Home selected in the Properties list, a list of items that belong to Home, and the "Add Item" button.

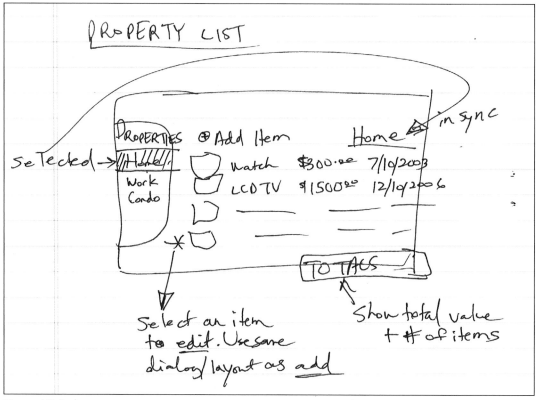

Figure 15-4

The final screen that I've hand-drawn (see Figure 15-5) shows the Add/Edit Item dialog.

At this point, I have a good understanding of how my application is going to flow and even have a couple of animations in mind. I could spend more time thinking things through at this level, but I'm really anxious to move along to doing real mockups in my design tool.

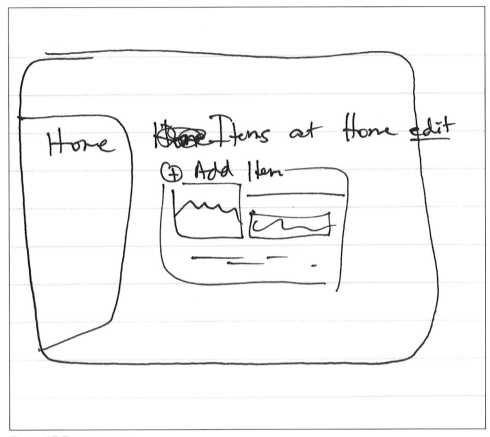

Figure 15-5

Design/Dev Part Ways

In the third phase of this process, I'm going to pretend that there is actually a design team and a development team, even though it's just me stepping through this process. We are now at a point where both teams have an understanding of what this application is going to do, roughly how it's going to be laid out, and what the various states of the application are. It is now time for the two teams to part ways. The designers will begin creating mockups in their design applications, and the developers will begin building a working infrastructure.

It doesn't really matter at this point whether you are a member of a large team putting this process into place or a single designer/developer hybrid capable of doing both.

Design Creates Mockups

With our hand-drawn mockups in hand, it's finally time to start pushing pixels! This is where the application starts to take on a personality. (I'll probably say this through each of the following phases.) I'm going to begin my design work in Adobe Fireworks because I've found it to be the right tool for the job. It gives me bitmap-level precision (pixel-perfect, that is) with vector-based drawing tools. I'll show you how I use Firework's page-based metaphor to create a walk-through, then how I use the Fireworks to XAML exporter to translate this artwork directly into Silverlight-based XAML.

> *I could do all of this in Blend, or another design tool for that matter, but I find that working in Fireworks at this stage is faster. Many designers in the WPF/Silverlight space use this same workflow.*

And just to be clear, this is not going to be a Fireworks tutorial — the techniques and thought process I'm presenting here are valid no matter what tool you're using.

First Pass

Let's jump right in by taking a look at my first round of mockups. The first round definitely feels like a first round, and normally I wouldn't show these to anyone, but I want to reinforce the fact that this is an iterative process. In the following screenshots, you can see how the original hand-drawn workflow is starting to take form on the design surface.

In Figure 15-6, I've started experimenting with branding at the top of the page, including a logo treatment for *schtüff*. The panel highlighted with blue on the right side of the application is the Pages panel. The Pages panel lets me quickly organize artwork by logical pages in my application.

Figure 15-7 shows this panel in more detail.

The first page in the Pages List is designated as a "Master Page." I define all of the artwork that stays fixed throughout the application on the Master Page, such as the header and footer artwork, then use additional pages to add the foreground elements, such as the LOG in screen just seen. Figure 15-8 shows the Home property selected, with a list of items defined for Home. Notice in this mockup that I am using the term *Catalog* instead of the final term *Property* that I ended up with.

The final screenshot, Figure 15-9, in this initial round of designs shows the Edit Item layout. Notice I've grayed out the background to draw attention to the foreground dialogs.

As I created this Edit dialog, I realized that I would want it to fade in or animate into place in some way. We didn't make a note of this prior to parting paths with the development team. I can either communicate that now or wait until the first round of integration. The key takeaway here is that the development team will be responsible for starting and stopping storyboards as the state of the application changes. These two teams need to decide on a name for the storyboard, then the development team will start and stop the storyboard, and the design team can define the storyboard. We'll dig into this in more detail in a couple of sections.

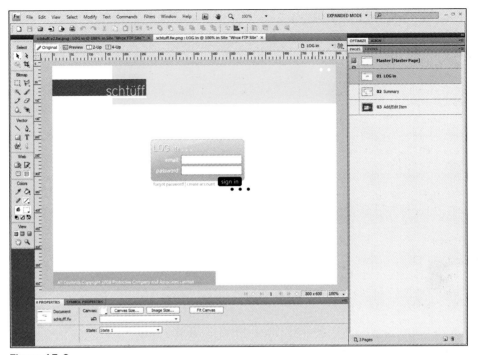

Figure 15-6

Figure 15-7

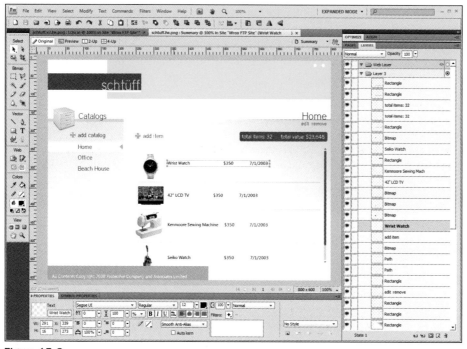

Figure 15-8

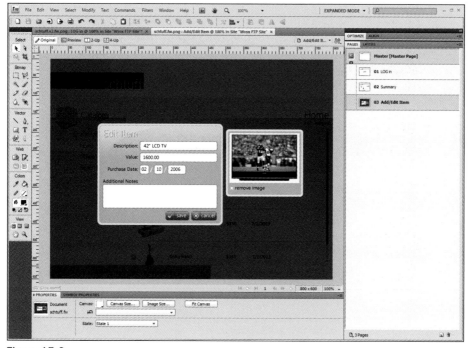

Figure 15-9

Second Pass

The first round of mockups in Fireworks put all of the major pieces into place and got me thinking about transitions from state to state, but that was just a warm-up. Now I know how much real estate I have after adding all of the required elements, and I'm ready to push the polish to the next level and make this app something to remember.

Figure 15-10 shows my enhanced Master Page. The header remained pretty true to the original, only with minor modification to the blue box behind the logo. The darker background is what adds the drama to this new layout, though. I went from the original solid white to a radial gradient with black and blue Gradient stops. I also added some texture to the background using the Fireworks Twist and Fade command (Commands ➪ Creative ➪ Twist and Fade) on two circles, similar to those seen over the "u" in *schtüff*.

Figure 15-10

I'm trying to avoid using any bitmap effects in my layout (such as blur or glow) to avoid the need to export artwork as images. So far, all of my layout elements, with the exception of the item photos, are vector-based and will translate directly to XAML.

Figure 15-11 shows the revised login screen. The text *log in* is now much more legible, and the "sign in" button really contrasts nicely against the blue background.

Figure 15-11

Figure 15-12 shows the revised Properties page, now using the term *properties* instead of *catalogs*. In this revised version, the relationship between the child grid of items is reinforced by making the item's container appear to have slid out from behind the Property List. In fact, while creating this mockup, I realized that I would need another storyboard to start when a property is selected from the list. I'll need to communicate this need to the development team so that they can add this to the application logic.

The final of the revised series of screenshots is shown in Figure 15-13. Here, we see the updated "edit item" layout. This layout will also serve as the "add item" layout. I've borrowed elements from both the "log in" layout (see Figure 15-11) and the revised "properties listing" scene (see Figure 15-12). Where the first version of this layout had the image dialog container floating by itself, this version uses the same technique as the "properties listing" to reinforce the relationship between parent and child containers.

I feel pretty good about this second round of layouts. I think I've established a cohesive, branded look across all of the screens of this simple application, and I've managed to keep everything in vector format, which means I'm ready for the first round of integration.

> *I'm omitting some states, such as login failure and account creation, to keep the scope of this discussion manageable. In a real application, all of those small states and screens would be taken into account.*

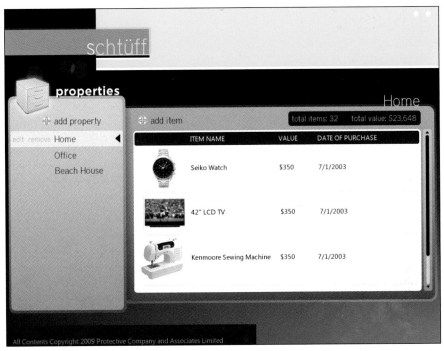

Figure 15-12

Figure 15-13

Development Creates Working Model

While the design team focuses on establishing a polished layout, the development team creates a working model of the application based on the initial requirements and specifications. Because this chapter is really about styling and less about coding, I'm going to avoid the details of what it would take to implement this application programmatically in Silverlight, and instead focus on the outcome of this phase.

The development team should create a fully functional application prior to the integration phase. They won't focus on layout or beauty; they'll just make sure everything is in place and working. Let's consider the login form as an example. The development team would create a simple XAML layout that includes two TextBoxes, a "Sign In" button, a "Forgot Password" button, and a "Create Account" button. They will add event listeners to the buttons, add a storyboard named sbFadeOutLogin, and start that storyboard when a user logs in successfully.

Figure 15-14 shows the login screen created by the development team during this phase. It looks nothing like our Fireworks mockups, but it does include all of the functional elements we're expecting.

Figures 15-15 through 15-17 show the additional development-created layouts.

Figure 15-14

Figure 15-15

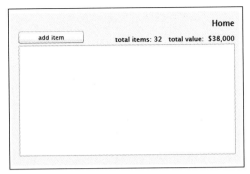

Figure 15-16

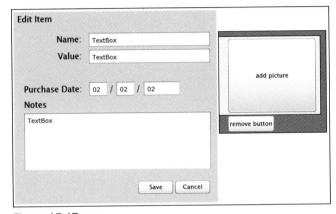

Figure 15-17

With all of the pieces in place, the development team/developer can test the application and ensure that all requirements have been met. The application is now ready for the first round of styling integration.

I want to point out that this minimal approach to styling by the development team speeds the integration process when the application is handed over to the design team. The less developer styling that has to be ripped out, the faster this stage goes.

Integration Phase

We are now at a point where we have a working model of the application and a set of highly styled mockups. These two pieces and their respective teams are about to collide in one of the most rewarding and exciting phases of the process — the Integration phase. We now get to see the Integrator role at work. The integrator will take the source Fireworks file and use the Fireworks to XAML Exporter panel (www .granthinkson.com/tools/fireworks) to export each layout/state to XAML that can be integrated into the live application, using Blend. So, I'll put my Integrator hat on now and step you through the process.

If your designers aren't using Fireworks, fear not! Blend 3 introduces new native Photoshop and Illustrator importers accessible directly from the File menu.

Assessing the Pieces

As the integrator, I first need to review both the application and the mockups. I need to understand the controls that the development team used to create the working model and assess how my artwork can be applied to those controls. I need to see if custom controls have been defined, if UserControls have been defined, and consider the way elements in my layout will need to animate. Knowing all of these things will affect the way I export my artwork and ultimately the way I group items in Blend.

When I open the working project in Blend, I first notice that several UserControls have been created by the development team. Fortunately, these UserControls map closely to the Pages in my Fireworks mockup (funny how that happened). Figure 15-18 shows the Object tree in Blend for Page.xaml. Notice the four UserControls: EditItemControl, ItemListingControl, PropertiesControl, and LoginControl.

Figure 15-18

Looking to the Solution Explorer in Figure 15-19, I can see XAML files for each of these controls. I will open each of these files individually to apply my custom styling.

Figure 15-19

This organization is going to work well for me. I will be able to apply my background styling at the Page.xaml level, then position, style, and animate each of the individual pieces. Let's start by exporting the Master Page artwork to Page.xaml. This will give us a chance to look at the options available with the Fireworks to XAML Exporter.

Using the Fireworks to XAML Exporter

Shifting back to Fireworks, select the page named *Master*. Figure 15-20 shows both the Master Page selected and the FW to XAML Exporter panel.

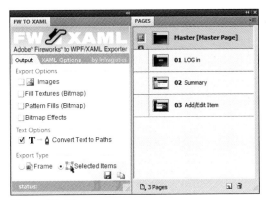

Figure 15-20

The Output Tab

The Fireworks to XAML Exporter panel is divided into two tabs: Output and XAML Options. The options of both of these tabs are further categorized into related sections.

Export Options

The Export Options section of the Output tab contains options that are bitmap-specific. The first checkbox, Images, when enabled will export Bitmap objects on the surface in Fireworks as Image controls in XAML and render the Source property with a full, absolute path. The next two options, when enabled, will attempt to define ImageBrushes based on Fireworks' Texture Fill and Pattern Fill features. Owing to differences between the Fireworks and Silverlight rendering engines, the results of these two options have to be tweaked in Blend nearly 100 percent of the time. The fourth option, Bitmap Effects, is currently WPF-specific. Silverlight does not currently support BitmapEffects on UIElements as WPF does.

Text Options

The Text Options section contains a single option, "Convert Text to Paths." When enabled, all text in the export operation will be converted to Path objects. Enable this option for text-based artwork (such as logos) whose look needs to be preserved without embedding a font.

Export Type

You can either export the entire current Frame (in Fireworks CS4 the name *Frame* has changed to *State*) or you can export the current selection. I generally use the "Selected Items" option here, as it lets me quickly bring specific artwork into Blend.

The XAML Options Tab

The XAML Options tab, shown in Figure 15-21, includes several settings that affect the final XAML that is rendered when exporting.

Figure 15-21

Outer Panel Type

When artwork is exported as XAML, it always has a root Panel that can either be a Grid or a Canvas. When Grid is selected, items are positioned by setting HorizontalAlignment="Stretch" and VerticalAlignment="Stretch" and applying left, right, top, and bottom margins to enforce the original size. This is useful if you want your application to stretch as it is resized, but you will still have to make changes in Blend to ensure the correct resizing behavior.

When Canvas is selected, all items are exported with fixed heights and widths and positioned using Canvas.Left and Canvas.Top.

Syntax

The first option in the Syntax section, "Convert Rectangles to Borders," is useful if you want individual control over the roundness of each corner. See Chapter 9 to get a better understanding of why you might want to enable this option. I always enable the second option in this section, "Use Condensed Path Syntax." When enabled, the PathData notation you were introduced to in previous chapters ("M X,Y CX,Y X,Y X,Y...") is used for the Path.Data property, instead of the longhand <PathGeometry> syntax.

Element Names

Enable the "Write when Specified" option when you want object names specified in the Layers panel to be rendered as x:Name in XAML. Using this option may cause problems if you have multiple items defined with the same name in Fireworks. Silverlight does not allow multiple items to share the same x:Name value, whereas Fireworks does not enforce uniqueness.

Resources

When "Export Fills as Resources" is enabled, all Fills used in the export operation will be converted to Brush resources and added to the outer panel's Resources collection. For example, if you select Grid as the Outer Panel Type, a Grid.Resources collection will be defined that houses all Brushes used in the layout. Exported elements use the {StaticResource brushName} notation to reference the defined brush.

Saving or Copying

Once you're finished customizing all of your export options, it's time to actually export. You can either export directly to a XAML file or copy XAML directly to the clipboard, using either the Save or the Copy icon located in the lower-right corner of the Fireworks to XAML Exporter panel. I usually copy directly to the Clipboard, as it makes for a really fast workflow between Fireworks and Blend.

Exporting the Master Page

Now that you have an idea of the options available when exporting, let's export the Master Page to XAML and add it directly to Page.xaml. I'm going to export the Selected Items, Convert Text to Paths, and export using a Grid as my Outer Panel Type. I press [Ctrl]+A on my keyboard to select all elements on my Master Page, click on the Copy button on the Exporter panel, and then switch to Blend.

In Blend, I select the Design/XAML Split view and select the LayoutRoot grid in the Object tree to scroll directly to its location in XAML. I then place my cursor in the Split view after the LayoutRoot definition and press [Ctrl]+V to paste my XAML into place. Figure 15-22 shows a snippet of the exported XAML pasted in place.

Figure 15-22

Figure 15-23 shows the layout with the new XAML copied into place. The artwork that was just imported is represented by the unnamed grid in the Object tree.

Not bad for a straight copy! Everything looks pretty much the same as it did in Fireworks. I do see that the footer text of my layout is being clipped. The mockup layout was sized at 800 × 600, so my exported XAML has that size set. It's being clipped either by Height and Width settings on LayoutRoot, the UserControl, or the preview area in Blend. After selecting these items, I see that the UserControl is set to 640 pixels wide by 480 pixels tall. I really want it to stretch to fill the full window, so I clear those values and let the design surface size itself based on its content. With those values cleared, I can now see all of my imported artwork.

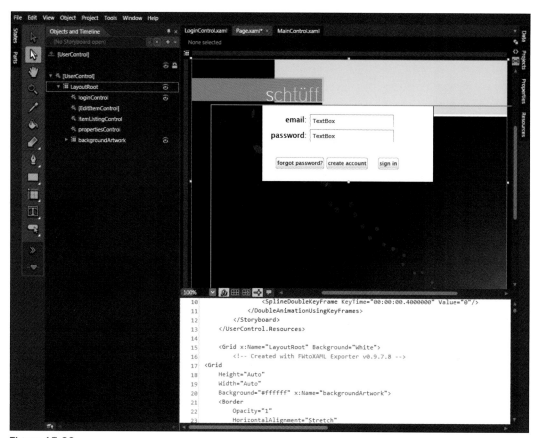

Figure 15-23

Setting Resize Behavior

I can use a design-time feature of Blend to help me get a feeling for how my layout will resize at run time. Figure 15-24 shows the Design-Time sizing adorner handle. As I resize my layout, I can see that my background artwork is not stretching to fill as I want it to (the white background is showing).

So, just like my layout was being clipped because it was set to 800 × 600, it's also *staying* at 800 × 600 as the form is resized. I now need to dig into the grid of elements that was brought over from Fireworks and individually set `HorizontalAlignment`, `VerticalAlignment`, `Height`, `Width`, and `Margin` properties on individual elements to ensure that they stretch when I want them to, don't stretch when I don't want them to, and remain anchored to the side I want them anchored to. Figure 15-25 demonstrates how I want each of the elements in this background to behave.

What I didn't call out in Figure 15-25 was the background rectangle. It should be clear that I want it to stretch to fill the entire window. The "bubbles" in the background are already grouped into two separate elements (Groups come over from Fireworks as `Grids`). I will anchor the group set that looks like a trail of bubbles to the top-left corner and anchor the cluster to the lower-right corner.

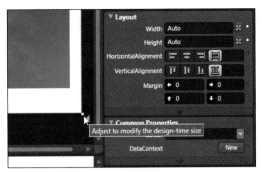

Figure 15-24

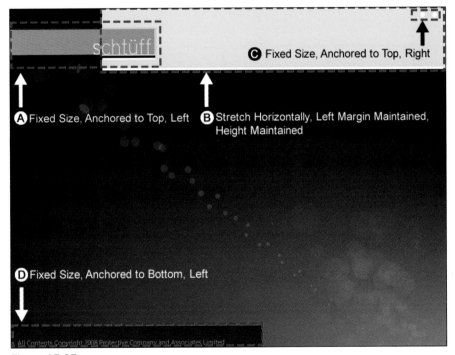

Figure 15-25

Achieving the desired behavior requires a combination of settings on each set of items. First, I will step through the imported grid and group each set of items that logically belong together, if they are not already grouped. I could also have done this in Fireworks. Once I've identified and grouped the target elements, I will set the `Height`, `Width`, `Margin`, `HorizontalAlignment`, and `VerticalAlignment` properties on each element. The following table shows the values for each of the items called out in Figure 15-25.

Element	Height	Width	HorizontalAlignment	VerticalAlignment	Margin
A	57	269	Left	Top	0,34,0,0
B	110	Auto	Stretch	Top	169,0,0,0
C	9	31	Right	Top	0,9,16,0
D	38	Auto	Left	Bottom	0,0,0,0
Background	Auto	Auto	Stretch	Stretch	0,0,0,0
Bubbles top-left	510	640	Left	Top	41,90,0,0
Bubbles bottom-right	278	264	Right	Bottom	0,0,25,-23

Originally, the footer text was a sibling of its rectangle background. Since I enabled "Convert Rectangles to Borders," I decided to make the `TextBlock` a child of the `Border`. I gave the `Border` a fixed height and no width, then aligned the `TextBlock` to the bottom of the `Border` and gave it a left, bottom, and right margin. This way, if the text length changes, the background will resize with it. Figure 15-26 shows the `copyrightFooter` `Border` and its nested `txtCopyright` `TextBlock`.

Figure 15-26

After stepping through the artwork and organizing the imported elements, grouping and naming them, the resulting object tree looks like the one shown in Figure 15-27.

Figure 15-27

Now, as I resize the design surface using the Design-Time size adjuster shown earlier, everything behaves exactly as I had in mind. It took me a little while to step through all of the imported objects and group them. Next time, I'll make sure that my design team groups and names everything for me instead of just giving me a big, unorganized layout.

Exporting the Login Form

With the background in place, it's now time to integrate the Login Form artwork into the `LoginControl UserControl`. Refer back to Figure 15-6 to see what the login mockup in Fireworks looks like and review Figure 15-14 to see the developer-created version of the control in place on the design surface. The working version of the layout includes two `TextBlocks` representing the labels *Email* and *Password*, and two `TextBoxes` for text input. Three buttons represent "Forgot Password?," "Create Account," and "Sign In."

We are now going to import the login artwork in its entirety. We'll use the fake `TextBoxes`, defined with Rectangles in Fireworks, to size and position the real `TextBoxes`. We'll then convert the "Sign In" artwork to a `Button Style`, and assign that `Style` to the existing, working `Button` on the form. We'll do the same thing for the other two `Buttons`, creating `Styles` that look like text links.

Figure 15-28 shows the first import of the artwork, with the original buttons and elements in the foreground. I toggled the visibility of the original Rectangle that the development team put in place as a background.

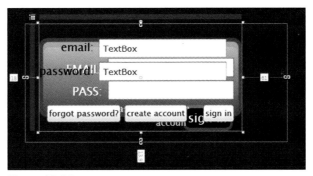

Figure 15-28

I know this looks like a mess, but we're about to take care of it. I'm going to position the `TextBoxes` on top of the imported `Rectangles`, then delete the imported `Rectangles`. I'll then remove the original labels and move on to creating the "sign in" `Button Style`. In Figure 15-29, I've hidden the current buttons and selected the sign-in artwork.

I made sure the sign-in artwork was grouped in Fireworks before it was exported and named as `btnSignIn`, so it came over as a grid with two child `Borders` and a child `TextBlock`. With the `btnSignIn` grid selected, I selected Tools ➪ Make Into Control from the main menu in Blend. Figure 15-30 shows the resulting Make Into Control dialog.

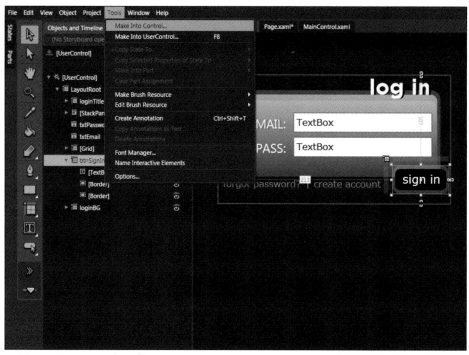

Figure 15-29

Figure 15-30

I selected Button from the list of available controls (to designate that this Style will target Button), named the new `Style` *ButtonSignIn* and chose to define the `Style` in "This document." After clicking OK, several things happen:

❑ A new `Style` is created and added to `UserControl.Resources` that targets `Button` and has a Key of `ButtonSignIn`.

❑ The elements that were selected on the stage are now set as the `ControlTemplate` of the new `Button` Style.

❑ A `ContentPresenter` is added to the new `ControlTemplate` as the foremost element.

❑ The items selected on the stage are replaced with a `Button` whose `Style` is set to `{StaticResource ButtonSignIn}`.

Before I consider this `Style` complete, I need to remove the `ContentPresenter` that was automatically added and `TemplateBind` the `Text` property of the sign-in `TextBlock` to the `Content` property of the `Button`. Figure 15-31 shows the `TextBlock` selected on the Blend design surface. Using the property marker next to the `Text` property, I have selected the TemplateBinding submenu and selected the Content property.

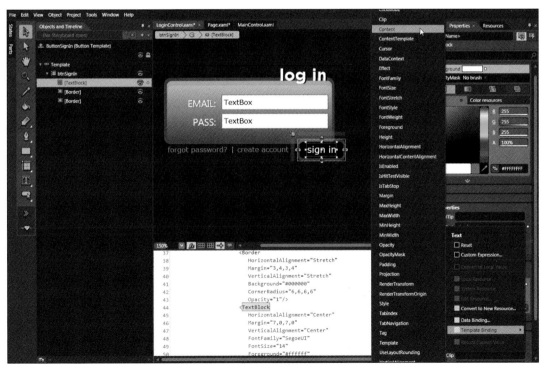

Figure 15-31

With `TemplateBinding` now in place for the `TextBlock`, I can delete the `ContentPresenter` that was automatically created. I will now click on the `btnSignIn` button in the breadcrumb toolbar at the top of the design surface to return to the `LoginControl` User Control on the design surface. At the `LoginControl` level, I'll make sure that my `btnSignIn` button is selected and set its `Content` property to `sign in`. The button should be updated on the design surface and look like the original button I had in mind.

I've gone through these extra steps to ensure that if I later change my mind and want *sign in* to read *log in*, all I have to do is set the `Content` property of my `Button`. (This also paves the way for localization, should I choose to localize my application.)

Now that I have a style that looks like the "sign in" button I defined, I have a couple of options. I can either set the `Style` of the original "sign in" button to the style I just created, position and size it correctly, then delete the newly created button; or I can rename my new button to match the name of the original button and review the original button's XAML and copy to my new button any event handlers that were predefined by the development team. The goal here is to ensure that I don't break any of the work that the development did to make this button work correctly. Figure 15-32 shows the final "sign in" button in place.

Figure 15-32

The last thing I need to do with this login form is create a `Style` that makes `Buttons` look like text links. I'll use the `Make Button` command again to create a `Style` quickly. First, I'll create a new `TextBlock` on the design surface, then select Tools ➪ Make Button. I'll name the new style `ButtonTextLink` and define it within the `UserControl` again. I'll then edit the template and delete the newly created `ContentPresenter`. As I did with the `ButtonSignIn` style, I'll `TemplateBind` the `Text` property of my `TextBlock` to the `Content` property of the `Button`.

I'm going to do a couple of additional things with this style to make it feel like a link. First, I'm going to underline the text when the button is in its `MouseOver` state. I'll also set the `Cursor` to `Hand` in the `MouseOver` state. Figure 15-33 shows the `MouseOver` state selected in the States panel of Blend.

Figure 15-33

With the `MouseOver` state selected, I now select the `TextBlock` and turn `Underline` on. I also set `Cursor` to `Hand`. With those properties selected, I move back to the `Base` state. I need to do one more thing to ensure correct behavior with this button: I need to set the `Background` property of the containing grid to a transparent brush. I do this to ensure that the `MouseOver` state is entered smoothly as the mouse moves over the control. Without setting the `Background` property of the grid, the text is the only thing in the button that will pick up the `HitTest`. Since the text does not fill the entire background, the cursor will toggle erratically between the arrow and the hand as you move over the text. Setting the grid's background solves this problem.

OK, with that style out of the way, let's delete the temporary button and assign the `Style` to the two `Buttons` created by the development team. Figure 15-34 shows the "forgot password?" button selected on the design surface. I'm using the Style property marker to assign the newly created `Style` to this `Button`.

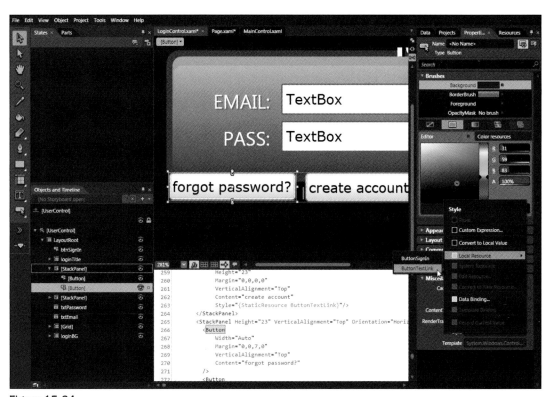

Figure 15-34

After setting the `Style` for both of the `TextLink` buttons, I return to Page.xaml and rebuild the solution. Figure 15-35 shows the final login `UserControl` styled and in place on Page.xaml.

Figure 15-35

With the login `UserControl` styled and positioned, the only thing left for me to do with this part of the application is customize the `sbLoginSuccess` storyboard. In Figure 15-36, I've clicked on the Storyboards dropdown and see the `sbLoginSuccess` storyboard already defined.

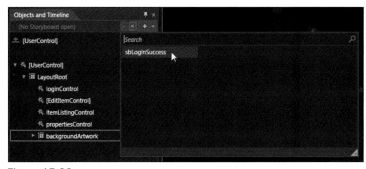

Figure 15-36

After selecting this storyboard, I drag the timeline marker to 0.400 second and select the `loginControl` in the Object tree as shown in Figure 15-37.

Figure 15-37

I then set its opacity to 0 percent and scale it to both the X-axis and Y-axis to 75 percent using the Transform panel, shown in Figure 15-38.

Figure 15-38

Now that I have the opacity and scale set, I want to customize the easing so that the animation slows as it reaches its destination. This final customization step adds that extra level of polish that users can feel when using the application. To do this, I select the keyframe that was just added to display the Easing panel shown in Figure 15-39. I then select the EasingFunction mode from the list of easing options. This mode lets me select from a number of preset easing functions. I've selected "Cubic Out", which will result in an animation that slows down as it reaches its destination value.

Figure 15-39

Additional `UserControls`

With the `Login` control finished, we now have three additional controls to style: `EditItemControl`, `ItemListingControl`, and the `PropertiesControl`. I'm not going to step through each of these controls, as the process is the same you just witnessed for the `Login` control. For each additional control, I will need to:

- ❑ Assess resize behavior.

- ❑ Group logical objects in Fireworks.

- ❑ Export XAML from Fireworks and Import into Blend.

- ❑ Tweak the Layout settings to support your desired resize behavior.

- ❑ Use the Make Button command or create custom Styles for other control types.

Continuous Iteration

Once the integrator has completed his first integration pass, it is time to assess additional UI requirements that were overlooked at the beginning of the planning phase. We've already identified several additional storyboards that we want started throughout the application. These can now be communicated to the development team. While the designers or the integrator are building the storyboard, the dev team can update the application logic to start and stop the storyboard at the appropriate time. The integrator may have identified additional properties that are needed to support the UI fully. Again, the development team can add those while the design team updates the layout in anticipation of those properties.

This process can continue for quite some time until both sides have everything they need in place. Often, the integrator has the requisite skills to add simple properties and perform other minor programming tasks to keep the process moving. He can then notify the development team of the changes he made, and they can review the changes for quality and robustness. He acts as an enabler for both teams, but understands that his changes may be temporary. At this point in the process, it works best if the designer and integrator, or designer and developer, are working closely together, with changes made very quickly.

Final Polish/Cleanup

After the fast-paced iteration stages are out of the way, the code churn should be slowing down, and both sides (design and development) should be focusing on quality and cleanup. The design team may have added images to the project that are no longer used and now need to be removed, or they may have created a number of resources early on that are now no longer referenced. They can use the freely available resource analyzer *Pistachio* (`www.granthinkson.com/tools/wpf`) to identify all unused resources in their project. Furthermore, the design team needs to continue stepping through the application, ensuring that their styles work correctly for all of the various states of the application and the controls used therein.

Summary

You should now have a solid understanding of a common Silverlight application–styling workflow. You've seen how an application can move from planning to designer mockups to working model to integrated artwork to final application. You've been introduced to the team members (designers, developers, integrators), seen how they work together, and learned what their various roles are throughout the development cycle. You can now reflect on how this workflow can fit within your current organization, hopefully picturing the faces of your coworkers who will step in and fill these roles. Or maybe it's your face in all three slots!

16

Making the Application Come Alive

Now that you have a good understanding of Silverlight application structure and architecture, have learned how to hook up your data, and have a good grasp on creating and styling your UI, it's time to take it to the next level and really make your application come alive. In this chapter, we dive into the facilities that Silverlight provides for you to make your application interactive.

Events

To start off, we'll dive into eventing, particularly event interop between JavaScript and your managed code.

Most of the interop with the browser (from managed code) is achieved through the `Browser` namespace, so you'll want to include using a `System.Windows.Browser;` statement when using it, as I've done in the samples in this chapter.

> Before moving on, many of the samples in the rest of this chapter do not require a corresponding web site, so we're not going to generate or use a web app (or site) for our Silverlight solutions. By default, the other option when creating a Silverlight Application in Visual Studio is to dynamically generate a test HTML page for the Silverlight app. This would be fine, except that we need to write some JavaScript and other interaction, so what we'll do is tweak the default single-project Silverlight setup.

Raising and Handling Managed Events in Script

If you've done any .NET development, you're already familiar with handling managed events, so here we're going to focus on two things: raising managed events and handling those events in JavaScript. Of all of this, the only particularly Silverlight-specific feature is handling them in JavaScript, so we're going to focus on that mainly.

First, though, we'll talk about raising managed events. There is a well-known pattern for this that holds true in Silverlight. I'm not talking about the Observer pattern (of which .NET eventing is an implementation); I'm talking about a pattern — maybe *convention* would be a better word — for how to declare and raise events in .NET.

Initially, you want to determine what, if any, special values you want to pass as arguments. If you need to, you can create a data transfer object (DTO) that can serve to pass data (usually simply aggregate objects) around for eventing. In this case, I have created a simple `User` type.

```
public class User
{
    public string Name { get; set; }
    public string Password { get; set; }
}
```

This could be anything — whatever you want to pass in your events. The next thing is to create a specialized `EventArgs` derivative. If you only have simple types (such as `string`, `int`, etc.), you can skip the first step and just do this one. Derive a new class from `EventArgs` and implement a constructor that takes the data you want to ship to your event handlers.

```
public class UserEventArgs : EventArgs
{
    public UserEventArgs(User user)
    {
        _User = user;
    }

    User _User;
    public User User { get { return _User; } }
}
```

The constructor is a convenience, but it is particularly useful for event args because they are so transitory — you usually don't want to go to the trouble of creating and then setting properties. Also, event args should be immutable, so using the constructor with Read Only properties enables this approach.

Now you've got your event args ready to go, so you can declare your event (you used to have to further declare a delegate to specify your event handler signature, but with generic `EventHandler<T>`, we get to skip that step — Yeah, generics!). By the way, you don't have to use the generic version here for Silverlight — when it is surfaced in JavaScript, it doesn't matter, but it certainly makes it nicer for anyone handling the event in managed code. Remember, it could be handled either way.

```
public event EventHandler<UserEventArgs> UserSelected;
```

> **All event signatures must use** `EventHandler` **or** `EventHandler<T>`, **as we did above.**

So now the event is all ready, you just have to raise it. Again, the convention is to use an `OnEvent` method to centralize raising of the event:

```
void OnUserSelected(User user)
{
    if (this.UserSelected != null)
        this.UserSelected(this,
            new UserEventArgs(user));
}
```

Again, this is pretty conventional — nothing Silverlight-specific yet. We just check if there are any observers (handlers) on our event and, if so, raise the event, passing the context-specific data/objects (via the event arguments). Voila! We're all set to start using our event.

Now to sprinkle on the Silverlight magic. First, we mark all the stuff we want to surface to JavaScript with the `ScriptableTypeAttribute`. You don't have to mark all types used as input parameters or return values on a type that you register (see below), but it may help to make your intent explicit to other programmers. Any type you mark with that attribute needs to be public, and Silverlight assumes that you want to expose all public properties, events, and methods on that type to JavaScript; that is, you don't need to mark all members with the `ScriptableMemberAttribute`, but it is worth noting that these attributes are not inherited (so derivative types need to declare themselves as scriptable as well). There is one exception to this, which is `HtmlEventArgs`, but again, you'll likely want to mark such a type as well to make your intent clear and to expose any new members you add.

```
[ScriptableType]
public sealed partial class Page : UserControl
{ ... }
[ScriptableType]
public class UserEventArgs : EventArgs
{ ... }
[ScriptableType]
public class User
{ ... }
```

The next thing you need to do is register any instances you want to access directly from the Silverlight `plugin` object in JavaScript. You can do this in the application startup event or at least somewhere before you need to access it. In our case, since we're registering the `Page` type, which is the root visual for the application and only created once in the application startup, we can just stick it in our `Page` type constructor. (If you needed to expose multiple instances, you wouldn't want to use the constructor because you couldn't give them unique names.)

```
public Page()
{
    InitializeComponent();
    HtmlPage.RegisterScriptableObject("Page", this);
}
```

Now you're all set to consume this event in JavaScript. You should be able to attach to it pretty much any time after the loaded event, and, in fact, that's what I do in this sample. So, first, write a simple JavaScript Silverlight loaded handler:

```
function onSilverlightLoad(sender, args) {
}
```

Then you need to specify it for the Silverlight instance. Depending on how you create your Silverlight object, you may do this in any number of ways. If you declare the object tag directly, as I am doing, you simply add a `param` tag to the object declaration:

```
<param name="onload" value="onSilverlightLoad"
```

If you're using the JavaScript `CreateObject` or `CreateObjectEx`, you specify in the call to those methods. If you're using the ASP.NET control, use the `onPluginLoaded` event. However you are creating the object, you can handle its loaded event and then do the following:

```
function onSilverlightLoad(sender, args) {
    var plugin = sender.getHost();
    plugin.Content.Page.UserSelected = userSelected;
}
```

The first thing is to get a reference to the Silverlight plug-in. Now, you'd think that the sender of the loaded event would be that, but it isn't. So you call `getHost`, and that will get a reference to the plug-in instance. (You could also use `document.getElementById`.) All types that are registered using `HtmlPage`.`RegisterScriptableObject` should be available on the plug-in's `Content` property, using the string identifier you provide as the first parameter to that method. We used *Page*, but we could've picked *fantabulous* or anything else we want.

Then, you can attach a JavaScript event handler to the managed event by simply setting a reference to the JavaScript function on the event (as was done above). This will allow you to set one handler; if you need multiple handlers, you should use the auto-generated `addEventListener` method on the registered object's JavaScript proxy like this:

```
plugin.Content.Page.addEventListener('UserSelected', userSelected);
```

> There is a corresponding `removeEventListener` **method with the same signature (string name, object method) that is generated to remove such listeners.**

Here's the `userSelected` function that the line above attaches to the event:

```
function userSelected(sender, userArgs) {
    alert("Username: " + userArgs.User.Name + "\nPassowrd: " +
    userArgs.User.Password);
}
```

Now everything is in place — you can just raise the event from anywhere in managed code, and your JavaScript handler should be called. Note that I named the second parameter `userArgs`. It's good practice to use a specific name if the args are more than the standard event args. Since our args have the `User` property and related data, I picked `userArgs`.

The last thing to do is actually raise the event, so just, for instance, add a `Button` to the Page XAML and create a `Click` event handler for it.

```
<UserControl x:Class="EventsAndUserActivity.Page"
    xmlns="http://schemas.microsoft.com/client/2007"
```

```
       xmlns:x="http://schemas.microsoft.com/winfx/2006/xaml"
       Width="400" Height="300">
       <Grid x:Name="LayoutRoot" Background="White">
           <Button Click="Button_Click" Content="Click Me" />
       </Grid>
</UserControl>
```

The Visual Studio tools have a nice facility to create the event handler stub while writing the XAML; then you can right-click on that and pick "Navigate to Event Handler" from the context menu. That's where you can add your code, in the example, to raise the managed event:

```
private void Button_Click(object sender, RoutedEventArgs e)
{
    User u = new User();
    u.Name = "Ambrose";
    u.Password = "youWish";
    this.OnUserSelected(u);
}
```

Now if you run the sample, it should give you a nice big button that says *Click Me*, and clicking it will give you what is shown in Figure 16-1.

Figure 16-1

That seems like a lot to do in order to bubble an event to JavaScript. It can be, but you probably won't need to do it very often. A big part of it is just implementing the standard .NET eventing conventions. Then you just need to decorate your types with ScriptableTypeAttribute and attach to and handle them in script.

Probably the most common need for this would be if you, say, created a reusable Silverlight island (such as an ad) that you wanted to reuse in multiple contexts and needed to expose events to JavaScript. Events give you a nice, loose coupling if that's what you need, but if you don't mind tighter coupling, you could just directly call a JavaScript method from your managed code. That is covered later in this chapter.

> There is another way to handle the standard user input (i.e., the universal ones like MouseMove, MouseLeave, KeyDown, etc.) managed events in JavaScript. If you try to handle a managed event that isn't available to script, such as the Click event on the Microsoft Button, it throws an AG_E_RUNTIME_ADDEVENT error.

In the Silverlight loaded handler you created, add the following:

```
var managedButton = plugin.content.findName("ManagedButton");
managedButton.addEventListener("MouseMove", managedButtonHover);
```

That's all you have to do to handle events like these in JavaScript. Let's look at how we could use this. We're going to show the mouse coordinates while hovering over the button. To do this, first create a bit of HTML to display the values:

```
<div id="MouseTracking">
    <div>X: <span id="MouseX"></span></div>
    <div>Y: <span id="MouseY"></span></div>
</div>
```

Put this right at the top of your test page, just inside the body tag. Then add the `managedButtonHover` function:

```
var mouseX, mouseY;
function managedButtonHover(sender, mouseArgs) {
    if (!mouseX)
        mouseX = document.getElementById("MouseX");
    if (!mouseY)
        mouseY = document.getElementById("MouseY");

    var coords = mouseArgs.getPosition(null);
    mouseX.innerHTML = coords.X;
    mouseY.innerHTML = coords.Y;
}
```

Define the global `mouseX` and `mouseY` variables for faster reference. The first thing in the function is to find the corresponding HTML elements if they're not set yet. Then you can call the `getPosition` method (`GetPosition` in managed code on the `MouseEventArgs` type, which is what you get as the args in JavaScript). This method returns a `Point` type, which gives you the X- and Y-coordinates, so then just set the `innerHTML` accordingly. Run it, and now you see that when you hover, the mouse coordinates are reported as expected (see Figure 16-2), with one caveat: The coordinates will be relative to the Silverlight root element in that instance.

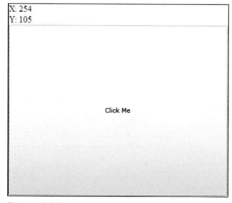

Figure 16-2

So if you just need to handle the basic events, this is another option that could work for you.

Handling Scripted Events from Managed Code

Handling JavaScript events in managed code is pleasantly easy. Continuing on from the last example, first add an HTML `Button` to the test page, just inside the body tag:

```
<button id="myHtmlButton">Click Me! [HTML]</button>
```

Now, inside of our `Page` type constructor, add the code to attach to that button's `Click` event:

```
HtmlElement btn = HtmlPage.Document.GetElementById("myHtmlButton");
btn.AttachEvent("onclick", HtmlButton_Click);
```

First you just use the `Document.GetElementById` (much as you would in HTML) to get a reference to the HTML element. There is no specific HTML `button` type in Silverlight — you just get the `HtmlElement` type, which is just fine and dandy. Once you have the reference, you simply use the `AttachEvent` method, giving it the JavaScript method name and an event handler with the appropriate signature:

```
void HtmlButton_Click(object sender, HtmlEventArgs e)
{
    User u = new User();
    u.Name = "Hamilton";
    u.Password = "HTML";
    this.OnUserSelected(u);
}
```

The `HtmlEventArgs` type gets you extra info, mostly around cursor positioning and key information. We're not using that here. Instead, the preceding code actually demonstrates how you can reuse your event raising (and handling) code, as alluded to previously. When you create a new user and call the `OnUserSelected` event already defined, the same managed `UserSelected` event will be raised, and the JavaScript code we had will handle it just as before, showing the info as in Figure 16-3.

Figure 16-3

> We're not covering raising scripted events because you're most likely not going to do that directly yourself, as you might with managed code. To raise scripted (browser or HTML) events, just do what you'd normally do, for example, trigger them via the usual ways.

You can imagine how raising and handling events between managed code and JavaScript could be essential to a "mixed-mode" application (one in which you have some DHTML and some Silverlight). Events are central to interactive, responsive applications, and understanding how to integrate managed and script events and handling should enable you to bring these kinds of apps to life. There are also facilities for invoking managed methods (as we did with `GetPosition`) from script and vice versa to further enhance such applications, and we'll get into that later in this chapter.

Responding to User Activity

While events, in and of themselves, are useful for building loosely coupled applications, the most interesting kinds of events, from an interactive application point of view, are those generated in some way by users. This section covers the essentials of effectively handling user activity in an application through the various input and control mechanisms, from most common to least.

Mouse Events

In the world of GUIs, a mouse is indispensable (at least for most apps). Obviously, a technology that is targeted at creating rich interactive (or Internet, if you prefer) applications needs thorough support for mouse input, and Silverlight gives you plenty. The following are the Silverlight mouse-related events that you can consume.

- ❏ `MouseEnter` — When the mouse enters the bounds of an element
- ❏ `MouseMove` — When the coordinates of the mouse change [Routed]
- ❏ `MouseLeave` — When the mouse leaves the bounds of an object
- ❏ `MouseLeftButtonDown` — When the mouse's left button is down [Routed]
- ❏ `MouseLeftButtonUp` — When the mouse's left button goes back up after a down event [Routed]

Using a combination of these events, you can do pretty much anything you should need to do in an interactive application. However, you may have a few questions (such as those addressed in the following sections) on your mind.

What about Click and Double-Click?

Click is essentially equivalent to `MouseLeftButtonUp`, so that shouldn't be an issue. If you need double-click, you could implement it in a helper class like the one described here: `http://weblogs.asp.net/ aboschin/archive/2008/03/17/silverlight-2-0-a-double-click-manager.aspx`.

What about Right-Click?

The convention is for plug-ins to use the right-click for general plug-in configuration and information, as you will see if you right-click a Silverlight instance. This is not necessarily set in stone, but it seems unlikely to change any time soon.

What Is This [Routed] of Which You Speak?

WPF introduced this name of *routed events*, although the concept is known elsewhere. The idea is that there is a visual hierarchy (e.g., the HTML DOM or the WPF/Silverlight UI element tree) such that an event can be routed through the hierarchy. In WPF, routed events are provided for two ways — *tunneling* down the tree, conceptually before the event happens, and *bubbling* up the tree once the event has happened. Silverlight only uses the bubbling half of that — tunneling is not supported.

The net effect is that you can, say, handle the MouseLeftButtonUp event for the top-level, root UI element and thereby handle all MouseLeftButtonUp events for the entire tree, without having to attach handlers to each individual element that you're interested in. This can come in really handy if you need to handle the same event for many objects in a generic way.

Routed events have a special OrinalSource property and Handled property. The OriginalSource property will get you a reference to the most specific element that registered the event. The Handled property lets you inform other handlers that you consider the event to have been taken care of. Setting Handled to true prevents further, normal bubbling, so you need to be aware of what events the controls you are using may swallow. For instance, Button swallows MouseLeftButtonUp and supplies Click instead.

Mouse Event Arguments

As you've seen already, there are specialized event arguments for mouse events. They are:

- ❏ MouseEventArgs — Non-button mouse events
- ❏ MouseButtonEventArgs — Button-related events

Interestingly enough, although MouseButtonEventArgs derives from MouseEventArgs and adds semantic value, no additional functionality is provided. Because there is effectively only one mouse button (the left one) and there is no double-click, there's nothing more it could add. It is pretty much only there for compatibility with WPF, but who knows, maybe it'll come in handy down the line, eh?

There is only one added bit of functionality for mouse event arguments over a standard routed event — the GetPosition method. (There are actually two more, ink-related events we'll cover later in this section.) You've already seen this in action in the last section. If you want to get the mouse coordinates relative to the content root (the Silverlight plug-in bounds), you can just pass null to this method.

GetPosition returns a Point structure (that's right, it's a value type) with two members of type Double — the X-coordinate and the Y-coordinate. These will be relative to the element that you pass into the method or (as noted) the root. If you do specify a relative element, the resultant coordinates will be relative to the top and left coordinate of the given element. This means, for instance, that if the pointer is above and to the left of the given element, the resultant Point will have negative X and Y values.

Common Mouse Scenarios

OK, so now you have a good overview of what Silverlight gives you in terms of mouse events, and it is time to apply that knowledge in meaningful ways. The following are common scenarios that you'll likely need to deal with while building interactive applications.

Hovering

Hovering is when the mouse cursor is over an element. On the Web today, in HTML, hovering is often used to provide visual feedback to indicate that an action is available (such as the mouse cursor changing to a hand if a link can be clicked and often some other indicator such as underline, changing color, etc.); it is also used to provide basic tooltips, and, occasionally, it is used to trigger the display of some nearby, related content, as on the Infragistics homepage (see Figure 16-4).

Figure 16-4

Silverlight gives you a few basic helpers to implement hover scenarios. First, there are the `MouseEnter` and `MouseLeave` events. When the mouse enters the target element, you activate your hover state. When the mouse leaves the target element, you deactivate the hover state, if applicable. The next one is the `Cursor` property that is available on all `FrameworkElement` types; this is a super-simple way of providing some basic visual feedback while hovering over an element. You may also need the `MouseMove` event — this continues to fire as you move the mouse over an element. It's more useful for click-and-drag type operations, although you may also have the occasional need for cursor tracking. The last hover-related facility in the box is the `ToolTip` control.

The `ToolTip` is key for providing transitory, contextual information. The most common use is to provide simply a short bit of text to answer an implicit question. For instance, if it is a link, button, or other command-type control, you typically want to tell the user what clicking on it will do. Another common use is to elaborate on a word, term, or visual/image — to further describe it and help users understand it.

In HTML, tooltips are built into several elements, but they're limited to textual information (which is good for accessibility and SEO, such as the `alt` tag for images). The tooltips are displayed in the system style, so if you want a styled or richer tooltip, you have to create your own or use a third-party control. In Silverlight, you can just use the standard text-based approach, but you can also completely customize the tooltip content by using a control template (or just use styles to change basic visual attributes). Either way, it does the heavy lifting of detecting mouse hovering, showing, timing, and hiding the tooltip via the `ToolTipService` class, which you can also use to programmatically attach tooltips.

Most controls don't have a `ToolTip` property, but, thankfully, you can just use the `ToolTipServer.ToolTip` attached property to effectively set a tooltip on pretty much any visual element. You can set it in one of two ways on related visuals (in XAML). First, if you just want the default look, you can set it on the element XAML directly, like this:

```
<Grid x:Name="LayoutRoot" Background="White"
    ToolTipService.ToolTip="Howdy, Folks!">
```

That will give you the default look and feel, as shown in Figure 16-5. This works because the `ToolTipService` will automatically wrap a string in a `ToolTip` instance for you.

Figure 16-5

If you want to customize it, you can use this alternative approach, placing the declaration just inside the tag of the element you want the tooltip to apply to:

```
<ToolTipService.ToolTip>
    <ToolTip Background="Black">
        <Border Background="White"
          BorderThickness="1" CornerRadius="4">
            <TextBlock Foreground="Maroon" FontSize="11"
              Margin="3,3,3,3" Text="Howdy, Folks!" />
        </Border>
    </ToolTip>
</ToolTipService.ToolTip>
```

The result is shown in Figure 16-6.

Figure 16-6

Note that you can style various properties about what is *in* the tooltip, even on the `ToolTip` control itself. The properties it exposes are, of course, stylable using standard Silverlight styling. It will even let you supply inner content that is basically anything you want — you could have a `StackPanel` with images and beyond. But it will always wrap it in that little silverish border. If you want to completely change it, you'll have to use a control template. Here's how.

First, you want to define your template. You can do it from scratch or you can use Reflector or a tool like Delay's default style browser (`http://blogs.msdn.com/delay/archive/2008/03/22/improved-access-to-silverlight-2-s-generic-xaml-resources-silverlightdefaultstylebrowser-available-via-clickonce.aspx`) to find and copy the default style and templates as a starting point, to simplify your customization. Here's what a custom tooltip style and template look like:

```xml
<Style x:Key="FaceOutToolTip" TargetType="ToolTip">
  <Setter Property="FontFamily" Value="Verdana" />
  <Setter Property="FontSize" Value="10" />
  <Setter Property="Foreground" Value="#FFC6DD5B" />
  <Setter Property="Template">
    <Setter.Value>
      <ControlTemplate>
        <Border HorizontalAlignment="Left" VerticalAlignment="Center"
          CornerRadius="4" BorderBrush="#FFFFFFFF"
          BorderThickness="1,1,1,1">
          <Border Background="#FF424542" Name="RootElement"
            CornerRadius="4" Padding="4">
            <Border.Resources>
              <Storyboard x:Key="Visible State"  />
              <Storyboard x:Key="Normal State"  />
            </Border.Resources>
            <ContentPresenter Content="{TemplateBinding Content}"
              ContentTemplate="{TemplateBinding ContentTemplate}" />
          </Border>
        </Border>
      </ControlTemplate>
    </Setter.Value>
  </Setter>
</Style>
```

You'll notice all the template bindings; these maintain most of the bindings that are in the default template, but we do force some of the properties for consistency's sake within the application. You could probably even do without maintaining all the template bindings if you know you don't need them to be customizable in your application.

You can put your templates and styles in your page/user control, but if you're going to reuse them, as is often the case, it is better to put them in the `app.xaml Application.Resources` tag to simplify the management of your look-and-feel and better ensure visual consistency. Doing that in the current sample, you can rework the tooltip usage like this:

```xml
<ToolTipService.ToolTip>
    <ToolTip Style="{StaticResource FaceOutToolTip}"
      Content="Howdy, Folks!" />
</ToolTipService.ToolTip>
```

You can see how using a template, especially applied over multiple uses of ToolTip, could greatly improve the manageability, consistency, and legibility, for that matter, of your XAML. You could also apply the template as follows:

```
ToolTip tt = new ToolTip();
tt.Style = App.Current.Resources["FaceOutToolTip"] as
  Style;
tt.Content = "Howdy, Folks!";
ToolTipService.SetToolTip(this.LayoutRoot, tt);
```

This would have the net same effect as the previous XAML for the given element.

So that's one important hover service for your apps. Changing the mouse cursor is another very common one, and that's easy enough. The simplest thing is to set the Cursor property in XAML, directly or via a style or template. Here you'll want to follow the standard cursor usage. This means, typically, if it is a command (link, image button, and content area/row being the most common) that isn't necessarily obviously a command, it helps to switch the cursor to Hand to indicate that the user can take some action — then you'd want to complement that with a tooltip describing the action.

You might also need to consider using the Busy cursor if you do something that ties up the UI for any length of time or if you simply want to indicate that the user's command input had an effect when it isn't immediately obvious. Arrow is going to be the default, and there is an IBeam, but applicability of that will be narrow outside of TextBox for the current version because it implies that you can manipulate text, and the TextBlock won't let you even select text in v2. Last, there are a couple of stylus-related cursors, but those apply in inking situations that we'll cover later.

If you do nothing else but use the Cursor and ToolTip, you'll handle the most common hover scenarios. However, if you need to kick it up a notch, that's when the MouseEnter and MouseLeave events become your friends.

Clicking

Probably the most common mouse input that application developers care about is clicking. As noted, Silverlight gives you the MouseLeftButtonUp event for this scenario, and some controls, such as Button, CheckBox, and so on (derived from ButtonBase) actually create a Click event for you, since that's what we're all more used to. (MouseLeftButtonUp seems so abstract.)

The point of clicking, of course, is to indicate selection, a commitment from the user that he or she wants whatever command is represented to be executed. Most often this will be one of three things: *Select* (as in selecting a row in a grid or some other list or a checkbox/radio button), *Go* (some navigational command, such as a link or menu item), and *Execute* (most often a button, menu item, or link that acts like a button).

The key thing here is to look at the control you're using. If it has a Click event, use that, because it is more likely to provide arguments that you're interested in (or none) and the "sender" will more likely be the control itself, rather than a visual in the control. If you handle, say, the MouseLeftButtonUp, the sender is likely going to be a specific visual element within the control rather than the control itself, and it may be hard to get at the control information from that.

If there is no Click event, then you can just use MouseLeftButtonUp or create some abstraction for yourself in a user control.

Drag-and-Drop

In some ways, this could be considered an advanced scenario, but it is also a pretty common one. You'd hope that the Popup control in the box would give you some basic window-like functionality, but it pretty much just gives you offset (vertical and horizontal) and an IsOpen property to open/close (by setting it to true/false). This is not especially helpful, but it *does* live in the Primitives namespace, so I suppose you can't be too surprised.

That said, it's a decent place to start with implementing some drag-and-droppiness to your application. There are three key events in the life of a drag-and-drop: mouse button down, mouse move, and mouse button up. So what you want to do is create another user control in your Silverlight app; call it Drag-n-Drop. (You could also just start a new project if you want.) Then reset the application to use that as the root visual in the App.xaml.cs startup.

```
private void Application_Startup(object sender, StartupEventArgs e)
{
    // Load the main control
    // this.RootVisual = new Page();
    this.RootVisual = new Drag_n_Drop();
}
```

Since the TestPage.html has some Page-specific script, you'll need to modify it like this:

```
function onSilverlightLoad(sender, args) {
    var plugin = sender.getHost();
    try // swallow exceptions for when Page doesn't exist
    { plugin.Content.Page.UserSelected = userSelected; } catch(e) {}

    // attach to mouse enter for button
    var managedButton = plugin.content.findName("ManagedButton");
    if (managedButton)
        managedButton.addEventListener("MouseMove",
            managedButtonHover);
}
```

This ignores any error on setting when the Page scriptable type doesn't exist and checks to ensure there is a ManagedButton found. You could just as easily clear out the onSilverlightLoad event, but this enables you to switch back to using Page as the root visual if you want. The other thing you may want to change on the HTML page is the height/width of the Silverlight instance — to 100 percent. This gives more room to drag stuff around because you'll only be able to drag inside the Silverlight plug-in bounds.

Now in your Drag-n-Drop.xaml, remove the default height/width, and add a button with a Click event handler. Your XAML should look something like this:

```
<UserControl x:Class="EventsAndUserActivity.Drag_n_Drop"
    xmlns="http://schemas.microsoft.com/client/2007"
    xmlns:x="http://schemas.microsoft.com/winfx/2006/xaml">
    <Grid x:Name="LayoutRoot" Background="White">
        <Button
            Width="80" Height="25"
            HorizontalAlignment="Left" VerticalAlignment="Top"
```

```
                    Content="Open Popup" Click="Button_Click" />
        </Grid>
    </UserControl>
```

Now you need to set up your pop-up. This is the meat of the Drag-n-Drop scenario. Create a new user control — call it RealPopup (as opposed to the fake one you get in the box). What you're going to do is create a basic title bar and content layout with a Close button in the top right. There are a few ways you could do this with XAML; here is one:

```
<UserControl x:Class="EventsAndUserActivity.RealPopup"
    xmlns="http://schemas.microsoft.com/client/2007"
    xmlns:x="http://schemas.microsoft.com/winfx/2006/xaml">
    <Border
        MinHeight="30" MinWidth="80" HorizontalAlignment="Left"
        VerticalAlignment="Bottom" CornerRadius="4"
        BorderBrush="#FFFFFFFF" BorderThickness="1,1,1,1">
        <Border
            Background="#FF424542" Name="RootElement"
            CornerRadius="4">
            <Grid>
                <Grid.RowDefinitions>
                    <RowDefinition Height="25" />
                    <RowDefinition Height="*" MinHeight="50" />
                </Grid.RowDefinitions>
                <Grid Grid.Row="0" Background="Black"
                  Cursor="Hand"
                  MouseLeftButtonDown="MouseDragStart"
                  MouseMove="MouseDrag"
                  MouseLeftButtonUp="MouseDragStop">
                    <Grid.ColumnDefinitions>
                        <ColumnDefinition Width="*" />
                        <ColumnDefinition Width="16" />
                    </Grid.ColumnDefinitions>
                    <TextBlock Grid.Column="0" Text="Title"
                        Foreground="White"
                        HorizontalAlignment="Center"
                        VerticalAlignment="Center" />
                    <Button Grid.Column="1" x:Name="CloseButton"
                        HorizontalAlignment="Right"
                        VerticalAlignment="Top" FontSize="9"
                        Width="16" Height="16"
                        Click="CloseButton_Click" Content="X" />
                </Grid>
                <Grid Grid.Row="1">
                    <TextBlock
                        Foreground="White" FontSize="9"
                        Margin="4">
                        <Run>This is the content area.</Run>
                    </TextBlock>
                </Grid>
            </Grid>
        </Border>
    </Border>
</UserControl>
```

The Borders were copied from the ToolTip style; it uses a basic top-bottom grid layout (25 pixels high for the title, everything else for the content, with a minimum height of 50 just to look proportional). The Close button is just a regular 16 × 16 button with an *X* as its content. The interesting bits for drag-and-drop are the `MouseLeftButtonDown`, `MouseMove`, and `MouseLeftButtonUp` handlers; and it sets the `Cursor` property to `hand` in order to indicate that you can do something with it. That's all there is to the XAML — the magic happens in the code.

What you need to do in code is:

1. Determine the position of the mouse relative to the top-left corner of the element being dragged — the drag offset.

2. Capture the mouse.

3. Update the top and left coordinates of the element being dragged. The value here will be the absolute coordinates of the mouse minus the drag offset.

4. Release the mouse when dragging stops.

First things first — handle the mouse down event.

```
bool _DragInProgress = false;
Point _DragOffset;
private void MouseDragStart(object sender, MouseButtonEventArgs e)
{
    FrameworkElement grabElement = sender as FrameworkElement;
    _DragOffset = e.GetPosition(this);
    _DragInProgress = true;
    this.BringToFront();
    grabElement.CaptureMouse();
}
```

Define the class fields of _DragInProgress and _DragOffset. The first one tracks whether or not there is a drag in progress, which is important because the mouse move event will fire even when the mouse button is not down — you don't want to have the sticky element problem, whereby the element tracks the mouse even if the user is not pressing down the button. The drag offset just records the location of the mouse relative to the upper-left corner of the element when the mouse is pressed down. The last thing to do is to capture the mouse. This is important because if the user drags the element under another one, you could lose the mouse input, and capturing ensures that the mouse events keep being sent to your element until you release it.

> **You can, optionally add the `BringToFront` feature; that will be covered later in this section.**

Next, you need to handle the mouse move event:

```
private void MouseDrag(object sender, MouseEventArgs e)
{
    if (_DragInProgress)
        this.ProcessDrag(e.GetPosition(null));
}

void ProcessDrag(Point location)
```

```
    {
        this.Move(new Point(location.X - _DragOffset.X,
            location.Y - _DragOffset.Y));
        if (this.Opacity == 1)
            this.Opacity = 0.6;
    }

    public void Move(Point targetLocation)
    {
        this.Popup.HorizontalOffset = targetLocation.X;
        this.Popup.VerticalOffset = targetLocation.Y;
    }
```

The first thing you do is ensure that there is a "drag in progress"; again, that's just a check that the mouse is depressed. Then you process the drag by moving the control to the new location — the mouse position relative to the plug-in bounds minus the offset. Here is where the built-in Popup control can come in handy; it has a HorizontalOffset and a VerticalOffset that you can use to update the X- and Y-coordinates. Without this, you could use a TranslateTransform; they both seem to work equally well, but this way makes your code a bit simpler and easier to understand. The Popup property is just a convenience property:

```
Popup _Popup;
Popup Popup
{
    get
    {
        if (_Popup == null)
        {
            _Popup = new Popup();
            _Popup.Child = this;
        }
        return _Popup;
    }
}
```

You just use a class field to store a Popup instance for the control and set the Popup.Child property to be this control, much as you would if you were using the Popup directly outside a custom control.

You may have noted the Opacity change in the ProcessDrag method. This is a nifty UI feature; it enables users to see what is behind the element while dragging it, which can be very useful for helping position it exactly where they want it. You don't have to do it for Drag-n-Drop if you don't want to.

The last bit is to respond when the user releases the mouse button and stop the dragging process.

```
private void MouseDragStop(object sender, MouseButtonEventArgs e)
{
    if (_DragInProgress)
        this.StopDrag();
}

void StopDrag()
{
    _DragInProgress = false;
```

399

```
        this.ReleaseMouseCapture();
        this.Opacity = 1;
    }
```

All you need to do here is update the _DragInProgress flag so that further mouse moves won't continue to change the element's location. Then release the mouse capture so that mouse events trigger normally again on all elements, and, finally, if you are changing the Opacity, set it back to full.

That is all you have to do to make elements drag-and-droppable. But there is still the question of showing and hiding the pop-up, though, so for that, you can just add simple Show and Hide methods like this:

```
public void Show()
{
    this.Popup.IsOpen = true;
    this.BringToFront();
}

public void Hide()
{
    this.Popup.IsOpen = false;
}
```

Mainly, this exercises the other feature built into Popup — you can just toggle the IsOpen property to toggle the visibility of the control. The other thing you see here is the use of BringToFront again. This should look familiar to Windows developers, but there is no built-in mechanism in Silverlight for this purpose. You can easily extend FrameworkElement, however, by just adding an extension class to your project.

```
public static class FrameworkExtensions
{
    internal static int LastZIndex = 1000;

    public static void BringToFront(this FrameworkElement element)
    {
        element.SetValue(Canvas.ZIndexProperty, LastZIndex++);
    }
}
```

This uses the new .NET 3.5 language feature called *extension methods*. Declare a static class and declare static methods and use the special this keyword on the first parameter. Then just use/import the namespace, and any elements of the type you specify can use those methods as if they were declared on the instance's class directly. Because our RealPopup control derives from FrameworkElement (as do almost all visual elements in Silverlight), we're able to use BringToFront as if it were a member of our class. Cool, huh?

Oh, and all it does is keep track of a shared z-index and increment/set it on the target element, making sure (in most cases) that it will be on top of other visual elements. We use it when you first show the pop-up and also when you click to drag it, both of which, from a user perspective, seem like the natural/right thing to have happen.

The last thing you need to do is to use the pop-up, which takes us back to our button click handler in Drag-n-Drop.xaml.cs:

```
private void Button_Click(object sender, RoutedEventArgs e)
{
    RealPopup p = new RealPopup();
    p.Show();
}
```

See? Easy. Makes sense. Once you bring it all together and run it, you can click on the "Show Popup" button a few times and end up with something like you see in Figure 16-7.

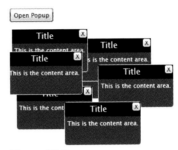

Figure 16-7

> If your interface has a high potential for having many of these "windows," you will want to have some sort of organizational tool — this is what the taskbar in Windows does and tabs do in multidocument interfaces like Visual Studio. Otherwise, the windows get overwhelming and hard to keep track of.

Keyboard Events

Next to mousing, of course, is keyboarding when it comes to interaction devices in apps today. Silverlight provides the two events that you need — KeyDown and KeyUp, both of which are routed events. As the names imply, the first is raised when a key is pressed down and the second when the key is released (up). They both use KeyEventArgs to give you information about the keys involved in the event.

In addition to OriginalSource and Handled, KeyEventArgs provides these members:

❑   Key — This is a facility provided to make handling common key entry easier — it is an enumeration value that represents so-called portable (cross-platform) keys, which are most of what you see on a standard 101-key keyboard. One of the members is Unknown, which means it's not one of the standard keys, and you need to look at the PlatformKeyCode.

❑   PlatformKeyCode — This is an integer that represents the platform-specific key code. You have to reference platform docs to make use of this.

Silverlight provides an additional facility for handling the case when, for example, the [Alt] or [Ctrl] key is pressed. For that, you use the static (Shared) property `Keyboard.Modifiers` property and compare it to the `ModifierKeys` flag enumeration. It's a flag enumeration because multiple modifier keys can be pressed at once.

Common Key Scenarios

As with mouse, there are a few scenarios with keys that will be very common for application developers. They can be boiled down to two basic categories — text input and control (e.g., navigation and commands).

Text Input

This one barely bears mentioning because it is the default and is often just taken for granted, but those two little events — `KeyDown` and `KeyUp` — enable things like the `TextBox` to receive the key input and reflect it as a string of characters in its display area. This is absolutely essential to pretty much any application that involves data (which is most in the business world).

In Silverlight 3, you pretty much just get the standard single-line textbox, although there are embellishments such as masking for passwords (`PasswordBox`). Unfortunately, there is no rich text editor, so text input scenarios in "native" Silverlight are limited; however, you can overlay HTML-based editors on Silverlight if you need that. Certainly the future will hold solutions for rich text editing.

To get a feel for `TextBox`, you can just add one to your `Popup` control from the drag-and-drop scenario covered in the mouse section. Actually, you'll probably want to add a `StackPanel` around the `TextBlock` and the new `TextBox` as follows (this is in RealPopup.xaml, if you recall):

```
<StackPanel>
    <TextBlock
        Foreground="White" FontSize="9"
        Margin="4">
        <Run>This is the content area.</Run>
    </TextBlock>
    <TextBox x:Name="TextInput" />
</StackPanel>
```

Run that sample again now, and you get something like Figure 16-8.

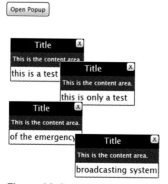

Figure 16-8

There are four very common text input scenarios, in addition to the basic textbox: masked text input, structured text input, multiple-line text input, and rich text input.

Masked Text Input

Out-of-the-box, you get the `PasswordBox` control, which enables you to mask sensitive information as it is being typed-in by users. This handles the majority of cases with this need, but other types of masking serve to further structure input and cross the line into structured text input.

Structured Text Input

Common examples where structured text input is used are phone numbers, tax identifiers, dates, and credit cards. These are used because the system needs to treat these numbers specially, potentially even storing the pieces of the numbers separately, so it helps to guide users to enter them in the format that the system needs.

Thus, you'll commonly see these numbers broken out into separate textboxes or a masking device used to constrain user input to the expected format. Third-party vendors like Infragistics usually supplement the platform controls with these kinds of masked text editors, and, no doubt, we'll see that for Silverlight as well. I recommend that you use one of these rather than rolling your own; they seem simple on the surface, but using them can get complicated rather quickly.

To do a simple implementation of the broken-apart structured format, you can use the following example. You'll make a simple US-based phone number input element, and by adding to the `RealPopup` example, you can add a `StackPanel` and put three `TextBox` controls in it, separated by two `TextBlock` controls, like this:

```
<StackPanel
    x:Name="PhoneNumber"
    Orientation="Horizontal">
    <TextBox
        x:Name="AreaCode"
        MaxLength="3"
        TabIndex="1"
        KeyUp="Structured_KeyUp"
        FontSize="9"
        Width="25" />
    <TextBlock
        Foreground="White" FontSize="9"
        Text="-" />
    <TextBox
        x:Name="Prefix"
        MaxLength="3"
        TabIndex="2"
        KeyUp="Structured_KeyUp"
        FontSize="9"
        Width="25" />
    <TextBlock
        Foreground="White" FontSize="9"
        Text="-" />
```

```
<TextBox
    x:Name="Number"
    MaxLength="4"
    TabIndex="3"
    FontSize="9"
    Width="33" />
</StackPanel>
```

Width and FontSize work together to create a visual feel that looks like a phone number, with the Width being proportionate to the maximum number of characters (MaxLength). The TabIndex is used both by the Silverlight tabbing mechanisms and our code, which follows. The MaxLength property is useful for both limiting text input length and creating a sort-of-generic method for moving between the parts — the Structured_KeyUp method that follows:

```
private void Structured_KeyUp(object sender, KeyEventArgs e)
{
    TextBox box = (TextBox)e.OriginalSource;
    if (box.Text.Trim().Length == box.MaxLength)
    {
        foreach (UIElement elem in ((Panel)box.Parent).Children)
        {
            Control c = elem as Control;
            if (c != null && c.IsTabStop &&
                c.TabIndex == box.TabIndex + 1)
            {
                c.Focus();
                break;
            }
        }
    }
}
```

First, notice the method signature — the same for all key-based events, taking an object as the sender of the event and the KeyEventArgs. We're not doing key detection here, but we do use the routed event argument OriginalSource to get the TextBox that triggers the event. This lets us use the same method for multiple boxes.

The first thing we do with the box is check that its length is equivalent to the expected MaxLength (maximum number of characters). If it is, we then attempt to find the next tab stop in its parent. We do this by assuming that the parent is a Panel (it is — a StackPanel), and we iterate through its Children (a UIElementCollection), trying to cast each element as a Control. If the cast is successful, c will be not null, and we can then check first that it is a tab stop and second that its tab index is the next in line, in which case, we focus on it and exit.

The net effect of this is that as users are typing, once they get to the expected length for the box, they'll automatically tab over to the next box in the sequence. This approach is fairly common on the Web, especially for things like phone numbers. You can see the end result in Figure 16-9, although, of course, you'll have to try it out to get the full effect.

Figure 16-9

Multiple-Line Text Input

Next to plain old single-line textboxes, probably the next most common input control is for multiple-line input. HTML defines a special TEXTAREA element for it, but in Silverlight, as in WinForms and WPF, you just modify the TextBox to accept multiline input. Key to doing this are the following properties:

❑ Height/Width — Use these just to define the viewable area — with a single line, you typically let the control manage the height; but for multiple lines, you set it to three lines, at a minimum. This will vary based on your font size.

❑ AcceptsReturn — This lets users use the [Enter] key as a carriage-return line feed (CRLF, which is like a \r\n in C# string syntax and VbCrLf in VB). More often than not, you want to let users do this in a multiline input. By default, it is off/false for TextBox.

❑ TextWrapping — Use this to wrap the text input at the end of the visible textbox area. This is again, more often than not, likely what you want to do as it is what users are used to; otherwise, you'll have horizontal scrolling, and the height setting won't really matter.

❑ VerticalScrollBarVisibility — If you want to show a scrollbar, you should set this property. Auto is a good one if you don't expect to need it most of the time; otherwise, you might want to set it to Visible so that its sudden appearance doesn't distract users.

```
<TextBox
    x:Name="TextInput"
    Width="200"
    Height="75"
    AcceptsReturn="True"
    FontSize="9"
    TextWrapping="Wrap"
    VerticalScrollBarVisibility="Auto"
    KeyDown="TextInput_Measure"
    KeyUp="TextInput_Measure" />
```

In addition to setting the normal multiline settings, the code above uses a TextInput_Measure method. This is done to allow us to provide feedback to users in terms of how many characters they've typed. If you have a back-end system that limits the length of the text being entered, it is a good experience to provide that feedback to help users proactively control the length of their input. For example, twitter limits tweets to 140 characters, so if you were implementing that, the TextInput_Measure method might look like the following:

```
const int MAX_INPUT = 140;
private void TextInput_Measure(object sender, KeyEventArgs e)
{
```

```
TextBox box = (TextBox)e.OriginalSource;
int actual = box.Text.Length;

this.ContentArea.Text =
    string.Format("{0} of {1} characters used. ",
        actual, MAX_INPUT);
int diff = MAX_INPUT - actual;
Run counter = new Run();

if (diff >= 0)
    counter.Text =
        string.Format("{0} characters left.", diff);
else
{
    counter.Text =
        string.Format("{0} characters too many.", Math.Abs(diff));
    counter.Foreground = new SolidColorBrush(Colors.Red);
}
this.ContentArea.Inlines.Add(counter);


if (e.Key == Key.A &&
    (Keyboard.Modifiers & ModifierKeys.Control)
        == ModifierKeys.Control)
{
    box.SelectionStart = 0;
    box.SelectionLength = actual;
}
}
```

First, we grab the reference to the originating (OriginalSource) TextBox and then grab the current length of its text and store it in the actual integer. We use our ContentArea TextBlock to report the number of characters versus the max. Some implementations of this pattern stop there, which leaves it to the user to figure out the difference, but to make it more usable, we go ahead and do the math for them (subtracting the actual from the max). If the difference is zero or more, we just append a message telling them how many characters they have left; however, if they are exceeding the maximum, we want to change the message to tell them that they have too many characters (and how many too many), as well as go ahead and reinforce that message by using red, indicating an unacceptable state.

> A Run is a Silverlight (and WPF) document object used to group a succession of characters (similar to a string). The benefit is that it lets you apply distinct styling to that group of characters, which is why we use it here — in case we want to change the color of that message to red.

The last bit actually has nothing to do with the measurement. Silverlight doesn't have an implementation of CTRL-A (select all), so this is a simple way to implement that. Using the Keyboard.Modifiers property, you can check to see which (if any) modifiers are pressed. It's a flags enumeration, which enables more than one of its values to be true at once. While we could simply check for equivalence to ModifierKeys.Control (e.g., Keyboard.Modifiers == ModifierKeys.Control), the syntax in the listing shows how you check for multiple values, and, in fact, this will register a select all even if you have more than just [Ctrl] pressed, as I do in Figure 16-10.

Figure 16-10

Rich Text Input

Unfortunately, Silverlight 3 still does not have good support for rich text. It has a very limited subset of the document API that you get with WPF. However, it does support font embedding, so that's one up on HTML. There are some free rich-text emulators that, for example, will take XHTML and attempt a conversion to Silverlight markup, but since Silverlight markup is inherently limited, the success of these will be inherently limited. There's the further consideration that the lingua franca for the Web today (and in the foreseeable future) is HTML, so you probably don't want to be storing Silverlight markup for your rich text.

One option in the current version will be to overlay an HTML editor on your Silverlight application. You do this by setting the Silverlight plug-in to windowless mode and then using the CSS z-index to layer the HTML elements on top of your Silverlight. The problem here is if you have draggable objects in your Silverlight app, the HTML will always be on top of those.

To deal with this layering problem, you can host two Silverlight plug-ins on your HTML page. You then layer them as follows: One Silverlight plug-in contains the main/background Silverlight objects; on top of that, you layer HTML overlays, and finally, you add another Silverlight layer where you host your objects that may need to overlie the overlaid HTML.

Another option for including rich HTML is to create a fixed transparent area of the Silverlight plug-in, underlay your HTML in that area, and, if you need to, shuttle input events to the underlying HTML. And last, there is always the option to not do full-page Silverlight — reserve part of your page for HTML content, and keep it there. This last approach will be the easiest and possibly best from an experience perspective, if it works to have the HTML and Silverlight completely separate. Otherwise, you're stuck with one of the other, less than optimal, options.

Now don't forget that the purpose of this whole discussion about HTML overlaying is to enable rich text editing in the context of this section. Obviously, it also affects other rich interactions such as HTML-based mashup elements or just plain HTML displaying. The bottom line is that rich text is a tough scenario in Silverlight 3, so if it is central to your application, you will have to think about these issues and decide which approach makes the most sense for you.

Navigation and Commands

Two other very common keyboard issues are navigation and commands. We actually already covered commands at the end of the "Multiple-Line Text Input" section, in which we added a `Select All` command mapped to pressing [Ctrl]+A (a very common mapping for that command). Other common commands are [Ctrl]+C (`Copy`), [Ctrl]+X (`Cut`), and [Ctrl]+V (`Paste`) — these work in Silverlight 3 and are the only way for your Silverlight app to get access to the system clipboard (for security reasons).

407

The thing to note here is that you can use the same technique we used for [Ctrl]+A to create your own keyboard commands, which are especially useful for heavily used applications in which you don't want your users to constantly have to switch between typing and using the mouse. A very common example (in Windows) is to use [Alt]+<*key*> to provide keyboard access to menu commands (known as keyboard accelerators). You need to be mindful that some modifier keys are platform-specific.

Keyboard navigation can be very useful, particularly in graphical applications in which you want to move graphical elements using the keyboard. There are plenty of Silverlight-based games that use this approach. For our purposes, we'll add basic keyboard movement capabilities to our pop-up.

To do this is actually pretty easy. First, you want to add a couple of event handlers to your `RealPopup` user control. You can do it in XAML or code (e.g., in the constructor). This is what the XAML will look like for your `UserControl`:

```
<UserControl x:Class="EventsAndUserActivity.RealPopup"
    xmlns="http://schemas.microsoft.com/client/2007"
    xmlns:x="http://schemas.microsoft.com/winfx/2006/xaml"
    IsTabStop="True"
    MouseLeftButtonUp="UserControl_MouseLeftButtonUp"
    KeyDown="UserControl_KeyDown">
```

You need to add the `MouseLeftButtonUp` and `KeyDown` event handlers. The `KeyDown` is probably obvious, but to make the navigation seem right, you have to do a few extra things besides just handling the `KeyDown`. The first of those tangential things is to enable the control to receive focus, and for that, it needs to be `Visible`, be in the visual tree, and be considered a tab stop. We get the last two for free just by showing the pop-up, but you need to set `IsTabStop` to `True` (as shown in the last listing).

That will make the control able to receive focus; then you need to do a couple of things to actually give it focus. First, in the `Show` method, add `this.Focus()`:

```
public void Show()
{
    this.Popup.IsOpen = true;
    this.BringToFront();
    this.Focus();
}
```

This means that when it shows, it will automatically have focus and be navigable (movable) with the keyboard. The next thing to address is the `MouseLeftButtonUp` handler:

```
private void UserControl_MouseLeftButtonUp(object sender,
    MouseButtonEventArgs e)
{
    this.Focus();
}
```

This gives the focus back to the control when you click anywhere that doesn't grab focus itself (such as a `TextBox`). In our pop-up, we have a few textboxes, so we want to be able to click back out of them, as it were, to give focus back to the control (otherwise, you can only click in other textboxes).

So that enables the not-so-obvious part of making the control keyboard navigable. Now you just need to do the actual keyboard navigation.

```
private void UserControl_KeyDown(object sender, KeyEventArgs e)
{
    if (e.OriginalSource == this)
    {
        switch (e.Key)
        {
            case Key.Right:
                this.Move(new Point(this.Popup.HorizontalOffset + 1,
                    this.Popup.VerticalOffset));
                break;
            case Key.Left:
                this.Move(new Point(this.Popup.HorizontalOffset - 1,
                    this.Popup.VerticalOffset));
                break;
            case Key.Down:
                this.Move(new Point(this.Popup.HorizontalOffset,
                    this.Popup.VerticalOffset + 1));
                break;
            case Key.Up:
                this.Move(new Point(this.Popup.HorizontalOffset,
                    this.Popup.VerticalOffset - 1));
                break;
        }
    }
}
```

The scenario you're enabling is to move the pop-up right, left, down, or up by 1 pixel using the natural mapping of those arrow keys. The way you can do it, again thanks to the offset properties that Popup provides, is to simply increment or decrement the appropriate offset using the Move method you created previously. You could, of course, just set the offsets directly (since that is all Move does), but it is a better practice to use the appropriate, semantically correct method if one is available to keep that code centralized. The kinky thing to remember is that you're acting on the coordinates from the top and left, so even though it may seem right to decrement the vertical offset to go down, it's actually the opposite.

The only other thing you'll want to do here is only move if it is the user control that has focus and, ergo, is the source of the event, so wrap the switch statement in a check against the OriginalSource of the event arguments. This is good so that you won't move the thing around while the focus is in, say, the textboxes.

> Be aware that keyboard input is disabled when in Full-Screen mode except for navigational type keys. This is a security feature to prevent phishing type applications — for example, you could design a Silverlight app to mimic the OS login screen to steal their login credentials (and that's just the beginning). If you need other keyboard input in Full-Screen mode, you need to consider a visual keyboard such as on iPhone, Xbox, and so forth. Here's a list of available key inputs in full-screen mode: Up Arrow, Down Arrow, Left Arrow, Right Arrow, Spacebar, [Tab], [Page Up], [Page Down], [Home], [End], [Enter].

That's the essentials of keyboard navigation and wraps up this section on keyboard input. You should be able to apply the concepts covered here to do pretty much anything you need to with keyboard input.

Other Inputs: Ink

Although this section is called "Other Inputs," essentially the only other user-initiated inputs that Silverlight handles are ink-related. While you may have other hardware devices that a user may use, they will need to translate to mouse, keyboard, or ink to work in Silverlight. So in this last user-interactivity section, we'll focus on ink stuff.

As noted in the mouse section, ink information is attached to mouse event arguments. This is important because you can use the mouse for basic ink input, but it won't support pressure sensitivity directly.

In any case, thankfully, Silverlight 3 makes cross-platform inking a breeze. In some ways, it resembles handling standard drag-and-drop mouse functionality; you just add an InkPresenter and take advantage of the Stylus-related stuff on the mouse event args.

First, add an InkPresenter to your RealPopup, at the bottom, under your structured input (phone) StackPanel:

```xml
<Border Background="Black" BorderThickness="1,1,2,2">
    <InkPresenter
        x:Name="Inker"
        Background="White"
        Width="200" Height="200"
        MouseLeftButtonDown="InkPresenter_MouseLeftButtonDown"
        MouseMove="InkPresenter_MouseMove"
        MouseLeftButtonUp="InkPresenter_MouseLeftButtonUp"
        />
</Border>
```

Well, you might want to add a Border around it to add a bit of definition. Just declare an InkPresenter, give it a name, set the background to something (white, if you want it to be like a standard drawing canvas), and give it some substantial height and width; finally, you need to handle the three usual suspects for drag-and-drop operations: left mouse button down, mouse move, and button up.

```csharp
System.Windows.Ink.Stroke _Stroke;
private void InkPresenter_MouseLeftButtonDown(object sender,
  MouseButtonEventArgs e)
{
    _Stroke = new System.Windows.Ink.Stroke();
    _Stroke.StylusPoints.Add(
      e.StylusDevice.GetStylusPoints(this.Inker));
    _Stroke.DrawingAttributes.Color = Colors.Black;
    this.Inker.Strokes.Add(_Stroke);
}
```

You'll need to define a class member of type Stroke. This serves two purposes: First, it provides an indicator of whether or not there is a current drag in progress (similar to the Boolean field used in the pop-up drag-and-drop), and second, it is what the inking infrastructure will use to record the actual drawing, on a per-stroke basis.

So in the mouse down handler, you create a new stroke and add the initial stroke information using the event argument's `StylusDevice.GetStylusPoints` method. You then just add the returned value to the stroke's `StylusPoints` collection. Finally, you may want to modify the `DrawingAttributes` (things like width, color, etc.); the code above just sets the color to black. And, last, add the new stroke to the `InkPresenter`'s `Strokes` collection for it to display the stroke.

Note that you don't need to capture the mouse. If you do, Silverlight will allow you to draw out of the `InkPresenter`'s bounds, which is almost certainly not what you want. But if you did, that's how you'd get it to do that.

```
private void InkPresenter_MouseMove(object sender, MouseEventArgs e)
{
    if (_Stroke != null)
    {
        _Stroke.StylusPoints.Add(e.StylusDevice.GetStylusPoints
            (this.Inker));
    }
}
```

As the mouse moves inside the presenter, its `MouseMove` handler is called. In that handler, you check to see if there is a current stroke using the `_Stroke` field you defined before. Recall that it serves a dual purpose of recording the stroke and that there is a current drag in progress. If there is a current stroke, you just add the new stylus points to the stroke's collection as you did for the initial mouse down handler.

The last thing you do is clear out the current stroke when the mouse button is released:

```
private void InkPresenter_MouseLeftButtonUp(object sender,
    MouseButtonEventArgs e)
{
    _Stroke = null;
}
```

Although this is a rather simplistic inking example, it demonstrates the essential facilities that Silverlight provides to ink-enable your applications on the Web. For Tablet PC (and other inking fans), this is a great addition to their Web toolkit. You can also use it to create basic drawing applications if your scenarios demand it.

> **An interesting use of this feature is shown at** www.tabletpcpost.com/search. **It uses Silverlight's ink capabilities along with character recognition to allow handwritten (ink-written) searches of Google. The recognition doesn't seem to be as good as Vista's, but it is cool nonetheless!**

Once you have added the `InkPresenter` and related code, you'll be able to do neat stuff like write (or mousepad, in my case!) messages to the world, as shown in Figure 16-11.

Figure 16-11

That wraps it up for responding to user input in your Silverlight applications. Every application you build in Silverlight will draw on these techniques and facilities. The stuff we covered here is fundamental and essential to user interaction, and everything else is derived from it. Obviously, you will want to take advantage of the more advanced controls provided to speed development and keep maintenance costs low. Microsoft has a pretty good offering out-of-the-box and in their supplemental toolkit, and third-parties like Infragistics will definitely be adding even more value on top of that.

Personalization

One of the surest ways to make your application come alive to your users is to personalize it for them. There are good ways and not so good ways to do this, of course. There is the idea of an *adaptive interface* that learns from the user and modifies itself according to the user's habits. The problem with this is that it can be very difficult to get right and very easy to get wrong — just remember the feature in Office that would try to hide rarely used commands in the menus?

More common (and reliable) forms of personalization lean on the user to explicitly opt in to choices. For some time, it has been popular to allow users to change the theme of their applications; you'll want to think about whether or not this is good. The theme can definitely affect a user's experience, and it certainly has an impact on their perception (or lack of perception) of your brand.

Probably the single most useful personalization feature across all applications is simply sharing a user's settings across multiple installations of the same application. After all, if you allow users to change settings, it is almost certain they don't want to reset the same settings over and over again. Since Silverlight 3 doesn't inherently have a personalization framework (or even basic user settings), the onus will be on you to make one. Making these settings persist across browsers, machines, and the like will involve storing them on your servers, but since Silverlight is a Web technology, this shouldn't come as a surprise.

You could create your own personalization store, or you could build on what you started in Chapter 13 and take advantage of the ASP.NET Profile provider and corresponding ready-made WCF service. So if you start with that, you already have your authentication framework in place. All you need to do now is add the profile stuff.

First, you need to add a new service file in your web site's Services directory. An easy way to do this is to just copy the Authentication.svc and rename it *Profile.svc* and then update the ServiceHost declaration:

```
<%@ ServiceHost Language="C#"
      Service="System.Web.ApplicationServices.ProfileService" %>
```

Next, as you did for the other services, add the service to the system.serviceModel/services section in the web.config:

```
<service
    name="System.Web.ApplicationServices.ProfileService"
    behaviorConfiguration="ProfileServiceTypeBehaviors">
  <endpoint
    contract="System.Web.ApplicationServices.ProfileService"
    binding="basicHttpBinding" bindingConfiguration="userHttp"
    bindingNamespace="http://asp.net/ApplicationServices/v200"/>
</service>
```

Notice that you're reusing the same basicHttpBinding you already defined. And then add the behavior definition to the system.serviceModel/behaviors/serviceBehaviors section:

```
<behavior name="ProfileServiceTypeBehaviors">
  <serviceMetadata httpGetEnabled="true"/>
</behavior>
```

Now, if you don't already have a profile section defined, add one to the system.web section. For example:

```
<profile>
  <properties>
    <add name="PreferredTheme"
         type="string" defaultValue="Orange Smoothy" />
  </properties>
</profile>
```

In real apps, of course, you will most likely have a whole host of things — whatever extra information you want to store about your users. For this example, we're just keeping it simple and doing a theme setting.

The last thing on the server side is that you need to enable the profile functionality to be accessed via the service, so in the system.web.extensions/scripting/webservices section, add the following:

```
<profileService
  enabled="true"
  readAccessProperties="PreferredTheme"
  writeAccessProperties="PreferredTheme" />
```

Now, to test out your config, right-click on your Profile.svc and select "View in Browser." If there are no errors, you're ready to move on to the client. Right-click on the Silverlight application, choose "Add Service Reference," and click Discover. You should see the services you have configured; select the Profile service and give it a namespace, for example, Services.Profile. Visual Studio should generate your proxies for you.

Now, before you move on, it is probably best to define your profile client-side class, so add a *Personalization* (or whatever you want to call it) folder and in it add an AppProfile.cs class like the following:

```csharp
public sealed class AppProfile
{
  AppSettings _Settings = new AppSettings();
  public AppSettings Settings
  {
    get
    {
      return _Settings;
    }
  }

}

public sealed class AppSettings : INotifyPropertyChanged
{
  ThemeInfo _Theme = Themes.Default;
  public ThemeInfo Theme
  {
    get
    {
      return _Theme;
    }
    set
    {
      if (value != _Theme)
      {
        _Theme = value;
        this.OnPropertyChanged("Theme");
      }
    }
  }

  #region INotifyPropertyChanged Members
  public event PropertyChangedEventHandler PropertyChanged;
  internal void OnPropertyChanged(string propertyName)
  {
    if (this.PropertyChanged != null)
    {
      this.PropertyChanged(this,
        new PropertyChangedEventArgs(propertyName));
    }
  }
  #endregion
}
```

The actual profile class is simple at this point. The idea is that you would expand it for things like user information (names, contact, etc.). For this example, you can just add a Settings property and the AppSettings class. This class will be used to store application settings/preferences. For now, just add a

Theme property (we'll look at the Theme types shortly). Make it implement INotifyPropertyChanged so that any bindings to its members will be updated; this will come in handy, as you'll see.

Next, add a ThemeInfo.cs file and put the following in it:

```
public sealed class ThemeInfo
{
  public ThemeInfo(string name, Brush background,
    Brush foreground, Brush dialogBackground,
    Brush buttonBackground)
  {
    this.Name = name;
    this.Background = background;
    this.Foreground = foreground;
    this.DialogBackground = dialogBackground;
    this.ButtonBackground = buttonBackground;
  }

  public string Name { get; private set; }
  public Brush Background { get; private set; }
  public Brush Foreground { get; private set; }
  public Brush DialogBackground { get; private set; }
  public Brush ButtonBackground { get; private set; }


}
```

Pretty straightforward — this class defines various properties that can be used to change the visual appearance of the application. Next, you should define some themes; one way to do that is adding a Themes class with some convenience properties and methods as follows:

```
public static class Themes
{
  const string BlackIceName = "Black Ice";
  public static ThemeInfo BlackIce
  {
    get
    {
      return new ThemeInfo(BlackIceName,
          new SolidColorBrush(Colors.Black),
          new SolidColorBrush(Colors.White),
          Gradient(Colors.White, Colors.Black, 0.07d),
          Gradient(Colors.White, Colors.Black, 0.3d));
    }
  }

  const string OrangeSmoothyName = "Orange Smoothy";
  public static ThemeInfo OrangeSmoothy
  {
    get
    {
      return new ThemeInfo(OrangeSmoothyName,
        new SolidColorBrush(Colors.Orange),
        new SolidColorBrush(Colors.White),
        Gradient(Colors.White, Colors.Orange, 0.07d),
```

```
                   Gradient(Colors.White, Colors.Orange, 0.3d));
        }
    }

    static GradientBrush Gradient(Color start, Color end,
      double endOffset)
    {
        LinearGradientBrush gb = new LinearGradientBrush();
        gb.StartPoint = new Point(0.5d, 0);
        gb.EndPoint = new Point(0.5d, 1);
        GradientStop stop = new GradientStop();
        stop.Color = start;
        stop.Offset = 0d;
        gb.GradientStops.Add(stop);
        stop = new GradientStop();
        stop.Color = end;
        stop.Offset = endOffset;
        gb.GradientStops.Add(stop);
        return gb;
    }

    public static ThemeInfo Default
    {
        get
        {
            return OrangeSmoothy;
        }
    }

    public static ThemeInfo GetThemeByName(string name)
    {
        switch (name)
        {
            case OrangeSmoothyName:
                return OrangeSmoothy;
            case BlackIceName:
                return BlackIce;
            default:
                return Default;
        }
    }
}
```

This class defines two preset themes, *Orange Smoothy* and *Black Ice*. It also provides a default as well as a facility to get theme information by name. If you were to go much further with this, you might want to consider creating, say, an XML schema that you can use to specify them, but this keeps it simple, maintaining the basic look-and-feel that you've designed but allowing users to select among a few different color palettes that you design. This addresses the concern about branding and experience because you retain full control of the theme options.

Now you need to plug your new profile goodness into your existing framework from Chapter 13. To do this, add a Profile property to your AppPrincipal class:

```
Personalization.AppProfile _Profile =
  new Personalization.AppProfile();
```

```
public Personalization.AppProfile Profile
{
  get
  {
    return _Profile;
  }
}
```

Now the profile (and app settings) will be available from the static App.CurrentUser property defined in Chapter 13. The next thing to do is update the SignIn user control to load the new profile settings, so in that control's code-behind, update the LoginCompleted method to — instead of displaying a success message and closing — tell the user that you are loading settings and make the call to do so:

```
void LoginCompleted(object sender,
    Services.Authentication.LoginCompletedEventArgs e)
{
  if (e.Error != null)
    [snipped]
  else
  {
    bool success = e.Result;
    if (!success)
      [snipped]
    else
    {
      App.CurrentUser =
        new Security.AppPrincipal((string)e.UserState, true);
      this.UserMessage.Text = "Loading your settings...";
      this.LoadProfile();
    }
  }
}
```

The LoadProfile method creates an instance of your new profile service proxy and calls to load all properties for the current user:

```
void LoadProfile()
{
  Services.Profile.ProfileServiceClient profile =
    new Services.Profile.ProfileServiceClient();
  profile.GetAllPropertiesForCurrentUserCompleted +=
    ProfileRetrieved;
  profile.GetAllPropertiesForCurrentUserAsync(false);
}
```

And the last thing in this class is to handle the callback for the profile properties loaded request:

```
void ProfileRetrieved(object sender,
    Services.Profile.GetAllPropertiesForCurrentUserCompletedEventArgs e)
{
  if (e.Error != null)
  {
    this.UserMessage.Text = "There's a problem loading " +
      "your settings. Default settings loaded instead.";
  }
```

```
   else
   {
     object val;
     if (e.Result.TryGetValue("PreferredTheme", out val))
       App.CurrentUser.Profile.Settings.Theme =
         Personalization.Themes.GetThemeByName((string)val);
     this.UserMessage.Text = "Settings loaded. Sign in complete.";
     this.Close();
   }
 }
```

Here, if there is success, you load the properties into the new `AppProfile` class. In this case, the code is just loading the one `Theme` setting.

So now you're all set with a fully loaded profile, what are you going to do with it? Since Silverlight 3 allows you to reuse resources at run time, there are a couple of ways to implement this style change. For this example, we'll go about implementing a custom theme provider that will give you a complete example of how you can use service calls and the profile service in ASP.NET in a complete personalization example.

As you saw in the `ThemeInfo` class, currently the app will only support changing the `Background`, `Foreground`, and more subtle control over dialog and button backgrounds.

First, change the background and foreground. To do that (and make it relatively easy to use in your app), you have to do a little prep work. First, create what I call a façade class; this class will serve as an instance to stick in your application `ResourceDictionary`:

```
public class AppSettingsStaticResource : INotifyPropertyChanged
{
  public AppSettingsStaticResource()
  {
    App.CurrentUserChanged += new EventHandler(App_CurrentUserChanged);
  }

  void App_CurrentUserChanged(object sender, EventArgs e)
  {
    this.OnPropertyChanged("Current");
  }

  public AppSettings Current
  {
    get
    {
      return App.CurrentUser.Profile.Settings;
    }
  }

  #region INotifyPropertyChanged Members
  public event PropertyChangedEventHandler PropertyChanged;
  internal void OnPropertyChanged(string propertyName)
  {
```

```
        if (this.PropertyChanged != null)
        {
          this.PropertyChanged(this,
            new PropertyChangedEventArgs(propertyName));
        }
      }
    #endregion
  }
```

Apart from implementing the INotifyPropertyChanged (again, so bindings will detect changes), this class simply exposes the current instance of the user's AppSettings. It subscribes to the App.CurrentUserChanged event (created in Chapter 13) so that when the user signs in or out, it will let any bindings know about the change by raising the OnPropertyChanged event specified in the INotifyPropertyChanged interface, which is what bindings look for to keep an eye on things.

Next, you need to stick this into your application ResourceDictionary, so in App.xaml, add an XML namespace pointing to your Personalization namespace where this class should be:

```
    xmlns:settings="clr-namespace:AppServices.Personalization"
```

Then add the façade class to its ResourceDictionary:

```
    <Application.Resources>
      <settings:AppSettingsStaticResource x:Key="Settings" />
    </Application.Resources>
```

What all this does is make your settings usable in XAML so that you can set up bindings against them and have changes be detected. To do such a binding, open Page.xaml, and on the UserControl element, add:

```
    Foreground="{Binding Current.Theme.Foreground, Source={StaticResource Settings}}"
```

(The line break is the result of the width constraint of the printed page and should be removed in the code.)

What this is doing is telling the binding to look for a static resource (*static* here means that it doesn't change, not that it is static as in C#, i.e., "shared") that has the key of "Settings" and, if it is found, bind it to the property path you specify, so the net result is that it will bind to App.CurrentUser.Profile .Settings.Theme.Foreground because, if you recall, the "Settings" resource you defined in App.xaml points to your façade (i.e., creates an instance of it and sticks it in that ResourceDictionary) that provides a Current property pointing to App.CurrentUser.Profile.Settings. Clear as mud, right?

Now, similarly bind your LayoutRoot grid's background like this:

```
    Background="{Binding Current.Theme.Background, Source={StaticResource Settings}}"
```

Now if you run your app, you should see these settings applied so they look something like Figure 16-12.

Figure 16-12

This is the Black Ice theme in action! But that only gets you part way because the SignIn XAML from Chapter 13 defines a specific look-and-feel that you want to "theme enable." So open up the SignIn.xaml file, and first update the Background on the Border to bind to the current theme's `DialogBackground`:

```
<Border CornerRadius="4,4,4,4" BorderThickness="1"
    Background="{Binding Current.Theme.DialogBackground, Source={StaticResource Settings}}">
```

That's one more step in the right direction, but you'll still have the stock button style, which is, well, stock. So why not spice it up a bit and at least match the theme? This is where the limitation of not being able to set `Style` properties more than once really bites. What you can do to work around that is create a new custom style (and template) for `Button` that effectively will bind to the button's `Background` property.

It takes some tweaking that would just take too much space here. Be sure to read Chapter 8 to understand how to do that; you can grab the `ThemeableButton` style out of the accompanying sample code (it's in App.xaml). But once you bind a gradient background to the `Button`'s `Background` property, you can then bind your buttons to your theme's `ButtonBackground` as follows:

```
<Button Height="23" Width="73.5"
    Canvas.Left="24" Canvas.Top="118.5"
    Content="Sign In!" x:Name="SignInButton"
    Click="SignInButton_Click"
    Background="{Binding Current.Theme.ButtonBackground, Source={StaticResource Settings}}"
    Style="{StaticResource ThemableButton}" >
</Button>
<Button Height="16" Width="17"
    Canvas.Left="267" Canvas.Top="4"
    Content="X" x:Name="CloseButton"
    Click="CloseButton_Click"
    Background="{Binding Current.Theme.ButtonBackground, Source={StaticResource Settings}}"
    Style="{StaticResource ThemableButton}" />
```

The net result is that now, if you run and sign in, the application will take on the new theme color palette. By default, if you refer back to the profile section you added to the web.config, it specifies a default preferred theme of Orange Smoothy, so when you log in with a user that has yet to specify one (all of them at this point), the theme will change from Black Ice (the default for the app) to Orange Smoothy, which looks like Figure 16-13, which is what shows just before the sign-in dialog fades out.

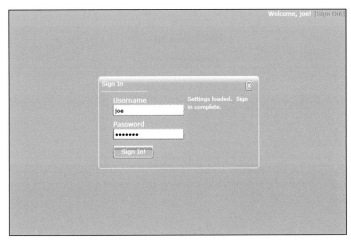

Figure 16-13

The next and final step is to save personalization settings back to the profile service. To enable this, add some UI to let the user pick a theme explicitly. A simple way is to just add the following to your Page.xaml:

```
<StackPanel HorizontalAlignment="Left" VerticalAlignment="Top"
  Orientation="Horizontal">
  <TextBlock Text="Theme" />
  <RadioButton
    x:Name="OrangeSmoothy" Content="Orange Smoothy"
    Foreground="{Binding Current.Theme.Foreground,
      Source={StaticResource Settings}}"
    GroupName="ThemeChoice" Margin="20,0,0,0"
    Click="RadioButton_Click" />
  <RadioButton
    x:Name="BlackIce" Content="Black Ice"
    Foreground="{Binding Current.Theme.Foreground,
      Source={StaticResource Settings}}"
    GroupName="ThemeChoice" Margin="20,0,0,0"
    Click="RadioButton_Click" />
</StackPanel>
```

This sets up a theme selector at the top-left of the screen. Figure 16-14 gives you an idea of what that looks like.

Figure 16-14

Then in your code-behind, update the `Page` constructor to select the current theme:

```
RadioButton rb =
  this.FindName(App.CurrentUser.Profile
  .Settings.Theme.Name.Replace(" ", ""))
  as RadioButton;
if (rb != null)
  rb.IsChecked = true;
```

And now add the `click` handler to update the theme based on the selection:

```
private void RadioButton_Click(object sender, RoutedEventArgs e)
{
  RadioButton r = sender as RadioButton;
  Personalization.ThemeInfo ti =
    Personalization.Themes.GetThemeByName((string)r.Content);
  App.CurrentUser.Profile.Settings.Theme = ti;
  if (App.CurrentUser.Identity.IsAuthenticated)
    App.CurrentUser.Profile.Save();
}
```

That's not quite enough, since you need to detect when something else changes the theme, which could happen in one of two ways — the theme is changed or the user signs in or out. So handle the relevant events as follows. First, you should refactor the selection code into its own method and add a check to see if it is checked (to avoid resetting the theme):

```
void SyncTheme()
{
  RadioButton rb =
    this.FindName(App.CurrentUser.Profile
```

```
        .Settings.Theme.Name.Replace(" ", ""))
      as RadioButton;
    if (rb != null && !(rb.IsChecked ?? false))
      rb.IsChecked = true;
  }
```

Then update your constructor to use that and subscribe to the change events for themes:

```
public Page()
{
  InitializeComponent();

  App.CurrentUserChanged += App_CurrentUserChanged;
  App.CurrentUser.Profile.Settings.PropertyChanged +=
    Settings_PropertyChanged;
  this.SyncTheme();
}
```

In the handler for the UserChanged event, you'll need to resubscribe to the theme change (because it will be a new instance) and sync up the theme:

```
void App_CurrentUserChanged(object sender, EventArgs e)
{
  App.CurrentUser.Profile.Settings.PropertyChanged +=
    Settings_PropertyChanged;
  this.SyncTheme();
}
```

In the settings Changed handler, check to see if it was the theme that changed and, if so, sync:

```
void Settings_PropertyChanged(object sender,
  System.ComponentModel.PropertyChangedEventArgs e)
{
  if (e.PropertyName == "Theme")
    this.SyncTheme();
}
```

Now you're all set to save the settings. Since you have only one property, it is lightweight enough to just do this each time the user changes the theme, but if you had many properties, as part of a dialog, you would probably have a Save button of some sort. In the theme change handler shown previously, you see that there is a check to see if the user is authenticated and, if so, to call Save on the profile. To implement this, open your AppProfile class and add a Save method like this one:

```
public void Save()
{
  Services.Profile.ProfileServiceClient profile =
    new Services.Profile.ProfileServiceClient();
  Dictionary<string, object> properties =
    new Dictionary<string,object>(1);
  properties["PreferredTheme"] =
    App.CurrentUser.Profile.Settings.Theme.Name;
  profile.SetPropertiesForCurrentUserAsync(properties, false);
}
```

You see that you do the inverse of what you did for loading (naturally!). There is a completion handler for this method as well, but since the app is saving in the background, it wouldn't make sense to notify the user of saving success or error. If you were explicitly requiring a user to press a Save button, though, you would want to handle the completion, ensure that there wasn't an error, and give the user feedback accordingly.

That wraps it up for personalization. It's hard to generalize about what you'd want to do for this aspect of your application, but it is important to keep in mind that adding personalization can definitely enhance the user experience, and persisting those settings across users' machines and browsers is preferable to just saving them locally in, for example, a cookie or IsolatedStorage.

Internationalization

Since Silverlight is a Web technology, being able to internationalize applications is extremely important. This section covers various facilities that Silverlight provides to make that possible. The run time itself is being provided in several (nine at writing) languages, including East Asian support with input via IME. This section covers a few aspects of internationalization; first, you'll see how to detect and change the current culture, then you see what facilities are there for globalizing your applications, and, finally, you'll see how you can localize it for specific locales you want to support.

Detecting Culture

Detecting the culture works the same way it does in standard .NET coding — you use the current thread's Culture and UICulture properties. For example, add this XAML to your page:

```
<StackPanel>
    <TextBlock x:Name="Culture"
               TextWrapping="Wrap" />
    <TextBlock x:Name="UICulture"
               TextWrapping="Wrap" />
    <Button
        x:Name="ColorButton"
        Width="200"
        VerticalAlignment="Top"
        HorizontalAlignment="Left" />
</StackPanel>
```

Then in your code, you can set these like this:

```
this.Culture.Text =
  "Current Culture: " +
    System.Threading.Thread.CurrentThread.CurrentCulture.DisplayName;
this.UICulture.Text =
  "Current UI Culture: " +
    System.Threading.Thread.CurrentThread.CurrentUICulture.DisplayName;
```

By default, Silverlight will inherit the OS's culture settings, but you can override those in one of two ways. First, you can set the culture and uiculture via param tags on the Silverlight object itself:

```
<param name="culture" value="en-GB" />
<param name="uiculture" value="en-GB" />
```

You can also do this in code:

```
System.Threading.Thread.CurrentThread.CurrentUICulture =
    new System.Globalization.CultureInfo("en-GB");
System.Threading.Thread.CurrentThread.CurrentCulture =
    new System.Globalization.CultureInfo("en-GB");
```

Overriding the culture may come in handy if you are making assumptions about the culture, for example, in your formatting and parsing operations. In those cases, you may want to override just the default culture, as it won't make sense to let your app break — at least it will work, even if you don't localize it.

One area, in particular, that can act a bit odd is currency formatting. By default, the .NET string formatting will use the locale's currency symbol, but if you are not actually converting your currency amounts to the user's locale, this can be misleading. Actually, it's almost certainly going to be just plain wrong. In that case, you'd want to override the culture or use culture-insensitive formatting for those specific situations, as covered in the next section.

Globalization

The idea of globalization is that you prepare your application to be localized as much as possible. If you do it from the get-go, you won't have to go back and rework things when you are ready to localize. Two of the core aspects of globalization in Silverlight (the same in .NET) are using resource files for string literals and any image resources that need to be localized, as well as using (or not using) the current culture info for formatting, parsing, and sorting.

Of course, these facilities will only get you so far. Your architecture may need to be even more global-aware in the sense of being able to adapt to different layout needs, such as making sure you use top label alignment (putting labels above inputs) to allow for changing widths of localized labels, and even differing input needs. For example, it is common to accept input of East Asian strings as well as Latin-based strings for things like addresses and names.

A complete course in globalization is outside the scope of this book, so if you are intending to localize, be sure to invest time up front to research the needs of your target locales and design your application accordingly. Then familiarize yourself with the features built into Silverlight/.NET that can help.

Resource Files

One such feature is the use of RESX files for resources that may need to be localized. As with .NET, you can simply add them to your projects, using the Add New Item dialog, selecting "Resources File," and entering the name you want. I typically create a *Common.resx* for common resources used throughout the application; another typical file I create is *Exceptions.resx* to store exception messages. Then you may want to create RESX files for individual user controls in your project, using a naming scheme like *MyControl.xaml.resx* to clearly associate a file with the control in question and limit its scope. You should create whatever makes sense for your needs.

> **You may need to manually set the Custom Tool property to** `ResXFileCodeGenerator` **by selecting the file and pressing [F4].**

If you get into the habit up front of using these, you will save yourself a lot of headache later when it comes time to localize.

Using Culture for String Operations

You also need to watch out for times when you need to override the user's locale. As mentioned previously, you may need to override things like sorting, parsing, and formatting. For instance, if you have a data source that has date values stored as strings in a local format (e.g., MM/DD/YYY, a U.S. format), you would need to take that into account in code that parses from that source into a `DateTime` object. For instance, if you have sales information stored in XML using U.S. date formats, when parsing it, you need to tell .NET to override the user's culture with a different format provider. Something like the following should work:

```
IFormatProvider usDates =
    System.Globalization.CultureInfo.GetCultureInfo(1033).DateTimeFormat;
```

Get the format provider from the English-US culture (1033), and then pass that into your parsing calls:

```
LastOrderReceived = DateTime.Parse(
    c.Element("SalesNote").Attribute("LastOrderReceived").Value, usDates)
```

Another case in which you may need to override is in formatting when displaying currency values. To do this, set up a static property on the App type like this:

```
static NumberFormatInfo _defaultNumberFormat;
public static NumberFormatInfo DefaultNumberFormat
{
    get
    {
        if (_defaultNumberFormat == null)
        {
            _defaultNumberFormat =
                (NumberFormatInfo)NumberFormatInfo.CurrentInfo.Clone();
            _defaultNumberFormat.CurrencySymbol = "$";
        }
        return _defaultNumberFormat;
    }
}
```

If all you want to do is override the currency symbol, you can grab a clone of the current number format and overwrite the `CurrencySymbol` with the U.S. dollar sign. Then use that in formatting currency values for display, for example:

```
total.ToString("c", App.DefaultNumberFormat)
```

Another case in which you may want to override culture is when sorting. If your data source is not culture-sensitive, you may want to force sorting operations to align with the data source's culture, in which case, you can pass in the desired culture info much as in the two previous examples.

Again, these sorts of things only get you so far. You will need to do research and understand your target locales and try to design flexibly enough to support them without much tweaking/specialization per locale.

Localization

Assuming that you spent the time to design your application for globalization, localizing into a specific culture should be much easier. If you didn't, you may have a lot of rework to do. In any case, it is almost certain that you won't have anticipated everything, but it's certain that trying to anticipate as much as possible will be worth your time.

The main effort of localization involves translation of resources (usually text and images with text), but you can certainly go deeper to understand and cater to particular locales. The facilities in Silverlight follow pretty closely those of the full .NET Framework, although there are a few extra steps required to get the packaging right:

1. You use RESX files as discussed previously to create your localized resources.

2. Add an assembly-level attribute to your AssemblyInfo file to specify the default, culture-neutral language for your application. For example:

    ```
    [assembly:NeutralResourcesLanguage("en")]
    ```

3. Unload the project in Solution Explorer and find the `SupportedCultures` tag. List in it any cultures that you intend to support, separated by semicolons.

4. Reload the project.

Now when you compile, the XAP should include subdirectories for each supported culture with satellite assemblies following the `<assemblyname>.resources.dll` naming convention. Then you use `ResourceManager` or the strongly typed wrappers as usual to get access to the localized resources.

> If you intend to support a lot of cultures or have a lot of resources, you may want to create separate build configurations for each language and then load the language-specific XAPs for the user. This part isn't built-in — you'll want to do it by detecting the user's language and/or letting her select it before loading the corresponding localized Silverlight application XAP file.

Dates and Times

Working with dates and times can become complex, but, thankfully, .NET and Silverlight have some facilities to help with that.

Retrieving Current Time

Any .NET programmer has probably done this one: `DateTime.Now`. The thing is, `DateTime` doesn't really do much for you in terms of dealing with time zones and differences in those. If that's not important to you, using it is fine. If not, you probably should think about `DateTimeOffset`.

Adjusting for Time Zones

The main tool for working with specific points in time, where differences in time zone matter, is `DateTimeOffset`. You can use `TimeZoneInfo`, but it is basically limited to `Local` and `Utc` (which just might be enough). If you need more, though, `DateTimeOffset` is the tool to use.

For example, let's say that you have a server in a different time zone and you want to know what that time zone is and potentially adjust for it to let the user know what time it is in terms of his time zone. This is a common need for applications that display logging where times are stored using the server time. In that case, using the `DateTimeOffset` can come in handy. To see what that is like, create a new Silverlight application and call it *DatesAndTimes*, and include the generated web app for the server time.

On the server app (the web site), right-click and add a Silverlight-enabled WCF Service, as shown in Figure 16-15.

In its code file, add the following operation:

```
[OperationContract]
public DateTimeOffset GetServerTime()
{
    return new DateTimeOffset(
        new DateTime(DateTime.Now.Ticks, DateTimeKind.Unspecified) +
            TimeSpan.FromHours(8).Add(TimeSpan.FromSeconds(73)),
            DateTimeOffset.Now.Offset + TimeSpan.FromHours(8));
}
```

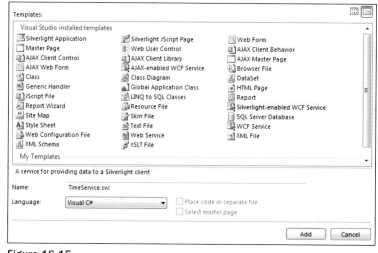

Figure 16-15

This is a bit goofy, but it's trying to emulate a server in another time zone that has a slightly different time from the real local time. You have to create a DateTime using DateTimeKind.Unspecified because .NET is smart and doesn't like it if you try to create a DateTimeOffset for a different time zone using a local DateTime object. Obviously, you'd rarely, if ever, need to do this in real apps.

Now, on your client, right-click and add a service reference to this service, putting it in a Services namespace. In your Page.xaml, add some text blocks to show different times:

```
<StackPanel>
    <TextBlock x:Name="LocalTime" />
    <TextBlock x:Name="ServerTime" />
    <TextBlock x:Name="ServerAdjustedTime" />
</StackPanel>
```

And in your code-behind, add a couple of class-level fields to keep an instance of a timer and one for the service proxy. Keeping the proxy at the class level is just for performance, so you don't to keep re-creating proxies (as it will be called every second).

```
System.Threading.Timer _TickTock;
Services.TimeServiceClient _ServerTime;
```

Then add a Loaded handler in the Page constructor:

```
public Page()
{
    InitializeComponent();

    this.Loaded += new RoutedEventHandler(Page_Loaded);
}
```

In your loaded handler, set up your proxy instance and start your timer:

```
void Page_Loaded(object sender, RoutedEventArgs e)
{
    _ServerTime = new Services.TimeServiceClient();
    _ServerTime.GetServerTimeCompleted +=
        ServerTime_GetServerTimeCompleted;
    _TickTock =
        new System.Threading.Timer(TimerTick, null, 0, 1000);
}
```

Now, every time the timer ticks (every second), the TimerTick callback will be called, as follows:

```
void TimerTick(object data)
{
    _ServerTime.GetServerTimeAsync();
    this.LocalTime.Dispatcher.BeginInvoke(
        delegate { this.LocalTime.Text = "Local Time: " +
            DateTime.Now.ToLongTimeString(); });
}
```

This calls the server's time service method to get the server time we set up previously. Then it sets the local time. Because the timer is set up on a background thread, you have to invoke changes to the UI using a UI object dispatcher (such as the one on `LocalTime` here).

The callback for the server time method is like this:

```
void ServerTime_GetServerTimeCompleted(object sender,
    DatesAndTimes.Services.GetServerTimeCompletedEventArgs e)
{
    this.ServerTime.Dispatcher.BeginInvoke(
        delegate
        {
            this.ServerTime.Text = "Server Time: " +
                e.Result.DateTime.ToLongTimeString() + " " +
                e.Result.Offset.ToString();
        });
    this.ServerAdjustedTime.Dispatcher.BeginInvoke(
        delegate
        {
            this.ServerAdjustedTime.Text = "Adjusted Server Time: " +
                e.Result.LocalDateTime.ToLongTimeString();
        });
}
```

It's doing two things. First, it shows the server time as is, including its UTC offset. Second, it uses the `DateTimeOffset`'s `LocalDateTime` property, which automatically calculates the local time based on its time and offset. The result of this is shown in Figure 16-16.

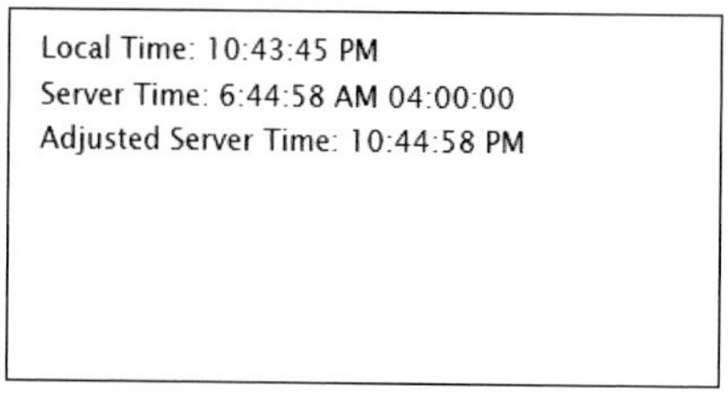

Local Time: 10:43:45 PM
Server Time: 6:44:58 AM 04:00:00
Adjusted Server Time: 10:44:58 PM

Figure 16-16

Astute readers will now be able to determine the author's time zone.

The reason that being aware of `DateTimeOffset` is important is that Silverlight is an n-tier technology by default — that is, the code running on the client will be running in the user's local time zone with the local settings, and it is going to be very likely that the server that backs up the application will be in another time zone. Web developers who are not used to thinking about this will need to keep that in mind, and if dealing with precise times is important to your application, you will definitely prefer using the `DateTimeOffset` over `DateTime`.

Summary

We covered a lot in this chapter. You dug in depth into the various ways that Silverlight receives user input and saw some techniques to enrich that. You saw how to add personalization services based on ASP.NET's profile provider and service. You saw how to make your application ready for the world and how to specialize it for particular locales, and, finally, you saw how to deal with dates and times in an RIA app that could have different time zones for its servers. All of these things combine toward enabling you to make your applications more interactive, adaptive, and resilient to enhance your users' experiences.

17

Creating Custom Controls

Silverlight 3 introduces an extensible control model, which you can leverage to encapsulate logic and common functionality. Custom controls allow you to follow the Silverlight pattern of separation between the presentation and logical functionality of the control. This architecture allows you to reuse functionality, while allowing a designer to completely change out the user interface displayed by the control.

In this chapter, you will discover how to:

❑   Create a Silverlight Class Library with a basic control.

❑   Reference a custom control from a Silverlight application.

❑   Work with the Parts Control Model.

❑   Take advantage of visual states.

❑   Create a dependency property.

❑   Build a content control.

Setting Up a Control Project

Start by creating a new Silverlight Class Library (SCL) in Visual Studio. This project can contain as many custom controls as you wish. For each custom control, create a new class that extends from `Control` or one of its subclasses.

Creating a `Control` Class

Silverlight exposes a handful of `Control` classes that you can extend. Selecting an appropriate class to extend will save you time when implementing the control and make your control easier to use. The following table lists a few of the base classes you can consider:

Class	Common Usage
Control	Provides only the essential functions for a control.
ContentControl	Used by controls that are expected to host content
Panel	Layout controls such as Grid, Canvas, StackPanel
ItemsControl	Used to display lists of items, often in data-bound scenarios

You can also extend from higher-level controls, such as a `ToggleButton`, if you find that the scenario your control targets is similar to another control in the framework.

For simplicity, the following example extends the core `Control` class; however, if you were creating a fully functional button, you would be well served to extend an existing button class such as `ButtonBase`.

```
namespace Wrox.Silverlight30.Controls
{
  public class CustomButton : Control
  {

  }
}
```

Defining a Default Control Template

You can associate a default Control Template with your control, which will provide default rendering when placed in a Silverlight application. As with any Silverlight control, a developer can choose to override this template. Three steps are required to set things up:

1. Create and embed a XAML resource in the assembly.

2. Define a resource dictionary that sets the Control Template.

3. Specify the `DefaultStyleKey` in your control's constructor.

Creating generic.xaml

To provide a default rendering for your control, you will need to create a new XAML filename — generic.xaml. This file must be located in a folder named *themes* off the root of your control project. Since Visual Studio does not offer "XAML file" from the Add New Item Wizard, select new "Text File," and name it *generic.xaml* (see Figure 17-1).

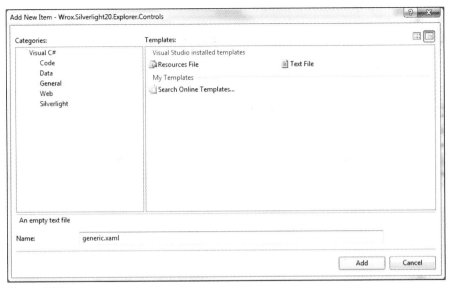

Figure 17-1

Next, adjust the project properties for generic.xaml so that it is included as a resource in the output assembly, and clear out the associated "Custom Tool," as shown in Figure 17-2.

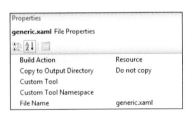

Figure 17-2

Providing a Style for the Control

Generic.xaml should include a resource dictionary with a Control Template defined for each control in your project. Begin by including a custom namespace reference to the document:

```
<ResourceDictionary
    xmlns="http://schemas.microsoft.com/winfx/2006/xaml/presentation"
    xmlns:x="http://schemas.microsoft.com/winfx/2006/xaml"
    xmlns:wrox="clr-namespace:Wrox.Silverlight30.CustomControls.
        Button;assembly=Wrox.Silverlight30.CustomControls.Button"
    >
</ResourceDictionary>
Silverlight30Silverlight30
```

Next, define a style that sets the template property to a new Control Template. Note that the `TargetType` for both the `Style` and `ControlTemplate` reference your control class:

```xml
<ResourceDictionary
    xmlns="http://schemas.microsoft.com/winfx/2006/xaml/presentation"
    xmlns:x="http://schemas.microsoft.com/winfx/2006/xaml"
    xmlns:wrox="clr-namespace:Wrox.Silverlight30.CustomControls.
        Button;assembly=Wrox.Silverlight30.CustomControls.Button"
>

    <Style TargetType="wrox:CustomButton">
      <Setter Property="Width" Value="100" />
      <Setter Property="Height" Value="32" />
      <Setter Property="Template">
        <Setter.Value>
          <ControlTemplate TargetType="wrox:CustomButton">
            <Grid x:Name="LayoutRoot">
            </Grid>
          </ControlTemplate>
        </Setter.Value>
      </Setter>
    </Style>
</ResourceDictionary>Silverlight30Silverlight30
```

As discussed in Chapter 8, you are free to specify other information in your style such as a more complex `ControlTemplate`, `StoryBoards`, `VisualStateGroups`, and other property setters. For instance, you can specify a size for the control and a basic rendering:

```xml
<ResourceDictionary
    xmlns="http://schemas.microsoft.com/winfx/2006/xaml/presentation"
    xmlns:x="http://schemas.microsoft.com/winfx/2006/xaml"
    xmlns:wrox="clr-namespace:Wrox.Silverlight30.CustomControls.
        Button;assembly=Wrox.Silverlight30.CustomControls.Button"
>

    <Style TargetType="wrox:CustomButton">
      <Setter Property="Width" Value="100" />
      <Setter Property="Height" Value="32" />
      <Setter Property="Template">
        <Setter.Value>
          <ControlTemplate TargetType="wrox:CustomButton">
            <Grid x:Name="LayoutRoot">
              <Rectangle HorizontalAlignment="Stretch"
                  VerticalAlignment="Stretch"
                  Stroke="#FF000000" StrokeThickness="5" RadiusY="5"
                  RadiusX="5"/>
            </Grid>
          </ControlTemplate>
        </Setter.Value>
      </Setter>
    </Style>
</ResourceDictionary>Silverlight30Silverlight30
```

Attaching the Style to the Control

The final step is to let your control know what key it should look for in generic.xaml for its default Control Template. This is achieved by setting the `DefaultStyleKey` property in your constructor:

```
namespace Wrox.Silverlight30.CustomControls.Button
{
  public class CustomButton : Control
  {
    public CustomButton() : base()
    {
      this.DefaultStyleKey = typeof(CustomButton);
    }
  }
}
```

Using a Custom Control in an Application

Now that you have a basic custom control, the next logical step is going to be checking it out in a running Silverlight application. Begin by adding a reference to the assembly that contains your control. As shown in Figure 17-3, to keep things simple, we will use a project reference.

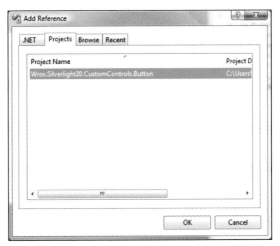

Figure 17-3

Now from Page.xaml, include the namespace for your control and include an instance of our custom control:

```
<UserControl x:Class="Wrox.Silverlight30.CustomControls.ButtonApp.Page"
    xmlns="http://schemas.microsoft.com/winfx/2006/xaml/presentation"
    xmlns:x="http://schemas.microsoft.com/winfx/2006/xaml"
```

```
    xmlns:wrox="clr-namespace:Wrox.Silverlight30.CustomControls.
        Button;assembly=Wrox.Silverlight30.CustomControls.Button"
    Width="400" Height="300">

  <Grid x:Name="LayoutRoot" Background="White">
    <StackPanel>
      <wrox:CustomButton />
    </StackPanel>
  </Grid>
</UserControl>Silverlight30Silverlight30Silverlight30
```

Voilà! We have a custom control rendering in our Silverlight application (see Figure 17-4).

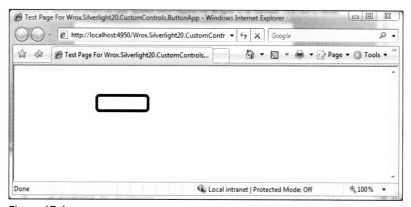

Figure 17-4

Styling the Custom Control

A custom control can be manipulated just like any other Silverlight control. For instance, you can override the default template and replace it with something a bit more visually interesting by setting the template with one defined in a style resource:

```
<UserControl x:Class="Wrox.Silverlight30.CustomControls.ButtonApp.Page"
    xmlns="http://schemas.microsoft.com/winfx/2006/xaml/presentation"
    xmlns:x="http://schemas.microsoft.com/winfx/2006/xaml"
    xmlns:wrox="clr-namespace:Wrox.Silverlight30.CustomControls.
        Button;assembly=Wrox.Silverlight30.CustomControls.Button"
    Width="400" Height="300">

  <UserControl.Resources>
    <LinearGradientBrush x:Key="StarBrush"
          StartPoint="0.3089005235602094,0.07222222222222222"
          EndPoint="0.9947643979057592,1.238888888888889">
      <LinearGradientBrush.GradientStops>
        <GradientStopCollection>
          <GradientStop      Color="#FFffff00"   Offset="0" />
          <GradientStop      Color="#FFf0f0f0"   Offset="0.9944" />
        </GradientStopCollection>
```

```
      </LinearGradientBrush.GradientStops>
    </LinearGradientBrush>
    <ControlTemplate x:Key="StarControlTemplate">
      <Grid>
        <Path    Margin="0,0,0,0"
         HorizontalAlignment="Left" VerticalAlignment="Top"
         Stretch="Fill" Opacity="1"
         Data="M 96,0 C96,0 117,70 117,70 117,70 191,69 191,69 191,69 130,111
130,111 130,111 154,180 154,180 154,180 96,136 96,136 96,136 37,180 37,180 37,180
61,111 61,111 61,111 0,69 0,69 0,69 74,70 74,70 74,70 96,0 96,0 z"
         Fill="{StaticResource StarBrush}"
         Width="{TemplateBinding Width}"
         Height="{TemplateBinding Width}"  />
      </Grid>
    </ControlTemplate>
  </UserControl.Resources>

  <Grid x:Name="LayoutRoot" Background="White">
    <StackPanel>
      <wrox:CustomButton />
      <wrox:CustomButton Template="{StaticResource StarControlTemplate}"
          Width="100" Height="100" />
    </StackPanel>
  </Grid>
</UserControl>Silverlight30Silverlight30Silverlight30
```

When run, this application shows the same control with two distinct rendering styles (see Figure 17-5).

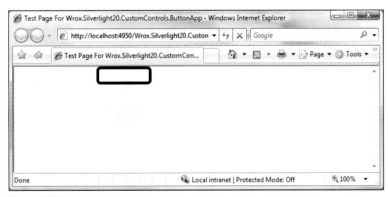

Figure 17-5

The Parts Control Model

So far, we have looked at a control that was essentially composed of one visual element, and there was no logic to handle interaction with that element. More sophisticated controls can be segmented into logically different visual elements. Silverlight addresses the need to have distinct visual areas of a control and still be able to completely customize its rendering with the Parts Model.

When creating a control, there are three steps to taking advantage of the Parts Model:

1. Attributing the control class with the names and types of the Template Parts that are expected
2. Overriding OnApplyTemplate to identify Template Parts within the supplied Control Template
3. Creating a Control Template with elements that correspond to the expected Template Parts

Identifying Control Template Parts

The TemplatePart class attribute is used to specify which parts a control expects. These attributes come in handy when a Design Surface, such as Blend, wishes to expose the expected Template Parts to a developer.

Two parameters are expected by the TemplatePart attribute: name and type. The name corresponds to the x:Name attribute that is applied in XAML to the element that represents the Template Part. The type parameter specifies the type of element that the control expects. This type could be as general as FrameworkElement or could be a specific control type such as CheckBox. When deciding which type to expect for each part, it is best to be as general as is feasible. Specifying a granular type will reduce the flexibility that a designer will have in providing a custom template.

To demonstrate the Parts Model, let's walk through building a PartButton control that expects one Template Part, defining the visual element that should be used to indicate a Button click:

```
[TemplatePart(Name = "ClickRegion", Type = typeof(FrameworkElement))]
public class PartButton : Control
```

In this case, we have no specific needs from the Template Part aside from exposing Mouse Events, so selecting FrameworkElement as the type of the part allows for the most flexibility.

Since we are going to be referencing the string identified for this part elsewhere in our control, it will help to make a static member to hold this value:

```
[TemplatePart(Name = PartButton.ClickRegionPartName,
              Type = typeof(FrameworkElement))]
public class PartButton: Control
{
    // The Name of the Element expected for our Click Region
    private const string ClickRegionPartName = "ClickRegion";
```

Mapping Template Parts in OnApplyTemplate

OnApplyTemplate is called whenever ApplyTemplate is invoked on a control. Normally, the Silverlight rendering framework handles invoking this method at the appropriate time. Custom controls that wish to take advantage of the Template Part Model need to perform the logic to find each Template Part within OnApplyTemplate. Finding the matching element can be accomplished with a call to GetTemplateChild:

```
// The Name of the Element expected for our Click Region
private const string ClickRegionPartName = "ClickRegion";

// Private member to hold our Click Region Template Part
```

```
private FrameworkElement _clickRegionElement;

public override void OnApplyTemplate()
{
  base.OnApplyTemplate();

  // Find our Click Region Template Part
  _clickRegionElement =
    GetTemplateChild(ClickRegionPartName) as FrameworkElement;
}
```

Hooking Up Event Handlers to Template Parts

In the case of our PartButton, we are going to want to hook up an event handler for when the Template Part is clicked. Be mindful that ApplyTemplate can be called multiple times, so it is important to clear out any existing event handlers before grabbing the Template Part.

Silverlight controls are expected to gracefully handle missing Template Parts, so make sure to add some null reference checks after looking for a particular part.

```
public override void OnApplyTemplate()
{
  base.OnApplyTemplate();

  // Clear out event hanlders if this is not the first template applied
  if (_clickRegionElement != null)
  {
    _clickRegionElement.MouseLeftButtonUp -=
      new MouseButtonEventHandler(clickRegion_MouseLeftButtonUp);
  }
  // Find our Click Region Template Part
  _clickRegionElement =
    GetTemplateChild(ClickRegionPartName) as FrameworkElement;

  if (_clickRegionElement != null)
  {
    // Hook up a new event handler for the Mouse LeftButtonUp
    _clickRegionElement.MouseLeftButtonUp +=
      new MouseButtonEventHandler(clickRegion_MouseLeftButtonUp);
  }
}
private void clickRegion_MouseLeftButtonUp(object sender,
  MouseButtonEventArgs e)
{
  // Mouse Click Logic
}
```

Before moving on, let's finally make this control exhibit the most basic functionality of a button, the Click event:

```
// Click Event
public event EventHandler<EventArgs> Click;

private void clickRegion_MouseLeftButtonUp(object sender,
```

```
                MouseButtonEventArgs e)
        {
          if (Click != null)
          {
            this.Click(this, EventArgs.Empty);
          }
        }
```

Using Template Parts in a Control Template

Now that we have a control exposing what Template Parts it expects and searching for them in `OnApplyTemplate`, we need to provide it with what it is asking for. Start by including the template parts in generic.xaml. All that is required is adding elements with a `Name` attribute that matches the Template Part name, and making sure that it is of the right type. For the `PartButton`, all that is required is a `FrameworkElement` with a name of `"ClickRegion"`.

```
<ResourceDictionary
    xmlns="http://schemas.microsoft.com/winfx/2006/xaml/presentation"
    xmlns:x="http://schemas.microsoft.com/winfx/2006/xaml"
    xmlns:wrox="clr-namespace:Wrox.Silverlight30.CustomControls.PartButton">
<Style TargetType="wrox:PartButton">
  <Setter Property="Width" Value="100" />
  <Setter Property="Height" Value="32" />
  <Setter Property="Template">
    <Setter.Value>
      <ControlTemplate TargetType="wrox:PartButton">
        <Grid x:Name="LayoutRoot">
          <Rectangle x:Name="ClickRegion"
                  HorizontalAlignment="Stretch"
                  VerticalAlignment="Stretch" Stroke="#FF000000"
              StrokeThickness="5"
                  RadiusY="5" RadiusX="5"/>
        </Grid>
      </ControlTemplate>
    </Setter.Value>
  </Setter>
</Style>
</ResourceDictionary>

Silverlight30
```

Providing a Custom Template for a Parts-Based Control

If you are looking to override the Control Template for a control that uses the Parts Model, make sure to include elements that match what the control expects. Just like in generic.xaml, all that is needed is an element with the appropriate name and type:

```
<UserControl x:Class="PartButtonApp.Page"
    xmlns="http://schemas.microsoft.com/winfx/2006/xaml/presentation"
    xmlns:x="http://schemas.microsoft.com/winfx/2006/xaml"
    xmlns:wrox="clr-namespace:Wrox.Silverlight30.CustomControls.
        PartButton;assembly=Wrox.Silverlight30.CustomControls.PartButton"
    Width="400" Height="300">

    <!-- Define a Brush and a Style containing a new template-->
```

```xml
<UserControl.Resources>
  <LinearGradientBrush x:Key="StarBrush"
        StartPoint="0.3089005235602094,0.07222222222222222"
        EndPoint="0.9947643979057592,1.238888888888889">
    <LinearGradientBrush.GradientStops>
      <GradientStopCollection>
        <GradientStop Color="#FFffff00"      Offset="0" />
        <GradientStop Color="#FFf0f0f0"      Offset="0.9944" />
      </GradientStopCollection>
    </LinearGradientBrush.GradientStops>
  </LinearGradientBrush>
  <ControlTemplate x:Key="StarControlTemplate">
    <Grid>
      <Path x:Name="ClickRegion" Margin="0,0,0,0" HorizontalAlignment="Left"
        VerticalAlignment="Top" Stretch="Fill" Opacity="1"
        Data="M 96,0 C96,0 117,70 117,70 117,70 191,69 191,69 191,69 130,111
130,111 130,111 154,180 154,180 154,180 96,136 96,136 96,136 37,180 37,180 37,180
61,111 61,111 61,111 0,69 0,69 0,69 74,70 74,70 74,70 96,0 96,0 z"
        Fill="{StaticResource StarBrush}"
Width="32"
Height="32"
        />
    </Grid>
  </ControlTemplate>
</UserControl.Resources>

<Grid x:Name="LayoutRoot" Background="White">
  <StackPanel>
    <!-- CustomButton with default control template-->
    <wrox:PartButton x:Name="PartButton1" />

    <!-- CustomButton with control template from a resource-->
    <wrox:PartButton x:Name="PartButton2" Template="{StaticResource
        StarControlTemplate}" />

    <TextBlock x:Name="ClickTextBlock" TextAlignment="Center"/>
  </StackPanel>
</Grid>
</UserControl>
Silverlight30Silverlight30
```

Let's also verify that our Click event is firing correctly:

```csharp
public partial class Page : UserControl
{
  public Page()
  {
    InitializeComponent();
    Loaded += new RoutedEventHandler(Page_Loaded);
  }

  void Page_Loaded(object sender, RoutedEventArgs e)
  {
    this.PartButton1.Click += new EventHandler<EventArgs>(Button_Click);
```

```
        this.PartButton2.Click += new EventHandler<EventArgs>(Button_Click);
    }

    void Button_Click(object sender, EventArgs e)
    {
        PartButton button = sender as PartButton;
        this.ClickTextBlock.Text = button.Name + " Clicked";
    }
}
```

When run, this application exhibits the behavior shown in Figure 17-6 when the user clicks within the control.

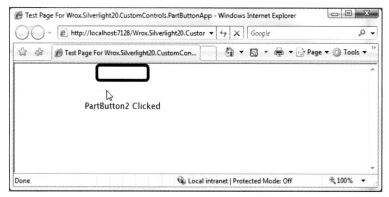

Figure 17-6

Taking Advantage of Visual States

Silverlight includes a new Visual State Model, which addresses the need to allow the control to have different visual representations for different logical states. This extensible model allows the control developer to offer common logical states such as MouseOver or MousePress as well as states related to the precise functionality of a control, such as the checked state of a CheckBox.

The VisualStateManager object provides the foundation and logic needed to transition fluidly between states. It allows the Control Template to define both the visual appearance for a particular state and how transitions should occur between states.

Adding Visual State support for a control can be accomplished in three steps:

1. Attributing the control class with information about the Visual States it supports
2. Leveraging the VisualStateManager object to specify the current state of the control
3. Creating a Control Template with display information for each Visual State

Identifying Visual States for a Control

The `TemplateVisualState` class attribute is used to identify what Visual States a control supports. Each state is defined by two strings, representing the unique state name and what logical group the state belongs to. Groups are used to identify Visual States that are mutually exclusive. A control can be in two logical states as long as those states are in different `StateGroups`. The following shows a new `StateButton` custom control with several states relating to mouse interaction:

```
// Visual State Definitions
[TemplateVisualState(Name = "Normal", GroupName = "CommonStates")]
[TemplateVisualState(Name = "MouseOver", GroupName = "CommonStates")]
[TemplateVisualState(Name = "Pressed", GroupName = "CommonStates")]
public class StateButton : Control
```

In a manner similar to the way we handled Template Part names, it will help to declare the Visual State identifiers as constants:

```
// Visual State Definitions
[TemplateVisualState(Name = NormalStateName,
  GroupName = CommonStatesGroupName)]
[TemplateVisualState(Name = MouseOverStateName,
  GroupName = CommonStatesGroupName)]
[TemplateVisualState(Name = PressedStateName,
  GroupName = CommonStatesGroupName)]
public class StateButton : Control
  {

    // Constants for Visual States
    private const string CommonStatesGroupName = "CommonStates";
    private const string NormalStateName = "Normal";
    private const string MouseOverStateName = "MouseOver";
    private const string PressedStateName = "Pressed";
```

Adjusting the Active Visual State

Now that you have identified the Visual States you expect, the control needs to ensure that it lets the `VisualStateManager` know when a logical state change occurs. It is highly recommended that this be done in centralized methods in your control to avoid unnecessary calls to the `VisualStateManager` and confusion as to the actual logical state of the control.

Begin by adding members to track the current logical state of the control:

```
// Members to track the current state
private bool _isMouseOver = false;
private bool _isPressed = false;
```

In the `StateButton` custom control, we also include a new `EnsureVisualState` method, which calls the `VisualStateManager`'s `GoToState` method. The `GoToState` method takes a parameter indicating if a transition should be used when moving to a new Visual State. Since our `VisualStates` are all in the same group, no two can be active at the same time. Here we make the decision that in the `StateControl`, the Pressed Visual State takes precedence over the `MouseOver` state:

```
private void EnsureVisualState(bool useTransitions)
{
  // Move to the appropriate State for the CommonStates group
  if (_isPressed)
  {
    VisualStateManager.GoToState(this,
      PressedStateName, useTransitions);

  }
  else if (_isMouseOver)
  {
    VisualStateManager.GoToState(this,
      MouseOverStateName, useTransitions);
  }
  else
  {
    VisualStateManager.GoToState(this,
      NormalStateName, useTransitions);
  }
}
```

Since we initially invoke our method from `OnApplyTemplate` and there is no state to transition from, we will not ask for a transition to take place. We also add event handlers to trigger changes in the Visual State.

```
// The Name of the Element expected for our Click Region
private const string ClickShapePartName = "ClickRegion";

// Private member to hold our Click Region Template Part
private FrameworkElement _clickRegionElement;

public override void OnApplyTemplate()
{
  base.OnApplyTemplate();

  // Clear out event hanlders if this is not the first template applied
  if (_clickRegionElement != null)
  {
    _clickRegionElement.MouseLeftButtonUp -=
      new MouseButtonEventHandler(clickRegion_MouseLeftButtonUp);
    _clickRegionElement.MouseEnter -=
      new MouseEventHandler(clickRegion_MouseEnter);
    _clickRegionElement.MouseLeave -=
      new MouseEventHandler(clickRegion_MouseLeave);
    _clickRegionElement.MouseLeftButtonDown -=
      new MouseButtonEventHandler(clickRegion_MouseLeftButtonDown);
  }
  // Find our Click Region Template Part
  _clickRegionElement =
    GetTemplateChild(ClickShapePartName) as FrameworkElement;
```

```
      if (_clickRegionElement != null)
      {
        // Hook up a new event handlers
        _clickRegionElement.MouseLeftButtonUp +=
          new MouseButtonEventHandler(clickRegion_MouseLeftButtonUp);
        _clickRegionElement.MouseEnter +=
          new MouseEventHandler(clickRegion_MouseEnter);
        _clickRegionElement.MouseLeave +=
          new MouseEventHandler(clickRegion_MouseLeave);
        _clickRegionElement.MouseLeftButtonDown +=
          new MouseButtonEventHandler(clickRegion_MouseLeftButtonDown);
      }

      // Reset the current state, no need to transition
      _isMouseOver = false;
      _isPressed = false;
      EnsureVisualState(false);
    }
```

Finally, we add logic to our event handlers to adjust the logical state of the control and trigger our EnsureVisualState method:

```
    // Click Event
    public event EventHandler<EventArgs> Click;

    void clickRegion_MouseLeftButtonDown(object sender,
      MouseButtonEventArgs e)
    {
      _isPressed = true;
      EnsureVisualState(true);
    }

    private void clickRegion_MouseLeave(object sender,
      MouseEventArgs e)
    {
      _isMouseOver = false;
      EnsureVisualState(true);
    }

    private void clickRegion_MouseEnter(object sender,
      MouseEventArgs e)
    {
      _isMouseOver = true;
      EnsureVisualState(true);
    }

    private void clickRegion_MouseLeftButtonUp(object sender,
      MouseButtonEventArgs e)
    {
      _isPressed = false;
      EnsureVisualState(true);

      if (Click != null)
```

```
    {
      this.Click(this, EventArgs.Empty);
    }
  }
```

Visual States in a Control Template

The last step in supporting visual states is adding them to our default Control Template in generic.xaml. Essentially, we need to provide a `StoryBoard` for each state and a `VisualTransition` that defines how the control visually moves between different states.

Start by declaring the Groups for the control on the root visual element of the Control Template:

```
<ResourceDictionary
    xmlns="http://schemas.microsoft.com/winfx/2006/xaml/presentation"
    xmlns:x="http://schemas.microsoft.com/winfx/2006/xaml"
    xmlns:vsm="clr-namespace:System.Windows;assembly=System.Windows"
    xmlns:wrox="clr-namespace:Wrox.Silverlight30.CustomControls.StateButton">
  <Style TargetType="wrox:StateButton">
    <Setter Property="Width" Value="100" />
    <Setter Property="Height" Value="32" />
    <Setter Property="Template">
      <Setter.Value>
        <ControlTemplate TargetType="wrox:StateButton">
          <Grid x:Name="LayoutRoot">
            <vsm:VisualStateManager.VisualStateGroups>
              <vsm:VisualStateGroup x:Name="CommonStates">
                <vsm:VisualState x:Name="Normal"/>
                <vsm:VisualState x:Name="MouseOver" />
              </vsm:VisualStateGroup>
            </vsm:VisualStateManager.VisualStateGroups>

            <Rectangle x:Name="ClickRegion"
                    HorizontalAlignment="Stretch"
                    VerticalAlignment="Stretch" Stroke="#FF000000"
               Fill="White" StrokeThickness="5" RadiusY="5"
                    RadiusX="5" />
          </Grid>
        </ControlTemplate>
      </Setter.Value>
    </Setter>
  </Style>
</ResourceDictionary>Silverlight30
```

VisualState Elements

For each state of the control, we now need to provide a matching `VisualState` element that includes the name of the state and an appropriate `StoryBoard`. If the `StoryBoard` has duration of zero, then the state will appear static; otherwise, the `StoryBoard` will repeat while the control is in that state.

```
<ResourceDictionary
    xmlns="http://schemas.microsoft.com/winfx/2006/xaml/presentation"
    xmlns:x="http://schemas.microsott.com/winfx/2006/xaml"
    xmlns:vsm="clr-namespace:System.Windows;assembly=System.Windows"
```

```
      xmlns:wrox="clr-namespace:Wrox.Silverlight30.CustomControls.StateButton">
  <Style TargetType="wrox:StateButton">
    <Setter Property="Width" Value="100" />
    <Setter Property="Height" Value="32" />
    <Setter Property="Template">
      <Setter.Value>
        <ControlTemplate TargetType="wrox:StateButton">
          <Grid x:Name="LayoutRoot">
            <vsm:VisualStateManager.VisualStateGroups>
              <vsm:VisualStateGroup x:Name="CommonStates">
                <vsm:VisualState x:Name="Normal"/>
                <vsm:VisualState x:Name="MouseOver">
                  <Storyboard>
                    <ColorAnimation
                      Storyboard.TargetName="ClickRegion"
                        Storyboard.TargetProperty="(Shape.Fill)
                        (SolidColorBrush.Color)"
                        To="#009933" Duration="0" />
                  </Storyboard>
                </vsm:VisualState>
                <vsm:VisualState x:Name="Pressed">
                  <Storyboard>
                    <ColorAnimation
                        Storyboard.TargetName="ClickRegion"
                        Storyboard.TargetProperty="(Shape.Fill)
                        (SolidColorBrush.Color)"
                        To="#33CCCC" Duration="0" />
                  </Storyboard>
                </vsm:VisualState>
              </vsm:VisualStateGroup>
            </vsm:VisualStateManager.VisualStateGroups>
            <Rectangle x:Name="ClickRegion"
                HorizontalAlignment="Stretch"
                VerticalAlignment="Stretch" Stroke="#FF000000"
              Fill="White" StrokeThickness="5" RadiusY="5"
                RadiusX="5" />
          </Grid>
        </ControlTemplate>
      </Setter.Value>
    </Setter>
  </Style>
</ResourceDictionary>


Silverlight30
```

Note that the normal state does not require a StoryBoard since it is represented by the appearance of the default Control Template.

Visual Transitions

Next, we specify the transitions for the transform that the VisualStateManager will apply between the states of each group. Each VisualTransition element contains a GeneratedDuration and optionally specifies the From and To states that are matched at run time based on the transition taking place.

In the `StateButton`, a default transition time of half a second seems appropriate for all transitions. Going from the `MouseOver` to `Pressed` state is something that should happen quickly, so we specify an almost immediate transition:

```xml
<ResourceDictionary
    xmlns="http://schemas.microsoft.com/winfx/2006/xaml/presentation"
    xmlns:x="http://schemas.microsoft.com/winfx/2006/xaml"
    xmlns:vsm="clr-namespace:System.Windows;assembly=System.Windows"
    xmlns:wrox="clr-namespace:Wrox.Silverlight30.CustomControls.StateButton">
  <Style TargetType="wrox:StateButton">
    <Setter Property="Width" Value="100" />
    <Setter Property="Height" Value="32" />
    <Setter Property="Template">
      <Setter.Value>
        <ControlTemplate TargetType="wrox:StateButton">
          <Grid x:Name="LayoutRoot">
            <vsm:VisualStateManager.VisualStateGroups>
              <vsm:VisualStateGroup x:Name="CommonStates">
                <vsm:VisualState x:Name="Normal"/>
                <vsm:VisualState x:Name="MouseOver">
                  <Storyboard>
                    <ColorAnimation
                        Storyboard.TargetName="ClickRegion"
                        Storyboard.TargetProperty="(Shape.Fill
                        (SolidColorBrush.Color)"
                        To="#009933" Duration="0" />
                  </Storyboard>
                </vsm:VisualState>
                <vsm:VisualState x:Name="Pressed">
                  <Storyboard>
                    <ColorAnimation
                        Storyboard.TargetName="ClickRegion"
                        Storyboard.TargetProperty="(Shape.Fill).
                        (SolidColorBrush.Color)"
                        To="#33CCCC" Duration="0" />
                  </Storyboard>
                </vsm:VisualState>
                <vsm:VisualStateGroup.Transitions>
                  <vsm:VisualTransition GeneratedDuration="0:0:1"/>
                  <vsm:VisualTransition To="Pressed"
                      GeneratedDuration="0:0:.25"/>
                  <vsm:VisualTransition From="Pressed"
                      GeneratedDuration="0:0:.5"/>
                  <vsm:VisualTransition From="MouseOver" To="Pressed"
                      GeneratedDuration="0:0:.1"/>
                </vsm:VisualStateGroup.Transitions>
              </vsm:VisualStateGroup>
            </vsm:VisualStateManager.VisualStateGroups>
            <Rectangle x:Name="ClickRegion"
                HorizontalAlignment="Stretch"
                VerticalAlignment="Stretch" Stroke="#FF000000"
            Fill="White" StrokeThickness="5" RadiusY="5"
                RadiusX="5" />
          </Grid>
        </ControlTemplate>
      </Setter.Value>
    </Setter>
  </Style>
```

```
    </ResourceDictionary>


    Silverlight30
```

End-User Customization

The `StateButton` custom control now fully supports some select Visual States. As with Template Parts, the actual rendering used to represent the distinct Visual States and the transitions that are applied between them can be configured in XAML through the Control Template property. Here, we include a `StateButton` in an application to check out its behavior:

```
<UserControl x:Class="Wrox.Silverlight30.CustomControls.StateButtonApp.Page"
    xmlns="http://schemas.microsoft.com/winfx/2006/xaml/presentation"
    xmlns:x="http://schemas.microsoft.com/winfx/2006/xaml"
    xmlns:wrox="clr-namespace:Wrox.Silverlight30.CustomControls.
        StateButton;assembly=Wrox.Silverlight30.CustomControls.StateButton"
    Width="400" Height="300">

  <Grid x:Name="LayoutRoot" Background="White">
    <wrox:StateButton ></wrox:StateButton>
  </Grid>

</UserControl>
Silverlight30Silverlight30Silverlight30
```

Including Dependency Properties

If you wish to have a property on a custom control fully participate in key Silverlight features such as data binding and styling, it should be implemented as a dependency property. Dependency properties are standard .NET properties that rely on the `DependencyProperty` system to store and retrieve their actual values. Adding a dependency property is accomplished in three stages:

1. Create and register a static member of type `DependencyProperty`.

2. Create a standard .NET property whose value is managed by the `DependencyProperty` system.

3. Handle updates to the property originating in the `DependencyProperty` system.

Registering a Dependency Property

A static member is needed on the control class to identify each dependency property the class offers. In addition, each property must be registered with the dependency property system. This is done by passing in:

❑ The static `DependencyProperty` member that identifies the property

❑ The type of the property

❑ The type of the object that contains the property

❑ Optional information used to identify an event handler for when the property changes

To demonstrate the concept, we will create a new `SelectButton` control, which has an `IsSelected` property indicating if the button has been clicked. Microsoft's naming convention on Boolean properties has shifted to using an `Is` prefix.

```
// Declare and register a Dependency Property
public static DependencyProperty SelectedProperty =
  DependencyProperty.Register("IsSelected", typeof(bool),
    typeof(SelectButton),
    new PropertyMetadata(new PropertyChangedCallback(OnSelectedPropertyChanged)));
```

The convention is to name the static `DependencyProperty` the same as the true property it represents with *Property* appended.

Declaring the Property

Next, create a standard .NET property that delegates management of its value to the Dependency Property system. This is done through the `GetValue` and `SetValue` methods that we inherit from `DependencyObject`:

```
// Create the actual Property
public bool IsSelected
{
  get
  {
    return ((bool)this.GetValue(SelectButton.SelectedProperty));
  }
  set
  {
    this.SetValue(SelectButton.SelectedProperty, value);
  }
}
```

Notice that we use the static `IsSelectedProperty` member to identify this property to the Dependency Property system.

Handling Updates

The last parameter we provided to `DependencyProperty.Register` was a Callback reference to an event handler. This will be invoked whenever the value of the property is adjusted. Since this is a dependency property, not all updates to the property will be sent through our setter; instead, updates may be made directly through mechanisms such as data binding.

In the event handler, invoke the `EnsureVisualState` helper method to transition to a new visual state:

```
// Handler for when our Dependency Propety Changes
private static void OnSelectedPropertyChanged(DependencyObject d,
  DependencyPropertyChangedEventArgs e)
{
```

```
  // Cast the Dependency Object to a SelectButton
  SelectButton sb = (SelectButton)d;

  // Update Visual State
  sb.EnsureVisualState(true);
}

private void EnsureVisualState(bool useTransitions)
{
  // Move to the appropriate State for the CommonStates group
  if (_isPressed)
  {
    VisualStateManager.GoToState(this,
      PressedStateName, useTransitions);
  }
  else if (_isMouseOver)
  {
    VisualStateManager.GoToState(this,
      MouseOverStateName, useTransitions);
  }
  else if (this.IsSelected)
  {
    VisualStateManager.GoToState(this,
      SelectedStateName, useTransitions);
  }
  else
  {
    VisualStateManager.GoToState(this,
      NormalStateName, useTransitions);
  }
}
```

After adjusting the Selected property, the control will appear in a new visual state (see Figure 17-7):

```xml
<UserControl x:Class="Wrox.Silverlight30.CustomControls.SelectButtonApp.Page"
    xmlns="http://schemas.microsoft.com/winfx/2006/xaml/presentation"
    xmlns:x="http://schemas.microsoft.com/winfx/2006/xaml"
    xmlns:wrox="clr-namespace:Wrox.Silverlight30.CustomControls.
        SelectButton;assembly=Wrox.Silverlight30.CustomControls.SelectButton"
  Width="400" Height="300">
  <Grid x:Name="LayoutRoot" Background="White">
    <StackPanel Background="White">
      <!-- CustomButton with default control template -->
      <wrox:SelectButton x:Name="SelectButton1" />
      <!-- CustomButton that is selected -->
      <wrox:SelectButton x:Name="SelectButton2" IsSelected="True" />
    </StackPanel>
  </Grid>
</UserControl>
Silverlight30Silverlight30Silverlight30
```

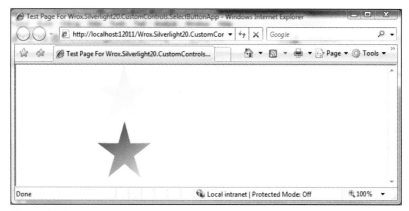

Figure 17-7

Building a Content Control

Content controls in Silverlight have the ability to host arbitrary content. Examples of content controls include `Button`, `TabItem`, and `CheckBox`. In the custom button controls developed so far in this chapter, there is no easy way to add elements within the button.

Creating a `ContentControl` is straightforward and requires the following steps:

1. Inherit from `ContentControl` or one of its subclasses.

2. Include a `ContentPresenter` in the Control Template.

Extending `ContentControl`

Start by creating a class that extends `ContentControl`:

```
namespace Wrox.Silverlight30.CustomControls.ContentButton
{
[TemplatePart(Name = ContentButton.ClickRegionPartName,
             Type = typeof(FrameworkElement))]
// Visual State Definitions
[TemplateVisualState(Name = NormalStateName,
  GroupName = CommonStatesGroupName)]
[TemplateVisualState(Name = MouseOverStateName,
  GroupName = CommonStatesGroupName)]
[TemplateVisualState(Name = PressedStateName,
  GroupName = CommonStatesGroupName)]
[TemplateVisualState(Name = SelectedStateName,
  GroupName = CommonStatesGroupName)]
public class ContentButton : ContentControl
{
    // The Name of the Element expected for our Click Region
```

```csharp
private const string ClickRegionPartName = "ClickRegion";

// Private members for Template Part Elements
private FrameworkElement _clickRegionElement;

// Constants for Visual States
private const string CommonStatesGroupName = "CommonStates";
private const string NormalStateName = "Normal";
private const string MouseOverStateName = "MouseOver";
private const string PressedStateName = "Pressed";
private const string SelectedStateName = "Selected";

// Members to track the current state
private bool _isMouseOver = false;
private bool _isPressed = false;

// Declare and register a Dependency Property
public static DependencyProperty SelectedProperty =
  DependencyProperty.Register("IsSelected", typeof(bool),
  typeof(ContentButton),
  new PropertyMetadata(new PropertyChangedCallback(OnSelectedPropertyChanged)));

// Create the actual Property
public bool IsSelected
{
  get
  {
    return ((bool)this.GetValue(ContentButton.SelectedProperty));
  }
  set
  {
    this.SetValue(ContentButton.SelectedProperty, value);
  }
}

// Events
public event EventHandler<EventArgs> Click;


public ContentButton()
  : base()
{
  this.DefaultStyleKey = typeof(ContentButton);
}

public override void OnApplyTemplate()
{
  base.OnApplyTemplate();

  // Clear out event hanlders if this is not the first template applied
  if (_clickRegionElement != null)
  {
    _clickRegionElement.MouseLeftButtonUp -=
      new MouseButtonEventHandler(clickRegion_MouseLeftButtonUp);
```

```csharp
      _clickRegionElement.MouseEnter -=
        new MouseEventHandler(clickRegion_MouseEnter);
      _clickRegionElement.MouseLeave -=
        new MouseEventHandler(clickRegion_MouseLeave);
      _clickRegionElement.MouseLeftButtonDown -=
        new MouseButtonEventHandler(clickRegion_MouseLeftButtonDown);
    }
    // Find our Click Region Template Part
    _clickRegionElement =
      GetTemplateChild(ClickRegionPartName) as FrameworkElement;
    if (_clickRegionElement != null)
    {
      // Hook up a new event handlers
      _clickRegionElement.MouseLeftButtonUp +=
        new MouseButtonEventHandler(clickRegion_MouseLeftButtonUp);
      _clickRegionElement.MouseEnter +=
        new MouseEventHandler(clickRegion_MouseEnter);
      _clickRegionElement.MouseLeave +=
        new MouseEventHandler(clickRegion_MouseLeave);
      _clickRegionElement.MouseLeftButtonDown +=
        new MouseButtonEventHandler(clickRegion_MouseLeftButtonDown);
    }
    // Reset the current state, no need to transition
    _isMouseOver = false;
    _isPressed = false;
    EnsureVisualState(false);

}


// Handler for when our Dependency Propety Changes
private static void OnSelectedPropertyChanged(DependencyObject d,
  DependencyPropertyChangedEventArgs e)
{
  // Cast the Dependency Object to a ContentButton
  ContentButton sb = (ContentButton)d;

  // Update Visual State
  sb.EnsureVisualState(true);
}

private void clickRegion_MouseLeftButtonDown(object sender,
  MouseButtonEventArgs e)
{
  _isPressed = true;
  EnsureVisualState(true);
}

private void clickRegion_MouseLeave(object sender,
  MouseEventArgs e)
{
  _isMouseOver = false;
  EnsureVisualState(true);
}

private void clickRegion_MouseEnter(object sender,
  MouseEventArgs e)
```

```
    {
      _isMouseOver = true;
      EnsureVisualState(true);
    }

    private void clickRegion_MouseLeftButtonUp(object sender,
      MouseButtonEventArgs e)
    {
      _isPressed = false;

      this.IsSelected = !this.IsSelected;

      if (Click != null)
      {
        this.Click(this, EventArgs.Empty);
      }
    }

    private void EnsureVisualState(bool useTransitions)
    {
      // Move to the appropriate State for the CommonStates group
      if (_isPressed)
      {
        VisualStateManager.GoToState(this,
          PressedStateName, useTransitions);
      }
      else if (_isMouseOver)
      {
        VisualStateManager.GoToState(this,
          MouseOverStateName, useTransitions);
      }
      else if (this.IsSelected)
      {
        VisualStateManager.GoToState(this,
          SelectedStateName, useTransitions);
      }
      else
      {
        VisualStateManager.GoToState(this,
          NormalStateName, useTransitions);
      }
    }
  }
}
```

Next, add a `ContentPresenter` to generic.xaml. The `ContentPresenter` is responsible for hosting elements in the control. Two properties inherited from `ContentControl` — `Content` and `ContentTemplate` — are set through a template binding.

```
<ResourceDictionary
    xmlns="http://schemas.microsoft.com/winfx/2006/xaml/presentation"
    xmlns:x="http://schemas.microsoft.com/winfx/2006/xaml"
    xmlns:vsm="clr-namespace:System.Windows;assembly=System.Windows"
```

```
          xmlns:wrox="clr-namespace:Wrox.Silverlight30.CustomControls.ContentButton">

   <Style TargetType="wrox:ContentButton">
     <Setter Property="Width" Value="100" />
     <Setter Property="Height" Value="100" />
     <Setter Property="Template">
       <Setter.Value>
         <ControlTemplate TargetType="wrox:ContentButton">
           <Grid x:Name="LayoutRoot">
             <vsm:VisualStateManager.VisualStateGroups>
               <vsm:VisualStateGroup x:Name="CommonStates">
                 <vsm:VisualState x:Name="Normal"/>
                 <vsm:VisualState x:Name="MouseOver">
                   <Storyboard>
                     <ColorAnimation Storyboard.TargetName="ClickRegion"
Storyboard.TargetProperty="(Shape.Fill).(GradientBrush.GradientStops)[0].
     (GradientStop.Color)"
To="#009933" Duration="0" />
                   </Storyboard>
                 </vsm:VisualState>
                 <vsm:VisualState x:Name="Pressed">
                   <Storyboard>
                     <ColorAnimation Storyboard.TargetName="ClickRegion"
Storyboard.TargetProperty="(Shape.Fill).(GradientBrush.GradientStops)[0].
     (GradientStop.Color)"
To="#33CCCC" Duration="0" />
                   </Storyboard>
                 </vsm:VisualState>
                 <vsm:VisualState x:Name="Selected">
                   <Storyboard>
                     <ColorAnimation Storyboard.TargetName="ClickRegion"
Storyboard.TargetProperty="(Shape.Fill).(GradientBrush.GradientStops)[0].
     (GradientStop.Color)"
To="#FF2C5DE2" Duration="0" />
                   </Storyboard>
                 </vsm:VisualState>
                 <vsm:VisualStateGroup.Transitions>
                   <vsm:VisualTransition GeneratedDuration="0:0:1"/>
                   <vsm:VisualTransition To="Pressed" GeneratedDuration="0:0:.25"/>
                   <vsm:VisualTransition From="Pressed" GeneratedDuration="0:0:.5"/>
                   <vsm:VisualTransition From="MouseOver" To="Pressed"
                        GeneratedDuration="0:0:.1"/>
                 </vsm:VisualStateGroup.Transitions>
               </vsm:VisualStateGroup>
             </vsm:VisualStateManager.VisualStateGroups>
             <Path x:Name="ClickRegion" HorizontalAlignment="Left"
             VerticalAlignment="Top" Stretch="Fill" Opacity="1" Width="100"
                 Height="100"
             Data="M 96,0 C96,0 117,70 117,70 117,70 191,69 191,69 191,69 130,111
130,111 130,111 154,180 154,180 154,180 96,136 96,136 96,136 37,180 37,180 37,180
61,111 61,111 61,111 0,69 0,69 0,69 74,70 74,70 74,70 96,0 96,0 z"
                 >
```

```
        <Path.Fill>
          <LinearGradientBrush
    StartPoint="0.3089005235602094,0.07222222222222222"
    EndPoint="0.9947643979057592,1.238888888888889">
            <LinearGradientBrush.GradientStops>
              <GradientStopCollection>
                <GradientStop    Color="#FFffff00"    Offset="0" />
                <GradientStop    Color="#FFf0f0f0"    Offset="0.9944" />
              </GradientStopCollection>
            </LinearGradientBrush.GradientStops>
          </LinearGradientBrush>
        </Path.Fill>
      </Path>
      <ContentPresenter x:Name="ContentPresenter"
  HorizontalAlignment="Center" VerticalAlignment="Center"
  Content="{TemplateBinding Content}"
  ContentTemplate="{TemplateBinding ContentTemplate}" />
      </Grid>
    </ControlTemplate>
  </Setter.Value>
  </Setter>
 </Style>
</ResourceDictionary>Silverlight30
```

Finally, include an element for the `Content` property when using the control in XAML (see Figure 17-8):

```
<UserControl x:Class="Wrox.Silverlight30.CustomControls.ContentButtonApp.Page"
    xmlns="http://schemas.microsoft.com/winfx/2006/xaml/presentation"
    xmlns:x="http://schemas.microsoft.com/winfx/2006/xaml"
    xmlns:wrox="clr-namespace:Wrox.Silverlight30.CustomControls.
        ContentButton;assembly=Wrox.Silverlight30.CustomControls.ContentButton"
    Width="400" Height="300">
  <Grid x:Name="LayoutRoot" Background="White">
    <StackPanel Background="White">
      <wrox:ContentButton x:Name="ContentButton1">
        <wrox:ContentButton.Content>
          <TextBlock Text="Star" TextAlignment="Center" Width="100" />
        </wrox:ContentButton.Content>
      </wrox:ContentButton>
    </StackPanel>
  </Grid>
</UserControl>Silverlight30Silverlight30Silverlight30
```

Because of the way that the XAML parser treats subelements of a `ContentControl`, you can also simply include the element as a child of the control, and it will be fed to the `Content` property (see Figure 17-8):

```
<wrox:ContentButton x:Name="ContentButton1">
  <TextBlock Text="Star" TextAlignment="Center" Width="100">
</wrox:ContentButton>
```

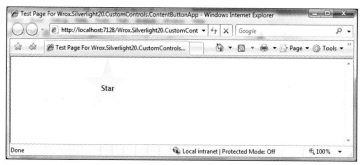

Figure 17-8

Since this is a `ContentControl`, you can also provide a `DataTemplate` for the `ContentTemplate` property (see Figure 17-9):

```
<UserControl x:Class="Wrox.Silverlight30.CustomControls.ContentButtonApp.Page"
    xmlns="http://schemas.microsoft.com/winfx/2006/xaml/presentation"
    xmlns:x="http://schemas.microsoft.com/winfx/2006/xaml"
    xmlns:wrox="clr-namespace:Wrox.Silverlight30.CustomControls.
        ContentButton;assembly=Wrox.Silverlight30.CustomControls.ContentButton"
    Width="400" Height="300">
  <Grid x:Name="LayoutRoot" Background="White">
    <StackPanel Background="White">
      <wrox:ContentButton x:Name="ContentButton2" IsSelected="True">
        <wrox:ContentButton.ContentTemplate>
          <DataTemplate>
            <Grid>
              <Ellipse Width="40" Height="20" Stroke="Blue"></Ellipse>
              <TextBlock Text="Star" TextAlignment="Center"
                  Width="100"></TextBlock>
            </Grid>
          </DataTemplate>
        </wrox:ContentButton.ContentTemplate>
      </wrox:ContentButton>
    </StackPanel>
  </Grid>
</UserControl>Silverlight30Silverlight30Silverlight30
```

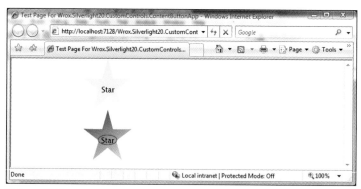

Figure 17-9

Summary

In this chapter, you learned the basics of creating a custom control project, leveraging the power of Template Parts and Visual States, and how to facilitate use of a control through Dependency Properties.

This foundation will prove useful as you develop in Silverlight and identify functionality that should be common across different applications. Silverlight's powerful, extensible model for creating custom controls allows you to tackle the challenge of providing functional controls that can offer radically different visual representations.

Appendices

Silverlight Base Class Libraries Reference

The .NET Framework for Silverlight class library is based on the same base class library (BCL) that you use in full desktop .NET applications. When building Silverlight Applications, you have the same experience as you would when building a full Windows Presentation Foundation (WPF) application. The difference between the full BCL and the Silverlight BCL lies in the namespaces and classes. The Silverlight BCL is much smaller than the .NET BCL. In order to be efficient for transport in a networked browser environment, many objects were removed that did not make sense. For example, many of the ASP.NET-specific classes have been removed, as well as `System.Security`, since the security model is completely different. In this appendix, you will see all of the namespaces that are included in the Silverlight BCL and the functions they perform.

Appendix A: Silverlight Base Class Libraries Reference

Namespace	Description
`Microsoft.Scripting.Silverlight`	Contains classes that enable Silverlight-based applications written in dynamic languages. Use the `DynamicApplication` class to gain access to visual elements from your dynamic language code. The `DynamicApplication` class also is used by the Silverlight host to start a dynamic language application.
`Microsoft.VisualBasic`	Contains classes that support the Visual Basic run time in Visual Basic.
`Microsoft.VisualBasic .CompilerServices`	Contains internal-use-only types that support the Visual Basic compiler.
`Microsoft.Win32.SafeHandles`	Contains classes that are abstract derivations of Safe Handle classes that provide common functionality supporting file and operating system handles.
`MS.Internal`	This namespace supports the .NET Framework for Silverlight infrastructure and is not intended to be used directly from your code.
`System`	Contains fundamental classes and base classes that define commonly used value and reference data types, events and event handlers, interfaces, attributes, and processing exceptions. Other classes provide services supporting data type conversion, method parameter manipulation, mathematics, remote and local program invocation, application environment management, and supervision of managed and unmanaged applications.
`System.CodeDom.Compiler`	Contains a class that identifies code that is generated by a tool.
`System.Collections`	Contains interfaces and classes that define various collections of objects, such as lists, queues, bit arrays, hash tables, and dictionaries.
`System.Collections.Generic`	Contains interfaces and classes that define generic collections, which enables users to create strongly typed collections that provide better type safety and performance than non-generic, strongly typed collections.
`System.Collections.ObjectModel`	Contains classes that can be used as collections in the object model of a reusable library. Use these classes when properties or methods return collections.

Namespace	Description
System.Collections.Specialized	Contains specialized and strongly typed collections.
System.ComponentModel	Provides classes that are used to implement the run-time and design-time behavior of components and controls.
System.Configuration.Assemblies	Contains classes that are used to configure an assembly.
System.Diagnostics	Provides classes that enable you to interact with system processes, event logs, and performance counters.
System.Data.Services.Client	Represents the classes and members that applications can use to interact with ADO.NET Data Services.
System.Data.Services.Common	Contains a class that indicates the key property or properties of an entity.
System.Diagnostics.CodeAnalysis	Contains classes for interaction with code analysis tools. These tools are used to analyze code for conformance to coding conventions such as naming or security rules.
System.Diagnostics.SymbolStore	Provides classes that enable you to read and write debug symbol information, such as source line to Microsoft Intermediate Language (MSIL) maps. Compilers targeting the .NET Framework can store the debug symbol information into programmer's database (PDB) files. Debuggers and code profiler tools can read the debug symbol information at run time.
System.Globalization	Contains classes that define culture-related information, including the language; the country/region; the calendars in use; the format patterns for dates, currency, and numbers; and the sort order for strings. These classes are useful for writing globalized (internationalized) applications.
System.IO	Contains types that enable reading and writing to files and data streams, and types that provide basic file and directory support.
System.IO.IsolatedStorage	Contains types for creating and using a virtual filesystem. Isolated storage provides safe client-side storage for partial trust applications. In Silverlight, all I/O operations are restricted to isolated storage and do not use the filesystem of the operating system.

Continued

Namespace	Description
System.Json	Provides standards-based support for the serialization of JavaScript Object Notation (JSON).
System.Linq	Contains classes and interfaces that support queries that use Language-Integrated Query (LINQ).
System.Linq.Expressions	Contains types that enable language-level code expressions to be represented as objects in the form of expression trees.
System.Net	Provides a simple programming interface for many of the protocols used on networks today. The WebRequest and WebResponse classes form the basis of pluggable protocols, which enable you to develop applications that use Internet resources without worrying about the specific details of the individual protocols.
System.Net.Sockets	Provides a managed implementation of the sockets networking interface for developers who need to tightly control access to the network. On Windows, this namespace provides a managed implementation of the Windows Sockets (Winsock) interface. On Apple Mac OS X, this namespace provides a managed implementation of the sockets interface based on Berkeley Software Distribution (BSD) UNIX.
System.Reflection	Contains types that retrieve information about assemblies, modules, members, parameters, and other entities in managed code by examining their metadata. These types also can be used to manipulate instances of loaded types, for example, to hook up events or to invoke methods.
System.Reflection.Emit	Contains classes that enable a compiler or tool to emit metadata and Microsoft Intermediate Language (MSIL) and optionally generate a PE file on disk. The primary clients of these classes are script engines and compilers.
System.Resources	Provides classes and interfaces that enable developers to create, store, and manage various culture-specific resources used in an application.
System.Runtime.CompilerServices	Provides functionality for compiler writers who use managed code to specify attributes in metadata that affect the runtime behavior of the Common Language Runtime (CLR).

Namespace	Description
System.Runtime.ConstrainedExecution	Defines a set of types that enumerate and define a contract for reliability between the author of some code and the developers who take a dependency on that code. The types are intended for use in constrained execution regions (CERs).
System.Runtime.InteropServices	Provides a wide variety of members that support COM interop and platform invoke services.
System.Runtime.Serialization	Contains classes that can be used for serializing and deserializing objects. *Serialization* is the process of converting an object or a graph of objects into a linear sequence of bytes for either storage or transmission to another location. *Deserialization* is the process of taking in stored information and recreating objects from it.
System.Runtime.Serialization.Json	Contains types for serializing objects to JavaScript Object Notation (JSON) and deserializing objects from JSON.
System.Runtime.Versioning	Contains advanced types that support versioning in side-by-side implementations of the .NET Framework.
System.Security	Provides the underlying structure of the .NET Framework security system, including base classes for permissions.
System.Security.Cryptography	Provides cryptographic services, including secure encoding and decoding of data, as well as many other operations, such as hashing, random number generation, and message authentication.
System.Security.Cryptography.X509Certificates	Contains the CLR implementation of the Authenticode X.509 v.3 certificate. This certificate is signed with a private key that uniquely and positively identifies the holder of the certificate.
System.Security.Permissions	Defines classes that control access to operations and resources based on policy.
System.Security.Principal	Defines a principal object that represents the security context under which code is running.
System.ServiceModel	Contains the types necessary to build Silverlight client applications that can be used to access distributed applications.

Continued

Namespace	Description
`System.ServiceModel.Channels`	Contains the types required to construct and modify the messages used by clients to communicate with services, the types of channels used to exchange messages, the channel factories used to construct those channels, and the binding elements used to configure them.
`System.ServiceModel.Description`	Contains the types required to construct and modify descriptions of services, contracts, and endpoints that are used to build service run times and to export metadata.
`System.ServiceModel.Dispatcher`	Contains the types necessary to modify the runtime execution behavior of client applications.
`System.ServiceModel.Syndication`	Contains the types that make up the Silverlight syndication object model.
`System.Text`	Contains classes representing Unicode and UTF-8 character encodings; abstract base classes for converting blocks of characters to and from blocks of bytes; and a helper class that manipulates and formats `String` objects without creating intermediate instances of `String`.
`System.Text.RegularExpressions`	Contains classes that provide access to the .NET Framework regular expression engine. The namespace provides regular expression functionality that can be used from any platform or language that runs within the .NET Framework.
`System.Threading`	Provides classes and interfaces that enable multi-threaded programming.
`System.Web.UI.Design.SilverlightControls`	Contains classes that provide design-time support of ASP.NET server controls for Silverlight.
`System.Web.UI.SilverlightControls`	Contains classes that enable ASP.NET developers to add Silverlight functionality to ASP.NET pages.
`System.Windows`	Provides general presentation classes for the Silverlight client, as well as the Silverlight base classes. These presentation classes are often analogous to classes that exist in the Windows Presentation Foundation (WPF).
`System.Windows.Automation`	Contains classes that provide support for WPF UI Automation clients.

Namespace	Description
System.Windows.Automation.Peers	Defines the `AutomationPeer` base class and a set of types that derive from it and that correspond to Silverlight controls. Each `AutomationPeer` exposes the corresponding Silverlight control to UI Automation.
System.Windows.Automation.Provider	Contains types for creating UI Automation providers.
System.Windows.Browser	Contains classes that enable the interaction between managed code and JavaScript in Silverlight-based applications. This functionality is referred to as the *HTML Bridge feature*.
System.Windows.Controls	Contains classes to create controls that enable a user to interact with an application.
System.Windows.Controls.Primitives	Contains base classes and controls that are intended to be used as part of other, more complex controls.
System.Windows.Data	Contains classes used for binding properties to data sources.
System.Windows.Documents	Contains classes that support basic document concepts in Silverlight.
System.Windows.Ink	Provides classes to interact with and manipulate ink in Silverlight.
System.Windows.Input	Contains classes that support the Silverlight client input system.
System.Windows.Interop	Contains classes that provide managed-code exposure for properties of the Silverlight plug-in, which otherwise exist in the HTML DOM of the hosting browser.
System.Windows.Markup	Contains classes that support Extensible Application Markup Language (XAML) processing in Silverlight.
System.Windows.Media	Contains classes that enable integration of rich media, including drawings, text, and audio/video content in Silverlight-based applications.
System.Windows.Media.Animation	Contains classes that support property animation functionality, including timelines, storyboards, and key frames.
System.Windows.Media.Imaging	Contains types used to encode and decode bitmap images.

Continued

Namespace	Description
System.Windows.Resources	Contains a class that provides resource stream information for application resources or other packages obtained through GetResourceStream.
System.Windows.Shapes	Contains a library of shapes that can be used in XAML or code.
System.Windows.Threading	Contains classes that support the Silverlight threading system.
System.Xml	Provides standards-based support for processing XML.
System.Xml.Linq	Contains the types for LINQ to XML, which is an in-memory XML programming interface that enables you to modify XML documents efficiently and easily.
System.Xml.Resolvers	Contains classes that provide support for prepopulating the cache with DTDs or XML streams.
System.Xml.Schema	Contains the XML classes that provide standards-based support for XML Schema definition language (XSD) schemas.
System.Xml.Serialization	Contains classes that are used to serialize objects into XML format documents or streams.

B

System.Windows Reference

The System.Windows namespace can be looked on as containing the code set of classes needed to render basic Silverlight content. It contains the critical classes that most other objects in Silverlight derive from to get their functionality.

In this appendix, you will learn about:

❏ The classes in System.Windows and what each property and enumeration gives you

❏ The DependencyObject class, which enables Silverlight Dependency Property system services on its derived classes, and what those derived classes are

❏ The FrameworkElement class, which enables layout, data binding, and lifetime management on its derived classes, and what those derived classes are

❏ The UIElement class, which is the base class for most visual elements that are rendered in Silverlight

System.Windows Classes

The following table describes the classes in the System.Windows namespace.

Class	Description
Application	Encapsulates a Silverlight application.
ApplicationIdentity	Represents information about an application that is configured for out-of-browser support.
ApplicationServiceContext	Represents the initial state of a Silverlight application when application services are started.
ApplicationUnhandledExceptionEventArgs	Provides data for the Application .UnhandledException event.
AssemblyPart	An *assembly part* is an assembly that is to be included in a Silverlight-based application's application package (.xap).
AssemblyPartCollection	Stores a collection of AssemblyPart objects. Provides collection support for the Deployment.Parts property.
DataTemplate	Describes the visual structure of a data object.
DependencyObject	Represents an object that participates in the Silverlight Dependency Property system.
DependencyProperty	Represents a dependency property that is registered with the Silverlight Dependency Property system. Dependency properties provide support for value expressions, data binding, animation, and property change notification.
Deployment	Provides application part and localization information in the application manifest when deploying a Silverlight-based application.
DurationConverter	Provides type conversion support for the Duration structure.
EventTrigger	Represents a trigger that applies a set of actions (animation storyboards) in response to an event.

Class	Description
ExceptionRoutedEventArgs	Provides event data for exceptions that are raised as events by asynchronous operations, such as `MediaFailed` or `ImageFailed`.
Expression	This type is not intended to be used from your code or to be derived from.
ExtensionPart	Represents a Silverlight platform extension that is required by your application.
ExternalPart	Represents a Silverlight platform extension that is used by your application but is not required.
ExternalPartCollection	Represents a collection of `ExternalPart` instances that indicate the Silverlight platform extensions used by an application.
FontStretches	Provides a set of predefined font stretches as static property values.
FontStyles	Provides a set of predefined font styles as static property values.
FontWeights	Provides a set of predefined font weights as static property values.
FrameworkElement	Provides a framework of common APIs for objects that participate in Silverlight layout. Also defines APIs related to data binding, object tree, and object lifetime feature areas in Silverlight.
FrameworkTemplate	Creates an element tree of elements.
HierarchicalDataTemplate	Represents a `DataTemplate` that supports `HeaderedItemsControl` objects, such as `TreeViewItem`.
Icon	Represents an icon that is used to identify an offline application.
IconCollection	Represents a collection of `Icon` instances.
LengthConverter	Converts instances of other types to and from instances of a `Double` that represent an object measurement such as a height or width.
MessageBox	Displays a message to the user and optionally prompts for a response.

Continued

Class	Description
NullableBoolConverter	Converts Nullable<(Of <(T>)>) types (using the Boolean type constraint on the generic) to and from strings.
PresentationFrameworkCollection<(Of <(T>)>)	Provides a common collection class for Silverlight collections.
PropertyMetadata	Defines certain behavior aspects of a dependency property, including the conditions it was registered with.
PropertyPath	Implements a data structure for describing a property as a path below another property, or below an owning type. Property paths are used in data binding to objects and in storyboards and timelines for animations.
PropertyPathConverter	Provides type conversion support for the PropertyPath type. Primarily exists to support specifying a PropertyPath as a string for XAML attribute usage of properties that take a PropertyPath.
ResourceDictionary	Provides a dictionary that contains keyed resources used by components of a Silverlight-based application.
RoutedEvent	Represents a routed event to the Silverlight event system.
RoutedEventArgs	Contains state information and event data associated with a routed event.
RoutedPropertyChangedEventArgs<(Of <(T>)>)	Provides data about a change in value to a dependency property as reported by particular routed events, including the previous and current value of the property that changed.
Setter	Applies a value to a property in a Style.
SetterBase	Represents the base class for value setters.
SetterBaseCollection	Represents a collection of objects that inherit from SetterBase.
SizeChangedEventArgs	Provides data related to the SizeChanged event.

Class	Description
StartupEventArgs	Contains the event data for the Startup event.
Style	Contains property setters, resources, and event handlers that can be shared between instances of a type.
StyleTypedPropertyAttribute	Represents an attribute that is applied to the class definition and reports the TargetType of the properties that are of type Style.
SystemColors	Contains system colors, system brushes, and system resource keys that correspond to system display elements.
SystemParameters	Contains properties that you can use to query system settings.
TemplateBindingExpression	Infrastructure. Supports template binding.
TemplatePartAttribute	Represents an attribute that is applied to the class definition to identify the types of the named parts that are used for control templating.
TemplateVisualStateAttribute	Specifies that a VisualState is a part of a control contract.
TextDecorationCollection	Provides the value for the TextDecorations and TextDecorations properties.
TextDecorations	Implements a set of predefined text decorations.
TriggerAction	Serves as the base class for BeginStoryboard.
TriggerActionCollection	Represents a collection of BeginStoryboard objects.
TriggerBase	Serves as the base class for EventTrigger.
TriggerCollection	Represents a collection of EventTrigger objects.
UIElement	Base class for most of the objects that have visual appearance and can process basic input in Silverlight

Continued

477

Class	Description
VisualState	Represents the visual appearance of the control when it is in a specific state.
VisualStateChangedEventArgs	Provides data for the CurrentStateChanging and CurrentStateChanged events.
VisualStateGroup	Contains mutually exclusive VisualState objects and VisualTransition objects that are used to go from one state to another.
VisualStateManager	Manages states and the logic for transitioning between states for controls.
VisualTransition	Represents the visual behavior that occurs when the control transitions from one state to another.

System.Windows Structures

The following table describes the structures in the System.Windows namespace.

Name	Description
CornerRadius	Describes the characteristics of a rounded corner, such as can be applied to a Border.
DependencyPropertyChangedEventArgs	Provides data for a PropertyChangedCallback implementation.
Duration	Represents the duration of time that a Timeline is active.
FontStretch	Describes the degree to which a font has been stretched compared to the normal aspect ratio of that font.
FontStyle	Represents the style of a font face (e.g., as normal or italic).
FontWeight	Refers to the density of a typeface, in terms of the lightness or heaviness of the strokes.
GridLength	Represents the length of elements that explicitly support Star unit types.
Point	Represents an X- and Y-coordinate pair in two-dimensional space. Can also represent a logical point for certain property usages.

Name	Description
Rect	Describes the width, height, and point origin of a rectangle.
Size	Describes the width and height of an object.
Thickness	Describes the thickness of a frame around a rectangle. Four `Double` values describe the `Left`, `Top`, `Right`, and `Bottom` sides of the rectangle, respectively.

System.Windows Enumerations

The following table describes the enumerations in the `System.Windows` namespace.

Name	Description
CrossDomainAccess	Defines values that specify the access that cross-domain callers have to a Silverlight-based application. **Values:** `NoAccess` — Cross-domain callers have no access to the Silverlight application. `FullAccess` — Cross-domain callers have full access to the Silverlight application. `ScriptableOnly` — Cross-domain callers have script access to the Silverlight application.
ExecutionStates	Defines constants that indicate the state of an application that can run offline. **Values:** `RunningOnline` — Returns if the application is running within its host Web page. `Detaching` — The application is in the process of detaching from its host Web page. `Detached` — The application is running in offline mode, detached from its host Web page. `DetachedUpdatesAvailable` — The application is running in offline mode, but a newer version of the application has been downloaded and will be used the next time that the application is launched. `DetachFailed` — The application could not be detached from its host Web page.

Continued

479

Name	Description
GridUnitType	Describes the kind of value that a GridLength object is holding. **Values:** Auto — Size is determined by the size properties of the content object. Pixel — Value is expressed as a pixel. Star — Value is expressed as a weighted proportion of available space.
HorizontalAlignment	Indicates where an element should be displayed on the horizontal axis relative to the allocated layout slot of the parent element. **Values:** Left — Element is aligned to the left of the layout slot for the parent element. Center — Element is aligned to the center of the layout slot for the parent element. Right — Element is aligned to the right of the layout slot for the parent element. Stretch — Element is stretched to fill the entire layout slot of the parent element.
LineStackingStrategy	Describes a mechanism by which a line box is determined for each line. **Values:** MaxHeight — The stack height is the smallest value that contains the extended block progression dimension of all the inline elements on that line when those elements are properly aligned. BlockLineHeight — The stack height is determined by the block element line-height property value.
MessageBoxButton	Specifies the buttons to include when you display a message box. **Values:** OK — Displays only the OK button. OKCancel — Displays both the OK and Cancel buttons.
MessageBoxResult	Represents a user's response to a message box. **Values:** None — This value is not currently used. OK — The user clicked on the OK button. Cancel — The user clicked on the Cancel button or pressed [Esc]. Yes — This value is not currently used. No — This value is not currently used.

Name	Description
TextAlignment	Specifies whether text is centered, left-aligned, or right-aligned. **Values:** Center — Text is centered. Left — Text is aligned to the left. Right — Text is aligned to the right.
TextWrapping	Specifies whether text wraps when it reaches the edge of its container. **Values:** Wrap — Line breaking occurs if a line of text overflows beyond the available width of its container. Line breaking occurs even if the standard line-breaking algorithm cannot determine any line break opportunity, such as when a line of text includes a long word that is constrained by a fixed-width container without scrolling. NoWrap — No line wrapping is performed.
VerticalAlignment	Describes how a child element is vertically positioned or stretched within a parent's layout slot. **Values:** Top — The child element is aligned to the top of the parent's layout slot. Center — The child element is aligned to the center of the parent's layout slot. Bottom — The child element is aligned to the bottom of the parent's layout slot. Stretch — An element stretched to fill the entire layout slot of the parent element.
Visibility	Specifies the display state of an element. **Values:** Visible — Display the element. Collapsed — Do not display the element, and do not reserve space for it in layout.

DependencyObject Class

The DependencyObject class enables Silverlight to compute the values of properties and to provide system notification about values that have changed.

The class hierarchy for DependencyObject is:

```
System.Object

  System.Windows.DependencyObject

    System.Windows.ApplicationIdentity

    System.Windows.AssemblyPart

    System.Windows.Automation.Peers.AutomationPeer

    System.Windows.Controls.ColumnDefinition

    System.Windows.Controls.DataFormField

    System.Windows.Controls.DataGridColumn

    System.Windows.Controls.MultiScaleSubImage

    System.Windows.Controls.RowDefinition

    System.Windows.Deployment

    System.Windows.Documents.Inline

    System.Windows.ExternalPart

    System.Windows.FrameworkTemplate

    System.Windows.Icon

    System.Windows.Ink.DrawingAttributes

    System.Windows.Ink.Stroke

    System.Windows.Input.InputMethod

    System.Windows.Media.Animation.ColorKeyFrame

    System.Windows.Media.Animation.DoubleKeyFrame

    System.Windows.Media.Animation.EasingFunctionBase

    System.Windows.Media.Animation.KeySpline
```

```
System.Windows.Media.Animation.ObjectKeyFrame

System.Windows.Media.Animation.PointKeyFrame

System.Windows.Media.Animation.Timeline

System.Windows.Media.Brush

System.Windows.Media.CacheMode

System.Windows.Media.Effects.Effect

System.Windows.Media.Effects.PixelShader

System.Windows.Media.GeneralTransform

System.Windows.Media.Geometry

System.Windows.Media.GradientStop

System.Windows.Media.ImageSource

System.Windows.Media.MultiScaleTileSource

System.Windows.Media.PathFigure

System.Windows.Media.PathSegment

System.Windows.Media.Projection

System.Windows.Media.TimelineMarker

System.Windows.Navigation.UriFragmentHelper.BrowserNavigationProxy

System.Windows.PresentationFrameworkCollection<(Of <(<'T>)>)>

System.Windows.ResourceDictionary

System.Windows.SetterBase

System.Windows.Style

System.Windows.TriggerAction

System.Windows.TriggerBase

System.Windows.UIElement

System.Windows.VisualState

System.Windows.VisualStateGroup
```

System.Windows
.VisualStateManagerDependencyObject Methods

The following table describes the methods that the DependencyObject exposes.

Name	Description
CheckAccess	Determines whether the calling thread has access to this object.
ClearValue	Clears the local value of a property.
Equals	Determines whether the specified object is equal to the current object (inherited from Object).
Finalize	Allows an object to attempt to free resources and perform other cleanup operations before the object is reclaimed by garbage collection (inherited from Object).
GetAnimationBaseValue	Returns any base value established for a Silverlight dependency property, which would apply in cases in which an animation is not active.
GetHashCode	Serves as a hash function for a particular type (inherited from Object).
GetType	Gets the Type of the current instance (inherited from Object).
GetValue	Returns the current effective value of a dependency property from a DependencyObject.
MemberwiseClone	Creates a shallow copy of the current object (inherited from Object).
ReadLocalValue	Returns the local value of a dependency property, if a local value is set.
SetValue	Sets the local value of a dependency property on a DependencyObject.
ToString	Returns a String that represents the current object (inherited from Object).

UIElement Class

The UIElement class defines the input behavior for UI elements, including the events for keyboard, mouse and stylus input, and focus events. Like WPF, Silverlight is a composite-UI rendering system; thus, it supports routed events, and many of the events in this class are routed events. This enables built-in event handling notification, so events from child elements bubble up to parent elements for handling.

The UIElement class has the following inheritance hierarchy:

```
System.Object

  System.Windows.DependencyObject

    System.Windows.UIElement

      System.Windows.FrameworkElement
```

UIElement Class Methods

The following table describes the methods that the UIElement class exposes.

Name	Description
AddHandler	Adds a routed event handler for a specified routed event, adding the handler to the handler collection on the current element. Specify handledEventsToo as true to have the provided handler be invoked for a routed event that had already been marked as handled by another element along the event route.
Arrange	Positions child elements and determines a size for a UIElement. Parent elements that implement custom layout call this method from their layout override implementations to form a recursive layout update.
CaptureMouse	Sets mouse capture to the element.
CheckAccess	Determines whether the calling thread has access to this object (inherited from DependencyObject).
ClearValue	Clears the local value of a property (inherited from DependencyObject).
Equals	Determines whether the specified object is equal to the current object (inherited from Object).
Finalize	Allows an object to attempt to free resources and perform other cleanup operations before the object is reclaimed by garbage collection (inherited from Object).
GetAnimationBaseValue	Returns any base value established for a Silverlight dependency property, which would apply in cases in which an animation is not active (inherited from DependencyObject).
GetHashCode	Serves as a hash function for a particular type (inherited from Object).
GetType	Gets the Type of the current instance (inherited from Object).

Continued

Name	Description
GetValue	Returns the current effective value of a dependency property from a DependencyObject (inherited from DependencyObject).
InvalidateArrange	Invalidates the arrange state (layout) for the element. After the invalidation, the element will have its layout updated, which will occur asynchronously.
InvalidateMeasure	Invalidates the measurement state (layout) for the element.
Measure	Updates the DesiredSize of a UIElement. Parent elements that implement custom layout call this method from their own MeasureOverride implementations to form a recursive layout update.
MemberwiseClone	Creates a shallow copy of the current object (inherited from Object).
OnCreateAutomationPeer	When implemented in a derived class, returns class-specific AutomationPeer implementations for the Silverlight automation infrastructure.
ReadLocalValue	Returns the local value of a dependency property, if a local value is set (inherited from DependencyObject).
ReleaseMouseCapture	Removes mouse capture from the object, which typically means that no object holds mouse capture.
SetValue	Sets the local value of a dependency property on a DependencyObject (inherited from DependencyObject).
ToString	Returns a String that represents the current object (inherited from Object).
TransformToVisual	Returns a transform object that can be used to transform coordinates from the UIElement to the specified object.
UpdateLayout	Ensures that all positions of child elements of this element are properly updated for layout.

UIElement Class Properties

The following table describes the properties of the UIElement class.

Name	Description
CacheMode	Gets or sets a value that indicates that rendered content should be cached when possible.
Clip	Gets or sets the Geometry used to define the outline of the contents of an element.

Name	Description
DesiredSize	Gets the size that this element computed during the measure pass of the layout process.
Dispatcher	Gets the Dispatcher this object is associated with (inherited from DependencyObject).
Effect	Gets or sets the pixel shader effect to use for rendering this UIElement.
IsHitTestVisible	Gets or sets whether the contained area of this UIElement can return true values for hit testing.
Opacity	Gets or sets the degree of the object's opacity.
OpacityMask	Gets or sets the Brush used to alter the opacity of regions of this object.
Projection	Gets or sets the perspective projection (3D effect) to apply when rendering this UIElement.
RenderSize	Gets the final render size of this element.
RenderTransform	Gets or sets transform information that affects the rendering position of this element.
RenderTransformOrigin	Gets or sets the origin point of any possible render transform declared by RenderTransform, relative to the bounds of the element.
UseLayoutRounding	Gets or sets a value that determines whether rendering for the object and its subtree should use rounding behavior that aligns rendering to whole pixels.
Visibility	Gets or sets the visibility of this element. Elements that are not visible do not render.

UIElement Class Events

The following table describes the events associated with the UIElement class.

Name	Description
GotFocus	Occurs when an element receives focus.
KeyDown	Occurs when a keyboard key is pressed while the element has focus.
KeyUp	Occurs when a keyboard key is released while the element has focus.
LostFocus	Occurs when the element loses focus.
LostMouseCapture	Occurs when the object loses mouse (or stylus) capture.

Continued

Name	Description
MouseEnter	Occurs when the mouse enters the bounding area of an element.
MouseLeave	Occurs when the mouse leaves the bounding area of an object.
MouseLeftButtonDown	Occurs when the left mouse button is pressed while the mouse pointer is over the element.
MouseLeftButtonUp	Occurs when the left mouse button is released while the mouse is over the element (or while the element holds mouse capture).
MouseMove	Occurs when the coordinate position of the mouse changes.

FrameworkElement Class

The FrameworkElement class extends the UIElement class and adds the following capabilities with layout capabilities, object lifetime events, and data-binding support.

The Framework element class has the following class hierarchy:

System.Object

　System.Windows.DependencyObject

　　System.Windows.UIElement

　　　System.Windows.FrameworkElement

　　　　System.Windows.Controls.Border

　　　　System.Windows.Controls.ContentPresenter

　　　　System.Windows.Controls.Control

　　　　System.Windows.Controls.Image

　　　　System.Windows.Controls.ItemsPresenter

　　　　System.Windows.Controls.MediaElement

　　　　System.Windows.Controls.MultiScaleImage

　　　　System.Windows.Controls.Panel

　　　　System.Windows.Controls.Primitives.Popup

　　　　System.Windows.Controls.TextBlock

```
System.Windows.Documents.Glyphs
```

```
System.Windows.Shapes.Shape
```

FrameworkElement Class Methods

The following table describes the methods that the FrameworkElement class exposes.

Name	Description
AddHandler	Adds a routed event handler for a specified routed event, adding the handler to the handler collection on the current element. Specify handledEventsToo as true to have the provided handler be invoked for a routed event that had already been marked as handled by another element along the event route (inherited from UIElement).
Arrange	Positions child elements and determines a size for a UIElement. Parent elements that implement custom layout call this method from their layout override implementations to form a recursive layout update (inherited from UIElement).
ArrangeOverride	Provides the behavior for the *Arrange* pass of Silverlight layout. Classes can override this method to define their own arrange pass behavior.
CaptureMouse	Sets mouse capture to the element (inherited from UIElement).
CheckAccess	Determines whether the calling thread has access to this object (inherited from DependencyObject).
ClearValue	Clears the local value of a property (inherited from DependencyObject).
Equals	Determines whether the specified object is equal to the current object (inherited from Object).
Finalize	Allows an object to attempt to free resources and perform other cleanup operations before the object is reclaimed by garbage collection (inherited from Object).
FindName	Retrieves an element that has the provided identifier name.
GetAnimationBaseValue	Returns any base value established for a Silverlight dependency property, which would apply in cases in which an animation is not active (inherited from DependencyObject).
GetBindingExpression	Returns any base value established for a Silverlight dependency property, which would apply in cases in which an animation is not active (inherited from DependencyObject).

Continued

Name	Description
GetHashCode	Serves as a hash function for a particular type (inherited from `Object`).
GetType	Gets the `Type` of the current instance (inherited from `Object`).
GetValue	Provides specialized property return value behavior for certain `FrameworkElement` properties [overrides `DependencyObject` `.GetValue(DependencyProperty)`].
InvalidateArrange	Invalidates the arrange state (layout) for the element. After the invalidation, the element will have its layout updated, which will occur asynchronously (inherited from `UIElement`).
InvalidateMeasure	Invalidates the measurement state (layout) for the element (inherited from `UIElement`).
Measure	Updates the `DesiredSize` of a `UIElement`. Parent elements that implement custom layout call this method from their own `MeasureOverride` implementations to form a recursive layout update (inherited from `UIElement`).
MeasureOverride	Provides the behavior for the *measure* pass of Silverlight layout. Classes can override this method to define their own measure pass behavior.
MemberwiseClone	Creates a shallow copy of the current object (inherited from `Object`).
OnApplyTemplate	When overridden in a derived class, is invoked whenever application code or internal processes (such as a rebuilding layout pass) call `ApplyTemplate`.
OnCreateAutomationPeer	When implemented in a derived class, returns class-specific `AutomationPeer` implementations for the Silverlight automation infrastructure (inherited from `UIElement`).
ReadLocalValue	Returns the local value of a dependency property, if a local value is set (inherited from `DependencyObject`).
ReleaseMouseCapture	Removes mouse capture from the object, which typically means that no object holds mouse capture (inherited from `UIElement`).
RemoveHandler	Removes the specified routed event handler from this `UIElement` (inherited from `UIElement`).
SetBinding	Attaches a binding to this element, based on the provided binding object.
SetValue	Sets the local value of a dependency property on a `DependencyObject` (inherited from `DependencyObject`).

Name	Description
ToString	Returns a `String` that represents the current object (inherited from `Object`).
TransformToVisual	Returns a transform object that can be used to transform coordinates from the `UIElement` to the specified object (inherited from `UIElement`).
UpdateLayout	Ensures that all positions of child elements of this element are properly updated for layout (inherited from `UIElement`).

`FrameworkElement` Class Properties

The following table describes the properties of the `FrameworkElement` class.

Name	Description
ActualHeight	Gets the rendered height of this element.
ActualWidth	Gets the rendered width of this element.
CacheMode	Gets or sets a value that indicates that rendered content should be cached when possible (inherited from `UIElement`).
Clip	Gets or sets the `Geometry` used to define the outline of the contents of an element (inherited from `UIElement`).
Cursor	Gets or sets the cursor that displays when the mouse pointer is over this element.
DataContext	Gets or sets the data context for an element when it participates in data binding.
DesiredSize	Gets the size that this element computed during the measure pass of the layout process (inherited from `UIElement`).
Dispatcher	Gets the `Dispatcher` this object is associated with (inherited from `DependencyObject`).
Effect	Gets or sets the pixel shader effect to use for rendering this `UIElement` (inherited from `UIElement`).
Height	Gets or sets the suggested height of the element.
HorizontalAlignment	Gets or sets the horizontal alignment characteristics applied to this element when it is composed within a parent element, such as a panel or items control.
IsHitTestVisible	Gets or sets whether the contained area of this `UIElement` can return true values for hit testing (inherited from `UIElement`).

Continued

Name	Description
Language	Gets or sets localization/globalization language information that applies to an element.
Margin	Gets or sets the outer margin of an element.
MaxHeight	Gets or sets the maximum height constraint of the element.
MaxWidth	Gets or sets the maximum width constraint of the element.
MinHeight	Gets or sets the minimum height constraint of the element.
MinWidth	Gets or sets the minimum width constraint of the element.
Name	Gets (or sets, in XAML only) the identifying name of the element. The name provides a reference so that code-behind, such as event handler code, can refer to a markup element after an XAML processor creates the object tree from markup.
Opacity	Gets or sets the degree of the object's opacity (inherited from UIElement).
OpacityMask	Gets or sets the brush used to alter the opacity of regions of this object (inherited from UIElement).
Parent	Gets the parent element of this element.
Projection	Gets or sets the perspective projection (3D effect) to apply when rendering this UIElement (inherited from UIElement).
RenderSize	Gets the final render size of this element (inherited from UIElement).
RenderTransform	Gets or sets transform information that affects the rendering position of this element (inherited from UIElement).
RenderTransformOrigin	Gets or sets the origin point of any possible render transform declared by RenderTransform, relative to the bounds of the element (inherited from UIElement).
Resources	Gets the locally defined resource dictionary. In XAML, you can establish resource items as child elements of the <object.Resources> property element, through XAML implicit collection syntax.
Style	Gets or sets an instance Style that is applied for this element during rendering.
Tag	Gets or sets an arbitrary object value that can be used to store custom information about this element.
Triggers	Gets the collection of triggers for animations that are defined for this object.

Name	Description
VerticalAlignment	Gets or sets the vertical alignment characteristics applied to this element when it is composed within a parent element such as a panel or items control.
Visibility	Gets or sets the visibility of this element. Elements that are not visible do not render (inherited from UIElement).
Width	Gets or sets the width of the element

FrameworkElement Class Events

The following table describes the events associated with the FrameworkElement class.

Name	Description
BindingValidationError	Occurs when a data validation error is reported by a binding source.
GotFocus	Occurs when an element receives focus (inherited from UIElement).
KeyDown	Occurs when a keyboard key is pressed while the element has focus (inherited from UIElement).
KeyUp	Occurs when a keyboard key is released while the element has focus (inherited from UIElement).
LayoutUpdated	Occurs when the layout of the various child elements associated with the current Silverlight plug-in instance changes.
Loaded	Occurs when the element has completed layout passes, has been rendered, and is ready for interaction.
LostFocus	Occurs when the element loses focus (inherited from UIElement).
LostMouseCapture	Occurs when the object loses mouse (or stylus) capture (inherited from UIElement).
MouseEnter	Occurs when the mouse enters the bounding area of an element (inherited from UIElement).
MouseLeave	Occurs when the mouse leaves the bounding area of an object (inherited from UIElement).
MouseLeftButtonDown	Occurs when the left mouse button is pressed while the mouse pointer is over the element (inherited from UIElement).
MouseLeftButtonUp	Occurs when the left mouse button is released while the mouse is over the element (or while the element holds mouse capture) (inherited from UIElement).

Continued

Name	Description
MouseMove	Occurs when the coordinate position of the mouse changes (inherited from `UIElement`).
SizeChanged	Occurs when either the `ActualHeight` or the `ActualWidth` properties change value on this element.

C

System.Windows.Media Reference

System.Windows.Media

The System.Windows.Media namespace contains the types that give Silverlight rich capabilities for media, audio, video, vector drawing, and text. In this section, we'll list all of the classes and dig deeper into some of the core classes that you'll need to bring richness to your Silverlight applications.

System.Windows.Media Classes

The following sections list and describe the classes in the System.Windows.Media namespace.

ArcSegment

ArcSegment draws an elliptical arc between two points. The ArcSegment has five properties that you can use to define an elliptical arc.

- ❏ IsLargeArc — A Boolean value that gets or sets whether the arc should be greater than 180 degrees. IsLargeArc is used in conjunction with SweepDirection to set one of four arcs that can be rendered. If IsLargeArc=True, then an arc with a 180 degree sweep or greater is rendered.

- ❏ Point — The Point structure that gets or sets the endpoint of where the elliptical arc is drawn. The default Point is 0,0.

- ❏ RotationAngle — A Double value that gets or sets the value in degrees by which the ellipse is rotated about the X-axis. The default RotationAngle is 0.

- ❏ Size — A Size structure that gets or sets the Width (X-radius) and Height (Y-radius) of the arc as a Size structure. The default value is a Size with value 0,0.

- ❏ SweepDirection — The value of CounterClockwise or Clockwise that gets or sets the value of how an arc is drawn.

Syntax

```
<Path Stroke="DarkOrange"
      StrokeThickness="4" Margin="10">
  <Path.Data>
    <PathGeometry>
      <PathFigure StartPoint="0,65">
        <ArcSegment
          SweepDirection="Clockwise"
          Size="2,9" Point="25,65"/>
        <ArcSegment
          SweepDirection="CounterClockwise"
          Size="2,18" Point="50,65"/>
      </PathFigure>
    </PathGeometry>
  </Path.Data>
</Path>
```

Example

BezierSegment

BezierSegment defines a cubic Bezier curve drawn between two points. This class has three properties that you can use to define the BezierSegment.

❑ Point1 — Point structure that gets or sets the first control point of the curve. The default value is 0.

❑ Point2 — Point structure that gets or sets the second control point of the curve. The default value is 0.

❑ Point3 — Point structure that gets or sets the endpoint of the curve

Syntax

```
<Path Stroke="Black" StrokeThickness="1" >
    <Path.Data>
        <PathGeometry>
            <PathFigure
              StartPoint="10,50">
                <BezierSegment
                    Point1="400,12"
                    Point2="100,200"
                    Point3="100,20"/>
            </PathFigure>
```

```
            </PathGeometry>
        </Path.Data>
    </Path>
```

Example

BitMapCache

BitMapCache enables the caching of XAML elements at run time for reuse by GPU acceleration. Using the CacheMode property of BitMapCache creates a bitmap of a XAML element that can dramatically improve the performance of elements on a page.

Syntax

```
CacheMode="BitMapCache"
```

In order for BitMapCache to work on cached items, the EnableGPUAcceleration property must be set to true on the Silverlight plug-in.

Syntax

```
<param name="EnableGPUAcceleration" value="true" />
```

Brush

Brush defines objects used to paint graphical objects. The XAML usage for setting a Brush can be one of several variances, based on how you are going to set the Brush color:

- ❑ `<object property="predefinedColorName"/>`
- ❑ `<object property="#rgb"/>`
- ❑ `<object property="#argb"/>`
- ❑ `<object property="#rrggbb"/>`
- ❑ `<object property="#aarrggbb"/>`
- ❑ `<object property="sc#scR,scG,scB"/>`
- ❑ `<object property="sc#scA,scR,scG,scB"/>`

The following figure demonstrates the full color table for the Brush object:

The Brush object can be one of the following five types:

❑ SolidColorBrush — Paints an area with a solid color.

❑ LinearGradientBrush — Paints an area with a linear gradient.

❑ RadialGradientBrush — Paints an area with a radial gradient.

❑ ImageBrush — Paints an area with an image.

❑ VideoBrush — Paints an area with a running video.

Note that SolidColorBrush is the only Brush that supports attribute and object element syntax; the remaining brushes all must be declared in XAML with the object element syntax.

❑ colorString — The color for a SolidColorBrush expressed as an attribute string. This includes:

    ❑ Named color

    ❑ RBG value (with optional Alpha information)

    ❑ ScRGB value (with optional Alpha information)

```
<object Fill="Red"/>
```

❑ singleBrush — Within opening and closing property elements for object.Fill, exactly one object element for a class that derives from Brush (LinearGradient, RadialGradient, Image, Video). For example:

```
<object>
  <object.Fill>
    singleBrush
  </object.Fill>
</object>
```

Syntax

```
<Rectangle Width="200" Height="100">
  <Rectangle.Fill>
    <LinearGradientBrush
        StartPoint="0,0"
        EndPoint="1,1">
      <GradientStop Color="Red"
                    Offset="0.0" />
      <GradientStop Color="Blue"
                    Offset="0.55" />
      <GradientStop Color="Yellow"
                    Offset="1.0" />
    </LinearGradientBrush>
  </Rectangle.Fill>
</Rectangle>
```

Colors

Colors defines a set list of color properties. The following table lists the system-defined colors and ARGB values that you can set/get on an object.

Color String	ARGB Value
Black	#FF000000
Blue	#FF0000FF
Brown	#FFA52A2A
Cyan	#FF00FFFF
DarkGray	#FFA9A9A9
Gray	#FF808080
Green	#FF008000
LightGray	#FFD3D3D3
Magenta	#FFFF00FF
Orange	#FFFFA500
Purple	#FF800080
Red	#FFFF0000
Transparent	#00FFFFFF
White	#FFFFFFFF
Yellow	#FFFFFF00

CompositionTarget

CompositionTarget represents the display surface of a Silverlight-based application. The purpose of this class is as the host of the Rendering event, which can be used as a per-frame callback for complex layout or composition scenarios. Handling CompositionTarget.Rendering and working with a DispatcherTimer are two possible ways to handle game loops or other lower-level timing tasks.

DeepZoomImageTileSource

DeepZoomImageTileSource sets the URI for the source of the MultiScaleImage object.

DoubleCollection

DoubleCollection defines an ordered collection of Double values.

Syntax

```
Dim dCollection As New DoubleCollection
dCollection.Add(6)

Dim rect As New Rectangle
With rect
  .StrokeDashArray = dCollection
  .Stroke = _
      New SolidColorBrush(Colors.Black)
  .SetValue(Canvas.TopProperty, _
          Convert.ToDouble(50))
  .SetValue(Canvas.LeftProperty, _
          Convert.ToDouble(50))
  .Height = 150
  .Width = 150
End With

LayoutRoot.Children.Add(rect)
```

Example

EllipseGeometry

EllipseGeometry represents the geometry of a circle or ellipse. Different from the Ellipse class in the System.Windows.Shapes namespace, this EllipseGeometry class defines the geometry of an ellipse and cannot render itself.

The following four properties are in the EllipseGeometry class:

❑   Bounds — Gets a Rect that specifies the axis-aligned bounding box of the Geometry. (Inherited from Geometry.)

❑   Center — Point structure that gets or sets the center point of the EllipseGeometry.

❑   RadiusX — Double value that gets or sets the X-radius value of the EllipseGeometry.

❑   RadiusY — Double value that gets or sets the Y-radius value of the EllipseGeometry.

Syntax

In the following XAML, notice the clipped Ellipse over the semitransparent image:

```
<Image Source="race.jpg"
       Opacity=".5" >
</Image>

<Rectangle>
```

```
    <Rectangle.Fill>
        <ImageBrush
         ImageSource="race.jpg" />
    </Rectangle.Fill>
    <Rectangle.Clip>
        <EllipseGeometry
            Center="175,175"
            RadiusX="50"
            RadiusY="50" />
    </Rectangle.Clip>
</Rectangle>
```

Example

FontFamily

FontFamily is a string that defines the family of related fonts in the Silverlight player. The following fonts are included:

- ❏ Arial
- ❏ Arial Black
- ❏ Comic Sans MS
- ❏ Courier New
- ❏ Lucida Grande
- ❏ Lucida Sans Unicode
- ❏ Times New Roman
- ❏ Trebuchet MS
- ❏ Verdana

GeneralTransform

GeneralTransform provides transformation support for objects, such as points or rectangles.

Geometry

`Geometry` provides a base class for objects that define geometric shapes for operations such as clipping and rendering two-dimensional (2D) data as a `Path` object. The following three key properties are used to define a `Geometry`:

- ❏ `Bounds` — `Rect` that specifies the axis-aligned bounding box of the `Geometry`
- ❏ `StandardFlatteningTolerance` — Gets the standard tolerance used for polygonal approximation.
- ❏ `Transform` — Gets or sets the `Transform` object applied to a `Geometry`, using a single transform or a transform group.

GeometryCollection

`GeometryCollection` defines a collection of `Geometry` objects that derive from `Geometry`.

GeometryGroup

`GeometryGroup` represents a composite geometry, composed of other `Geometry` objects. These are usually a combination of `EllipseGeometry`, `GeometryGroup`, `LineGeometry`, `PathGeometry`, and `RectangleGeometry`.

Syntax

```
<Path Stroke="Black"
      StrokeThickness="3"
      Fill="Yellow">
    <Path.Data>
        <GeometryGroup
            FillRule="Nonzero" >
            <EllipseGeometry
                Center="60,70"
                RadiusX="40"
                RadiusY="30" />
            <RectangleGeometry
                Rect="60,55 100 60" />
        </GeometryGroup>
    </Path.Data>
</Path>
```

Example

GradientBrush

An abstract class that describes a gradient, composed of gradient stops. Classes that derive from `GradientBrush`, such as `LinearGradientBrush` and `RadialGradientBrush`, describe different ways of interpreting gradient stops.

The following seven properties are exposed by GradientBrush:

❏ ColorInterpolationMode — Gets or sets a ColorInterpolationMode enumeration value that specifies how the gradient's colors are interpolated.

❏ GradientStops — Gets or sets a collection of the GradientStop objects associated with the Brush. Each GradientStop specifies a color and an offset along the Brush's gradient axis. The default is an empty GradientStopCollection.

❏ MappingMode — Gets or sets a BrushMappingMode enumeration value (Absolute or RelativeToBoundingBox) that specifies whether the positioning coordinates of the gradient brush are absolute or relative to the output area.

    ❏ Absolute — The coordinate system is not relative to a bounding box. Values are interpreted directly in local space.

    ❏ RelativeToBoundingBox — The coordinate system is relative to a bounding box: 0 indicates 0 percent of the bounding box, and 1 indicates 100 percent of the bounding box. For example, (0.5, 0.5) describes a point in the middle of the bounding box, and (1, 1) describes a point at the bottom right of the bounding box.

❏ Opacity — Gets or sets the degree of opacity of a Brush. (Inherited from Brush.)

❏ RelativeTransform — Gets or sets the transformation that is applied to the Brush using relative coordinates. (Inherited from Brush.)

❏ SpreadMethod — Gets or sets the type of spread method that specifies how to draw a gradient that starts or ends inside the bounds of the object to be painted.

❏ Transform — Gets or sets the transformation that is applied to the brush. (Inherited from Brush.)

GradientStop

GradientStop sets the location and color of a transition point in a LinearGradientBrush or RadialGradientBrush.

Syntax

```
<Rectangle Width="200" Height="100">
    <Rectangle.Fill>
        <LinearGradientBrush
            StartPoint="0,0"
            EndPoint="1,1">
            <GradientStop
                Color="Yellow"
                Offset="0.0" />
            <GradientStop
                Color="Red"
                Offset="0.25" />
            <GradientStop
                Color="Blue"
                Offset="0.75" />
```

```
        <GradientStop
            Color="LimeGreen"
            Offset="1.0" />
    </LinearGradientBrush>
  </Rectangle.Fill>
</Rectangle>
```

Example

GradientStopCollection

GradientStopCollection represents a collection of GradientStop objects that can be individually accessed by index.

ImageBrush

ImageBrush paints an area with an ImageSource, which is defined as a BitmapImage. An ImageBrush is used on an object such as a Rectangle or a TextBlock.

Syntax

```
<Rectangle>
  <Rectangle.Fill>
      <ImageBrush ImageSource="race.jpg"/>
  </Rectangle.Fill>
</Rectangle>
```

Example

ImageSource

ImageSource is an abstract type that is used in the signatures for Image.Source, MultiScaleImage .Source, and ImageBrush.ImageSource.

LinearGradientBrush

LinearGradientBrush paints an area with a linear gradient along a specific linear line defined by StartPoint and EndPoint properties. In the case of a LinearGradientBrush, its GradientStops are rendered along this line.

The default linear gradient is diagonal. In the default, the StartPoint of a linear gradient is a Point with value 0,0, the upper-left corner of the area being painted, and its EndPoint is a Point with value 1,1, the lower-right corner of the area being painted. The colors in the resulting gradient are interpolated along the diagonal path.

Syntax

```
<Rectangle Width="200"
        Height="100">
<Rectangle.Fill>
    <LinearGradientBrush
        StartPoint="0,0"
        EndPoint="1,0">
        <GradientStop
            Color="Yellow"
            Offset="0.25" />
        <GradientStop
            Color="Green"
            Offset="0.50" />
        <GradientStop
            Color="Red"
            Offset="0.75" />
    </LinearGradientBrush>
</Rectangle.Fill>
</Rectangle>
```

Example

LineGeometry

LineGeometry defines the geometry of a line used by a Path shape to render the line. Similar to the EllipseGeometry, the LineGeometry only defines the line — it depends on other objects to render itself.

Syntax

```
<Path Stroke="OrangeRed"
        StrokeThickness="5">
    <Path.Data>
        <GeometryGroup>
            <LineGeometry
                StartPoint="10,10"
```

```
                    EndPoint="100,10"/>
                <LineGeometry
                    StartPoint="100,10"
                    EndPoint="100,100"/>
            </GeometryGroup>
        </Path.Data>
    </Path>
```

Example

LineSegment

LineSegment defines a line drawn between two points, which can be part of a PathFigure within Path data. The LineSegment class does not contain a property for the starting point of the line. The starting point of the line is the endpoint of the previous segment or the StartPoint of the PathFigure if no other segments exist.

The simple shape of a line can also be generated using Line. LineSegment is particularly intended for drawing a line within what is typically a more complex geometry group.

The LineSegment has a single Point property, which gets or sets the endpoint of the line.

Syntax

```
<Canvas>
    <Path Stroke="Black" StrokeThickness="1">
        <Path.Data>
            <PathGeometry>
                <PathGeometry.Figures>
                    <PathFigure StartPoint="10,20">
                        <PathFigure.Segments>
                            <LineSegment Point="100,130"/>
                        </PathFigure.Segments>
                    </PathFigure>
                </PathGeometry.Figures>
            </PathGeometry>
        </Path.Data>
    </Path>
</Canvas>
```

MatrixTransform

MatrixTransform creates an arbitrary 2D X–Y plane that uses a 3 × 3 matrix for transformations. The following six property values are used in XAML to define the transform matrix on the X–Y plane.

❏   m11 — Double value at position (1, 1) of the transformation Matrix

❏   m12 — Double value at position (1, 2) of the transformation Matrix

❑ m21 — Double value at position (2, 1) of the transformation Matrix

❑ m22 — Double value at position (2, 2) of the transformation Matrix

❑ offsetX — Double value at position (3, 1) of the transformation Matrix

❑ offsetY — Double value at position (3, 2) of the transformation Matrix

Syntax

```
<Rectangle Width="75"
           Height="90"
           Fill="Blue">
    <Rectangle.RenderTransform>
        <MatrixTransform>
            <MatrixTransform.Matrix >
                <Matrix OffsetY="-50"
                        M12="1.4" />
            </MatrixTransform.Matrix>
        </MatrixTransform>
    </Rectangle.RenderTransform>
</Rectangle>
```

Example

MediaStreamDescription

MediaStreamDescription defines the media type needed to initialize the MediaElement and the underlying media pipeline. The following properties are specific to MediaStreamDescription:

❑ MediaAttributes — Gets a collection of attributes about the media stream. This collection only contains attributes that are used to initialize the media pipeline and the MediaElement.

❑ StreamId — Integer value that gets the stream ID of the stream being described

❑ Type — The MediaStream enumeration that contains the following:

   ❑ Audio — The stream is an audio stream.

   ❑ Video — The stream is a video stream.

   ❑ Script — The stream is a script stream.

Currently script commands are not supported in MediaStreamSource.

MediaStreamSample

MediaStreamSample defines a media sample in enough detail to allow the MediaElement and underlying pipeline to render the sample.

MediaStreamSource

MediaStreamSource enables MediaElement to use a container format other than ASF.

MultiScaleTileSource

MultiScaleTileSource specifies the source of Deep Zoom images. The DeepZoomImageTileSource, which derives from this class, is used to specify the source of a MultiScaleImage.

PathFigure

PathFigure defines a path geometry that can contain multiple PathSegments to make up a single, interconnected geometry.

- ❑ IsClosed — Boolean that gets or sets a value that specifies whether this figure's first and last segments are connected

- ❑ IsFilled — Boolean that gets or sets whether the contained area of this PathFigure is to be used for hit-testing, rendering, and clipping

- ❑ Segments — A PathsegmentCollection that gets or sets the collection of segments that define the shape of this PathFigure object

- ❑ StartPoint — Point structure that gets or sets the Point where the PathFigure begins

The key property for the PathFigure is its StartPoint, which is the point from which the first contained line segment starts. If you need a geometry in which the multiple segments are not connected, you can define multiple PathFigure objects in a PathFigureCollection. Each PathFigure would have a different StartPoint.

Usage

```
<PathFigure>
    oneOrMorePathSegments
</PathFigure>
```

where the PathSegments are objects that derive from PathSegment, such as ArcSegment, BezierSegment, LineSegment, PolyBezierSegment, PolyQuadraticBezierSegment, or QuadraticBezierSegment.

Notice in the following XAML that there are only three lines in the PathFigure.Segements collection, yet four lines are rendered. The IsClosed property automatically closed the geometry with a line connecting the first and third LineSegments. You can also omit the PathGeometries.Figures syntax, since you can use the implicit collection syntax in this case.

Syntax

```
<Path Stroke="DarkSalmon"
      StrokeThickness="3">
   <Path.Data>
      <PathGeometry>
         <PathGeometry.Figures>
            <PathFigure
                StartPoint="10,20"
                IsClosed="True" >
               <PathFigure.Segments>
                  <LineSegment
                      Point="100,130"/>
                  <LineSegment
                      Point="100,230"/>
                  <LineSegment
                      Point="200,50"/>
               </PathFigure.Segments>
            </PathFigure>
         </PathGeometry.Figures>
      </PathGeometry>
   </Path.Data>
</Path>
```

Example

PathFigureCollection

As demonstrated in the previous PathFigure example, this PathFigureCollection contains a collection of PathFigure objects that collectively make up the geometry of a PathGeometry.

Either you can use the Path mini-language, which is a collection of drawing commands, or you can define multiple geometries in a PathFigure.Segments collection.

PathGeometry

As demonstrated in the previous PathFigure example, a PathGeometry is a complex shape that may be composed of arcs, curves, ellipses, lines, and rectangles.

Appendix C: System.Windows.Media Reference

Syntax

```xml
<Path Stroke="Black"
      StrokeThickness="3"
      Fill="DodgerBlue">
    <Path.Data>
        <GeometryGroup
            FillRule="EvenOdd" >
            <EllipseGeometry
                Center="60,70"
                RadiusX="40"
                RadiusY="30" />
            <RectangleGeometry
                Rect="60,55 100 60" />
        </GeometryGroup>
    </Path.Data>
</Path>
```

Example

PathSegment

PathSegment defines a segment of a PathFigure object based on an instance of the ArcSegment, BezierSegment, LineSegment, PolylineSegement, PolyBezierSegment, PolyQuadraticBezierSegment, and QuadraticBezierSegment derived types.

Similarly to the previous PathFigure example, this XAML adds a BezierSegment and sets the IsClosed property to False.

Syntax

```xml
<Path Stroke="DarkSalmon"
      StrokeThickness="3">
    <Path.Data>
        <PathGeometry>
            <PathGeometry.Figures>
                <PathFigure
                    StartPoint="10,20"
                    IsClosed="False" >
                    <PathFigure.Segments>
                        <BezierSegment
                            Point1="100,0"
                            Point2="200,200"
                            Point3="300,100"/>
                        <LineSegment
                            Point="100,130"/>
```

```
                              <LineSegment
                                    Point="100,230"/>
                              <LineSegment
                                    Point="200,50"/>
                         </PathFigure.Segments>
                       </PathFigure>
                    </PathGeometry.Figures>
                 </PathGeometry>
              </Path.Data>
         </Path>
```

Example

PathSegmentCollection

PathSegmentCollection represents a collection of PathSegment geometries. Each PathSegment in the PathSegmentCollection can be accessed by index. See the previous PathFigure examples for the syntax on implementing a PathSegmentCollection.

PixelFormats

PixelFormats defines the values that represent the supported pixel formats:

❑ **Bgr32** — An sRGB format with 32 bits per pixel (BPP). Each color channel (blue, green, and red) is allocated 8 BPP.

❑ **Pbgra32** — An sRGB format with 32 BPP. Each channel (blue, green, red, and alpha) is allocated 8 BPP. Each color channel is pre-multiplied by the alpha value.

PlaneProjection

PlaneProjection is used to create a perspective transform (a 3D effect) on an object. For example, you can create the illusion that an object is rotated toward or away from you. You can apply a PlaneProjection to any UIElement, including controls. This class also enables you to animate the perspective transform properties to create moving 3D effects.

The following properties are in the PlaneProjection class:

❑ CenterOfRotationX — Double value that gets or sets the X-coordinate of the center of rotation of the object you rotate

❑ CenterOfRotationY — Double value that gets or sets the Y-coordinate of the center of rotation of the object you rotate

❑ CenterOfRotationZ — Double value that gets or sets the Z-coordinate of the center of rotation of the object you rotate

❑ GlobalOffsetX — Double value that gets or sets the distance the object is translated along the X-axis of the screen

❑ GlobalOffsetY — Double value that gets or sets the distance the object is translated along the Y-axis of the screen

❑ GlobalOffsetZ — Double value that gets or sets the distance the object is translated along the Z-axis of the screen.

❑ LocalOffsetX — Double value that gets or sets the distance the object is translated along the X-axis of the plane of the object

❑ LocalOffsetY — Double value that gets or sets the distance the object is translated along the Y-axis of the plane of the object

❑ LocalOffsetZ — Double value that gets or sets the distance the object is translated along the Z-axis of the plane of the object

❑ RotationX — Double value that gets or sets the number of degrees to rotate the object around the X-axis of rotation

❑ RotationY — Double value that gets or sets the number of degrees to rotate the object around the Y-axis of rotation

❑ RotationZ — Double value that gets or sets the number of degrees to rotate the object around the Z-axis of rotation

Syntax

```
<StackPanel Margin="35" Background="PapayaWhip">
    <StackPanel.Projection>
        <PlaneProjection RotationX="-25"
                         RotationY="35"
                         RotationZ="0"  />
    </StackPanel.Projection>

    <TextBlock Margin="10">First Name:</TextBlock>
    <TextBox Margin="10"></TextBox>

    <TextBlock Margin="10">Last Name:</TextBlock>
    <TextBox Margin="10"></TextBox>

    <Button Margin="10" Content="Submit" Width="100" />
</StackPanel>
```

Example

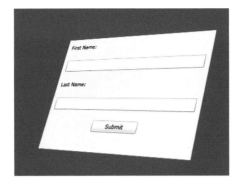

PointCollection

PointCollection represents a collection of Point values that can be individually accessed by index.

Syntax

```
<Path Stroke="DarkOliveGreen"
      StrokeThickness="3">
    <Path.Data>
        <PathGeometry>
            <PathGeometry.Figures>
                <PathFigureCollection>
                    <PathFigure
                            StartPoint="10,50">
                        <PathFigure.Segments>
                            <PathSegmentCollection>
                                <PolyBezierSegment
                                    Points="0,0 100,0
                                    300,100 400,10
                                    100,0 300,100" />
                            </PathSegmentCollection>
                        </PathFigure.Segments>
                    </PathFigure>
                </PathFigureCollection>
            </PathGeometry.Figures>
        </PathGeometry>
    </Path.Data>
</Path>
```

Example

PolyBezierSegment

PolyBezierSegment represents one or more cubic Bezier curves.

PolyLineSegment

PolyLineSegment defines a series of connected lines in a PathFigure, which contains a series of points that specify the endpoint of each line segment in a PointCollection.

The previous PathSegment example demonstrates a PolylineSegment.

PolyQuadraticBezierSegment

PolyQuadraticBezierSegment represents a set of quadratic Bezier segments that have one control point and an endpoint. Each PolyQuadraticBezierSegment can have an unlimited number of control points, with the values of these points and the endpoint given as the Points property value.

Syntax

```
<Path Stroke="Chocolate"
      StrokeThickness="4" >
    <Path.Data>
        <PathGeometry>
            <PathFigure
              StartPoint="10,100">
                <PolyQuadraticBezierSegment
                      Points="200,200 300,
                      100 0,200 30,250"/>
            </PathFigure>
        </PathGeometry>
    </Path.Data>
</Path>
```

Example

Projection

Projection provides a base class for projections, which describe how to transform an object in 3D space using perspective transforms. See PlaneProjection earlier in this appendix for usage.

QuadraticBezierSegment

QuadraticBezierSegment defines a quadratic Bezier curve between two points in a PathFigure. In a QuadraticBezierSegment, there is no property for the starting point of the line. The starting point of the line is the endpoint of the previous segment, or the StartPoint of the PathFigure if no other segments exist.

Syntax

```
<Path Stroke="Chocolate"
      StrokeThickness="4" >
    <Path.Data>
        <PathGeometry>
            <PathFigure
              StartPoint="10,100">
                <QuadraticBezierSegment
                    Point1="200,200"
                    Point2="300,100"/>
            </PathFigure>
        </PathGeometry>
    </Path.Data>
</Path>
```

Example

RadialGradientBrush

Using a focal point that defines the beginning of the gradient and a circle that defines the endpoint of the gradient, this class paints an area with a radial gradient.

Whereas the linear gradient has a start and an endpoint to define the gradient vector, the radial gradient has an ellipse along with a focal point (the GradientOrigin) to define the gradient behavior. The ellipse defines the endpoint of the gradient.

RadialGradientBrush is derived from GradientBrush, which is derived from Brush. The four properties unique to RadialGradientBrush are:

❑   Center — Point structure that gets or sets the center of the outer circle of the radial gradient

❑   GradientOrigin — Point structure that gets or sets the location of the focal point that defines the beginning of the gradient

❑   RadiusX — Double value that gets or sets the horizontal radius of the outer circle of the radial gradient

❑   RadiusY — Double value that gets or sets the vertical radius of the outer circle of the radial gradient

Syntax

```
<Rectangle Width="200"
                   Height="100">
    <Rectangle.Fill>
        <RadialGradientBrush
            GradientOrigin="0.5,0.5"
            Center="0.5,0.5"
            RadiusX="0.5"
            RadiusY="0.5">
```

```
            <GradientStop
                Color="Yellow"
                Offset="0" />
            <GradientStop
                Color="Red"
                 Offset="0.25" />
            <GradientStop
                Color="Blue"
                Offset="0.75" />
            <GradientStop
                Color="LimeGreen"
                Offset="1" />
        </RadialGradientBrush>
      </Rectangle.Fill>
  </Rectangle>
```

Example

RectangleGeometry

RectangleGeometry describes a 2D rectangular geometry. The RectangleGeometry has three properties that set its height, width, X location, Y location, and the X-radius and Y-radius of the geometry's ellipse.

❑   RadiusX — Double value that gets or sets the X-radius of the ellipse used to round the corners of the rectangle

❑   RadiusY — Double value that gets or sets the Y-radius of the ellipse used to round the corners of the rectangle

❑   Rect — Rect structure that gets or sets the dimensions of the rectangle in the form of Rect="x,y,width,height"

The value of RadiusX or RadiusY must be greater than or equal to 0 and less than half of the X-radius or Y-radius of the geometry. Anything greater than half of the X-radius or Y-radius value will be treated as half of the X-radius or Y-radius value. In the case of the example below, the X-radius and Y-radius of the geometry are both 150, so any RadiusX or RadiusY setting greater than 75 would be treated as 75.

Syntax

```
<Path Fill="Firebrick"
      Stroke="Green"
      StrokeThickness="4">
    <Path.Data>
        <RectangleGeometry
            Rect="100,100,150,150" />
    </Path.Data>
</Path>
```

Example

This XAML adds the RadiusX and RadiusY properties:

```
<Path Fill="Firebrick"
      Stroke="Green"
      StrokeThickness="4">
    <Path.Data>
        <RectangleGeometry
            RadiusX="30"
            RadiusY="30"
            Rect="100,100,150,150" />
    </Path.Data>
</Path>
```

resulting in the same geometry with rounded corners:

RenderOptions

RenderOptions provides options for controlling the rendering behavior of objects. By default, Silverlight optimizes text for readability, which can have a large performance impact when you animate text. This is because during animation, Silverlight is constantly re-drawing the optimized text, and this optimization takes significant resources. When animating text, you will likely get better performance by turning off this readability optimization by setting the TextRenderingMode property to RenderForAnimation and then setting it back to Default when the animation ends.

RotateTransform

RotateTransform rotates an object clockwise about a specified point in a 2D X–Y coordinate system by changing the Angle property, which rotates an object by that angle about the point CenterX, CenterY.

Syntax

In the following example, the `Angle` property is set to 90 degrees for the second `TextBlock`. Notice that the `Margin` is the same for both `TextBlock` elements.

```
<TextBlock Margin="100,30"
           Text="Rotated Text"
           FontSize="18" />
<TextBlock Margin="100, 30"
           Text="Rotated Text"
           FontSize="18" >
    <TextBlock.RenderTransform>
        <RotateTransform Angle="90" />
    </TextBlock.RenderTransform>
</TextBlock>
```

Example

ScaleTransform

`ScaleTransform` scales an object by changing the `ScaleX` and `ScaleY` properties in a `ScaleTransform`. The four properties that set how the `ScaleTransform` is rendered are:

- ❏ `ScaleX` — `Double` value that specifies the amount to stretch or shrink an object along the X-axis

- ❏ `ScaleY` — `Double` value that specifies the amount to stretch or shrink an object along the Y-axis

- ❏ `CenterX` — `Double` value that gets or sets the X-coordinate of the center point of this `ScaleTransform`

- ❏ `CenterY` — `Double` value that gets or sets the Y-coordinate of the center point of this `ScaleTransform`

All scale operations are centered on the point specified by the `CenterX` and `CenterY` properties.

The same XAML used in the `RotateTransform` example is used below. A `TransformGroup` is added, so we can use multiple transforms, and the `ScaleX` and `ScaleY` properties are changed on the `ScaleTransform` to grow the X and Y scale of the rotated text by 2. Note that when you change the font size of an object, the font is calculated independently to render the best resolution based on the size set. When scaling text with `ScaleTransform`, the text preserves the proportions of the original-sized text.

Syntax

```
<TextBlock Margin="100,30"
           Text="Rotated Text"
           FontSize="18" />
```

```
<TextBlock Margin="100, 30"
           Text="Rotated Text"
           FontSize="18" >
    <TextBlock.RenderTransform>
        <TransformGroup>
            <RotateTransform
                Angle="90" />
            <ScaleTransform
                ScaleX="2" ScaleY="2"/>
        </TransformGroup>
    </TextBlock.RenderTransform>
</TextBlock>
```

Example

Rotated Text

SkewTransform

SkewTransform represents a 2D skew that created the illusion of 3D depth in a 2D object. The four properties that set how the SkewTransform is rendered are:

- ❏ AngleX — Double value that gets or sets the X-axis skew angle, which is measured in degrees counterclockwise from the Y-axis

- ❏ AngleY — Double value that gets or sets the Y-axis skew angle, which is measured in degrees counterclockwise from the X-axis

- ❏ CenterX — Double value that gets or sets the X-coordinate of the transform center

- ❏ CenterY — Double value that gets or sets the Y-coordinate of the transform center

The following image illustrates the various effects the properties can have on an object:

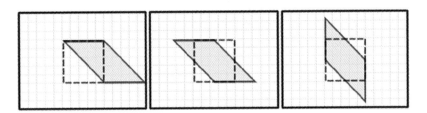

Syntax

```
<Image
        Source="race.jpg"
        Margin="50, 25">
    <Image.RenderTransform>
            <TransformGroup>
                <SkewTransform
                    AngleX="-15"
                    AngleY="0" />
                <ScaleTransform
                    ScaleX=".5"
                    ScaleY=".5"/>
            </TransformGroup>
    </Image.RenderTransform>
</Image>
```

Example

SolidColorBrush

SolidColorBrush paints an area with a solid color. For a complete description of the SolidColorBrush, refer to the beginning of the section for the Brush class.

TileBrush

TileBrush defines a way for the derived ImageBrush and VideoBrush classes to paint a region by using one or more tiles. The properties specific for its rendering are:

❑   AlignmentX — Gets or sets the horizontal alignment of content in the TileBrush base tile.

❑   AlignmentY — Gets or sets the vertical alignment of content in the TileBrush base tile.

❑   Opacity — Gets or sets the degree of opacity of a Brush. (Inherited from Brush.)

❑   RelativeTransform — Gets or sets the transformation that is applied to the Brush using relative coordinates. (Inherited from Brush.)

❑   Stretch — Gets or sets a value that specifies how the content of this TileBrush stretches to fit its tiles.

❑   Transform — Gets or sets the transformation that is applied to the Brush. (Inherited from Brush.)

TimelineMarker

TimelineMarker represents metadata associated with a specific point in a media file.

TimelineMarkerCollection

`TimelineMarkerCollection` represents a collection of `TimelineMarker` objects that can be individually accessed by index.

TimelineMarkerRoutedEventArgs

`TimelineMarkerRoutedEventArgs` provides event data for the `MarkerReached` event.

Transform

`Transform` defines functionality for creating transformation on a 2D plane. The following transform classes derive from the `Transform` class:

- ❑ System.Windows.Media — MatrixTransform
- ❑ System.Windows.Media — RotateTransform
- ❑ System.Windows.Media — ScaleTransform
- ❑ System.Windows.Media — SkewTransform
- ❑ System.Windows.Media — TransformGroup
- ❑ System.Windows.Media — TranslateTransform

TransformCollection

`TransformCollection` represents a collection of `Transform` objects that can be individually accessed by index. The `TransformCollection` element does not need to be included in your `TransformGroup` declaration, as it follows the implicit collection syntax.

TransformGroup

`TransformGroup` defines a series of transforms on an object. A `TransformGroup` is required if there is more than a single transform being applied to an object.

It is important to note that the order of the transforms matters in how the element renders. Rotating an object that is centered at the origin produces a different result from rotating an object that has been moved away from the origin based on the `CenterX` or `CenterY` property settings.

Syntax

```
<Image
        Source="race.jpg"
        Margin="110, 15">
    <Image.RenderTransform>
        <TransformGroup>
            <SkewTransform
                AngleX="-15"
                AngleY="0" />
            <ScaleTransform
                ScaleX=".5"
                ScaleY=".5"/>
```

```
                    <RotateTransform
                        Angle="25"/>
                </TransformGroup>
            </Image.RenderTransform>
        </Image>
```

Example

TranslateTransform

TranslateTransform translates (moves) an object in the 2D X–Y coordinate system.

VideoBrush

A VideoBrush is a type of Brush object similar to a LinearGradientBrush or an ImageBrush. However, instead of painting an area with a solid color, a gradient, or an image, it paints an area with video content. This video content is provided by a MediaElement. Just like the other brush types, you can use a VideoBrush to paint the Fill of a shape such as a Rectangle or the geometry contents of a Path, the Background of a Canvas, or the Foreground of a TextBlock or Run.

To use a VideoBrush, you create a MediaElement, apply the VideoBrush to the object that you want to paint, and set the VideoBrush object's SourceName property to the name of the MediaElement that you created. The following properties are in the VideoBrush class:

❑ AlignmentX — Gets or sets the horizontal alignment of content in the TileBrush base tile. (Inherited from TileBrush.)

❑ AlignmentY — Gets or sets the vertical alignment of content in the TileBrush base tile. (Inherited from TileBrush.)

❑ Opacity — Gets or sets the degree of opacity of a Brush. (Inherited from Brush.)

❑ RelativeTransform — Gets or sets the transformation that is applied to the Brush using relative coordinates. (Inherited from Brush.)

❑ SourceName — Gets or sets the name of the MediaElement to use as the source of the VideoBrush.

❑ Stretch — Gets or sets a value that specifies how the content of this TileBrush stretches to fit its tiles. (Inherited from TileBrush.)

❑ Transform — Gets or sets the transformation that is applied to the Brush. (Inherited from Brush.)

Syntax

```
<MediaElement
  x:Name="butterflyMediaEelment"
  Source="sampleMedia/Butterfly.wmv" IsMuted="True"
  Opacity="0.0" IsHitTestVisible="False" />

<TextBlock Canvas.Left="5" Canvas.Top="30"
  FontFamily="Verdana" FontSize="120"
  FontWeight="Bold" TextWrapping="Wrap"
  Text="Video">

  <TextBlock.Foreground>
    <VideoBrush SourceName="butterflyMediaElement"
                Stretch="UniformToFill" />
  </TextBlock.Foreground>
</TextBlock>
```

VisualTreeHelper

VisualTreeHelper provides utility methods that can be used to traverse object relationships (along child object or parent object axes) in the Silverlight visual tree.

System.Windows.Media Enumerations

The following sections describe the enumerations in the System.Windows.Media namespace.

AlignmentX

AlignmentX specifies how content is positioned horizontally in a container.

The values are:

- ❑ Left
- ❑ Center
- ❑ Right

AlignmentY

AlignmentY specifies how content is positioned vertically in a container.

The values are:

- ❑ Top
- ❑ Center
- ❑ Bottom

BrushMappingMode

BrushMappingMode specifies the coordinate system used by a Brush.

The values are:

- ❑ Absolute — The coordinate system is not relative to a bounding box. Values are interpreted directly in local space.

- ❑ RelativeToBoundingBox — The coordinate system is relative to a bounding box: 0 indicates 0 percent of the bounding box, and 1 indicates 100 percent of the bounding box.

ColorInterpolationMode

ColorInterpolationMode specifies how the colors in a gradient are interpolated.

The values are:

- ❑ ScRgbLinearInterpolation — Colors are interpolated in the scRGB color space.

- ❑ SRgbLinearInterpolation — Colors are interpolated in the sRGB color space.

FillRule

FillRule specifies how the intersecting areas of PathFigure objects contained in a Geometry are combined to form the area of the Geometry.

The values are:

- ❑ EvenOdd — Rule that determines whether a point is in the fill region by drawing a ray from that point to infinity in any direction and counting the number of path segments within the given shape that the ray crosses. If this number is odd, the point is inside; if even, the point is outside.

- ❑ Nonzero — Rule that determines whether a point is in the fill region of the path by drawing a ray from that point to infinity in any direction and then examining the places where a segment of the shape crosses the ray

GradientSpreadMethod

GradientSpreadMethod specifies how to draw the gradient outside a gradient brush's gradient vector or space.

The values are:

- ❑ Pad — The color values at the ends of the gradient vector fill the remaining space.

- ❑ Reflect — The gradient is repeated in the reverse direction until the space is filled.

- ❑ Repeat — The gradient is repeated in the original direction until the space is filled.

LogSource

LogSource indicates the reason that a media log was generated.

The values are:

- ❏ RequestLog — The RequestLog method was called.
- ❏ Stop — The media stopped.
- ❏ Seek — A seek operation occurred on the media; that is, playback was moved forward or backward.
- ❏ Pause — The media paused.
- ❏ SourceChanged — The source of the media changed.
- ❏ EndOfStream — The media reached the end of its stream.
- ❏ MediaElementShutdown — The runtime shutdown.
- ❏ RuntimeShutdown — The runtime shutdown.

MediaElementState

MediaElementState defines the potential states of a MediaElement object.

The values are:

- ❏ Closed — MediaElement contains no media. The MediaElement displays a transparent frame.
- ❏ Opening — MediaElement is validating and attempting to open the Uniform Resource Identifier (URI) specified by its Source property. While in this state, the MediaElement queues any Play, Pause, or Stop commands it receives and processes them if the media is successfully opened.
- ❏ Buffering — MediaElement is loading the media for playback. Its Position does not advance during this state. If the MediaElement was already playing video, it continues to display the last displayed frame.
- ❏ Playing — MediaElement is playing the media specified by its source property. Its Position advances.
- ❏ Paused — MediaElement does not advance its Position. If the MediaElement was playing video, it continues to display the current frame.
- ❏ Stopped — MediaElement contains media but is not playing or paused. Its Position is 0 and does not advance. If the loaded media is video, the MediaElement displays the first frame.

MediaSampleAttributeKeys

MediaSampleAttributeKeys is an enumeration that describes the media sample.

The values are:

- ❏ KeyFrameFlag — Data about the sample needed to decrypt it
- ❏ DRMInitializationVector — Boolean value describing whether or not the given video frame is a keyframe

MediaSourceAttributesKeys

`MediaSourceAttributesKeys` is an enumeration that describes the media source.

The values are:

- ❑   `CanSeek` — Boolean value describing whether or not this source can seek
- ❑   `Duration` — DRM data that the pipeline needs to initialize and decrypt correctly. This is the DRM header represented as a string.
- ❑   `DRMHeader` — The length of playback time of this source as an integer in 100-nanosecond increments

MediaStreamAttributeKeys

`MediaStreamAttributeKeys` is an enumeration that describes the media stream.

The values are:

- ❑   `CodecPrivateData` — Codec data that the pipeline needs to initialize and render correctly. For video, this is other `Header` information. For audio, this is the base16-encoded `WaveFormatEx` structure.
- ❑   `VideoFourCC` — This is data needed to instantiate a video codec. This is the 4 character value also known as `FourCC`.
- ❑   `Width` — This is the integer width a video frame is to be rendered at.
- ❑   `Height` — This is the integer height a video frame is to be rendered at.

MediaStreamSourceDiagnosticKind

`MediaStreamSourceDiagnosticKind` is an enumeration that describes the type of diagnostic information used by the media.

The values are:

- ❑   `BufferLevelInMilliseconds` — Download buffer in milliseconds
- ❑   `BufferLevelInBytes` — Download buffer in bytes

MediaStreamType

`MediaStreamType` is an enumeration that specifies the type of stream.

The values are:

- ❑   `Audio` — The stream is an audio stream.
- ❑   `Video` — The stream is a video stream.
- ❑   `Script` — The stream is a script stream.

PenLineCap

`PenLineCap` describes the shape at the end of a line or segment.

The values are:

- ❏ `Flat` — A cap that does not extend past the last point of the line. Comparable to no line cap.
- ❏ `Square` — A rectangle that has a height equal to the line thickness and a length equal to half the line thickness
- ❏ `Round` — A semicircle that has a diameter equal to the line thickness
- ❏ `Triangle` — An isosceles right triangle whose base length is equal to the thickness of the line

PenLineJoin

`PenLineJoin` describes the shape that joins two lines or segments.

The values are:

- ❏ `Miter` — Line joins use regular angular vertices.
- ❏ `Bevel` — Line joins use beveled vertices.
- ❏ `Round` — Line joins use rounded vertices.

Stretch

`Stretch` describes how content is resized to fill its allocated space.

The values are:

- ❏ `None` — The content preserves its original size.
- ❏ `Fill` — The content is resized to fill the destination dimensions. The aspect ratio is not preserved.
- ❏ `Uniform` — The content is resized to fit in the destination dimensions while it preserves its native aspect ratio.
- ❏ `UniformToFill` — The content is resized to fill the destination dimensions while it preserves its native aspect ratio. If the aspect ratio of the destination rectangle differs from the source, the source content is clipped to fit in the destination dimensions.

StyleSimulations

`StyleSimulations` describes the simulation style of a font.

The values are:

- ❏ `None` — No font style simulation
- ❏ `BoldSimulation` — Bold style simulation

❑   ItalicSimulation — Italic style simulation

❑   BoldItalicSimulation — Bold and Italic style simulation

SweepDirection

SweepDirection defines the direction in which an elliptical arc is drawn.

The values are:

❑   Counterclockwise — Specifies that arcs are drawn in a counterclockwise (negative-angle) direction.

❑   Clockwise — Specifies that arcs are drawn in a clockwise (positive-angle) direction.

System.Windows.Shapes Reference

System.Windows.Shapes Classes

The System.Windows.Shapes namespace contains the basic drawing elements that make up most of the rendered content in the player. The Ellipse, Line, Path, Polygon, Polyline, and Rectangle classes render vector-based resolution-independent lines and shape, so they can be resized appropriately no matter what size the shape is being rendered in. In this appendix, we'll go into detail on the classes in this namespace and cover how you can use the classes.

The following classes are in the System.Windows.Shapes namespace:

- ❑ Shape
- ❑ Ellipse
- ❑ Line
- ❑ Path
- ❑ Polygon
- ❑ Polyline
- ❑ Rectangle

We'll cover each in the next sections.

Shape Class

The Shape class is the base class for the Ellipse, Line, Path, Polygon, Polyline, and Rectangle classes. The following sections describe the properties of the Shape class that are not inherited from UIElement or FrameworkElement.

Appendix D: System.Windows.Shapes Reference

Fill

Fill gets or sets the color (Brush object in System.Windows.Media) that specifies how to paint the interior of the shape. Figure D-1 demonstrates the full color table for the Brush object.

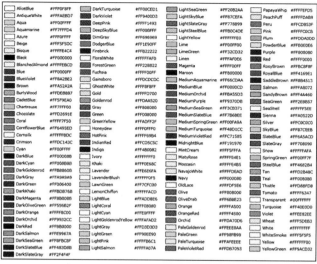

Figure D-1

The Brush object can be one of the following five types:

❑ SolidColorBrush — Paints an area with a solid color.

❑ LinearGradientBrush — Paints an area with a linear gradient.

❑ RadialGradientBrush — Paints an area with a radial gradient.

❑ ImageBrush — Paints an area with an image.

❑ VideoBrush — Paints an area with a running video.

Note that SolidColorBrush is the only brush that supports attribute and object element syntax; the remaining brushes all must be declared in XAML with the object element syntax.

❑ colorString — The color for a SolidColorBrush expressed as an attribute string. This includes:

❑ Named color

❑ RBG value (with optional Alpha information)

❑ ScRGB value (with optional Alpha information)

```
<object Fill="Red"/>
```

❑ singleBrush — Within opening and closing property elements for object.Fill; exactly one object element for a class that derives from Brush (LinearGradient, RadialGradient, Image, Video) For example:

```
<object>
  <object.Fill>
    singleBrush
  </object.Fill>
</object>
```

Stretch

Stretch gets or sets one of the following four values from the Stretch enumeration value that indicates how a shape is stretched within its parent.

❑ None — The content preserves its original size.

❑ Fill — The content is resized to fill the destination dimensions. The aspect ratio is not preserved.

❑ Uniform — The content is resized to fit in the destination dimensions while it preserves its native aspect ratio.

❑ UniformToFill — The content is resized to fill the destination dimensions while it preserves its native aspect ratio. If the aspect ratio of the destination rectangle differs from the source, the source content is clipped to fit in the destination dimensions.

Syntax

```
<Line Stroke="Black"
    Stretch="UniformToFill"
    StrokeThickness="10"
    X1="120" Y1="40"
    X2="200" Y2="20"/>
```

StrokeDashArray

StrokeDashArray is a collection of Double values that get or set values based on a specific grammar that indicate the pattern of dashes and gaps that is used to outline shapes.

The grammar follows this format:

```
StrokeDashArray="S[,G][,S*,G**]*"
```

❑ S — A Double value that defines the length of the first stroke in the sequence

❑ G — A Double value that defines the length of the first gap between strokes in the sequence. If G is not included, the gap length is identical to the preceding stroke length.

❑ S* — A Double value that defines the length of the additional strokes in the sequence

❑ G* — A Double value that defines the length of additional gaps between strokes in the sequence. If G* is omitted, the gap length is identical to the preceding stroke length.

Syntax

```
<Rectangle Stroke="Black"
    Margin="100,100,100,100"
    StrokeDashArray="3,2">
</Rectangle>
```

Example

StrokeDashCap; StrokeEndLineCap; StrokeStartLineCap

Each Stroke with the Cap suffix gets or sets one of the four PenLineCap enumeration values below that specify how the ends of a dash are drawn.

- ❑ Flat — A cap that does not extend past the last point of the line. Comparable to no line cap.

- ❑ Square — A rectangle that has a height equal to the line thickness and a length equal to half the line thickness

- ❑ Round — A semicircle that has a diameter equal to the line thickness

- ❑ Triangle — An isosceles right triangle whose base length is equal to the thickness of the line

Syntax

```
<Path Data="M 70, 150 A 60,
    60 0 0 0 170, 150"
    Stroke="Red"
    StrokeThickness="20"
    StrokeStartLineCap="Triangle"
    StrokeEndLineCap="Square"/>
```

Example

StrokeDashOffset

StrokeDashOffset is a Double value that gets or sets the distance within a dash pattern where a dash begins.

Syntax

```
<Rectangle Stroke="Green"
    Margin="100,100,100,100"
    StrokeThickness="15"
    StrokeDashArray="3,3"
    StrokeDashOffset="5"
    StrokeDashCap="Triangle" >
</Rectangle>
```

Example

StrokeLineJoin

StrokeLineJoin gets or sets one of the three PenLineJoin enumeration values below that specify the Join appearance used at the vertices of a Shape:

❑ Miter Line joins use regular angular vertices.

❑ Bevel Line joins use beveled vertices.

❑ Round Line joins use rounded vertices.

Syntax

```
<Path Height="200"
    StrokeLineJoin="Bevel"
    Fill="#FFFFFFFF"
    Stroke="Black"
    StrokeThickness="10"
    Data="M320,195 L325,65
         L411,192 L432,47"/>
```

Example

StrokeMiterLimit

StrokeMiterLimit is a Double value that gets or sets a positive number greater than or equal to 1 that limits the ratio of the miter length (the beveled end of two joined lines) to half the StrokeThickness of a Shape element.

Syntax

```
<Path Height="200"
    StrokeMiterLimit="50"
    Fill="#FFFFFFFF"
    Stroke="Black"
    StrokeThickness="10"
    Data="M320,195 L325,65
          L411,192 L432,47"/>
```

Example

Stroke

Stroke is a Brush that gets or sets how the Shape outline is painted. The Fill property explained in the beginning of this chapter uses the same Brush object. The same definition and rules apply to the Stroke property.

Syntax

```
<Rectangle
    Stroke="Black"
    StrokeThickness="6"
    StrokeDashArray="3,2"
    StrokeDashCap="Round"
    StrokeLineJoin="Round" >
</Rectangle>
```

Example

StrokeThickness

StrokeThickness is a Double value that gets or sets the width in pixels of a Shape outline.

Syntax

```
<Rectangle
    Stroke="Purple"
    StrokeThickness="6">
</Rectangle>
```

Example

Ellipse Class

The Ellipse class, whose purpose is to simply draw an ellipse, inherits all of its properties from Shape, UIElement, and FrameworkElement.

Syntax

```
<Canvas>
    <Ellipse Canvas.Top="30"
        Canvas.Left="30"
        Fill="Red"
        Height="150"
        Width="120"
        StrokeThickness="5"
        StrokeDashArray="3"
        StrokeDashCap="Triangle"
        Stroke="Black"/>
</Canvas>
```

Example

The above XAML returns this ellipse:

Line Class

The Line class, which draws a straight line between two points, has the following properties that determine where it should draw the line based on the parent it is rendering in:

❏ X1 — Gets or sets the X-coordinate of the Line start point.

❏ X2 — Gets or sets the X-coordinate of the Line endpoint.

❏ Y1 — Gets or sets the Y-coordinate of the Line start point.

❏ Y2 — Gets or sets the Y-coordinate of the Line endpoint.

The remaining properties of the Line class are inherited from Shape, FrameworkElement, and UIElement.

Syntax

```
<Line Stroke="Black"
    StrokeThickness="10"
    X1="120" Y1="40" X2="200" Y2="20" />
```

Example

The above XAML returns this line:

Path Class

The Path class is responsible for drawing a series of connected lines and curves. The line and curve dimensions are declared through the Data property, which is the only property of the Path class not inherited from Shape, UIElement, or FrameworkElement.

The Data property gets or sets a Geometry that specifies the shape to be drawn.

In XAML, the Data property is made up of a series of geometries (PathGeometry objects) based on the Path mini-language. Each PathGeometry is a collection of PathFigure objects that describe a discrete shape in the PathGeometry. Each PathFigure is composed of one or more PathSegment objects, which each describes a segment of the figure.

The following segments make up each PathFigure:

- ❏ ArcSegment — Creates an elliptical arc between two points.
- ❏ BezierSegment — Creates a cubic Bezier curve between two points.
- ❏ LineSegment — Creates a line between two points.
- ❏ PolyBezierSegment — Creates a series of cubic Bezier curves.
- ❏ PolyLineSegment — Creates a series of lines.
- ❏ PolyQuadraticBezierSegment — Creates a series of quadratic Bezier curves.
- ❏ QuadraticBezierSegment — Creates a quadratic Bezier curve.

Each segment in a PathFigure is connected to another segment to create a single, continuous shape. The segments are connected based on the initial StartPoint property of a PathFigure, and then subsequent segments are connected based on the endpoint of the previous segment.

In the Path mini-language, the PathSegments map to commands in the language. The following commands make up the Path mini-language:

- ❏ Move — Specifies the start point of a new figure, represented by an uppercase *M* and lowercase *m*. The uppercase *M* indicates that startPoint is an absolute value, while the lowercase *m* indicates that startPoint is an offset to the previous point.

❏ Draw — A Draw command can consist of several shape commands. The following shape commands are available:

Command	Mini-Language	Description
Line	L or l	Creates a straight line between the current point and the specified endpoint with an uppercase *L* or lowercase *l*. The endpoint is an X, Y value of the Point structure.
HorizontalLine	H or h	Creates a horizontal line between the current point and the specified X-coordinate with an uppercase *H* or lowercase *h*. The endpoint is the X-coordinate of the line.
VerticalLine	V or v	Creates a vertical line between the current point and the specified Y-coordinate with an uppercase *V* or lowercase *v*. The endpoint is the Y-coordinate of the line.
CubicBezierCurve	C or c	Creates a cubic Bezier curve between the current point (Point structure) and the specified endpoint (Point structure) by using the two specified control points with an uppercase *C* or lowercase *c*. The two control points and one endpoint are described as follows: ❏ controlPoint1 — The first control point of the curve, which determines the starting tangent of the curve ❏ controlPoint2 — The second control point of the curve, which determines the ending tangent of the curve ❏ endPoint — The point to which the curve is drawn
QuadraticBezierCurve	Q or q	Creates a quadratic Bezier curve between the current point (Point structure) and the specified endpoint (Point structure) by using the specified control points with an uppercase *Q* or lowercase *q*. The control point and endpoint are as follows: ❏ controlPoint — The control point of the curve, which determines the starting and ending tangents of the curve ❏ endPoint — The point to which the curve is drawn

Command	Mini-Language	Description
SmoothCubic BezierCurve	S or s	Creates a cubic Bezier curve between the current point (Point structure) and the specified endpoint (Point structure) by using the specified control points with an uppercase S or lowercase s. The control point is assumed to be the reflection of the control point of the previous command relative to the current point. The control point and endpoint are as follows: ❑ controlPoint — The control point of the curve, which determines the ending tangent of the curve ❑ endPoint — The point to which the curve is drawn
SmoothQuadraticBezierCurve	T or t	Creates a quadratic Bezier curve between the current point (Point structure) and the specified endpoint (Point structure) by using the specified control points with an uppercase T or lowercase t. The control point is assumed to be the reflection of the control point of the previous command relative to the current point. The control point and endpoint are as follows: ❑ controlPoint — The control point of the curve, which determines the ending tangent of the curve ❑ endPoint — The point to which the curve is drawn
EllipticalArc	A or a	Creates an elliptical arc between the current point and the specified endpoint. The values of the Elliptical Arc are set using: ❑ size — X, Y of the X-radius and Y-radius of the arc ❑ rotationAngle — Double value of the rotation of the ellipse, in degrees ❑ isLargeArcFlag — Set to 1 if the angle of the arc should be 180 degrees or greater; otherwise, set to 0 ❑ sweepDirectionFlag — Set to 1 if the arc is drawn in a positive-angle direction; otherwise, set to 0 ❑ endPoint — Point structure to which the arc is drawn

❑   `Close` — The uppercase Z or lowercase *z* close command ends the current figure and creates a line that connects the current point to the starting point of the figure. This command creates a line join (corner) between the last segment and the first segment of the figure.

Syntax

```
<Path Margin="96,64,157,110"
  Fill="#FFFFFFFF"
  Stretch="Fill"
  Stroke="CornflowerBlue"
  StrokeThickness="10"
  Data="M106,74 L111,368 L483,370"/>
```

Example

The above XAML results in this path:

Syntax

```
<Path Margin="80.5,72.5,88.5,64"
  Fill="#FFFFFFFF"
  Stretch="Fill"
  Stroke="Red"
  StrokeThickness="10"
  Data="M81,73
  L184.5,330.5
  L550.5,341.97769
  L495.05902,98.40345
  C495.05902,98.40345
    192.38138,413.20697
    192.38138,413.20697
  C547.00372,413.70438
    547.00372,358.99271
    546.00476,413.70438"/>
```

Example

The above XAML results in this path:

Polygon Class

The Polygon class handles the drawing of a connected series of lines that forms a closed shape. The Polygon class inherits its properties from the Shape, FrameworkElement, and UIElement classes, but it also exposes the same FillRule enumeration and Points property that the Polyline class has.

- ❏ FillRule — Has two enumeration options, EvenOdd or NonZero, which specify the interior fill of the polygon.

  - ❏ EvenOdd — Determines whether a point is in the fill region by drawing a ray from that point to infinity in any direction and counting the number of path segments within the given shape that the ray crosses. If this number is odd, the point is inside; if even, the point is outside.

  - ❏ NonZero — Determines whether a point is in the fill region of the path by drawing a ray from that point to infinity in any direction and then examining the places where a segment of the shape crosses the ray. Starting with a count of 0, add one each time a segment crosses the ray from left to right, and subtract one each time a path segment crosses the ray from right to left. After counting the crossings, if the result is 0, then the point is outside the path; otherwise, it is inside.

- ❏ Points — Gets or sets a collection that contains the vertex points of the polygon in the format *X,Y[X*,Y*]**

  - ❏ *X,Y* — A pair of double values that identify the X,Y initial point of the polygon

  - ❏ *X*,Y** — Subsequent pairs of double values that define additional points of this object

Syntax

```
<Polygon
    Points="10,10 10,110 110,110 110,10"
    Stroke="Black"
    StrokeThickness="10"
/>
```

Example

The above XAML returns this polygon:

PolyLine Class

The Polyline class handles the drawing of a connected series of lines that do not have to form a closed shape. The Polyline class inherits its properties from the Shape, FrameworkElement, and UIElement classes, but it also exposes the same FillRule enumeration and Points property that the Polygon class has.

❏   FillRule — Has two enumeration options, EvenOdd or NonZero, which specify the interior fill of the polygon.

    ❏   EvenOdd — Determines whether a point is in the fill region by drawing a ray from that point to infinity in any direction and counting the number of path segments within the given shape that the ray crosses. If this number is odd, the point is inside; if even, the point is outside.

    ❏   NonZero — Determines whether a point is in the fill region of the path by drawing a ray from that point to infinity in any direction and then examining the places where a segment of the shape crosses the ray. Starting with a count of 0, add one each time a segment crosses the ray from left to right, and subtract one each time a path segment crosses the ray from right to left. After counting the crossings, if the result is 0, then the point is outside the path; otherwise, it is inside.

    ❏   Points — Gets or sets a collection that contains the vertex points of the polygon in the format X, Y[X*, Y*] *.

    ❏   X, Y — A pair of Double values that identify the X,Y initial point of the polygon

    ❏   X*, Y* — Subsequent pairs of Double values that define additional points of this object.

Syntax

```
<Polyline
    Points="60,15 20,100 100,100 70,05"
    Stroke="Blue"
    Fill="Bisque"
    StrokeThickness="5" />
```

Example

The above XAML returns this polyline:

Rectangle Class

The Rectangle class handles the drawing of a rectangle shape, which can optionally have a Stroke and a Fill. The Rectangle class inherits its properties from the Shape, FrameworkElement, and UIElement classes, but it also exposes the RadiusX and RadiusY properties.

❏   RadiusX — A Double value that gets or sets the X-axis radius of the ellipse that is used to round the corners of the rectangle

❏   RadiusY — A Double value that gets or sets the Y-axis radius of the ellipse that is used to round the corners of the rectangle

The default value for both RadiusX and RadiusY is 0.

Syntax

```
<Rectangle
    Stroke="Green"
    Margin="50,50,50,50"
    StrokeThickness="5"
    StrokeDashArray="6,6"
    StrokeDashOffset="9"
    StrokeLineJoin="Round">
</Rectangle>
```

Example

The above XAML returns this rectangle:

Additional Resources

The following are some additional resources that we have found helpful in our own learning of Silverlight 3. We hope you find them useful!

- ❏ `http://community.infragistics.com/silverlight/default.aspx` — Infragistics community site for Silverlight
- ❏ `http://silverlight.net` — The Official Silverlight Community Site
- ❏ `http://msdn.microsoft.com/en-us/silverlight/default.aspx` — Silverlight SDK
- ❏ `www.infragistics.com/silverlight` — Infragistics Silverlight Resources
- ❏ `http://channel9.msdn.com` — The Ever-Present Channel9: lots of good stuff on Silverlight
- ❏ `www.silverlightshow.net` — Quality Independent Silverlight community site
- ❏ `www.wynapse.com` — Silverlight articles, blogs, examples, and more
- ❏ `http://msdn.microsoft.com/en-us/library/bb188743.aspx` — MSDN Library for Silverlight
- ❏ `http://tinyurl.com/ironruby-resources` — IronRuby resources
- ❏ `http://tinyurl.com/ironpython-project` — IronPython Project
- ❏ `www.shinedraw.com` — Shine Draw: Silverlight and Flash repository
- ❏ `www.projectrosetta.com` — From Flash to Silverlight

Some related Microsoft blogs:

- ❏ `http://Weblogs.asp.net/scottgu` — Scott Guthrie (a must for any .NET dev!)
- ❏ `http://Blogs.msdn.com/brada/` — Brad Abrams
- ❏ `http://Blogs.msdn.com/tims/` — Tim Sneath
- ❏ `http://adamkinney.com/` — Adam Kinney
- ❏ `http://silverlight.net/blogs/jesseliberty/` — Jesse Liberty

Index

Index

C